# UNEMPLOYMENT IN EUROPE

# Unemployment in Europe

Edited by

Joan Muysken
*Professor of Economics*
*University of Limburg*

and

Chris de Neubourg
*Associate Professor of Economics*
*University of Limburg*

M
MACMILLAN

First published 1989

Published by
THE MACMILLAN PRESS LTD
Houndmills, Basingstoke, Hampshire RG21 2XS
and London
Companies and representatives
throughout the world

Printed in China

British Library Cataloguing in Publication Data
Unemployment in Europe.
1. Unemployment—European Economic
Community countries
I. Muysken, Joan II. Neubourg, Chris de
331.13′794 HD5764.5.A6
ISBN 0-333-43800-0

# Contents

*List of Figures* viii

*List of Tables* xii

*Notes on the Contributors* xiv

Introduction 1
*Joan Muysken and Chris de Neubourg*

1 Unemployment and Female Labour Supply 9
*Richard Blundell, John Ham and Costas Meghir*

2 Unemployment and Labour Market Transition Probabilities 37
*Jules Theeuwes*

Comment on Chapters 1 and 2 56
*Ďaniel Weiserbs*

3 A Vintage Model of Labour Demand by UK Manufacturing 60
*J. Ansar, A. Ingham, M. Toker and A. Ulph*

4 Employment and Unemployment in the Netherlands, 1960–84: A Putty-Clay Approach 86
*Joan Muysken and A. H. van Zon*

Comment on Chapters 3 and 4 97
*E. R. de Regt*

5 Mass Unemployment in the United Kingdom: An Analysis of Causes and Possible Cures 124
*Jim Taylor*

6 Labour Hoarding, and Recorded Unemployment in OECD Countries 150
*Derek Bosworth and Tony Westaway*

7 Unidentified Floating Unemployment (UFU) and the Specification of the *UV*-curve 165
*Chris de Neubourg*

Comment on Chapters 5, 6 and 7 197
*David F. Heathfield*

8 Trade Unions, Investment and Employment in a Small Open Economy: A Dutch Perspective 200
*C. B. Mulder and F. van der Ploeg*

9 Wage Formation in a Two-sector Open Economy with Two Strong Unions 233
*Oddbjørn Raaum*

Comment on Chapters 8 and 9 263
*P. Keizer*

10 Unemployment in the European Community: Counting the Costs 269
*P. N. Junankar*

11 Job Creation Programmes in an International Comparison 281
*Marcia de Wachter and Yolanda Somers*

Comment on Chapters 10 and 11 306
*J. A. H. Maks*

12 Germany and the European Disease 316
*John Davis and Patrick Minford*

13 Keynesian Policies for Voluntary Unemployment 343
*William Peterson*

Comment on Chapters 12 and 13 357
*Victoria Chick*

14 Unemployment and Fiscal Activism in a Small Open Economy 361
*John Bradley*

15 Labour Market Flexibility: An Analysis with the DMS Model 397
*Laurence Bloch*

Comment on Chapters 14 and 15 418
*F. C. Palm*

16 Wage Flexibility and Labour Market 422
*Bernard Compaijen and Klaas A. Springer*

17 Rigidities and Employment in Belgium: An Econometric Analysis by Sectoral Employment Functions 439
*A. Bayer, N. Deimezis, Y. Guillaume and D. Meulders*

Comment on Chapters 16 and 17 452
*Peter de Gijsel*

*Index* 457

# List of Figures


| | | |
|---|---|---|
| 2.1 | Stock-flow model | 45 |
| 3.1 | Output | 62 |
| 3.2 | Labour demand | 63 |
| 3.3 | Real labour price | 64 |
| 3.4 | Choice of production techniques | 66 |
| 3.5 | The utilisation of vintages | 70 |
| 3.6 | Aggregate PSP - labour | 73 |
| 3.7 | Labour-demand forecasts - all models | 76 |
| 3.8 | *Ex ante* and *ex post* isoquants for labour and energy | 78 |
| 3.9 | Ranking the first fifteen vintages operating in 1973$Q$1 in order of operating costs | 79 |
| 4.1 | The determination of investment and demand for labour | 92 |
| 4.2 | The choice of equipment of vintage $T$ | 92 |
| 4.3 | Distribution of vintages according to productivity | 94 |
| 4.4 | [No caption] | 103 |
| 4.5 | [No caption] | 103 |
| 4.6 | Labour productivity - boundaries of new equipment | 106 |
| 4.7 | Percentage of production capacity scrapped for varying reasons | 107 |
| 4.8 | [No caption] | 108 |
| 4.9 | [No caption] | 110 |
| 5.1 | Registered unemployment and estimated vacancies: UK, 1953-85 | 130 |
| 5.2 | The U-V relationship | 131 |
| 5.3 | Percentage registered unemployed and percentage notified vacancies: UK, 1953-85 | 132 |
| 5.4 | Estimated mean duration of unemployment in months: UK | 133 |
| 5.5 | Unemployment and the CBI Labour Shortage Indicator, 1964-85 | 134 |
| 5.6 | CBI Indicator of Labour Shortage | 135 |
| 5.7 | Confirmed redundancies by sector in Great Britain, 1977-85 | 138 |
| 5.8 | Output growth and the change in unemployment, 1951-85 | 140 |

5.9 Demand *v.* supply constraints on output growth 141
5.10 Index of capacity utilisation 142
5.11 Relationship between labour shortage and capacity utilisation in the UK, 1964-85 143
5.12 Unemployment and the CBI index of capacity utilisation 144
5.13 Gross fixed investment in plant and machinery by manufacturing industry at 1980 prices, 1955-85 145
6.1 Average and frontier production functions 145
7.1 Unemployment and vacancies: The Netherlands, 1960-83 176
7.2 The decomposition of unemployment according to Muysken (1985) 180
8.1 Unemployment in The Netherlands, the EEC and OECD, 1966-83 217
8.2 The composition of the potential labour force in the Netherlands, 1955-84 218
8.3 Employment in the Netherlands, 1955-84 218
8.4 Investment in the Netherlands, 1955-84 219
8.5 Output growth in the Netherlands, 1955-84 220
8.6 Growth in wage rates and unit labour costs in the Netherlands, 1955-84 220
8.7 World trade growth, 1960-84 221
8.8 The real foreign interest rate, 1961-83 222
8.9 Government expenditure and budget deficit in the Netherlands, 1955-83 222
8.10 The real exchange rate for the Netherlands, 1959-84 223
8.11 Taxes and social security in the Netherlands, 1955-84 223
8.12 The wedge in the Netherlands, 1955-84 224
8.13 Changes in real benefits in the Netherlands, 1965-84 225
9.1 The non-cooperative equilibrium (*NCE*) 243
9.2 The non-cooperative equilibrium (*NCE*) and the leader-follower equilibrium (*LF*) 245
9.3 A positive shift in the $N$-sector reaction function ($R^N$) may reduce $T$-sector wages ($w^T$) 249
9.4 Pareto optimal collusive solutions are on the contract curve *PP* 250
9.5 The indifference curves change if a union attaches more importance to relative wages 252
9.6 The non-cooperative wages increase if the $N$-sector union gives more weight to relative wages 253

| | | |
|---|---|---|
| 9.7 | Wages may change in opposite directions in the *LF* equilibrium if the *N*-sector gives more weight to relative wages | 253 |
| 9.8 | Wages in both sectors increase if the *T*-sector union attaches more importance to relative wages | 254 |
| 11.1 | Cost of the 'pure' job-creation policy per unemployed, 1975–83, in guilder of 1983 | 291 |
| 11.2 | Percentage of unemployed persons reached through the measures, 1975–83 | 292 |
| 12.1 | [No caption] | 320 |
| 12.2 | [No caption] | 321 |
| 12.3 | [No caption] | 323 |
| 12.4 | Supply curves with flat rate and benefit ratio system of unemployment support | 325 |
| 12.5 | West Germany: unemployment and equilibrium unemployment | 330 |
| 12.6 | Logarithm of real unemployment benefits, including *sozialhilfe* | 330 |
| 12.7 | Unionisation rate: percentage of employees in unions | 331 |
| 12.8 | Employers' national insurance contributions and non-wage costs: indirect costs as proportion of gross wages | 331 |
| 12.9 | Employees' direct tax and national insurance contributions as a percentage of employees' gross income | 331 |
| 12.10 | Changes in prices and unemployment rates, 1954–79, and Phillips curves for USA | 334 |
| 12.11 | Actual unemployment - equilibrium unemployment as a percentage of the working population | 335 |
| 12.12 | Recent German monetary shocks (% change in real M1) | 336 |
| 12.13 | Recent German fiscal shocks (change in the real budget deficit as a % of real GNP) | 336 |
| 12.14 | Recent world trade shocks (% p.a. change in world trade) | 336 |
| 12.15 | Effect of recent shocks on unemployment, differences from base | 338 |
| 13.1 | [No caption] | 346 |
| 14.1 | Unemployment rate | 362 |
| 14.2 | Sectoral employment | 362 |
| 14.3 | Labour-force change and net migration abroad | 363 |

| | | |
|---|---|---|
| 14.4 | Tax rates, indirect, direct, payroll, corporate | 363 |
| 14.5 | Borrowing requirements and balance of payments | 364 |
| 14.6 | Domestic and foreign debt interest | 365 |
| 14.7 | Tax wedge | 379 |
| 14.8 | Total employment effect | 383 |
| 14.9 | Market sector employment effect | 383 |
| 14.10 | Industrial employment effect | 384 |
| 14.11 | Market services employment effect | 384 |
| 14.12 | Unemployment effect | 385 |
| 14.13 | Industrial exports effect | 386 |
| 14.14 | Borrowing requirement effect | 386 |
| 14.15 | Balance-of-payments effect | 387 |
| 15.1 | Scheme of supply effects in the DMS model, induced by a decrease in the real wage | 399 |
| 15.2 | Variant 1: 'Decrease of 1 per cent of the *per capita* real gross wage - fixed exchange rate - rate-wage-sensitive scrapping behaviour' | 404 |
| 15.A.1 | Real and nominal dynamics of accumulation in industry and construction | 409 |
| 15.A.2 | Hourly productivity of labour | 410 |
| 16.1 | Real wage rigidity and nominal wage rigidity | 429 |
| 16.2 | Short-run real wage rigidity and unemployment | 430 |
| 17.1 | Total employment 1967-81 | 448 |

# List of Tables


| | | |
|---|---|---|
| 1.1 | Parameter estimates and diagnostics for the Tobit model $L_1$ | 19 |
| 1.2a | Labour-supply estimates and diagnostics for Model $L_2$ | 20 |
| 1.2b | Estimated parameters of the employment probability index for model $L_2$ | 21 |
| 1.2c | Predictive performance | 22 |
| 1.3 | Wage elasticities (non-market time) | 23 |
| 1.4 | Employment elasticities with respect to demand side variables | 25 |
| 2.1 | Long-run steady-state values | 48 |
| 2.A.1 | Estimation results | 51 |
| 2.A.2 | Transition probabilities and labour-market status in the Netherlands, for five data points, in the period 1974–83 | 52 |
| 3.1 | Estimated parameters of the Fuss model | 71 |
| 3.2 | Tests of restrictions | 72 |
| 3.3 | Aggregate PSP stability test | 74 |
| 3.4 | Comparison of forecasts from three models | 75 |
| 3.5 | Marginal vintage details | 80 |
| 3.6 | Operating of vintage 1973 | 82 |
| 3.7 | Simulating a maintained employment level | 83 |
| 4.1 | The parameter estimates | 104 |
| 4.2 | Estimation results compared with KvZ and GWJ | 107 |
| 5.1 | Vacancies notified to employment offices or job centres and estimated total vacancies by region | 127 |
| 5.2 | The duration of unemployment in Great Britain, 1979 and 1985 | 133 |
| 5.3 | Changes in unemployment by broad sector, 1979–83 | 136 |
| 5.4 | Percentage change in manufacturing employment, 1979–83 | 137 |
| 5.5 | Redundancy rate by region, 1977–82 | 139 |
| 5.6 | The CBI index of capacity utilisation by industry | 146 |
| 6.1 | Recorded unemployment and hoarded labour: summary statistics | 158 |
| 10.1 | Growth of unemployment in the EC | 270 |
| 10.2 | Static output loss costs of unemployment (Okun's Law estimates) | 278 |

| | | |
|---|---|---|
| 11.1 | Evaluation criteria of job-creation measures | 284 |
| C.1 | Summary of Junankar's typology of costs | 306 |
| C.2 | Guestimate of the Okun parameters | 308 |
| C.3 | The development of the labour force and employment in the market sectors of various countries, 1962–79 | 310 |
| C.4 | Indicators of labour-market flexibility (1970s and early 1980s) | 313 |
| 12.1 | The German equations | 327 |
| 12.2 | Unemployment rates in major European countries | 332 |
| 12.3 | Shocks (unanticipated) simulated by the model | 337 |
| 12.A.1 | Source of variables used in German equations | 339 |
| 14.1 | Price elasticities of demand for Irish factors of production in the industrial sector | 369 |
| 14.2 | Block structure of model | 371 |
| 14.A.1 | [No caption] | 392 |
| 15.1 | Variant 1: 'Decrease of real wage – real-wage-sensitive scrapping behaviour – fixed exchange rate' | 402 |
| 15.2 | Employment and unemployment | 405 |
| 15.3 | Main macroeconomic effects of a 1 per cent decrease in real wage rate | 406 |
| 15.A.1 | Variant 2: 'Decrease in real wage – invariant scrapping behaviour – fixed exchange rate' | 413 |
| 15.A.2 | Variant 3: 'Decrease in real wage – real-wage-sensitive scrapping behaviour – flexible exchange rate' | 415 |
| 16.1 | Coefficients of variation for two periods | 426 |
| 16.2 | The real wage gap in manufacturing for selected periods and years | 427 |
| 16.3 | Real (RWR) and nominal wage rigidity (NWR) | 429 |
| 16.4 | SWVs of (nominal) compensation per employee per year for the period 1970–83 | 432 |
| 16.5 | Coefficients of variation (unweighted) of nominal hourly earnings and compensation | 433 |
| 17.1 | Branch breakdown of manufacturing industry | 440 |
| 17.2 | Employment in Belgian manufacturing industries, 1966–81 | 441 |
| 17.3 | Sectoral employment elasticities | 443 |
| 17.4 | Manufacturing employment: simulation results by branch | 447 |
| 17.A.1 | Estimation results for equation (17.10) | 449 |
| 17.A.2 | Estimation results for equation (17.11) | 450 |

# Notes on the Contributors

**Jasmin Ansar** is Lecturer in Economics and Econometrics at City University, London, and is currently visiting Purdue University, Indiana, USA

**Ali Bayar** is Assistant of Economics at the Free University of Brussels. He was formerly Researcher in Labour Economics at the Department of Applied Economics of the Free University of Brussels (DULBEA).

**Laurence Bloch** is an administrator of the INSEE since 1981. Presently she works in the Forecasting Department where she is in charge of the METRIC model (macroeconomic quarterly model). She has published on demand systems and macroeconomic modelling.

**Richard Blundell** graduated from the Econometrics Masters at The London School of Economics and Political Science in 1975 and moved directly into a Lectureship in Econometrics at Manchester. Professor of Economics at University College London in 1985 and Director of Research at the Institute for Fiscal Studies in 1986. Publications in econometrics, consumer behaviour and the microeconomics of labour markets.

**Derek Bosworth** is Principal Research Fellow at the Institute for Employment Research, University of Warwick. His interests span the areas of the economics of technological change and labour economics. He is author of a number of books on production functions, intellectual property, and employment theory. He is currently working on a number of projects within the Institute, including research for the manpower Services Commission on long-term unemployment and for the Engineering Industry Training Board on the prospects for the UK engineering sector.

**John Bradley** is a Senior Research Officer in the Economic and Social Research Institute in Dublin, Ireland. He was previously an economist in the Central Bank of Ireland. He holds a PhD from Dublin University (Trinity College) in applied optimisation theory. For the past ten years he has worked on the development of macroeconomic models and their application to policy analysis in small open economies.

**Victoria Chick** is Reader in Economics, University College London. She has also taught at McGill University and the Universities of Southampton (England), Aarhus (Denmark) and California at Berkeley and Santa Cruz, on various leaves from UCL, and part-time at the London School of Economics. She has been a Visiting Economist at the Reserve Bank of Australia and Federal Reserve Bank of New York, and a Visiting Fellow in the Université Catholique de Louvain (Belgium). She has published books on monetary policy and numerous articles on monetary theory and Keynesian economics.

**B. Compaijen** is attached to the Free University of Amsterdam since 1973 and is at present Associate Professor of Economics. He is a member of the Labour Market Research Group.

**J. G. Davis** is currently an Economist with Barclays Bank, having completed his doctorate at Liverpool University in 1987. Previously he obtained degrees in economics at Hull University and Warwick University and was a Tutor in economic statistics for one year at Exeter University.

**Nikitas Deimezis** is PhD in economics. He is Researcher in Applied Economic Modelling, at the Department of Applied Economics of the Free University of Brussels (DULBEA).

**Yvan Guillaume** is Professor of Macroeconomic Modelling, Economic Policy and Energy Economics at the Free University of Brussels. He is also Deputy Director of the Department of Applied Economics of the Free University of Brussels (DULBEA).

**Peter de Gijsel** is since 1985 Assistant Professor in Economics at the University of Limburg in Maastricht. He graduated with the PhD from University of Dortmund in 1980 and moved to the University of Regensburg where he stayed until 1985. His working fields are post-Keynesian Economics, labour market economics and the economics of the shadow economy.

**John Ham** graduated with a PhD from Princeton University in 1980 and moved to the University of Toronto where he is now an Associate Professor in Economics. He has published in the areas of econometrics and applied labour economics.

**David F. Heathfield** is Senior Lecturer in Economics at the University of Southampton. After ten years in engineering he graduated in economics and joined the econometric model building unit at Southampton. He has taught in the United States and was a DAAD visitor in Kiel in 1984. He is chairman of the European Production Study Group and has published several books and articles on production and econometric modelling.

**Alan Ingham** has been Lecturer in Economics at Southampton since 1973. Visiting appointments include Université Catholique de Louvain, and University of British Columbia. His main research interests lie in resource economics and models of production. At present he is a member of a research group working for the United Kingdom Department of Energy.

**P. N. Junankar** is a Lecturer in Economics at the University of Essex. He was a Principal Research Fellow at the Institute of Employment Research at the University of Warwick, 1984–85. He has been a Visiting Assistant Professor at Northwestern University, USA (1972–73), Visiting Associate Professor at Queen's University, Canada (1978–79), Visiting Fellow at the Indian Statistical Institute, New Delhi, India and at the Australian National University in Canberra, Australia. He has worked on labour economics, macroeconomics, development economics and Marxian economics. He has published books on Investment, Marx's Economics and Costs of Unemployment.

**Piet Keizer** is currently Associate Professor of Institutional Economics at the University of Limburg in Maastricht. He studied economics at the University of Groningen and wrote a dissertation on institutional aspects of wage and price inflation. He has published on wage theory, inflation theory and on the problem of the relation between economics, sociology and psychology.

**J. A. H. Maks** studied economics at the University of Amsterdam. He was Assistant and Associate Professor at the University of Groningen. Currently he is Professor of Economics, especially microeconomics, at the University of Limburg. His main research interests are the non-parametric approach, industrial economics and neo-Austrian economics.

**Costas Meghir** graduated with a PhD from Manchester University in 1984 and moved to University College London where he is now Lecturer in Economics. Publications in microeconometrics and labour economics.

**Daniele Meulders** is Professor of Labour Economics and Public Finance at the Free University of Brussels.

**Patrick Minford** is Edward Gonner Professor of Applied Economics at the University of Liverpool, where he has been since end 1976. He is the author of books on the exchange rate, and co-author of a textbook on rational expectations. He has also written widely in journals on trade and the economy. In 1979 he started the Liverpool Research Group in Macroeconomics, which publishes quarterly forecasts of the UK and a commentary on policy issues, both domestic and international.

**Christian Mulder** after completion of his Master's degree in Economics at Erasmus University, Rotterdam, he commenced his PhD studies at the London School of Economics. He has taught at Erasmus University, Tilburg University and the London School of Economics and has worked for a summer at the International Monetary Fund. Currently, he is an economist at the Dutch Ministry of Finance.

**Joan Muysken** is a professor of economics at the University of Limburg in Maastricht. He studied quantitative economics at the University of Groningen and received his PhD degree from the University of Groningen on the aggregation of production functions. He has published on aggregation and reduction in economic theory, development and estimation of putty-clay vintage models, production functions and technological progress, analysis of unemployment and vacancies, and the separation of unemployment into its components.

**Chris de Neubourg** studied economics and sociology at the Universities of Louvain and Antwerp. He lectured at the University of Groningen and is now teaching economics at the University of Limburg. His research efforts are concentrated on labour market issues, including unemployment and labour utilisation, studied in an international comparative context.

**Franz Palm** is currently professor of economics and econometrics at the University of Limburg in Maastricht. He studied economics and econometrics at the University of Louvain and the University of Chicago and received his PhD degree in economics from the University of Louvain. He taught econometrics at the University of Louvain and at the Free University in Amsterdam. He has published on econometric theory and applications in several leading journals including *Econometrica, European Economic Review, International Economic Review, Journal of Econometrics* and *Journal of Business and Economic Statistics*, of which he is an associate editor.

**William Peterson** is a University Lecturer in Economics at Cambridge, and a fellow of Christ's College. He has been associated for a number of years, as a member of the Cambridge Growth Project, in the construction of a dynamic disaggregated model of the UK economy for use in forecasting and policy analysis. His research interests include energy economics, applied econometrics and macroeconomic modelling.

**Frederick van der Ploeg** after completion of his BSc degree in Mathematics and Applied Sciences at Sussex University, he obtained a PhD from King's College, Cambridge University. He has worked as a Junior Research Officer on the Cambridge Growth Project, a member and consultant of Cambridge Econometrics Ltd, a teacher at various Cambridge colleges, a Fellow of Darwin College, a Research Fellow at the University of Amsterdam and the Cobbenhagen Visiting Professor at Tilburg Univeristy. Currently, he is a Lecturer at the London School of Economics, a Professor of Quantitative Economics at Tilburg University, and the Director of the National PhD Network for Quantitative Economics in the Netherlands. He is also an editor of *Economica*, an associate editor of *Computer Science in Economics and Management*, a fellow of the Centre for Economic Policy Research, and a senior member of the Centre for Labour Economics.

**Oddbjørn Raaum** has been working as a research fellow at the Department of Economics, University of Oslo, since graduation 1984 (MA in economics University of Oslo). At the present, he is working with his PhD thesis on trade union behaviour and wage bargaining as a part of the post-graduate programme at the department. A revised version of the paper to be published will probably be one part of his thesis.

**Erik de Regt** is currently Assistant Professor of Economics at the University of Limburg in Maastricht. He studied econometrics at the Erasmus University in Rotterdam. He taught economics at the Erasmus University from 1981 to 1985. He is mainly interested in theory and applications of labour economics.

**Yolanda Somers** is working as a research assistant at the University of Antwerp/SESO.

**K. A. Springer** is junior researcher at the Free University of Amsterdam since 1985. He is a member of the Labour Market Research Group.

**Jim Taylor** teaches at Lancaster University and previously worked at the Universities of Pennsylvania and British Columbia (Vancouver). He has published many articles on unemployment, inflation, regional policy and the geographical movement of industry. He has published books on unemployment and wage inflation and regional economic policy. He is currently editor of *Regional Studies.*

**J. J. M. Theeuwes** studied at the Universities of Antwerp and Louvain. He received his PhD from the University of British Columbia (Vancouver). He is professor of Economics at the Leyden Faculty of Law since December 1986. His research interests are mainly in the area of labour economics. He has published articles in economic journals on family labour supply and labour force participation decisions, on investments in human capital and the duration of unemployment.

**Mehmet Toker** joined the Department of Economics at Southampton University as a Temporary Lecturer in 1985.

**Alistair Ulph** joined the Economic Department at Southampton University in 1979 as Lecturer, and subsequently became Senior Lecturer, and in 1985, Professor of Economics. He has previously been a Research Fellow in Resource and Environmental Economics at Australian National University, Canberra, for three years, following a four-year period as Lecturer in Economics at the University of Stirling.

**Marcia de Wachter** is an Economic Advisor of the Prime Minister of Belgium and Associate Professor at the University of Antwerp/SESO. Her expertise and research are oriented towards macroeconomic policy making and labour problems.

**Daniel Weiserbs** is Professor of Economics at the Université Catholique de Louvain. He is editor of *Recherches Economique de Louvain* and vice-chairman of the European Production Study Group. He published among others on demand analysis, applied econometrics and macroeconomic policy.

**Tony Westaway** is Lecturer in Economics at Loughborough University. He is also Associate Research Fellow at the Institute for Employment Research, University of Warwick. He has been a consultant to both industrial companies and government departments. He has also written on a wide range of subjects in economics.

**Adriaan van Zon** is currently employed at the Department of Economics of the University of Limburg in Maastricht. His main interest lies in the field of macroeconomic production modelling, especially vintage modelling and its empirical implementation.

# Introduction

## Joan Muysken and Chris de Neubourg

In April 1986 the European Production Study Group and the Department of Economics of the University of Limburg organised a conference on 'Unemployment in Europe' in Maastricht, the Netherlands.[1] The aim of this conference was to discuss papers on all aspects of labour market research, and to relate them to the unemployment situation in Europe. Papers, starting often from different theoretical inspirations, were presented on the following topics:

- labour supply and unemployment;
- demand for labour;
- unemployment and discrepancies on the labour market;
- wage formation and wage flexibility;
- policy measures with respect to unemployment, both on the macrolevel and on the microlevel.

In this introduction we summarise the chapters within the context of these topics.

The topic of labour supply and unemployment is first discussed by Richard Blundell, John Ham and Costas Meghir in Chapter 1. They argue that when modelling labour supply one should not only account for those persons supplying positive hours but one should also include in the analysis those searching for work, and discouraged workers. The resulting double-hurdle model offers a framework for studying the effects of macroeconomic variables on labour force participation. This model also allows one to test the hypothesis behind the traditional labour-supply model that all individuals not supplying positive hours of work have set their reservation wage above their perceived market wage. The authors apply their model - and some extensions - to a sample of married women drawn from the UK Family Expenditure Survey of 1982. They find that the traditional labour supply model should be rejected. Moreover, the presence of discouraged workers turns out to be significant.

The other chapter (Chapter 2) on this topic is by Jules Theeuwes, who proposes a research programme to study the inefficiencies and inequities of unemployment, based on a stock-flow model of the labour market. In this model individual transition probabilities are modelled as functions of supply and demand side and policy variables. Distributional aspects then can be studied by analysing how individual experiences with respect to unemployment change over time and with policy measures. The individual experiences can also be aggregated into a dynamic stock-flow model of the labour market. Then the efficiency aspects can be studied by simulating different long-run steady-state distributions of unemployment, employment and non-participation, using different assumptions about characteristics of the supply, demand and policy side. The main problem in implementing this research programme is the lack of a sizeable amount of good data. Although Theeuwes is also confronted with this problem, he demonstrates the applicability of his approach to a Dutch sample of unemployed youngsters in May and November 1984.

The topic of demand for labour is discussed by J. Ansar, A. Ingham, M. Toker and A. Ulph. In Chapter 3 demand for labour is analysed employing a vintage production model for the UK manufacturing sector, 1970–85. Energy is distinguished as a separate factor of production which enables the authors to pay explicit attention to the problems of adjustment to the oil price shocks in 1973 and 1979. The authors conclude that increasing unemployment in the early 1980s was not due to real wages increases: if output levels could have been maintained, unemployment would have increased only fractionally.

Joan Muysken and Adriaan van Zon also use a vintage production model to analyse demand for labour and unemployment in Chapter 4. Their model is applied to the manufacturing sector in the Netherlands, 1960–84. The authors stress the importance of a proper specification of technical progress, both embodied and disembodied. Their analysis enables them to distinguish between cyclical and structural (both quantitative and qualitative) unemployment; moreover, labour hoarding is analysed explicitly. The main finding is that whereas unemployment in the early and mid-1970s is caused by a high real wage, which induces scrapping of equipment because of economic obsolescence, in the late 1970s and thereafter unemployment is because of severe underutilisation of capacity, which causes both cyclical unemployment and scrapping due to underutilisation.

Whereas the previous two topics dealt with supply and demand separately, the next two topics cover the interaction of supply and demand. These topics are discrepancies on the labour market and wage formation. Chapter 7 by Chris de Neubourg emphasises various types of imbalances on the labour market and their relation with various ways to subdivide aggregate unemployment according to type and origin. Unemployment is subdivided in order to diagnose the causes of unemployment as a basis for remedial action. Several classifications of unemployment (voluntary-involuntary, demand-deficient-non-demand-deficient, seasonal-frictional-structural) are discussed. De Neubourg concludes that it appears to be extremely difficult to define and to measure the relative importance of the various types of unemployment independently of each other, on the basis of a taxonomic labour-market framework only. In Chapter 6 Derek Bosworth and Tony Westaway stress that in order to analyse the slack on the labour market one should not only take into account observed unemployment, but also hidden unemployment due to labour hoarding. They measure labour hoarding in a rather crude way by means of a Cobb-Douglas production function, distinguishing between persons employed and number of hours worked. The analysis is applied to the twelve EEC countries, Japan and the USA in the period 1959–83 (for most countries). For the European countries they find that hoarded labour grew in the late 1970s. Moreover, they observe that during the late 1970s and early 1980s underutilisation of labour due to labour hoarding was replaced by increasing unemployment.

Jim Taylor, in Chapter 5, explores the underlying nature of the UK's unemployment problem. This is done by examining the relationship between unemployment and vacancies in the UK during the period 1953–1985 together with other labour-market information. Attention is focused upon the importance of gaining a better understanding of the relationship between unemployment stocks and flows (and similarly for vacancies). The final section emphasises primarily the demise of the manufacturing sector. It is argued that a conventional demand expansion may face severe obstacles due to the large-scale scrapping of plant and machinery in the early 1980s.

The second topic in which interaction between demand and supply on the labour market is discussed is wage formation and wage flexibility. In their contribution (Chapter 16) Bernard Compaijen and Klaas A. Springer emphasise international differences in wage flexibility (or wage rigidity). Having discussed several measures of wage flexibility, they compute rankings of some EEC countries according to the degree of flexibility estimated by different methods. It appears that Japan and the USA have a high wage flexibility relative to the EC countries. The latter group is rather homogeneous, although the Netherlands stands out by a high real-wage gap in manufacturing and a low dispersion of sectoral wages. Finally an alternative indicator of wage flexibility is constructed.

Chapter 17 by A. Bayar, *et al.*, also relates to the flexibility issue. However, the authors discuss 'numerical flexibility' only. Numerical flexibility is defined as the possibility for firms to adjust actual employment to its desired level immediately and completely. It implies policies of reducing employment when the economy slackens and increasing employment when the economy grows. Numerical flexibility (quantity adjustment) is favoured by partial (un)employment, fixed-term contracts, overtime, subcontracting, temporary work, etc. The study estimates the direct effect of the introduction of 'total' numerical flexibility in the labour market upon employment in the manufacturing industry. Estimates are made by means of sectoral employment functions for Belgium. It is concluded that, contrary to what is usually claimed, 'total' numerical flexibility would have reduced employment.

The topic of wage formation is analysed by Oddbjørn Raaum in Chapter 9 in the context of a theoretical model of a small open economy (e.g. Norway) in which two sectors are distinguished, producing tradable and non-tradable goods, respectively. In both sectors a strong trade union is supposed to be able to set nominal wages. Both unions attach importance to relative wages with respect to each other. With respect to the wage formation two possibilities are distinguished: a non-cooperative solution and a leader–follower solution, in which the tradable goods sector is leading. The latter solution implies lower wages and higher employment, and is preferred by both unions.

C. B. Mulder and F. van der Ploeg also analyse wage formation in Chapter 8 in the context of a model of a small open economy. They do not distinguish between two sectors and assume one dominant trade union which has monopoly power on the labour market and looks after the interests of both employed and unemployed workers. In choosing its wage the union is completely rational since it takes account of the investment and employment decisions of firms and of the aggregate demand side of the economy. An interesting feature of the model is that it contains various policy variables such as employers and employees social security contributions, direct and indirect taxes and investment subsidies. The reason is that the model is intended to describe the Dutch rise in unemployment. Although the model is not estimated, the authors present stylised facts on the Dutch economy for the post-war period and analyse these facts in terms of their model. The rise in unemployment is explained by two factors. First the role the government played by enlarging the wedge between producers and consumers wage rates and by increasing the level of real benefits. Second the breakdown in social contract between employers and the trade union at a time when the government lost most of its direct institutional impact on the wage setting process.

A model of a small open economy is also presented by J. Bradley in Chapter 14. His main concern is to analyse macroeconomic policies to combat unemployment, which brings us to the next topic of the conference. Bradley distinguishes between four sectors in his model: industrial, services (both marketed and non-marketed) and agricultural. This last sector is included since the model is estimated for Ireland, 1965–82. The conclusion of the analysis is that policy-makers in Ireland failed to understand the crucial relationship between fiscal activism, taxation and competitiveness. As a consequence resources shifted from the exposed industrial sector to the non-marketed sectors and left the economy less responsive to any improvement in world conditions than it might otherwise have been.

In Chapter 15 Laurence Bloch analyses the effects of a uniform decrease of the per capita real gross wage. The effects are estimated by means of a simulation study with the official French DMS-model. The exercise reveals that for the firms all effects would be favourable, while a uniform decrease of the real gross wage per capita would be unfavourable for the households. Exports would rise, so would GDP after the second year. Employment and unemployment effects would become positive in the second year, although unemployment would only decline with more than 1 per cent after the fifth year. Bloch, however, warns against too much optimism, since the effects are sensitive for changes in the basic assumptions of the model and the additional assumptions necessarily made in order to allow for a change in one of the endogenous variables (gross wage per capita).

Discussing macroeconomic policies Patrick Minford and John Davis argue in Chapter 12 that the 'European Disease' is crucial in understanding labour-market imbalances in Germany. The disease is characterised by high unemployment and low output growth, these being systematic rather than the consequence of some temporary phenomenon such as the downphase of the business cycle. Consequently they present a 'natural rate' explanation as an underlying determinant of unemployment with consideration given to the role of the business cycle in recent German unemployment. Their full macroeconomic model is neo-classical, including the assumption of rational expectations as well as the endogenous determination of natural rates. The authors conclude that Germany may have caught the now familiar 'British disease' – that is, the prevention of real-wage adjustment via unemployment benefits and social aid.

William Peterson, on the other hand, starts Chapter 13 with the assumption that unemployment is entirely voluntary. His paper analyses how a single classical model of the labour market should be modified to allow for the existence of a government which is compelled to finance its activities by distortionary taxes. The need for such taxes can lead to an equilibrium where unemployment is persistently above the natural rate and where a Pareto-improving policy is attainable. Such a policy requires the government to cut taxes and its existence can explain how the application of Keynesian measures to macroeconomic forecasting models may offer the policy-maker a 'free lunch'. The paper discusses how far such a policy could contribute to a reduction of unemployment in the UK.

In discussing in Chapter 11 the final topic of the conference, microeconomic policies, Marcia de Wachter and Yolanda Somers, present empirical evidence on the application of job creation policies in five European countries (Belgium, France, Germany, the Netherlands, the UK) and the USA. The authors compare the effectiveness and efficiency of these instruments as they appear from existing investigations in the different countries. It appears that of all categories of measures, the education policy is evaluated as the most successful. Marginal labour-cost subsidies do not result in an actual improvement of the labour-market position of the participants. De Wachter and Somers conclude that stimulating workers to set up private enterprises, however, gives positive results in all countries that have applied this policy.

In Chapter 10, P. N. Junankar discusses the other side of the coin by looking at the economic, social and political costs of unemployment. He argues that the total costs of unemployment seem to have risen considerably in the 1980s, especially because of the growth of youth unemployment as well as the increase in long-term unemployment. Estimates for the (static) output loss resulting from unemployment (based on Okun's law) are provided. It appears that output losses in Germany, France, Italy and the UK were significant and exceeded 10 per cent of GDP.

All in all the conference covered a broad spectrum of topics from different points of view which were not only brought forward in the papers presented but also by the discussants. For that reason we thought it worthwhile to include the contributions of the discussants too. Considering the state of the art of economic theory and the intricacies in its empirical application the reader should not be surprised that the causes and cures of unemployment in Europe may be the subject of many future conferences. Nonetheless we hope that the insights forwarded in this conference contribute to a future convergence in unemployment analysis.

## Note

1. The conference was sponsored by the European Investmentbank.

# 1 Unemployment and Female Labour Supply

Richard Blundell, John Ham and Costas Meghir*

ABSTRACT

The definition of labour-force participation in the standard labour-supply model stands in sharp contrast to that used in compiling the labour-force statistics. In the labour-supply models only those supplying positive hours of work are considered to be labour-force participants. On the other hand, participation in the labour-force statistics is often defined to include not only those supplying positive hours but also those actively searching for work. This paper is an attempt to reconcile these concepts by allowing 'unemployed' workers to enter a generalisation of the standard labour-supply model. This turns out to be a convenient way to enter demand-side factors directly into the determination of an individual's labour market position. The model is applied with some success to the working behaviour of married women in the UK Family Expenditure Survey.

## 1.1 INTRODUCTION

In the basic empirical model of female labour supply (see Heckman (1974), Hausman (1981), Layard, Barton and Zabalza (1980) for example) any woman reporting zero hours of work is assumed not to want to work at the going market wage. Labour-supply parameters are estimated from a likelihood function where the probability of an individual recording zero hours is equivalent to the probability of her not having positive desired hours of work. All non-participants in this 'Tobit' model are assumed not to want to work.

* A previous version of this paper appeared in the *Economic Journal.* We thank the editors for allowing us to reproduce this paper. We should like to thank George Jakubson, Ian Walker and a referee for helpful comments. Javad Emami provided excellent research assistance. Finance for this research was provided by the ESRC and the Leverhulme Trust. All errors remain our responsibility.

The assumptions of the Tobit model stand in sharp contrast to those made in calculating the labour-force statistics. In particular, those reporting zero hours of work but seeking work are considered to be labour-market participants, and a measure of the unemployment rate is often formed from data on such individuals. Our purpose in this paper is to modify the standard model of female labour-supply to allow for unemployed workers who want to work at their perceived market wage but cannot find a job.

We believe this extension to the standard labour-supply model is important for two reasons. First, it provides a more realistic model of the labour market. Second, in the presence of unemployed workers, the standard Tobit model produces inconsistent estimates of labour-supply parameters, since these individuals are mis-classified as non-participants. Thus our work is a natural complement and extension of previous work on unemployment and labour supply, which has focused on prime aged males (e.g. Ham (1982, 1986)) or utilised aggregate data (e.g. Ashenfelter (1980)).

In any labour supply study, assumptions concerning functional form and the distribution of unobservables play a critical role. In this chapter, we are careful to specify a general functional form for preferences and to employ diagnostic tests for distributional assumptions. We do this to minimise the possibility that differences between our model and the standard model represent misspecification in the standard model unrelated to unemployment.

We should note that the fixed cost literature developed by Cogan (1981) and Hausman (1980) provides an alternative mechanism for relaxing the Tobit model. Thus both the model presented here and the fixed cost model provide an explanation for the results reported in Mroz (1987), who finds that the Tobit model is rejected in favour of a model with an unrestricted specification for the participation decision.[1] In principle, fixed costs can be incorporated into the unemployment model estimated in this chapter. This would provide an extremely useful extension for future work. However, combining fixed costs and unemployment in one model is a difficult task, and here we concentrate solely on the unemployment issue.

Allowing for unemployment provides a natural mechanism for the introduction of demand side variables which vary across time and regions.[2] Moreover, the use of such demand side variables generates a fairly direct link between observables and the economic model; this link appears much closer than that between the theory and the variables that we usually have to proxy fixed costs. Finally, the introduction of unemployment into our labour-supply model offers the potential to increase considerably the stability of our estimates across different years of data, since the demand variables provide a natural means of controlling for a changing economic environment.

Our application is to a sample of women in the UK Family Expenditure Survey. This survey has the distinct advantage of allowing regional and time variation in the date of interview. It has also been subjected to a number of favourable reliability checks (Atkinson, Micklewright and Stern (1982)).

The paper proceeds as follows. In section 2 we review the standard Tobit model of labour supply and participation. In section 3 we generalise the Tobit model to allow for unemployment. Section 4 contains our empirical results. We find that the Tobit model is decisively rejected by the data. In section 5 we conclude the paper and discuss topics for further research.

## 1.2 THE STANDARD LABOUR SUPPLY MODEL

In this subsection we briefly review the standard labour supply model where an individual, $i$, is assumed to be able to work as many hours as is desired at her market wage $w_i$. Given other income $y_i$, demographic characteristics $d_i$ and unobservable characteristics $u_i$, desired hours of work are described by some function

$$h_i = g(w_i, y_i, d_i; \beta) + u_i \tag{2.1}$$

derived from the first order conditions for utility maximisation. In (2.1) $\beta$ represents the vector of unknown preference parameters and $u_i$ represents unobservable taste variation.

In this model anyone with positive desired labour supply works. It is important for the analysis that follows to note that conditional on the wage there are no 'demand side' variables entering the hours or participation decision. Hence the probability of observing zero hours of work is

$$\begin{aligned} Pr[h_i \leqslant 0] &= 1 - Pr[h_i \geqslant 0] \\ &= 1 - F_i. \end{aligned} \tag{2.1a}$$

In order to define (2.1) and (2.1a), one needs to choose an explicit form for $h_i$ and a distribution for $u_i$. It is quite common (see Heckman, 1974 and Hausman, 1979, for example) to adopt the following normal linear specification

$$h_i = \beta_1' \cdot x_i + \beta_2 w_i + u_i \tag{2.2}$$

where $u_i \sim N(0, \sigma^2)$ and $x_i = (1, y_i, d_i)'$. Although convenient for estimation purposes, the linear model rules out some quite plausible types of labour supply responses (see Stern, 1986). In particular, the linear model excludes the joint occurrence of forward-sloping and backward-bending labour-supply behaviour. In our empirical work we utilise a more general specification which is consistent with life-cycle utility maximisation and which allows for considerably greater flexibility in substitution behaviour.

Given a general functional form for $g(\cdot)$ in (2.1), and making a normality assumption on $u_i$, the probability of observing a woman not working in this model is simply:

$$\begin{aligned} Pr[h \leqslant 0] &= Pr[u_i \leqslant -g(w_i, x_i; \beta)] \\ &= F(-g(w_i, x_i; \beta)/\sigma_i) \\ &= 1 - F(g(w_i, x_i; \beta)/\sigma_i) \end{aligned} \tag{2.3}$$

where $F(\cdot)$ is the cumulative normal distribution function. We show below that our choice of preference structure and the random taste interpretation of $u_i$ implies a particular form of heteroscedasticity in $\sigma_i$. In what follows below we shall simply write the probability of an individual not wanting to work as

$$Pr[h_i \leqslant 0] = 1 - F(w_i, x_i; \beta, \sigma_i) \tag{2.4}$$

where $F(\cdot)$ will depend on the particular functional form chosen for $g(\cdot)$.

When $w_i$ is known for all individuals, or when the decision to work is made on the basis of an expected wage which can be predicted perfectly, the likelihood for a random sample is described by the standard Tobit model. Identifying the workers by '+' and the non-participants by '0', the Tobit likelihood is

$$L_1 = \Pi_+ f(h_i | w_i, x_i,; \beta, \sigma_i) \cdot \Pi_0 (1 - F(w_i, x_i, \beta, \sigma_i)) \tag{2.5}$$

where $f(\ )$ is the normal density for $u_i$.

Consider, as an alternative, the case where individuals recording zero hours of work know their market wage but the analyst does not. The parameters of a wage equation are now required to specify the sample likelihood. Assume that the wage equation takes the form

$$w_i = \delta r_i + \tau_i \tag{2.6}$$

where $r_i$ represents a vector of individual characteristics, $\delta$ represents the corresponding unknown parameters and $\tau_i \sim N(0, \sigma_\tau^2)$. For simplicity we assume $\tau_i$ to be independent of $u_i$. The likelihood function is now

$$L_1^* = \Pi_+ f(h_i|w_i, x_i; \beta, \sigma_i) \cdot q(w_i|r_i; \delta, \sigma_\tau) \cdot \Pi_0(1 - F^R(x_i, r_i; \delta, \beta, \sigma_i, \sigma_\tau)) \tag{2.7}$$

where $q(\ )$ is the density of $w_i$ and $F^R(\ )$ is the cumulative distribution function of the reduced form equation for $h_i$ given $x_i$ and $r_i$. In the linear labour-supply model $F^R(\cdot)$ represents the cumulative normal distribution of $u_i + \beta_2\tau_i$, and (2.7) involves explicit restrictions between the parameters of $f(\cdot)$, $q(\cdot)$ and $F^R(\cdot)$. For the non-linear labour-supply function, such as that considered here, imposing such cross-equation restrictions is, as a practical matter, computationally infeasible. Thus in our empirical work we maximise the likelihood (2.5) using predicted wages for the non-workers from a wage equation based on (2.6).

## 1.3 UNEMPLOYED WORKERS

In section 2 we made the standard labour-supply assumption that an individual can find employment at her market wage with certainty. In this section we relax this assumption and consider the case where some individuals who want to work at their market wage do not find employment. We introduce an index function, $z_i$, which depends on a variety of macroeconomic and microeconomic factors and determines whether an individual who wishes to work is in employment. If

$$E_i = \theta z_i + v_i > 0 \tag{3.1}$$

the individual would obtain employment whereas if

$$E_i = \theta z_i + v_i \leq 0 \tag{3.1'}$$

she would not. The probability of finding employment is then simply

$$P^E(z_i; \theta) = Pr(v_i > -\theta z_i) = Pr(v_i < \theta z_i). \tag{3.2}$$

assuming $v_i$ is drawn from a symmetric distribution with mean zero.

Since the time at which individuals are interviewed varies (by year or month), elements of $z_i$ representing demand factors in the economy also will vary over time.

It is worth noting that $P^E(\cdot)$ is a reduced form equation and does not represent explicitly a lay-off rate or a rate of job arrivals. To see this, consider a simple example of an individual who leaves school at the end of period $t-2$. Assume that $\alpha$ represents the probability of receiving an acceptable job offer in a given period, that $\partial$ represents the probability of being laid off from a job in a given period and that if the individual is laid off in a period she must stay unemployed for at least that period. Then there are two ways in which this person can be employed at the end of period $t$. The first possibility occurs if she finds a job in period $t-1$ and is not laid off in period $t$. This event has probability $\alpha(1-\partial)$. The second possibility occurs if she does not find a job in period $t-1$ but does find one in period $t$. This event has probability $(1-\alpha)\alpha$. (This assumes that you cannot be laid off in the same period that you accept a job.) Then in period $t$ the probability $P^E$ equals $\alpha(1-\partial)+(1-\alpha)\alpha$ which is a combination of both the lay-off and job arrival rates.

In the presence of unemployment, two groups of individuals will record zero hours of work. The first group consists of those who do not want to work at their market wage. The second group consists of those who want to work but remain unemployed. The first event has probability $(1-F_i)$ while the second event has probability $(1-P_i^E)F_i$. The probability of an individual reporting zero hours is then given by:

$$(1-F_i)+(1-P_i^E)F_i = 1-P_i^E F_i. \tag{3.3}$$

In writing down this probability we have assumed a normal distribution for $v_i$ and $u_i$ and independence between their distributions. However, in our empirical application we test this assumption as well as other assumptions that affect the consistency of our results. The likelihood for a random sample is the following generalisation of the Tobit model:

$$L_2 = \Pi_+ P_i^E f_i \cdot \Pi_0(1-P_i^E F_i). \tag{3.4}$$

This model relates directly to Cragg's double-hurdle model (Cragg, 1971) and has been considered by Atkinson, Gomulka and Stern (1984) and by Deaton and Irish (1984) in the context of modelling individual household-commodity expenditures.

When $L_2$ is the correct model specification, the standard Tobit model $L_1$ attributes the wrong probability to unemployed and working women. This will generate inconsistent labour-supply parameters. Moreover, by modelling $P_i^E$ it is possible to introduce aggregate and local demand factors directly into the labour-market model. The impact of these factors over time and regions provides us with potentially useful information on the degree to which zero hours of work reflect unemployment as opposed to desired non-participation. It is interesting to note that, under independence of $v_i$ and $u_i$, the truncated model (Blundell and Walker, 1986; Meghir, 1985; and Blundell and Meghir, 1986), which considers positive hours of work only, provides consistent estimates of the labour supply parameters whether $L_1$ or $L_2$ is the appropriate likelihood for the full sample.

It is useful to contrast the probability defined in (3.3) with that in a standard probit equation for participation, and in particular the influence of demand variables in the respective probabilities. The probit equation implicit in (3.4) takes the form

$$L_p = \Pi_+ P_i^E F_i \Pi_0 (1 - P_i^E F_i) = \Pi_+ P_i^* \Pi_0 (1 - P_i^*), \tag{3.5}$$

where $P_i^* - P_i^E F_i = Pr[h_i > 0]$. Demand variables will affect $P_i^*$ directly through $P_i^E$ and indirectly through their effect on the wage rate. For example, a negative demand shock may reduce market wages and decrease the probability that a woman has positive desired hours. Second, it will reduce the probability that she finds a job. Thus dropping the subscript $i$, we know that

$$\frac{\partial P^*}{\partial x_k} = \frac{\partial F}{\partial w} \cdot \frac{\partial w}{\partial x_k} \cdot P^E + \frac{\partial P^E}{\partial x_k} \cdot F \tag{3.6}$$

where $x_k$ is a demand variable that influences labour supply only through the wage. A standard probit equation on participation which includes demand variables captures *both* effects in (3.6) and does not allow one to separate these effects. Equations (3.4) and (3.5), because they incorporate labour-supply behaviour conditional on market wages, allow one to estimate the two effects separately in (3.6). Thus use of (3.4) allows one to assess the impact of demand variables on the probability of working, above and beyond that due to changing wages. Further, the presence of significant demand effects in $P^E(\cdot)$ is not compatible (at least to a first approximation) with using a fixed-cost model to relax the Tobit specification since demand variables should enter $P^*$ in a fixed costs model only through the wage effect on labour supply.

## 1.4 EMPIRICAL RESULTS

The empirical results presented here refer to a sample of 2011 married women from the 1981 UK Family Expenditure Survey. Precise details of the sample selection and information on each of the variables used are provided in the Data Appendix. The sample split is 1076 recording positive hours and 935 recording zero hours.

As noted above we believe that it is crucial to provide a general specification of preferences. Otherwise, one faces the problem that allowing for unemployment 'makes a difference' simply because the assumed hours equation is too restrictive. The overall specification of the hours-of-work equation is taken from Blundell and Meghir (1986). That study was concerned only with individuals currently in work and used the truncated model. The labour supply model is a generalisation of the Linear Expenditure System that possesses a number of desirable features. In particular, it allows for quite general substitution effects and demographic interactions. The specification is derived from the following indirect utility function defined over wages ($w$), prices ($p$), other income ($y$) and is conditional on several demographic (and taste shifter) variables ($d$)

$$V(w, p, y; d) = \frac{y + a(w, p; d)}{b(w, p; d)} \tag{4.1}$$

Wage rates for participants refer to marginal rates after accounting for the impact of the tax and benefit system using the procedure described in Blundell, Meghir, Symons and Walker (1986). Wage rates for nonparticipants are derived from the wage equation presented in Appendix A.[3] The other income variable $y$ is defined as the difference between expenditures and net earnings to ensure the life-cycle consistency of the estimated labour-supply model (see Blundell and Walker (1986)). This variable may be negative or positive although $y + a(\cdot)$ is strictly positive for all individuals in our estimated model. Choosing the form for $a(w, p; d)$ to be

$$a(w, p; d) = a_{ff}(d)w - 2\alpha_{fc}(d)w^{1/2}p^{1/2} - \alpha_{cc}(d)p \tag{4.2}$$

and by writing

$$\ln b(w, p; d) = \beta_f(d) \ln w + (1 - \beta_f(d)) \ln p \tag{4.3}$$

we ensure the zero homogeneity of $V(\cdot)$ in $w$, $p$ and $y$. As economic theory tells us very little about the way demographic characteristics affect preferences over paid work and consumption, we shall allow the parameters of $V(\cdot)$ to depend fairly generally on the demographic variable $d$.

Using Roy's Identity, the corresponding hours of work equation takes the form:

$$h = \alpha_{ff}(d) - \alpha_{fc}(d) p^{1/2}/w^{1/2} - \beta_f(d)(y + a(w, p; d))/w. \tag{4.4}$$

The specifications of $a(w, p; d)$ and $b(w, p; d)$ in (4.2) and (4.3) ensure a wide variety of shapes for this function. For example, when $\alpha_{fc}$ is zero, preferences are represented by the popular Stone-Geary utility function and generate a linear earnings function corresponding to the Linear Expenditure System. The Stone-Geary model provides a useful illustration of the restrictiveness of simple models of labour supply since the sign of the wage coefficient (somewhat crucial in policy analysis) is determined by the signs of $(y - \alpha_{cc} p)$ and $\beta_f$. If leisure is a normal good, $\beta_f$ is positive, the labour-supply curve is forward sloping everywhere for $y > \alpha_{cc} p$ and backward bending everywhere for $y < \alpha_{cc} p$. Our more general specification allows for both forward and backward bending labour supply to coexist independently of $y$. The flexibility of our general form is probably best illustrated through the wage derivative

$$\partial h/\partial w = \tfrac{1}{2}\alpha_{fc}(1 - 2\beta_f) p^{1/2}/w^{3/2} + \beta_f (y - \alpha_{cc} p)/w^2. \tag{4.5}$$

In the additive Linear Expenditure System specification, the wage derivative consists only of the second term.

In order to allow a random preference interpretation to the stochastic specification of the labour supply model derived in the previous section, we introduce random variation in the $\beta_f$ parameter. This parameter represents the marginal budget share of non-market time or the marginal value of time. We assume that a normal distribution approximates unobservable taste variation; this assumption is tested below. In modelling unobservable random preference errors, we cannot simply add a homoscedastic error to (4.4), since the model will no longer integrate back to the underlying indirect utility function. After suitable rearrangement, our labour supply function for individual $i$ corresponding to (2.1) with random unobservable taste errors may be written

$$h_i = \alpha_{ff}(d_i) - \alpha_{fc}(d_i)p^{1/2}/w_i^{1/2} - (\beta_f(d_i) - \mu_i)(y_i + a(w_i, p_i, d_i))/w_i \tag{4.6}$$

where $\mu_i \sim N(O, \sigma^2)$. Hence $u_i$ in (2.1) takes the form $\mu_i(y_i + a(\cdot))/w_i$.

It is important to subject the distributional assumptions on $\mu_i$ (the labour-supply disturbance) and $v_i$ (the disturbance on the employment equation) to diagnostic testing. Following Bera, Jarque and Lee (1984) and Blundell and Meghir (1986), we use the Pearson family to derive score tests against skewness and kurtosis. These are equivalent to the score tests using generalised residuals developed in Chesher and Irish (1987) and Gourieroux, Monfort, Renault and Trognon (1987). A similar score test based on generalised residuals is used to test independence between $u_i$ and $v_i$.[4]

As described above demographic characteristics are allowed to enter through both the $\alpha$ and $\beta$ parameters. That is, we specify

$$\alpha_{ff}(d) = \alpha_{ff}^0 + n_1\alpha_{ff}^1 + D_2\alpha_{ff}^2 + D_3\alpha_{ff}^3$$

$$\alpha_{fc}(d) = \alpha_{ff}^0 + n_1\alpha_{fc}^1 + \sqrt{(n_2D_2)}\alpha_{fc}^2 + \sqrt{(n_3D_3)}\alpha_{fc}^3$$

$$\alpha_{cc}(d) = \alpha_{cc}^0 + n_1\alpha_{cc}^1 + n_2\alpha_{cc}^2 + n_3\alpha_{cc}^3$$

$$\beta_f(d) = \beta_f^0 + \beta_f^1 D_1 + \beta_f^2 D_2 + \beta_f^3 D_3 + \beta_f^A AGE + \beta_f^{AA} AGE^2 + \beta_f^{ed}\, education$$

where

$n_1$ = number of children with $0 < \text{age} \leq 2$

$n_2$ = number of children with $3 \leq \text{age} \leq 10$

$n_3$ = number of children with $11 \leq \text{age} \leq 18$

and where $D_i$ are conditional dummies such that

$D_1 = 1$ if $n_1 > 0$, zero otherwise

$D_2 = 1$ if $n_2 > 0$ and $n_1 = 0$, zero otherwise

$D_3 = 1$ if $n_3 > 0$ and $n_1 = n_2 = 0$, zero otherwise.

As described in the data appendix, age is the female age while education is her age at the end of schooling. The conditional dummies $D_1$, $D_2$ and $D_3$ are used in some parts of the specification rather than the actual number of children to account for the importance of the age of the youngest child in the time requirement of children.

Given the specification of the hours equation, we can turn to the estimation of the standard Tobit model $L_1$ described in section 2. This model does not allow for the possibility of unemployment and therefore does not require a specification for the employment probability index function $P^E(\cdot)$. Model $L_1$ is simply based on the desired hours equation of (4.6) and the reservation wage condition. The wage equation is provided in Appendix A and the model estimates are presented in Table 1.1.

*Table* 1.1 Parameter estimates* and diagnostics for the Tobit model $L_1$

| | | | | | |
|---|---|---|---|---|---|
| $\alpha^0_{ff}$ | 38.466 | (2.878) | $\beta^{AA}_f \times 100$ | 0.046 | (0.008) |
| $\alpha^1_{ff}$ | 11.296 | (13.978) | $\beta^1_f$ | 0.544 | (0.079) |
| $\alpha^2_{ff}$ | −4.929 | (4.677) | $\beta^2_f$ | 0.219 | (0.044) |
| $\alpha^3_{ff}$ | −1.147 | (3.997) | $\beta^3_f$ | 0.086 | (0.043) |
| $\alpha^0_{fc}$ | −8.909 | (3.403) | $\beta^{ed}_f$ | −0.014 | (0.004) |
| $\alpha^1_{fc}$ | 1.037 | (11.821) | $\beta^{servs}_f$ | 0.093 | (0.018) |
| $\alpha^2_{fc}$ | −6.803 | (3.345) | $\beta^{manu}_f$ | −0.025 | (0.017) |
| $\alpha^3_{fc}$ | −2.720 | (2.249) | $\sigma$ | 0.274 | (0.012) |
| $\alpha^0_{cc}$ | 31.065 | (3.134) | Log *L* | −5201.68 | |
| $\alpha^1_{cc}$ | −6.383 | (10.218) | Skewness (1)† | 85.345 | |
| $\alpha^2_{cc}$ | 2.199 | (2.170) | Kurtosis (1) | 2.547 | |
| $\alpha^3_{cc}$ | 10.017 | (1.242) | | | |
| $\beta^0_f$ | 0.338 | (0.0318) | | | |
| $\beta^A_f \times 10$ | 0.054 | (0.0085) | | | |

* Standard errors in parentheses throughout the following Tables.
† Under the null hypothesis all test statistics are distributed as $\chi^2$ with degrees of freedom as indicated in parentheses.

On the whole the $\alpha$ and $\beta$ estimates appear quite plausible. The $\beta_f$ parameters are generally well determined and show an expected (albeit quite large) increase in the value of female time with age and young children. However, turning to the diagnostic tests we see that normality is very strongly rejected through the skewness test. From the results in Blundell and Meghir (1986), it is interesting to note that skewness often picks up general model misspecification. To provide an insight into which directions this standard labour supply model may be misleading we turn next to the general 'unemployment' specification based on (3.4).

The labour supply estimates in Table 1.2(a) refer to this more general unemployment or 'double-hurdle' model and stand in contrast to the simple Tobit model estimates. The estimates of the parameters of the employment probability index function $P^E(\cdot)$ are provided in Table 1.2(b). In specifying the arguments of this probability function we have tried to allow for both individual and demand side characteristics. Precise definitions of the variables are given in the Data Appendix.

Turning first to the parameters of this probability index in Table 1.2(b), we find a strong impact of the demand side characteristics directly related to the female both through the age specific unemployment rate, the industry specific unemployment rate and the industry specific vacancy rate. Among those non-participants that record an industry (the majority of these also report that they are actively seeking work) the vacancy rate is on average 20 per cent lower and the redundancy rate is 50 per cent higher than that for participants. Interestingly, there is also a significant direct effect of young children (D1 and D2) possibly reflecting the importance of fixed costs associ-

*Table* 1.2(a) Labour supply estimates and diagnostics for model $L_2$

| | | | | | |
|---|---|---|---|---|---|
| $\alpha^0_{ff}$ | 29.328 | (2.104) | $\beta^{AA}_f \times 100$ | 0.013 | (0.005) |
| $\alpha^1_{ff}$ | −20.112 | (7.495) | $\beta^1_f$ | 0.256 | (0.067) |
| $\alpha^2_{ff}$ | −15.441 | (3.327) | $\beta^2_f$ | 0.095 | (0.032) |
| $\alpha^3_{ff}$ | −2.838 | (3.591) | $\beta^3_f$ | 0.079 | (0.033) |
| $\alpha^0_{fc}$ | −16.242 | (2.796) | $\beta^{ed}_f$ | −0.007 | (0.003) |
| $\alpha^1_{fc}$ | −27.527 | (7.606) | $\beta^{servs}_f$ | 0.082 | (0.011) |
| $\alpha^2_{fc}$ | −16.591 | (2.979) | $\beta^{manu}_f$ | 0.059 | (0.011) |
| $\alpha^3_{fc}$ | −6.342 | (2.703) | $\sigma$ | 0.156 | (0.008) |
| $\alpha^0_{cc}$ | 29.206 | (2.308) | Log $L$ | | −4835.760 |
| $\alpha^1_{cc}$ | 26.630 | (8.056) | Skewness (1) | | 5.267 |
| $\alpha^2_{cc}$ | 4.520 | (2.297) | Kurtosis (1) | | 9.192 |
| $\alpha^3_{cc}$ | 11.968 | (1.552) | | | |
| $\beta^0_f$ | 0.161 | (0.022) | Independence (1) | | 20.896 |
| $\beta^A_f \times 10$ | 0.025 | (0.006) | | | |

*Table* 1.2(b) Estimated parameters of the employment probability index for model $L_2$

| | | |
|---|---|---|
| Intercept | 3.3372 | (0.8467) |
| Education | −0.0249 | (0.0291) |
| Age | −0.0319 | (0.0068) |
| Regional unemployment | −0.0132 | (0.0249) |
| Unemployment by age | −0.0675 | (0.0197) |
| Unemployment by industry | −0.3218 | (0.0206) |
| Vacancy by region | −0.0591 | (0.1162) |
| Redundancy by region | −0.0030 | (0.0284) |
| Vacancy by industry | 0.9149 | (0.0722) |
| Redundancy by industry | 0.0055 | (0.0031) |
| D1 | −1.5060 | (0.1495) |
| D2 | −0.5869 | (0.1162) |
| London | 0.2241 | (0.2450) |
| Other south | 0.1050 | (0.1673) |
| Manual worker | −0.5466 | (0.1467) |
| Services industry | −5.2387 | (0.3856) |
| Unemployment by industry (male) | 0.0217 | (0.0090) |
| Manual worker (male) | −0.0932 | (0.1099) |
| Services industry (male) | 0.1461 | (0.1240) |
| Skewness (1) 41.086 | | |
| Kurtosis (1) 14.479 | | |

ated with child care (not observed in our data) or alternatively the impact of recently having been out of the labour market. Both age and the industry and occupation specific dummies are significant.[5] The range of $P^E(\cdot)$ for non-working women in the sample is 0.031–0.993 with a mean and standard deviation of 0.313 and 0.236 respectively while for workers the corresponding figures are 0.003–0.999, 0.822 and 0.254 respectively. The standard 'Tobit' labour supply model assumes that this probability is identically unity for all individuals and on the basis of a likelihood ratio test $(-2\log(L_1/L_2)=732.26)$ the Tobit model is strongly rejected. In Table 1.2(c), a classification of individuals according to whether their predicted probability is higher as a non-participant or participant points also to a superior performance from the double-hurdle model. In this classification an individual is predicted to work if $P_i^*$ from (3.5) exceeds 0.5. For the Tobit model this reduces to $F_i$ exceeding 0.5.

The impact of introducing this employment probability function on the determination of hours of work and desired participation is quite dramatic. Many of the labour-supply parameters in Table 1.2(a) have changed significantly from those reported for the Tobit model in Table

*Table* 1.2(c) Predictive performance

| | (*actual*) | |
|---|---|---|
| (*predicted*) | *non-workers* | *workers* |
| (i) *Tobit* | | |
| non-workers | 601 | 210 |
| workers | 335 | 866 |
| (ii) *Double-hurdle* | | |
| non-workers | 822 | 203 |
| workers | 114 | 873 |

1.1. The additivity assumption behind the LES preference specification (measured by non-zero $\alpha_{fc}$ terms) is now much more strongly rejected. Moreover, the impact of young children, although still very important on participation through a combination of effects on $F_i$ and $P_i^E$, has reduced its impact through the $\beta_f^1$ term from the rather large figure in Table 1.1. The diagnostic tests now appear more reasonable – the skewness test statistic has fallen dramatically. The independence test on the stochastic processes determining the two hurdles is quite large and would suggest reestimation under dependence.

Estimates for the double-hurdle under dependence are presented in Appendix B and display broadly similar properties to those in Table 1.2. The likelihood ratio test and the Wald test for a zero correlation ($\tau = 0$) between the stochastic terms in the two hurdles take the values 20.14 and 22.79 respectively. As in the case of the score test this implies a rejection of independence. If the two latent variables underlying the double-hurdle model were both continuously observed then a non-zero correlation would only affect the efficiency of the estimates. However, in this model with the two hurdles jointly determining the observability of working hours, consistency will be affected. Despite this, it is apparent from Appendix B that the labour-supply parameters are affected only marginally although their standard errors are often slightly larger. The significant parameters of the employment probability index remain of the same sign and display a similar pattern to those reported in Table 1.2(b).[6]

In Table 1.3 we present a description of the distribution of the wage elasticities (for non-market time) over the whole sample in the estimated Tobit and double-hurdle models from Tables 1.1 and 1.2(a). Participants are evaluated at their actual labour supply hours by including the estimated random preference error in the marginal value

*Table* 1.3 Wage elasticities (non-market time)*

| | *Participants* | | *Non-participants* | |
|---|---|---|---|---|
| | *Tobit* | *Double-hurdle* | *Tobit* | *Double-hurdle* |
| Mean | 0.040 | 0.087 | −0.207 | −0.095 |
| Standard Deviation | 0.147 | 0.125 | 0.116 | 0.123 |
| Minimum | −1.299 | −1.937 | −0.671 | −0.593 |
| $M_{25}$ | −0.045 | 0.013 | −0.270 | −0.151 |
| $M_{50}$ | 0.040 | 0.096 | −0.189 | −0.095 |
| $M_{75}$ | 0.122 | 0.155 | −0.128 | −0.038 |
| Maximum | 1.254 | 0.541 | 0.180 | 1.460 |
| Proportion positive | 0.610 | 0.784 | 0.010 | 0.153 |

* $M_i$ is the $i$th percentile.

of time $\beta_f$. For non-participants a random preference error is drawn from the appropriately truncated normal distribution. Despite the fact that we use the same flexible preference structure in each case, the double-hurdle model displays considerably more backward bending behaviour, denoted by a positive elasticity in Table 1.3. These results could have important implications for policy analysis in general and in particular for the analysis of the incentive effects of reforms to the tax and benefit system. These differences occur because the Tobit model forces the reservation wage to exceed the market wage for all non-participants and misallocates the observations on non-participants.

We also can contrast the Tobit and double-hurdle models through the effect that demand side variables have on actual employment. While the Tobit model accounts for demand side effects only via their influence on the wage rate, in the double-hurdle model these variables also have a direct impact through the first hurdle employment probability index $P^E$. The effects may counteract or reinforce each other, and thus it is of some interest to explicitly consider the two effects and analyse their relative size and magnitude. Noting that $\log(Pr[h>0]) = \log(P^E(\cdot)) + \log(F(\cdot))$ the elasticity of the positive hours probability with respect to some demand side variable $z_k$ can be conveniently decomposed as

$$\frac{\partial \log Pr(h>0)}{\partial \log z_k} = \frac{\partial \log F}{\partial \log w}\frac{\partial \log w}{\partial \log z_k} + \frac{\partial \log P^E}{\partial \log z_k} \tag{4.7}$$

where the first term on the right-hand side is the elasticity of participation while the second term is the elasticity of the employment probability index. The Tobit model sets this second term to zero. Rewriting the labour-supply model (2.1) as

$$h_i = g(w_i, y_i, d_i; \beta) + \mu_i(y_i + a(\cdot))/w_i \tag{4.8}$$

allows the desired participation probability to be expressed as

$$F(\cdot) = Pr[\mu_i < w_i g(w_i, y_i, d_i; \beta)/(y + a(\cdot))]. \tag{4.9}$$

Consequently, the derivative of this participation probability is given by

$$\partial F(\cdot)/\partial w_i = \varphi(\cdot)[w_i \partial g(\cdot)/\partial w_i + g(\cdot) \tag{4.10}$$

$$- w_i g(\cdot)(y_i + a(\cdot))^{-1}(\partial a(\cdot)/\partial w_i)](y_i - a(\cdot))^{-1}$$

here $\varphi(\cdot)$ is the standard normal density function evaluated at the same point as $F(\cdot)$ and $\delta g(\cdot)/\delta w_i$ is defined by the labour supply derivative (4.5). From (4.10) it is clear that the sign of the first term on the right-hand side of (4.7) is not necessarily positive for those with positive desired hours, giving rise to the possibility that the wage derivative of the participation probability is negative for some workers.[7]

In Tables 1.4(a) and 1.4(b) we present a description of the distribution of these elasticities over all participants and non-participants in our sample for two important demand-side variables: female unemployment by age and female unemployment by industry. The effect of the demand-side variables on the wage rate were obtained by a regression of the (gross) wage rate which controls only for the variables appearing in the employment probability index $P^E$. The column 'participation' refers to the first term on the right-hand side of (4.7), the column $P^E$ refers to the second term on the right-hand side and the column 'Total' to the left-hand side of (4.7). In the double-hurdle model most of the impact of the demand-side variables comes through their direct effect on the first hurdle probability $P^E$. The indirect effect which works through the wage rate is quite small. In contrast the Tobit model sets the direct effect to zero and forces the demand variables to work entirely through the wage rate. For this reason the Tobit model gives a misleading picture of both the channels through which demand-side variables affect the number of people in employment and the magnitude of these effects. The double-hurdle model allows us both to obtain a more accurate picture of the *total* effect of a change of a macro variable on the expected numbers of people in work as well as to decompose the effect into a direct one via the employment probability index and an indirect one via the wage in the labour-supply function.

*Table* 1.4 Employment elasticities with respect to demand side variables

| | Participation | $P^E$ | Total |
|---|---|---|---|
| **(a) Female unemployment by age** | | | |
| **(i) Participants** | | | |
| *Double-hurdle* | | | |
| Mean | −0.003 | −0.148 | −0.151 |
| Standard deviation | 0.039 | 0.247 | 0.252 |
| $M_{25}$ | −0.001 | −0.172 | −0.175 |
| $M_{50}$ | 0.000 | −0.047 | −0.049 |
| $M_{75}$ | 0.000 | −0.014 | −0.016 |
| *Tobit* | | | |
| Mean | −0.009 | 0 | −0.009 |
| Standard deviation | 0.041 | 0 | 0.041 |
| $M_{25}$ | −0.010 | 0 | −0.010 |
| $M_{50}$ | −0.001 | 0 | −0.001 |
| $M_{75}$ | 0.000 | 0 | 0.000 |
| **(ii) Non-participants** | | | |
| *Double-hurdle* | | | |
| Mean | −0.003 | −0.680 | −0.683 |
| Standard deviation | 0.007 | 0.508 | 0.508 |
| $M_{25}$ | −0.004 | −0.951 | −0.951 |
| $M_{50}$ | −0.001 | −0.525 | −0.530 |
| $M_{75}$ | 0.000 | −0.291 | −0.293 |
| *Tobit* | | | |
| Mean | −0.037 | 0 | −0.037 |
| Standard deviation | 0.041 | 0 | 0.041 |
| $M_{25}$ | −0.052 | 0 | −0.052 |
| $M_{50}$ | −0.021 | 0 | −0.021 |
| $M_{75}$ | −0.008 | 0 | −0.008 |

(*Continued*)

Table 1.4 (*continued*)

(*b*) *Female unemployment by industry*

(*i*) *Participants*

| | *Participation* | $P^E$ | *Total* |
|---|---|---|---|
| *Double-hurdle* | | | |
| Mean | −0.005 | −0.985 | −0.990 |
| Standard deviation | 0.071 | 2.084 | 2.087 |
| $M_{25}$ | −0.003 | −1.048 | −1.048 |
| $M_{50}$ | 0.000 | −0.220 | −0.227 |
| $M_{75}$ | 0.000 | −0.072 | −0.075 |
| *Tobit* | | | |
| Mean | −0.016 | 0 | −0.016 |
| Standard deviation | 0.074 | 0 | 0.074 |
| $M_{25}$ | −0.018 | 0 | −0.018 |
| $M_{50}$ | −0.001 | 0 | −0.001 |
| $M_{75}$ | 0.000 | 0 | 0.000 |

(*ii*) *Non-participants*

| | | | |
|---|---|---|---|
| *Double-hurdle* | | | |
| Mean | −0.007 | −3.846 | −3.853 |
| Standard deviation | 0.014 | 1.633 | 1.632 |
| $M_{25}$ | −0.010 | −5.227 | −5.237 |
| $M_{50}$ | −0.003 | −3.654 | −3.671 |
| $M_{75}$ | 0.0 | −2.942 | −2.951 |
| *Tobit* | | | |
| Mean | −0.068 | 0 | −0.068 |
| Standard deviation | 0.062 | 0 | 0.062 |
| $M_{25}$ | −0.100 | 0 | −0.100 |
| $M_{50}$ | −0.050 | 0 | −0.050 |
| $M_{75}$ | −0.022 | 0 | −0.022 |

## CONCLUSIONS

In this chapter we have discussed ways of extending the standard model of labour-supply and participation. In particular we introduced the possibility that zero hours of work represent unemployment and not simply non-participation. This was achieved by modelling the probability that a particular individual obtains a job at his/her perceived market wage. The resulting double-hurdle model offers a framework for studying the effects of macroeconomic variables on labour-force participation. Moreover the model nests the traditional

Tobit model and hence the hypothesis underlying the basic labour-supply model can easily be tested using the likelihood ratio test.

We applied our proposed methodology to a sample of married women drawn from the UK Family Expenditure Survey of 1981. We found that demand variables have an important impact in the $P^E$ function, which in turn plays a role in determining the probability of working. Moreover, the Tobit model was strongly rejected using a likelihood ratio test and the non-normality diagnostics for the labour-supply model improved considerably when this model is generalised.

Although the double-hurdle model presented here seems to offer an improved framework over the Tobit model for analysing both participation and hours of work, there is room for improvement in future research. First, the model would benefit from qualitatively better information relating to demand side constraints. This is suggested by the relatively large normality statistic reported in Table 1.2(b) that points to some remaining misspecification. Second, in future, it would be fruitful to exploit the information separating the non-workers into job seekers and non-seekers and explicitly accounting for discouraged workers. Third, our approach may offer a useful framework for analysing the stability of the parameter estimates from several years of FES data. Finally, we could investigate the challenging problem of incorporating fixed costs and unemployment in a single model.

## Appendix A: The Wage Equation

Dependent variable: Log (gross wage rate in tenth of pence/hour)

| *Variable* | *Parameter* | *Standard error* |
|---|---|---|
| 1. Intercept | 5.271 | .903 |
| 2. Children (0–2) | −.182 | .132 |
| 3. Children (3–4) | −.101 | .077 |
| 4. Children (5–10) | −.069 | .026 |
| 5. Children (11+) | −.036 | .019 |
| 6. Regional unemployment[1] | .052 | .030 |
| 7. London | .569 | .217 |
| 8. South East | .485 | .241 |
| 9. Yorkshire | .260 | .122 |
| 10. East Midlands | .360 | .192 |
| 11. East Anglia | .407 | .240 |
| 12. South West | .340 | .180 |
| 13. Wales | .008 | .052 |

*(Continued)*

**Appendix A** (*continued*)

| *Variable* | *Parameter* | *Standard error* |
|---|---|---|
| 14. West Midlands | .184 | .086 |
| 15. North West | .063 | .061 |
| 16. Tenure dummy 1[2] | −.024 | .023 |
| 17. Tenure dummy 2 | −.019 | .043 |
| 18. Male Occupation dummy 1[3] | −.045 | .036 |
| 19. Male occupation dummy 2 | −.083 | .028 |
| 20. Male occupation dummy 3 | −.061 | .032 |
| 21. Male age | .026 | .012 |
| 22. Male age squared | −.00028 | .0001 |
| 23. Male education | .00074 | .0262 |
| 24. Male education squared | −.00023 | .0008 |
| 25. Female education | −.087 | .032 |
| 26. Female education squared | −.002 | .001 |
| 27. Female age | −.043 | .019 |
| 28. Female age squared | .00016 | .0002 |
| 29. Conditional child dummy 1[4] | .064 | .151 |
| 30. Conditional child dummy 2 | −.109 | .099 |
| 31. Conditional child dummy 3 | −.037 | .049 |
| 32. Conditional child dummy 4 | −.086 | .042 |
| 33. Male industry dummy 1[5] | .0503 | .0307 |
| 34. Male industry dummy 2 | .0119 | .068 |
| 35. Male industry dummy 3 | .0396 | .031 |
| 36. Male industry dummy 4 | .016 | .032 |
| 37. Female industry dummy 1[6] | .069 | .075 |
| 38. Female industry dummy 2 | −.072 | .085 |
| 39. Female industry dummy 3 | −.036 | .053 |
| 40. Female industry dummy 4 | −.484 | .079 |
| 41. Female occupation dummy 1[7] | −.333 | .032 |
| 42. Female occupation dummy 2 | −.398 | .052 |
| 43. Female occupation dummy 3 | −.514 | .034 |
| 44. January | .045 | .090 |
| 45. February | −.023 | .086 |
| 46. March | .046 | .079 |
| 47. April | −.025 | .075 |
| 48. May | −.019 | .067 |
| 49. June | −.039 | .056 |
| 50. July | −.075 | .048 |
| 51. August | −.091 | .041 |
| 52. September | −.063 | .040 |
| 53. October | −.013 | .042 |
| 54. Female unemployment by age | −.011 | .008 |
| 55. Female unemployment by industry | −.015 | .005 |
| 56. Vacancy (region) | .162 | .073 |
| 57. Redundancy (region) | .026 | .014 |

**Appendix A** (*continued*)

| *Variable* | *Parameter* | *Standard error* |
|---|---|---|
| 58. Vacancy (industry/female) | .052 | .013 |
| 59. Redundancy (industry/female) | −.001 | .001 |
| 60. Male unemployment (age) | −.006 | .004 |
| 61. Female age *x* education | .002 | .001 |

*Definitions*:

| | |
|---|---|
| Vacancy (redundancy) by region: | Proportion of vacancies (redundancies) to regional population per/1000. |
| Vacancy (redundancy) by industry:[8] | Proportion of vacancies (redundancies) to the employee in Industry per/1000. |
| Source for population: | *Annual Abstract of Statistics* (1984). |
| Source for vacancies and redundancies: | *Employment Gazette* (1983) |

*Notes*:

1. Male unemployment by region and month.
2. Tenure dummy 1: council rented accommodation.
   Tenure dummy 2: other rented accommodation.
3. Occupation dummy 1: clerical workers and shop assistants.
   Occupation dummy 2: skilled manual worker.
   Occupation dummy 3: semi-skilled and unskilled manual worker.
4. Conditional child dummies constructed as described in the text for the four age groups.
5. Male industry dummies:
   1. FES (1981) industry codes 3–12.
   2. FES (1981) industry codes 13–15.
   3. FES (1981) industry codes 16–23.
   4. FES (1981) industry codes 24–28.
6. Female industry dummies as in 5.
7. Female occupation dummies as in 3.
8. For those non-workers where industry was not recorded the weighted average figure was used.

**Appendix B**

(a) Labor supply estimates and diagnostics for model $L_2$ with dependence

| | | | | | |
|---|---|---|---|---|---|
| $\alpha_{ff}^{0}$ | 28.527 | (2.105) | $\beta_f^{AA} \times 100$ | 0.012 | (0.006) |
| $\alpha_{ff}^{1}$ | −19.770 | (7.502) | $\beta_f^{1}$ | 0.231 | (0.069) |
| $\alpha_{ff}^{2}$ | −14.767 | (3.371) | $\beta_f^{2}$ | 0.101 | (0.033) |
| $\alpha_{ff}^{3}$ | −3.306 | (3.551) | $\beta_f^{3}$ | 0.076 | (0.034) |
| $\alpha_{fc}^{0}$ | −17.036 | (2.790) | $\beta_f^{ed}$ | −0.005 | (0.003) |
| $\alpha_{fc}^{1}$ | −27.510 | (7.610) | $\beta_f^{servs}$ | 0.082 | (0.011) |

**Appendix B** (*continued*)

(a) Labor supply estimates and diagnostics for model $L_2$ with dependence

| | | | | | |
|---|---|---|---|---|---|
| $\alpha^2_{fc}$ | −16.959 | (3.043) | $\beta_f^{manu}$ | 0.068 | (0.012) |
| $\alpha^3_{fc}$ | −6.494 | (2.698) | $\sigma$ | 0.159 | (0.009) |
| $\alpha^0_{cc}$ | 30.198 | (2.318) | $\tau$ | −0.335 | (0.070) |
| | | | Log $L$ | −4825.688 | |
| $\alpha^1_{cc}$ | 25.612 | (8.048) | | | |
| $\alpha^2_{cc}$ | 5.152 | (2.296) | | | |
| $\alpha^3_{cc}$ | 12.118 | (1.545) | | | |
| $\beta^0_f$ | 0.146 | (0.023) | | | |
| $\beta^A_f \times 10$ | 0.023 | (0.006) | | | |

(b) Estimated Parameters of the employment probability index for model $L_2$ with dependence

| | | |
|---|---|---|
| Intercept | 3.0344 | (0.8163) |
| Education | −0.0156 | (0.0274) |
| Age | −0.0304 | (0.0067) |
| Regional unemployment | −0.0089 | (0.0238) |
| Unemployment by age | −0.0646 | (0.0194) |
| Unemployment by industry | −0.3189 | (0.0199) |
| Vacancy by region | −0.0406 | (0.1109) |
| Redundancy by region | 0.0110 | (0.0268) |
| Vacancy by industry | 0.8568 | (0.0705) |
| Redundancy by industry | −0.0079 | (0.0030) |
| D1 | −1.4534 | (0.1550) |
| D2 | −0.5338 | (0.1165) |
| London | 0.2951 | (0.2348) |
| Other South | 0.1033 | (0.1608) |
| Manual worker | −0.5015 | (0.1446) |
| Services industry | −4.8604 | (0.3830) |
| Unemployment by industry (male) | 0.0203 | (0.0087) |
| Manual worker (male) | −0.0964 | (0.1053) |
| Services industry (male) | 0.1331 | (0.1186) |

## Notes

1. See also Cogan (1981) and Blank (1985). Heckman (1980) finds that his data reject the restrictions that the Tobit specification places on the constant term of the participation equation, but do not reject the restrictions that the Tobit model places on the slope coefficients in a linear participation equation.

2. Blank (1985) finds that a state unemployment rate is statistically significant in her reduced-form hours per week and weeks per year equations. However, as she notes, this variable may enter these equations simply as a determinant of the wage.
3. We allowed for a selection adjustment term in the wage equation for participants but this was found to be insignificant.
4. Further details of these tests are given in Blundell and Meghir (1987).
5. Omitting the industry dummy leads to an increase in the weight given to industry unemployment, vacancy and redundancy rates but does not affect the overall conclusions from this section. Similarly, the conclusions are little affected by the omission of the services and manual dummies from the labour-supply model.
6. A worrying aspect of the results presented in Table 1.2(b) is the large normality test statistics. As these tests are conditional on independence they could simply be 'picking up' the failure of that assumption. In future work we investigate this issue by deriving appropriate statistics for non-normality in the double-hurdle model with dependence.
7. In fact it is possible for the derivative (4.10) to be negative for workers even when labour supply is forward-sloping. This could occur as $y + a(\cdot)$ becomes very small and the last term in the expression dominates.

## Data Appendix

The data was drawn from the Family Expenditure Survey 1981. The following sample selection was applied

1. occupation: FES variable A210 with value 2, 3, 4, 5, 6, 7, 8.
2. age: Women with $16 \leq \text{Age} < 60$ Men with $16 \leq \text{Age} < 65$
3. hours: Female hours $\leq 80$, Male hours $\leq 80$
4. two adult households with the two adults being a married couple.

*Sample Size*:

1. households with working women 1076 (A201 = 1);
2. households with non-working women 935 (A201 = 2, 3, 4, 5, 7).

(i) *Analysis for household with working women*

| *Variable* | *Mean* | *Standard deviation* | *Minimum* | *Maximum* |
|---|---|---|---|---|
| Female hours | 25.961 | 11.835 | 1 | 80.00 |
| Male hours | 38.762 | 8.939 | 9.00 | 77.00 |
| Children 0–2 | 0.068 | 0.269 | 0 | 2 |
| Children 3–4 | 0.064 | 0.259 | 0 | 2 |

(i) *Analysis for household with working women*

| *Variable* | *Mean* | *Standard deviation* | *Minimum* | *Maximum* |
|---|---|---|---|---|
| Children 5–10 | 0.437 | 0.709 | 0 | 3 |
| Children 11+ | 0.474 | 0.767 | 0 | 4 |
| Female wage | 1.363 | 1.206 | 0.012 | 10.817 |
| Male wage | 2.022 | 0.747 | 0.295 | 5.392 |
| Expenditure | 71.601 | 34.307 | 18.748 | 331.093 |
| Other income | 39.292 | 34.682 | −37.025 | 232.761 |
| Female age | 36.930 | 10.554 | 17.000 | 59.0 |
| Education (female) | 15.674 | 1.959 | 14.000 | 24.0 |

Wages are in £/hour. This unit of measurement was used in estimation. The low minimum wage reflects the impact of the tax and benefit system.

*Education*: Female age at the end of education (FES Variable A010).

*Breakdown of households by numbers and age of children*

| | *Number of children* | | | | |
|---|---|---|---|---|---|
| Age | *0* | *1* | *2* | *3* | *4* |
| 0–2 | 1008 | 63 | 5 | 0 | 0 |
| 3–4 | 1011 | 61 | 4 | 0 | 0 |
| 5–10 | 735 | 219 | 114 | 8 | 0 |
| 11+ | 728 | 205 | 125 | 17 | 1 |

*Breakdown of households by number of children and female hours*

| | *Female hours* | | | | |
|---|---|---|---|---|---|
| Children (age<3) | 1–10 | 11–20 | 21–30 | 31–40 | 41+ |
| 0 | 115 | 265 | 178 | 426 | 24 |
| 1 | 21 | 30 | 5 | 5 | 2 |
| 2 | 1 | 4 | 0 | 0 | 0 |

| | *Female hours* | | | | |
|---|---|---|---|---|---|
| Children (age 3–4) | 1–10 | 11–20 | 21–30 | 31–40 | 41+ |
| 0 | 113 | 276 | 178 | 421 | 23 |
| 1 | 20 | 23 | 5 | 10 | 3 |
| 2 | 4 | 0 | 0 | 0 | 0 |

*Breakdown of households by number of children and female hours* (continued)

| | *Female hours* | | | | |
|---|---|---|---|---|---|
| Children (age 5–10) | 1–10 | 11–20 | 21–30 | 31–40 | 41+ |
| 0 | 59 | 151 | 129 | 373 | 23 |
| 1 | 45 | 97 | 35 | 41 | 1 |
| 2 | 31 | 47 | 18 | 16 | 2 |
| 3 | 2 | 4 | 1 | 1 | 0 |

| | *Female hours* | | | | |
|---|---|---|---|---|---|
| Children (age > 10) | 1–10 | 11–20 | 21–30 | 31–40 | 41+ |
| 0 | 101 | 166 | 114 | 327 | 20 |
| 1 | 20 | 86 | 39 | 57 | 3 |
| 2 | 14 | 41 | 28 | 40 | 2 |
| 3 | 1 | 6 | 2 | 7 | 1 |
| 4 | 1 | 0 | 0 | 0 | |

*Female occupation*

| *Occupation* | *Frequency* |
|---|---|
| Clerical and professional | 510 |
| Shop assistants | 79 |
| Skilled manual | 60 |
| Semi-skilled manual | 278 |
| Unskilled manual | 149 |

*Female industry by 32 FES sub-groupings*

| *FES code* | *Frequency* | *FES code* | *Frequency* |
|---|---|---|---|
| 1 | 6 | 17 | 5 |
| 2 | 3 | 18 | 27 |
| 3 | 37 | 19 | 9 |
| 4 | 2 | 20 | 16 |
| 5 | 13 | 21 | 10 |
| 6 | 5 | 22 | 1 |
| 7 | 13 | 23 | 41 |
| 8 | 3 | 24 | 179 |
| 9 | 24 | 25 | 84 |
| 11 | 20 | 26 | 245 |
| 12 | 9 | 27 | 18 |
| 13 | 14 | 28 | 170 |
| 14 | 2 | 30 | 33 |
| 15 | 32 | 31 | 5 |
| 16 | 7 | 32 | 40 |

*Regional breakdown*

| *Region* | *Frequency* |
|---|---|
| Northern | 67 |
| Yorks | 103 |
| East Midlands | 91 |
| East Anglia | 43 |
| Greater London | 115 |
| South East | 196 |
| South West | 61 |
| Wales | 48 |
| West Midlands | 117 |
| North Western | 130 |
| Scotland | 105 |

(ii) *Analysis for households with nonworking wives*
(A201 = 2, 3, 4, 5, 7)

| *Variable* | *Mean* | *Standard deviation* | *Minimum* | *Maximum* |
|---|---|---|---|---|
| Male hours | 35.906 | 14.065 | 0 | 80 |
| Children 0–2 | 0.475 | 0.635 | 0 | 4 |
| Children 3–4 | 0.251 | 0.465 | 0 | 2 |
| Children 5–10 | 0.525 | 0.786 | 0 | 4 |
| Children 11+ | 0.344 | 0.711 | 0 | 4 |
| Female wage | 1.254 | 1.389 | 0.339 | 5.307 |
| Male wage | 2.227 | 1.040 | 0.149 | 6.924 |
| Expenditure | 65.398 | 36.175 | 14.817 | 390.631 |
| Female age | 34.667 | 10.853 | 16.0 | 59.0 |
| Education | 15.634 | 2.177 | 14.0 | 24.0 |

*Breakdown of households by numbers and age of children*

| | *Number of children* | | | | |
|---|---|---|---|---|---|
| *Age* | *0* | *1* | *2* | *3* | *4* |
| 0–2 | 560 | 308 | 66 | 0 | 1 |
| 3–4 | 713 | 209 | 13 | 0 | 0 |
| 5–10 | 588 | 227 | 100 | 16 | 4 |
| 11+ | 722 | 123 | 74 | 13 | 3 |

*Regional breakdown*

| *Region* | *Frequency* |
|---|---|
| Northern | 68 |
| Yorks | 105 |
| East Midlands | 75 |
| East Anglia | 42 |
| Greater London | 61 |
| South East | 163 |
| South West | 54 |
| Wales | 59 |
| West Midlands | 91 |
| North West | 99 |
| Scotland | 18 |

## References


ASHENFELTER, O. (1980) 'Unemployment as Disequilibrium in a Model of Aggregate Labor Supply', *Econometrica*, 48, pp. 547–64.

ATKINSON, A. B., GOMULKA, J. and STERN, N. (1984) 'Household Expenditure on Tobacco 1970–1980', London School of Economics (LSE) ESRC Programme on Taxation, Incentives and the Distribution of Income, Discussion Paper 57.

ATKINSON, A. B., MICKLEWRIGHT, J. and STERN, N. H. (1982) 'A Comparison of the Family Expenditure Survey and the New Earnings Survey: Part II, Hours and Earnings', LSE Taxation and Incentives Discussion Paper 32.

BERA, A. K., JARQUE, C. M. and LEE, L. F. (1984) 'Testing for the Normality Assumption in Limited Dependent Variable Models', *International Economic Review*, 25, pp. 563–78.

BLANK, R. (1985) 'Simultaneously Modelling the Supply of Weeks and Hours of Work Among Female Household Heads', Working Paper 197, Industrial Relations Section, Princeton University.

BLUNDELL, R. W. and WALKER, I. (1986) 'A Life Cycle Consistent Empirical Model of Labour Supply using Cross Section Data', *Review of Economic Studies*, LIII, pp. 539–58.

BLUNDELL, R. W. and MEGHIR, C. (1986) 'Selection Criteria for a Microeconometric Model of Labour Supply', *Journal of Applied Econometrics*, 1, pp. 55–81.

BLUNDELL, R. W. and MEGHIR, C. (1987) 'Bivariate Alternatives to the Tobit Model', *Journal of Econometrics*, 34, pp. 179–200.

BLUNDELL, R. W., MEGHIR, C., SYMONS, E. and WALKER, I. (1986) 'A Labour Supply Model for the Simulation of Tax and Benefit Reforms', in R. Blundell and I. Walker (eds), *Unemployment Search and Labour Supply* (Cambridge: Cambridge University Press).

CHESHER, A. and IRISH, M. (1987) 'Residuals and Diagnostics for Probit, Tobit and Related Models', *Journal of Econometrics*, 34, pp. 33–61.

COGAN, J. F. (1981) 'Fixed Costs and Labor Supply', *Econometrica*, 49, 945–64.

CRAGG, J. G. (1971) 'Some Statistical Models for Limited Dependent Variables with Applications to the Demand for Durable Goods', *Econometrica*, 39, pp. 829–44.

DEATON, A. S. and IRISH, M. (1984) 'Statistical Models for Zero Expenditures in Household Budgets', *Journal of Public Economics*, 23, pp. 59–80.

GOURIEROUX, C., MONFORT, A., RENAULT, E. and TROGNON, A. (1987) 'Generalised Residuals', *Journal of Econometrics*, 34, pp. 5–32.

HAM, J. (1982) 'Estimation of a Labor Supply Model with Censoring due to Unemployment and Underemployment', *Review of Economic Studies*, 49, pp. 335–354.

HAM, J. (1986) 'Testing Whether Unemployment Represents Life-Cycle Labor Supply Behaviour', *Review of Economic Studies*, LIII, pp. 559–78.

HAUSMAN, J. A. (1981) 'Labor Supply' in H. Aaron and J. Peckman (eds) *How Taxes Affect Economic Behaviour* (Washington DC: Brookings Institution).

HAUSMAN, J. A. (1980) 'The Effect of Wages, Taxes and Fixed Costs on Women's Labor Force Participation', *Journal of Public Economics*, 14, pp. 161–94.

HECKMAN, J. J. (1974) 'Shadow Prices, Market Wages and Labor Supply', *Econometrica*, 42, pp. 679–94.

HECKMAN, J. J. (1980) 'Sample Selection Bias as a Specification Error', in J. Smith (ed.) *Female Labor Supply* (Princeton: Princeton University Press).

LAYARD, R., BARTON, M. and ZABALZA, A. (1980) 'Married Women's Participation and Hours', *Economica*, 47, pp. 51–72.

MEGHIR, C. (1985) 'The specification of Labour Supply Models and their use for the Simulation of Tax and Benefit Reforms', Ph.D. thesis, University of Manchester.

MROZ, T. (1984) 'The Sensitivity of an Empirical Model of Married Women's Hours of Work to Economic and Statistical Assumptions', *Econometrica*, 55, pp. 765–80.

STERN, N. (1986) 'On the Specification of Labour Supply Functions', in R. W. Blundell and I. Walker (eds) *Unemployment, Search and Labour Supply* (Cambridge: Cambridge University Press).

# 2 Unemployment and Labour Market Transition Probabilities*

Jules Theeuwes

## 2.1 ANALYSING UNEMPLOYMENT: A RESEARCH PROGRAMME

There are many kinds of unemployment. An average economist should be able to enumerate at least a dozen without forward notice.[1] This embarrassing abundance of definitions gives a clear indication of the trouble we have pinning unemployment down.

Unemployment is generally considered to be an undesirable quantity in a market economy. Although not all of it. Part of it is unavoidable and even considered necessary for an efficient matching of jobs and workers. In this sense one could define - although this would not be easy - an optimal quantity of unemployment taking into account the institutions and stochastics of the labour market. Unemployment under and above this optimum would be inefficient. Can one avoid too much or too little unemployment through policy measures at reasonable costs? There is no definite answer to that. A lot of heated discussion in macroeconomics focuses on this subject.

Apart from efficiency there is also the problem of distribution. Who carries the burden of unemployment at a point in time and over time? Does everybody have an equal chance in becoming and remaining unemployed? Are certain groups more unemployment-prone than others? What about recurrence of unemployment over one's life cycle?

The study of the inefficiencies and inequities of unemployment and the possible trade-off between them has only just begun. Yet these are essential problems. In this chapter I will propose a research programme

* Thanks are due to W. Kloek for letting me use the aggregate data in section 3. I would also like to thank R. van Opstal for his permission to use the estimation results in section 2. They come out of our 1985 report for the Organisation for Strategic Labour Market Research (OSA) in The Hague. Participants of the Conference on 'Unemployment in Europe' in Maastricht, April 1986 and especially Daniel Weiserbs gave very valuable comments on a previous version of this paper. Without implicating them, I would like to thank them all.

that has a lot of potential for analysing these aspects of unemployment. The programme consists of two parts: a first part explaining individual unemployment experiences (and other labour-market experiences), and a second aggregate part describing the dynamics of the labour market. This chapter contains an introduction to this research programme and some empirical applications that fit into it. The central concept is a stock-flow model of the labour market which describes the dynamic flows between labour-market states (in this chapter: employment ($e$), unemployment ($u$) and non-participation ($n$)) in a given period for an individual or a group of individuals.

Stock-flow analysis of the labour market enables one to be more precise in describing the dynamics of unemployment and at the same time allows one to say something about the efficiency and distributional issues. At least that is what I want to illustrate. Stock-flow analysis of the labour market has been around for some time already, but I think that all its potentials have not been used or stressed enough.

The essential tool for a stock-flow analysis of the labour market is the transition rate probability, i.e. the probability of moving from one labour-market state to another (during a given time interval). I will first of all show (in section 2) how individual probabilities can be estimated. I will thereby concentrate on the probability of moving out of unemployment into employment. With the same procedure one could, in principal, estimate transition probabilities for all relevant transitions in the labour market. In section 3 I will illustrate how one could make use of information on labour-market transition rates to analyse aggregate unemployment. I will thereby concentrate more specifically on the determinants of the long-run, steady-state rate of unemployment. Section 4 contains a summary as well as a brief discussion of the efficiency and equity issues in the context of a stock-flow model.

## 2.2 INDIVIDUAL TRANSITION PROBABILITIES

The aggregate transition probabilities that I will describe in the next section are the result of thousands of individual decisions to move from state $i$ to state $j$ in a given period. If the aggregate transition probabilities change, it is because the individual decision units have acted differently.

It is, in principle, possible to define for each individual $k$ a transition probability given his or her personal and labour-market characteristics and relevant government regulations. An individual transition probability gives the probability that individual $k$ will move from $i$ to $j$ in the given period. One usually models these individual probabilities as consisting of a deterministic part and a stochastic part. If the specification of the deterministic part is adequate, then the stochastic part should on average be zero. Information on the deterministic part of the transition probability could then be used for simulation purposes by averaging the individual transition probabilities into aggregate ones. I will take up this issue in section 3.

But first: how would one go about and estimate these individual transition probabilities? An obvious answer is to use a logit or a probit model. These models were developed to deal with probabilities. If one observed a sample of individuals that in a given period either changed or did not change a particular labour-force status one could fit a logit or probit model to estimate the probability that person $k$ with given characteristics vector $x$ and facing policy-vector $z$, will have changed status in the period under consideration. For instance, one observes a group of people who are unemployed at a given point in time and follows them, say during the following half-year, (i.e. reinterviews them half a year later). During that period some will have found work, while others will have remained unemployed. Using this information one could estimate a probit or logit model explaining the individual probabilities of finding a job.

Suppose however that one also knows the date at which a person made the change and hence one also knows the duration, $t$, of his or her unemployment. For those who remain unemployed during the whole period of observation, one knows that their unemployment spell has lasted at least so many months. It would be a waste if one did not take this information on completed and incompleted duration along. Here however the probit or logit model fails. These are discrete dependent variable models, unfit for this continuous type of information. The appropriate model now is the hazard function. In what follows I will briefly explain the workings of a hazard function as it is usually found in the literature. I will concentrate on the individual transition probability of moving from unemployment into employment. In principle hazard functions can be developed for all transition probabilities (see, for example, Flinn and Heckman (1982a, b)).

The hazard rate, or in this case the employment probability, can be expressed in the following form:

$$\theta(t)\,\mathrm{d}t = \mathrm{Prob}[t < T < t + \mathrm{d}t \mid T > t]. \tag{2.1}$$

The hazard or transition rate, after $t$ periods of unemployment is equal to the probability that the completed unemployment duration (stochast $T$) is between $t$ and $t+\mathrm{d}t$, conditional on the fact that the unemployment spell already lasts $t$ periods. This conditional probability can be written as:

$$\theta(t)\,\mathrm{d}t = \text{Prob}[t < T < t+\mathrm{d}t]/\text{Prob}[T > t]. \tag{2.2}$$

Hence the following holds:

$$\theta(t)\,\mathrm{d}t = g(t)\,\mathrm{d}t/(1 - G(t)) \tag{2.3}$$

where

$g(t)\,\mathrm{d}t$ = the probability of a spell of unemployment of length $t$;

$1 - G(t)$ = the probability of still being unemployed after $t$ periods;

$t$ = the duration of the current spell of unemployment.

$g(\cdot)$ is the probability density function of (completed) unemployment durations and $G(\cdot)$ is the corresponding distribution function. These functions are related to the hazard as follows:

$$G(t) = 1 - \exp\left\{-\int_0^t \theta(u)\,\mathrm{d}u\right\} \tag{2.4}$$

$$g(t) = \theta(t)\exp\left\{-\int_0^t \theta(u)\,\mathrm{d}u\right\}. \tag{2.5}$$

Given data on complete spells of unemployment one can use the density function (2.5) to study the probability of leaving unemployment for employment. For incomplete spells of unemployment distribution function (2.4) can be used. One often has a mixture of persons who have found a job in the given period and for whom we observe a completed spell, and of persons who are still unemployed at the end of the period. The likelihood function for such a sample will therefore be a mixture of density and distribution functions, very similar to the Tobit model.

In the hazard model the transition rate is usually written as the product of three separate functions: a function which depends on actual spell duration ($t$), a function of a set of personal and economic variables $x$ and policy variables $z$ (define $x = x, z$) and finally a function of the error term (e):

$$\theta(t \mid x, \mathrm{e}) = \theta 1(t) \cdot \theta 2(x) \cdot \theta 3(\mathrm{e}). \tag{2.6}$$

The $\theta 1(t)$ function measures duration dependence, i.e. the effect of the duration of the ongoing spell on the probability of escaping from the unemployment state. This can either be positive, if the person becomes more willing to accept a job offer as unemployment lasts longer, or negative, if the probability of obtaining a job offer declines with $t$. For the $\theta 1(t)$ function I will use the following functional form, known as the Weibull model, which is quite popular in the empirical literature:

$$\theta 1(t) = at^{a-1} \quad \text{with } a > 0. \tag{2.7}$$

For $a < 1$ there is negative duration dependence and vice versa for $a > 1$.[2]

The second function $\theta 2(x)$ captures the influence of personal and labour-market characteristics and policy variables. The set of explanatory variables is defined in Appendix B. The functional form that is always used for this second part is simply $\exp(x'b)$ whereby $b$ is the vector of coefficients to be estimated.

As one cannot possibly observe and incorporate all the relevant explanatory variables that might shift the hazard, a third function $\theta 3(e)$ is finally added. The effect of adding such a term is to control, at least partially, for unrecognised heterogeneity which might otherwise bias the parameters of the model. Not only the duration dependence process, but also the coefficients measuring the influence of the explanatory variables will be affected if one omits relevant regressors (see Lancaster and Nickell (1980)). The usual way to control for heterogeneity is to assume that $e$ consists of drawings from a distribution function, with parameter vector $d$. These distributional parameters are then estimated together with the other parameters ($a$, $b$) of the model.

Theory does not provide any clue whatsoever as to which distribution should be used for the heterogeneity term. Hence practical considerations prevail in the literature. In the case of the proportional hazard function the gamma distribution is very convenient. It has been used in this context by Lancaster (1979), Kooreman and Ridder (1983) and Lynch (1985).[3]

Writing the error term of the hazard $\theta 3(e)$ as $v = \exp(e)$, there exist closed solutions for the expectation of $G(t \mid x, e)$ and $g(t \mid x, e)$ with respect to the distribution of $e$ when assuming that $v$ is gamma distributed.

To estimate this hazard model a national sample is used which was drawn randomly at the end of May 1984 from the population of unemployed youngsters (15–26 years old) who were registered at one of twenty-six regional labour bureaus and were willing to work at least 20 hours per week. Those selected for the sample in May were then interviewed during the months October and November 1984 (sample size was 1142 persons). Between May and October–November some of them (about 11 per cent) had found work but most of them remained unemployed. For the first group one observes a completed unemployment spell. After discarding observations for which essential variables were missing or for whom it was not clear whether they were really unemployed in May 1984 (registration at the regional labour bureau is not the same as being unemployed) a sample of 797 persons remained, 85 of whom had found a job before the interview date.

For each person in the subsample information is available on personal characteristics (such as gender, nationality, place of living, level of education, marital status, age, employment experience) and on familial background (the educational background of parents, the unemployment of family members). We also know their after-tax unemployment benefit levels while unemployed and could predict after-tax monthly earnings for each of them. This was done by means of a predicted net earnings equation which was estimated on the subsample of those who had found work and for whom net earnings were observed. Corrections for selectivity bias were made while estimating the earnings equation. It turns out that observed earnings follow closely the minimum youth wage levels which are differentiated by age in the Netherlands.

The estimation results are presented in Appendix A, Table 2.A.1. In the first column I present the results for the probit model, in the second and third column the results for the hazard model first without and then with correction for heterogeneity. The variables used are the same in each column, except for the variable measuring duration dependence. In the probit model duration dependence is measured as the coefficient that belongs to a variable measuring duration of unemployment at the moment of selection (May 1984).

Neglecting for the moment the third column, it is quickly seen that the results of the probit and the hazard model are, qualitatively speaking, very similar.

Females and foreigners have a smaller chance of finding a job than males and Dutchmen. The gender variable is significant in both columns. Married people have a greater escape rate than singles. People with higher education and secondary vocational schooling have a significantly better chance than other educational groups. The difference with youngsters who had a general secondary education is especially remarkable. Extended primary schooling has no significant effect. Household variables such as parents' education and unemployment of other members of the household are generally not significant. The regional vacancy/unemployment ratio ($v/u$) is assumed to measure labour-market conditions. The sign is right but the variable is not significant. The same holds for the previous job dummy variable.

The effect of the income variables is at the same time surprising and disturbing. One would expect, within the framework of search theory, a negative effect of benefit levels and a positive effect of expected earnings (or, taking both variables, a negative effect of the 'replacement ratio'). The only significant effect that was found is a negative expected-earnings effect! The explanation could be that this is a demand side effect. In a slack labour market (as was the case in the Netherlands in 1984) an employer will offer a job to the cheapest unemployed, everything else remaining the same. Because of the strong positive correlation between minimum youth wages and age this would imply that the employer will choose the 'youngest' unemployed.

Turning now to the estimation results for the duration dependence it is not surprising that the results in both columns correspond. The $a$-coefficient is negative in the probit case and smaller than 1 in the Weibull model of the second column. This indicates negative duration dependence.

Up to now all seems to be well. However results become very different quantitatively (not qualitatively for the $x$-variables!) if one adds the heterogeneity term in column 3. Although one would theoretically expect the estimates to be higher in absolute value when correcting for heterogeneity (see Lancaster, 1979), the coefficients in the third column are inflated to an uncomfortable magnitude. Especially the estimates for duration dependence $a$ and for the variance of the error distribution $\sigma^2$ are improbably high. Neither of the two is significant (for the $a$-coefficient this means: significantly different from 1).

An explanation for these confusing results is not easily found, and only suggestions can be made. The first thing one must realise is that the data are not very informative. Almost 90 per cent of the unemployment durations are not completed. One observes only 85 persons with a complete spell. Only the later data contain 'hard' information. This paucity of information seems to lead to an identification problem of the duration dependence effect and the heterogeneity effect.

Presumably, given better data - e.g. data that stretch out over a longer period such that one would observe more completed spells of unemployment - one could estimate duration dependence and the variance of unmeasured heterogeneity more precisely. Until then however one can still work with the qualitative results measuring the influence of the explanatory variables on the individual transition probabilities. These results are useful for the aggregate model in the next section.

## 2.3 AGGREGATE STOCK-FLOW ANALYSIS

Suppose one has estimated individual transition probabilities for all possible flows between employment, unemployment and non-participation. These transition probabilities vary across individuals depending on their personal characteristics, the labour market in which they operate and the levels of relevant policy variables. For a given sample one could determine aggregate transition probabilities based on these individual rates. The aggregate transition probabilities will then depend on the distribution of characteristics and levels of policy variables in the sample. If the estimated hazard model is adequately specified then the average predicted transition probability for the sample should be very close to the observed proportion of transitions. For instance, if we predict for each individual his probability of moving from unemployment into employment in the given period, on the basis of his vector of explanatory variables ($x$) and the estimated coefficients ($b$) and next average these individual probabilities over the sample, then this average should be close to the observed proportion of people in the sample that moved from unemployment to employment. Once this relationship is established, one can exploit it for simulation purposes. One can now change a policy variable (e.g. decrease all unemployment benefits by 10 per cent), recalculate all individual transition probabilities, average them over the sample and derive in this way a new aggregate transition probability. Through simulation one establishes the dependence of the aggregate transition probabilities on the distribution of characteristics and levels of policy variables. Recently Blau and Robins (1986) published results obtained with a similar kind of model in which they traced the effects of welfare programmes on labour supply.

In this section I will show what one could do with an aggregate stock-flow model of the labour market once one has derived it. In order to do that I have to introduce the aggregate stock-flow models that are customarily based on aggregate-time-series data for flows between labour-market states.

The first influential stock-flow analysis is presumable C. C. Holt's 1969 article. The original article in which the framework was, to my knowledge, first presented is Holt and David (1966). A seminal article in this area is Clark and Summers (1979). The stock-flow analysis has some similarities with the circular-flow analysis of an economy as can be judged from the simplified version pictured in Figure 2.1.

*Figure* 2.1 Stock-flow model

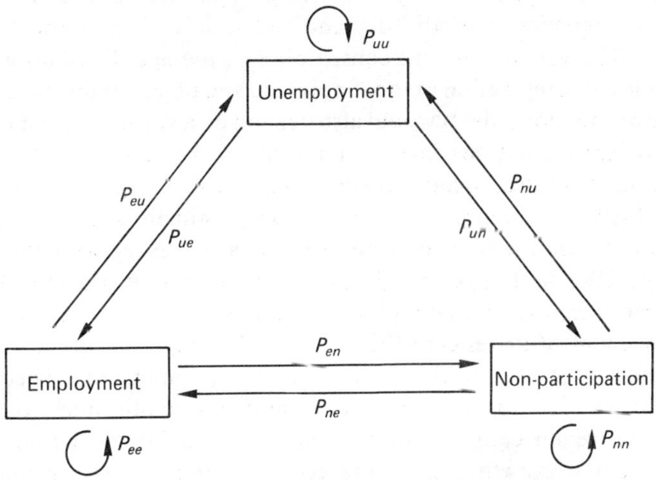


There are three stocks and six flows between them. For completeness I also added the 'flows' of people who stayed in their original stock.[4] Aggregate stock-flow analysis is always a dynamic analysis. In a given period of time, stocks change between the first and the last date due to the flows within a given period. If one defines $P_{ij}(t)$ as the probability of flowing from stock $i$ to stock $j$ during period $t$,[5] then the following holds for the system pictured in Figure 2.1:

$$\begin{bmatrix} E(T) \\ U(T) \\ N(T) \end{bmatrix} = \begin{bmatrix} P_{ee}(t) & P_{ue}(t) & P_{ne}(t) \\ P_{eu}(t) & P_{uu}(t) & P_{nu}(t) \\ P_{en}(t) & P_{un}(t) & P_{nn}(t) \end{bmatrix} \begin{bmatrix} E(T-1) \\ U(T-1) \\ N(T-1) \end{bmatrix} \tag{2.8}$$

or written more compactly:

$$S(T) = P(t)S(T-1) \tag{2.9}$$

whereby $S(T)$ stands for the vector of stocks and $P(t)$ for the matrix of transition probabilities $P_{ij}(t)$. This is a simple Markov chain and hence can be analysed as a dynamic system in this sense.

If the $P_{ij}(t)$'s are known functions of time, or even more simply constants, we can trace the time-paths of the stocks of unemployment, employment and non-participation. In this way one can study the short-run behaviour of these three labour-market states.

I would suggest writing each $P_{ij}(t)$ as consisting of a structural part that is time-invariant and a cyclical part that is dependent on time or better still on a cyclical index. The structural part would be determined by characteristics $x$ of the demand-and-supply side of the labour market. The vector $x$ would consist of, e.g., the age distribution and educational composition of the supply side and of technological details on the production side. It would also depend on a vector $z$ summarising government regulations that are relevant for the labour market such as income-tax rates, social security premiums and benefits, etc. Ehrenberg (1980) and Junankar and Price (1984) estimate a similar type of relationship on the basis of time-series data for respectively the USA and the UK. As I suggested in the beginning one could also derive them from cross-section data through simulation. In that case one can take account of the effect of distributional changes on the transition probabilities. The cyclical part would have as a property that it becomes zero in what could be defined as a short-run equilibrium situation. For instance one could let the cyclical part depend on deviations from the potential growth rate of the economy and make sure that the function becomes zero when the economy is on a potential growth path. Or let it depend on the log of the vacancy/unemployment ratio, and define short-run equilibrium as equality of unemployment and vacancies. On the basis of this assumption I rewrite $P_{ij}(t)$ as:

$$P_{ij}(x,z,t) = P_{ij}(x,z) + P_{ij}(t). \tag{2.10}$$

The dynamic system in (2.8) could then be split in the same two parts. Using only the structural part one could define long-run, steady-state values for the stocks as follows. First normalise the stocks by dividing them through with Population (sum of $U$, $N$ and $E$, constant in the long run). Call these proportions $u$, $n$ and $e$ respectively and the vector containing them $s$. In the steady state the following holds:

$$s^* = P(x, z) \cdot s^*. \tag{2.11}$$

Whereby $s^*$ stands for the steady-state distribution over the states. System (2.11) cannot be solved as $P$ is a singular matrix, because $P_{ie} + P_{iu} + P_{in} = 1$, for all $i$. However the following system of three equations can be solved for the three unknowns $e^*$, $u^*$ and $n^*$:

$$e^* = P_{ee}(x,z) \cdot e^* + P_{ue}(x,z) \cdot u^* + P_{ne}(x,z) \cdot n^* \tag{2.12.1}$$

$$u^* = P_{eu}(x,z) \cdot e^* + P_{uu}(x,z) \cdot u^* + P_{nu}(x,z) \cdot n^* \tag{2.12.2}$$

$$1 = e^* + u^* + n^*. \tag{2.12.3}$$

It is clear from system (2.12) that the long-run, steady-state values of unemployment $u^*$, employment $e^*$ and non-participation $n^*$ depend on all the transitions in the labour market and on the characteristics $x$ and policy variables $z$. Changing $x$ or $z$ will change these steady-state values.

As an illustration of how these calculations are done I will use aggregate data for the Netherlands on yearly transitions between the three states $U$, $N$, and $E$. The data are given in Table 2.A.2 in Appendix A. They are aggregated from individual data from a nation-wide sample (the individual data are not available for all the years). In a bi-annual labour market survey (Arbeidskrachtentellingen, CBS) a question is asked on the labour-market status in the survey week and one year earlier. The answers to these questions are the basis of Table 2.A.2. All kinds of horrible things are wrong with these data, going from changes of definitions over time, to selective memory losses of the respondents (easier to forget very short spells, especially unemployment spells). These data should therefore not be used for anything fancy, and hence I will not do that. All calculations done with them can be seen only as mere illustrations.

As an illustration then of system (2.12) let me assume that the average of the five $P$-matrices that are presented in Table 2.A.1 is a good representation of what I meant with the structural part in (2.10). Substituting these averages in (2.12) and solving we get Table 2.1.

Note that $u^*$ is not the unemployment rate that one usually encounters as it stands for the proportion of total population which is unemployed. Unemployment as a proportion of the labour force is defined as: $u^{**} = u^*/(u^* + e^*)$, which in the example would be 7.3

*Table* 2.1 Long-run steady-state values

| | *Men* | *Women* |
|---|---|---|
| $e^*$ | 67.7 | 23.9 |
| $u^*$ | 5.3 | 1.6 |
| $n^*$ | 27.0 | 74.5 |

per cent for men and 6.2 per cent for women. These numbers and the ones in Table 2.1 are intuitively acceptable. The interesting thing of course would be to play around with different specifications for the demand and supply characteristics and for the government regulations and to simulate and compare the corresponding steady-state distributions $s^*$.

I would consider the steady-state value $u^{**}$ to be a good summary measure of all that goes on in the labour market. Obviously $u^{**}$ is determined by all the transition probabilities $P_{ij}$ and hence anything that changes the structural $P_{ij}$ will eventually change $u^{**}$. It is only through studying movements in the $P_{ij}$ that we can say something about the steady state rate of unemployment.

The relationship between $u^{**}$ and the $P_{ij}$'s can be made even more directly clear (see Marston (1976)). To do this one has to rewrite the first two equations of system (12) as follows:

$$(1-P_{ee})\cdot e^* = P_{ue}\cdot u^* + P_{ne}\cdot n^* \tag{2.13.1}$$

or:

$$(P_{eu}+P_{en})\cdot e^* = P_{ue}\cdot u^* + P_{ne}\cdot n^*. \tag{2.13.1'}$$

In going from (2.13.1) to (2.13.1′) we use the equality ($\sum P_{ij}=1.$). Equation (2.13.1′) has an attractive interpretation. It states that the long-run steady state is attained if the outflow from employment (left-hand side of (2.13.1′)) is equal to the inflow into employment (right-hand side).

Similarly equation (12.2) can be rewritten as:

$$(P_{ue}+P_{un})\cdot u^* = P_{eu}\cdot e^* + P_{nu}\cdot n^* \tag{2.14}$$

which is an outflow=inflow equilibrium condition as well, this time for unemployment.

One can solve $n^*$ out of equations (2.13.1′) and (2.14) to get one equation in terms of $e^*$ and $u^*$. Combining this with the definition for $u^{**}$ one obtains after some manipulation:

$$u^{**} = 1/(1+R) \tag{2.15}$$

whereby:

$$R = \frac{[(P_{ne}+P_{nu}) \cdot P_{ue} + P_{ne} \cdot P_{un}]}{[(P_{ne}+P_{nu}) \cdot P_{eu} + P_{en} \cdot P_{nu}]}. \tag{2.16}$$

For easier interpretation of (2.15) or (2.16) it is convenient to define $P_{se}$, the probability of successful labour market entry, as:

$$P_{se} = P_{ne}/(P_{ne}+P_{nu}). \tag{2.17}$$

$R$ then becomes:

$$R = [P_{ue} + P_{se} \cdot P_{un}]/[P_{eu} + (1-P_{se}) \cdot P_{en}]. \tag{2.16.1′}$$

It follows from (2.15) and (2.16) that whatever has a positive effect on $R$ will have a negative effect on $u^{**}$. Hence the long-run steady-state rate of unemployment is influenced positively by transitions into it: $P_{eu}$, $(1-P_{se})$, and negatively by transitions out of it: $P_{ue}$ and $P_{un}$, which is not a big surprise. It is however also influenced negatively by the transition from out of the labour force into employment ($P_{ne}$) and positively by the reverse flow ($P_{en}$).

Looking down the columns of Table 2.A.2 to what happens with the $P_{ij}$'s over time, one can discern for the men, something approaching a negative time-trend in $P_{ue}$ and $P_{ne}$ and a positive one in $P_{nu}$. The combination of these trends in $P_{ne}(-)$ and $P_{nu}(+)$ means that $P_{se}$ would have decreased. The latter combined with the reduction in $P_{ue}$, would imply, if it were structural, that $u^{**}$ would have increased in this period. The increase in $u^{**}$ would then be mainly due to the lack of inflow into employment. This should be contrasted with the other possibility where $u^{**}$ could increase due to increased turnover from quitting jobs ($P_{eu}$ and $P_{en}$).

For the women one could say that there is a positive trend in $P_{nu}$ and $P_{eu}$ which would increase the steady-state unemployment rate if it were structural. Furthermore there seems to be a strong increase in $P_{ue}$ which would again imply a higher unemployment in the long run. The only offsetting tendency is the decreasing trend in $P_{en}$. All in all these developments suggest that women get stuck in the unemployment state: they flow in vigorously ($P_{eu}$ and $P_{nu}$) but not out any more ($P_{ue}$ declines).

As was suggested in the beginning of this section one can define aggregate $P_{ij}$'s on the basis of cross-section data with the help of estimated hazard functions. Through simulation exercises one can relate this aggregate transition rates to the distribution of characteristics in the sample. In this section it was shown that the steady state unemployment rate differs depending on all the underlying transition rates.

## 2.4 RECOMMENDATIONS AND CONCLUSIONS

To study the dynamics of unemployment in a more satisfying way than has mostly been done until now I would make the following recommendations for the appropriate research project. Gather sufficient high-quality (panel) data on individual labour-market history. On the basis of this estimate individual transitions probabilities for all labour-market flows. Individual transition probabilities should be modelled as functions of supply-and-demand side and public-sector variables. This will require a lot of good data.

Given this individual data base and the empirical regularities in the transition probabilities one can study equity and efficiency problems of unemployment with the help of micro-simulation models. First, the distributional aspects: because one has available data on individuals one can easily identify and classify problem cases and also analyse how individual $u$–$n$–$e$ experiences change over time and with policy measures.

Aggregating the individual experiences into the dynamic stock-flow model of the labour market one can simulate different long-run steady-state distributions for $u^*$–$n^*$–$e^*$ using different assumptions about characteristics of the supply, demand and policy sides. The latter is important for tackling the efficiency question of unemployment. Although it is very hard to define exactly the most efficient $u$–$n$–$e$ distribution for individuals and the population, I would think that policy measures that minimise unemployment and maximise employment are desirable in this respect. Different policy vectors will generate different stationary rates of unemployment. Using simulation results one could search for policies with minimal steady-state unemployment rates.

The framework of stock-flow analysis is a very flexible one. It can incorporate many extensions and embellishments. It is surprising that it has not been used more often before. The only obstacle appears to be the large number of data required.

## Appendix A

*Table* 2.A.1 Estimation results

| | | Hazard model | |
|---|---|---|---|
| | *Probit model* | *No heterogeneity term* | *With gamma-distributed heterogeneity term* |
| GENDER | −0.782 (0.170)** | −1.325 (0.286)** | −4.006 (1.733)** |
| NON-DUTCH | −0.573 (0.313)* | −0.953 (0.600) | −2.840 (1.893) |
| MARRIED | 0.242 (0.163) | 0.383 (0.266) | 2.846 (2.110) |
| HIGHER ED | 0.622 (0.309)** | 1.119 (0.503)** | 6.050 (3.404)* |
| SEC GEN ED | −0.141 (0.311) | 0.134 (0.530) | 1.443 (1.835) |
| SEC VOC ED | 0.615 (0.241)** | 1.110 (0.396)** | 2.272 (1.846) |
| XPRIM. GEN. ED. | 0.283 (0.216) | 0.539 (0.365) | 2.266 (1.481) |
| XPRIM. VOC. ED. | 0.164 (0.183) | 0.394 (0.321) | 0.889 (1.308) |
| HOUSEH. UNEMPL. | −0.175 (0.157) | −0.343 (0.278) | −1.555 (1.194) |
| PARENTS>SEC. ED. | 0.055 (0.178) | 0.119 (0.288) | −0.789 (1.056) |
| PARENTS: XPRIM. ED. | −0.010 (0.162) | −0.049 (0.279) | −0.555 (1.151) |
| PREVIOUS JOB | 0.122 (0.158) | 0.332 (0.263) | 1.821 (1.411) |
| ln *V*/*U* PROVINCE | 0.122 (0.216) | 0.320 (0.346) | 1.211 (1.645) |
| ln BENEFITS | 0.015 (0.016) | 0.011 (0.026) | −0.004 (0.077) |
| ln PRED. EARNINGS | −0.756 (0.325)** | −1.201 (0.511)** | −2.519 (2.039) |
| CONSTANT | 5.197 | 7.811 | 16.862 |
| $\alpha$ | −0.342 (0.057)** | 0.473 (0.119)* | 2.103 (1.126) |
| $\sigma$ | | | 5.016 (3.546) |
| Latent $R^2$ | 0.280 | | |
| Log Likelihood | | −310.845 | −308.801 |

Asymptotic standard errors are between brackets.
**: significant at 5 per cent level.
*: significant at 10 per cent level.

*Table* 2.A.2 Transition probabilities and labour-market status in the Netherlands, for five data points, in the period 1974–83

*A. Men*

| | | *Employment* | | | | *Employment* | | | | *Not in the labour force* | | | |
|---|---|---|---|---|---|---|---|---|---|---|---|---|---|
| | $POP_{t-1}$ | $E_{t-1}$ | $P_{ee}$ | $P_{eu}$ | $P_{en}$ | $U_{t-1}$ | $P_{ue}$ | $P_{uu}$ | $P_{un}$ | $N_{t-1}$ | $P_{ne}$ | $P_{nu}$ | $P_{nn}$ |
| 1974–5 | 4837 | 0.703 | 0.951 | 0.023 | 0.026 | 0.011 | 0.340 | 0.566 | 0.094 | 0.286 | 0.073 | 0.014 | 0.913 |
| 1976–7 | 4992 | 0.630 | 0.960 | 0.015 | 0.025 | 0.018 | 0.374 | 0.560 | 0.066 | 0.302 | 0.066 | 0.013 | 0.921 |
| 1978–9 | 5134 | 0.666 | 0.962 | 0.013 | 0.025 | 0.015 | 0.325 | 0.597 | 0.078 | 0.319 | 0.067 | 0.011 | 0.922 |
| 1980–1 | 5304 | 0.656 | 0.948 | 0.029 | 0.023 | 0.021 | 0.264 | 0.600 | 0.136 | 0.323 | 0.053 | 0.017 | 0.930 |
| 1982–3 | 5425 | 0.611 | 0.932 | 0.042 | 0.026 | 0.051 | 0.205 | 0.727 | 0.068 | 0.338 | 0.057 | 0.032 | 0.911 |

*B. Women*

| | | *Employment* | | | | *Unemployment* | | | | *Not in the labour force* | | | |
|---|---|---|---|---|---|---|---|---|---|---|---|---|---|
| | $POP_{t-1}$ | $E_{t-1}$ | $P_{ee}$ | $P_{eu}$ | $P_{en}$ | $U_{t-1}$ | $P_{ue}$ | $P_{uu}$ | $P_{un}$ | $N_{t-1}$ | $P_{ne}$ | $P_{nu}$ | $P_{nn}$ |
| 1974–5 | 4874 | 0.235 | 0.837 | 0.016 | 0.147 | 0.003 | 0.461 | 0.385 | 0.154 | 0.762 | 0.029 | 0.003 | 0.968 |
| 1976–7 | 5056 | 0.231 | 0.889 | 0.014 | 0.097 | 0.005 | 0.435 | 0.435 | 0.130 | 0.764 | 0.029 | 0.003 | 0.968 |
| 1978–9 | 5221 | 0.243 | 0.897 | 0.014 | 0.089 | 0.006 | 0.375 | 0.469 | 0.156 | 0.751 | 0.027 | 0.005 | 0.968 |
| 1980–1 | 5406 | 0.268 | 0.905 | 0.020 | 0.075 | 0.011 | 0.383 | 0.450 | 0.167 | 0.721 | 0.026 | 0.008 | 0.966 |
| 1982–3 | 5549 | 0.270 | 0.905 | 0.022 | 0.073 | 0.019 | 0.269 | 0.577 | 0.154 | 0.711 | 0.030 | 0.011 | 0.959 |

*Note* $POP_{t-1}$ is the sum total of people employed ($E_{t-1}$), unemployed ($U_{t-1}$) or not in the labour force ($N_{t-1}$) in the first of the two years given. The relative distribution over these three labour market states in the same years is given by $e_{t-1}$, $u_{t-1}$ and $n_{t-1}$. $P_{ij}$ refers to the proportion of people moving from labour market status $i$ in the first year to labour market status $j$ in the second (defined as a proportion of the status in the first year).

*Source* CBS, Arbeidskrachtentellingen 1975, 1977, 1979, 1981 and 1983. These tables are aggregated from individual data on the labour market status in both years. The second year is always the year of the interview. Only people living in the Netherlands are counted. People drafted for military service are considered to be out of the labour force. Some other, small, adjustments were always balanced through the out-of-the-labour-force group.

## Appendix B Definition of Variables

*Dummy Variables: equal to 1 if:*

| | |
|---|---|
| GENDER | female |
| NON-DUTCH | persons with nationality other than Dutch or with Dutch nationality but born in Suriname or the Dutch Antilles |
| MARRIED | married or living together |

EDUCATION (highest level obtained)

| | |
|---|---|
| HIGH.ED | higher academic or vocational schooling |
| SEC.GEN.ED | secondary level, general schooling |
| SEC.VOC.ED | secondary level, vocational schooling |
| XPRIM.GEN.ED | extended primary level, general schooling |
| XPRIM.VOC.ED | extended primary level, vocational schooling |
| PARENT>SEC.ED | primary income earner (father or mother) has at least secondary level of education |
| PARENT.XPRIM.ED | primary income earner (father or mother) has extended primary level of education |
| HOUSEH.UNEM | one or more persons in the household (besides person interviewed) is/are unemployed |
| PREVIOUS JOB | whether one has had a job (of at least 20 hours a week) prior to June 1984 |
| 32–39 HOURS | works between 32 and 39 hours a week |
| 24–31 HOURS | works between 24 and 31 hours a week |
| 20–23 HOURS | works between 20 and 23 hours a week |
| CIVIL SERVANT | works in a (lower or central) governmental agency |

*Continuous variables*

| | |
|---|---|
| ln AGE | logarithm of age at moment of interview |
| ln *V*/*U* PROVINCE | logarithm of the ratio between registered vacancies ($V$) and number of unemployed ($U$) in the province where interviewed person lives (source: Central Bureau of Statistics/Sociaal-Economische Maandstatistiek, July 1984) |
| ln BENEFITS | logarithm of the after-tax unemployment benefit income per month. For those unemployed the benefits at interview month are used; for those working the benefits of the last unemployment period are relevant. In a few cases there were no benefits. To avoid computational problems the value of this variable was then set equal to 0.01 |
| ln PRED.EARNINGS | logarithm of predicted after-tax monthly earnings. Prediction was done with the earnings equation in (R. van Opstal and J. Theeuwes |

| | |
|---|---|
| | (1985)). For the hours worked dummies in that equation a variable stating the desired number of working hours per week was inserted for prediction purpose for those unemployed at interview. |
| ln REPLACEMENT RATIO | logarithm of ratio of BENEFITS and PRED.EARNINGS |

## Notes

1. For some help: seasonal; frictional; structural; cyclical; hard core; deficient demand; long term; natural; non-accelerating inflation rate of; full employment; equilibrium; growth gap; Keynesian; classical; voluntary; involuntary; wait; search; hidden.
2. A second functional form that has been used in the literature to study duration dependence in hazard functions is the Gompertz model. This is specified as follows:

   $$\theta(t) = \exp(a \cdot t)$$

   The Gompertz model has a 'problem' however. When there is negative duration dependence in this model, i.e. $a < 0$, this implies that the related distribution function is defective. This means that there exists a probability, not equal to zero, that someone might remain indefinitely unemployed. In our OSA-report (van Opstal and Theeuwes, 1985) we present estimation results with the Gompertz model.
3. Flinn and Heckman (1982a) assume a log-normal density for the heterogeneity term. Results with this density function are also discussed in van Opstal and Theeuwes (1985).
4. For simplicity reasons I dropped the 'birth, migration and death' flows into and out of the state 'Not in the labour force'.
5. Actually in this section the $P_{ij}$'s are defined as the flow from $i$ to $j$ divided by the initial stock of $i$. It is the gross number of persons that left $S_i$ for $S_j$ during the period $t$ as a proportion of the initial stock $S_i(t-1)$.

## References

BLAU, D. M. and ROBINS, P. K. (1986) 'Labor supply response to welfare programs: a dynamic analysis', *Journal of Labor Economics*, 4, 1, pp. 82–104.

CLARK, K. B. and SUMMERS, L. H. (1979) 'Labor market dynamics and unemployment: a reconsideration', *Brookings Papers on Economic Activity*, 1, pp. 13–60.

EHRENBERG, R. G. (1980) 'The demographic structure of unemployment rates and labor market transition probabilities', in *Research in Labor Economics*, 3, pp. 241–91.

FLINN, C. J. and HECKMAN J. J. (1982a) 'Models for the analysis of labor force dynamics', in Basmann and Rhodes (eds) *Advances in Econometrics*, 1, pp. 35–95.

FLINN, C. J. and HECKMAN, J. J. (1982b) 'New methods for analyzing structural models of labor force dynamics', *Journal of Econometrics*, 18, pp. 115–68.

HOLT, C. C. (1969) 'Improving the labor market trade-off between inflation and unemployment', *American Economic Review*, 59 (2).

HOLT, C. C. and DAVID M. H. (1966) 'The concept of vacancies in a dynamic theory of the labour market', in *Measurement and Interpretation of Job Vacancies* (New York: NBER), pp. 73–141.

JUNANKAR, P. J. and PRICE, S. (1984) 'The dynamics of unemployment: structural change and unemployment flows', *Economic Journal*, Conference Supplement, pp. 158–65.

KOOREMAN, P. and RIDDER, G. (1983) 'The effects of age and unemployment percentage on the duration of unemployment', *European Economic Review*, 20, pp. 41–57.

LANCASTER, T. (1979) 'Econometric methods for the duration of unemployment', *Econometrica*, 47, pp. 939–56.

LANCASTER, T. and NICKELL, S. (1980) 'The Analysis of Re-employment Probabilities for the Unemployed', *Journal of the Royal Statistical Society A*, 143, pp. 141–65.

LYNCH, L. M. (1985) State dependence in youth unemployment: a lost generation?, in *Journal of Econometrics*, 28, pp. 71–84.

MARSTON, S. (1976) 'Employment Stability and High Unemployment Rates', *Brookings Papers on Economic Activity*, pp. 169–203.

VAN OPSTAL, R. and THEEUWES, J. (1985) *Jeugdige werklozen en hun kans op een baan* (The Hague: Organisatie voor Strategisch Arbeidsmarktonderzoek (OSA), working paper 14).

## COMMENT ON CHAPTERS 1 AND 2

**Daniel Weiserbs**

1. These two chapters provide important and to some extent complementary contributions to the analysis of the position of an individual in the labour market. The study of Blundell, Ham and Meghir (in short B–H–M) is an impressive generalisation of previous econometric studies based on classical consumer-demand analysis while Theeuwes sheds light on the methodological problems involved in applying individual probabilities to the study of the dynamics of aggregate unemployment.
2. The extension of neoclassical demand analysis to the modelling of a labour-supply function is a rather controversial issue and, indeed, it has quite often yielded meaningless or misleading results especially in an aggregate time-series context. However, the neoclassical model of labour supply is by far more realistic and therefore more useful when applied to the participation decision of individuals.

   Basically, an individual $h$, described by a vector of characteristics, $d_h$, participates if the wage rate offered to him, $w_h$, exceeds his implicit price of leisure (shadow wage) $w_h^*$. To proceed to the estimation of the participation probability several problems have to be tackled.
3. The first and obvious one is the specification of a household objective function theoretically plausible with the least possible *a priori* restrictions. B–H–M choose the generalised linear expenditure system whose cost function is:

$$C = ub(\cdot) + a(\cdot)$$

with

$$b(\cdot) = \Pi_i p_i^{bi} \text{ and } a(\cdot) = \Sigma_i \Sigma_j a_{ij} (p_i p_j)^{1/2}$$

where

$$i, j = 0, n;\ p_o = w \text{ and } a_{ij},\ b_i \text{ are function of } d_h.$$

This flexible form together with the quite general specifications of $a_{ij}$ and $b_i$ amounts to a substantial progress with respect to previous empirical studies in the field which very often have used rather *ad hoc* linear forms. In particular their model allows for any plausible shape of the labour-supply function. However, for practical reasons, all households are assumed to face the same prices. Consequently, $n$ is set equal to 1(one) which rules out complementarity between leisure and any of the consumption goods. Yet, one may hope that the regional dummies will capture most of the price differences.

4. A second problem is that wages offered to non-participants are unobservable. B–H–M avoid this difficulty by modelling a wage equation (equation 1.6). This is likely to be the best if not the only way to proceed. However, introducing in this equation the same characteristics as those entering in the $a_{ij}$ and $b_i$ functions creates a problem of identification. Moreover, it is not clear why the wage offered to a women should depend on her family's size, her husband's level of education, her husband's age, etc.
5. The third problem is that the neoclassical model assumes that any individual who wishes to work does find a job, i.e. only 'voluntary unemployment' exists.

   The methodology proposed by B–H–M to distinguish among non-participants those who do not want to work from those willing to work is straightforward. It consists in decomposing the probability of observing zero hours of work by modelling the probability of finding a job as a function of a vector of macroeconomic and local variables. As B–H–M correctly point out the standard tobit model is no longer an adequate econometric tool. Quite ingeniously they use the 'double-hurdle' model introduced by Cragg in the context of demand for durable goods. This also yields a quite satisfactory way to analyse the effects of the demand-side variables on the participation rate.
6. To conclude there is no doubt in my mind that B–H–M contribute an excellent and important chapter and I am pleased to hear that further research is on its way, which is to take into account, among other features, the problem of discouraged workers. I would also suggest that they should examine the possibility of simultaneity in the household's decisions regarding hours of work and children. Concerning the econometric part, the report would benefit from a search for a more parsimonious representation of the model, especially given the fact

that some specifications of demographic characteristics (e.g. conditional dummies) appears rather *ad hoc* and perhaps unnecessarily complicated.

7. The data available to Theeuwes is far more limited. Nevertheless, it has the advantage of containing information on the same sample at two points of time. This permits one to examine an additional question with respect to the previous analysis: the probability of moving from one category (employed, unemployed, not participating) to another between time $t$ and time $t+1$. If everything remains constant, this could be described by an appropriate hazard function. Theeuwes selects the Weibull distribution which is particularly appropriate for describing the failure functions in situations where failure is essentially due to the most serious flaw among a large number of flaws in the system. In fact, its success was originally due to its capacity to describe well the malfunctioning characteristics of the B52 aircraft.

8. Theeuwes incorporates a second functional form, $e^{x'b}$, where $x$ is a set of personal characteristics and economic variables that might shift the hazard. However there is no mention of the constraints this form must satisfy if $\theta$ is to remain a probability.

   Here also I wonder why the author did not examine either the implication of statistically acceptable restrictions or the possible relationships between some characteristics. For instance, if it is true that a primary level of education reduces the probability of an individual's escaping from unemployment, this should also apply to his parents, inducing collinearity between 'househ. unempl.' and 'parents prim.ed'.

9. In the second part of his paper, Theeuwes describes and illustrates what could be a sensible methodology which aggregates individual transition probabilities. Such an ambitious exercise would indeed be of great importance in examining the impact of various policy measures, not so much, in my opinion, on the steady-state level of unemployment but rather on its distribution between individual categories (if the purpose of the study is only the level of unemployment, I believe that a good macroeconometric model is simpler and more efficient).

   I would like to emphasise that aggregate transition probabilities should not simply consist of averaging individual probabilities but requires a lot of care. For example, as individual probabilities depend on the regional unemployment rate, simple aggregation will end up with a tautology. Another problem is that one cannot explain individual probabilities by all the variables which affect at least one group. But several measures amount in fact to 'export' unemployment from one group to another one. Although possibly desirable on some equity grounds, such measures hardly affect aggregate probabilities. Simple aggregation will yield misleading impacts.

# 3 A Vintage Model of Labour Demand by UK Manufacturing

J. Ansar, A. Ingham, M. Toker and A. Ulph

## 3.1 INTRODUCTION

The conventional model of factor demand has firms choosing the technique of production and mix of factor inputs to minimise the cost of producing some given level of output for an exogenously determined set of factor prices and a given set of technical know-how. In this simple model, firms are free to vary the mix of factors each period. Unemployment then occurs as a feature of labour-market failure. For otherwise wage rates would adjust so that supply equalled demand. A vintage model takes account of the fact that some factors are durable, and this means that it is important to take account of two different decisions on factor choice. Firms will make an *ex ante* choice of techniques at the time that new capital is installed – e.g. will firms use automated energy-intensive or labour-intensive production methods? Once that piece of capital is installed, firms may be able subsequently to alter the mix of factors, but their ability to do so is now constrained by the *ex ante* choice of technique. This second decision is the *ex post* decision.

At any moment of time, then, the ability of firms to respond to a change in factor prices, or a change in the demand for their output, will depend precisely on which kinds (or vintages) of capital they invested in previously. In the short run, the substitution possibilities are given by the extent of substitution available for each vintage of capital, and the extent to which firms can vary the amount of output they produce on each vintage. In the long run firms can also change the structure of capital stock by new investment, so the vintage approach will lead naturally to long-run responses being greater than short. Crucial in policy questions will be how long the long run is, or alternatively the degree of flexibility that exists. The aim of this paper is to measure this degree of flexibility in labour usage. This is also important in comparing this degree of flexibility in labour usage. This is also important in comparing alternative models of production and their implications for the underlying causes of unemployment, and actions that can be taken to reduce such levels.

The neoclassical model of smooth strictly convex isoquants in which wage rigidities, and other similar phenomena, are usually blamed for unemployment has already been mentioned. One alternative to this is the case of Leontief isoquants in which relative prices play no role at all, and the level of employment is purely determined by demand. The model we estimate includes both of these as nested special cases. It is therefore possible to test for the validity of these against the more general structure in which there is some flexibility at the operation stage, but not as much as at the design stage. For obvious reasons this is referred to as a putty-semi-putty model. Such a model was first estimated in Fuss (1977) for electricity generation in the USA. The model reported here does a similar analysis but for manufacturing industry in the UK. The fact that we are dealing with an aggregate sector for which data on individual vintage operation is not available (unlike electricity generation) causes some obstacles. However as aggregate manufacturing employment is of some policy interest, and recent work by Muellbauer (1984) and Mendis and Muellbauer (1984) has pointed to the way changes in labour productivity and demand are related to a changing capital stock, we believe that attempts to overcome these obstacles are of some importance.

There is certainly quite a lot to be explained in the data. Figures 3.1, 3.2 and 3.3 show the paths of output, labour demand and the real wage rate over the period 1955–83. The relatively smooth growth in output in the first two-thirds of the period was followed by a period of zero trend growth and then fall in output levels. This has been accompanied by a more or less continuous fall in employment, of considerable magnitude in the final quarters. Real wages have also shown considerable change in behaviour, changing from a smooth exponential path to one of considerable variability. These variable patterns provide a challenge to any model. In fact many have broken down during this period. The large variability in the data should provide evidence on the degree of substitutability, which is of some policy importance in the current era of large factor price changes. For example, whether the current large falls in oil prices will lead to increases in employment through stimulation to demand, or whether to reduced employment due to energy/labour substitution will hinge on this.

*Figure* 3.1 Output

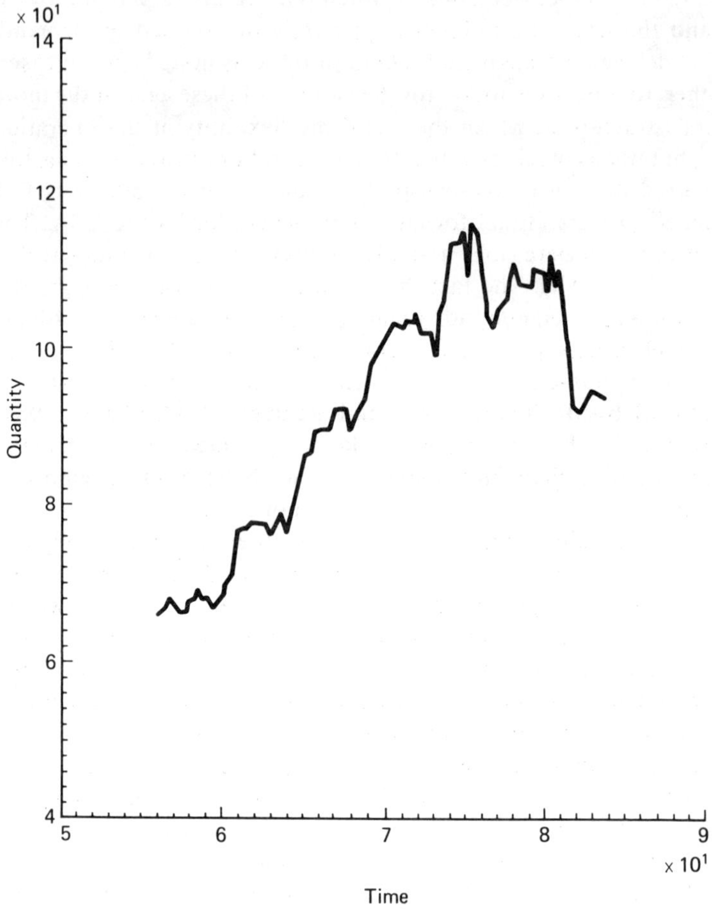

*Figure* 3.2 Labour demand

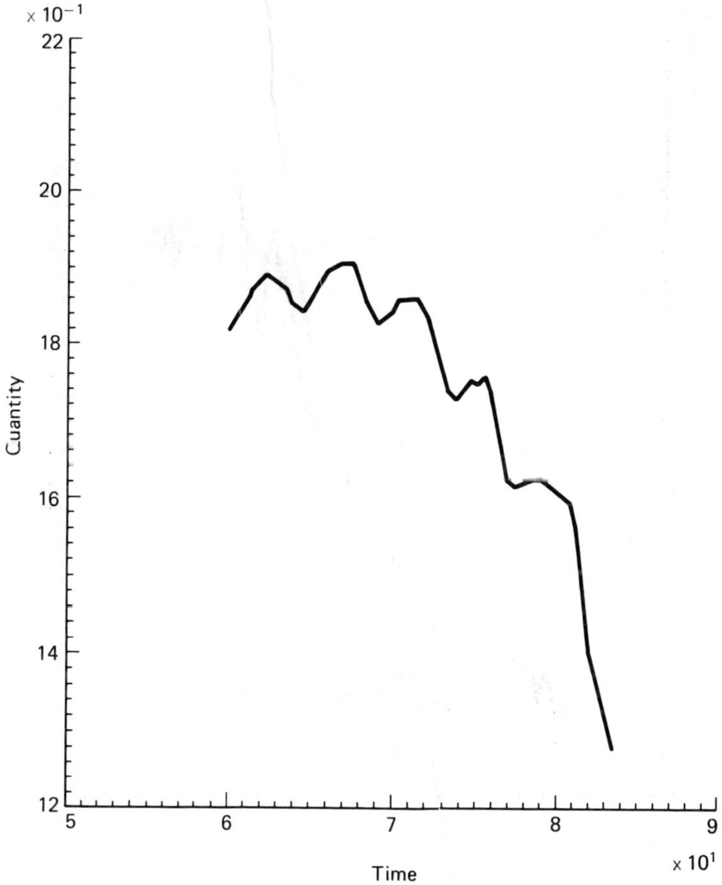

*Figure* 3.3 Real labour price

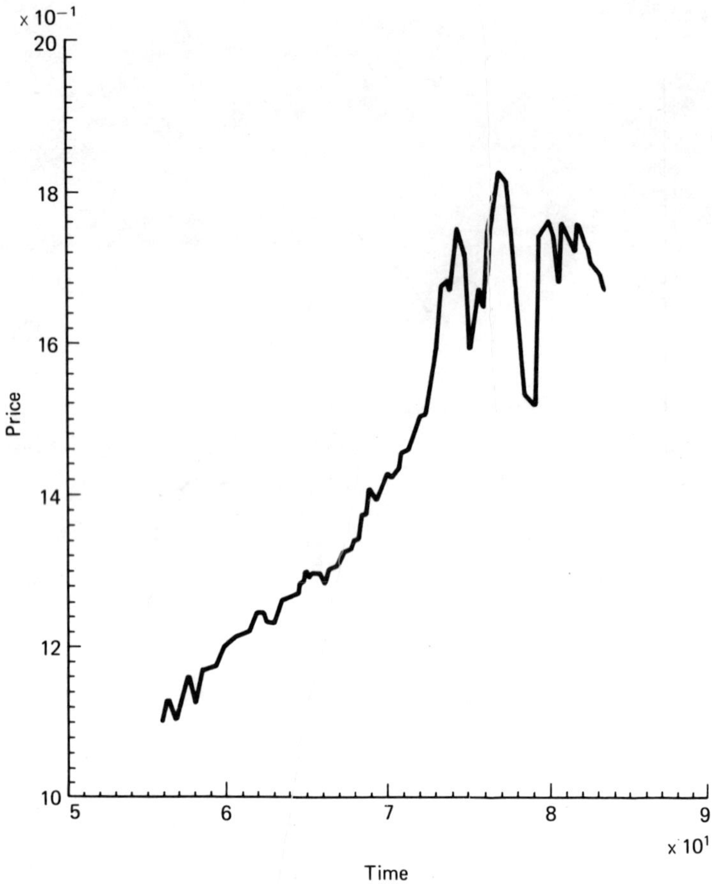

Section 3.2 gives a brief view of the working of the model and how it is estimated. Section 3.3 gives the results of estimation and reports the hypothesis-testing on the nested models. Details of the implications of the model for labour demand are contained in section 3.4.

## 3.2 A DESCRIPTION OF THE VINTAGE MODEL

In this section, we shall give an overview of the model and how it is estimated. For fuller descriptions of the problems and methods involved see Ansar, Ingham, Leon, Toker and Ulph (1986a and b). The model reported on here is one of a variety of models examined and the experience gained with those has influenced the assumptions that have been made. In particular our treatment of technical progress is due to these results.

Output is produced using capital, labour and energy. (It had been intended to include materials in this list. However there is not sufficient reliable data to allow this to be done.) It is possible to vary the capital, labour and energy output ratios at the design stage, but at the operation stage the capital output ratio is fixed and only the labour and energy output ratios may be varied, albeit to a lesser extent. The model is illustrated in Figure 3.4.

Suppose it has been decided to install capital designed to produce an output level $y^*$. *Ex ante* it has to be decided which technique is to be used. The *ex ante* set of available techniques is given by isoquant $AA$. Given expected factor prices $Ep_E$, $Ep_k$ technique $X$ is selected. In practice, actual factor prices, $P_E$ and $P_k$, turn out to be different from those expected, but whilst firms can make some changes in the quantities of factors that they use the choice open to them *ex post* is more restrictive than *ex ante.* The appropriate *ex post* isoquant for choice of techniques is then $BB$, and cost minimisation occurs at point $Y$. Of course had factor prices been accurately predicted, firms would have been able to operate at $Z$.

Thus the actual cost of production depends on actual factor prices, the nature of the *ex post* isoquant, the *ex ante* choice which determines which *ex post* isoquant is being operated on, which in turn depends on the *ex ante* isoquant and the expected prices. Suppose that *ex ante* the firm has to choose a vector $d$ of design coefficients. At time, $v$, a choice $d^v$ is made. At time $t > v$, firms have to choose a vector of factor-demands, $x$, to minimise costs of producing actual output $y_t$ given a vector of factor prices $p_t$ and the *ex ante* choice $d^v$. This generates an *ex post* cost function $C_{vt}(p_t, y_t : d^v)$.

*Figure* 3.4 Choice of production techniques

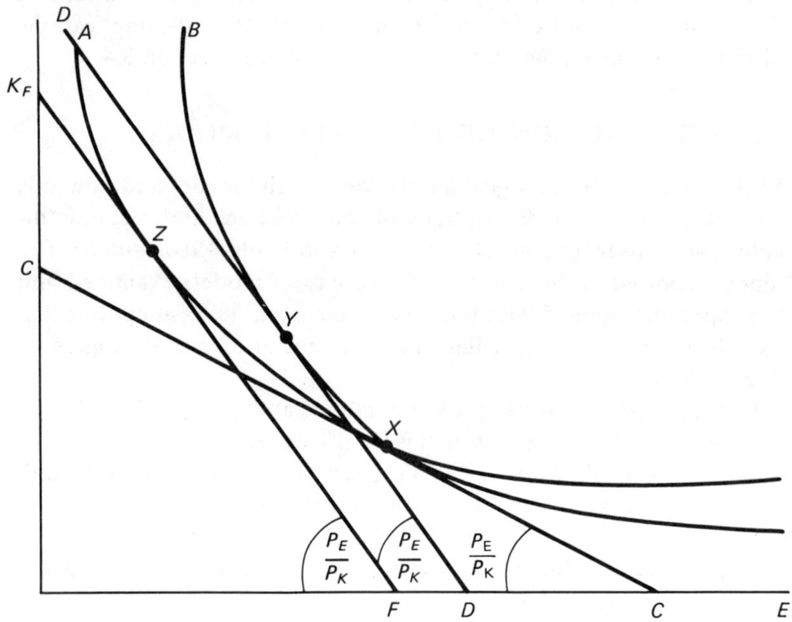


To link the *ex post* and *ex ante* decisions, firms choose $d^v$ to minimise present value expected future costs; i.e. firms choose $d^v$ to minimise

$$V(d^v) = \sum_{t=v}^{t=v+2} \rho_{t-v} C_{vt}(Ep_t, Ey_t : d^v) \tag{3.1}$$

subject to some restrictions on $d^v$ given by $f(d^v) = 0$, where $\rho_{t-v}$ is the relevant discount factor, and $L$ is the expected horizon of the decision.

One immediate aspect of the vintage model is that it requires us to model the formation of price expectations, and it turns out to be crucial how this is done. Unfortunately it is not possible to use perfect foresight as this would use up too many observations, and so the estimated model uses simple time-series-based expectations. Even with these some difficulties are experienced, due to the sharp real energy price falls that occurred in the first half of the sample. There are also two important theoretical implications. First, it may well be that the sluggish response to changing factor prices is not due to technical constraints, but to the slow response of expectations to shifts in current prices. Secondly the variance of price forecasts will determine the amount of *ex post* variability that firms may want to make, in other words the degree of flexibility that they will choose. This is something which we do not model, but hope to do in further work.

We now specify the functions $C$ and $f$. In choosing these we follow the forms used by Fuss (1977) for similar reasons. These are the generalised Leontief form, which have three advantages: (i) they are a flexible functional form; (ii) parameter restrictions allow the putty–semi-putty model to be restricted to putty–clay, putty–putty, and clay–clay subcases; (iii) perhaps most importantly, all the calculations which follow from this functional form are linear, which enables the vast number of calculations which have to be done for the model to be estimated using maximum likelihood methods, to be done quickly. This allows for feasible estimation using existing computing power. This point should be remembered in connection with some of the restrictions that have been imposed.

$C$ therefore has the form:

$$C_{vt}(p_t, y_t) = y_t \Sigma_i \Sigma_j b^v_{ij}(p_{it} p_{it})^{1/2} \tag{3.2}$$

From this we can calculate *ex post* factor demands:

$$x^v_{it} = y_t [\Sigma b^v_{ij}(p_{jt}/p_{it})^{1/2}] \tag{3.3}$$

At the *ex ante* stage firms choose the parameters $b^v_{ij}$, which corresponds to the vector $d^v$. They also choose the capital stock. This is discussed later. The separate time-series models for price expectations provide $Ep^v_{it}$, where this is the expected price of factor $i$ at time $t$, the expectation being formed at time $v$. Firms use a planning horizon for capital of $L$, and a depreciation factor of $\delta_{t-v}$. These are both parameters to be estimated, the estimation procedure being a simple grid search.

More complex to handle is the inclusion of technical progress. This has been allowed for so far by the inclusion of a subscript $t$ in the cost function $C_{vt}$. In fact it has not proved possible so far to allow for this, due to the increased computational burden imposed, and the fact that a technical progress parameter could not be estimated in the relatively straightforward way that the depreciation term can be. Support for exclusion of this term is provided by the fact that when a technical progress term was included in a Cobb–Douglas Leontief vintage model, for which these complications do not arise, it was extremely small.

Given initial investment at time $v$, there will be an initial level of installed capacity output $y_v^v$, so that in year $t$ output will be given by

$$y_v^t = \delta_{t-v} y_v^v$$

We now come to the specification of the function $f$. Firms will choose the parameters $b_{ij}^v$ to minimise the present value of expected future costs subject to a Generalised Leontief relationship. Fuss (1977) shows that the solution to this problem is:

$$b_{ij}^v = \Sigma_k \Sigma_l \{q_{kl}^v / q_{ij}^v\}^{1/2} \alpha_{ijkl} \tag{3.4}$$

where

$$q_{ij}^v = \Sigma \rho_{t-v} \delta_{t-v} (Ep_{it}^v Ep_{it}^v)^{1/2} \tag{3.5}$$

$q_{ij}^v$ can be thought of as a present value expected price. Eliminating $b_{ij}^v$ from the factor demand equation gives a factor demand equation in terms of the parameters $\alpha$

$$x_{it}^v = y_t \Sigma\Sigma\Sigma \{q_{kl}^v / q_{ij}^v)^{1/2} \{p_{jt} / p_{it})^{1/2} \alpha_{ijkl} \tag{3.6}$$

The model is now characterised by the parameters $\alpha_{ijkl}$ which determine both the *ex ante* and *ex post* isoquants, and it is these parameters that we wish to estimate. These parameters will satisfy certain theoretical restrictions which will allow us to reduce their number considerably. Symmetry restrictions imply that:

$$\alpha_{ijkl} = \alpha_{jikl} = \alpha_{jilk} = \alpha_{ijlk}$$

The maintained hypothesis is that of putty–semi-putty, that is that *ex ante* and *ex post* isoquants differ, but neither is Leontief. Further restrictions on the $\alpha$ parameters yield the following special cases:

clay–clay $\alpha_{ijkl} = 0$ unless $i = j = k = l$

putty–putty $\alpha_{ijkl} = 0$ unless $i, j = k, l$

putty–clay $\alpha_{ijkl} = 0$ unless $i = j, k = l$

The problem with the estimation of the factor demand equations, given above, is that it is specified in terms of individual vintages whereas the only data available on factor demands and output is at an aggregate level. To overcome this problem it is necessary to specify how the output on individual vintages is determined at each moment of time. We make the conventional assumption that vintages will be employed in decreasing order of the rents that they earn, or equivalently in order of increasing variable cost. Let factor 3 be capital which we have assumed to be fixed *ex post* apart from depreciation. This is shown by Fuss to imply that $b_{i3}^{v}=0,\ i\neq 3$. The demand for capital services on vintage $v$ at time $t$ is given by:

$$x_{3t} = b_{33}^{v} y_{v} \tag{3.7}$$

Now it is assumed that $x_{3t}^{v} \leq I^{v}\delta_{t-v}$ where $I^{v}$ is the amount of investment made in vintage $v$ equipment. Apart from a marginal vintage it will be the case that either $y_v = 0$ or that

$$y_v = I^{v}\delta_{t-v}/b_{33}^{v}. \tag{3.8}$$

Vintages will be used either at full capacity or not at all.

Whether or not a vintage is used will depend on its variable cost. This is given by

$$VC_t^{v} = \sum_{i,j\neq 3} b_{ij}^{v}(p_{it}p_{it})^{1/2} \tag{3.9}$$

Vintages will be used in order of increasing cost until the total aggregate output is produced. In Figure 3.5 vintages $v_1$ and $v_2$ are used up to full capacity. Vintage $v_3$ is the marginal vintage. No other vintages are used, being either idle or scrapped. Of course in the variable cost expressions there appear $b$ parameters which in turn depend on $\alpha$ parameters to be estimated. This is then done in an iterative way which can be briefly summarised as follows:

1. Calculate present value expected prices $q_{ij}^{v}$ for all $i, j, v$ as given by equation (3.5).
2. Use current $\alpha$ estimates and the $q_{ij}^{v}$ to calculate the $b_{ij}^{v}$ as given by equation (3.4).
3. Calculate variable costs on all vintages as done by equation (3.9).
4. Decide on which vintages will be used.
5. Calculate predicted factor demands using equation (3.6).
6. Obtain errors in prediction.

*Figure* 3.5 The utilisation of vintages

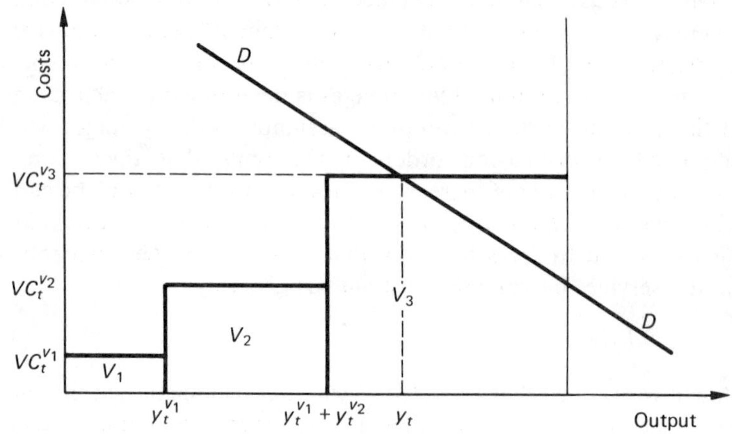


7. Use function minimisation algorithm to recalculate $\alpha$.

In this way it is possible to avoid having to have data on individual vintages, although calculating which vintages to use is non-trivial in terms of computing time.

## 3.3 ESTIMATED RESULTS

This section presents the results from maximum likelihood estimation. Equation (3.6) for $i = l, e$ gives a system of two equations, which correspond to a system of seemingly unrelated regressions. Because of the non-linearity in the equations they should not be estimated using *OLS*. It can be shown that the correct maximand is $|uu'|$. The model in (3.6) has potentially 34 parameters $\alpha_{ijkl}$. Symmetry restrictions reduce this number considerably to 36. Further restrictions that capital is fixed *ex post* eliminate a further 12 parameters. These are presented in the following way.

Let the three *ex post* input–output coefficients for labour, energy and capital be $\lambda_1, \lambda_2, \lambda_3$. The structure of the model shows that these have the form

$$\lambda_1(v, t) = A_1(v) + A_4(v)(p_{0t}/p_{1t})^{1/2}$$

$$\lambda_2(v, t) = A_2(v) + A_4(v)(p_{1t}/p_{0t})^{1/2}$$

$$\lambda_3(v, t) = A_3(v)$$

Each of the functions $A_1$, $A_2$, $A_3$, $A_4$ is linear in present value expected prices corresponding to price ratios of the six pairs of factors, *KK*, *LL*, *EE*, *KL*, *KE*, *LE*. The coefficients are presented as elements $a_{ij}$ of a $4 \times 6$ matrix *A*, where the rows correspond to the functions $A_1$, $A_2$, $A_3$, $A_4$ and the columns to the ratio of present value expected prices. Parameter estimates for the period 1966*Q*1 to 1982*Q*3 are shown in Table 3.1, together with those for the subcases to which we now turn.

*Table* 3.1 Estimated parameters of the Fuss model

| | | *Model* | | |
|---|---|---|---|---|
| *Parameter* | *PSP* | *PC* | *PP* | *CC* |
| $a_{11}$ | −0.0033 | −0.0069 | 0.0161 | 0.0160 |
| $a_{12}$ | 0.0529 | 0.0569 | — | — |
| $a_{13}$ | −0.0770 | −0.0545 | — | — |
| $a_{14}$ | −0.0761 | −0.0682 | — | — |
| $a_{15}$ | −0.3561 | −0.2938 | — | — |
| $a_{16}$ | 0.0480 | 0.0415 | — | — |
| $a_{21}$ | −0.0216 | −0.0194 | — | — |
| $a_{22}$ | −0.0312 | −0.0295 | 0.0181 | 0.0175 |
| $a_{23}$ | −0.5421 | −0.6618 | | — |
| $a_{24}$ | −0.1194 | −0.1181 | — | — |
| $a_{25}$ | −0.0664 | −0.0658 | — | — |
| $a_{26}$ | 0.1005 | 0.1010 | — | — |
| $a_{31}$ | 3.9233 | 4.2677 | — | — |
| $a_{32}$ | 2.3363 | 2.8816 | — | — |
| $a_{33}$ | −3.4851 | 5.5634 | — | — |
| $a_{34}$ | 1.1244 | −0.8828 | — | — |
| $a_{35}$ | −2.3507 | −0.6071 | — | — |
| $a_{36}$ | −1.5765 | 2.8284 | — | — |
| $a_{41}$ | −0.0016 | — | — | — |
| $a_{42}$ | 0.0026 | — | — | — |
| $a_{43}$ | 0.0716 | — | — | — |
| $a_{44}$ | −0.0015 | — | — | — |
| $a_{45}$ | 0.0193 | — | — | — |
| $a_{46}$ | −0.0008 | — | −0.0003 | — |
| $SS^2$ Total | 0.4193 | 0.5990 | 1.9603 | 1.9611 |
| $SS^2$ Labour | 0.2003 | 0.2996 | 1.5122 | 1.5007 |
| $SS^2$ Energy | 0.2190 | 0.2994 | 0.4481 | 0.4604 |
| *RSQ* Total | 0.9989 | 0.9984 | 0.9948 | 0.9948 |
| *RSQ* Labour | 0.9988 | 0.9983 | 0.9912 | 0.9912 |
| *RSQ* Energy | 0.9989 | 0.9985 | 0.9978 | 0.9978 |

It can now be seen how the restrictions of the full putty-semi-putty model (*PSP*) to its subcases can be made. The putty-clay (*PC*) model assumes substitution *ex ante* but not *ex post*, therefore expected prices at the time of installation enter the equations for *ex post* input-output coefficients but not current prices. This imposes the restriction on $A$ that $a_{4j} = 0\ j = 1, 6$. Next most restricted is the putty-putty model (PP) which assumes that factors can be substituted to the same extent *ex post* as *ex ante*. The only prices to enter the equations will be the current ones, and thus the only non-zero elements will be constant terms, which turn out to be $a_{11}, a_{22}, a_{33}, a_{46}$. This last term being the only non-zero parameter in $B(v)$ will determine the degree of substitutability. In the clay-clay case (*CC*) this will be zero. The four models are nested as follows:

$$PSP \supset PC \supset CC$$

$$PSP \supset PP \supset CC$$

and it is possible to test which of the restrictions can be accepted. These tests are reported in Table 3.2.

Grid search on $L$ and $\delta$ gave values of 20 and 0.0001. One final point is that within the *PP* and *CC* models the capital-output ratio $a_{33}$ plays no effective role as all machines are identical. This value is therefore fixed and consequently not reported.

Turning to the results, we can note that the sums of squares are in the order suggested by the nesting. To test whether they correspond to valid restrictions of the general model we conduct a likelihood ratio test assuming that 61 observations are sufficient for us to use large-sample theory so that $-2 \log \lambda$ is distributed as $\chi^2(m)$ where $\lambda$ is the

*Table* 3.2 Tests of restrictions

| *Models* | | | | |
|---|---|---|---|---|
| *Unrestricted* | *Restricted* | $-2 \log \lambda$ | *Degrees of freedom* | *Critical value* $\chi^2_{0.995}(m)$ |
| *PSP* | *PC* | 21.757 | 6 | 18.5 |
| *PSP* | *PP* | 94.078 | 20 | 40.0 |
| *PSP* | *CC* | 94.102 | 21 | 41.4 |
| *PC* | *CC* | 72.346 | 15 | 32.8 |
| *PP* | *CC* | 0.025 | 1 | 7.88 |

restricted-to-unrestricted likelihood ratio $L_R/L_u$ and there are $m$ degrees of freedom. It is clear from Table 3.2 that the only restriction that can be accepted is that of clay–clay as a special case of putty–putty; we shall return to this finding. All other restrictions are quite easily rejected, even using a very tight significance level. The maintained hypothesis is therefore that of putty–semi-putty, and at the aggregate

*Figure* 3.6 Aggregate PSP – labour

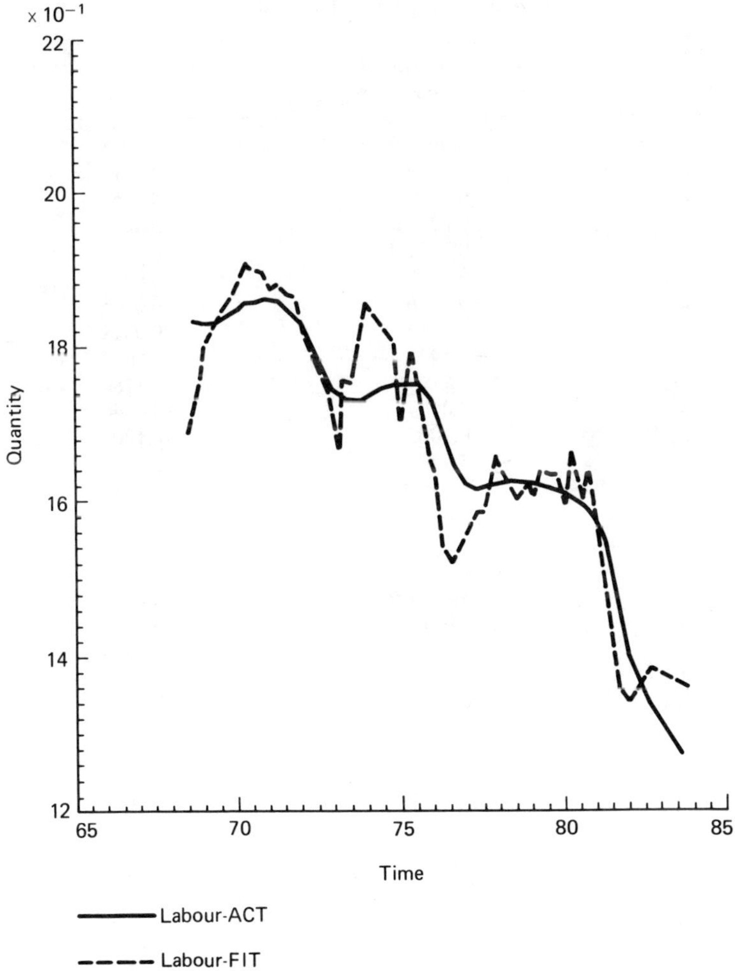

level we overwhelmingly reject the assumption that there is no vintage structure to production and factor demands. It also appears that some *ex post* substitution does take place.

These findings are reinforced by carrying out stability tests. As mentioned in the introduction, one of the problems that models have faced is adequately explaining the falls in factor demands in the later part of the sample period. The tracking performance is presented in Figure 3.6. This shows a pattern the reverse of what one usually sees

*Table* 3.3 Aggregate PSP stability test

| | *Parameter* | *Coefficients estimated on complete data set* | *Coefficients estimated on restricted data set* |
|---|---|---|---|
| | $a_{11}$ | −0.0033 | −0.0028 |
| | $a_{12}$ | 0.0529 | 0.0516 |
| | $a_{13}$ | −0.0770 | −0.0666 |
| | $a_{14}$ | −0.0761 | −0.0781 |
| | $a_{15}$ | −0.3561 | −0.3535 |
| | $a_{16}$ | 0.0480 | 0.0485 |
| | $a_{21}$ | −0.0216 | −0.0215 |
| | $a_{22}$ | −0.0312 | −0.0311 |
| | $a_{23}$ | −0.5421 | −0.5374 |
| | $a_{24}$ | −0.1194 | −0.1186 |
| | $a_{25}$ | −0.0664 | −0.0640 |
| | $a_{26}$ | 0.1005 | 0.1007 |
| | $a_{31}$ | 3.9233 | 3.7595 |
| | $a_{32}$ | 2.3363 | 2.3540 |
| | $a_{33}$ | −3.4851 | −2.3287 |
| | $a_{34}$ | 1.1244 | −0.7396 |
| | $a_{35}$ | −2.3507 | −1.7874 |
| | $a_{36}$ | −1.5765 | −1.5715 |
| | $a_{41}$ | −0.0016 | −0.0023 |
| | $a_{42}$ | 0.0026 | 0.0027 |
| | $a_{43}$ | 0.0716 | 0.0834 |
| | $a_{44}$ | −0.0015 | −0.0006 |
| | $a_{45}$ | 0.0193 | 0.0183 |
| | $a_{46}$ | −0.0008 | −0.0006 |
| *SS* | Total | 0.4193 | 0.4136 |
| | Labour | 0.2003 | 0.1999 |
| | Energy | 0.2190 | 0.2136 |
| $R^2$ | Total | 0.9989 | 0.9989 |
| | Labour | 0.9988 | 0.9998 |
| | Energy | 0.9989 | 0.9990 |

- the actual series being quite smooth, but the fitted values showing some variation about this path. This is particularly marked for the period 1974–6. Some variation of this type should be expected. The model assumes that firms will be able to make the adjustments they desire, and that workers work equally hard in all periods. Thus we do not allow for labour-hoarding and increased intensity of effort. However we do capture the fall in employment since 1979 well. This is a within-sample result though. For this reason the model was estimated on data up to 1979*Q*3, which is just before the sharp drop took place, and then used to forecast for the period 1979*Q*4–1982*Q*3. Table 3.3 presents a comparison of the two sets of estimates. It is not possible to make definite statments comparing them. This is because standard errors of the estimates are not yet available. These standard errors are normally obtained from the information matrix, which will be obtained from the likelihood maximisation algorithm. However, because of non-linearities inherent in the vintage structure, it was not possible to use a Gauss–Newton algorithm and a simplicial one devised by Nelder and Mead, which does not require derivatives, was used. Of course such an algorithm does not provide derivatives either.

It can be seen that the parameter estimates, apart from the $a_{3j}$ parameters, are close, in particular $a_{34}$. These parameters correspond to the capital/output ratio which we would not expect to be particularly robust given that we do not have either an investment or a scrapping equation.

*Table* 3.4 Comparison of forecasts from three models

| | *Labour* | | | | *Energy* | | | |
|---|---|---|---|---|---|---|---|---|
| *Quarter* | *Actual* | *B–J* | *CDL* | *PSP* | *Actual* | *B–J* | *CDL* | *PSP* |
| 1979*Q*4 | 1.5848 | 1.5903 | 1.5574 | 1.6402 | 1.8358 | 1.9058 | 1.8385 | 1.8687 |
| 1980*Q*1 | 1.5652 | 1.5726 | 1.5032 | 1.5885 | 1.9138 | 1.9292 | 1.7786 | 1.8068 |
| 1980*Q*2 | 1.5350 | 1.5526 | 1.4279 | 1.5146 | 1.6792 | 1.7960 | 1.6921 | 1.7267 |
| 1980*Q*3 | 1.4928 | 1.5268 | 1.3508 | 1.4385 | 1.6006 | 1.6864 | 1.6030 | 1.6316 |
| 1980*Q*4 | 1.4445 | 1.5056 | 1.2775 | 1.3668 | 1.6488 | 1.8794 | 1.5187 | 1.5183 |
| 1981*Q*1 | 1.4052 | 1.4871 | 1.2531 | 1.3495 | 1.6320 | 1.7096 | 1.4945 | 1.4770 |
| 1981*Q*2 | 1.3735 | 1.4725 | 1.2542 | 1.3554 | 1.5110 | 1.6722 | 1.5020 | 1.5025 |
| 1981*Q*3 | 1.3494 | 1.4699 | 1.2736 | 1.3837 | 1.5022 | 1.6583 | 1.5329 | 1.5374 |
| 1981*Q*4 | 1.3328 | 1.4735 | 1.2732 | 1.3956 | 1.6030 | 1.7224 | 1.5393 | 1.5241 |
| 1982*Q*1 | 1.3162 | 1.4777 | 1.2603 | 1.3908 | 1.5926 | 1.7327 | 1.5299 | 1.5116 |
| 1982*Q*2 | 1.2996 | 1.4807 | 1.2489 | 1.3822 | 1.4566 | 1.6357 | 1.5222 | 1.5222 |
| 1982*Q*3 | 1.2814 | 1.4882 | 1.2348 | 1.3745 | 1.4742 | 1.6064 | 1.5111 | 1.5145 |

A further test is to compare the model performance to that of others. Table 3.4 and Figure 3.7 show comparisons with two other models that we have estimated. One is a Cobb–Douglas–Leontief vintage model(*CDL*), which is of some interest as it is the version of vintage model normally considered, the other model is a Box–Jenkins type time series model (*B–J*). This uses all the information available to the vintage model, and a specification obtained by time series methods.

*Figure* 3.7 Labour-demand forecasts – all models

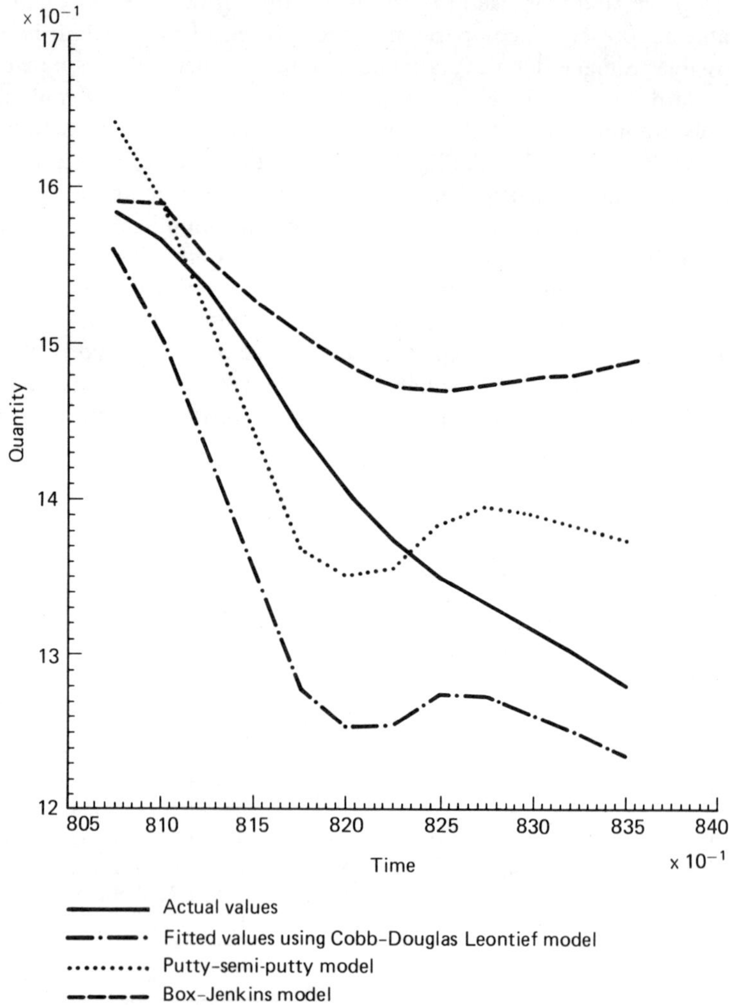

Whilst improvements undoubtedly could be made to this model it does combine all the same information but in a non-structural way. It was this type of comparison that we particularly wanted to make.

All the models were then estimated on the same data prior to 1979*Q*3, and then used to forecast up to 1982*Q*3. It is clear from Table 3.4 and Figure 3.7 that only the *PSP* model provides reasonable forecasts for labour demand, the *B–J* model overpredicting throughout and the *CDL* model underpredicting.

## 3.4 APPLYING THE MODEL TO LABOUR DEMAND CHARACTERISTICS

We now look at the results of the estimation on various ways in order to pull out the implications for labour demand. We begin by plotting the graphs of the *ex ante* and *ex post* isoquants for labour and energy. The *ex ante* isoquant is labelled *AA* in Figure 3.8. This will be the same for all periods. Curve *BB* in this figure is the *ex post* isoquant corresponding to machines installed in 1973*Q*1. Although the units of both labour and energy are in index form it can be seen that the *ex post* isoquant, while displaying some curvature, is close to a Leontief isoquant. This is confirmed by calculating the elasticity of substitution for the *ex post* isoquant. The *ex post* labour-output and energy-output ratios, $\lambda_1(t)$, $\lambda_2(t)$ for 1973*Q*1 capital can be obtained by using the price expectations current at that time. They are

$$\lambda_1(t) = 0.01446 + 0.001468(p_{et}/p_{1t})^{1/2}$$

$$\lambda_2(t) = 0.01457 + 0.001468(p_{1t}/p_{et})^{1/2}$$

These give an elasticity of substitution at the 1973*Q*1 prices of the order of 1/20. This in part explains why the putty–putty model is rejected in favour of the clay–clay model. The distinct appearance of the *ex ante* isoquant explains why both these are rejected in favour of the putty–semi-putty model.

Just as we have produced an exact version of Figure 3.4 it is possible to produce an exact version of Figure 3.5. This is done in Figure 3.9, where the ordering of vintages in 1973*Q*1 is provided. Variable cost is plotted on the vertical axis and output on the horizontal. Only the first fifteen vintages are plotted but it can be seen how variable cost begins to increase at a rapid rate.

The changes in the operation of the marginal vintage can be used to see how a marginal-cost index changes over time and how the marginal-labour output ratio changes. This is done in Table 3.5 and Figure 3.9. One can see here a continuous reduction in marginal cost and increase in labour productivity. Alternatively we could focus on the operation of a single vintage. The one we shall consider is that of

*Figure* 3.8 *Ex ante* and *ex post* isoquants for labour and energy

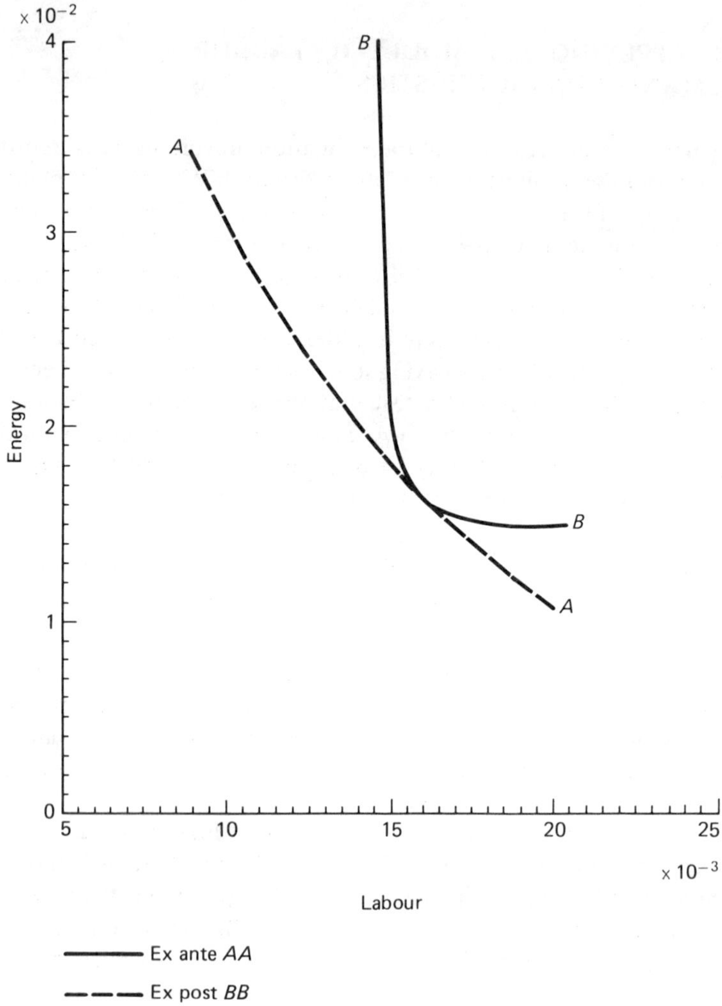

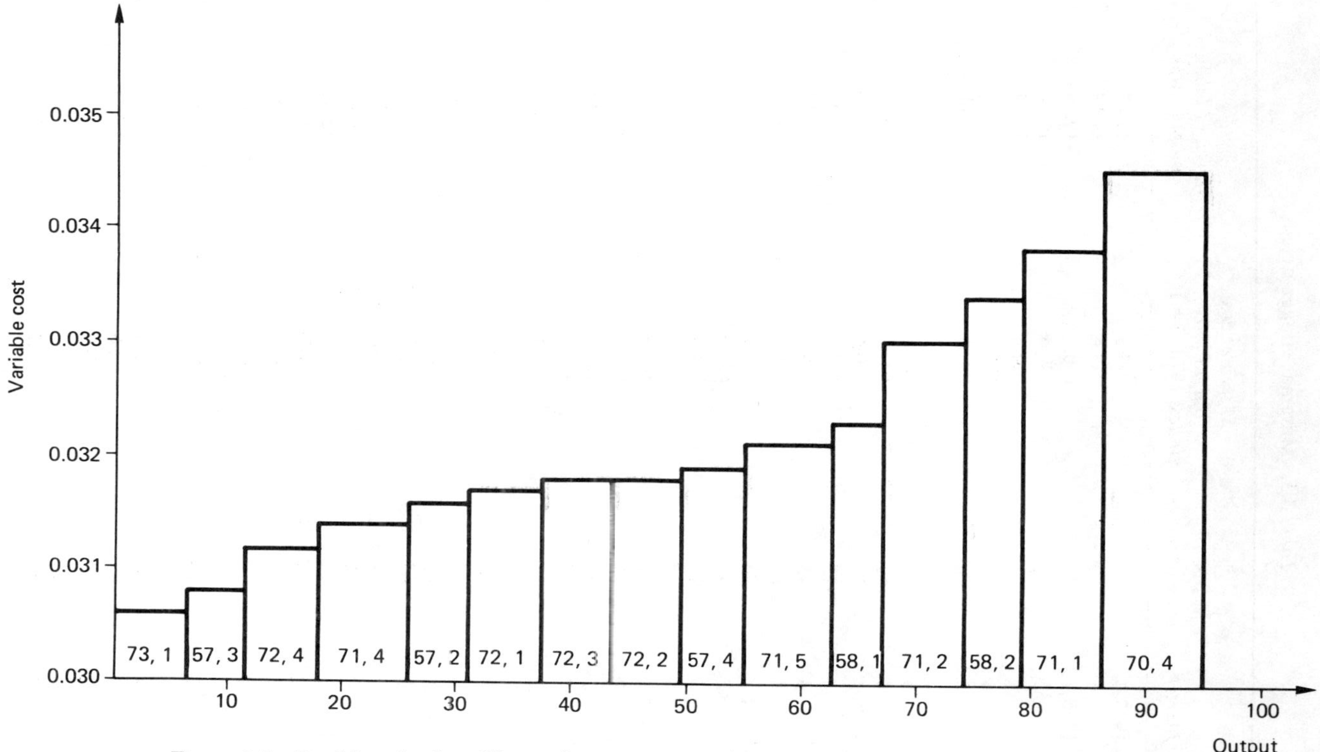


*Figure* 3.9 Ranking the first fifteen vintages operated in 1973*Q*1 in order of operating costs

*Table* 3.5 Marginal vintage details

| *Quarter* | *Marginal vintage no.* | *Marginal cost output price (index* 1970, 2 = 100) | *Marginal labour/ output ratio* |
|---|---|---|---|
| 1967,3 | 50 | 98.3 | 19.64 |
| 4 | 50 | 98.6 | 19.64 |
| 1968,1 | 21 | 100 | 19.54 |
| 2 | 21 | 99.4 | 19.54 |
| 3 | 21 | 99.4 | 19.54 |
| 4 | 44 | 100.3 | 19.69 |
| 1969,1 | 44 | 100.9 | 19.68 |
| 2 | 44 | 100.3 | 19.68 |
| 3 | 50 | 100 | 19.56 |
| 4 | 50 | 100.3 | 19.57 |
| 1970,1 | 18 | 100.6 | 19.46 |
| 2 | 15 | 100 | 19.40 |
| 3 | 45 | 99.7 | 19.24 |
| 4 | 60 | 100 | 18.88 |
| 1971,1 | 46 | 101.1 | 19.09 |
| 2 | 48 | 100.6 | 18.98 |
| 3 | 14 | 101.1 | 18.97 |
| 4 | 47 | 102.8 | 18.96 |
| 1972,1 | 61 | 104.6 | 18.56 |
| 2 | 61 | 105.1 | 18.54 |
| 3 | 62 | 106 | 18.13 |
| 4 | 62 | 105.4 | 18.10 |
| 1973,1 | 13 | 102.8 | 18.15 |
| 2 | 64 | 102.9 | 17.16 |
| 3 | 63 | 106.6 | 17.60 |
| 4 | 64 | 103.4 | 17.19 |
| 1974,1 | 65 | 96.6 | 16.84 |
| 2 | 65 | 93.7 | 16.83 |
| 3 | 11 | 96.5 | 16.89 |
| 4 | 10 | 95.7 | 16.44 |
| 1975,1 | 70 | 93.7 | 15.88 |
| 2 | 71 | 96.9 | 15.81 |
| 3 | 69 | 98 | 15.82 |
| 4 | 7 | 99.4 | 16.09 |
| 1976,1 | 7 | 101.4 | 16.10 |
| 2 | 69 | 101.1 | 15.82 |
| 3 | 69 | 98.9 | 15.82 |
| 4 | 69 | 95.7 | 15.85 |
| 1977,1 | 69 | 92.6 | 15.87 |
| 2 | 69 | 88.3 | 15.86 |
| 3 | 69 | 86.6 | 15.86 |
| 4 | 69 | 87.1 | 15.88 |

*Table* 3.5 (*continued*)

| *Quarter* | *Marginal vintage no.* | *Marginal cost output price (index* 1970, 2 = 100) | *Marginal labour/ output ratio* |
|---|---|---|---|
| 1978,1 | 69 | 87.7 | 15.90 |
| 2 | 69 | 96.3 | 15.81 |
| 3 | 69 | 95.7 | 15.81 |
| 4 | 69 | 95.7 | 15.83 |
| 1979,1 | 69 | 98.9 | 15.84 |
| 2 | 71 | 95.4 | 15.80 |
| 3 | 7 | 92.3 | 16.08 |
| 4 | 68 | 97.4 | 15.71 |
| 1980,1 | 99 | 95.4 | 15.85 |
| 2 | 84 | 93.1 | 15.29 |
| 3 | 82 | 91.7 | 15.17 |
| 4 | 73 | 94.6 | 15.13 |
| 1981,1 | 73 | 95.4 | 15.15 |
| 2 | 81 | 91.4 | 14.95 |
| 3 | 81 | 90.3 | 14.93 |
| 4 | 81 | 92 | 14.97 |
| 1982,1 | 81 | 92.6 | 14.98 |
| 2 | 108 | 89.1 | 15.11 |
| 3 | 108 | 88.3 | 15.11 |

1973*Q*1 which we have already examined in part. This vintage is of interest as it was installed just before the sharp increase in oil prices. One might expect some variability in its subsequent use. We have already presented the relationship between the input–output coefficients and the current factor prices in the equations above, and changes in these factor prices will correspond to movements along the isoquant *BB* in Figure 3.8. These coefficients and the real operating cost are presented in Table 3.6. As energy prices rose after 1973*Q*1, labour was substituted for energy, although the amount of substitution did not keep operating costs down, and real costs rose by 10 per cent between quarters 1973*Q*1 (period 73 in the table) and 1976*Q*1 (period 85). Operating costs then dropped back to below initial operating cost until a sudden jump in 1978, when the reaction to increasing wage costs brought a relatively large substitution of energy for labour, although again it was not possible to prevent an increase in operating cost.

The model suggests that the vintage would have been retired in 1981*Q*1. This would have been due to increases in capacity and

Table 3.6 Operating of vintage 1973

| Period, $t$ | $\lambda_2(73, t) \times 100$ | $\lambda_3(73, t) \times 100$ | Real operating cost × 100 |
|---|---|---|---|
| 73 | 1.508 | 1.805 | 3.06 |
| 74 | 1.508 | 1.802 | 3.15 |
| 75 | 1.509 | 1.789 | 3.28 |
| 76 | 1.510 | 1.790 | 3.21 |
| 77 | 1.512 | 1.783 | 3.06 |
| 78 | 1.511 | 1.787 | 2.97 |
| 79 | 1.511 | 1.789 | 3.10 |
| 80 | 1.514 | 1.772 | 3.18 |
| 81 | 1.515 | 1.768 | 3.16 |
| 82 | 1.512 | 1.785 | 3.26 |
| 83 | 1.512 | 1.784 | 3.31 |
| 84 | 1.513 | 1.779 | 1.38 |
| 85 | 1.513 | 1.777 | 3.45 |
| 86 | 1.512 | 1.784 | 3.41 |
| 87 | 1.512 | 1.785 | 3.33 |
| 88 | 1.514 | 1.772 | 3.23 |
| 89 | 1.517 | 1.762 | 3.12 |
| 90 | 1.515 | 1.768 | 2.98 |
| 91 | 1.515 | 1.768 | 2.92 |
| 92 | 1.518 | 1.757 | 2.95 |
| 93 | 1.519 | 1.750 | 2.97 |
| 94 | 1.511 | 1.785 | 3.25 |
| 95 | 1.511 | 1.787 | 3.28 |
| 96 | 1.513 | 1.779 | 3.32 |
| 97 | 1.514 | 1.774 | 3.34 |
| 98 | 1.512 | 1.791 | 3.22 |
| 99 | 1.511 | 1.786 | 3.14 |
| 100 | 1.514 | 1.774 | 3.32 |
| 101 | 1.512 | 1.784 | 3.29 |
| 102 | 1.510 | 1.789 | 3.23 |
| 103 | 1.510 | 1.789 | 3.20 |
| 104 | 1.513 | 1.778 | 3.31 |
| 105 | 1.515 | 1.770 | 3.34 |

the state of demand rather than increases in operating cost as the operating cost for the next six quarters would have been 3.20, 3.18, 3.25, 3.26, 3.15, 3.12. So costs would have been less than for most of the time that the vintage was operated. This suggests that had the government been able to maintain demand levels at that time then the level of manufacturing employment could have been maintained.

To examine this type of question the model has been simulated in the following way. Employment is kept at the 1979$Q4$ level by increasing output until that level would be reached by cost-minimising producers. We then calculate the level of output necessary, the marginal vintage that would have been used and the cost of operating this marginal vintage. The results of this simulation are contained in Table 3.7. This should allow us to answer the question as to whether unemployment was entirely due to workers pricing themselves out of jobs as some observers indicated at that time. In fact the increases in marginal operating cost is slight in that the necessary marginal operating cost is always in the range of the actuals for that period. Thus it cannot be asserted that increasing unemployment was due to real wage increases. Alternatively, if output levels could have been maintained unemployment would have increased only fractionally.

*Table* 3.7 Simulating a maintained employment level

| *Period necessary* | *Output level* | *Actual output level* | *Marginal vintage* | *Marginal operating cost Necessary* | *Marginal operating cost Actual* |
|---|---|---|---|---|---|
| 99 | 106.508 | 108.1 | 68 | 0.0322 | 0.0323 |
| 100 | 106.847 | 110.1 | 72 | 0.0339 | 0.0341 |
| 101 | 107.112 | 107.0 | 99 | 0.0334 | 0.0334 |
| 102 | 107.102 | 102.4 | 84 | 0.0326 | 0.0326 |
| 103 | 107.440 | 97.6 | 8 | 0.0321 | 0.0321 |
| 104 | 107.711 | 93.0 | 8 | 0.0322 | 0.0321 |
| 105 | 107.757 | 91.8 | 83 | 0.0335 | 0.0334 |
| 106 | 107.772 | 92.4 | 82 | 0.0324 | 0.0320 |
| 107 | 107.739 | 94.3 | 82 | 0.0320 | 0.0316 |
| 108 | 107.467 | 94.8 | 83 | 0.0325 | 0.0322 |
| 109 | 107.347 | 94.4 | 8 | 0.0327 | 0.0324 |
| 110 | 107.743 | 94.1 | 73 | 0.0315 | 0.0312 |
| 111 | 107.370 | 93.6 | 73 | 0.0312 | 0.0309 |

So in answer to the question that we initially posed it seems that the labour demand model is very close to the Leontief fixed coefficient model in the short run (periods of up to three years at least). Adjustment to factor price changes does take place, but this is relatively slight on an *ex post* basis. More important will be the adjustment due to the installation of new equipment. Of course this adjustment will correspond to changes in price expectations, rather than prices themselves.

## 3.5 CONCLUSIONS

Clearly a vintage model is necessary to model labour demand, but one cannot restrict oneself to clay–clay types as *ex post* flexibility does exist. This flexibility does appear to be used in practice, although the proportionate changes in input–output coefficients are relatively small. Crucial to this model is the modelling of the formation of expectations. Whilst the model performs well in fitting, prediction and stability tests, for the case of a simple expectational model, any simulation results will depend on the validity of this part of the model. For this reason we have not produced the price elasticities that one would normally expect in a labour demand model, and would wish to stress caution in such exercises.

The model incorporates time effects by using the differing expectations at different periods. If expectations never changed then, apart from depreciation, all machines would be alike and it would not matter which were used. In just the same way if the expectational model allows the path of future prices to be modelled very well at one time but not so well at another, then the former vintage will be used a lot of the time whilst the latter vintage will be used hardly at all. Thus whilst aggregate characteristics such as factor demands, marginal cost, and labour/output ratios can be plausibly modelled, detailed vintage information will be very sensitive to the expectational model used.

In looking at the simulation results several important points emerge. Holes do exist in the stock of vintages used. This contrasts with the continuous spectrum assumption used by several previous workers in this field. Second, vintages are retired and brought back into use. The possibility of this depends on them being temporarily retired and kept in place awaiting further use. This is particularly important for employment-policy simulation. Whilst the model suggests that 1979 levels of employment would be achieved by returning output to its 1979 level, this does require that such vintages are still available to be used.

It has been suggested that current declines in manufacturing output have been accompanied by the sale or scrapping of much of the capital stock. If this is the case then such policies are not open, and require the installation of new machinery. As this will correspond to different price expectations it may well be less labour-intensive and so even greater output increases may be needed. Such increases in output will increase total operating costs, but this should not affect profitability as the mark-up on the marginal vintage is of the order of 20 per cent. Indeed it may be the case that employment problems in the UK are due in part to the degree of industrial concentration and the consequent mark-up of price over cost.

## References

ANSAR, J., INGHAM, A., LEON, H., TOKER, M. and ULPH A. (1986a) 'Demand for Energy and Capacity Utilisation in a Vintage Model of UK Manufacturing' in D. Bosworth and D. Heathfield (eds) *Working below Capacity* (London: Macmillan).

ANSAR, J., INGHAM, A., LEON, H., TOKER, M. and ULPH, A. (1986b) 'A Vintage Model of the Demand for Energy in the UK Manufacturing Sector', final report on UK Dept. of Energy Project (unpublished).

FUSS, M. (1977) The Structure of Technology over time' *Econometrica* 45, no. 8.

MENDIS, L. and MUELLBAUER, J. (1984) 'British Manufacturing Productivity 1955–83', CEPR discussion Paper no. 32.

MUELLBAUER, J. (1984) 'Aggregate Production Functions and Productivity Measurement: A New Look', CEPR discussion paper no. 34.

# 4 Employment and Unemployment in the Netherlands, 1960–84: A Putty-Clay Approach*

Joan Muysken and A. H. van Zon

## 4.1 INTRODUCTION

Since the mid-1970s vintage models have played an important role in the analysis of the Dutch economy.[1] Although earlier vintages of these models were of a clay-clay nature, technical progress in economic analysis and in estimation methods enabled more recent vintages to be of a putty-clay nature. Examples of the latter are Kuipers and van Zon (1982) and Gelauff, Wennekes and de Jong (1985). We shall further refer to them as KvZ and GWJ, respectively. Our model fits in with this putty-clay tradition. However, before highlighting several features of our model, some general remarks should be made.

In the period 1950–70 employment in the private sector in the Netherlands increased from 3400 to 4130 thousand man-years. It remained at a more or less constant level of 4100 thousand man-years till 1980 and then decreased rapidly to a level of 3800 thousand in 1983, at which it remained for the years 1984 and 1985. Likewise, unemployment increased slowly from 70 thousand man-years in 1970 to 325 thousand man-years in 1980. Then unemployment accelerated towards a level of 800 thousand man-years in 1983, at which it remained for the years 1984 and 1985. The unemployment rate is nowadays about 17 per cent. Muysken and Meijers (1985) explain that the earlier developed clay-clay vintage models cannot adequately deal with these turbulent developments in the period 1980–5. With respect to the putty-clay models, KvZ estimate their model for the period 1950–77 and GWJ for the period 1960–82. As we shall explain later on, their models do not describe the aforementioned turbulent developments adequately. Moreover, although investment is in

* We thank H. Meijers for his computational assistance.

principle endogenous in a putty–clay model, as it is in a clay–clay model, both KvZ and GWJ treat it as an exogenous variable.[2] Finally, while KvZ do not distinguish explicitly between demand for labour and employment in discussing unemployment, GWJ do not discuss employment or unemployment at all and only explain demand for labour.

As we explain in section 4.2, investment is an endogenous variable.[3] Furthermore, demand for labour and employment are distinguished explicitly. For that purpose an employment function is introduced into the analysis. Finally, both employment and scrapping of equipment are dealt with in different ways. Whereas all previous vintage models assume that all equipment is utilised at the same utilisation rate once it has been installed, we assume that equipment is utilised at full capacity in decreasing order of efficiency. Hence, when aggregate demand is below full-capacity output, equipment of least efficient vintages is laid-off. This also leads to labour hoarding, which is explicitly incorporated into the model. As a consequence, vintages can also be scrapped when they have not been used for several years even though they have a positive quasi-rent: Apart from economic obsolescence we also allow for obsolescence caused by excess capacity.

In section 4.3 we estimate the parameters of the model for the period 1960–82 and, in order to check the reliability of the results, forecast for the years 1983 and 1984. We use the results to analyse unemployment, distinguishing between structural unemployment (of both a qualitative and a quantitative nature) on the one hand, and cyclical unemployment on the other.

Finally, some concluding remarks are made in section 4.4.

## 4.2 THE MODEL

### The Production Structure *ex ante*

The production structure *ex ante* in year $T$ is described by means of a linearly homogeneous CES-function with both capital- and labour-augmenting technical progress. The function is:

$$X_{T,T} = [\{A \cdot (1+\mu_n)^T \cdot h_{nT} \cdot N_{T,T}\}^{-\rho} + \{B \cdot (1+\mu_i)^T \cdot h_{iT} \cdot I_{T,T}\}^{-\rho}]^{-1/\rho} \tag{4.1}$$

where $X_{t,T}$, $N_{t,T}$ and $I_{t,T}$ stand for productive capacity, labour and investment of vintage $T$ in year $t$, respectively.[4] Since labour is expressed in man-years, $N_{T,T}$ is corrected by an index for effective working hours, $h_{nT}$. As a consequence, investment is also corrected by an index for effective working hours, $h_{iT}$. Embodied labour and capital augmenting technical progress are expressed by the parameters $\mu_n$ and $\mu_i$, respectively. Disembodied technical progress shows up in the production structure *ex post.* The elasticity of substitution is $\sigma = 1/(1+\rho)$.

We assume that behaviour of entrepreneurs can be described as follows. Expecting a certain need for capacity $(X_{T,T})$, man-years $(N_{T,T})$ and capital $(I_{T,T})$ are chosen as to maximise the present value of expected rent of equipment of vintage $T$ over its expected lifetime, $P_T$. That is:

$$\Phi = \sum_{t=T}^{T+P_T-1} \frac{\{p^e(t)_T \cdot X_{t,T} - w^e(t)_T \cdot N_{t,T}\}}{(1+r^e(t)_T)^{t-T}} - p_T^i \cdot I_{T,T} \tag{4.2}$$

is maximised subject to (4.1). In equation (4.2) $p^e(t)_T$, $w^e(t)_T$ and $r^e(t)_T$ represent expectations of output prices, wages (wage sum per man-year) and the rate of interest in year $t$, respectively, formed in year $T$. $p_T^i$ stands for the price of investment.

As can be seen from equation (4.2), the choice of a certain production technique from the production function *ex ante*, requires information both about the production structure *ex post* and about expectations with respect to output, lifetime and factor prices. We first discuss the production structure *ex post.*

### The Production Structure *ex post*

It is assumed that once the machines of vintage $T$ have been installed, substitution between labour and capital is no longer possible. Nonetheless, both labour productivity and capital productivity of that vintage will change over time for two reasons: changes in effective working hours and in disembodied technical progress. This can be expressed as follows:

$$\frac{X_{t,T}}{N_{t,T}} = \frac{h_{nt}}{h_{nT}} \cdot (1+\gamma_n)^{t-T} \cdot \frac{X_{T,T}}{N_{T,T}} \tag{4.3}$$

$$\frac{X_{t,T}}{I_{t,T}} = \frac{h_{it}}{h_{iT}} \cdot (1+\gamma_i)^{t-T} \cdot \frac{X_{T,T}}{I_{T,T}} \tag{4.4}$$

where $\gamma_n$ and $\gamma_i$ stand for labour augmenting and capital augmenting disembodied technical progress, respectively. Moreover, due to wear and tear, $I_{t,T}$ will decrease relative to $I_{T,T}$ in the course of time. This is expressed by:

$$I_{t,T} = \Omega_{t-T} \cdot I_{T,T} \tag{4.5}$$

where $\Omega_{t-T}$ represents the technical survival fraction of equipment of vintage $T$ in period $t$.

### Expectations with Respect to Lifetime, Factor Prices and Output

As we mentioned above, the choice of a production technique is influenced by expectations with regard to lifetime, factor prices and output.

Expected lifetime is treated in different ways in putty-clay models. It can be considered as 'an endogenous variable intricately determined in the maximisation procedure in relation to, by all means, uncertain expectational values of wage rates, prices and discount rates'.[5]

We share den Hartog's implicit reservations against this approach. In the face of so much uncertainty entrepreneurs are more apt to rely on simple rules of thumb. However, we think that it is too simple to assume that expected lifetime is constant throughout the whole estimation period, as for instance both KvZ and GWJ do. In fact, we do not agree with KvZ's statement that 'an expected lifetime is independent of the actual lifetime'.[6] On the contrary, a plausible approach seems to us that expected lifetime is proportional to actual lifetime: KvZ found that actual lifetime decreased from 45 years in the early 1950s to 15 years in 1977, nonetheless they find an expected lifetime of 13 years throughout the whole period. We think that in the face of actual lifetime decreasing by two-thirds, expected lifetime must have decreased as well and therefore postulate:

$$P_t = \alpha \cdot L_t \qquad \alpha \leqslant 1 \tag{4.6}$$

as a suitable approach to the entrepreneurial rule of thumb. $L_t$ stands for actual lifetime at year $t$.

With respect to expected prices and wages we follow common practice in assuming:

$$\begin{aligned} pe(t)_T &= [1+g^e(p)_T]^{t-T} \cdot P_T \\ w^e(t)_T &= [1+g^e(w)_T]^{t-T} \cdot w_T \end{aligned} \tag{4.7}$$

where $p^e(t)_T$ and $w^e(t)_T$ represent expected prices and wages for year $t$, with expectations formed in year $T$, and $g^e(p)_T$ and $g^e(w)_T$ stand for the expected rates of growth of prices and wages, respectively. We assume that the expected rate of growth is equal to the average rate of growth over the past four years.[7] Moreover, we make the same assumption with respect to the expected interest rate, i.e. $r^e(t)_T$ is equal to the average interest rate over the past four years.

It is obvious that expectations with respect to capacity output of vintage $T$ depend on expectations formed in year $T$ with respect to aggregate demand for year $t$, $D^e(t)_T$. Essentially, these latter are formed in the same way as in the case of factor prices:

$$D^e(t)_T = [1 + g^e(D)_T]^{t-T} \cdot D_T \tag{4.8}$$

where $D_T$ stands for aggregate demand at year $T$ and $g^e(D)_T$ is the expected rate of growth of demand at year $T$. Again we assume that the expected rate of growth is equal to the average rate of growth over the past four years.

We furthermore assume that investment behaviour of entrepreneurs is such that aggregate demand is met by employing equipment at a desired rate of utilisation, $q_t^d$, which is smaller than unity.[8] In this case desired aggregate capacity output in year $t$ is:

$$X^d(t) = D^e(t)_{t-1} / q_t^d. \tag{4.9}$$

By definition desired capacity output of vintage $T$, $X^d_{T,T}$, should fill the gap between desired aggregate capacity output in year $T$ and aggregate capacity output which can be produced by equipment still in existence at the end of year $T-1$, $X^-(T-1)$.[9] That is:

$$X^d_{T,T} = X^d(t) - X^-(T-1). \tag{4.10}$$

We assume that in the choice of the production technique entrepreneurs adjust productive capacity to desired capacity output with a factor $\pi$, i.e.:

$$X_{T,T} = \pi \cdot X^d_{T,T} \qquad 0 < \pi \leq 1. \tag{4.11}$$

Essentially this implies that actual aggregate capacity output is a weighted average of desired capacity and capacity already existing at the end of the previous period.

**The Choice of the Production Technique**

Having specified the production structure *ex post* and expectations with respect to lifetime, factor prices and output, the choice of the production technique can be elaborated.

Substitution of equations (4.3), (4.4), (4.5) and (4.7) into equation (4.2) yields the expression for the present value of expected rent of equipment of vintage $T$ over its expected lifetime:

$$\Phi = X_{T,T} \cdot p_T \cdot S_{1,T} - N_{T,T} \cdot w_T \cdot S_{2,T} - p_T^i \cdot I_{T,T} \tag{4.12}$$

with

$$S_{1,T} = \sum_{t=T}^{T+P_T-1} \left\{ \frac{[1+g^e(p)_T] \cdot [1+g^e(h_i)_T] \cdot [1+\gamma_i]^{t-T}}{[1+r^e(t)]} \right\} \cdot \Omega_{t-T}$$

$$S_{2,T} = \sum_{t=T}^{T+P_T-1} \left\{ \frac{[1+g^e(w)_T] \cdot [1+g^e(h_i)_T] \cdot [1+\gamma_i]^{t-T}}{[1+r^e(t)_T] \cdot [1+g^e(h_n)_T] \cdot [1+\gamma_n]} \right\} \cdot \Omega_{t-T}. \tag{4.13}$$

For a certain level of desired capacity output, $X_{T,T}$, maximisation of equation (4.12) with respect to labour, $N_{T,T}$, and investment, $I_{T,T}$, subject to equation (4.1) yields:[10]

$$\frac{N_{T,T}}{I_{T,T}} = \left( \frac{w_T \cdot S_{2,T}}{p_T^i} \right)^{-\sigma} \cdot \left[ \frac{A \cdot (1+\mu_n)^T \cdot h_{nT}}{B \cdot (1+\mu_i)^T \cdot h_{iT}} \right]^{\sigma-1}. \tag{4.14}$$

And the optimal levels of labour and investment corresponding to the desired level of capacity output can be derived from equations (4.1) and (4.14). This is illustrated in Figure 4.1, where $X_{T,T}$ determines the isoquant of the CES-production function (4.1), and, together with other variables, the ratio $w_T/p_T^i$ determines the optimal labour intensity according to equation (4.14). We elaborate this later on.

Up to this point we discussed the investment decisions for each vintage as if they were taken by one single entrepreneur who has specific expectations with regard to future developments. However, by their very nature, entrepreneurs will have different expectations with respect to the future and for that reason they will take different investment decisions at a given moment of time. As a consequence, we cannot expect that a vintage is characterised by a single value of its labour intensity, as is the case in Figure 4.1. The labour intensity depicted in this figure should be interpreted as the average value of

*Figure* 4.1 The determination of investment and demand for labour.

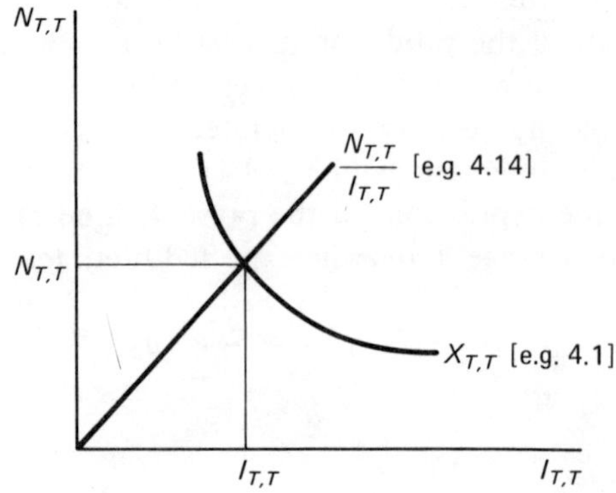


the outcomes of different entrepreneurial decisions, whereas the individual outcomes are distributed around this average value.[11]

For analytical purposes we assume that entrepreneurial decisions differ in such a way that the amount of capital embodied in a unit of equipment varies uniformly on a range $I_b \cdots I_u$. If we furthermore approximate the isoquant segment *PQ* using the line-segment *PQ*,[12] it follows that each point *I* on the range $I_b \cdots I_u$ is associated with a point *N* on the range $N_b \cdots N_u$, such that *N* is uniformly distributed over the range $N_b \cdots N_u$,[13] this is depicted in Figure 4.2. Since we assume that each unit of equipment can produce the same amount of output regardless of its capital intensity, it follows furthermore that the labour coefficients corresponding to different units of equipment vary uniformly on the range $N_b/X \cdots N_u/X$.

*Figure* 4.2 The choice of equipment of vintage *T*.

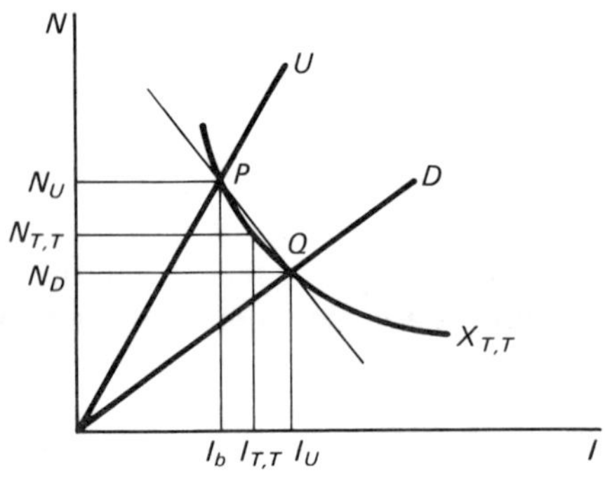

The values of capacity demand for labour and for investment can be found by integration of the uniform distributions over these ranges, i.e.:

$$N_{T,T} = \frac{1}{N_u - N_b} \cdot \int_{N_b}^{N_u} N \cdot \mathrm{d}N = 1/2 \cdot (N_b + N_u) \tag{4.15}$$

$$I_{T,T} = \frac{1}{I_u - I_b} \cdot \int_{I_b}^{I_u} I \cdot \mathrm{d}I = 1/2 \cdot (I_b + I_u). \tag{4.16}$$

These values correspond to the values found in the analysis using Figure 4.1.[14] Hence, the analysis of the production structure *ex ante* does not change.[15]

Nonetheless, the notion of a distribution in expectations can have far-reaching consequences compared with traditional vintage models. For in these models whole vintages are scrapped at a time, and this frequently gives rise to serious discontinuities in the model. Such discontinuities are implausible and can yield computational problems.[16] In our model, however, these discontinuities are less pronounced. Moreover, as we shall demonstrate, the utilisation of equipment is treated in a far more plausible way.

**Utilisation and Scrapping of Equipment**

An obvious scrapping condition, which is used in almost every vintage model, is negative quasi-rent – that is when, for equipment of a certain vintage:

$$p_t \cdot X_{t,T} - w_t \cdot N_{t,T} < 0 \tag{4.17}$$

holds, the equipment becomes obsolete.[17] However, it is also possible that equipment that is able to generate a positive quasi-rent is laid-off because of a slackening in aggregate demand. In that case aggregate demand is met by employing more efficient equipment. When the slackening in aggregate demand is persistent, the inefficient equipment will be scrapped because of underutilisation. GWJ also allow for scrapping because of excess capacity, although in a different way. When the three-year moving average of the rate of capacity utilisation is below the normal rate, a certain percentage of all vintages over two years of age is scrapped.[18] However, we prefer to assume that equipment which is laid-off first is also scrapped first. As a consequence, we assume that when the rate of capacity utilisation is below the normal rate for several consecutive years, a certain percentage of equipment which has been laid-off is scrapped in such a way that scrapping occurs to the least productive equipment.[19]

Since we assume that labour productivity of equipment installed in a certain year varies over a certain range, equipment is not scrapped according to its year of installation as is usually assumed. This is illustrated in Figure 4.3 which shows equipment of different vintages (1–5) in increasing order of productivity. The range over which productivity varies for vintage $T$ at moment $t$ is indicated on the $X/N$-axis by the lowerbound $P_b(t, T)$ and the upperbound $P_u(t, T)$.[20] The size of the rectangle which represents vintage $T$ indicates the productive capacity corresponding to that vintage.[21]

*Figure* 4.3 Distribution of vintages according to productivity.

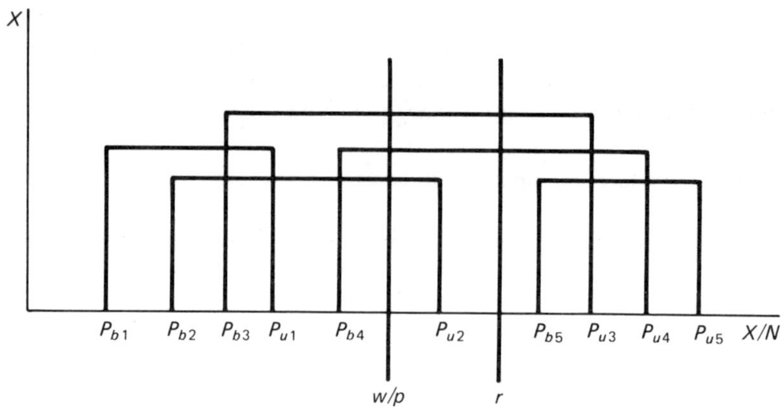


When we indicate the fraction of productive capacity of vintage $T$ which has been scrapped for economic reasons in year $t$ by $1 - Q(t, T)$, we find that $Q(t, T)$ will lie between 0 and 1 for some vintages. In Figure 4.3 the real wage-rate, $w/p$, is indicated on the $X/N$-axis. It is clear that $Q(t, 5)$ is equal to 1 and $Q(t, 1)$ is equal to 0. However, equipment from vintages 2, 3 and 4 is only scrapped in so far as its productivity lies in the ranges $(P_b(t, 2), w/p)$, $(P_b(t, 3), w/p)$ and $(P_b(t, 4), w/p)$, respectively. Hence for these years $Q$ will lie between 0 and 1.

The discussion above implies that $Q(t, T)$ is defined in the following way:[22]

$$Q(t, T) = \begin{cases} 1 & P_b(t-1, T) > w_t/p_t \\ \dfrac{\dfrac{P_u(t-1)}{w_t/p_t} - 1}{\dfrac{P_u(t-1)}{P_b(t-1)} - 1} & P_b(t-1, T) < w_t/p_t < P_u(t-1, T) \\ 0 & P_u(t-1, T) < w_t/p_t. \end{cases} \tag{4.18}$$

Since less productive equipment is scrapped first, the fraction of labour of vintage $T$ which is scrapped for economic reasons, $1 - Q_n(t, T)$ will exceed that of output. The amount of labour which is not scrapped can be found by integration of $N$ in equation (4.15) from $N_b(t-1, T)$ to $N^*(t, T)$, where:

$$N^*(t, T) = N_b(t-1, T) + Q(t, T) \cdot (N_u(t-1, T) - N_b(t-1, T)). \tag{4.19}$$

As a consequence we find:

$$Q_n(t, T) = Q(t, T) \cdot Q_n^*(t, T) \tag{4.20}$$

where

$$Q_n^*(t, T) = Q(t, T) + [1 - Q(t, T)] \cdot \frac{2 \cdot N_b(t-1, T)}{N_u(t-1, T) + N_b(t-1, T)}.$$

Obviously $Q_n^*$ is smaller than 1, since $N_b$ is smaller than $N_u$. The resulting divergence between $Q$ and $Q_n$ is a consequence of the assumption that entrepreneurs will buy different equipment of a certain vintage.

For investment the opposite holds, since equipment that has lowest labour productivity in a certain vintage also has highest capital productivity. Denoting the fraction of investment of vintage $T$ which is scrapped for economic reasons by $1 - Q_i(t, T)$, we find:

$$Q_i(t, T) = Q(t, T) \cdot Q_i^*(t, T) \tag{4.21}$$

where:

$$Q_i^*(t, T) = Q(t, T) + [1 - Q(t, T)] \cdot \frac{2 \cdot I_u(t-1, T)}{I_u(t-1, T) + I_b(t-1, T)}.$$

Obviously $Q_i^*$ exceeds 1, since $I_u$ exceeds $I_b$, and hence $Q_i$ exceeds $Q$.

As we mentioned above, vintages can also be scrapped because of persistent underutilisation. When the utilisation rate has been below its normal level for at least two consecutive years, least productive equipment will be scrapped until a percentage $\theta$ of excess capacity is scrapped. In the context of Figure 4.3 this would mean that all equipment for which labour productivity lies below $r$ but above $w/p$, is scrapped.[23] Let the fraction of profitable capacity of vintage $T$ which is scrapped in year $t$ because of underutilisation be $1-R(t, T)$. In the same way $1-R_n(t, T)$ and $1-R_i(t, T)$ refer to labour and investment, respectively. Then it is obvious that $R$, $R_n$ and $R_i$ are defined analogously to $Q$, $Q_n$ and $Q_i$. That is:

$$R(t, T)=\begin{cases} 1 & P_b(t-1, T)>r_t \\ \dfrac{1}{Q(t, T)}\cdot\dfrac{P_u(t-1, T)/r_t-1}{P_u(t-1, T)/P_b(t-1, T)-1} & P_b(t-1, T)<r_t<P_u(t-1, T) \\ 0 & P_u(t-1, T)<r_t \end{cases} \tag{4.22}$$

and

$$R_n(t, T)=R(t\cdot T)\cdot R_n^*(t, T) \tag{4.23}$$

where:

$$R_n^*(t, T)=R(t, T)+[1-R(t, T)]\cdot\frac{2\cdot N_b(t-1, T)}{N^*(t, T)+N_b(t-1, T)}$$

and

$$R_i(t, T)=R(t, T)\cdot R_i^*(t, T) \tag{4.24}$$

where:[24]

$$R_i^*(t, T)=R(t, T)+[1-R(t, T)]\cdot\frac{2\cdot I_u(t-1, T)}{I_u(t-1, T)+I^*(t, T)}.$$

In equations (4.18)–(4.24) we use the boundary values of the previous period. The reason is that we refer to equipment which has survived scrapping in the previous period. Finally, as a consequence of this scrapping, the upper boundary of labour and the lower boundary of investment will change. Moreover, both boundaries of labour will change because of disembodied technical progress and changes in working-time.[25] Therefore we find:

$$
\begin{aligned}
I_u(t, T) &= I_u(t-1, T) \\
I_b(t, T) &= I_u(t-1, T) - R(t, T) \cdot Q(t, T) \\
&\quad \cdot (I_u(t-1, T) - I_b(t-1, T)) \\
N_b(t, T) &= N_b(t-1, T) \cdot \frac{1+\gamma_i}{1+\gamma_n} \cdot \frac{h_{it}/h_{it-1}}{h_{nt}/h_{nt-1}} \\
N_u(t, T) &= N_u^*(t-1, T) \cdot \frac{1+\gamma_i}{1+\gamma_n} \cdot \frac{h_{it}/h_{it-1}}{h_{nt}/h_{nt-1}} \\
N_u^*(t, T) &= N_b(t-1, T) \\
&\quad + R(t, T) \cdot Q(t, T) \cdot (N_u(t-1, T) - N_b(t-1, T)).
\end{aligned} \tag{4.25}
$$

When we take into account both the influence of variation in entrepreneurial expectations and the influence of scrapping, equations (4.3)-(4.5) should be replaced by:[26]

$$
I(t, T) = I(t-1, T) \cdot \Omega_{t,T}/\Omega_{t-1,T} \cdot R_i(t, T) \cdot Q_i(t, T) \tag{4.26}
$$

$$
\frac{X(t, T)}{I(t, T)} = \frac{X(t-1, T)}{I(t-1, T)} \cdot (1+\gamma_i) \cdot \frac{h_{it}}{h_{it-1}} \cdot \frac{1}{Q_i^*(t, T) \cdot R_i^*(t, T)} \tag{4.27}
$$

$$
\frac{X(t, T)}{N(t, T)} = \frac{X(t-1, T)}{N(t-1, T)} \cdot (1+\gamma_n) \cdot \frac{h_{nt}}{h_{nt-1}} \cdot \frac{1}{Q_n^*(t, T) \cdot R_n^*(t, T)} \tag{4.28}
$$

These equations differ from equations (4.3)-(4.5) due to the presence of the various factors $Q$ and $R$, which is not remarkable since these factors reflect differences in entrepreneurial expectations and scrapping due to economic obsolescence and underutilisation.

### Aggregation and Hoarding of Labour

It is obvious that capacity output and demand for labour, $X_t^c$ and $N_t^c$, respectively, are defined by:

$$
\begin{aligned}
X_t^c &= \sum_{T \in V(r)} X_t, T \\
N_t^c &= \sum_{T \in V(r)} N_{t,T}.
\end{aligned} \tag{4.29}
$$

$V(r)$ is the set of vintages consisting of equipment which labour productivity is at least equal to $r$. If $X_t^c > X_t$ then we define the value $Q'$ for labour productivity such that:

$$\sum_{T \in V(Q')} X_{tT} = X_t \tag{4.30}$$

holds. This enables us to define the amount of labour which would have been exactly sufficient to produce actual demand $X_t$, as:

$$N_t' = \sum_{T \in V(Q')} N_{t,T}. \tag{4.31}$$

Idle labour, $N_t^i$, is then equal to:

$$N_t^i = N_t^c - N_t'. \tag{4.32}$$

We assume that there are two types of labour hoarding, i.e. desired hoarding and forced hoarding. The first type of labour hoarding may be regarded as a tactical reserve of idle labour which may be activated at any time, while the second type of labour hoarding is caused by institutional factors which inhibit an instantaneous adjustment of the demand for labour to its optimum level. Actual labour hoarding is equal to the maximum of both types of hoarding. Assuming that desired hoarding is equal to a fraction $\zeta_1$ of idle labour, and furthermore assuming that forced hoarding equals a fraction $\zeta_2$ of actual labour hoarding in the previous period, it follows that demand for labour is equal to:

$$N = N' + \max\,(\zeta_1 \cdot (N^c - N'), \zeta_2 \cdot (N_{-1} - N'_{-1})) \tag{4.33}$$

**Investment**

From the discussion of Figure 4.1 one can conclude that both investment and capacity demand for labour are endogenous in the model. In this paragraph we will concentrate on investment only, however, since capacity labour demand associated with new investment follows directly both from the amount of investment and the optimal labour intensity of new investment (cf. equation [4.14]).

From equations (4.1) and (4.14) the following investment function can be derived:[27]

$$I_{T,T} = X_{T,T} \cdot [A' \cdot \Psi^{(\sigma-1)/\sigma} + B']^{\sigma/(1-\sigma)} \tag{4.34}$$

where

$$A' = (A \cdot (1+\mu_n)^T \cdot h_{nT})^{(\sigma-1)/\sigma}$$

$$B' = (B \cdot (1+\mu_i)^T \cdot h_{iT})^{(\sigma-1)/\sigma}$$

$$\Psi = \left( \frac{B' \cdot w_T \cdot S_{2,T}}{A' \cdot p_T^i} \right)^{-\sigma} \qquad \text{(cf. equation [4.14])}$$

The first argument in equation (4.34) represents the influence of expected demand on investment and the second argument represents the influence of expected factor-price developments. Both expected demand and the ratio of expected wages to the price of investment exert a positive influence on investment.

However, one should recall from equation (4.10) that $X_{T,T}$ does not only represent expected demand, but also aggregate capacity output which can be produced by equipment installed at the end of year $T-1$, $X^{-}(T-1)$. From equation (4.29) it can be seen that $X^{-}(t-1)$ is defined as follows:

$$X^{-}(t-1) = \sum_{T \in V'(r,t)} X_{t,T} \tag{4.35}$$

where $V'(r, t)$ is the set of vintages older than $t$ with equipment which labour productivity is at least equal to $r$. Hence, factor-price developments also influence investment via $X_{T,T} = \pi \cdot [X^d(T) - X^{-}(T-1)]$, because $V'(r, t)$ is influenced by factor prices. This will increase the negative impact on employment of a relative wage increase.

Investment is also influenced by unutilised capacity, even in two different ways. First, persistent excess capacity will lead to scrapping of equipment. As a consequence the capital stock and hence $X^{-}(T-1)$ will decrease. This has a positive influence on investment, given desired aggregate capacity output. However, both components of this latter variable – expected demand and the desired rate of utilisation – will probably be influenced by persistent excess capacity. Excess capacity indicates that in the past too high a demand has been expected. Hence, future expected demand will be negatively influenced by excess capacity. The influence on the rate of capacity utilisation is not clear, however, because persistent excess capacity will not decrease the desired rate of utilisation when it is already so low as to allow for this excess capacity. On the whole we expect that the negative influence of excess capacity on investment dominates the positive influence because of its impact on expected demand.

**Employment, Unemployment and Labour Hoarding**

As we stated in the introduction, one of our motivations for developing the putty-clay model is to analyse unemployment. However, up to now we have only explained actual demand for labour, whereas an analysis of unemployment requires an explanation of employment. Hence, the relation between actual demand for labour and employment has to be elaborated. For this purpose we use the concept of an employment function which relates employment in year $t$, $E_t$, to demand for labour, $N_t$, and supply of labour, $N_t^s$. In general this function can be defined as:

$$E_t = F(N_t, N_t^s) \tag{4.36}$$

It is assumed to be linearly homogeneous in both arguments.[28] We follow Muysken (1987) in the use of this function to distinguish between qualitative and quantitative structural unemployment on the one hand and cyclical unemployment on the other.[29] Qualitative structural unemployment, $U_t^q$, results from qualitative discrepancies between supply of and demand for labour. Usually it is measured by the amount of unemployment where unemployment and vacancies are equal, and hence $E_t = N_t^s \cdot F(1, 1)$ holds. As a consequence we find:

$$U_t^q = N_t^s\{1 - F(1, 1)\} \tag{4.37}$$

Quantitative structural unemployment, $U_t^c$, is the unemployment that results, apart from qualitative structural unemployment, when all equipment is used at normal capacity. Employment is then given by:

$$E_t^c = F(q_{n,t}^n \cdot N_t^c, N_t^s)$$

and:

$$U_t^c = N_t^s\{F(1, 1) - F(q_{n,t}^n \cdot N_t^c / N_t^s, 1)\} \tag{4.38}$$

holds. $q_{n,t}^n$ equals the normal rate of utilisation of labour ($q_{n,t}^n = N_t^n / N_{c,t}$, where $N_t^n$ is equal to the amount of labour associated with the most productive equipment which would have been used to produce an amount of output exactly equal to $q_t^n \cdot X_{c,t}$). Obviously, quantitative structural unemployment is due to a shortage of capacity demand for labour.

Finally, the remaining unemployment, $U'_t$, is of a cyclical nature, and can be written as follows:

$$U'_t = N^s_t \cdot \{F(q^n_{nt} N^c_t / N^s_t, 1) - F(q_{N,t} \cdot N^c_t / N^s_t, 1)\} \tag{4.39}$$

where $q_{N,t}$ is the rate of utilisation of labour. Equation (4.39) shows that cyclical unemployment varies inversely with the rate of utilisation of labour. Furthermore, since most productive equipment is used first, it follows that, *ceteris paribus*, a rise in the rate of capacity utilisation generates a more than proportional rise in the rate of labour utilisation. Therefore cyclical changes in unemployment tend to be more outspoken than changes in the rate of capacity utilisation itself.

## 4.3 THE ESTIMATION OF THE MODEL

We have estimated the model for the period 1960–82,[30] and in order to check the reliability of the estimation results, we forecast for the years 1983–4. Although investment is endogenous in our model, we treat it as exogenous in the estimation process in order to keep this process manageable.[31] However, we feel that the estimation results with exogenous investment are already interesting enough to be presented in more detail. Before presenting the estimation results, we will first discuss the data and the estimation method used.

### The Data and the Estimation Method

For the period 1905–84 data for value added excluding natural gas and housing, investment in equipment and means of transportation, wages, prices of investment and of value added, and the long-term interest rate were obtained from GWJ upon request.[32] Moreover, for the period 1947–84 data were obtained from the same source on employment, vacancies and the rate of capacity utilisation.[33] With respect to technical scrapping the assumptions from den Hartog and Tjan (1980) have been followed.[34] Finally we do not distinguish between working hours for equipment and personnel, but use the same data for both, as KvZ do.[35]

With respect to the estimation procedure it seems sensible to define the objective function in terms of the two strategic variables of the model: capacity output and actual demand for labour.[36] Capacity output is defined as actual output divided by the rate of capacity utilisation, and demand for labour is defined as employment plus vacancies. The estimation procedure should minimise the following objective function:[37]

$$F = \sum_{t=1960}^{1982} (X_t^{c\prime}/X_t^c - 1)^2 + (N_t'/N_t - 1)^2 \qquad (4.40)$$

where $X_t^c$ and $N_t$ are observed capacity output and actual demand for labour, respectively, and $'$ denotes computed values. The objective function is minimised by means of a non-linear search procedure over all parameters to be estimated. For this purpose we used a quasi-Newton algorithm (E04JBF from the NAG library).

**The Estimation Results**

Before presenting the estimation results, some comments should be made on the role of technical progress. The computed values of capacity output and demand for labour appear to be very sensitive to changes in the rate of technical progress. Hence the specification of technical progress is important. From that point of view efforts to endogenise technical progress may be considered to be very useful. However, there is no strong tradition in this field and thus far only modest results have been obtained with endogenous technical progress in empirical models. It should therefore not be too surprising that we have not been able to find a specification for technical progress that is satisfactory from both a theoretical and an empirical point of view.[38] From our estimation results, though, it was clear that the assumption of a constant rate of technical progress during the entire estimation period could be held responsible for some misfits, in particular in the periods 1964–71 and 1975–81. As a consequence we introduced dummy-variables for the rate of technical progress in these two sub-periods.[39] Furthermore, we followed the tradition of setting the rate of embodied labour augmenting technological progress before 1948 at a constant fraction of its post-war value.[40]

The fits of the computed values of the rate of capacity utilisation and demand for labour to their observed counterparts are presented in Figures 4.4 and 4.5, respectively. From these figures it can be seen that the model fits the data well.[41] Moreover, when we extrapolate the model for the years 1983–4, it turns out that the predicted value of the rate of capacity utilisation reverses its downward trend to an upward trend as is the case with its actual value, although the turning-

*Figure* 4.4

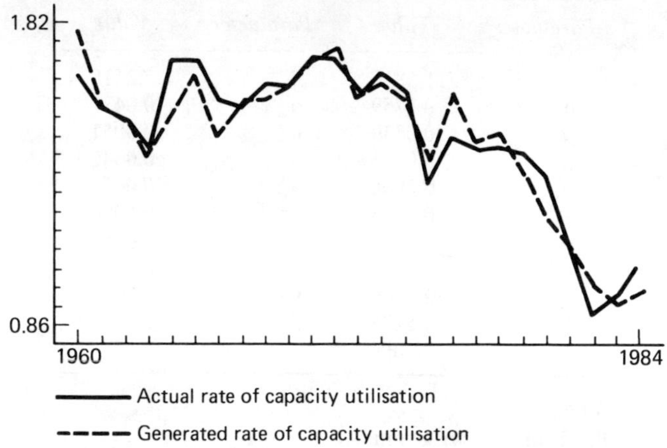


*Figure* 4.5

point is predicted one period late. Moreover, the actual value is slightly underestimated - by 1.5 percentage points in 1984. The reverse in the downward trend of demand for labour is also predicted quite well, but actual demand for labour is overestimated - by about 128 thousand man-years in 1984. We will comment on that later.

The estimation results for the parameter values are presented in Table 4.1. Those results which are comparable with the results found

*Table* 4.1 The parameter estimates

| *Parameter* | *Value* | *Parameter* | *Value* |
|---|---|---|---|
| A | 11.5810 | B | 2.2518 |
| $\sigma$ | 0.3759 | $\mu_n^1$ | 0.0477 |
| $\mu_n^2$ | 0.0539 | $\mu_n^3$ | 0.0051 |
| $\mu_i$ | 0.0113 | $\gamma_n^1$ | 0.0040 |
| $\gamma_n^2$ | 0.0000 | $\gamma_n^3$ | 0.0000 |
| $\gamma_i^1$ | 0.0125 | $\gamma_i^2$ | 0.0000 |
| $\gamma_i^3$ | 0.0000 | $\alpha$ | 0.6950 |
| $\mu_u^{pb}$ | 0.1926 | $\theta$ | 0.4579 |
| $sp^{a,c}$ | 2.0000 | $i$-range[d] | 0.2928 |
| $\zeta_1$ | 0.5178 | $\zeta_2$ | 0.3921 |
| $F^e$ | 0.0066 | | |

*Notes*:
[a] fixed on *a priori* grounds
[b] multiplication factor of embodied labour-augmenting technical progress, i.e.

$$\mu_n^{1\prime} = \mu_u^p \cdot \mu_n^{1\prime\prime}$$

where $''$ denotes the value of embodied labour-augmenting technical progress from 1948 onwards, and $'$ denotes its pre-1948 equivalent.
[c] lag with respect to scrapping on account of underutilisation, i.e. if the (initial) rate of capacity utilisation is smaller than the normal rate of capacity utilisation for a period of *sp* years, then part of excess capacity is scrapped.
[d] the amount of capital varies uniformly over a range $i' +/- 0.145 \cdot i'$, where $i'$ is equal to the average amount of capital embodied in a certain vintage.
[e] value of objective function.

in KvZ and GWJ are also presented in Table 4.2, together with these alternative estimates.

With respect to the parameters describing the production structure, the elasticity of substitution and the nature and rate of technical progress should be considered as the most interesting ones. The estimated value of the elasticity of substitution is 0.38, which is close to the values found by KvZ and GWJ. However, with respect to technical progress we find somewhat different results.

Taking embodied and disembodied labour-augmenting technical progress together, we find approximately the same results – almost 5

*Table* 4.2 Estimation results compared with KvZ and GWJ

| | *KvZ* | *GWJ* | *MvZ* |
|---|---|---|---|
| estimation period | 1950–77 | 1960–82 | 1960–82 |
| elasticity of substitution | 0.32 | 0.44 | 0.38 |
| embodied technical progress (%) | | | |
| labour-augmenting | 4.75 | 2 – 3[a] | 4.77 (5.38, 0.50)[b] |
| fraction in pre-war period[c] | 0.25 | 0.1 – 1[a] | 0.195 |
| capital augmenting | 0 | 0 | 1.13 |
| disembodied technical progress (%) | | | |
| labour-augmenting | 0[d] | 2 – 3[a] | 0.40 (0, 0)[c] |
| capital-augmenting | 0[d] | 0 | 1.25 (0, 0)[b] |
| expected lifetime (years) | 13 | 15 | 25 – 8[e] |

*Notes*
[a] approximate range of variation of endogenous technical progress in the post-war period,
[b] values for the periods 1964–71 and 1975–81, respectively;
[c] fraction of the post-war rate of labour-augmenting embodied technical progress;
[d] for the 1950s a value of – 1.75 per cent is found;
[e] a fraction 0.7 of actual lifetime. Actual lifetime decreases from 45 years in 1960 to 12 years in 1982. See also note 42.

per cent – as both KvZ and GWJ do – except for the late 1970s where we find technical progress to be almost absent. But while GWJ find similar magnitudes for both embodied and disembodied technical progress, we find labour-augmenting technical progress to be almost totally embodied, which is also the case in KvZ. On the other hand, neither KvZ nor GWJ find any capital-augmenting technical progress, whereas we find rates of technical progress, both embodied and disembodied, of over 1 per cent. One should realise, however, that according to our results there is no disembodied capital-augmenting technical progress in the late 1960s or the late 1970s. As a consequence of these differences, we find that, compared with our results, both KvZ and GWJ slightly overestimate the labour intensity of new equipment. But they also overestimate the rate of decrease over time of the labour intensity of equipment installed, which partly compensates the previous overestimation.

With respect to the parameters describing entrepreneurial behaviour, we distinguish between the choice of the production technique, scrapping and labour hoarding. With regard to the choice of the production technique we find that expected lifetime of equipment is a fraction 0.7 of actual lifetime. As a consequence, expected lifetime decreases from 25 years to 8 years in the estimation period, compared with a fixed number of 13 and 15 years estimated by KvZ and GWJ, respectively.[42]

We also find that entrepreneurial behaviour differs such that the labour intensity of new equipment is distributed over an interval of 29 per cent around its average value. In 1950 the labour intensity chosen varied in the range 5.83–8.33 and in 1984 in the range 2.40–3.46. This is quite considerable, hence differences in entrepreneurial behaviour should not be ignored. The importance of differences in entrepreneurial behaviour can also be seen in Figure 4.6 where the upper and lower boundaries of labour productivity of new equipment are presented. From that figure one sees that a certain level of labour productivity can be found in equipment of several vintages, in particular in the late 1970s. Hence, when the wage-rate corresponds to that level of labour productivity, equipment of several vintages will be scrapped. For instance, from Figure 4.6 it can be seen that in the period 1973–81 new equipment was installed with labour productivity

*Figure* 4.6 Labour productivity – boundaries of new equipment

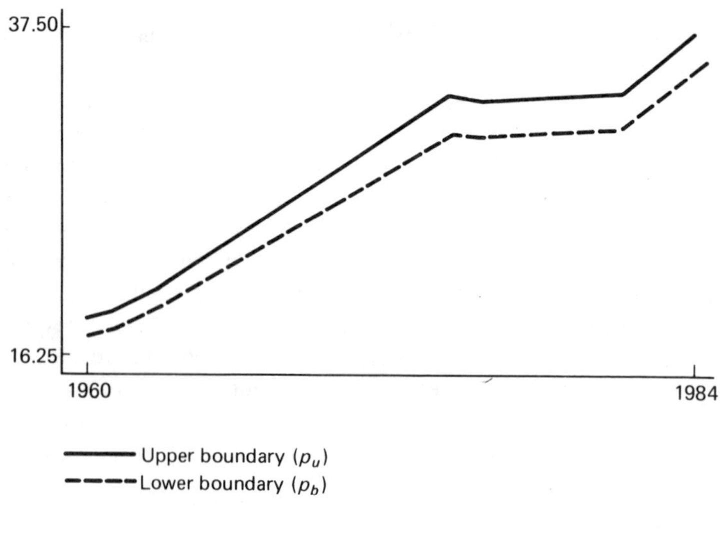

ranges which were virtually the same. So, when at some moment of time the real wage rate lies within these productivity ranges, it follows that all these vintages will be partially scrapped at the same time.[43]

With respect to scrapping behaviour, the parameters to be estimated concern scrapping as the result of excess capacity. We find that when the rate of capacity utilisation is below its normal level of 98 per cent for two consecutive years, a fraction 0.46 of least productive equipment that has been laid-off is scrapped. In Figure 4.7 we show equipment scrapped for various reasons as a percentage of total production capacity. A more or less constant proportion of 2 to 3 per cent over the estimation period is scrapped because of technical obsolesence.

*Figure* 4.7 Percentage of production capacity scrapped for technical, technical plus economic, and technical, economic and underutilisation reasons.

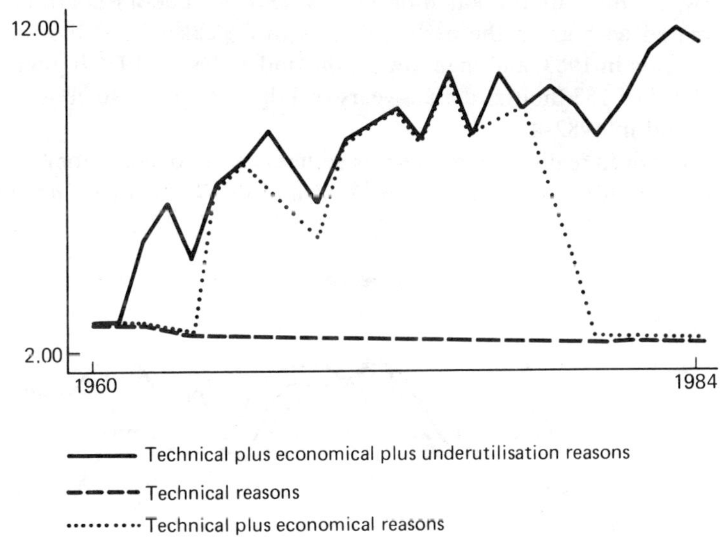


An additional 5–7 per cent is scrapped because of negative quasi-rent in the years 1965–79. In the early 1960s and from 1976 on equipment was scrapped because of underutilisation. In particular from 1980 onwards, this scrapping because of excess capacity is high, varying between 8 and 10 per cent. This reflects the sharp decline in the rate of capacity utilisation. Finally, one should realise that scrapping because of underutilisation occurs to the least productive equipment.

Therefore this is often accompanied by a zero rate of scrapping because of negative quasi-rent in subsequent periods.[44]

The parameters to be estimated with regard to labour hoarding concern the fraction of idle labour to be hoarded, which is estimated to be 52 per cent, and the fraction of labour hoarded in the previous period which cannot be discarded, which turns out to be 38 per cent. Actually, it turns out that labour hoarding in the previous period led to involuntary labour hoarding in the subsequent period in only a few years.[45] Hence, in most years demand for labour is described by:

$$N_t = N'_t + 0.52\{N^c_t - N'_t\} \tag{4.41}$$

where $N'_t$ stands for labour necessary to produce current output, employing the most efficient equipment.

The development of labour hoarding, $N_t - N'_t$, can be seen in Figure 4.8, where data are presented on $N^c_t$, $N_t$ and $N'_t$. Labour hoarding is estimated as high in the early 1960s, with a peak of 159 thousand man-years in 1963, and then low till the mid-1970s. In 1975 it jumped to a level of 157 thousand man-years and then increased to about 300 thousand in 1982–4.

One should realise that our results with respect to demand for labour differ markedly from the ones of KvZ and GWJ, for they find that

*Figure* 4.8

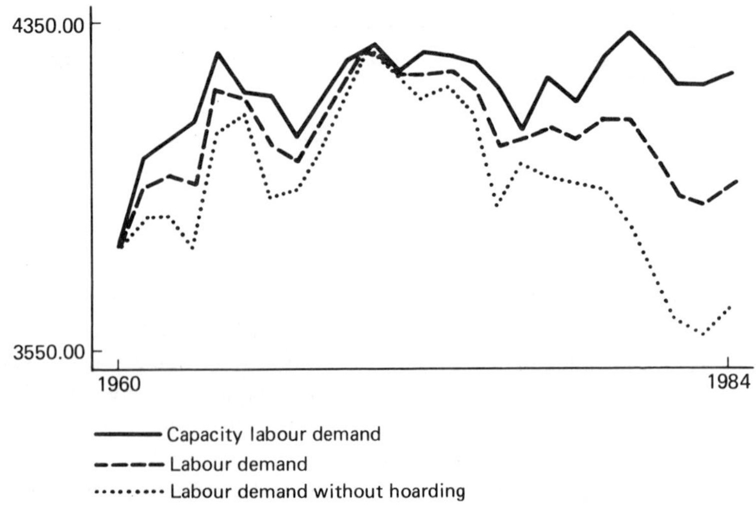

past employment or demand for labour influence current employment or demand for labour strongly, by a factor of proportion of 0.8 and 0.75, respectively.[46] The motivation of their specifications is that hoarding in the previous period is carried over to the present period. Our results, though, indicate that this kind of hoarding is not very relevant for the period under study.

Equation (4.41) can also be used to explain the error in the prediction of the demand for labour, which can be seen in Figure 4.5. From Figure 4.4 one can see that the rate of capacity utilisation is estimated to be 87.7 per cent instead of 89.2 per cent in 1984. Hence capacity output should be estimated to be 1.7 per cent lower and as a consequence capacity demand for labour should be estimated at least 1.7 per cent lower. However, according to equation (4.41) capacity demand for labour should be about 6 per cent lower, provided that $N_t'$ does not change, in order to eliminate the prediction error in actual demand for labour. A possible reason for the prediction errors in both capacity output and capacity demand for labour then is that disembodied capital-augmenting technical progress has been overestimated after 1981 and that disembodied labour augmenting technical progress has been underestimated.[47] But instead of trying to solve this by means of the introduction of another dummy variable for the rate of technical progress, this should be regarded as an additional stimulus to look for a satisfactory way to endogenise technical progress.

**Cyclical and Structural Unemployment**

As we explained earlier, the estimation results can be used to decompose unemployment in its cyclical and structural components, according to equations (4.37)–(4.39). For the employment function we used the function that has been derived in Kooiman and Kloek (1979) and which is used in the FREIA-model.[48] The results are presented in Figure 4.9.

From the figure one sees that qualitative structural unemployment grew from about 70 thousand man-years in 1960 to about 120 thousand man-years in 1984. Quantitative structural unemployment was negative during the first half of the 1960s, reaching its lowest value of −53 thousand man-years in 1964. Then it climbed, slowly at first, to a level of 354 thousand man-years in 1984. This result is in line with the conclusion found in many vintage models for the Netherlands that the 1960s were characterised by labour shortage while the 1970s and early 1980s were characterised by capital shortage.[49] But there is one

*Figure* 4.9

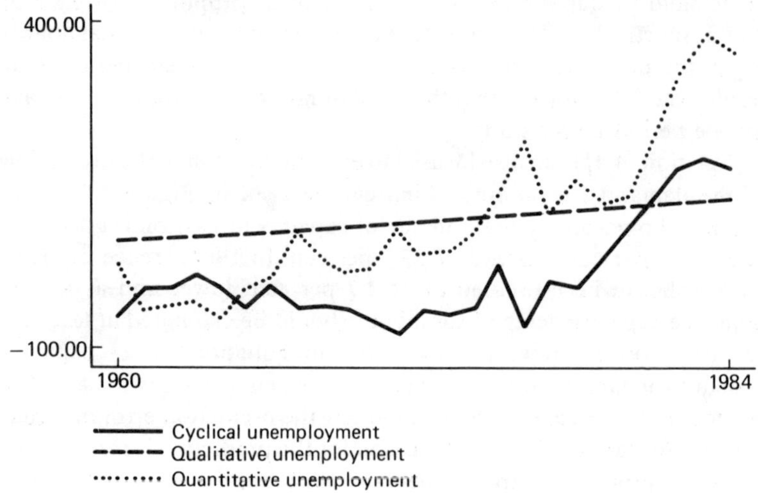


important difference. Most models explain capital shortage by a high real wage-rate which induces scrapping due to economic obsolescence. As can be seen from Figure 4.7 this is consistent with the present model for the situation in the early and mid-1970s. But it can also be seen from this figure that in the late 1970s and early 1980s capital shortage was caused by a persistent low rate of capacity utilisation which led to scrapping due to underutilisation. Hence, the cause of quantitative structural unemployment has changed from a high wage-rate to a low rate of capacity utilisation.

Cyclical unemployment was low in the 1960s and the first half of the 1970s. Its cyclical movements follow the business cycle of the economy which can be inferred from the time-series of the rate of capacity utilisation, presented in Figure 4.4. Booms appear in 1960, 1971 and 1976. Moreover, the rise in cyclical unemployment from a level of 67 thousand man-years in 1976 to 190 thousand man-years in 1983 mirrors the decrease in the rate of capacity utilisation during that period.

With respect to the nature of unemployment we conclude that the rise in unemployment from 325 thousand man-years in 1980 to 800 thousand man-years in 1983 and 1984 is explained both by a deterioration of the cyclical situation and an insufficient level of capacity demand for labour relative to labour supply.[50] The latter was caused by the low level of capacity utilisation which led to scrapping of equipment (due to idleness) to about 10 per cent of productive capacity, as can be seen from Figure 4.7.

## 4.4 CONCLUSIONS

The analysis presented in this paper contains some theoretical innovations with respect to earlier putty–clay vintage models. As a consequence the development of employment and unemployment in the Netherlands is explained in a different way from models like KvZ and GWJ. This applies in particular to the development of unemployment in the last decade.

The main theoretical innovations in our putty–clay vintage model are the consistent use of the notion of efficient utilisation of equipment and the assumptions that a range of labour intensities of a certain vintages is chosen of which the distribution is known. Moreover, the model is complemented with an employment function, which enables us to integrate the various components of unemployment in a coherent way in our model. The assumptions of a distribution of labour intensities, together with an efficient utilisation of equipment are very useful; for instance, hoarding of labour can be studied explicitly.

An interesting empirical finding in this context is that hoarding in a certain period has less spillover to the next period than is usually assumed. Another interesting empirical finding is that in the late 1970s and early 1980s scrapping due to excess capacity turns out to have been relevant. As a consequence of it, the low level of the rate of capacity utilisation not only caused a high level of cyclical unemployment, but due to the persistence of its low level, it also caused a high level of quantitive structural unemployment. Therefore the latter was no longer caused by a high wage-rate, as was the case in the early and mid-1970s.

Although our model does fit the data well and yields plausible results, several questions still remain to be answered. An important conclusion of our empirical analysis is that technological change should no longer be considered as a constant rate of change. This implies that an explanation of the rate of technological change is required. It remains to be seen whether such an explanation will provide a better prediction for the years 1983–4 of demand for labour and the rate of capacity utilisation. But whatever these results are, we think that the explanation of demand for labour could be improved anyway, by incorporating the notion of labour hoarding in the analysis of aggregation by integration which underlies the employment function. Finally, an obvious shortcoming of our empirical analysis is that we treated investment as exogenous.

We think that our analysis has provided not only interesting questions for further research, but also indicated new directions for such research. This holds in particular for the notion of efficient utilisation of equipment in combination with the insight that entrepreneurial behaviour, by its very nature, leads to a spectrum of choices which are realised at a certain moment of time, and which outcomes are distributed in a certain way. These insights have already been proved to be worthwhile in the present analysis.

## Notes

1. An excellent survey is given in den Hartog (1984).
2. Compare Gelauff *et al.*, p. 336 and Kuipers and van Zon (1982) p. 48.
3. We treat it as exogenous in the estimation process, however, in order to keep this process manageable.
4. These variables are defined at maximum-capacity utilisation, where the utilisation rate is equal to 1.
5. Den Hartog (1984), pp. 339–40.
6. Kuipers and van Zon (1982) p. 45.
7. In Kuipers and van Zon (1982) this period is a parameter to be estimated, they find as a result four years (p. 51). Gelauff *et al.*, p. 337, assume this period to be ten years, which seems rather long to us.
8. Both Kuipers and van Zon and Gelauff *et al.* assume a normal rate of capacity utilisation which is constant during the entire estimation period, cf. Kuipers and van Zon (1982) p. 48, where $q^N = 1$ and the rate of capacity utilisation is allowed to exceed 1, and Gelauff *et al.*, p. 337 where $q^N = 0.98$ and $q$ cannot exceed 1. Like Gelauff *et al.*, we have taken $q^N$ to be equal to 0.98. We have, however, experimented with a variable normal rate of capacity utilisation which is equal to the average rate of capacity utilisation over the past eight years. The outcomes were virtually the same as the ones obtained using a fixed normal rate of capacity utilisation. This is not too surprising however, since on the one hand the actual rate of capacity utilisation lies below the normal rate of capacity utilisation in the late 1970s and early 1980s in both cases. On the other hand the rate of scrapping due to underutilisation is not related to the degree of underutilisation. See also note 19.
9. $X^{-}(T-1)$ is defined in equation (4.35).
10. This function is similar to Kuipers and van Zon, equation (2.12). We treat expectations with regard to $h_i$ and $h_n$ analogously to those with regard to $r$.

11. This notion is inspired by the distribution approach to the aggregation of production functions; cf Johansen (1972), Sato (1975) and Muysken (1987).
12. Otherwise the CES-function should be included in the integrand.
13. The values of $N_b$ and $N_u$, can be derived in a straightforward manner by substitution of $I_{bT}$ and $I_{uT}$ in equation (4.1). For instance:

$$Nb_{T,T} = \left(\frac{(X_{T,T})^{-\rho} - (B(1+\mu_i)^T h_{iT} \cdot I_{uT})^{-\rho}}{(A \cdot (1+\mu_n)^T h_{nT})^{-\rho}}\right)^{-1/\rho}$$

14. Actually, these values hold only approximately, because of the linear approximation of the isoquant segment *PQ*. We correct for this approximation error by rescaling $N_b$ and $N_u$ such that $(N_b + N_u)/2 = N_{T,T}$ holds exactly. For instance, the lowerbound becomes $N_b = N_{T,T} - (N_u - N_b)/2$.
15. However, now we can explain why investment takes place at the same time that equipment is scrapped due to underutilisation: Successful and unsuccessful entrepreneurs coexist and while the unsuccessful entrepreneurs scrap their equipment, the successful ones expand.
16. See for instance Gelauff *et al.*, p. 13.
17. However, we assume that when labour productivity is compared with the real wage rate, entrepreneurs do not consider the real wage rate of that year, but the average real wage rate of the past two years and the current year. Compare Kuipers and van Zon, p. 18 and Gelauff *et al.*, p. 334, who do the same.
18. Cf. Gelauff *et al.*, p. 333.
19. A possible future extension of the model is the assumption of a variable proportion of excess capacity to be scrapped, for it seems likely that in times of severe underutilisation a larger proportion of excess capacity will be scrapped than in times of a relatively small amount of excess capacity.
20. $P_b(t, T) = X(t, T)/N_u(t, T)$ and $P_u(t, T) = X(t, T)/N_b(t, T)$. We discuss the time-indices of these boundaries later. For the purpose of calculating the labour productivity boundaries, $X(t, T)$, $N_u(t, T)$ and $N_b(t, T)$ are evaluated exclusive of the influence of technical decay. See also note 25.
21. Hence the indication of $X$ on the vertical axis should be interpreted carefully, cf. Muysken (1985).
22. One should realise that $N/X$ is distributed uniformly over the range $(1/P_u(t, T), 1/P_b(t, T))$.
23. Hence $r$ is determined such that aggregate productive capacity of all equipment for which $r > X/N > w/p$ is equal to the amount of productive capacity to be scrapped.
24. $I^*(t, T) = I_u(t-1, T) - Q(t, T) \cdot (I_u(t-1, T) - I_b(t-1, T))$.
25. Scrapping due to technical obsolescence will not affect the boundaries because this occurs to all equipment of a certain vintage simultaneously.
26. These equations are similar to equations (2.23)–(2.25) of Gelauff *et al.*, except for the presence of the factors $Q'_i$, $Q^*_n$, $R^*_i$ and $R^*_n$. Since

Gelauff *et al.* do not allow for different expectations, they assume these factors to be equal to 1.

27. Equation (4.34) refers to the average amount of capital embodied in equipment of vintage *T*. We assume that expectations among entrepreneurs differ such that aggregation over the different types of equipment yields the average values of *I* and *N*.
28. For an extensive discussion of this function we refer to Muysken (1986) pp. 5–7.
29. Cf. Muysken (1986) section 2.
30. We ignored the development in the 1950s which are notoriously difficult to describe. See for instance the results of Kuipers and van Zon (1982) for this period.
31. Incorporation of investment in the analysis would increase the number of parameters to be estimated simultaneously and would probably require a refinement of the assumptions underlying the modelling of investment behaviour. We consider this as a matter of future research.
32. Gelauff *et al.* refer to the data used by the Central Planning Bureau for the Dutch annual model FREIA (CPB, 1983).
33. With respect to the rate of capacity utilisation one should note that the data used by Gelauff *et al.* in their publication differ from those published by the Central Bureau of Statistics, in particular from 1980 on. For that reason we extrapolated these data for the period 1983–4 using the CBS-data.
34. i.e. we used the same technical survival scheme ($\Omega$) and we assume that war damage on vintages installed before 1946 is 40 per cent – these assumptions are common in most Dutch empirical vintage models.
35. Cf. Kuipers and van Zon (1982) p. 42. Gelauff *et al.* (1985) pp. 337–8, do distinguish between both types of working hours, using rather elaborate measures.
36. When investment is endogenous this would be the third strategic variable.
37. A penalty is given when the estimated value of $N^c$ drops below 99 per cent of actual demand for labour, *N*.
38. Gelauff *et al.* (1985) pp. 331–2, assume that, apart from an autonomous component, embodied technical progress depends on the structural rate of change in the export share, whereas disembodied technical progress depends on the sum of the rates of growth of exports and national product. These particular functional specifications are hardly justified, however. Efforts to include the influence of relative factor-prices failed either because of identification problems (embodied) or because of poor empirical results (disembodied).
39. An exception is made for the rate of embodied capital augmenting technical progress, for which the model appeared to be less sensitive.
40. This tradition is initiated by den Hartog and Tjan (1974), who use a fraction of 0.25, motivated on *a priori* grounds.
41. These results are better than those of Gelauff *et al.*: in particular with respect to the fit of the rate of capacity utilisation. This can be seen when we compare our Figure 4.4 with their Figure 3.1. Gelauff *et al.* underestimate the rate of capacity utilisation during the period 1960–9

and overestimate it in the period 1973–8, while our estimate does not show such systematic errors.

42. We have imposed an upper limit on expected lifetime of 25 years.
43. We ignore the influence of disembodied technical progress, which is low.
44. This explains one difference from the results presented by Gelauff *et al.* in their Figure 3.5. Part of the difference between our results and the ones of Gelauff *et al.* is caused by the fact that we have defined scrapping in terms of productive capacity rather than in terms of the capital stock, as Gelauff *et al.* have done. Because of disembodied technical progress, capital productivity increases over time. Therefore, in our case, old vintages may be more important from a scrapping point of view than is the case with Gelauff *et al.* which only consider the amount of capital embodied in those vintages. In addition to this, the (relative) amount of capital scrapped because of underutilisation is effectively bounded from above to about 4 per cent in the case of Gelauff *et al.* (see Gelauff *et al.*, 1985, pp. 334–5) while such an upper limit does not exist in our case. But apart from these differences, the results are quite comparable.
45. These are the years 1965, 1970, 1971 and 1976.
46. Cf. Kuipers and van Zon (1982), p. 54; and Gelauff *et al.* (1985) p. 336.
47. It turns out that when disembodied capital-augmenting technical progress remains zero, as it was till 1982, and disembodied labour-augmenting technical progress is increased to a level of 1.65 per cent, both the computed rate of capacity utilisation and computed demand for labour fit the observed values in 1982–4 very well.
48. CPB (1983) p. 23; we also used the parameter values presented in that publication, since the model was estimated for approximately the same period. One drawback of this particular specification is that the friction parameter has been estimated with a linear time-trend. As a consequence, qualitative structural employment as a percentage of the labour force grows along a linear time-path.
49. Cf. Kuipers and van Zon (1985) p. 61.
50. Note, however, that because of the overestimation of labour demand in 1983 and 1984, unemployment is underestimated in those years.

## References

CENTRAL PLANNING BUREAU, *FREIA* (1983) 'Een macro-economisch model voor de middellange termijn', The Hague.

DRIEHUIS, W. (1985) 'Unemployment in the Netherlands, 1960–1983', *Research Memorandum* no. 8521, University of Amsterdam.

GELAUFF, G. M. M., WENNEKERS, A. R. M. and DE JONG, A. H. M. (1985) A Putty-Clay Model with Three Factors of Production and Partly Endogenous Technical Progress', *De Economist*, 133, no 3, pp. 327–51.

HARTOG, H. DEN (1984) 'Empirical Vintage Models for the Netherlands: A Review in Outline', *De Economist*, 132, no 3, pp. 326–49.

HARTOG, H. DEN and TJAN, H. S. (1980) 'A Clay–Clay Vintage Model Approach for Sectors of Industry in the Netherlands', *De Economist*, 128, no 2, pp. 129–88.

JOHANSEN, L. (1972) *Production Functions* (Amsterdam: North-Holland).

KUIPERS, S. K. and VAN ZON, A. H. (1982) 'Output and Employment Growth in the Netherlands in the Post-war Period: A Putty-Clay Approach', *De Economist*, 130, no 1, pp. 38–70.

KOOIMAN, P. and KLOEK, T. (1979), Aggregation of Micro Markets in Disequilibrium. Working paper of the Econometric Institute of Erasmus University, Rotterdam.

MUYSKEN, J. (1985) 'Representation and Estimation of the Capacity Distribution: The Case of the Swedish Dairy Industry, 1964–1973', in F. R. Forsund, M. Hoel, S. Longra. (eds) *Production, Multisectoral Growth and Planning* (Amsterdam: North-Holland) pp. 43–64.

MUYSKEN, J. (1987) 'The Distribution Approach to the Aggregation of Production Functions', Working Paper, no 85-008, University of Limburg, *Recherches Economique de Louvain*, Vol. 4, pp. 269–82.

MUYSKEN, J. (1987a) 'Full Capacity Employment, Unemployment and Labour Hoarding', in D. Bosworth, and D. Heathfield (eds) *Measuring Capacity and Factor Utilization* (London: Macmillan).

MUYSKEN, J. and MEIJERS, H. (1986) 'Conjunctuur- en structuurwerkloosheid in Nederland, 1970–1985', *Working Paper*, no 86-009, University of Limburg, Maastricht.

SATO, K. (1975) *Production Functions and Aggregation* (Amsterdam: North-Holland).

## COMMENT ON CHAPTERS 3 AND 4

**E. R. de Regt**

### INTRODUCTION

The two papers by Ansar *et al.* and by Muysken and van Zon (further referred to as AITU and MvZ respectively) extend existing putty-clay vintage labour demand models into different, though related, directions. AITU focus on long-run and short-run substitution possibilities between the production factors. The dual approach adopted allows the authors to test the often-used putty-clay, putty-putty or clay-clay production models against their maintained hypothesis of a putty-semi-putty model. The latter vintage model allows for both *ex ante* and *ex post* substitution possibilities, though the *ex post* substitution characteristics for each vintage are reduced by the *ex ante* choice of production technique. Nevertheless, for active vintages factor proportions are, among other things, influenced by actual factor prices.

A more or less similar property holds in the approach suggested by MvZ. They retain the assumption of a putty-clay vintage technology, but introduce additional heterogeneity in the capital stock: The capital-labour ratio varies not only between vintages, but also within a vintage. Starting-point for their analysis is the observation that no representative firm exists; on the contrary, by their very nature entrepreneurs have diverging expectations, and, accordingly, diversified investment decisions are taken. In the MvZ paper this is modelled by the assumption that the capital-labour ratio, and labour productivity as a consequence, are stochastically distributed at the level of the firm. For the variable under consideration aggregate values are then obtained by integration over the relevant range.

This innovative aspect of the MvZ paper - inspired by the distribution approach to the aggregation of production functions - has an important implication for aggregate scrapping behaviour. Whereas in existing putty-clay models a vintage is fully scrapped once its labour productivity falls below real wage costs, the efficient use of equipment in the MvZ model requires a more differentiated behaviour: at the level of the firm, equipment with labour productivity below actual real wage costs is indeed scrapped, whereas equipment of the same vintage but with a labour productivity level exceeding real wage costs is retained. Because of the aggregation procedure, scrapping behaviour at the aggregate level is smoothed, the survival fraction of a vintage being a decreasing function of real wage costs. As a consequence, the aggregate capital–labour ratio of a vintage is positively related to actual real labour costs.

Having briefly outlined the focal point of both papers, I will now discuss them separately in some more detail.

## LABOUR DEMAND IN UK MANUFACTURING

Let me first consider the AITU model for UK manufacturing. The theoretical model used is taken from Fuss (1977): Diewert's generalised Leontief cost function is introduced for the *ex post* decision stage, and a further parameterisation is added to link *ex ante* and *ex post* behaviour. The resulting vintage specific factor demand functions for labour, energy and capital are given in equation 3.6. The 'present value expected factor price ratios' summarise *ex ante* considerations, whereas *ex post* substitution possibilities account for the occurrence of the actual price ratios.

Theoretical considerations reduce the number of parameters to 36. Moreover, notice that sufficient parameter restrictions for global concavity of the cost function are $\alpha_{ijkl} \geqslant 0$, see Fuss (1977).

Unfortunately data are, as usual, only available at an aggregate level. Hence, to obtain total factor demand, the aforementioned demand equations have to be aggregated over the active vintages. Given the additional assumption that the capital stock is fixed *ex post* (which reduces the number of parameters to 24), vintages are used in order of increasing variable costs until the exogenous output restriction is satisfied. The remaining vintages, with the highest variable costs, are idle. Obviously, this procedure allows for holes to occur in the vintage structure, although this complication has not been dealt with in the *ex ante* decision model: the vintage specific demand equations are derived under the assumption that a vintage will be used throughout its fixed planning horizon.

A related and more serious problem is that only physical deterioration of capital is included in the model, but there is no scrapping for economic reasons. Thus a particular vintage, with relatively high *ex post* variable costs, might remain idle for several years without being scrapped. Therefore it still adds to productive capacity, even though this vintage might have a negative quasi rent. This problem seems closely related to the determinants of new investment in the model. Beside cost considerations, output expectations relative to capacity constraints, should play an important role in this respect. Unfortunately, the paper does not address this question, and the empirical analysis carried out is conditional upon investment behaviour.

Let me now proceed with the empirical analysis for UK manufacturing as presented by AITU. I then felt slightly uncomfortable, as some links between the theoretical and the empirical part of the paper have remained quite implicit. As a minor example, it is stated in the introduction that there is quite a lot to be explained in the data; Figures 3.1, 3.2 and 3.3 present annual data over the period 1955–83 (including *real* labour costs which have no direct role in a cost-minimising framework), whereas parameter estimates are obtained using quarterly data covering 1966$Q$1 to 1982$Q$3. What is the reason for this difference? More seriously, however, there is a non-trivial reparameterisation from $\alpha_{ijkl}$ $(i, j, k, l = 1, 2, 3)$ to $a_{ij}$ $(i = 1$ to 4 and $j = 1$ to 6). Moreover, the deterioration parameter $\delta$ is not explicitly linked with $\delta_{t-v}$; but I suppose that $\delta_{t-v} = (1-\delta)^{t-v}$. In that case, however, there is an enormous discrepancy between the planning horizon $L$ of 20 quarters and expected lifetime of equipment, as implicitly defined by $\delta = 10^{-4}$.

Obviously, the estimates are conditional upon the specification of expected prices included in the 'present value expected prices'. The only information available in the AITU paper is that a separate time-series model is used, but even no summary information about the performance of this model is presented.

As stated before, investment is treated as exogenous in the empirical analysis. Nevertheless, the parameters of the investment function ($a_{3j}$, $j = 1$ to 6) appear in the list of estimates for the labour and energy demand equations, as they influence the aggregation procedure over vintages. As *mutatis mutandis* the interpretation of the $a_{ij}$ parameters is similar for any $i = 1, 2, 3$, it is then puzzling to observe the diverging pattern of the $a_{3j}$ estimates in Table. This raises some doubts with respect to the relevance of the estimates. However, it is difficult to assess the importance of this argument, as no standard errors of the estimates are provided.

A final difficulty with the estimates is that they do not seem to satisfy the sufficient conditions for global concavity of the cost function. The authors should then check for local concavity.

With respect to the presentation of the model characteristics, I would have preferred some summary information in terms of *ex ante* and *ex post* price and substitution elasticities, instead of the various figures and tables used by AITU. Both approaches are conditional upon the validity of the expectational price model, but the latter would facilitate comparison with alternative models.

Given their parameter estimates, AITU then test alternative hypotheses with respect to the structure of production technology. There seems to be strong evidence in favour of a vintage structure of the capital stock allowing for *ex ante* substitution possibilities. Moreover, it also appears that some *ex post* substitution does exist, although I suspect that the latter conclusion might be due to the absence of technological progress from the model: the parameters of the rising factor price ratios might pick up part of this impact. AITU argue against the inclusion of technical progress on the basis of preliminary estimates of a Cobb–Douglas–Leontief production model. However, that model assumes a large impact of factor prices in the *ex ante* stage. If in reality *ex ante* substitution elasticities are significantly below 1 (one), we might expect a more pronounced influence of technological progress. Summarising, I am not convinced that the rejection of the putty–clay hypothesis is a robust funding.

Let me conclude the comments on the AITU paper with a remark on unemployment, the topic of this conference. On the basis of their analysis the authors suggest that increasing unemployment in recent years is essentially due to depressed output levels, and not to too high a level of labour costs. I think the above-mentioned arguments raise some doubts with respect to this conclusion. For example, scrapping of capital for economic reasons might have reduced productive capacity, reducing the scope for demand management. Moreover, *ex ante* investment decisions then become more important and there is no doubt that this has led to the use of labour-saving techniques on new vintages as a reaction to high relative labour costs.

## LABOUR DEMAND IN THE NETHERLANDS

Let me switch my attention to the MvZ paper. Unlike AITU, they do not consider energy as a production factor in their analysis of the Dutch business sector: they focus on capital–labour substitution, although again estimates are conditional upon investment behaviour. On the other hand, MvZ do explicitly deal with scrapping behaviour for economic behaviour, and their model illustrates why investment and scrapping due to under-utilisation might occur simultaneously:

in the distribution approach successful firms may coexist with unsuccessful ones.

Unfortunately, the elaboration of the distribution approach is not always very lucid. The distinction between the level of the firm and the aggregate level especially is sometimes ambiguous (see, for example, the figures 4.1 and 4.2 where the former refers to the aggregate level and the latter to the entrepreneurial level). Nevertheless, since the distribution approach leads to smoothed scrapping behaviour, the idea seems promising, but a more formal treatment would be clarifying.

Moreover, the link between diverging expectations and different choices of technique at the level of the firm could then be elaborated. In this respect, I also suspect that a link should exist between aggregate expected prices and the underlying distribution of expectations at the firm level. However, MvZ do not even hint at such a relation. Expectations are modelled *ad hoc* by the use of four-year moving averages of growth rates. This leads to fairly long lags, which might be questionable given that the estimation period (1960–82) includes both oil shocks.

MvZ extend the model by the introduction of additional scrapping due to persistent excess capacity. Unfortunately, the specification is rather *ad hoc*: after two consecutive years of under-utilisation, a fixed percentage of excess capacity is scrapped; again a link with an underlying distribution of demand expectations at the level of the firm is missing. Moreover, with respect to this scrapping behaviour of profitable capacity, as described in equation (4.22), three more technical remarks should be made. First, an explicit equation for the critical value of labour productivity ($r$) is missing. Second, I suspect that the lower bound $Pb$ should be replaced by real wage costs, as $R$ is the fraction of profitable capacity. Third, I doubt whether the timing of the upper- and lower boundaries of labour productivity ($P_u$ and $Pb$, respectively) is correct. Obviously, these bounds refer to equipment having replaced scrapping in previous periods, but they should be corrected for disembodied technical progress. A similar remark also applies to equation (4.18).

The final extension to the theoretical model is the introduction of labour hoarding, although in a rather unconventional way: actual labour demand is essentially a weighted average of capacity labour demand and of the efficient level of employment needed to produce actual output; dynamic aspects, due, for example, to adjustment costs, only play a role if hoarding in the previous year has been high.

Turning to the empirical part of the MvZ paper, the model has been estimated for the Dutch private sector, the two strategic variables being productive capacity and labour demand, the latter being defined as employment plus vacancies. Unfortunately, the choice of the objective function is rather obscure: The underlying stochastic structure is not mentioned, but the errors are certainly not normally distributed. Had the latter choice been made, it would also have enabled the authors to compute the now missing asymptotic standard errors.

Whereas AITU have fully ignored technological progress, MvZ seem to have gone to an other extreme. They have introduced as much as ten parameters for technological progress, dividing the twenty-three years into three subperiods. Ultimately, six of these parameters have non-zero estimated values.

The abundant use of parameters for technological progress makes it almost impossible to identify the empirical content of the smoothed scrapping model. For example, the post-sample performance of the model seems quite respectable, predicting the turning-points in the early 1980s. But I wonder whether this is due to the assumed heterogeneity of vintages - and, consequently, to the smoothed scrapping - or to the specification of technical progress. The evidence of Table 4.5, where parameter estimates are compared with rival models, suggests that the latter plays a non-negligible role.

Similarly, the specification of the expected lifetime of equipment seems important. Contrary to the rival models, expected lifetime is directly linked to actual lifetime in the MvZ model. However, the interpretation of the latter variable seems ambiguous, as capital is heterogeneous within vintages.

Finally, it is difficult to evaluate the overall performance of the MvZ model, as no summary statistics are provided. However, inspection of the Figures 4.4 and 4.5 suggests that some autocorrelation in the errors exists. This might point at misspecification of the model, perhaps with regard to the dynamic specification of the labour demand equation.

The MvZ paper ends with a decomposition of unemployment into its structural and cyclical components. Thereto, the estimates of capacity and actual labour demand are inserted in an existing employment function. Essentially, this exercise amounts to an UV-analysis of the labour market, but the use of capacity labour demand figures also allows for a distinction between non-frictional unemployment due to capital shortages or to insufficient demand. Both types of unemployment appear to be fairly large in the 1980s. However, I have some doubt with respect to the relevance of the distinction. Had firms correctly anticipated goods demand, capacity and actual labour demand would have been more or less in balance, at least ignoring adjustment lags. Hence, the strong increase in cyclical unemployment starting in 1979 seems essentially due to persistent inappropriate expectations. Once more, this conclusion stresses the need for a further development of the expectational structure underlying the MvZ model.

## CONCLUSION

The two papers by Ansar *et al.* and by Muysken and van Zon elaborate on putty-clay vintage labour demand models. Essentially, *ex post* factor proportions are allowed to vary with actual factor price ratios. The empirical models, however, seem not yet to have provided sufficient evidence in favour of such a possible extension, and call for further research in this area.

### Reference

FUSS, M. A. (1977) 'The Structure of Technology over Time: A Model for Testing the 'Putty-Clay' Hypothesis', *Econometrica*, 45, pp. 1797–1821.

# 5 Mass Unemployment in the United Kingdom: An Analysis of Causes and Possible Cures

Jim Taylor

## INTRODUCTION

Until 1975, unemployment in the UK had remained below the 1 million mark for over thirty years. Between 1979 and 1982 it rose from under 1.5 million to over 3 million and remained above 3 million until 1987. The 1980s have certainly been a disaster as far as unemployment is concerned and a question of paramount importance to policy-makers is whether the government can do anything to reduce unemployment significantly in the foreseeable future. The answer to this question depends on the causes of unemployment and whether these causes can be affected by government action. Unfortunately, the causes of current unemployment are not clearly understood and there is a startling lack of consensus amongst policy-makers and their economic advisers over what can (or should) be done to tackle the unemployment problem.

One of the issues about which there is substantial disagreement amongst economists is whether unemployment is currently high because of a deficiency in the aggregate demand for goods, or whether it is high for other reasons. These other reasons include: the existence of disincentives to take jobs because unemployment benefit is too high relative to net take-home pay; a serious mismatch between labour demand and labour supply; excessively high real wages relative to labour productivity; the sudden structural collapse of large sections of UK manufacturing industry; and a combination of these factors. It is not the purpose of this paper to examine the relative merits of the various explanations of high unemployment which have been offered in recent years. The aim is more limited, namely to investigate the extent to which unemployment *cannot* be removed in the short run by simply raising the aggregate demand for goods. This task can be approached in several ways, one of which is to use unemployment and vacancy data in order to establish whether there exists a serious mismatch between labour demand and labour supply. An alternative (and in my view more valuable) approach is to investigate the extent to which the UK economy is capable of responding to a demand injection in order to create more jobs.

The chapter is in three sections. Section 1 discusses and evaluates the approach to measuring a mismatch between the demand for labour and the supply of labour based upon unemployment and vacancy data disaggregated by occupation and region. It is concluded that such methods have very little value. Section 2 investigates the time-series relationship between aggregate unemployment and aggregate vacancies. This suggests that structural unemployment in the UK has increased substantially in the 1980s. Finally, Section 3 examines the collapse of the manufacturing sector and its critical role in determining the severity of structural unemployment in the UK at the present time.

## 1 THE U–V METHOD OF CATEGORISING THE UNEMPLOYED

Numerous attempts have been made to divide total unemployment into separate categories using unemployment and vacancy data. One of these is referred to in the literature as the U–V method.[1] Provided that unemployment and vacancy data are available by occupation and by geographical area, three main categories of unemployment can be distinguished and measured:

(i) Demand-deficient unemployment exists when national unemployment exceeds national vacancies.

(ii) Frictional unemployment exists when job vacancies and unemployment occur within the same geographical labour market area and within the same occupational category.

(iii) Structural unemployment exists when a mismatch occurs between job vacancies and unemployment. A mismatch can occur for three reasons:

(a) job vacancies and unemployment occur in the same occupation but in different labour market areas: this is the geographical component of structural unemployment.

(b) job vacancies and unemployment occur in the same geographical area but in different occupations; this is the occupational component of structural unemployment.

(c) job vacancies and unemployment occur but in different geographical areas and in different occupations; this is the mixed occupational/geographical component of structural unemployment.

Estimates of the number of unemployed persons falling into each of these categories can be obtained by using a simple procedure based upon matching job vacancies and unemployment. Both vacancies and unemployment must be available by occupation and by geographical area (i.e. a vacancy matrix and an unemployment matrix are required with occupation and geographical area as the two dimensions). Calculating the number of unemployed persons in each category simply involves allocating the vacancies among the unemployed.[2] Frictional unemployment is calculated by matching unemployment and vacancies in corresponding cells. Structural unemployment is calculated by reallocating vacancies either between occupations within regions (to obtain the occupational component) or between regions within occupations (to obtain the geographical component). The mixed occupational/geographical component is obtained by reallocating vacancies between regions and occupations simultaneously. Finally, demand-deficient unemployment is the amount left over after the other components have been calculated (assuming that total unemployment exceeds total vacancies).

This method of categorising the unemployed by matching vacancies with unemployment appears at first sight to be an attractive and useful device. There are, however, several critical problems which reduce its practical value considerably. First, the method relies on the unemployment and vacancy data being of reasonable accuracy. This condition is not met. In January 1986, for example, the official unemployment count recorded 3.3 million unemployed persons. But this figure includes only those claiming unemployment benefit. It has been estimated that if unemployment were calculated on the same basis as it was before October 1982 (when all those registering as unemployed were included in the unemployment total irrespective of whether or not they were claiming benefit), the unemployment total would have been 3.8 million.[3] In addition, a substantial number of persons may be looking for work but would not be registered as unemployed even under the pre-October 1982 registration rules. These are the hidden unemployed. On the other hand, it has been argued that a significant proportion of the unemployed are not seriously interested in finding a job since they regard themselves as being better off on the dole (partly because some of the unemployed have part-time jobs). The upshot of the matter is that the official unemployment count should be treated simply as an accurate measure of the number of unemployed persons claiming unemployment benefit post-1982. Whether this corresponds closely with the definition of unemployment which is needed for explaining why unemployment occurs is a matter for debate and careful analysis.

The official vacancy data is also of doubtful value for calculating different types of unemployment. According to a 1977 survey by the Department of Employment, vacancies notified to job centres were estimated to be about one-third of total (i.e. 'true') vacancies. The degree of underestimation, however, was found to vary considerably between regions, as can be seen from Table 5.1 (e.g. notified vacancies varied between 22 per cent of estimated total vacancies in the West Midlands and 50 per cent in the East Midlands at the survey date).

*Table* 5.1 Vacancies notified to employment offices or job centres and estimated total vacancies by region

| *Region* | *Notified vacancies* | *Estimated total vacancies* | *Notified as % of estimated* |
|---|---|---|---|
| West Midlands | 9 000 | 41 000 | 22 |
| North-west | 14 000 | 51 000 | 27 |
| South-west | 11 000 | 31 000 | 34 |
| Wales | 7 000 | 20 000 | 35 |
| South-east | 69 000 | 196 000 | 35 |
| Yorkshire and Humberside | 14 000 | 35 000 | 40 |
| East Anglia | 5 000 | 12 000 | 42 |
| Scotland | 18 000 | 39 000 | 46 |
| North | 9 000 | 19 000 | 47 |
| East Midlands | 11 000 | 22 000 | 50 |
| Great Britain | 167 000 | 465 000 | 36 |

*Source*: *Employment Gazette*, May 1980, p. 507.

The underestimation of true vacancies is also likely to be more serious during recessions when recruitment of new workers will be much easier. The matrix of notified vacancies cannot therefore be used with any confidence for categorising the unemployed. In particular, the under-recording of vacancies means that structural unemployment is likely to be seriously underestimated.

Even if the vacancy matrix were accurate, however, there would still be serious problems with the U–V method. One of these concerns the sensitivity of the results to the level of demand in the economy. As the demand for labour falls, vacancies decline and this leads to the disappearance of the structural component. According to the U–V method, structural unemployment increases during booms and declines during slumps. This is somewhat counter-intuitive in so far as it implies that fundamental structural problems are present only in periods of high economic activity. A further problem with the U–V method is that the results are sensitive to the delineation of occupations and geographical areas. As the number of occupations and geographical areas increases, for example, the frictional component will decline and the structural component will increase. This can be illustrated by considering the geographical component of structural unemployment. Delineating Scotland as a labour-market area means that an unemployed person in the south of Scotland (in a particular occupational category) would be classified as frictionally unemployed if a job vacancy existed within the same occupation in the north of Scotland – over 300 miles away. If Scotland were divided into travel-to-work areas, however, this unemployed person would be reclassified as belonging to the geographical component of structural unemployment.

Finally, the U–V method of categorising unemployment can be criticised on the grounds that the degree of mismatch is measured on a one-to-one basis between the unemployed and vacant jobs. Frictional plus structural unemployment cannot therefore exceed the total number of vacancies (in the case where total unemployment exceeds total vacancies). Jackman and Roper (1985) reject this approach and argue instead that structural unemployment exists when the relative distribution of unemployed workers between sectors does not match the relative distribution of vacancies. They measure structural unemployment by calculating 'the number of unemployed workers who need to be moved from one sector to another in order to achieve structural balance' (p. 6), where structural balance is defined as a situation in which $U_i/U = V_i/V$ for all sectors ($U_i$ is unemployment in sector $i$, $V_i$ is vacancies in sector $i$, and $U$ and $V$ are total unemployment and total vacancies respectively). The following equation is used by Jackman and Roper to calculate the proportion of total unemployment which is structural:

$$\frac{SU}{U} = \tfrac{1}{2}\sum \left| \frac{U_i}{U} - \frac{V_i}{V} \right|$$

The main point to note about this measure of structural unemployment is that the absolute number of vacancies has no effect on the calculated value of structural unemployment. Thus, in a simple two-sector economy in which all unemployed persons are in sector 1 and none is in sector 2, then all unemployment would be classified as structural (irrespective of the total number of vacancies) if all vacancies were in sector 2. An obvious drawback of this measure of structural unemployment is that it may provide quite bizarre estimates of structural unemployment. If, for example, there are 100 unemployed persons in sector 1 and no unemployed persons in sector 2, while there are no vacancies in sector 1 and there is 1 vacancy in sector 2, the Jackman–Roper measure indicates that all unemployment is structural since 100 per cent of the unemployed are in the 'wrong' sector. If the vacancy in sector 2 suddenly disappeared structural unemployment would fall to zero.

The notion that dividing unemployment into separate categories is meaningful and useful for policy-formation has recently been challenged by de Neubourg (1986). He argues that attempts to categorise unemployment are fraught with methodological problems, one of the foremost of these being that such attempts imply that each category has a separately identifiable cause (or cure) and is often regarded as being independent of the other categories. This criticism certainly applies to the U–V method discussed in the present section.

## 2 UNEMPLOYMENT AND VACANCIES OVER TIME

Empirical work on the time-series relationship between unemployment and vacancies dates back to Dow and Dicks-Mireaux (1958) who observed (and provided an explanation for) the existence of an inverse relationship between unemployment and vacancies. This inverse relationship is evident from Figure 5.1. Unemployment was assumed to reflect the excess supply of labour; and vacancies were assumed to reflect the unsatisfied demand for labour. Both unemployment and vacancies could therefore be expressed as a function of excess labour demand:

$$U = f(XD) \qquad f^1 < 0$$

$$V = g(XD) \qquad g^1 > 0$$

where $U$ = unemployment, $V$ = vacancies and $XD$ = excess labour

*Figure* 5.1 Registered unemployment and estimated vacancies: UK, 1953–85

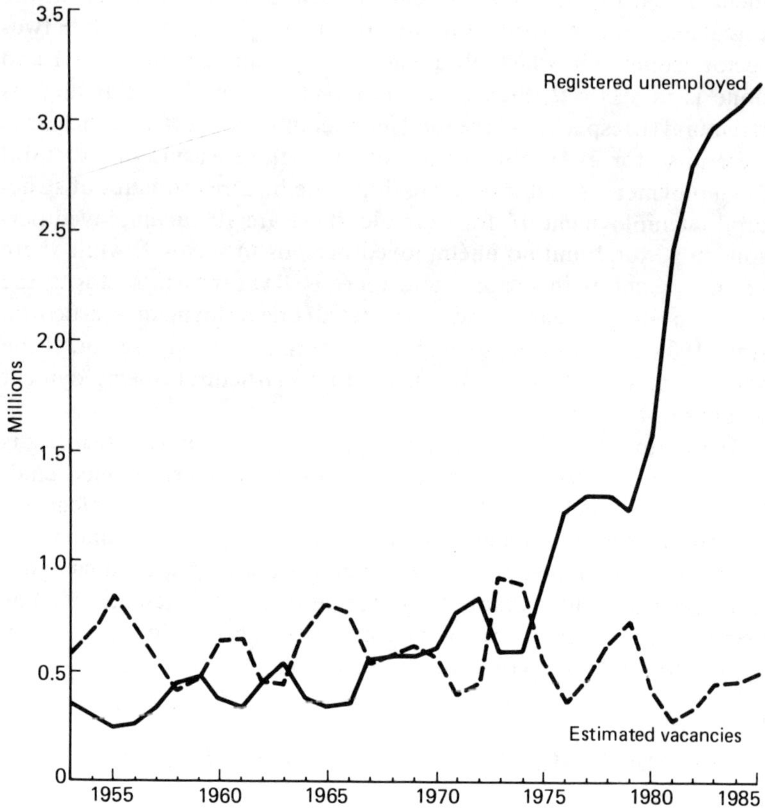


*Note*: Estimated vacancies = notified vacancies × 3.
*Sources*: *Economic Trends*; *Employment Gazette.*

demand. Combining (1) and (2), a smooth inverse relationship between unemployment and vacancies is obtained (see Figure 5.2). When $XD = x_1$ unemployment is at $u_1$ and vacancies are at $v_1$. As $XD$ increases to $x_2$ unemployment falls to $u_2$ and vacancies rise to $v_2$. This derivation of the U–V relationship is agnostic as to the factors determining the excess demand for labour, which may change, for example, because of a change in real wages or because of a change in the demand for goods. Any movement along the U–V relationship will reflect a change in excess labour demand regardless of its origin.

*Figure* 5.2 The U–V relationship

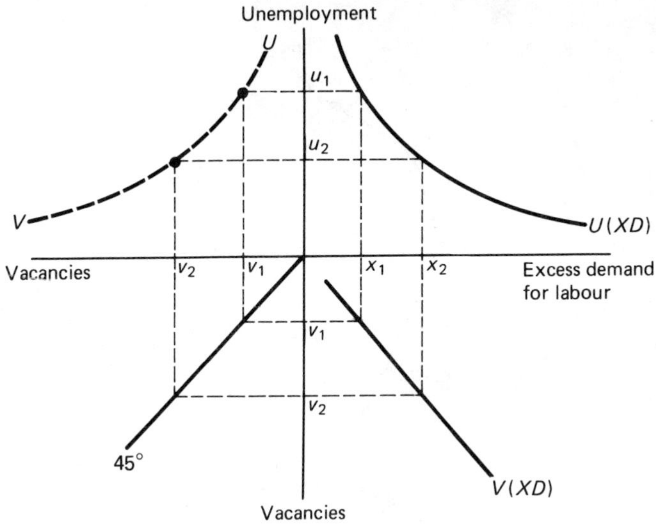


The relationship between unemployment and vacancies was regarded as little more than an interesting curiosity until the whole relationship began to shift upwards after 1967 (see Figure 5.3). Although the upward shift in the U–V relationship has been occurring since the mid-1960s, the shift was particularly well-marked during 1976–9 and again during 1981–5. Between 1976 and 1979, vacancies doubled whilst unemployment changed very little; and between 1981 and 1985, unemployment and vacancies were increasing simultaneously. Both these shifts indicate that fundamental changes have occurred in the relationship between unemployment and vacancies during the past decade. It is certainly the case, for instance, that an expansion of labour demand does not now guarantee a reduction in unemployment in the way that it did during the first two post-war decades. This lack of responsiveness of the unemployment rate to significant increases in the demand for labour suggests that unemployment is structural rather than due to a demand deficiency.

The view that structural unemployment has increased substantially in the UK since the mid-1970s is supported by other evidence. First, there has been a substantial increase in long-term unemployment. Between 1979 and 1985, for example, the number of persons unemployed for over one year increased from 337 000 to 1 294 000 (see

*Figure* 5.3 Percentage registered unemployed and percentage notified vacancies: UK, 1953–85

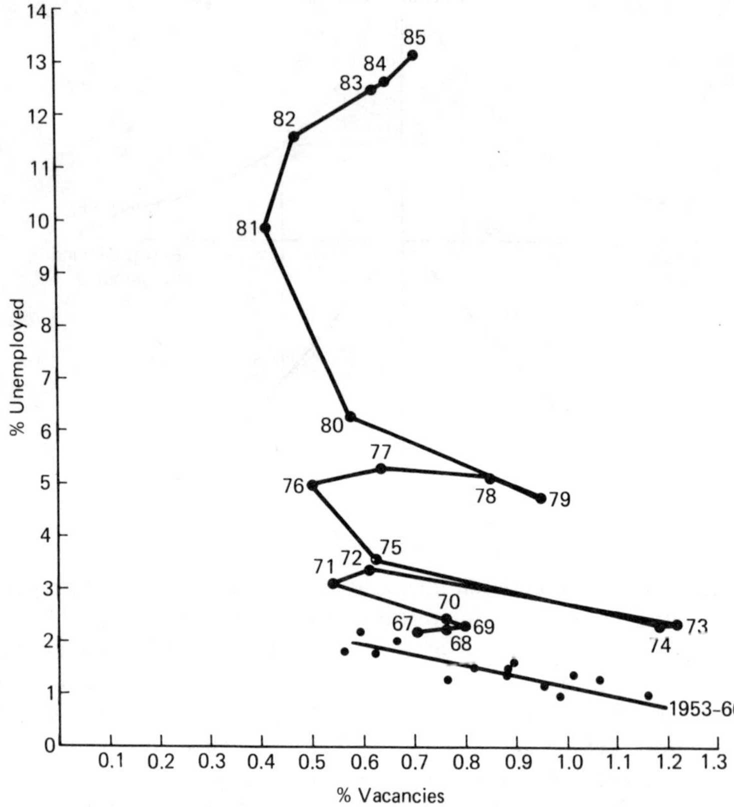


Table 5.2); and over half a million persons had been unemployed for over three years in 1985. Moreover, the mean duration of unemployment has risen sharply since the mid-1970s (see Figure 5.4).

How does an increase in the duration of unemployment help to explain the increase in structural unemployment? The critical factor is the link between the duration of unemployment and the skill-level of unemployed persons. The gap between the skills possessed by the unemployed and those possessed by those in work will widen as the duration of unemployment increases. Not only will the unemployed tend to lose some of their skills when these skills are not being used, but those in work will also be enhancing their skill level as a result of continuous on-the-job training. In many occupations, skills are

*Table* 5.2 The duration of unemployment in Great Britain 1979 and 1985

| *Duration in years* | *Number unemployed (October each year)* 1979 | 1985 |
|---|---|---|
| 0–1/2 | 772 | 1347 |
| 1/2–1 | 194 | 515 |
| 1–2 | | 510 |
| 2–3 | 337 | 279 |
| 3 and over | | 505 |
| Total | 1303 | 3156 |

*Source*: *Employment Gazette*, August 1980; *Labour Market Quarterly Report*; Manpower Services Commission, November 1985.

*Figure* 5.4 Estimated mean duration of unemployment in months: UK

*Note*: The mean duration was estimated by dividing the unemployment stock by the monthly inflow into the stock. See Armstrong and Taylor (1985) for details.

constantly having to be changed as new products appear and as new production techniques are adopted. The need for constant re-skilling does not cause problems provided workers are in work since new skills will be learnt on the job. This on-the-job enhancement of skills is only possible, of course, for those in work with the result that the longer the time spent on the dole, the greater will be the relative de-skilling of the person concerned.[4]

Second, information obtained from the CBI's Industrial Trends Survey offers further support to the view that structural unemployment has increased substantially during the study period. The CBI asks

*Figure* 5.5 Unemployment and the CBI Labour Shortage Indicator, 1964–85

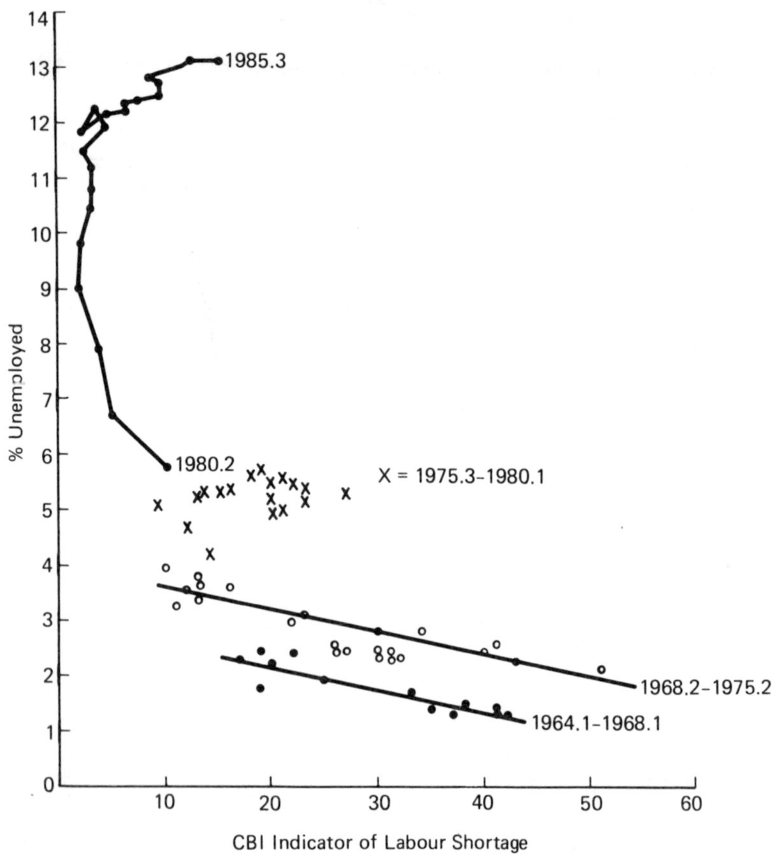


*Sources*: *Main Economic Indicators OECD*; *CBI Industrial ds Survey*

firms to state which factors are likely to limit their output over the next few months. Since 'skilled labour' is one of seven possible answers (the others being 'orders or sales, other labour, credit or finance, materials and components, and other factors') it is possible to construct an indicator of labour shortage based upon the number of firms identifying skilled labour as a factor likely to limit output. The shortage of skilled labour can therefore be used as proxy for excess labour demand. Figure 5.5 indicates that a substantial upward shift in the unemployment rate occurred against the CBI's labour shortage indicator (see Figure 5.6) during the study period and that this upward shift was particularly large during the 1980s. The picture we obtain is certainly consistent with an increase in structural unemployment during the 1980s.

*Figure* 5.6 CBI Indicator of Labour Shortage, 1964–85

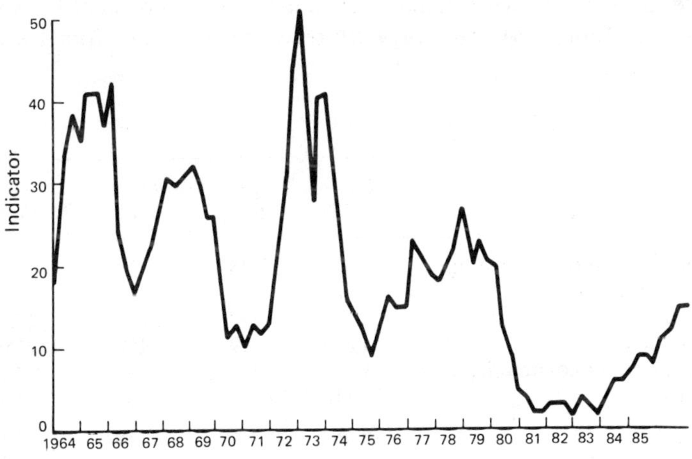


*Source*: CBI, *Industrial Trends Surveys* (1964–85).

## 3 STRUCTURAL UNEMPLOYMENT IN THE UK: THE COLLAPSE OF THE MANUFACTURING SECTOR

The simultaneous increase in unemployment and vacancies in the UK between 1981 and 1985 is consistent with the view that mismatch unemployment increased during this period. The increase in vacancies, however, was minute compared with the increase in unemployment. (Notified vacancies increased by under 100 000 while registered unemployment increased by over 1 million.) The view that structural unemployment increased substantially in the 1980s because of an increase in the mismatch between the demand and supply for labour does not therefore receive much support. Is there an alternative explanation of the increase in structural unemployment after 1981? One plausible alternative explanation is that structural unemployment increased substantially because of the unprecedented collapse of the manufacturing sector.

There is no doubt that the manufacturing sector suffered disproportionately from the 1979–81 recession, both in relation to other sectors in the UK and in relation to manufacturing elsewhere in the industrialised world. A comparison of sectoral employment levels in 1979 and 1983, for example, reveals stark disparities in employment change between sectors. Manufacturing lost over 20 per cent of its workforce while the service sector actually expanded its employment by 2 per cent (see Table 5.3). The 1979–81 recession was therefore heavily

*Table* 5.3 Changes in employment by broad sector, 1979–83 (thousands)

| Sector | Total employed 1979 | 1983 | Change | % change |
|---|---|---|---|---|
| Agriculture, forestry, fishing | 658 | 628 | −30 | −4.6 |
| Energy and water supply | 723 | 660 | −63 | −8.7 |
| Manufacturing | 7 400 | 5 757 | −1 643 | −22.2 |
| Construction | 1 605 | 1 429 | −176 | −11.0 |
| Transport and communications | 1 560 | 1 417 | −143 | −9.2 |
| Services | 13 116 | 13 383 | 267 | 2.0 |
| Total | 25 062 | 23 274 | −1 788 | −7.1 |

*Source*: 'Employment in the Public and Private Sectors 1978 to 1984', I. G. Richardson in *Economic Trends*, March 1985, Table 2.

biased against the manufacturing sector. It could be argued that the decline in manufacturing employment between 1979 and 1983 was simply the continuation of a long-run trend. Between 1969 and 1979, for example, manufacturing employment fell by 116 000 per annum. The annual job-loss leapt up to 400 000 per annum, however, between 1979 and 1983. Moreover, the job-losses in manufacturing between

1969 and 1979 were more than offset by job-gains of 170 000 per annum in non-manufacturing whereas during 1979–83 job-losses also occurred in non-manufacturing (around 90 000 per annum).

To what extent was the decline of the manufacturing sector in the UK simply a reflection of what was happening in the rest of the industrialised world? Comparison with the UK's main trading partners suggests that manufacturing in the UK suffered disproportionately (see Table 5.4). From 1979 to 1983, for instance, manufacturing

*Table* 5.4 Percentage change in manufacturing employment, 1979–83

| *Country* | *% change in manufacturing employment 1979–83* |
|---|---|
| UK | −22 |
| Netherlands | −13 |
| Canada | −13 |
| USA | −12 |
| France | −10 |
| Germany | −9 |
| Sweden | −8 |
| Australia | −7 |
| Italy | −6 |
| Japan | 3 |

*Source*: *Main Economic Indicators,* Historical Statistics OECD, 1984.

employment fell by 12 per cent in the USA, 10 per cent in France, 9 per cent in Germany, 7 per cent in Australia and 6 per cent in Italy; and perhaps not surprisingly it increased by 3 per cent in Japan. No other industrialised nation suffered such a large decline in manufacturing employment in such a short time.

Further evidence of the severity of the 1979–82 recession is provided by redundancy data. Redundancies increased from around 15 000 per month in 1979 to 50 000 per month at the end of 1980. The vast majority of these occurred in the manufacturing sector (see Figure 5.7).[5] This huge leap in redundancies in such a short time indicates just how quickly the recession hit the UK manufacturing sector.

A further aspect of the 1979–81 recession which is pertinent to an explanation of the sharp increase in structural unemployment during the 1980s is the differential regional impact of the recession. Table 5.5

clearly shows that the southern and eastern regions of the UK suffered far less from redundancies than did the regions of the north and west. The redundancy rate in the South-east, and in East Anglia was lower in fact during the recession than it had been in the traditionally depressed regions *before* the recession.

Is there any evidence that the industrial and geographical bias in job-losses has led to greater structural unemployment? Current unemployment would have to be regarded as being predominantly structural if an increase in output growth quickly ran into production bottlenecks. The critical question to be answered then is whether a faster rate of output growth would face any serious supply constraints. To what

*Figure* 5.7 Confirmed redundancies by sector in Great Britain, 1977–85 (monthly averages)

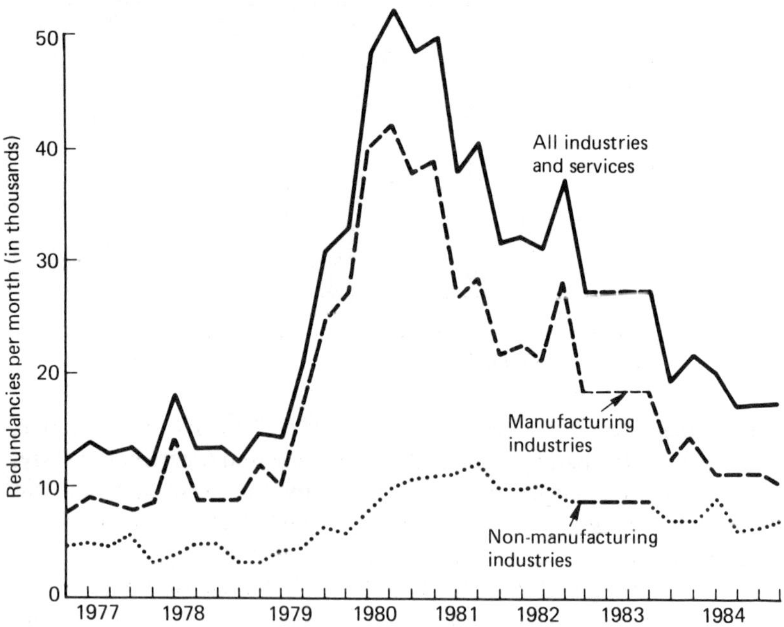


*Notes*:

1. Confirmed redundancies only include redundancies involving ten or more employees in single establishment. The service sector is more likely to be affected than other sectors. See *Employment Gazette*, June 1983, pp. 245–6 for a more detailed explanation.
2. For 1983 only data of confirmed redundancies were published.

*Sources*: *Employment Gazette*, June 1983, page 247; *Employment Gazette*, November 1985, page S43.

*Table* 5.5 Redundancy rate by region, 1977–82

| Region | Redundancies per 1000 employees 1977–9 | 1980–2 | Increase 1977/9–1980/2 |
|---|---|---|---|
| South-east | 3.5 | 11.9 | 8.4 |
| East Anglia | 5.0 | 12.4 | 7.4 |
| South-west | 7.6 | 17.8 | 10.2 |
| East Midlands | 4.4 | 23.2 | 18.8 |
| West Midlands | 5.3 | 27.1 | 21.8 |
| Yorkshire and Humberside | 7.7 | 28.7 | 21.0 |
| Scotland | 14.0 | 27.5 | 13.5 |
| North | 14.0 | 30.8 | 16.8 |
| North-west | 13.8 | 33.4 | 19.6 |
| Wales | 14.0 | 37.2 | 24.2 |
| Great Britain | 7.8 | 22.2 | 14.4 |

*Source*: *Employment Gazette*, June 1983, p. 249.

extent is faster output growth constrained by supply factors at the present time in the UK? This depends upon:

(i) the speed at which output will have to grow in order to reduce unemployment;
(ii) capacity output and its rate of growth.

How fast does output have to grow in order to reduce the unemployment rate? This question can be answered by looking at past experience. An examination of unemployment and output data for the UK over the period 1951–85 indicates a close relationship between *changes* in the unemployment rate and changes in real GDP (see Figure 5.8). According to this relationship output growth has to reach at least 3 per cent per annum for the unemployment rate to stand still.[6] A sustained growth in output of 5 per cent would be required to bring the unemployment rate down by one percentage point per annum. This is clearly bad news for the unemployed, since a sustained output growth of 5 per cent would require a miracle if previous experience is anything to go by. Could output growth be maintained at a level between 3 per cent and 4 per cent per annum over a number of years? Output growth, after all has, been around 3 per cent per annum since 1982. Is there any reason for doubting whether an even faster rate can be maintained during the next few years? A necessary

*Figure* 5.8 Output growth and the change in unemployment, 1951–85

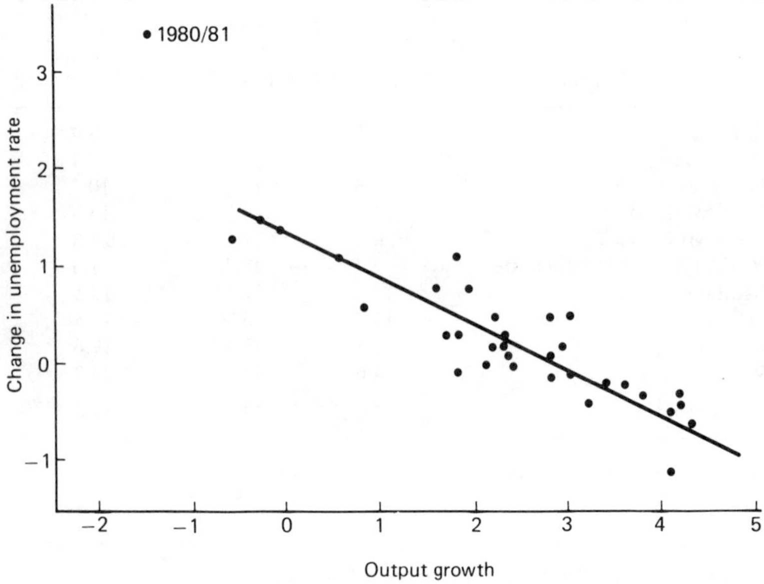


*Note*: Output growth is a distributed lag of current and past rates of change of GDP at factor cost. The weights were obtained by regressing $\Delta u_t$ on $\dot{y}_t$, $\dot{y}_{t-1}$ and $\dot{y}_{t-2}$ and then using the estimated coefficients on these three variables as weights.

condition is that producers must be capable of producing the extra output.

A cursory examination of economic data suggests that there must be plenty of spare capacity around. After all, we have over 3 million unemployed and output in manufacturing is still less than it was in 1979. This view is supported by the CBI's *Industrial Trends Survey*, which indicates that the manufacturing sector is constrained not by supply factors but by a lack of demand (see Figure 5.9). Supply factors in general do not pose any serious threat to a rapid expansion of output. But this general (or composite) index of the balance of demand and supply constraints on growth does not tell the whole story. If we dig a little deeper we find that there is, in fact, a serious constraint on output growth in the manufacturing sector, namely a lack of adequate plant capacity. This is clearly indicated by the CBI's indicator of capacity utilisation, which was higher in 1985 than it was in 1979 in spite of the drop in output over this period (see Figure 5.10).

*Figure* 5.9 Demand *v.* supply constraints on output growth

*Note*: This index was obtained by subtracting an index of supply constrained output growth from an index of demand constrained output growth. A high value indicates that output growth was constrained by a demand shortage; and conversely for a supply shortage. The two indices were obtained from answers to the following question: 'what factors are likely to limit your output over the next four months?' The index supply constrained growth included the following categories: skilled labour, other labour, plant capacity, credit or finance, materials or components. The index of demand-constrained growth included only one category: orders or sales. The sum of the percentage of firms in each category can exceed 100 per cent because more than one factor can be indicated.
*Source*: CBI, *Industrial Trend Surveys* (1964–85).

How is it possible for the manufacturing sector to be suffering from a shortage of capacity in 1985 when output has still not regained its pre-recession level? The obvious and indeed only answer is that productive capacity was cut back as plants were closed down because of the severity of the recession and these plants have not yet been replaced by new capacity. Although there is no direct information about the amount of productive capacity lost during 1979–82, some

*Figure* 5.10 Index of capacity utilisation

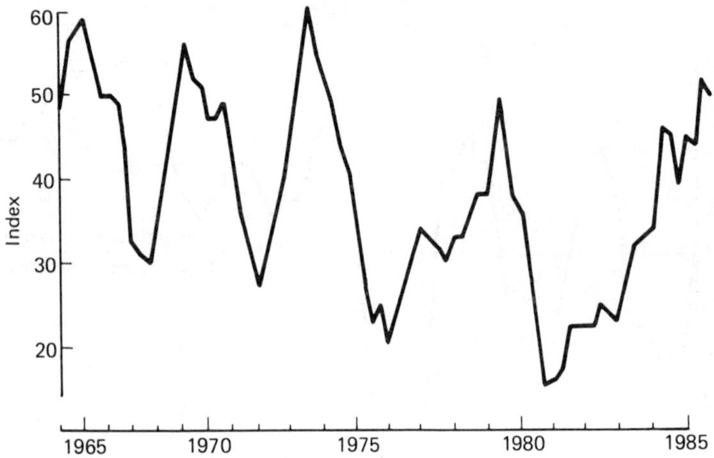


*Note*: This index is the percentage of respondents who said that they were not working below a satisfactory full rate of operation. The responses are weighted by the employment level in each industrial sector.
*Source*: CBI, *Industrial Trends Surveys* (1964–85).

indirect evidence is available which is consistent with a sharp reduction in plant capacity.[7] First, a given level of labour demand (as measured by the CBI's labour shortage indicator) was associated with a considerably higher level of capacity utilisation *after* 1981 than it was *before* 1981 (see Figure 5.11). This is exactly what would have happened if there had been a reduction in plant capacity. Second, unemployment and capacity utilisation were increasing simultaneously between 1981 and 1985, indicating the coexistence of labour abundance and a shortage of capital stock (see Figure 5.12). Third, gross fixed investment in plant and machinery fell from £7.5 billion to £4.9 billion between 1979 and 1982 (and remained well below the 1979 level until 1985). This suggests that additions to productive capacity are likely to have failed to match the rate at which existing machinery was being scrapped (see Figure 5.13).

It has been suggested that the sharp fall in gross investment in the manufacturing sector after 1979 may have resulted from the greater use of leased assets (i.e. plant and machinery acquired on rental from the financial sector). This does not appear to have happened to any great extent, however, during the period 1979–83. The amount of new

*Figure* 5.11 Relationship between labour shortage and capacity utilisation in the UK, 1964–85

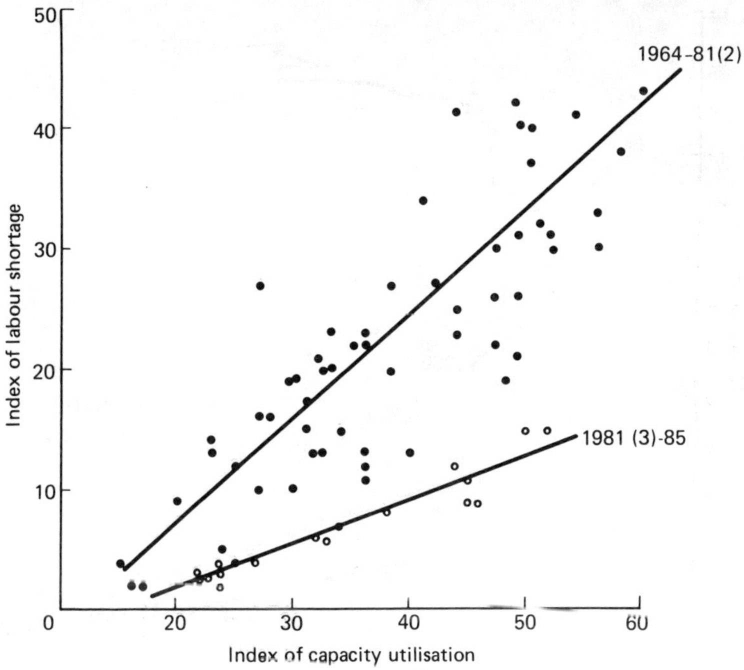


*Source*: CBI, *Industrial Trends Surveys* (1964–85).

assets leased per annum to all UK industry remained stable at around £2 billion during this period.[8] The sharp fall in gross manufacturing investment during 1979–82 is therefore unlikely to have been offset to any considerable extent by a sudden switch into asset leasing.

The sharp reduction in plant capacity during the early 1980s now means that the ability of the manufacturing sector to respond to an increase in the demand for its output is extremely limited in the short run. If the CBI's estimates of capacity utilisation are to be believed, the situation facing the UK in 1986 is one of capital shortage coupled with labour abundance.[9] The UK is therefore faced with a conflict between:

(i) the need to raise output growth beyond 3 per cent per annum in order to reduce unemployment, and

*Figure* 5.12 Unemployment and the CBI index of capacity utilisation, 1964–85

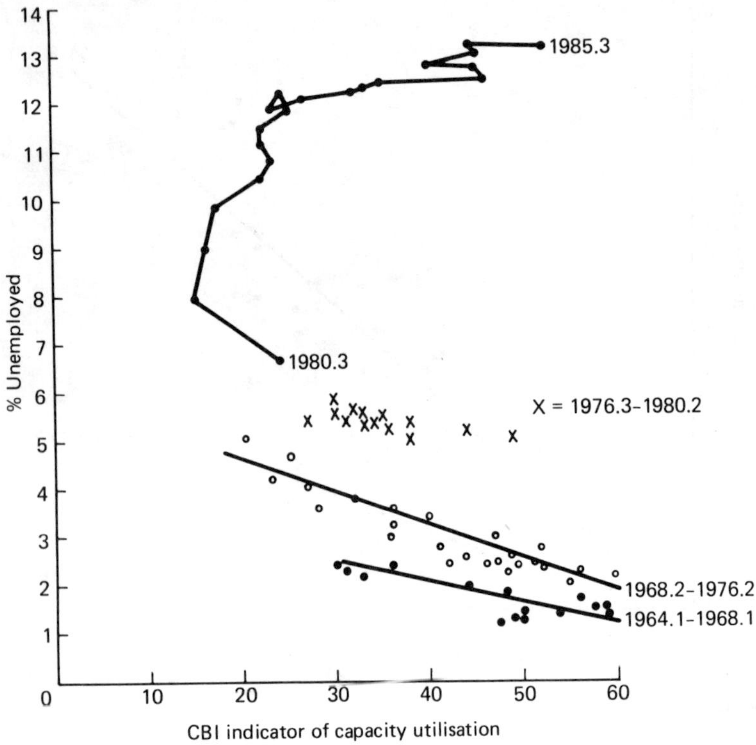


*Sources*: OECD, *Main Economic Indicators*; CBI, *Industrial Trends Survey*

(ii) the possibility that raising output growth above 3 per cent may quickly run into production bottlenecks.

The coexistence of a capacity constraint on output growth and mass unemployment therefore suggests that a considerable proportion of current unemployment must be regarded as structural. Reducing unemployment is likely to be far more difficult than it was to increase it in the first place. If output growth is to be increased, however, some way must be found to do this without running into production bottlenecks.

Although the CBI's indicator of capacity utilisation suggests that the manufacturing sector is now pressing against its output ceiling (compared with previous cyclical peaks), this does not necessarily

*Figure* 5.13 Gross fixed investment in plant and machinery by manufacturing industry at 1980 prices, 1955–85

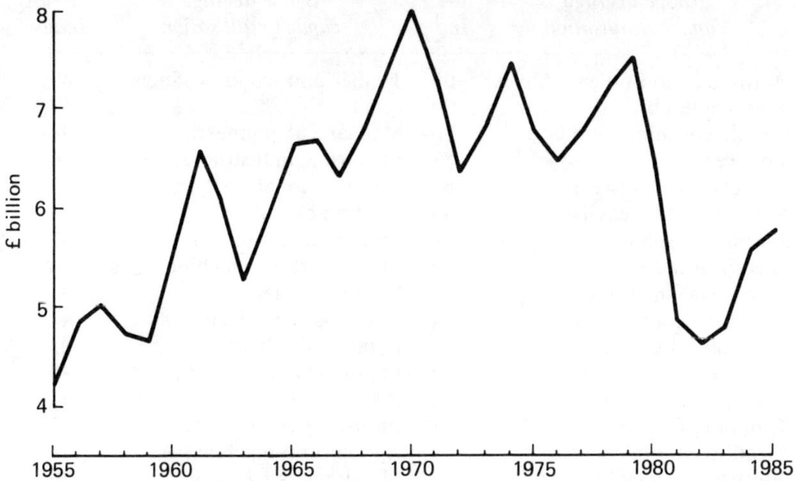


*Note*: The figure for 1985 is provisional.
*Source*: *Economic Trends*, Annual Supplement 1985 and November 1985.

mean that manufacturing is not capable of responding to a faster growth in demand. First, productive capacity can be increased fairly quickly in some industries by simply installing new plant and equipment. Second, existing plant and machinery can be utilised more intensively in the short term by adding extra shifts. Third, although manufacturing as a whole may be facing capacity constraints, this is certainly not true of all parts of the manufacturing sector. Capacity utilisation indices calculated for individual industry groups, for example, indicate that capacity constraints are not operative in all sectors. Capacity utilisation rates are high in footwear, furniture, electrical goods, textiles, clothing and pharmaceuticals; but they are low in metals, building materials, plastic products and parts of the engineering industry (see Table 5.6). This suggests that a *general* demand expansion would be more likely to run into production bottlenecks than a *selective* demand expansion (e.g. based on those manufacturing industries which supply the construction sector with inputs such as timber, constructional steelwork, contractors' plant, and building materials).

*Table* 5.6 The CBI index of capacity utilisation by industry

| *Above-average capacity utilisation* | *Index* | *Below-average capacity utilisation* | *Index* |
|---|---|---|---|
| Aerospace and other vehicles | 95 | Timber and wood products | 49 |
| Man-made fibres | 90 | Food | 49 |
| Textile consumer goods | 86 | Mechanical engineering | 48 |
| Footwear | 83 | Electronic industrial goods | 46 |
| Hosiery and knitwear | 82 | Constructional steel work | 46 |
| Spinning and weaving | 80 | Contractors' plant | 46 |
| Furniture, upholstery, bedding | 79 | Printing and publishing | 45 |
| Electrical industrial goods | 79 | Metal-working machine tools | 44 |
| Engineers' small tools | 75 | Motor vehicles | 43 |
| Electrical consumer goods | 74 | Industrial chemicals | 42 |
| Pharmaceuticals, etc. | 74 | Drink and tobacco | 41 |
| Wool textiles | 72 | Instrument engineering | 40 |
| Glass, ceramics | 72 | Plastic products | 38 |
| Clothing, fur | 65 | Industrial engines, etc. | 33 |
| Heating equipment, etc. | 59 | Agricultural machinery | 30 |
| Electrical and instrument | | Metal goods n.e.s. | 29 |
| engineering | 59 | Building materials | 29 |
| Other mechanical engineering | 58 | Foundaries, forging, etc. | 28 |
| Paper and board products | 58 | Coal and petroleum products | 25 |
| Leather and leather goods | 55 | Industrial machinery | 21 |
| Hand tools and implements | 53 | Ferrous metals | 19 |
| Office equipment | 53 | Rubber products | 8 |
| Shipbuilding | 51 | Non-ferrous metals | 3 |
| Pulp, paper and board | 51 | | |

*Source*: *Industrial Trends Survey 98*, October 1985, Confederation of British Industries.

## CONCLUSION

The purpose of this chapter was to examine the relationship between unemployment and vacancies in the UK in order to gain a better understanding of the current high level of unemployment. In particular, the aim was to examine the potential usefulness of methods designed to produce estimates of structural unemployment. The main conclusions are as follows.

First, the methods of measuring structural unemployment based on unemployment and vacancy data are open to serious criticism, not least because different methods are capable of producing conflicting estimates of structural unemployment.

Second, the mismatch view of structural unemployment is extremely limited since it ignores the possibility that structural unemployment can exist for reasons other than a mismatch. A broader view of structural unemployment includes unemployment that cannot be removed in the short run through a *general* demand expansion. This chapter has argued that a considerable proportion of UK unemployment may now fall under this broader definition of structural unemployment. It has been argued that large-scale scrapping of plant and machinery in the manufacturing sector in the early 1980s has led to the coexistence of a capital shortage and labour abundance in many manufacturing industries. Faster output growth is needed in order to reduce unemployment, yet this may not be possible in many industries because of the existence of capacity constraints on output growth.

Third, the existence of wide disparities in capacity utilisation rates between industries in the UK suggest that there may be scope for reducing unemployment in the medium term. But this is only likely to be achieved if increases in demand are selective so that the first round of expenditure is directed at those industries which are not pressing against their capacity limits. The alternative strategy is to let market forces induce an expansion of labour demand by encouraging investment in more labour-intensive production methods. There seems little sign that mass unemployment has so far had much effect on labour costs in the UK, however, and there must be considerable doubt whether this classical adjustment mechanism will have a significant impact on unemployment in the foreseeable future.

## Notes

1. See Perlman (1969), Thirlwall (1969, 1974), Hughes (1974), Gleave and Palmer (1979), Armstrong and Taylor (1981), King (1986).
2. See Armstrong and Taylor (1985) for a simple explanation of this method.
3. This estimate was calculated by the Unemployment Research Unit which publicises its 'adjusted' unemployment estimate each month immediately after the official figures are released.
4. Hargreaves-Heap (1980) suggests that this is one of the reasons why the 'natural' rate of unemployment will increase during periods of prolonged recession.
5. Confirmed redundancies understate actual redundancies since they include only those redundancies occurring in establishments with ten or more employees. The degree of underestimation is likely to be greater in the non-manufacturing sector since the vast majority of manufacturing establishments are likely to employ more than ten people.

6. When production sector output is used instead of real GDP, an output growth of 4 per cent is required in order to maintain the same level of unemployment.
7. The official capital stock estimates are based on the perpetual inventory method, which assumes a 'normal' rate of depreciation and does not take account of any premature scrapping that might have occurred (such as is believed to have happened during 1980–2). See de Neubourg (1986) for a brief discussion of research on the relationship between structural unemployment and the scrapping of plant and machinery in the Netherlands.
8. See the *Annual Abstract of Statistics 1985*, Table 14.16.
9. The OECD arrives at the same conclusion using a different measure of capacity utilisation (OECD 1986, pp. 26–8). See also Record (1985).

## References


ARMSTRONG, H. and TAYLOR, J. (1981) 'The Measurement of Different Types of Unemployment' in John Creedy (ed.) *The Economics of Unemployment in Britain* (London: Butterworth) pp. 99–127.

ARMSTRONG, H. and TAYLOR, J. (1982) 'The U–V Method of Categorising the Unemployed: An Amendment', *Bulletin of Economic Research*, 34, May, pp. 77–8.

ARMSTRONG, H. and TAYLOR, J. (1985) *Regional Economics and Policy*, (Deddington, Oxford: Philip Allan).

DEPARTMENT OF EMPLOYMENT (1980) 'A Review of Unemployment and Vacancy Statistics', *Employment Gazette*, May, pp. 497–503.

DEPARTMENT OF EMPLOYMENT (1983) 'Statistics of Redundancies and Recent Trends', *Employment Gazette*, June, pp. 245–9.

DOW, J. C. R. and DICKS-MIREAUX, L. A. (1958) 'The Excess Demand for Labour: A Study of Conditions in Great Britain, 1946–56', *Oxford Economic Papers*, 10, pp. 1–33.

GLEAVE, D. and PALMER, D. (1979) 'Spatial Variations in Unemployment Problems: A Typology', papers of the *Regional Science Association*, 44, 1980, pp. 57–71.

HARGREAVES-HEAP (1980) 'Choosing the wrong 'natural' rate: accelerating inflation or decelerating employment and growth?' *Economic Journal*, 90, September, pp. 611–20.

HUGHES, J. J. (1974) 'The Use of Vacancy Statistics in Classifying and Measuring Structural and Frictional Unemployment in Great Britain, 1958–72', *Bulletin of Economic Research*, 26, pp. 12–33.

JACKMAN, R. and ROPER J. (1985) 'Structural Unemployment', discussion paper no. 233, Centre for Labour Economics, London School of Economics, October.

KING, J. E. (1986) 'How Large is the Structural Element in the Current Unemployment?', *Australian Bulletin of Labour*, March.

NEUBOURG, C. de (1986) 'Unspecified Floating Unemployment and the Specification of the U–V Curve', European Production Studies Group Conference, University of Limburg, Maastricht.

OECD (1986) *United Kingdom,* OECD Economic Surveys 1985/86 (January) (Paris: OECD).

PERLMAN, R. (1969) *Labor Theory* (New York: Wiley).

RECORD, N. (1985) 'Manufacturing Capacity', unpublished paper, C. and J. Clark, Street, Somerset.

THIRLWALL, A. P. (1969) 'Types of Unemployment with Special Reference to Non-deficient-demand Unemployment in Great Britain', *Scottish Journal of Political Economy,* 16, pp. 20–49.

THIRLWALL, A. P. (1974) 'Types of Unemployment in the Regions of Great Britain', *Manchester School,* 42, pp. 325–39.

# 6 Labour Hoarding, and Recorded Unemployment in OECD Countries*

D. Bosworth and T. Westaway

## 1 INTRODUCTION

There has been an intense, often heated debate about the 'true' level of unemployment in European economies (see for example, Lipsey, 1983, and Metcalf, 1984). Most of the discussion has a political element concerned with the niceities of the official definitions of unemployment, including views about what should (or should not) be included within the measure and even about the timing of unemployment counts. The debate is clearly important, particularly if comparisons are to be valid over time or across countries.

This chapter focuses on an omission that has interested economists, but which is much more rarely considered in the political arena. The question addressed here is the extent to which a particular form of hidden unemployment or underemployment might modify our views about the 'true' rate of unemployment. Here we concentrate on hoarded labour, although it is recognised that other forms of underemployment, such as disguised unemployment and discouraged workers, may also be relevant and important. In this sense, the work draws on an already extensive literature (Taylor, 1970; Fair, 1969; Evans, 1974; Hauser, 1974 and 1977; Greer and Rhodes, 1977; Deaton, 1977; Deaton and Bowers, 1977 and 1978; Maddison, 1980; Stricker and Sheehan, 1981; Neubourg, 1984, 1985a and 1985b; Mangan, 1984; Muysken, 1986; Rimler, 1985, and Bosworth, 1985). Apart from the debate about the 'true' magnitude of the unemployment problem, accurate measures of these dimensions of labour utilisation might help to resolve a number of other mainly empirical problems. In particular, we know that, over the past twenty years or more, the rate of

* This research is an extension of work undertaken on the Australian economy during a visit to the National Institute for Labour Studies at Flinders University, South Australia during 1985. It also represents some preliminary ideas about further work on capacity utilisation in Europe.

unemployment has shown a tendency to drift steadily upwards in most industrialised countries. By implication, it might be concluded that there has been growing underutilisation of labour and that the labour market has become increasingly slack. In contrast, however, a number of other labour market variables, such as hours of work and wage inflation, have not always suggested the same degree of slackness.

This sort of problem appears to have been at the heart of the associated 'breakdown' of a number of statistical relationships, such as the Phillips curve (Phillips, 1958). One possibility therefore is that the overall unemployment rate is a poor indicator of the 'true' level of pressure in the labour market (Gregory and Smith, 1983, and Dawkins and Wooden, 1985). In addition, some understanding of the role of hidden unemployment and underemployment might be necessary in constructing more meaningful measures of the dependent variables for modelling unemployment in a number of countries (Bean *et al.*, 1985).

## 2 RECORDED UNEMPLOYMENT AND HOARDED LABOUR

### 2.1 Recorded Unemployment

This paper takes the official estimates of recorded unemployment, $U(1)$, as given. This will clearly upset some researchers who feel that official measures under or over estimate the level of unemployment. The differences between estimates based on various, mainly political, views can be large (see Lipsey, 1983). On the other hand, recent empirical work for the UK does not, on balance, indicate a 'true' figure that is too different from the official estimate (see Metcalf, 1984). Nevertheless, there are clearly some people who are recorded as unemployed but are not actively seeking work and *would not do so at any position of the cycle.* In the long run, these people will appear as *a component* of the long-term unemployed and should, in principle, be netted out from the measures reported below. This is a point that we will bear in mind, but, in this chapter at least, take no direct action about.

A second major point about the level of recorded unemployment is that different countries use slightly different definitions of unemployment, methods of collecting data, etc. Again, most countries, with some - often minor - modifications, tend to follow the ILO guidelines for labour statistics and no direct adjustment is made for such differences in the calculations contained in this chapter. The question of the method of collecting data, for example, sample surveys *versus* registered unemployment, is also a potential problem. *A priori* one might expect the survey level of unemployment to be higher than registered unemployment if discouraged workers allocate themselves to the unemployed but feel there is no point in registering. In practice there is evidence that many discouraged workers do not see themselves as unemployed (women classify themselves as housewives rather than unemployed). In practice, comparison of registered and survey estimates of the unemployment rate - at least for a number of European countries - do not differ markedly from one another, although there are differences between the two measures across countries and over time (Sorrentino, 1978; Moy and Sorrentino, 1982; and Neubourg, 1984). According to Neubourg (1984, pp. 16–17), the survey figures tend to be greater than the registration figures in the Netherlands and UK, but smaller in France and West Germany. However, the main impression is that the two types of estimates move closely together and even in the country and time periods where the differences are greatest we are probably talking about 1 to 2 percentage point differences in the rate of unemployment.

## 2.2 Hoarded Labour

Labour hoarding is by no means easy to define. Solow (1964) suggests that, it is 'a catch-phrase for all the frictions involved in meeting transitory variations in output with variations in employment' and Taylor (1970) simply argues that it occurs 'When employed labour is not fully utilised' (Evans, 1974, p. 16). Here we suggest that labour hoarding occurs when there are increases in the input of labour services not matched by commensurate increases in output or there are decreases in output not matched by commensurate reductions in the input of labour services, consistent with the underlying technology of production. In trying to pin labour hoarding down, it should be remembered that, in addition to occupational/educational/etc. changes in the workforce, we must consider the level of employment, hours of work and worker effort.

Earlier work in this area has tended to treat the underlying production function as separable with regard to its capital and labour service inputs (Fair, 1969; Taylor, 1970; Evans, 1974) of the following type:

$$Y = f(KS, LS) = \min f(KS, LS) \tag{6.1}$$

where $Y$ denotes output, $KS$ are capital services and $LS$ are labour services. If we denote the limiting factor,*, then where $KS = KS^*$ is a constraint on output, then $LS \geqslant LS^*$ and labour hoarding occurs. Where $LS = LS^*$, then $KS \geqslant KS^*$ and capital services are underutilised. Taken to its natural conclusion, $Y/g(LS)$ is a measure of labour productivity. Clearly, if the production function is not separable in this way, then the productivity of labour will not be independent of the input of capital services. We return to this point below.

If, for a moment, we examine labour productivity in more detail, there are a number of outstanding questions. Labour services are a combination of employment, $E$, hours of work, $H$, and worker effort, $WE$. Thus, productivity can be written $Y/g(E, H, WE)$. Taylor focused on $Y/E$, and clearly, variations in this measure over the cycle are caused, in part, by changes in hours and worker effort. This measure was criticised by Evans (1974, p. 17), although it was added that the Taylor measure is more easily compared with unutilised labour in the internal labour market (i.e. with hidden and recorded unemployment). In practice, however, it is relatively easy to accommodate hours of work (Fair, 1969; Bosworth, 1985). An index based on $Y/EH$ suggests that the residual variation in productivity should be caused by the intensity of worker effort.

There are several caveats that should be made clear. The first is that $H$ (and possibly $E$) may pass through periods of over-, as well as underutilisation. Certainly, as a recent Australian Bureau of Statistics, ABS, survey showed, both the employed and the unemployed have a view of their optimal hours input at the going wage and premia levels that often do not correspond with actual hours of work (ABS, 6220.0 and 6341.0; Bosworth, 1985, pp. 136–65). At the time of the survey, the majority of individuals in employment would have preferred to have worked longer hours. On the other hand, there were a minority of people who wanted shorter hours. The balance was different between males and females (with the latter showing a much greater preference for shorter rather than longer hours) and also between age groups (following a life-cycle pattern). Almost certainly the balance also changes over time and the observed preference for longer hours reflected the depressed state of the Australian economy at that stage. Thus, in the estimates reported below, we accept the idea that there may be a trend value of hours, $H_t^*$, which reflects the normal utilisation level and that deviations from this trend may reflect a tendency to overutilise ($H_t > H_t^*$) or underutilise ($H_t < H_t^*$) the labour input (Gregory and Smith, 1983; Dawkins and Wooden, 1985; Bosworth, 1985; and Bosworth and Westaway, 1985, 1986a and 1986b).

The second consideration concerns what message $Y/g(E, H, WE)$ might convey, assuming that the production function is appropriately specified. An index of productivity of this type would require a measure of worker effort, but, for some countries, such measures do exist (Bennett and Smith-Gavine, 1986). *A priori* one would imagine that there would be little cyclical movement remaining, leaving a trend. this seems a promising line for future investigations, but is not followed up in this chapter where we are attempting to obtain broadly comparable measures across a number of countries. In practice, some residual variation will almost certainly remain, for example, caused by changes in industrial or occupational structure over the cycle.

Finally, we return to the specification of the production function and the choice of measure. The implicit production function underlying the work of Taylor (1970) is rather restrictive. The discussion is made easier if, for the moment, we focus on points of full capacity working in each period. The production function is written,

$$Y_t = aj(t)KS_t^* = bh(t)LS_t^* \qquad (6.2)$$

where * denotes the minimum values of factor services required in the production of $Y$, and $j(t)$ and $h(t)$ represent factor-augmenting technological change. If $h(t)$ is linear,

$$h(t) = x + yt \qquad (6.3)$$

then,

$$\left(\frac{Y}{LS}\right)_t^* - \left(\frac{Y}{LS}\right)_{t-1}^* = bh(t) - bh(t-1) = by \qquad (6.4)$$

Thus, hoarded labour services can be written,

$$HL = \left[\left(\frac{LS}{Y}\right)_t - \left(\frac{LS}{Y}\right)_t^*\right] Y_t \qquad (6.5)$$

From equation (6.5), we can write a hoarded labour as a multiple of fully employed labour and an index of labour utilisation,

$LU = LS/LS^* - 1,$

$$HL = [LU_t - 1]LS_t^* \qquad (6.6)$$

where $LU_t = 1$, and by implication $U(2) = 0$, denotes full utilisation of labour.

Even if the micro production functions are fixed coefficient, the chances are that the aggregate production function will exhibit substitution possibilities between capital and labour, even if the aggregate function is not well behaved (Fisher, 1969, 1971; Johansen, 1972). Substitution possibilities present important problems for the measure-

*Figure* 6.1 Average and frontier production functions

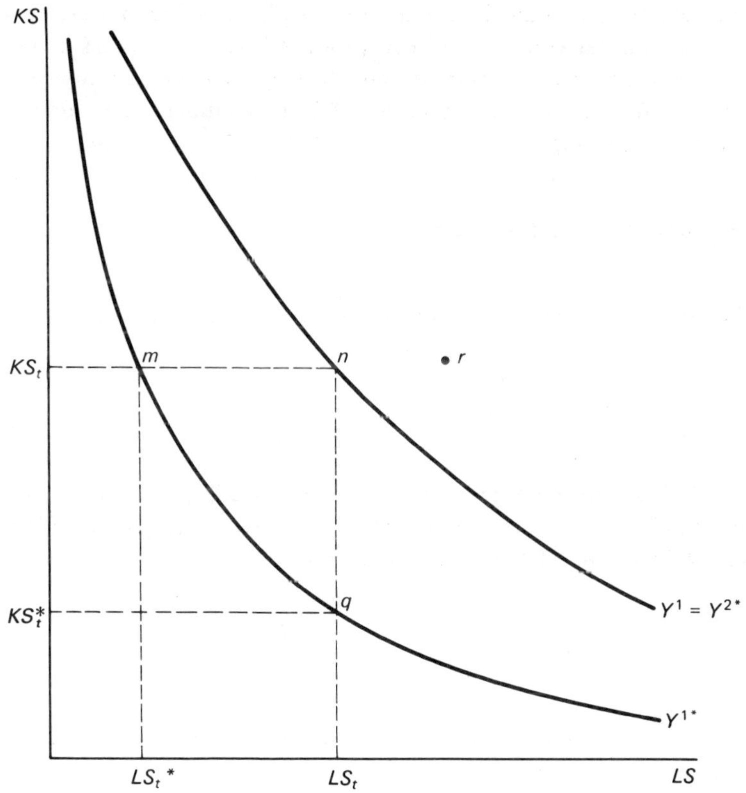


*Legend*: $Y^1$ = average isoquant, level 1. $Y^{1*}$, $Y^{2*}$ = frontier isoquants, levels 1 and 2.

ment of labour hoarding. It is possible, for example, that the highest observed peak output per unit of total input could occur when *neither* capital or labour is fully utilised.

The situation becomes slightly easier if it can be assumed that *both* inputs are used to their full extent when total factor productivity is at its peak. Thus, we might fit a 'frontier' production function, illustrated by the isoquant map shown in Figure 6.1. At time $t$, the economy is at point $n$, paying for $KS_t$ and $LS_t$ of factor services but producing only $Y^1$ of output. Inputs are clearly underutilised as $KS_t$ and $LS_t$ could produce $Y^2$ of output at peak use, or $Y^1$ could be produced with smaller amounts of one or both inputs. We know that the firm uses $KS_t$ of capital services at this time, so with peak labour use, it could have produced $Y^1$ (with $m-n$ less of labour services). This gives an estimate of the maximum labour hoarding. Alternatively, at the other extreme, it could be argued that, with $LS_t$ of labour services, the same output could have been produced with $(n-q)$ less capital services. Thus, as a minimum, the model suggests that labour hoarding is zero. In this paper we estimate $(m-n)$ the maximum possible amount of labour hoarding.

### 2.3 Revised Unemployment Rates

The rate of recorded unemployment is represented by:

$$\mu(1) = \mu(R) = \frac{R}{E+R} = \frac{R}{LF} \tag{6.7}$$

where $R$ is the recorded number unemployed, $E$ is the number employed and $LF$, the labour force. A revised unemployment rate including hoarded labour, $HL$, is given by:

$$\mu(2) = \mu(R+HL) = \frac{R+HL}{E+R} = \frac{R}{LF} + \frac{HL}{LF} = \mu(R) + \mu(HL) \tag{6.8}$$

and as $\mu$ $(HL)$, the rate of hoarded labour must be greater than or equal to zero then clearly:

$$\mu(R+HL) > \mu(R) \tag{6.9}$$

## 3. ESTIMATES OF HOARDED LABOUR

### 3.1 Data Sources

Annual data were collected for fourteen different countries which included the twelve member-states of the EEC, Japan and the USA. A complete data series was available for the period 1959–83 for France, Germany, Ireland, the Netherlands, the UK, USA and Japan whereas for Belgium it was slightly curtailed to the period 1961–83 and for Italy to 1959–82. The data series for the remaining countries were more restricted, with missing observations limiting a complete data set for Denmark to the period 1969–83. For more detail see the final column of Table 6.1.

Output was measured as GDP in purchaser's values at constant, own currency, prices and was taken from the Organisation for Economic Cooperation and Development (OECD), *National Accounts.* Data for civilian employment, the number recorded as unemployed and the population of working age were taken from OECD, *Labour Force Statistics*, whereas the hours of work in manufacturing was taken from the International Labour Organisation (ILO), *Yearbook of Labour Statistics.* Finally, capital services were measured by electricity production, which was taken from the OECD *Yearbook* until 1980 and the OECD *Energy Yearbook* thereafter.

### 3.2 Hoarded Labour: Method of Estimation

The number of hoarded employees was estimated from a Cobb-Douglas production function of the form:

$$ln\ Y_t = a + bln(LS)_t + cln(KS)_t + rt \qquad (6.10)$$

where employee hours *EH*, were used as a measure of labour services, *LS*, and electricity production as a measure of capital services, *KS*. The parameters *a*, *b*, *c* and *r* were estimated using ordinary least squares and the residuals obtained. This production function was then shifted out until it passed through its trended full capacity value which was assumed to occur at the point where the residual was at a maximum, $e_{max}$. Trended, full capacity output, $Y^*$, is thus obtained from:

$$ln\ Y^*_t = (a + e_{\max}) + bln(LS)_t + cln(KS)_t + rt \qquad (6.11)$$

*Table* 6.1 Recorded unemployment and hoarded labour: summary statistics

| | $\mu$ (*HL*) *Hoarded labour* | | | $\mu$ (*R*) *Recorded unemployment* | | | *HIL* *Hoarded index of labour* | | | |
|---|---|---|---|---|---|---|---|---|---|---|
| | *Mean* | *Max* | *SD* | *Mean* | *Max* | *SD* | *Mean* | *Max* | *SD* | *Data period* |
| Belgium | 2.58 | 4.81 | 1.23 | 4.57 | 13.22 | 3.56 | 1.87 | 3.19 | 0.63 | 1961–83 |
| Denmark | 2.99 | 5.43 | 1.48 | 5.44 | 11.55 | 3.91 | 2.35 | 8.45 | 2.01 | 1969–83 |
| France | 4.45 | 7.85 | 2.16 | 3.43 | 8.48 | 2.38 | 3.10 | 6.62 | 1.66 | 1959–83 |
| Germany | 2.81 | 9.51 | 1.80 | 2.34 | 8.39 | 2.12 | 3.11 | 6.32 | 1.66 | 1959–83 |
| Greece | 1.28 | 2.56 | 0.98 | 3.69 | 7.85 | 2.37 | 1.46 | 2.14 | 0.39 | 1977–83 |
| Ireland | 2.63 | 7.48 | 1.78 | 6.63 | 14.21 | 2.30 | 1.44 | 2.63 | 0.37 | 1959–83 |
| Italy | 3.65 | 7.72 | 2.50 | 5.96 | 9.18 | 1.45 | 1.63 | 2.57 | 0.46 | 1959–82 |
| Luxembourg | 3.05 | 8.72 | 2.64 | 0.61 | 1.25 | 0.38 | 7.92 | 17.85 | 5.70 | 1974–82 |
| Netherlands | 1.71 | 3.62 | 1.04 | 3.63 | 13.98 | 3.57 | 1.96 | 4.99 | 1.02 | 1959–83 |
| Portugal* | 10.42 | 13.68 | 2.59 | 6.77 | 8.23 | 2.06 | 2.67 | 3.90 | 0.59 | 1974–81 |
| Spain | 2.24 | 6.51 | 1.39 | 5.19 | 18.55 | 5.46 | 1.91 | 5.31 | 0.98 | 1960–83 |
| UK | 2.46 | 4.54 | 1.05 | 3.60 | 11.28 | 2.89 | 2.08 | 4.02 | 0.85 | 1959–83 |
| Japan | 2.71 | 6.33 | 1.81 | 1.64 | 2.65 | 0.47 | 2.67 | 4.91 | 1.05 | 1959–83 |
| USA | 4.12 | 11.01 | 3.01 | 5.93 | 9.69 | 1.69 | 1.68 | 2.99 | 0.50 | 1959–83 |

* The large mean values of $\mu$ (*HL*) for Portugal result from the fact that the production function was fitted for the period 1974–81. It was not possible to obtain $\mu$ (*HL*) for 1959–73, the period when $\mu$ (*HL*) would have been at its lowest.

which, when divided by $EH$, will given an estimate of trended full capacity labour productivity, $(Y/EH)^*$. Inverting this expression thus gives the minimum labour service required to produce the given output on the assumption that the output mix and capital services are at full capacity. An estimate of *maximum* hoarded labour can therefore, be obtained from:

$$HL_t = [(EH/Y)_t - (EH/Y)_t^*]Y_t/H_t^* \tag{6.12}$$

where $H_t^*$ is a measure of the normal utilisation of hours. The part of the equation within the square brackets can be taken to measure the distance $(m-n)$ in Figure 6.1. Given the method of calculation $HL_t$ will equal zero when the residual is at its maximum.

Equation (6.12) uses $H_t^*$ the trended value of hours rather than actual hours as deviations from this trend may reflect a tendency to overutilise or underutilise the labour input. Estimates of $H_t^*$ were obtained from both linear and quadratic trends but, as the alternatives gave measures of $HL$ that showed few differences, we present the results using linear trends. Finally, it should be noted that this regression-based approach will be inappropriate if the data set contains outliers, particularly if these occur at the beginning or end of the time-series. Casual observation showed that such outliers were not present.

### 3.3 Recorded Unemployment and Hoarded Labour: OECD Comparison

Summary statistics of the measures of hoarded labour and recorded unemployment are given in Table 6.1. Limited space prevents a more complete presentation, which can be found in Bosworth and Westaway (1986b). For most European countries examined the level of hoarded labour appears to reach a trough in the early-mid-1970s with Germany (trough in 1967) being a notable exception. A further general conclusion for the European countries is that a peak occurs in the late 1960s although for Germany peaks occur earlier in 1959 and 1963. In general, however, the 1960s appear to be a period when there were relative high and stable levels of hoarded labour, the exception to this latter observation being Italy which shows the most erratic behaviour with six major peaks and five major troughs in the period 1959–82. The final point to note for the European countries is the growth in hoarded labour that occurred in the late 1970s.

Comparing the European countries with Japan and the USA we can see some similarity. Japan exhibited peaks in 1960, 1973 and the late 1970s with troughs in the late 1960s and 1975. The USA, on the other hand, showed peak values in 1962 and 1979 with a major trough in the late 1960s. This is similar to Germany with its troughs and peaks generally predating those in the rest of Europe. The peak in late 1979, however, appears to have been world wide. Therefore, despite having the lowest and most stable level of recorded unemployment throughout the period, Japanese hoarded labour exhibited similarities in both patterns and magnitude with the other countries studied.

Comparing the measures of hoarded labour with recorded unemployment we can see that those countries with a relatively small variation in recorded unemployment, as measured by its standard deviation, tend to have a relatively large variation in hoarded labour. The final columns present summary statistics for an index which gives the ratio of the composite index of unemployment, $\mu(R+HL)$, to recorded unemployment, $\mu(R)$. This 'hoarded index of labour', *HIL*, will be one when *HL* is zero as can be seen from:

$$HIL = \frac{\mu(R+HL)}{\mu(R)} = \frac{\mu(R)+\mu(HL)}{\mu(R)} = 1 + \frac{\mu(HL)}{\mu(R)} \tag{6.13}$$

A large mean value for the *HIL* implies that recorded unemployment is a poor indicator of the magnitude of the underemployment of labour whereas a large standard deviation will occur if recorded unemployment exhibits a pattern different from the composite index. It should be noted that variations in the standard deviation can occur when the two measures of unemployment have coincidental peaks and troughs but the gaps between them fluctuate and so the use of the standard deviation should be treated with caution.

The countries with the largest mean values for *HIL* are France and Germany, while Ireland and Italy have the smallest values. (The value for Luxembourg can be taken as unrepresentative as it results from the near-zero value for recorded unemployment at the beginning of the period.) We can also note that the mean value of *HIL* for Japan is 2.67 indicating that, on average, the combined $\mu(R)$ and $\mu(HL)$ is larger than recorded unemployment by a factor of 2.67. Small variations in the *HIL* are to be noted for Greece, Ireland, Italy and the USA all of which have a standard deviation of 0.5 or less. On the other hand relatively large variations are exhibited by Denmark, France and Germany. Thus of the countries for which a relatively large data set was available it is only Belgium, Ireland, Italy, the UK and the USA for whom the recorded level of unemployment exhibits a similar pattern to the composite level of underemployment that includes hoarded labour.

## 4 CONCLUDING REMARKS

For most countries examined recorded unemployment appears to be a poor indicator of the pattern of underutilisation of labour. It is apparent that labour hoarding is likely to form a major component of the underutilisation of labour and that the peaks and troughs in the labour-hoarding series do not, for most countries, correspond to the peaks and troughs in the recorded unemployment series. This study also points to the need to estimate the other components of the underutilisation of labour if appropriate international comparisons are to be made. European countries can point to the very large discrepancy between recorded and 'composite' unemployment rates for Japan and hence question whether Japan is really enjoying such low levels of underemployed labour services as suggested by the recorded unemployment statistics. In addition, when recorded unemployment was low for most countries it is clear that other elements of underemployment were relatively high. The evidence is therefore consistent with the exchange of one type of underutilisation of labour (hoarded labour) for another (recorded unemployment) during the late 1970s to early 1980s.

It would be foolish to suggest that problems do not still remain within the estimating procedure adopted. The measure of hoarded labour could be developed by constructing a more appropriate 'frontier' production function. In addition, consideration of how to allow for the underutilisation of both capital and labour services is required because it is unclear which, if any, of the factor services is at their peak use on the chosen point on the frontier.

This Chapter presents estimates of the hoarded labour force and taken at face-value they indicate, that, for most countries, recorded unemployment is an inadequate indicator of the pattern of labour utilisation. Until the recent recession hoarded labour accounted for the major share of the composite index of underutilisation presented here. Only in a small number of countries, including the USA and to a lesser extent the UK, was the pattern of recorded unemployment similar to the composite index of underutilisation of labour.

## References

ABS, *Persons in the Labour Force (Including Discouraged Job Seekers)* (Canberra: Australian Bureau of Statistics) Cat. 6220.0.

ABS, *Alternative Working Arrangements, Australia, March to May* (Canberra: Australian Bureau of Statistics) Cat. no. 6341.0.

BEAN, C. R., LAYARD, P. R. G. and NICKELL S. J. (1985) 'The Rise in Unemployment: An Overview', Working Paper no. 795, (London: London School of Economics, Centre for Labour Economics).

BENNETT, A. and SMITH-GAVINE, S. A. N. (1986) 'The PUL Index', in D. Bosworth and D. Heathfield (eds) *Working Below Capacity* (London: Macmillan).

BOSWORTH D. (1985) *The Economics of Labour Utilisation*, Preliminary Report by the National Institute of Labour Studies to the South Australian Department of Labour (November).

BOSWORTH D. L. and WESTAWAY, A. J. (1985) 'The Demand for Hours', mimeo, (Coventry: University of Warwick, Institute for Employment Research).

BOSWORTH, D. L. and WESTAWAY, A. J. (1986a) 'Hours of Work in British Manufacturing Industry: An Empirical Analysis' in R. Wilson (ed.) *Hours of Work*, Research Report (Coventry: University of Warwick, Institute for Employment Research).

BOSWORTH, D. L. and WESTAWAY A. J. (1986b) 'Labour Hoarding, Discouraged Workers and Recorded Unemployment in OECD Countries: Some Preliminary Results', mimeo, (Loughborough University of Technology, Department of Economics).

DAWKINS, P. and WOODEN, M. (1985) 'Labour Utilisation and Wage Inflation in Australia: An Empirical Examination', *Australian Economic Record*, 61, pp. 516–21.

DEATON, D. R. (1977) 'Employment Functions, Labour Hoarding and the Theory of Adjustment', Discussion Paper no. 11, (Coventry: Warwick University, Industrial Relations Research Unit).

DEATON, D. R. and BOWERS, J. K. (1977), 'Employment Functions and the Measurement of Labour Hoarding', Discussion Paper no. 12, (Coventry: Warwick University, Industrial Relations Research Unit).

DEATON, D. R. and BOWERS J. K. (1978) 'The Period of Labour Hoarding in the Presence of Quits', Discussion Paper no. 13, (Coventry: Warwick University, Industrial Relations Research Unit).

EVANS, G. J. (1974), 'The Labour Market Mechanism and the Hoarding of Manpower' in J. Wabe *et al.*, *Problems in Manpower Forecasting* (Farnborough: Saxon House) pp. 97–152.

FAIR, R. C. (1969) *The short Run Demand for Workers and Hours* (Amsterdam: North Holland).

FISHER, F. M. (1969) 'The Existence of Aggregate Production Functions', *Econometrica*, 37, pp. 553–77.

FISHER, F. M. (1971) 'Aggregate Production Functions and the Explanation of Wages: A Simulation Experiment', *Review of Economics and Statistics*, LIII, no. 4, pp. 305–25.

GREER, J. and RHODES, S. R. (1977) 'A Test of the Reserve Labour Hypothesis', *Economic Journal*, 87, pp. 290–9.

GREGORY, R. G. and SMITH, R. E. (1983) 'Unemployment, Inflation and Job Creation Policies in Australia', paper presented to the Conference on Government Policies Toward Inflation and Unemployment in Developed Countries, Macquarie University (September).

HAUSER, P. M. (1974) 'The Measurement of Labour Utilisation', *Malaysian Economic Review*, 19, no. 1, pp. 1–15.

HAUSER, P. M. (1977) 'The Measurement of Labour Utilisation - More Empirical Results', *Malaysian Economic Review*, 22, no. 1, pp. 10–25.

JOHANSEN, L. (1972), *Production Functions: An Integration of Micro and Macro, Short-Run and Long-Run Aspects*, Amsterdam: North Holland.

LIPSEY D. (1983) 'Why You Can't Count the Jobless', *Financial Times*, (6 November).

MADDISON, A. (1980) 'Monitoring the Labour Market: A Proposal for a Comprehensive Approach in Official Statistics (illustrated by recent developments in France, Germany and the UK)', *Review of Income and Wealth* (June), pp. 175–217.

MANGAN, J. (1984) 'Labour Hoarding in Australian Manufacturing: An Inter-Industry Analysis', *Australian Bureau of Labour*, 7, no. 4 (September) pp. 219–35.

METCALF, D. (1984) 'On the Measurement of Employment and Unemployment', *National Institute Economic Review*, 109, 3, pp. 59–67.

MOY, J. and SORRENTINO, C. (1982) 'Unemployment and Labour Force: Trends in Ten Industrial Nations: an Update', *Monthly Labour Review* (November) pp. 17–21.

MUYSKEN, J. (1987) 'Full Employment, Unemployment and Labour Hoarding', in D. Bosworth and D. Heathfield (eds) *Working Below Capacity* (London: Macmillan) pp. 219–45.

NEUBOURG, C. de (1984) *Labour Market Accounting and Labour Utilisation: Theory and Measurement*, National Programma Arbeidsmarktonderzoek, Publication no. 16.

NEUBOURG, C. de (1985a) 'The Dough, the Doughnut and the Hole: Unemployment, Labour Utilisation and Labour Market Accounting', (Maastricht: Limburg University) Research Memorandum, Faculty of Economics (RM 85-002).

NEUBOURG, C. de (1985b) 'Aggregate Unemployment and Labour Slack as Indices of Labour Utilisation', (Maastricht: Limburg University, Research Memorandum, Faculty of Economics) (RM 85-011).

PHILLIPS, A. W. (1958) 'The Relation Between Unemployment and the Rate of Change of Money Wage Rates in the United Kingdom 1861–1957', *Economica*, 25, pp. 283–99.

RIMLER, J. (1985) 'An International Comparison of Industrial Capacity Utilisation: on Dutch, Australian and Hungarian Examples', Discussion Paper no. 102 (Vienna: Vienna Institute for Comparative Economic Studies).

SOLOW, R. M. (1964) 'Draft of Presidential Address on the Short-Run Relations of Employment and Output', mimeograph.

SORRENTINO, C. (1978), *International Comparisons of Unemployment*, Washington: Bureau of Labour Statistics.

STRICKER, P. and SHEEHAN, P. (1981) *Hidden Unemployment; The Australian Experience* (Melbourne: Institute of Applied Economic and Social Research).

TAYLOR, J. (1970) 'Hidden Unemployment, Hoarded Labour, and the Phillips curve', *Southern Economic Journal*, 37, pp. 1–16.

# 7 Unidentified Floating Unemployment (UFU) and the Specification of the *UV*-curve

Chris de Neubourg*

Conceptually, unemployment may originate in various types of (temporary) imbalances on the labour market. Five types of origins are broadly to be distinguished[1] (given the real wage level and the volume of labour supply):

$U_k$ unemployment originating in very short term - seasonal - fluctuations in economic activity;

$U_l$ unemployment originating in the underutilisation of the existing physical production capacity;

$U_m$ unemployment originating in a shortage of new investment, that fails to compensate for the loss of employment due to the ongoing scrapping of older vintages of production capacity. Two dimensions can be distinguished (a) production capacity may increase too slowly and (b) the new capacity may be too capital-intensive to guarantee the absorption (utilisation) of the (given) labour force;

$U_n$ unemployment due to labour-market imperfections leading to real mismatches of supply and demand. Market imperfections in turn, originate in the behavioural reactions of workers and employers to incomplete information and in the fact that adjustments are seldom immediate and necessarily take time (see de Neubourg, 1985a, for details);

$U_o$ unemployment originating in the unemployability of certain specific groups for specific jobs, because of real characteristics of suppliers belonging to those groups (given the level of real

* I wish to thank Angus Maddison, David Heathfield, Joan Muysken and Peter de Gijsel for their critical and valuable comments on earlier drafts of the paper.

wages). Their unemployability may be due to various characteristics ranging from physical handicaps to the lack of relevant skills or education.

The main purpose of subdividing aggregate unemployment according to type and origin is to diagnose the causes of unemployment as a basis for remedial action. More specifically, the analysis should allow an estimate of the relative weight of each type of unemployment, in order to decide on the policy-mix that is expected to be successful in combating the empirically found type of unemployment. To be useful a classification of unemployment needs to satisfy two main conditions. First, it should be based on clearly defined criteria, that permit an unambiguous distinction of the various categories on the basis of mutually independent definitions. Second, it should lend itself to the possibility of measurement. In this article it will be argued that none of the classifications found in the literature, nor the distinction made at the beginning of this section, satisfy these two conditions. It appears to be impossible to define and to measure the relative importance of the various types of unemployment independently from each other, on the basis of a taxonomic labour market framework only. The nature of unemployment cannot be discussed unless decisive references to an underlying 'general theory' are made. In other words, analysis of the nature of unemployment implies necessarily the introduction of the dilemmas and unresolved questions related to the actual state of unemployment theory.[2]

## 1 VOLUNTARY AND INVOLUNTARY UNEMPLOYMENT

The concepts of 'voluntary' and 'involuntary unemployment' were introduced in the unemployment debate between Pigou and Keynes. Pigou (1933) defined all unemployment as voluntary. This expressed his basic idea that the acceptance of lower real wages by the workers would make all unemployment disappear (if the market and price mechanisms are not hampered by government or labour union action). Keynes (1936), on the other hand, accepted the idea of voluntary unemployment, but argued that unemployment was most likely to be of an involuntary nature due to inadequate final demand.[3]

However, his definition of involuntary unemployment is confusing and makes the demarcation between voluntary and involuntary unemployment 'embarrassingly vague' (Maddison, 1980).[4] The fuzziness on the distinction between voluntary and involuntary unemployment is due to two reasons. The first is the introduction of an element of individual behaviour (accepting a lower wage) into definition that is essentially macro in character. This in turn can be seen as a logical consequence of the very words 'voluntary' and 'involuntary' (and their use in more popular texts) and of the definitions explicitly given by Pigou and Keynes, that refer to the individual decision-making. It should, however, be acknowledged (as done by Keynes)[5] that real wages are often beyond individual control (due to legal and social restraints). It is, therefore, not surprising to find the distinction unhelpful in empirical investigations (see e.g. Hill *et al.* 1973, Hill 1976, Hahn 1978). The second, and more important, reason, for the inadequacy of the voluntary–involuntary distinction, is to be attributed to the fact that the classification was not introduced to divide empirically found volumes of unemployment into two categories, but to serve as signposts in a debate between those who favour macroeconomic policy and those who reject it. This idea is illustrated by the observation that all the types of $U$ discussed formerly ($U_k, \ldots U_o$) can be seen as either voluntary or involuntary depending on whether or not the analysts expect a lower real wage to cure the resulting unemployment.

Until recently, the distinction was commonly used in the rhetoric sense, reflecting rather ideological and fundamentally theoretical differences between the authors. The revival of the Pigouvian (neoclassical) analysis, as reflected in the search-theory and its complements, however, has resulted in a renewed emphasis on the voluntary nature of all unemployment. This emphasis is now based on a firmer microeconomic underpinning of macroeconomic theory. However important conceptually, the distinction between voluntary and involuntary unemployment nevertheless does not meet the crucial conditions set at the beginning of the section and, therefore, is not very useful in diagnosing the actual character of unemployment and contributing to remedial action. This seems to be a widely accepted idea (Robinson, 1937, Hahn 1976, Maddison 1980, Standing 1981).[6,7]

## 2 DEMAND DEFICIENT AND NON-DEMAND-DEFICIENT UNEMPLOYMENT

If the idea of the compatibility of unemployment (of a type different from frictional and voluntary as defined by Pigou) with a (non-market-clearing) wage rate equilibrium is accepted, the resulting unemployment may be caused by deficient demand and may be cured by stimulating aggregate demand. In principle, the distinction between demand-deficient unemployment and non-demand-deficient unemployment has the same virtues and deficiencies as the distinction between voluntary and involuntary unemployment. However, the concepts may be defined more rigorously and may lend themselves to unambiguous measurement. Therefore a discussion of the classification, under the explicit and, in my opinion, reasonable assumption that demand-deficient unemployment may exist, is necessary and useful.

Two ways to distinguish demand-deficient from non-demand-deficient unemployment are found in the literature: one on an *ex ante* causal base and the other on an *ex post* base (Addison and Siebert, 1979, pp. 376–94; Thirlwall, 1969). Under the first method demand-deficient unemployment is defined *a priori* as the amount of unemployment that is attributable to the fact that total expenditures in an economy are not sufficient to generate jobs for all those willing to work at the equilibrium wage (see e.g. Davidson, 1967). Strictly speaking, demand deficient unemployment is thus the amount of unemployment in excess of the unfilled demand for labour (vacancies).[8] Classifying unemployment in this way makes the measurement of the different types of unemployment extremely difficult. The information required for the measurement consists not only of an index for the demand for labour, but also of data on the wage-responsiveness of labour supply (and demand). This is more information than governments and researchers normally have at their command. This kind of distinction between demand-deficient and non-demand-deficient unemployment is not operationally meaningful.

Another approach to this practical problem of measurement is to divide unemployment into a demand-deficient and a non-demand-deficient component according to the possible means of reducing it, assuming certain constraints on action. Demand-deficient unemployment, according to this definition, is defined as the part of unemployment which might be removable by successful macro policy, as distinct from the other component, which can only be mitigated by other measures (as will be discussed further). The constraint on action commonly accepted relates to the level of inflation considered to be 'tolerable'. This constraint, however, is defined in various ways, according to the subjective preferences of individual researchers or the arbitrariness of *a priori* target-setting. The constraint is introduced recognising that if the demand for labour were strong enough almost all unemployment could probably be eliminated but only at the cost of substantial upward pressure on wages and prices. Without doubt it is legitimate to assume a relation between unemployment and inflation. It is nevertheless, conceptually very confusing to need a necessarily arbitrary inflation-target in order to define and to calculate how much of the observed unemployment can be explained by demand-deficiency and can therefore be removed by stimulating aggregate demand.

The difficulty of delimiting the volume of demand-deficient unemployment can be illustrated also by considering the types of unemployment listed at the beginning of the section. Closer examination of $U_k \cdots U_o$ teaches us that at least $U_1$ and $U_m$ are strongly affected by the level and the development of aggregate demand. While $U_1$ (unemployment originating in the underutilisation of the existing physical production capacity) is traditionally recognised as demand-deficient, only a part (but how much?) of $U_m$ (unemployment originating in the lack of new investment) has to be seen as demand-deficient.[9] The literature does not provide a clear-cut operational answer on the demarcation of demand-deficient *versus* non-demand-deficient unemployment.

It is important to notice that the sum of all other types of unemployment (covered by the concept 'non-demand-deficient unemployment') is treated as a residual after 'demand-deficient unemployment' is deducted from aggregate unemployment. Since the definition and measurement of the former is troublesome, a viable solution may be found either by defining and measuring other types of unemployment first and treating demand deficient unemployment as the residual, or by defining all types of unemployment simultaneously.

## 3 SEASONAL, FRICTIONAL AND STRUCTURAL UNEMPLOYMENT

The classification of aggregate unemployment into four categories seasonal, frictional, structural and demand-deficient – is now common practice rather than the use of the dubious dichotomies voluntary–involuntary, demand-deficient – non-demand deficient. The definitions of seasonal and frictional unemployment are the oldest and intuitively the least controversial.

## Seasonal Unemployment

Seasonal unemployment is often considered of minor importance for three reasons. First, its significance diminished historically in the capitalist world due to the very big decline in agricultural employment, to new social security acts such as income compensation for bad weather and winter-time work-losses (which excludes beneficiaries from the count of unemployed), and to a larger degree of labour hoarding. Second, most statistical offices provide regular unemployment estimates corrected for seasonal fluctuations and these estimates are considered to be trustworthy indicators of business cycles. Third, the era of mass unemployment that began in the late 1970s drew attention away from smaller temporary fluctuations. If seasonal unemployment is defined as the difference between actual annual average unemployment and what it would have been if the same seasonal adjustment factor was most favourable to employment, then for the 1970s, seasonal unemployment was far less than 1 per cent in most capitalist countries (Maddison, 1980; Gilpatrick, 1966). The definition of these authors is commonly accepted and operational; an estimate of seasonal unemployment is provided and can be deducted from aggregate unemployment in order to obtain a figure that is more suited for medium- and long-term analysis. In terms of the concepts introduced at the beginning of the section, seasonal unemployment equals $U_k$.[10]

## Frictional Unemployment

Frictional unemployment was already accepted and defined by Pigou and Keynes, who regarded it as that portion of unemployment that is related to the normal functioning of the labour market and which policy should accept. Keynes:

> legitimately allows for various inexactnesses of adjustment which stand in the way of continuous full employment: for example, unemployment due to a temporary want of balance between the relative quantities of specialised resources as a result of miscalculation or intermittent demand; or to time-lags consequent on unforeseen changes; or to the fact that the change-over from one employment to another cannot be effected without a certain delay, so that there will always exist in a non-static society a proportion of resources unemployed 'between jobs' (Keynes, 1936, p. 6).

Clarity requires that the concept should be used only to indicate unemployment due to normal search-time irrespective of the situation on the labour market. Frictional unemployment should be considered as fairly stable over time, although some corrections according to the labour-force volume may be necessary when an extended time-span is studied. However, the exact definition of frictional unemployment is a matter of pragmatic judgement on which opinions differ.

A growing number of authors tend to ignore the distinction between frictional and 'structural' unemployment. Influenced by the new micro-economics of (job search) unemployment they argue that 'normal' search-time has been lengthened recently by increasing wage rigidity, extended unemployment insurance and/or the changing demographic composition of the labour force (see e.g. Hall 1970; Scott and Laslett, 1978; Maddison, 1980; Klaasen and Heyke, 1977). Introducing these elements into the definitions of frictional unemployment means that its intial meaning is ignored. If frictional unemployment changes when wage rigidity or social security arrangements alter, it can no longer be regarded as beyond the control of policy and should therefore not be accepted *a priori*. In order to reserve the conceptual clarity and the initial meaning, which is intuitively plausible, it therefore seems to be useful to adopt a pragmatic definition of frictional unemployment, which defines it operationally as an *a priori* and unchanging absolute minimum number of unemployment that is to be considered as irreducible.

Such a definition has the advantage that it acknowledges the existence of unemployment due to the normal working of the labour market, which should not be of policy concern, while it avoids mixing up frictional unemployment and that which originates in labour market imperfections that is classified as 'structural unemployment'. It is clear, that this is but a pragmatic solution that states that 'some' unemployment will always exist. It does not solve the underlying conceptual problems. In terms of the types of unemployment at the beginning of the section, frictional unemployment is a part of $U_n$.

## Structural Unemployment

As argued, it is possible to define and to estimate seasonal and frictional unemployment on pragmatic grounds. What is left is the most important part of unemployment both in quantitative terms and in relation to policy concern. This main part consists (if we adopt the commonly used classification) of structural unemployment and demand-deficient unemployment. Given the impossibility of defining and measuring the latter in an operationally meaningful way (as explained above), the main question is whether structural unemployment can be defined and measured in order to estimate the volume of demand-deficient unemployment as a residual.

The demarcation problem of structural *versus* demand-deficient unemployment is not new. The relatively high levels of unemployment that persisted from 1957 until the early 1960s in the USA did raise the question whether unemployment was of a structural type or has to be seen as the result of an inadequate level of demand for goods and services. The disappearance of unemployment during the period of prosperous economic growth that followed, more or less settled the matter in favour of the latter point of view. But in the 1970s a renewed and sharper debate resulted, fed by the new microeconomics of search theory and new high unemployment rates pressing governments to act in one way or another.

Structural unemployment has to be understood as unemployment due to labour-market imperfections leading to mismatches of supply and demand (i.e. $U_n$ in terms of the subdivision given at the beginning of this section). In the – largely American – debate at the end of the 1950s and during the early 1960s, empirical investigations intended to indicate that the overall volume of unemployment due to market imperfections was either significant or non-significant rather than to estimate the well-defined part of unemployment that could be attributed to market imperfections. Empirical tests relied upon the study of the dispersion of unemployment according to type of job, geographical area and/or demographic group (see Simler, 1964, for a review). The relation between the growing importance of imperfections and the average duration of unemployment, was emphasised and documented by Simler (1964). More recently Gordon (1967), Jenness (1978) and Cramer *et al.* (1976) used similar methods to discuss the importance of unemployment due to market imperfections (not to estimate its exact impact). More sophisticated empirical contributions can be found in Hughes, 1974; Armstrong and Taylor, 1981; Maneval, 1977; Riese, 1980; Hartog, 1980, and Muysken *et al.*, 1982. In their studies disaggregated unemployment – and vacancy – figures are used to estimate the impact of unemployment due to labour market imperfections. These estimates, however, are based on the fairly simple assumption that the volume of structural unemployment on a submarket is given by the minimum of $U$ (unemployment) and $V$

(vacancy). This type of calculation yields but a crude approximation of the part of unemployment to be attributed to structural mismatches since it can be shown that the results are, by definition, not independent from the cyclical situation. This seems rather inappropriate when a structural phenomenon is studied (See Muysken and de Neubourg, 1981, for an explanation).

*UV*-analysis, outlined by Brown (1975), Hansen (1970), Holt (1970) and Phelps (1970) and partly suggested in the earlier contributions of Dow and Dicks-Mireaux (1988) and Thirlwall (1969) avoids this inconsistency by articulating theoretically the relationship between unemployment and vacancies. After estimating the *UV* curve, the volume of unemployment due to labour-market imperfections can be defined as the value of $U$ (and $V$) for which $U = V$. Numerous studies have estimated the volume of structural unemployment by this method especially for the UK (Gujarati, 1972; Taylor, 1972; Foster, 1973; Holden and Peel, 1975; Bowers, 1976; Evans, 1977; Warren, 1977; Parick, 1977) and for the Netherlands (Kuipers and Buddenberg, 1977; Siegers, 1980; Muysken, de Neubourg and van der Burg, 1978; van der Berg, 1983; de Neubourg, 1985) (see also Jenness, 1978, and Driehuis, 1978, for several OECD countries).

Although, the *UV*-analysis defines the volume of unemployment (vacancies) due to labour-market imperfections conceptually in a way which guarantees its independence from the cyclical situation, serious problems are met when it comes to the empirical specification of the *UV*-curve. From most of the specifications it became clear that the cyclical situation (either in the form of lagged unemployment or in a more direct way) should enter the equation in order to obtain a good fit. This applied to the early contributions of Phelps (1970) and Hansen (1970) and became strikingly apparent when the period of observation was extended after 1975 for the Netherlands (see de Neubourg, 1985a, for a detailed survey). The specifications used by Kuipers and Buddenberg (1978) and Driehuis (1978) did not yield satisfactory fits when post-1975 data were included. The specifications used by Muysken *et al.* (1982) and van den Berg (1982) accounted for the cyclical influence by incorporating lagged unemployment and the capacity utilisation rate respectively. In an attempt to detect simultaneously the underlying causes of the assumed and observed upward shift of the *UV* curve (hence of the rise of structural unemployment due to labour-market imperfections) and to ameliorate the specification of the equation, de Neubourg (1985a) experimented with various specifications. The specification which gives the best fit can be written ($t$-values between brackets) as:

$$\ln U = 32.4 - 0.97 \ln S + 0.21\, WA + 1.8 AGE - 2.45 C - 1.52 V \quad (7.1)$$
$$(24.8)(-4.3) \quad (2.31) \quad (2.8) \quad (-2.5)\ (-13.7)$$

$$R^2 = 0.98$$

$$DW = 1.84$$

where:

$U$ = unemployment;
$S$ = the share of vacancies open to workers younger than 19 years as a percentage of total vacancies;
$WA$ = weighted benefit-wage ratio measured as the quotient of the weighted average of the mean unemployment benefit multiplied by the number of beneficiairies and the mean disability act (WAO) benefit multiplied by the number of beneficiaries, and the modal wage multiplied by the number of employees.
$AGE$ = the ratio 'labour-market-entering population' to labour-market-leaving population' measured as the ratio of male population aged 20–24 years to male population 50–59 years;
$C$ = capacity utilisation rate;
$V$ = vacancies.

From this specification of the *UV*-curve it becomes clear that the increase in unemployment due to labour-market imperfections cannot be interpreted as a structural problem, in the sense that it can be attributed solely to the malfunctioning of the labour market. A close inspection of the variables in the equation shows that, besides a hard core of constantly emerging frictional unemployment *strictu sensu* of about 55 000 persons and a relatively small influence of the structural shift in the age-composition of the potential labour force, the other three underlying causes of the upward shift since 1967 clearly bear a cyclical character. The number of vacancies open to workers younger than 19 years and the capacity utilisation rate do not refer to the assumed growth of labour-market imperfections. Nor is the weighted benefit–wage ratio to be regarded as an indicator of structural changes. It is clear that the quotient of the weights – respectively the number of beneficiaries and the number of employed workers – is influenced by cyclical rather than by structural factors. This result is consistent with the findings for other countries for which it was established that structural changes are unlikely to provoke crises at the economy-wide level nor that an accentuation of structural problems caused by labour-market imperfection can be found since 1970 (Maddison, 1983; Turvey, 1977; Cramer *et al.*, 1976; Abraham, 1983; OECD, 1982).

In the context of the present discussion, aiming at finding a method to define and measure structural unemployment due to labour market imperfections, the failure to specify the *UV*-curve independently from the cyclical situation lends weight to the remarks of Gilpatrick (1966). She argues that there are significant sources of interaction of structural change and final demand and that the two kinds of unemployment causes (structural mismatches and deficient demand) can reinforce or offset each other depending on the particular combination of circumstances. 'In addition', she concludes, 'the unemployment categories themselves are not rigidly separated. There is interaction among structural, frictional and "demand" unemployment' (Gilpatrick, 1966, p. 211). From the discussion it can be concluded that, although it is conceptually possible to define the volume of unemployment due to labour-market imperfections independently from the cyclical circumstances by means of *UV* analysis, it seems impossible to specify the *UV*-curve statistically in a way that guarantees the assumed independence. This raises questions about interrelations between the parts of unemployment to be attributed to different causes; we will return to these questions later.

The statistical difficulty of specifying the *UV*-curve after 1975 and deriving an estimate of unemployment due to labour-market imperfections from it, is also illustrated by Figure 7.1. The graphs depict aggregate unemployment and the number of vacancies respectively for the Netherlands. The estimation of the *UV*-curve is based on the position of the intersection of the two curves. As no such point can be observed after 1971, the position of the curve that shows the time-path of unemployment due to labour-market imperfections ($U^*$), depends highly on the projection of a future intersection., this is implicitly defined by the chosen specification of the *UV*-curve. The figure shows two possible future positions of the intersection: it can be clearly seen that the estimate of $U^*$ highly depends on which point is chosen. In this respect, it is highly relevant that although unemployment may rise - statistically speaking - infinitely, the vacancies can not fall below the *x*-axis (and *vice versa*). This asymmetry implies automatically that when unemployment increases sharply and vacancies fall to their minimum level, the position of the *UV*-curve is bound to be pushed upwards. The resulting rise in structural unemployment is then the result of a statistical delusion.

*Figure* 7.1 Unemployment and vacancies: The Netherlands 1960–83

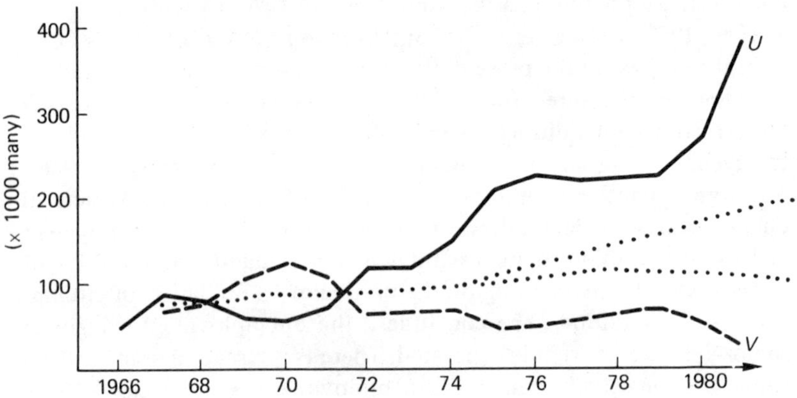


Even if there were a method to measure the volume of genuinely qualitative structural unemployment, i.e. caused by labour market imperfections, the question whether the residue (after deducting the former from aggregate unemployment) should be regarded as an adequate estimate of the volume of demand-deficient unemployment (as suggested by Abraham, 1983) remains open. Some authors state that besides cyclical fluctuations, structural problems of another type, namely the quantitative shortage of the capacity demand for labour, are important in explaining current unemployment rates. This type of unemployment can be indicated by the concepts 'neo-structural unemployment' or 'capital shortage unemployment'. The underlying theory relates to the vintage theory of economic growth and is particularly popular in the Netherlands and in some circles in Germany (den Hartog and Tjan, 1976; Fels and Weiss, 1978). It states that recovery to full employment would be impossible because of capital shortage. The suggestion is that excessive wage claims over a long period have forced entrepeneurs to scrap old equipment, so that there is now a shortage of capital which prevents full employment from being retained because, even if wages declined, there would be no suitable capital available to provide extra employment. Empirically the volume of capital-shortage unemployment is estimated by macroeconomic models with a vintage structure (such as the official Dutch models Vintaf II and FREIA). The impact of this type of structural imbalance upon unemployment, however, strongly depends on the specifications of the scrapping conditions. Real wages are a decisive element in this context and serious criticism has been made on the hypotheses that have been made concerning this interrelation (Maddison, 1983; Driehuis, 1979; Gruen, 1978; de Klerk *et al.*, 1977).

The Dutch official Planning Bureau (CPB) uses the notion of capital-shortage unemployment (indicated quite unfortunately as 'quantitative structural unemployment') to subdivide aggregate unemployment into four major components:

- frictional unemployment, which is defined as constant over time;
- cyclical unemployment which is related to the underutilisation of the existing capital stock;
- capital-shortage unemployment defined by scrapping and investment conditions; and
- a residue, which is said to represent the part of unemployment due to labour market imperfections.

It is clear that defining cyclical unemployment strictly as the part of aggregate unemployment that disappears when the existing capital stock is fully used and the specification of the scrapping conditions, in which real wages are dominant, are problematic when the reliability of the subdivision is considered. The weights attached to fluctuations in final demand on the one hand and changes in the real wages on the other hand, are, moreover, settled in a way which is unsatisfactory when decisions have to be made concerning the causes of unemployment. Additionally, the definition of unemployment due to labour-market imperfections as the residue after the other types of unemployment are measured, is unnecessarily inaccurate, as will be explained under the next heading. Summarising, it may be concluded that no solid ground may be found to distinguish frictional, structural and demand-deficient unemployment empirically in a trustworthy way. The reasons for this impossibility will be discussed at the end of the section. Preceding the discussion, however, it should be investigated whether it is not possible to define the different types of unemployment simultaneously.[11]

## 4 SIMULTANEOUS DEFINITION OF ALL TYPES OF UNEMPLOYMENT

In a recent contribution, Muysken (1984) integrates *UV* and macroeconomic vintage analysis, to distinguish three major types of unemployment simultaneously (after seasonal and frictional unemployment are deducted from aggregate unemployment). The central concept of the analysis is the employment function. On the one hand a *UV*-curve is derived from the employment function. Thus the volume of structural unemployment due to market imperfections can be determined. On the other hand the employment function is also used in the estimation of the vintage models, which allows him to distinguish employment from actual demand for labour and full-capacity demand for labour. As a consequence unemployment due to capacity-underutilisation and capital-shortage unemployment can be defined and labour hoarding can be determined. His analytical framework can be summarised by the following set of equations:

$$U = U' + U^c + U^* \tag{7.2}$$

$$U' = (\bar{N} - \tilde{N}) + (E^c - E) \tag{7.3}$$

$$U^c = E^* - E^c \tag{7.4}$$

$$U^* = \tilde{N} - E^* \tag{7.5}$$

wherein:

$U$ = aggregate unemployment;
$U'$ = unemployment due to the underutilisation of the existing production capacity;
$U^c$ = capital shortage unemployment;
$U^*$ = structural-unemployment due to labour market imperfections;

note: that $U' = U_e$; $U^c = U_m$ and $U^* = U_n$ in terms of the subdivision of $U$ given at the beginning of this section.

further:

$\tilde{N}$ = demand for labour;
$\bar{N}$ = supply of labour corrected for cyclical influences;
$N$ = actual supply of labour;
$E^c$ = employment at full capacity level;
$E$ = actual employment;
$E^*$ = employment consistent with structural labour market imperfections = $U^*$;

$$E = g(N, \bar{N}) \tag{7.6}$$

while it is assumed that the function is homogeneous of the first degree in $N$ and $\bar{N}$, hence:

$$g\left(\frac{N}{E}, \frac{\bar{N}}{E}\right) = 1 \tag{7.6a}$$

$$\frac{E}{N} = f\left(\frac{N}{\bar{N}}\right) = g\left(\frac{N}{\bar{N}}, 1\right) \tag{7.6b}$$

$$\tilde{N} = N^* \tag{7.7}$$

wherein:

$N^*$ = demand for labour at which structural imperfections on the labour market occur at the level $U^*$; i.e. = the demand for labour for which holds $U = V$;

$$E^* = \tilde{g}(N^*, \tilde{N}) \tag{7.8}$$

wherein: $\tilde{g} = g$ corrected for capacity underutilisation.

$$E^c = \tilde{g}(\tilde{q}N^c, \tilde{N}) \tag{7.9}$$

wherein $N^c$ = demand for labour at full capacity level.

This analytical framework can also be summarised graphically as is done in Figure 7.2. The figure represents a typical situation in the downswing of the cycle, assuming $N$ and $E$ to be given. The function $\bar{g}$ represents a cyclically neutral situation with labour supply at $\bar{N}$. The capacity demand for labour, $N^c$, and the utilisation rate, $q$, are generated by the vintage model. Actual demand for labour, $N$, and the corresponding employment, $E$, can now be derived. The employment at full capacity level, $E^c$, is derived from equation (7.9); labour demand ($N^*$) and employment ($E^*$) consistent with structural labour-market imperfections (where $U = V$) are given by equation (7.8).

It can now be seen from the figure that aggregate unemployment (after corrections are made for seasonal and frictional factors) can be subdivided into three components: using the existing production capacity at a full capacity level would increase $E$ up to $E^c$. Therefore, accounting for a cyclical influence in the supply of labour, the corresponding unemployment equals $(E^c - E) - (N - \tilde{N})$. A further reduction of residual unemployment would require an extension of production capacity. When capacity is increased up to the point where the demand for labour equals its supply, employment would increase

*Figure* 7.2 The decomposition of unemployment according to Muysken (1985)

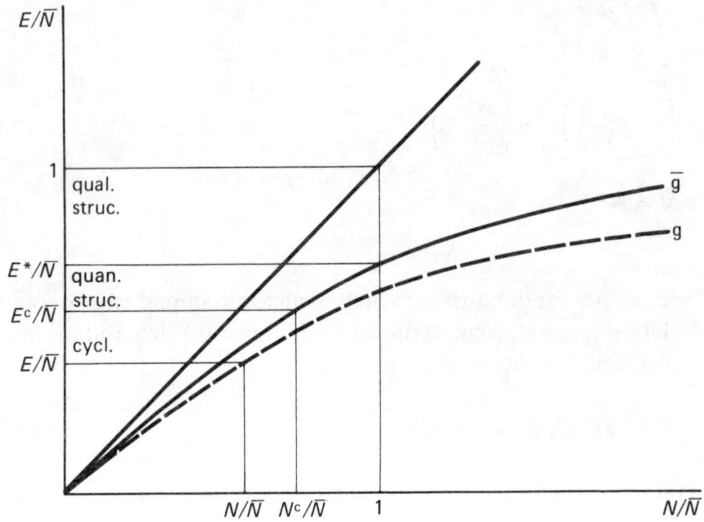


further from $E^c$ to $E^*$; hence capital shortage unemployment is $E^* - E^c$. The remaining unemployment, $N - E^*$, is due to market imperfections and is consistent with the position on a *UV*-curve where $U = V$.

The analytical framework developed by Muysken has unmistakable advantages compared with the previous work on the subdivision of unemployment. Its main innovative feature is the definition of a consistent framework in which the three major components of unemployment are defined simultaneously and independently.

There remains, however, a fundamental and important problem when the analysis of Muysken is regarded as a solution to the initial problem raised at the beginning. The main purpose of subdividing aggregate unemployment according to type and origin was said to be the establishment of a diagnosis concerning the causes of unemployment as a basis for remedial action. More specifically, the analysis should allow one to estimate the relative weight attached to each type of unemployment, in order to decide on the policy-mix that is expected to be successful in combating the type of unemployment found empirically. The discussion focused on the distinctions between voluntary–involuntary and demand-deficient–structural unemployment. These types of unemployment are judged to be important since their causes and the policy recommendations related to them are said to be significantly different. However, the analytical frameworks and their empirical applications, are not very successful, in that no consistent and clear-cut subdivision of unemployment could be found.[12] It should be noted that we sought so far to subdivide unemployment by means of statistical demarcation without theoretical modelling.

The analysis proposed by Muysken is different in this respect and indeed yields a consistent definition and demarcation of the types of unemployment. However, the types of unemployment distinguished by the analytical framework no longer have a direct link either with the causes of unemployment or with the policy recommendations. The link between the subdivision proposed by Muysken and the causes of unemployment can only be made via the theories underlying the specification of the general and the labour market model. That is not to suggest that the types distinguished by Muysken are not relevant.

Unemployment due to the underutilisation of capital equipment defines and measures that part of aggregate unemployment that would disappear if the existing capital stock were utilised fully.[13] Capital-shortage unemployment defines and measures the part of unemployment that would disappear if the existing capacity were extended. Unemployment due to labour-market imperfections define and measure the part of unemployment that is to be attributed to the mismatch of supply and demand. The analysis, however, does not reveal why the existing capital stock is underutilised, why the volume of new investments is insufficient to compensate for the loss of employment due to the scrapping of older vintages of capital stock or why labour market imperfections exist (grow, decline). This means that the analytic framework of Muysken leaves the question of the causes of unemployment unanswered.[14] It is impossible to provide an answer to these questions without a general model.

Equally, the framework itself does not by itself provide an answer to the question what type of policy is bound to be successful in combating the three types of unemployment. It can easily be argued that stimulating effective final demand may not only diminish unemployment due to the underutilisation of the existing capacity, but also increase new investment or delay the scrapping of existing equipment and thus diminish capital shortage unemployment. If the empirical interrelation between cyclical factors and unemployment due to labour-market imperfections, as discussed in the previous paragraph, holds, the latter may also be diminished by a Keynesian type of policy. The same reasoning, however, applies when a real-wage cut is considered as policy option. A decline in real wages may stimulate employers to use their capital equipment more effectively, may stimulate new investment or render older vintages of the capital stock more profitable and may provide workable incentives to employers and workers to limit the impact of market imperfections.

Summarising, a wage cut as well as demand management may diminish all types of unemployment distinguished by Muysken.[15] Without a general model no choice between them can be made.

It may be concluded that Muysken (1985) provides a useful and interesting analysis of unemployment leading to the subdivision of it into three types. However, each of the types finally distinguished, miss a direct link with a well-defined cause and a clear-cut policy recipe to combat it. The framework, therefore, cannot be regarded as a diagnostic statisical instrument that provides direct insights in the causes of unemployment and ways to combat it. It has to be supplemented by a general model specifying both the relations between the variables assumed relevant and the adjustment processes.

This conclusion, however, is not recognised explicitly by Muysken himself. Quite on the contrary, the concepts he uses to indicate the three types of unemployment, each refer implicitly to a certain type of cause and policy. Unemployment due to the underutilisation of existing capacity is named 'cyclical unemployment'; capital shortage unemployment and unemployment due to labour-market imperfections are indicated respectively as 'quantitative structural unemployment' and 'qualitative structural unemployment'. He acknowledges that the relevance of a decomposition of unemployment 'lies in the differences between underlying causes and the implied consequences for economic policy' (Muysken, 1985, p. 1), but on the other hand he does not make any attempt to explain why the definition of cyclical unemployment should be limited to the unemployment resulting 'from deviations in capacity utilisation from the level of full capacity due to changes in effective demand' (p. 10). This is, however, very important since it leads further (p. 13) to the (implicit) conclusion that stimulation of effective demand can only be used to combat that part of unemployment which is due to the underutilisation of existing capacity.

This is a very limited interpretation of the effects of a Keynesian type of policy, as argued previously. More fundamentally it can be argued that the volumes of capital shortage unemployment and unemployment due to labour-market imperfections are not independent from cyclical factors. Not because no attempt has been made (by

Muysken) to define them independently but because cyclical factors have an influence on their definition via the underlying general model.[16]

## 5 UNIDENTIFIED UNEMPLOYMENT

Summarising the previous paragraphs, it seems extremely difficult to subdivide aggregate unemployment into types which fulfill the following requirements simultaneously. They should be defined independently from each other, within a consistent framework by means of definitions that can be operationalised. Moreover, each type should correspond to a particular cause and to specific policy consequences. It is interesting to consider the reasons for the failure to achieve these goals. Three main elements should be considered: first, the fundamental problem of modelling dynamic processes within a static framework; second, the mixed character of unemployment, and third the logical gap between explanation and policy.

### Dynamics in a Static Framework

The very concepts 'unemployment due to labour-market imperfections' and 'capital-shortage unemployment' refer to adjustment processes that are essentially dynamic in their nature. In both cases they refer to a (temporary) failure of adjustment. The concepts relate to adjustments to technological change and to permanent shifts in the composition of final demand.

More specifically both shifts may take the form of changes in production techniques, changes in consumer demand, in industrial location or changes in skill requirements. Since the economic structure is in permanent flux,[17] and the composition of productive activity is constantly changing, there is always a part of unemployment that can be attributed to these changes. However, the estimate of the exact amount of unemployment that can be attributed to structural changes and the determination of this part of unemployment as genuinely structural or as a matter of inadequate demand, is highly dependent on the assumptions concerning the invariability of the coefficients in the production function and the transferability of skills. Or, as Gilpatrick (1966) puts it, 'whether one admits the possibility of structural and/or demand unemployment is clearly related to one's view of the nature of economic adjustment' (Gilpatrick, 1966, p. 207).[18]

The assumed nature of economic adjustment is also important when capital-shortage unemployment is considered. Whether this type of unemployment is defined as demand-deficient or structural, depends upon the specification of the interrelations between the strength of final demand, profitability and expectations on the one hand and investment and scrapping behaviour on the other hand. When investment and scrapping are modelled as a function of real-wage changes only, the conclusion that will emerge will be different from that found if final demand is assumed to play an important role in investment and scrapping decisions. These interrelations, however, cannot be modelled in a partial-labour-market analysis. This conclusion, is implicitly accepted in the analytic framework proposed by Muysken, in which the distinction between the three major types of unemployment can only be made by means of a general (vintage) model. The causal links between certain types of unemployment and specific variables, however, is then no longer a matter of definition and independent demarcation only, but essentially depends upon the assumed adjustment processes embodied in the models. The subdivision of unemployment into different types is consequently no longer a measurement matter, but becomes an essential part of the underlying 'general' theory.

This is recognised by Malinvaud, who states that it should not be believed that structural unemployment is clearly distinguishable from, and causally independent of, demand-deficient unemployment. 'The distinction is concerned rather with our analytical method for approaching a complex phenomenon than with two identifiable components of statistical unemployment' (Malinvaud, 1977, p. viii).

## The Mixed Character of Unemployment

Depending on the theoretical preferences of the analysts, it can easily be argued that all the types of unemployment distinguished at the beginning of this article and defined by the consistent framework of Muysken, are sensitive both to changes in the strength of final demand and in the level of real wages. Confining ourselves to the three major types defined by the *UV*-vintage approach, we can illustrate the plausibility of this statement. Assume that the level and the rate of change of final demand is an important factor for employers when making decisions on the degree of utilisation of their productive capacity, scrapping existing capital equipment, investing in new capacity and providing facilities in order to adapt the available human capital to demand (e.g. by on-the-job training, etc.). Stimulating final demand accordingly can be considered to be a viable policy-option to combat unemployment. To the extent, however, that the behaviour of employers (employees) concerning the decisions mentioned above, is assumed to be a function of the level and the rate of change of real wages, the unemployment which results from the actual behaviour can be seen as structural or even voluntary in the Pigouvian sense. A real-wage cut is to be considered as the policy measure to follow.

Concluding, it may be said that the diagnosis of the nature of unemployment is coloured by the underlying theory concerning final demand elasticities and the degree of wage responsiveness of demand and supply. It is, therefore, not a matter of measurement only, whether one weighs either elasticity larger than the other one.[19]

As to the analysis, it seems impossible to distinguish unemployment due to one cause, from unemployment due to other causes without a general model. The precise demarcation between the types of unemployment and the related estimates of the relative importance of the types is highly dependent on the theoretical assumptions and the (partly arbitrary) operational decisions made within or on behalf of the models. The main theoretical schools have many unresolved problems. An undisputed analysis of the nature of unemployment is therefore not within our means, if ever.

As to the policy recommendations it seems wise to regard 'total' unemployment as a policy-problem either of an economic or a social nature. Various instruments, combined in various policy-mixes, may and can be used to combat unemployment. Judgements on the actual mix that is expected to be the most successful, cannot be provided by analysis alone. 'Neither economic theory nor macro econometric models can give today the kind of clear-cut answers that would be directly useful for policy-makers' (Malinvaud, 1982, p. 1).

## The Link between the Causes of Unemployment and Policy

Since it seems difficult to hunt down the ultimate causes of unemployment by simple measurement, the question may be raised whether it is indeed important to establish causes in order to formulate viable policy options. The answer to that question contains two elements.

In the first place it can be argued that it is not always necessary to establish causes in order to diminish total unemployment. This holds especially when unemployment due to labour market imperfections is concerned, but may apply also to other types of unemployment.

Most types of unemployment tend to disappear when the labour market becomes tighter. This observation is partly a tautology, since unemployment will be low in a tight labour market by definition, but it was remarkable that unemployment in the early 1960s, which was defined by a significant number of authors as due to labour market imperfections disappeared without special measures taken to divert the imperfections. The explanation for this phenomenon must be sought in the fact that the situation on the labour market itself is an important determinant of the behaviour of employers and workers; especially of that part of the behaviour that determines the existence and persistence of labour market imperfections. In general, it is plausible to say that as long as the behaviour of entrepreneurs and workers is of a complex nature, i.e. as long as the behaviour is not determined by a single variable, the political manipulation of one of the relevant variables (e.g. real wages or final demand) may cause a change in unemployment that is larger than one might expect from estimates of the part of unemployment that may be attributed to the cause that is related to the manipulated variable. The fact that it is analytically difficult to diagnose the ultimate causes of unemployment, therefore, does not imply that no political choice can be made.

There is, however, a second reason why there must not necessarily be a direct link between the causes of unemployment and the policy recommendations formulated to combat unemployment. This reason is linked to the observation that the character of unemployment may change, especially when a significant number of the unemployed are out of work for a long period. Two examples illuminate the relevant processes.

Assume that a worker is dismissed because his or her employer changes the production process and the worker's qualifications no longer fit the technical requirements. The worker then belongs to the 'structurally unemployed'. Whether or not the worker will stay unemployed depends on a lot of factors among which the overall state of the labour market is an important one. Suppose mass unemployment already exists and demand for labour is very weak. In that case, the chances that the worker will find a job in a new firm or be retrained by his previous employer is very small. Hence, he or she is at least partially to be seen as belonging to the cyclically unemployed.

The reverse is even more likely to occur. Assume that a school-leaver (new entrant) who is perfectly trained, does not find a job (e.g. because more experienced colleagues of older cohorts are preferred). If the new entrant stays without a job for a long time, his or her qualifications, not being used and exercised and not brought up to date by experience, are likely to deteriorate. In the end the qualifications, both in skills and attitudes, will no longer fit the actual demand for labour. Hence the unemployed person has moved into 'structural' unemployment.

The two examples illustrate that even if the precise origin and character of unemployment may be established and measured, this does not automatically imply that the most successful economic policy can be derived. It is safe to state that a policy intended to absorb the largest possible share of labour supply, is likely to be more successful than other types of measures. This conclusion relates to the question on the target rate of unemployment.

## 6 LABOUR SLACK AND THE ART OF FULL EMPLOYMENT

Having argued in the previous sections that it is difficult to diagnose the ultimate causes of unemployment and that this prevents mechanical derivation of policy prescriptions, we will discuss the impact of these conclusions for the definition of the full-employment policy target in this last section.

In 1909, William Beveridge published a book entitled *Unemployment: A Problem of Industry*. Unemployment is described in that book as a product of the business cycle, although part of it can be removed by better organisation of the labour market. Business cycles could be ameliorated by improving business planning with the help of statistical information. Although evening out local public construction would help, the role of the central government should be kept modest. The conclusions of the 1909 book of Beveridge are representative for the general view of economists until the Great Depression.

In 1944, William Beveridge published his classic *Full Employment in a Free Society*, wherein he states 'the ultimate responsibility for seeing that outlay as a whole, taking public and private outlay together, is sufficient to set up a demand for all the labour seeking employment, must be taken by the State' (Beveridge, 1944, pp. 134–5). In that book Beveridge, and other authors elsewhere[20] tried to establish the meaning and definition of full employment and to formulate why and how economic policy should be used to guarantee full employment in a free society. The theoretical underpinning for the government's assuming such responsibility was provided by Keynes's *General Theory* and let loose a flood of literature on the meaning of full employment and on how to maintain a full-employment level of aggregate demand.[21]

It is clear that neither Beveridge nor any other analyst would defend a literal interpretation of 'full employment'.[22] 'Full employment means that unemployment is reduced to short intervals of standing by, with the certainty that very soon one will be wanted in one's old job again or will be wanted in a new job that is within one's power', is the definition that Beveridge gives (Beveridge, 1944, p. 18). He further states that it means always having more vacant jobs than unemployed persons. The argument to sustain that target is rather primitive since it assumes that the labour force is a fixed number of persons. It states that the margin of vacancies is necessary, since without it' no undertaking . . . could expand its labour force to meet growing needs, except by finding another undertaking which at the same moment was ready to release a workman who was qualified for the work and either was living in the right place or was able and willing to move to it' (Beveridge, 1944, p. 125). Later, however, he relaxes his assumption, saying that this 'test of full employment . . . means that the margin of unemployment is very small' (Beveridge, 1944, p. 126). Beveridge, and the majority of his colleagues after him, tried then to define the full-employment rate of unemployment, since full employment does not mean that there is absolutely no unemployment. 'Some margin for change and movement is needed' (Beveridge, 1944, p. 126).

This margin is defined by two factors, according to Beveridge, and the second of these factors gives rise to serious differences in the specification of the amount of unemployment that should be tolerated and defined as the full-employment rate of unemployment. The first of these factors involves seasonal unemployment; the second factor for which allowance must be made is 'the margin for change of employment incidental to progress' (Beveridge, 1944, p. 127). The question 'what is the irreducible minimum of unemployment in a community with adequate effective demand for labour?' is answered by various scholars in different ways. Beveridge himself saw fluctuations in overseas demand and industrial frictions originating in changes in the composition of the production, as the main elements. '3 per cent appears as a conservative rather than an unduly hopeful, aim to set for the average unemployment rate of the future under conditions of full employment' (Beveridge, 1944, p. 128).

It can now be understood that subject of the former section is highly relevant in this context. The irreducible and thus tolerable volume of unemployment is determinated (in modern terms) by the volume of frictional and part of structural unemployment. The empirical questions are how to define and to measure frictional unemployment, how to distinguish it from structural unemployment and what part of structural unemployment is to be considered as irreducible by public policy? These questions have been discussed at large in the previous section and are left without clear-cut answers.

Two interrelated tools are nowadays used to calculate the target rate of unemployment: the *UV*-curve (the relation between unemployment and vacancies) and the Phillips-curve (the relation between unemployment and wage-inflation). The former is discussed in the previous section. The Phillips-curve, on the other hand, does not yield a single estimate of the target rate of unemployment. This can only be calculated if an indifference curve, reflecting the policy-maker's marginal rate of substitution between a little less unemployment and a slightly faster rise in prices, is introduced (Gordon, 1967, p. 71). This means that the target rate of unemployment should be calculated assuming policy preferences on the combination of unemployment and target rates of inflation. Moreover, recent empirical investigation raise doubt, about the stability or even the existence (relevance) of the Phillips curve.

In discussions on the target rate of unemployment after 1970, it has often been suggested that it has to be set higher in the 1970s and 1980s than it was in the 1950s and 1960s. In both *UV*- and Phillips-curve analysis this is reflected by an upward shift of the empirically observed curves. Two kinds of factors are held responsible for these upward shifts. First the predominant role of expectations of inflation on wages in the recent decades and second, changes in the nature of the labour market, i.c. the influence of higher unemployment benefits and changes in the (sex- and age-) composition of labour supply.[23] A recent attempt to estimate the impact of the latter factors on the unemployment rate target is found in Scott and Laslett (1978).

Assumptions and theories on the impact of expected changes in prices on money wages, led to the introduction of the 'natural rate of unemployment' or the 'non-accelerating inflation rate of unemployment (NAIRU)'. The rate is defined as that rate of unemployment 'ground out by the Walrasian system of general equilibrium equations' (Friedman, 1968) and is determined by real factors: in particular by the costs of gathering information about job vacancies in a given market (thus, by the level of frictional and structural unemployment). Since the nominal wages that the workers are willing to accept depends in the model on the price level that they expect to prevail,[24] unemployment can only be reduced temporarily below the natural rate by expanding aggregate demand. Once workers recognise that the induced price increases lower their real wage, they demand and obtain higher nominal wages. The reduction of the real wages below the equilibrium level can be maintained only by a further increase in prices. Workers come to anticipate the inflation and act on their anticipations. Accordingly wages and prices are rising together, with real wages remaining constant and employment falling back to its equilibrium level. Hence attempts to maintain a level of unemployment below the natural rate imply an accelerating inflation.[25]

Empirical estimates of the natural rate of unemployment are based on the so called 'expectations-augmented Phillips curve'. Thirlwall (1983) convincingly argues that the natural rate derived from the expectations-augmented Phillips curve reflects not only real (structural) influences but also monetary (demand) influences. In other words that the natural rate of unemployment is influenced by factors that vary cyclically with the pressure of demand. This conclusion is consistent with our own conclusions on the specification of the *UV*-curve (see previous section).

Our imperfect knowledge of the nature of unemployment does not allow us to formulate on non-theoretical grounds a useful policy advice beyond the general and vague rule that unemployment and labour slack should be kept 'as small as possible'. Judgements on what should be seen as 'possible', in particular in combination with other policy targets, can of course be formulated, but are not the outcome of economic analyses. They imply the formulation of an hierarchy of policy targets or the specification of policy-preference curves as introduced earlier.

The unarticulated target that unemployment and labour slack should be as small as possible can be interpreted as an economic or a social imperative (or both). Economically spoken it is wise and accepted to try to use the available factor resources (including labour) as fully as possible and to maximise welfare both collectively and individually. Moreover, unemployment may diminish final demand giving rise, in turn, other things being equal, to more unemployment. Unemployment, however, is often seen in the first place as a social problem. The arguments and descriptions given by Beveridge are still valid and serve as implicit guidelines for modern analysts and politicians. Beveridge introduced his *Full Employment in a Free Society* under a theme chosen (by his wife)[26] from *Shirley* by Charlotte Brontë, 'Misery generates hate', and expresses his concern over the social, and thus economic, stability of a society characterised by mass unemployment. He explains further:

> A person who has difficulty in buying the labour that he wants, suffers inconvenience or reduction of profits. A person who cannot sell his labour is in effect told that he is of no use. The first difficulty causes annoyance or loss. The other is a personal catastrophe. This difference remains even if an adequate income is provided, by insurance or otherwise, during unemployment: idleness even on an income corrupts; the feeling of not being wanted demoralises (Beveridge, 1944, p. 19).

It is important to note that it matters whether unemployment is interpreted as an economic or a social problem. In the latter case policy-options that redistribute unemployment, e.g. by work-sharing, are effective, although they do not alter the rate of utilisation of labour resources; hence the economic problem remains.

## Notes

1. The types are abbreviated as $U_k$, $U_1, \ldots, U_0$ in order to avoid confusion with the more commonly used subscripts that refer to specific definitions, discussed further or with the statistical definitions of $U_1, U_2, \ldots, U_6$ used by the US Bureau of Labor Statistics.
2. For critical discussion de Neubourg 1988 chapter I, 'Between Pigou and Malinvaud Unemployment Theory Revisited'.
3. Both Pigou and Keynes acknowledged the existence of 'frictional unemployment', though they were not interested in its fluctuations, if any. The definition of 'frictional unemployment' will be discussed further.
4. The definition is as follows: 'Men are involuntarily unemployed if, in the event of a small rise in the price of wage-goods relatively to the money-wage, both the aggregate supply of labour willing to work for the current money-wage and the aggregate demand for it at that wage would be greater than the existing volume of employment' (Keynes, 1936, p. 15).
5. Voluntary unemployment due to the refusal or inability of a unit of labour, as a result of legislation of social practices or of combination for collective bargaining or of allow response to change or of more human obstinacy, to accept a reward corresponding to the value of the product attributable to its marginal productivity' (Keynes, 1936, p. 6).
6. 'It was puzzling to see the apparent calmness with which the conference accepted that the distinction was unhelpful' (Worswick, 1976, pp. 311–12).
7. This is not to say that lowering real wages is not a viable policy recommendation, as will be discussed in the next section.

8. The remaining part is provisionally defined as 'non-demand deficient'; the subdivision of that type of unemployment will be discussed further.
9. We will argue further that $U_n$ and $U_0$ are also strongly influenced by the level and changes in the level of aggregate demand.
10. It should be noted that seasonal unemployment is higher in recessions, due to obvious reasons related to labour dishoarding when recovery is not expected in the short term.
11. The discussion of the definition of structural unemployment should not be concluded without a reference to attempts to define the 'natural rate of unemployment' within the monetarist tradition. The natural rate of unemployment or the 'non-accelerating inflation rate of unemployment' (NAIRU) can be regarded as a proxy for the volume of unemployment due to market imperfections. It is, however, defined by means of a Phillips-curve type of analysis and therefore relates more specifically to the target rate of unemployment, which will be discussed in the next section.
12. It is interesting to consider the reasons for this failure as will be done at the end of this section.
13. Theoretically this part can also be negative, in which case, labour hoarding is measured.
14. This is not fully true. Since the vintage models regularly assume a relation between the real wages and the scrapping or the investment decisions, they regard excessive wage claims as one of the main underlying causes for at least the capital shortage unemployment.
15. One restriction has to be made in this context. Micro-oriented labour-market policy, intended to diminish structural unemployment due to labour-market imperfections, is usually not capable of reducing unemployment stemming from other origins. In this sense the Muysken-framework provide an estimate of the part of unemployment that may be combated successfully by this type of policy.
16. The volume of unemployment due to labour-market imperfections is partly a function of the cyclical situation; employers and employees are more inclined to adjust their behaviour in order to facilitate the matching process when the cyclical situation is more favourable. It is also clear that new investments decisions or decisions to make existing capital idle, are not independent from the cyclical situation. It is therefore, reasonable to state that both $U^*$ and $U^c$ have a cyclical component (see also de Neubourg 1985a, Muysken–de Neubourg 1982).
17. Resulting in perpetual transformations with economic activities and their related productive units emerging, growing and disappearing 'like trees in a forest'. 'One tree will last longer in full vigour and attain a greater size than another, but sooner or later age tells on them all' (A. Marshall, 1890, p. 315).
18. For an outspoken view in this context see Fitoussi and Georgescu-Roegen (1980).
19. Econometric models cannot provide decisive answers either, since their outcomes are very sensitive to the underlying theoretical assumptions.

20. Simultaneously with Beveridge study another was published by members of the Institute of Statistics at Oxford, who investigated the economic problems related to full-employment policy: among the authors we find F. A. Burchardt, M. Kalecki, G. D. N. Worswick, E. F. Schumacher, T. Balogh and K. Mandelbaum (F. A. Burchardt *et al.*, 1945).
21. In Sweden these issues had been discussed since the beginning of the 1930s; see E. Lundberg (1957).
22. Pigou (1945, pp. 1-3) is one of the rare exceptions. He, however applies that definition in a rather provocative way, acknowledging that 'certain economists . . . have come to use the term full employment in a special technical way' (p. 1).
23. For a critique on the assumed impact of higher unemployment benefits (see de Neubourg 1985).
24. If they anticipate an increase in the price level in the future, they will compensate for this factor by increasing their wage aspirations.
25. A compact summary of the theory in found in Addison and Siebert (1979); see also Phelps 1970.
26. Beveridge, 1944, p. 15.

## References

ABRAHAM, K. 'Structural/Frictional *vs* Deficient Demand Unemployment: Some New Evidence', *American Economic Review*, LXXIIV, (1983) pp. 708–24.

ADDISON, J. T. and SIEBERT, W. S. *The Market for Labor* (Goodyear, Santa Monica, 1979).

ARMSTRONG H. and H. TAYLOR, 'The Measurement of Different Types of Unemployment', in J. Creedy (ed.) (1981) pp. 99–127.

BERG, D. VAN DEN, 'Specification and Estimation of the Unemployment-Vacancy Curve in The Netherlands', *De Economist* (1982) pp. 397–419.

BEVERIDGE, W., *Unemployment: A Problem of Industry* (1909) republished with a new part II, (London: Longmans & Green 1930).

BEVERIDGE W., *Full Employment in a Free Society* (London: Allen Unwin, 1944).

BOWERS, J. K., 'Some Notes on Current Unemployment' in G. D. N. Worswick (ed.) *The Concept and Measurement of Involuntary Unemployment* (London: Allen & Unwin, 1975) pp. 109–33, 1976.

BROWN, A. J., 'UV-analysis' in G. D. N. Worswick, *The Concept and Measurement of Involuntary Unemployment* (London: 1975) pp. 134–45.

BURCHARDT, F. A., *et al.*, *The Economics of Full Employment* (Oxford: Blackwell, 1945).

CRAMER, U., KLAUDER, W., MERTENS, D., REIJHER, L. and SPITZNAGEL, E., 'Zum Problems der Strukturellen Arbeitslosigkeit', *Mitteilungen IAB*, 1976, I.

CRAMER, U. and EGLE, F., Zur durchschnittlichen Dauer der Arbeitslosigkeit, *Mitteilungen aus der Arbeitsmark – und Berufsforschung*, 9, Jg. 2/1976, pp. 482–95.

DAVIDSON, P., 'A Keynesian View of Patinkin's Theory of Employment', *Economic Journal*, September, 1967.

DOW, J. C. R., and DICKS-MIREAUX, L. A., 'The Excess Demand for Labour', *Oxford Economic Papers*, 10, pp. 1-33, February 1958.

DRIEHUIS, W., 'Labour Market Imbalances and Structural Unemployment', *Kyklos*, 31, 1978, pp. 638-61.

DRIEHUIS, W., 'Capital-Labour Substitution and Other Potential Determinants of Structural Employment and Unemployment', OECD, *Structural Determinants of Employment and Unemployment* (Paris: OECD, 1979).

EVANS, A. A., 'Notes on the Changing Relationship between Registered Unemployment and Notified Vacancies: 1961-1966 and 1966-1971', *Economica*, vol. 44, May 1977, pp. 179-96.

FELS, G. and WEISS, F., 'Structural Change and Employment: The Lesson of West Germany', in H. Giersch (ed.) *Capital shortage and Unemployment in the World Economy* (Tübingen 1978) pp. 31-53.

FITOUSSI, J. P. and GEORGESCU-ROEGEN, N., 'Structure and Involuntary Unemployment', in E. Malinvaud and J. P. Fitoussi, *Unemployment in Western Countries* (London: Macmillan, 1980) pp. 206-77.

FOSTER, J. I., 'The Behaviour of Unemployment and Unfilled Vacancies: Great Britain 1958-1971 - A Comment', *Economic Journal*, 83, no. 329, pp. 192-201, March 1973.

FRIEDMAN, M. (1968), 'The Role of Monetary Policy', *American Economic Review*, 58, pp. 1-17.

GILPATRICK, E. G., 'Structural Unemployment and Aggregate Demand' (John Hopkins, 1966).

GORDON, R. A., *The Goal of Full Employment* (New York: Wiley, 1967).

GRUEN, F. H., 'Structural Unemployment as a Rival Explanation - A Survey of an Inconclusive Argument', in H. Giersch (ed.) *Capital Shortage and Unemployment in the World Economy* (Tubingen: Mohr 1978).

GUJARATA, D., 'The Behaviour of Unemployment and Unfilled Vacancies', *Economic Journal*, March 1972, pp. 195-204.

HAHN, F. H. (1978) 'On Non-Weberian Equilibria', *Review of Economic Studies*, pp. 1-17.

HALL, R. E., 'Why is Unemployment Rate so High at Full Employment?' *Brookings Papers on Economic Activity*, 3: 1970, pp. 369-402.

HANSEN, B., 'Excess Demand, Unemployment, Vacancies and Wages', *The Quarterly Journal of Economics*, 1970, 84, no. 1, pp. 1-23.

HARTOG, H. DEN and TJAN, H. S., 'Investments, Wages, Prices, and Demand for Labour, A Clay-clay Vintage model for the Netherlands', *De Economist*, 1976, 1/2 issue.

HARTOG, J., *Tussen vraag en aanbod* (Leiden: Stenfert Kroese, 1980).

HILL, M. J., HARRISON, R. M., SARGEANT, A. V. and TALBAT, V., *Men out of Work: a Study of Unemployment in Three English Towns* (Cambridge University Press, 1973).

HILL, M. J., 'Can we Distinguish Voluntary from Involuntary Unemployment?' in G. D. N. Worswick (ed.) *The Concept and Measurement of Involuntary Unemployment* (London: Allen & Unwin, 1976).

HOLDEN, K. and PEEL, D. A., 'The Determinants of Unemployment and the UV-relationship', *Applied Economics*, 1975, p. 7.

HOLT, C. C. and SEARCH J., 'Phillips' Wage Relation and Union Influence: Theory and Evidence' in E. S. Phelps *et al. Micro Foundations of Employment and Inflation Theory* (London: 1970) pp. 53–123.

HUGHES, J. J., 'The Use of Vacancy Statistics in Classifying and Measuring Structural and Frictional Unemployment in Great Britain, 1958–1972', in *Bulletin of Economic Research*, 26pp. 12–33, 1974.

JENNESS, R. A., *Manpower and Employment: Problems and Prospects* (Paris: OECD, 1978).

KAHN, G. A., 'International Differences in Wage Behaviour: Real, Nominal, or Exaggerated?' *American Economic Review*, 1984, no. 2, papers and proceedings, pp. 155–9.

KEYNES, J. M., *The General Theory of Employment Interest and Money*, (London: Macmillan, 1936).

KLAASSEN, C. and HEYKE, H. 'Economic Growth and Employment' in G. R. Denton and J. J. N. Cooper (eds) *The European Economy beyond the Crisis: From Stabilisation to Structural Change* (Brugge: 1977).

KLERK, R. A. de, LAAN, H. B. M. VAN DER and THIO, K. B. T., 'Unemployment in the Netherlands: a Criticism of the den Hartog–Tjan Vintage Model', *Cambridge Journal of Economics*, 1977.

KUIPERS, S. K., and BUDDENBERG, F. H., 'Unemployment on Account of Market Imperfections in The Netherlands since the Second World War', *De Economist*, 126, 1978, pp. 380–412.

MADDISON, A., 'Monitoring the Labour Market: A Proposal for a Comprehensive Approach in Official Statistics', *Review of Income and Wealth*, June 1980.

MADDISON, A., 'Why Do Unemployment Rates Differ?', *Shell Lecture*, University of Buckingham, 25 October 1983.

MALINVAUD, E., 'The Theory of Unemployment Reconsidered', *Yrjö Johnsson Lectures* (Oxford: Basil Blackwell, 1977).

MALINVAUD, E., 'Wages and Unemployment', *Economic Journal*, 1982, no. 365, pp. 1–12.

MANEVAL, H., 'Arbeitslosigkeit'; *Handwörterbuch der Wirtschaftswissenschaft*, hrsg. von W. Albers *et al.*, Stuttgart, pp. 267–79, 1977.

MUYSKEN, J. and NEUBOURG, C. DE, 'Qualitative Structural Unemployment in the Netherlands 1955–1979', memorandum from the Institute of Economic Research, no. 75, Groningen, 1981.

MUYSKEN J., NEUBOURG, C. DE and DEN BURG, H. VAN 'Qualitative Structural Unemployment in the Netherlands 1955–1980, in Van der burg *et al. The Volume and Composition of Structural unemployment in the Netherlands* 1950–1980, N.P.A.O. publication no. 11 (Den Haag: Staatsuitgeverij, 1982).

NEUBOURG, C. DE, 'The Origin and Insignificance of Unemployment due to Labour Market Imperfections', *Economist*, 1985, 1.

NEUBOURG C. DE, *Unemployment, Labour Utilisation and Labour Market Accounting: Theory, Evidence, and Policy* (Amsterdam, New York: North-Holland, 1988).

OECD, *Labour Supply, Growth Constraints and Work Sharing* (Paris: OECD, 1982).

PARICK, A., 'The Relation between Unemployment and Vacancies: A Comment', *Applied Economics*, 1977, pp. 77–90).

PHELPS, E. S. (ED.) *Microeconomic Foundations of Employment and Inflation Theory* (London, Macmillan, 1970).
PIGOU, A. C., *The Theory of Unemployment* (London: 1933).
RIESE, M., 'Ursachen und Erscheinungsformen der Arbeitslosigkeit; Veröffentlichungen des Osterreichischen Instituts für Arbeitsmarktpolitik', Heft XXVI, Linz, 1980.
ROBINSON, J., '*Essays in the theory of Employment*' (New York: 1937).
SCOTT, M. and LASLETT, R. A., 'Can We Get Back to Full Employment?' (London: Macmillan, 1978).
SIEGERS, J. J., 'On Kuipers' and Buddenberg's Estimation of Unemployment due to Market Imperfection in the Netherlands since the Second World War', *De Economist*, 128, 1980, pp. 563-58.
SIMLER, N. S., 'Long-Term Unemployment, the Structural Hypothesis and Public Policy', *American Economic Review*, 1964, no. 6, pp. 985-1001.
STANDING, G., 'The Nation of Voluntary Unemployment', *International Labour Review*, 1981, no. 5, pp. 563-79.
TAYLOR, J., 'The Behaviour of Unemployment and Unfilled Vacancies: Great Britain, 1958-71: An Alternative View', *Economic Journal*, 1972, pp. 1352-65.
THIRWALL, A. P., 'Types of Unemployment: With Special Reference to "Unemployment in Great Britain"', *Scottish Journal of Political Economy*, 1969, vol. 16, no. 1, pp. 20-49.
THIRLWALL, A. P., 'What are Estimates of the Natural Rate of Unemployment Measuring?', *Oxford Bulletin of Economics and Statistics*, 1983, pp. 173-9.
TURVEY, R., 'Structural Change and Structural Unemployment', *International Labour Review*, September/October, 1977.
WARREN, R. S., 'The Behaviour of Unemployment and Unfilled Vacancies in Great Britain, A Search-Turnover View', *Applied Economics*, 1977, pp. 237-42.

# COMMENT ON CHAPTERS 5, 6 AND 7

**David Heathfield**

Each of these three chapters deals with the inadequacies of measures of recorded unemployment. Taylor implicitly, and de Neubourg explicitly, suggest that we require a finer breakdown of unemployment data into categories which are useful for policy information. Any tool will be rough and ready and we are sure to be disappointed if we seek perfect idealised theoretical categories, empirically operational categories and politically useful categories of any economic variable. What needs to be demonstrated is that current methods can be improved upon and that these alternatives prove useful to some degree, for theoretical, empirical and policy analysis. Both Taylor and de Neubourg make much of the shortcomings of $U-V$ analysis but it is not easy to suggest an alternative. Neither writer seems to feel that input–output techniques may prove useful here.

In the case of Taylor's chapter the distinction between 'structural' and 'demand-deficient' unemployment is central. There is, he argues, no satisfactory way of sharply delineating them and that increasing aggregate demand can help to decrease them both. However, the word 'aggregate' provides some difficulties here. Both writers follow Keynes in suggesting that boosting *aggregate* demand may be inappropriate and that a sectoral approach may be necessary. Only those sectors with excess capacity (high elasticity of supply in Keynes's words) are suitable candidates for increasing demand. This is important since, once the disaggregated approach is admitted, the distinction between 'structural' and 'demand-deficient' unemployment virtually disappears.

Taylor's arguments about deficient demand lead him to estimate the growth of capacity necessary for full employment to be regained and maintained. This estimate is based on past experience but, as de Neubourg points out in his chapter, if technological progress is 'embodied' then any significant expansion in capacity may be more labour-saving than currently installed capacity. Thus growth rates would have to be rather higher than those estimated by Taylor. The choice of technique is clearly important but is not dealt with in these papers. What is surprising is that with high levels of unemployment and high real-interest rates the choice of technique should be labour-saving.

The switch from arguments about aggregate demand to arguments about growth rates implies some connection between them - either that or it is necessary to investigate the supply side much more fully. Unfortunately, neither writer deals with an explicitly open economy and hence the limitations which this 'openness' imposes on various policy options are not discussed.

de Neubourg goes somewhat further than Taylor in introducing the voluntary/involuntary distinction. This is clearly important in that it both colours and informs public attitudes to the unemployed. In particular, the costs of unemployment are allocated primarily to the tax-payer when it is deemed voluntary and allocated primarily to the unemployed when it is involuntary. It is not however very clear how these categories (voluntary/involuntary) match up to the analytical categories discussed above (frictional, structural, demand deficient, etc.). What is clear is that some involuntary unemployment may be necessary (i.e. frictional) and some may be unnecessary (i.e. due to deficient aggregate demand). It should be possible to agree that involuntary unnecessary unemployment should be reduced to a minimum. What is not clear is how this could be identified and rectified. Both chapters clear a great deal of ground and contain a number of interesting and potentially operational ideas.

The chapter by Bosworth and Westaway also deals with inadequacy of recorded unemployment but this is in terms of its failure truly to reflect underemployment by neglecting hidden unemployment or labour hoarding. The degree of underemployment is in some ways a more relevant variable than the identification of those wholly without a 'job'. But once again there are thorny definitional problems, not least among them the definition of hoarding itself.

Bosworth and Westaway approach the problem by identifying differences between 'capacity' and 'actual' labour-output ratios. This they agree is not easy to justify, particularly as, with substitution, we cannot say which factor is hoarded. Nor do we have any reliable guide to 'capacity labour output ratios'. Bosworth and Westaway argue that the appropriate measure of actual labour input is the product of number of men, average working hours and work effort. This last is rarely available and hence is omitted. Perhaps this is just as well since if effort could be measured then it would be the best indicator of labour hoarding - idle workers expend zero effort. Its inclusion into the labour-input measure would therefore have denied the authors' premise that 'hoarding' is part of the residual of their regression equation.

This assumption is anyway rather heroic but without this kind of heroism very little empirical work would get done in economics. That is not to say their approach could not be improved upon. As they themselves suggest, it may have been preferable to have estimated a frontier production function rather than impose the usual error term properties on 'hoarding' or undercapacity working.

What is clear from their chapter is that hoarding is often a substitute for unemployment - in some countries much more so than in others. This means that the degree of underemployment is not reliably indicated by recorded unemployment and, more importantly, a change in hoarding policy by firms would cause the recorded unemployment figures to change with no underlying economic counterpart.

# 8 Trade Unions, Investment and Employment in a Small Open Economy: A Dutch Perspective*

C. B. Mulder and F. van der Ploeg

ABSTRACT

A model of a small open economy with a well-developed supply-side and demand-side is presented. There are many firms engaged in monopolistic competition, who take the wage and aggregate demand as given, when deciding on their labour demand and investment decisions. Aggregate supply depends on capital, the producers' real wage and aggregate demand; investment depends on what firms expect the real wage, aggregate demand, real interest rates and investment subsidies to be in current and future periods. Aggregate demand depends on disposable income, wealth, public spending, foreign income, the real exchange rate and the world real-interest rate. There is one monopoly union, who chooses the consumers real wage to maximise a utilitarian utility function subject to the constraints describing the rest of the economy. Its behaviour is time inconsistent, since it has an incentive to announce a low wage and then, once capital has been accumulated, renege and cream off the quasi-rent of a more-or-less fixed factor by demanding a higher wage. The time-consistent behaviour is credible but is inefficient due to much lower levels of capital, employment and activity. The results of this analysis are used to describe the Dutch rise in unemployment. This analysis pays particular attention to the level of real benefits, to the wedge between producer and consumer wages, consisting of employers' and employees' social security contributions, direct and indirect taxes and the real exchange rate, to world trade, to investment subsidies and to

* An earlier version of this chapter was presented at a conference on 'Unemployment in Europe' at Limburg University, Maastricht, 17–19 April 1986. We are grateful for the comments of the participants and in particular thank Piet Keizer for his discussion of the paper.

demand management. Sociological changes, to explain a move from 'rules' to 'discretion', may also be important.

## 1 INTRODUCTION

As in most European countries, unemployment in Holland has increased considerably in the past ten to fifteen years. This phenomenon is of major concern and warrants explanation. This chapter sets out to explain employment and unemployment in a small open economy with powerful trade unions. It provides a framework in which various essential features of a small open economy, like that of Holland, are imbedded. World trade is a dominating factor on the demand side, whereas unions and long-run labour-supply are dominating factors on the supply side. The various instruments which the government has available (tax rates, levels of benefits, investment subsidies, public-sector expenditure and employment) affect both sides of the economy. The investment behaviour of firms is an important link between present and future.

The formal framework developed in this chapter consists of a model with a well-developed supply side and a demand side. The supply side is built around firms engaged in monopolistic competition. This provides a role for demand. The firms take the wage rates and aggregate demand as given when deciding on their labour demand and investment decisions. Aggregate supply depends on capital, the producer's real wage and aggregate demand; investment depends on what firms expect the real wage, aggregate demand and investment subsidies to be in current and future periods. Aggregate demand in turn depends, in a conventional way, on disposable income, wealth, public spending, foreign income, the real exchange rate and world interest rates. In combination with a money-demand equation and the various budget definitions this system can be solved for the real exchange rate, the producers' real wage, output and labour demand in terms of the exogenous variables (the various tax and social security contribution rates, investment subsidies, benefit levels, public-sector expenditure and employment, the real world-interest-rate, foreign income and labour supply) and in terms of the endogenous variables described by the state equations (the capital stock, wealth, and the marginal value of capital). The monopoly union, the Stackelberg leader in the underlying game chooses the consumers' real wage to maximise an expected utility function subject to the constraints describing the rest of the economy. In other words the interaction of the demand and supply side of the economy leads to a complicated intertemporal labour-demand schedule. This labour-demand schedule depends on the level of the consumers' real wage rate which the firms expect the union to set. From the point of view of the union this labour-demand schedule is the trade-off which it faces between employment and wages. The union will set current and future wage rates to maximise the expected utility of her reference group, subject to the labour-demand schedule. The more emphasis the union puts on employment, the lower will be the wage-rate it chooses and vice versa: the smaller the emphasis on employment the higher the wage rates.

In the absence of binding contracts the union's behaviour is time inconsistent (Kydland and Prescott, 1977) since it has an incentive to announce a low wage and then, once capital has been accumulated renege and cream off the quasi-rent of a more or less fixed factor by demanding a higher wage. The time consistent outcome is credible, but is inefficient due to much lower levels of capital, employment and activity. This is the paradox of the disadvantageous power of the monopoly union.

The results of this paper are used to analyse the major empirical tendencies of the past decades in Holland, in a coherent way; the rise in unemployment and the large drop in investment, the increase in the wedge between real producers' and real consumers' wages (consisting of the employers' and employees' social security contributions, the wage tax, indirect taxes and the real exchange rate), the large changes in world trade growth and real world interest rates, the continuous rise in public sector employment and real benefits. Attention is paid as well to sociological changes which might explain a move from the time inconsistent to the time consistent outcome.

The analysis put forward in this paper assumes a rational trade union, which uses its power to achieve its goals. Unemployment is henceforward the consequence of a rational choice by the union, a choice between wages and (un)employment. What does this approach imply for the causes of unemployment? First, it should be remarked that this assumption does not imply that the union ought to be blamed for the rise in unemployment experienced, for example, in Holland. If the union represents employees well, then employees should in general be satisfied with the choice and accept the consequences, of which unemployment is (the unpleasant) one. Next it does not imply that the unions caused the increase in unemployment. There are the other factors which influence the trade-off between (un)employment and wages and thereby the choice the unions make. These trade-off-influencing factors included the technology describing the production side of the economy, external influences such as real world-interest-rates and foreign income and government behaviour. By changing benefit levels, tax rates, investment subsidies, public-sector-employment and public expenditure, the government changes the labour-demand schedule. By changing the level of benefits and public-sector employment the government can change elements in the union's utility function in a direct way as well. For example reduced benefits will increase the emphasis which unions put on employment and induce them to reduce their wage claims which indeed will improve the employment situation. Another factor influencing unemployment is the solution concept of the model. For example a breakdown in the social contract between employers and trade union, to stick to the time-inconsistent solution and the other institutional features imbedded in the model (i.e. the unions have no direct say in the employment or investment decisions by the firms) may cause extra unemployment if the firms change their assessment of the credibility of unions and thereby make the time-consistent solution more appropriate.

In explaining the rise in unemployment in the Netherlands we will in particular stress the role the government played by enlarging the wedge between producers' and consumers' wage rates and by increasing the level of real benefits, and the breakdown in the social contract between employers and the trade union(s) at a time when the government had lost most of her direct institutional impact on the wage-setting process.

The chapter is organised as follows. The model is presented in sections 2–6. Section 2 deals with the behaviour of the monopolistically competitive firms notably their investment behaviour and demand for labour. In section 3 the macroeconomic aspects of aggregate demand are explained and the results of the interaction with the behaviour of firms is investigated. In section 4, unions enter the analysis, and the time-inconsistency of their behaviour is briefly discussed. Section 5 deals with credible wage formation. Confusion between real and nominal magnitudes is briefly discussed in section 6. The formal analysis of sections 2–6 is used in section 7 to explain the major empirical trends in the Netherlands. Section 8 concludes the chapter.

## 2 MONOPOLISTIC COMPETITION AND INVESTMENT BEHAVIOUR

Consider $N$ firms involved in monopolistic competition. To a certain extent each firm can carve out a part of the market as products are not homogeneous. The standard analysis (McDonald and Solow, 1981) is extended, since each firm also faces an investment problem with internal adjustment costs (Gould, 1968). The demand curve for the products of firm $n$ is given by:

$$y_n = D(y, P_n/P) = (y/N)(P_n/P)^{-\varepsilon(y)}, \qquad \varepsilon_y \geqslant 0 \tag{8.1}$$

where $y$ denotes aggregate demand in the economy, $P_n$ denotes the price charged by firm $n$ and $P$ denotes the average price level. The technology of firm $n$ is described by a concave production function, $y_n = f(k_n, l_n)$ where $k_n$ denotes the capital stock of firm $n$ and $l_n$ denotes employment in firm $n$, with constant returns to scale and the usual neoclassical properties. Adjustment of the capital stock is costly. The larger the adjustment the higher the costs incurred. This can be formalised by including a convex internal adjustment cost function $\phi(i_n)$ in the profit function of firm $n$, where $\phi(0)=0$, $\phi''>0$ and $i_n$ denotes gross investment of firm $n$. Firms have some monopoly power in the product market but not in the labour market and face a given wage. Each firm maximises the discounted value of its profit stream:

$$\underset{P_n, l_n, i_n}{\text{Max}} \int_0^\infty e^{-rt}\pi_n \, dt, \qquad \pi_n = P_n y_n - Wl_n - q[i_n + \phi(i_n)] \tag{8.2}$$

subject to the capital accumulation equation:

$$\dot{k}_n = i_n - \delta k_n, \qquad k_n(0) = k_n^0 \tag{8.3}$$

where $r$, $\delta$, $\pi_n$, $W$ and $q$ denote the rate of interest, the depreciation rate, profits of firm $n$, the nominal wage paid by the firm and the price of investment goods, respectively. If the Hamiltonian of firm $n$ is defined as

$$\begin{aligned} H_n \equiv\ & P_n f(k_n, l_n) - Wl_n - q[i_n + \phi(i_n)] \\ & - \chi_n[f(k_n, l_n) - D(y, P_n/P)] + \lambda'_n(i_n - \delta k_n) \end{aligned} \tag{8.4}$$

where $\chi_n$ is a Lagrange multiplier and $\lambda'_n$ is the nominal shadow price of capital for firm $n$, then the optimality conditions are $\partial H_n/\partial P_n = \partial H_n/\partial l_n = \partial H_n/\partial i_n = 0$ and $r\lambda'_n - \dot{\lambda}'_n = \partial H_n/\partial k_n$. They yield in symmetric equilibrium

$$P_n = P, \qquad l = Nl_n, \qquad k = Nk_n, \qquad \lambda'_n = \lambda', \qquad \chi_n = P/\varepsilon;$$
$$f_l(k, l) = W^P/[1-\varepsilon^{-1}(y)] \tag{8.5}$$

where $W^P = W/P$ is the producers' real wage, $\phi'(i_n) = (\lambda'_n - q)/q$ or

$$i = I\left[\frac{\lambda-(1-\sigma)}{1-\sigma}\right], \qquad I(0)=0, \qquad I' = N/\phi'' \tag{8.6}$$

where $q \equiv P(1-\sigma)$, $\sigma$ is the investment subsidy rate and $\lambda \equiv \lambda'/P$ is the real shadow price of capital, and

$$f_k(k, l)[1-\varepsilon^{-1}(y)] = (r+\delta-\dot{P}/P-\dot{\lambda}/\lambda)\lambda \tag{8.7}$$

Equation (8.5) says that the marginal revenue product of labour equals the real wage, so that the demand for labour can be written as

$$l = kh(W^P, y), \qquad h_{W^P} < 0, \qquad h_y \geqslant 0 \tag{8.8}$$

The advantage of a framework based on monopolistic competition is that the demand for labour not only decreases with the real producers' wage ($h_{W^P} < 0$) but also increases with the aggregate demand for goods ($h_y \geqslant 0$), since it is assumed that the elasticity of demand for each firm is an increasing function of aggregate demand ($\varepsilon'(y) \geqslant 0$). Nickell (1985) shows that the framework encompasses two interesting alternatives. Normal cost pricing assumes that the price mark-up;

$$P/W = [1-\varepsilon^{-1}(y)]^{-1}/f_l(1, \tilde{f}(y, k)) \tag{8.9}$$

where $y/k = f(l, l/k)$ yields $l/k = \tilde{f}(y/k)$, is independent of demand, so that $\varepsilon'(y) > 0$ and therefore $h_y > 0$ must hold. Perfect competition leads to price equals marginal cost, so that $\varepsilon(y) = \infty$ and therefore $h_y = 0$. Equation (8.6) says that, when the marginal value of capital exceeds the real cost of investment goods, investment takes place. Equation (8.7) says that the marginal revenue product of capital has to match the user cost of capital, where the latter consists of the rental charge plus the depreciation charge minus the capital gains term. Note that the firm will not, due to the presence of internal adjustment costs, adjust its capital stock instantaneously. The fact that adjustment costs increase with the absolute size of the rate of investment or disinvestment limits the size of the firm.

The behaviour of the firm can be described by the labour-demand curve, (8.8), the capital accumulation equation:

$$\dot{k} = I\left[\frac{\lambda-(1-\sigma)}{1-\sigma}\right] - \delta k, \qquad k(0) = k^0, \tag{8.10}$$

and the shadow price equation:

$$\dot{\lambda} = (r^* + \delta)\lambda - g(W^P, y), \qquad \lim_{t\to\infty} e^{-r^* t}\lambda(t)k(t) = 0 \tag{8.11}$$

where $r^* = r - \dot{P}/P$ is the real rate of interest given by the world real rate of interest and $g(W^P, y) \equiv f_k(l, h(W^P, y))(1-\varepsilon^{-1}(y))$, $g_{W^P} < 0$, $g_y \geqslant 0$ gives the marginal revenue product of capital.

The steady-state investment rate is just sufficient to provide for depreciation, $i(\infty) = \delta k(\infty)$, and this raises the shadow price of capital above the price of investment goods, $\lambda(\infty) = 1 - \sigma + \phi'(\delta k(\infty))$. Upon substitution in (8.11), one obtains the steady-state levels of the capital stock:

$$k(\infty) = K^{\infty}(\overset{-}{W}{}^P, \overset{+}{y}, \overset{-}{r}{}^*, \overset{+}{\sigma}), \tag{8.12}$$

and of output

$$y(\infty) = K^{\infty}(W^P, y, r^*, \sigma)f(1, h(W^P, y)) \equiv Y^{\infty}(\overset{-}{W}{}^P, \overset{+}{y}, \overset{-}{r}{}^*, \overset{+}{\sigma}) \tag{8.13}$$

Hence, an increase in the real wage which firms have to pay or the real interest rate and a reduction in investment subsidies or aggregate demand leads to higher levels of capital, employment and output. Capital formation clearly accentuates the adverse consequences of higher real wage rates on employment. The determinant of (8.10)–(8.11) is $-\delta(r^* + \delta) < 0$, so the steady-state is a saddlepoint. Hence, capital is a backward-looking variable and investment (or $\lambda$) is a forward-looking variable. It follows that investment today depends on expectations of the producers' real wage, investment subsidies and aggregate demand tomorrow.

## 3 THE DEMAND-SIDE OF A SMALL OPEN ECONOMY

Section 2 described the supply side of the economy. This section describes the demand side. The economy is a small open economy with highly integrated capital markets and perfect substitution between home and foreign bonds, so that the home real interest rate is pegged to the world real interest rate (as it is assumed that the expected depreciation of the real exchange rate is zero). The rest of the economy is described by the following equations:

$$y = c(\overset{+}{y}^{d}, \overset{-}{r}^{*}, \overset{+}{a}_{p}) + I\left(\frac{\lambda-(1-\sigma)}{1-\sigma}\right) + \phi(i) + g$$

$$+\, x\left(\overset{+}{y}^{*}, \frac{p^{*}\overset{+}{e}}{P}\right) - m\left(\overset{+}{y}, \frac{p^{*}\overset{-}{e}}{P}\right)$$

$$= y\left(\overset{+}{\lambda}, \overset{+}{a}_{p}, \overset{-}{t}_{1}, \overset{-}{t}_{2}, \overset{-}{t}_{3}, \overset{-}{t}_{4}, \overset{+}{\sigma}, \overset{+}{g}, \overset{+}{l}_{g}, \overset{+}{b}^{c}, \overset{+}{n}, \overset{-}{r}^{*}, \overset{+}{y}^{*}, \frac{p^{*}\overset{+}{e}}{P}, \overset{+}{W}^{p}\right) \tag{8.14}$$

$$M/P^{c} = l(y\overset{+}{P}/P^{c}, \overset{-}{r}, \overset{+}{a}_{p}) \tag{8.15}$$

$$P^{c} = P^{\beta}(p^{*}e)^{1-\beta}(1+t_{3}) \tag{8.16}$$

$$y^{d} = b_{c}(n-l-l_{g})\frac{P^{c}}{P} + W^{P}(l+l_{g})(1-t_{1})(1-t_{2}) + \pi\frac{(1-t_{4})}{P} + r^{*}a_{p} \tag{8.17}$$

$$\dot{a}_{p} \approx r^{*}a_{f} + W^{p}(l+l_{g})(1-t_{1}(1-t_{2}) + (n-l-l_{g})b^{c}\frac{P^{c}}{P}$$

$$+ (1-t_{4})\frac{\pi}{P} - (1+t_{3})c \tag{8.18}$$

$$a_{f} \approx y - [i+\phi(i)] - c - g_{c} + r^{*}a_{f} \tag{8.19}$$

$$W^{c}P^{c} = W^{p}P(1-t_{1})(1-t_{2}), \qquad t = \frac{W^{p}}{W^{c}} \tag{8.20}$$

$c$ real consumption[1]
$y^{d}$ real disposable income[2]
$a_{p}$ real private sector asset holdings ($a_{p} = a_{g} + a_{f}$)
$a_{g}$ real public sector debt
$a_{f}$ real Dutch asset holdings
$g$ real public sector expenditure (using $p$ as deflator)
$x$ real exports

$y^*$ world real income
$p^*$ foreign price level
$e$ nominal exchange rate
$\frac{p^*e}{P}$ real exchange rate
$m$ real imports[3]
$M$ nominal stock of high powered money
$P^c$ consumers price index (geometrically weighted)
$b^c$ the real level of unemployment benefits ($p^c$ is the deflator)
$n$ supply of labour
$l_g$ public sector employment
$t_1$ rate of employers and employees social security contributions
$t_2$ wage tax rate
$t_3$ rate of indirect taxation
$t_4$ profit tax
$W^c$ real consumers wage ($W^c = W/P^c$)
$t$ wedge between real producers' and consumers' wages

Equation (3.1) is the *IS*-curve, which shows that aggregate demand increases when, disposable income, real wealth, public spending (on goods), investment subsidies, the marginal value of capital, labour supply, public-sector employment or world income increases and when the real exchange rate depreciates. Equation (8.15) is the *LM*-curve, which shows that the real demand for cash balances increases with real income and wealth and decreases with the nominal interest rate. In the absence of any confusion between real and nominal magnitudes the monetary part of the model is separable from the real part, inflation is entirely a monetary phenomenon and therefore follows from the *LM*-curve. Equation (8.16) is based on Cobb–Douglas preferences and shows that the consumers' price index is a geometrically weighted average of the price of home and imported goods, plus a percentage to allow for the rate of indirect taxation. Equation (8.17) defines real disposable income, which consists of benefit income for the unemployed, after tax income for the private and public sector employed, after tax profit income and real income from asset holdings (private sector labour demand and profits can be solved from (8.2) and (8.8)). Equations (8.18) and (8.19) define respectively the private sector asset holdings and the net Dutch asset holdings. The increase in private-sector asset holdings corresponds to the increase in holdings of foreign assets and public debt. They follow from the private- and public-sector budget constraints.

Finally equation (8.20) defines the 'wedge' between what a firm pays a worker and what a worker receives in his pocket. The logarithm of this wedge can be approximated by:

$$\ln t = \ln \frac{W^p}{W^c} \approx t_1 + t_2 + t_3 + (1-\beta)\log\left(\frac{p^*e}{P}\right), \tag{8.21}$$

so that the wedge increases when the real exchange rate depreciates or when any of the three tax rates increases. Obviously a larger wedge will lead to more unemployment (see section 4).

Intersection of the aggregate demand schedule (8.14) and the aggregate supply schedule $y = kf(1, h(tW^c, y)) \equiv kF(tW^c)$ ensures goods market equilibrium and yields the equilibrium real exchange rate,

$$\frac{p^*e}{P} = \varepsilon(\overset{+}{k}, \overset{-}{\lambda}, \overset{-}{a_p}, \overset{+/-}{t_1}, \overset{+/-}{t_2}, \overset{+/-}{t_3}, \overset{+/-}{t_4}, \overset{-}{\sigma}, \overset{-}{g}, \overset{-}{l_g}, \overset{-}{b^c}, \overset{-}{n}, \overset{+}{r^*}, \overset{+}{y^*}, \overset{-}{W^c}) \tag{8.22}$$

producers real wage,

$$\begin{aligned} W^p &= tW^c \\ &= W^p(\overset{+}{k}, \overset{-}{\lambda}, \overset{-}{a_p}, \overset{+}{t_1}, \overset{+}{t_2}, \overset{+}{t_3}, \overset{+}{t_4}, \overset{-}{\sigma}, \overset{-}{g}, \overset{-}{l_g}, \overset{-}{b^c}, \overset{-}{n}, \overset{+}{r^*}, \overset{-}{y^*}, \overset{+}{W^c}) \end{aligned} \tag{8.23}$$

level of activities,

$$y = \tilde{y}(\overset{+}{k}, \overset{+}{\lambda}, \overset{+}{a_p}, \overset{-}{t_1}, \overset{-}{t_2}, \overset{-}{t_3}, \overset{-}{t_4}, \overset{+}{\sigma}, \overset{+}{g}, \overset{+}{l_g}, \overset{+}{b^c}, \overset{+}{n}, \overset{-}{r^*}, \overset{+}{y^*}, \overset{-}{W^c}) \tag{8.24}$$

and labour demand (by (8.8)),

$$l = L(\overset{+}{k}, \overset{+}{\lambda}, \overset{+}{a_p}, \overset{-}{t_1}, \overset{-}{t_2}, \overset{-}{t_3}, \overset{-}{t_4}, \overset{+}{\sigma}, \overset{+}{g}, \overset{+}{l_g}, \overset{+}{b^c}, \overset{+}{n}, \overset{-}{r^*}, \overset{+}{y^*}, \overset{-}{W^c}) \tag{8.25}$$

An increase in aggregate demand, caused by an increase in public spending, world activity, wealth, investment subsidies, benefits, labour supply, government employment or the marginal value of capital to the firm or caused by a fall in the rate of social security contribution, direct tax rate or the world real interest rate, and a reduction in aggregate supply, caused by a fall in the capital stock or an increase in any of the four tax rates or the real consumers' wage, leads to an incipient excess demand for goods, which is choked off by a real appreciation of the exchange rate. This leads to a fall in the wedge between the producers' and the consumers' real wage, over and above any changes in the wedge that causes the initial incipient excess demand for goods. Hence, the employment-generating effects of an increase in capital or a reduction in the wedge are attenuated by the associated depreciation of the real exchange rate. Also in a small open economy, increases in aggregate demand, e.g. due to increases in public spending or world income, increase employment and output, since the associated appreciation reduces the 'wedge'.

## 4 TIME-INCONSISTENCY OF THE OPTIMAL WAGES OF A MONOPOLY UNION

The small open economy has one dominant trade-union movement, which looks after the interests of both employed and unemployed workers. It has monopoly power on the labour market, so that it can effectively set any consumers' real wage it wishes. In choosing its wage the union takes account of the investment and employment decisions of the 'fringe' of monopolistically competitive firms and of the aggregate demand side of the economy, so the trade union is completely rational. It maximises a quasi-concave utility function:

$$\operatorname*{Max}_{W^c} \int_0^\infty e^{-r^* t} U(W^c, l)\, \mathrm{d}t \tag{8.26}$$

subject to the reduced-form relationships (8.8), (8.10), (8.11), (8.18) and (8.23). For example, the union may attempt to maximise the total wage bill (e.g. Dunlop, 1944), total rent, that is surplus income over the wage bill under perfect competition in the labour market (e.g. de Menil, 1971) or a more general Stone–Geary utility function that allows for subsistence levels of wages and employment and the importance of supernumerary wages and employment (e.g. Pencavel, 1984). Alternatively, the private-sector trade-union maximises the expected utility of a member of the reference group of the union (e.g. McDonald and Solow, 1981; Oswald, 1985) of the form:

$$U(W^c, l) = \frac{l}{n - l_g} u(W^c) + \frac{(n - l - l_g)}{n - l_g} u(b^c), \qquad u' > 0, \qquad u'' \leq 0 \tag{8.27}$$

where $n$ denotes labour supply, $l$ private sector employment, $l_g$ government sector employment and $b^c$ denotes the level of real unemployment benefits. $l/(n-l_g)$ is taken as the probability of a member of the reference group of being employed and $(n-l-l_g)/(n-l_g)$ as the probability of being unemployed. It is assumed that the trade unions reference-group includes all private-sector employees ($l$) and all unemployed $(n-l-l_g)$. The union effectively acts as a Stackelberg leader and the rest of the economy as followers.

It will be assumed, for simplicity, that the elasticity of demand for each firm is constant ($\varepsilon_y = 0$) and that wealth effects in consumption are, due to capital market imperfections, fairly small ($c_3 \cong 0$). The Hamiltonian for the monopoly union can then be defined as:

$$H^u = \frac{k}{n-l_g} h(W^p(\cdot))[u(W^c) - u(b^c)] + \mu\left[I\left(\frac{\lambda-(1-\sigma)}{1-\sigma}\right) - \delta k\right] + \eta[(r^* + \delta)\lambda - g(W^p(\cdot))] + \text{constant} \tag{8.28}$$

where $\mu$ and $\eta$ are the union's shadow-price for capital and the firm's shadow-price of capital. Hence, on the assumption of an interior solution, the following are necessary conditions for optimality: $\partial^2 H^u/\partial^2 W^c < 0$, $\partial H^u/\partial W^c = 0$, or

$$\frac{u(W^c) - u(b^c)}{u'(W^c)} = \frac{h(tW^c) - [\eta(n-l_g)g'(tW^c)/ku'(tW^c)]}{h'(tW^c)\, W^p_{15}(k, \lambda, a_p, t_1, t_2, t_3, t_4, \sigma, g, l_g, b^c, n, r^*, y^*, W^c)} > 0, \tag{8.29}$$

$$\dot{\mu} = r^*\mu - \partial H^u/\partial k = (r^* + \delta)\mu - \frac{[u(W^c) - u(b^c)]}{[n-l_g]}[h(tW^c) + kh' W^p_1] + \eta g' W^p_1,$$

$$\lim_{t\to\infty} e^{-r^* t}\mu(t)k(t) = 0 \tag{8.30}$$

and

$$\dot{\eta} = r^*\eta - \partial H^u/\partial\lambda = -\delta\eta - \mu I'\left(\frac{\lambda-(1-\sigma)}{1-\sigma}\right), \qquad \eta(0) = 0. \tag{8.31}$$

The marginal value to the union of the firms' shadow-price of capital must be equal to zero at the beginning of the planning period, because the firms' investment rate and shadow-price are free to jump at that point of time and therefore become effectively an additional policy instrument for the monopoly union.

**Definition 4.1** The optimal wage strategy is time inconsistent (Kydland and Prescott, 1977) if there is an incentive for the union to reoptimise its wage strategy at some later date, that is if $\exists s, t$ such that $W^c(t, s) \neq W^c(t, 0)$, $s > 0$ and $t \geqslant s$, where $W^c(t, s)$ is the optimal consumption wage at time $t$ when the planning period (re)starts at time $s$. □

**Proposition 4.1** The optimal wage strategy is time-inconsistent.

**Proof:** There is no time inconsistency if $\eta(t) = 0$, $\forall t \geqslant 0$. Assume therefore that this is the case and see whether this leads to a contradiction. Equation (8.31) shows that $\mu(t) = 0$, $\forall t \geqslant 0$ upon which equation (8.30) shows that *either* $W^c(t) = b^c$, $\forall t \geqslant 0$, *or* $h + kh'W_1^p = 0$, $\forall t \geqslant 0$. The former case implies, using equation (4.4), that $l(t) = 0$, $\forall t \geqslant 0$. This is inconsistent with the Inada conditions as $f_l \to \infty$ and not to $b^c$ as $l/k \to 0$. The latter case implies $u(W^c) - u(b^c) = -u'(W^c)kW_1^p/W_{15}^p < 0$ or $W^c(t) < b$, $\forall t \geqslant 0$, which can not hold either as, workers would then prefer to be on the dole rather than be employed. Hence, $\eta(t) = 0$, $\forall t \geqslant 0$ can not hold along the equilibrium path and therefore the optimal wage strategy must be time-inconsistent.

This time inconsistency is a familiar feature of open-loop Stackelberg equilibrium solutions to differential games. It implies that the optimal wage strategies must be backed up by binding contracts, otherwise the union will renege. There is an incentive for the union to renege, because by announcing the intention of demanding low wages in the future along the lines of the time-inconsistent solution, it can persuade the firms to invest in a relatively large capital stock. Once the machines are installed, the monopoly union has an incentive to cheat and to claim higher wages than promised in order to extract the rent of a quasi-fixed factor. Obviously, such cheating can be prevented by binding contracts. Grout (1984) and Bean (1983) find a similar time inconsistency in a two-period model with cooperative wage–employment contracts.

Equation (8.29) can be solved for $W^c$ and for $W^p$,

$$W^p = \bar{W}^p(\overset{+}{\eta}/k, \overset{-}{\lambda}, \overset{-}{a}_p, \overset{+}{t}_1, \overset{+}{t}_2, \overset{+}{t}_3, \overset{+}{t}_4, \overset{-}{\sigma}, \overset{-}{g}, \overset{+}{l}_g, \overset{+}{b}_c, \overset{-}{n}, \overset{+}{r}^*, \overset{-}{y}^*) \quad (8.32)$$

so that the wage firms have to pay increases when the level of unemployment benefits and public-sector employment increases or labour supply decreases, and furthermore when any of the four tax-rates increases or when there is a real appreciation (caused by an increase in $\lambda$, $\sigma$, $g$, $a$, or $y^*$ or by a reduction in $k$ or $r^*$). An increase in benefits reduces the gap between an employed and an unemployed person's utility and therefore reduces the marginal cost to the union from raising the wage. In other words, the union places at the margin, less value on jobs than on income and consequently demands a higher wage.

A reduction in labour supply or an increase in public-sector employment works in the same way as an increase in benefits. They reduce the utility attached to the gap between an employed and unemployed person's utility and therefore reduce the marginal benefits for the union from raising the wage. The supply effects of these variables dominate the opposite demand effects.

The marginal value to the union of the firms' investment rate, $\eta$, is typically negative, since the union and firms have conflicting objectives. For example in steady state $\mu(\infty) > 0$ so $\eta(\infty) < 0$ follows from (8.31). Hence, $-\eta$ can be interpreted as a marginal cost to the union. An increase in the marginal cost to the union of the firms' shadow-price increases the marginal cost to the union from raising the wage, because it worsens the adverse effects of a higher wage on the marginal productivity of capital. The monopoly union consequently values jobs, at the margin, more than income and lowers the optimal wage.

## 5 CREDIBLE WAGE FORMATION

The previous section showed that non-cooperative outcomes are time-inconsistent, so that binding contracts are required. However, in many countries such contracts are not available. In principle, it is possible that reputational forces may, when the discount rate is small enough and the game between the monopoly union and the rest of the economy is repeated indefinitely, ensure that the monopoly union does not renege even though there is a short-run incentive to do so (e.g. Barro and Gordon, 1983; Driffill, 1985; van der Ploeg, 1987; Horn and Persson, 1985). It is one of the conjectures of this paper (see Section 7) that, due to increased conflict between the trade union movement and firms in the early 1970s the trust and reputational forces have broken down. In such circumstances the optimal (but time-inconsistent) wage strategies of Section 4 are no longer credible, because the firms no longer believe that the union will not renege when it has an incentive to do so. The main purpose of this section is to argue that credible outcomes are Pareto-inferior to the optimal outcomes and are characterised by high wages and low levels of the capital stock, employment and output.

It can be shown that the consistent outcome or the feedback Stackelberg equilibrium solution for this particular problem can be obtained by replacing equation (8.31) by $\eta(t)=0,\ t\geqslant 0$ (see van der Ploeg, 1987), which avoids a rather cumbersome solution based on dynamic programming. It follows that the optimal wage rate to be paid by firms is given by:

$$W^p = \tilde{W}^p(0, \overset{+}{k}, \overset{-}{\lambda}, \bar{a}_p, \overset{+}{t}_1, \overset{+}{t}_2, \overset{+}{t}_3, \overset{+}{t}_4, \bar{\sigma}, \bar{g}, \overset{+}{l}_g, \overset{+}{b}^c, \bar{n}^*, \overset{+}{r}^*, \bar{y}) \qquad (8.33)$$

so that, *ceteris paribus*, the wage is higher than in the pre-commitment outcome of Section 4 where $\eta > 0$. It follows that the marginal productivity of capital, the shadow-value of capital and the labour–capital ratio are lower in the credible, consistent outcome than in the pre-commitment outcomes. Hence, less capital is accumulated and unemployment is high (because of both the higher producers' wage and the lower capital stock) when there are no binding contracts or reputational forces have broken down. The reason is that, in the absence of binding contracts, the monopoly union is unable to convince the firms that it will stick to a strategy of low wages. Consequently, firms accumulate less capital and jobs are lost. The introduction of long-term wage contracts or reputational forces leads to a Pareto improvement, since the lower cost of labour makes the firm better off and the union's utility is improved as there are many more jobs created. This paradox of the disadvantageous power of a monopoly union clearly demonstrates the desirability of a political, sociological and legal framework that ensures that announced wage strategies are enforced.

Note from (8.33) that an increase in benefits or in the wedge, due to an increase in any of the four taxes or due to real depreciation, increases the producers' wage and therefore leads to less capital and to more unemployment.

## 6 CONFUSION BETWEEN REAL AND NOMINAL MAGNITUDES

So far, we have given a detailed account of the interactions between a monopoly trade union and a fringe of monopolistically competitive producers in a small open economy under various institutional arrangements. It was found that unemployment increases when the direct tax rate, indirect tax rate, employers' and employees' social security contributions, the level of benefits or labour supply increases. Aggregate demand management only had a supply-side effect on unemployment through the wedge between the consumers' and producers' real wage. That is, a contraction of aggregate demand through an increase in the world real interest rate or a reduction in public spending or world income, leads to a long-run depreciation of the real exchange rate, lower prices for home produced goods, and therefore a larger wedge and more unemployment.

To give a more conventional role for aggregate demand, it is necessary to introduce some confusion between real and nominal magnitudes. For example, there may be asymmetric information so that the firm knows the price level exactly and the union has to form expectations of it (cf. Friedman, 1968). In that case (8.32) becomes:

$$W^p = \frac{p^e}{p}\,\tilde{W}^p(\eta/k, \lambda, a_p, t_1, t_2, t_3, t_4, \sigma, g, l_g, b^c, n, r^*, y^*) \quad (8.34)$$

and similarly for (5.1). With the assumption of adaptive expectations,

$$\frac{\mathrm{d}}{\mathrm{d}t}\left(\frac{\dot{p}^e}{p^e}\right) = \xi\left[\left(\frac{\dot{p}}{p}\right) - \left(\frac{\dot{p}^e}{p^e}\right)\right], \quad \xi > 0 \quad (8.35)$$

and the use of the *LM*-curve (8.15), to give the rate of inflation ($\dot{p}/p$), the model is complete. Under perfect foresight $\xi \to \infty$, the model becomes as in Sections 2–5. For finite $\xi$, it is possible for an expression of aggregate demand to lead to a temporary increase in employment over and above the increase in employment due to the associated contraction of the wedge.

## 7 SUPPLY, DEMAND AND INSTITUTIONAL FEATURES IN THE NETHERLANDS

In the previous sections the analytical framework in which the empirical trends will be discussed was set out. In this section we will present some of these trends and discuss the way they fit together.

The most concerning and significant trend in the past fifteen years in Holland, as in many countries, has been the rise in unemployment. The Dutch unemployment rate has changed relatively much. It remained below the EEC or OECD average until the early 1970s, equalled the increased average of the unemployment rate of these sets of countries in the mid-1970s and at the end of the 1970s it steeply rose above the rising trend of the EEC and OECD countries (see Figure 8.1). Even though the official unemployment figures have increased so much, they still underestimate the actual trends in unemployment because of the various measures arranged to reduce the *official* number of unemployed. In Holland these measures include increased compulsory enrolment in educational institutions and benefits for disabled workers which are granted partly on the basis of the employment perspectives of the participants.

Underlying the trend in unemployment are the trends in *employment* $(l+l_g)$ and *labour supply* $(n)$ (Figure 8.2). The rise in employment levelled off in the early 1970s whereas the labour force kept increasing. We have included in the figure *N* broad, a series for labour supply which includes the in-stream in the disabled benefits programme for employed since its major modification in 1969 and *N* potential, a series which is constructed by taking 70 per cent of the population in the age range 20–64. 70 per cent is roughly the Dutch participation ratio in the 1950s.

The number of employed is in fact a bad measure for *real employment*, total hours worked (see Figure 8.3), because hours worked per year per person and sick-leave have changed rather significantly over the years. Sick-leave and hours worked per year show a long-run upward trend, whereas the first moves pro- and the second counter-cyclically.

Another important trend is the one in investment (Figure 8.4). Comparing Figure 8.4 with Figure 8.3 illustrates why we have put so much emphasis or explaining employment and investment in relation to each other. The levelling off of employment growth ($l$) coincides with the drop in gross ($i$) and net investment as a percentage of the production of firms ($y$). If (proper) data on the capital stock had been available for the Netherlands, the labour-capital ratio ($l/k$, see equation (8.8)) would have provided valuable insights.

*Figure* 8.1 Unemployment in The Netherlands, the EEC and OECD, 1966–83

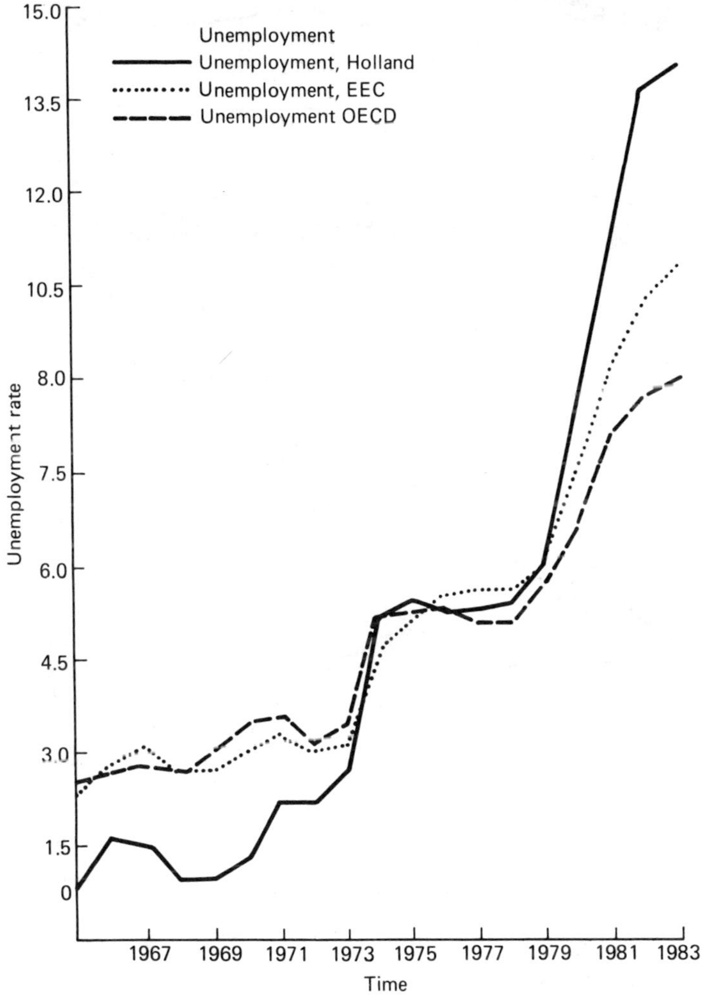

*Figure* 8.2 The composition of the potential labour force in the Netherlands, 1955–84

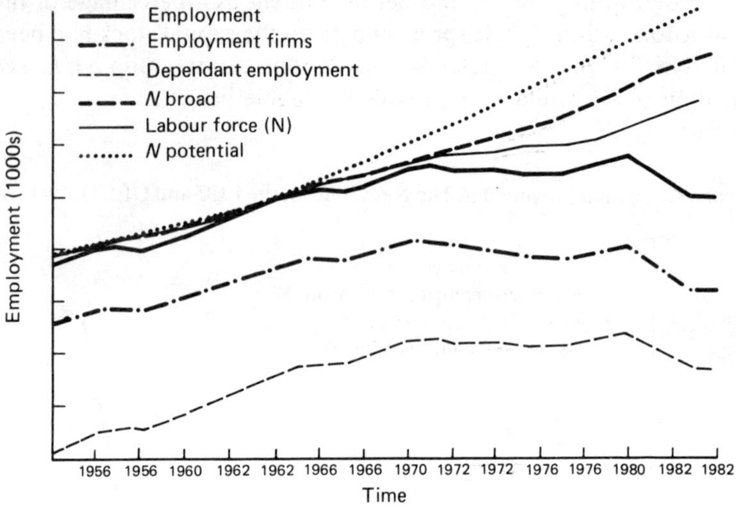


*Figure* 8.3 Employment in the Netherlands, 1955–84

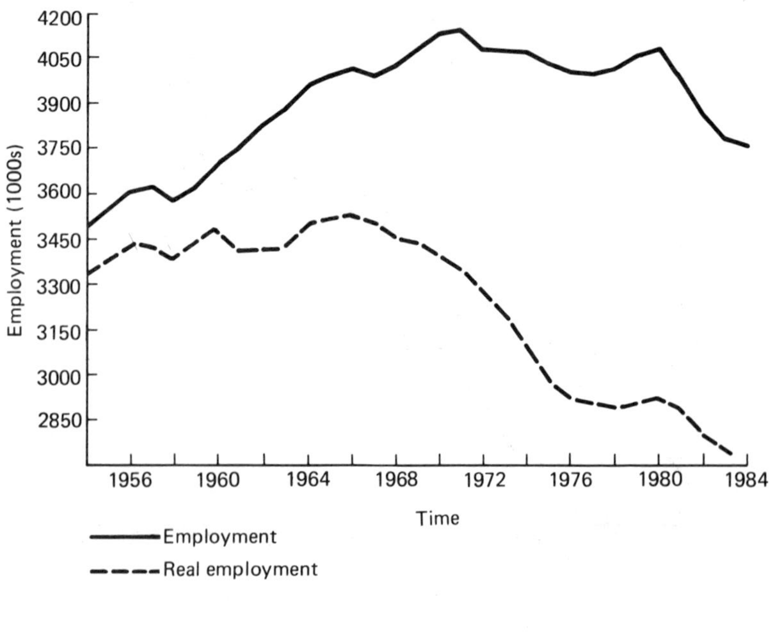

*Figure* 8.4 Investment in the Netherlands, 1955–84

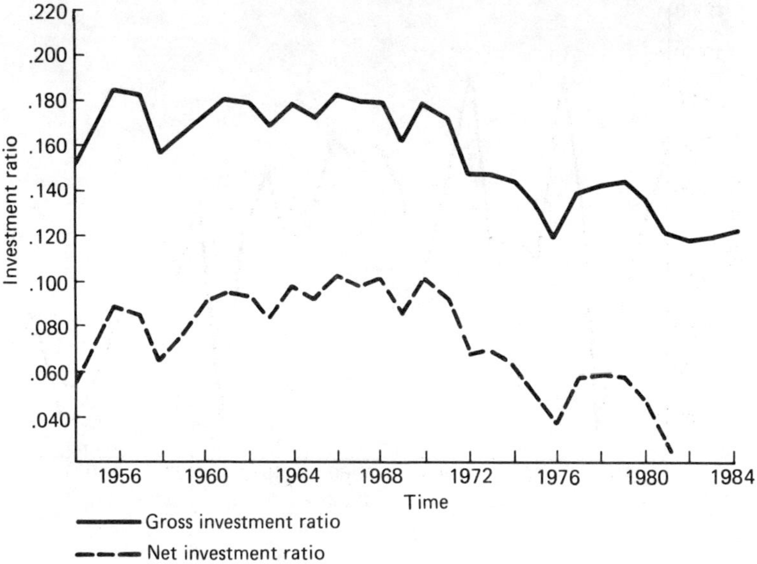


The change in output ($\dot{y}$), labour costs ($\dot{W}^p$) and labour productivity ($\dot{y} - \dot{l} - \dot{W}^p$) are the subjects of Figures 8.5 and 8.6 respectively.

A number of factors, to some extent specifically Dutch, may be responsible for these trends in output, (un)employment, investment and labour costs. In sections 2–6 we have set up a framework to analyse these factors. Various external factors, foreign income $y^*$, real foreign interest rates $r^*$, labour supply $n$, and government factors, government demand for goods $g$, various tax and social security contribution rates ($t_1$, $t_2$, $t_3$, $t_4$), investment subsidies, public sector employment and the real level of benefits were distinguished, besides the private sector stock of wealth, $a_p$, and capital stock, $k$. It is rather unfortunate that there are no proper data on the marginal value of capital, $\lambda$, or on Tobin's '$Q$', available. This co-state variable $\lambda$ is closely correlated with investment and both are complex functions of present, past and future versions of the exogenous variables. This makes analysis without exact observations on $\lambda$ rather hard. The same lack of data applies for investment subsidies (or negative taxes), $\sigma$.

Government demand for goods, $g$, and world trade or world activity, $y^*$, exert their influence mainly through the demand side.[4] The short-run effect, for given values of $a$, $k$, and $\lambda$, of an increase in world

*Figure* 8.5 Output growth in the Netherlands, 1955–84

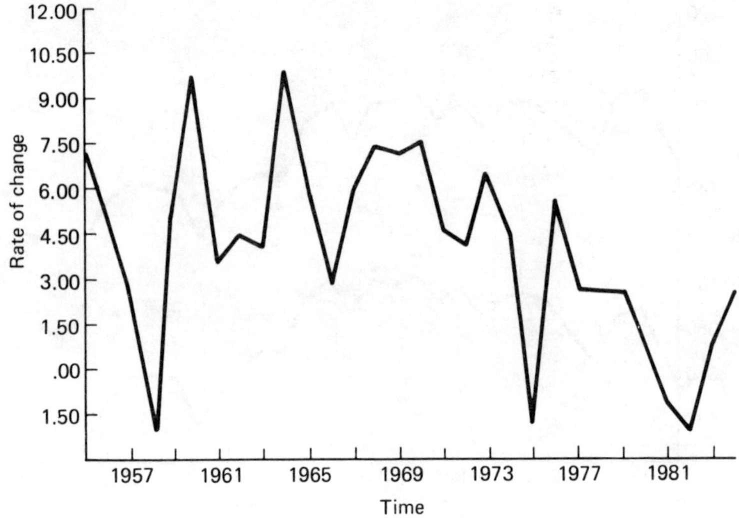


*Figure* 8.6 Growth in wage rates and unit labour costs in the Netherlands, 1955–84

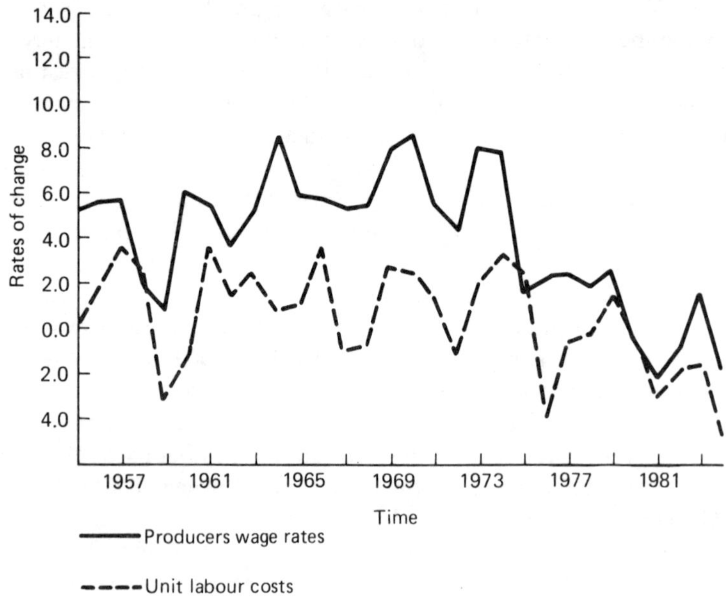

trade or government demand is an increase in the price or home-produced goods and therefore an appreciation of the real exchange rate ($p^*e/P$). An increase in the real foreign interest rate, $r^*$, for we used the deflated German call money rate, has the opposite effect on the real exchange rate. World-trade growth is depicted in Figure 8.7, real foreign interest rate in Figure 8.8, government expenditure in Figure 8.9 and the real exchange rate in Figure 8.10. The appreciation of the real exchange rate in the 1970s is fairly well explained by the short-run effects of the changes in world trade, real foreign interest rates and government demand. The appreciation of the real exchange rate reduced the wedge between producers' and consumers' real wage rates and this by itself must have stimulated output and labour demand and reduced unemployment.

The development of the 'wedge' was however dominated by other factors – the tax rates and rates of social security contribution. During the past two decades, direct and indirect tax rates ($t_2$, $t_3$) and the employers' and employees' rates of social security contribution ($t_1$) have increased at a breathtaking pace (Figure 8.11), and have enlarged the wedge considerably (Figure 8.12). Though part of the increased burden of taxes and social security contributions is borne by the wage-earners, a rational union will not make the members of its reference group bear the complete burden. It will reduce the consumer

*Figure* 8.7 World trade growth, 1960–84

*Figure* 8.8 The real foreign interest rate, 1961–83

*Figure* 8.9 Government expenditure and budget deficit in the Netherlands, 1955–83

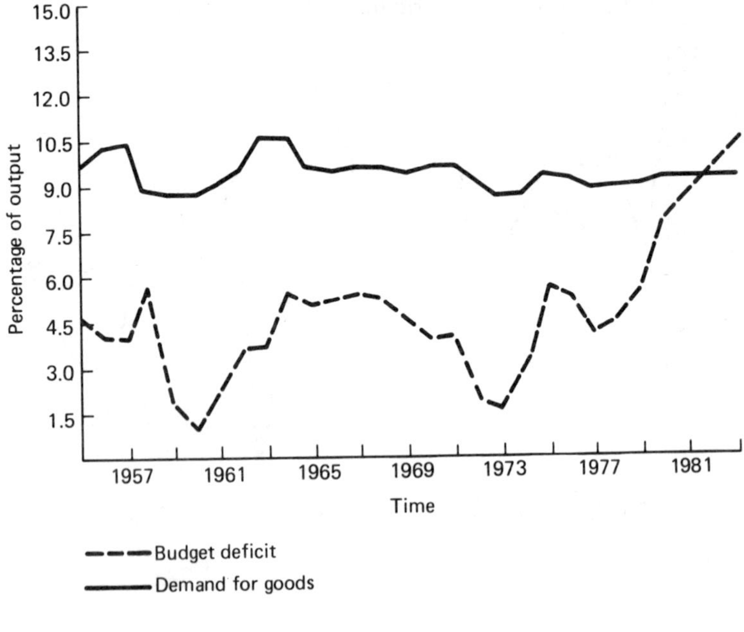

*Figure* 8.10 The real exchange rate for the Netherlands, 1959–84

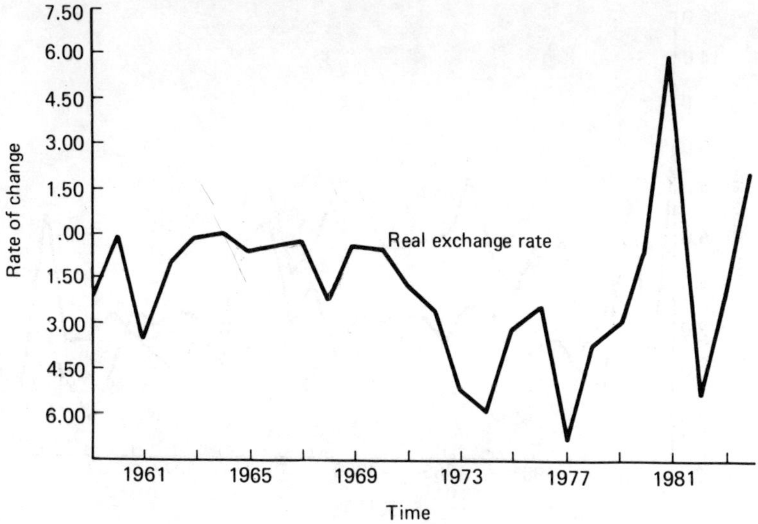


*Figure* 8.11 Taxes and social security in the Netherlands, 1955–84

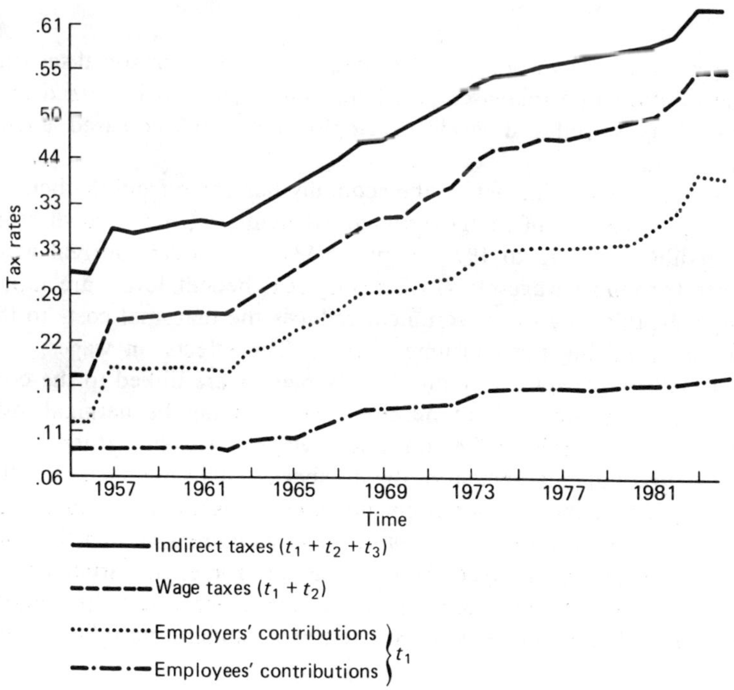

*Figure* 8.12 The wedge in the Netherlands, 1955–84

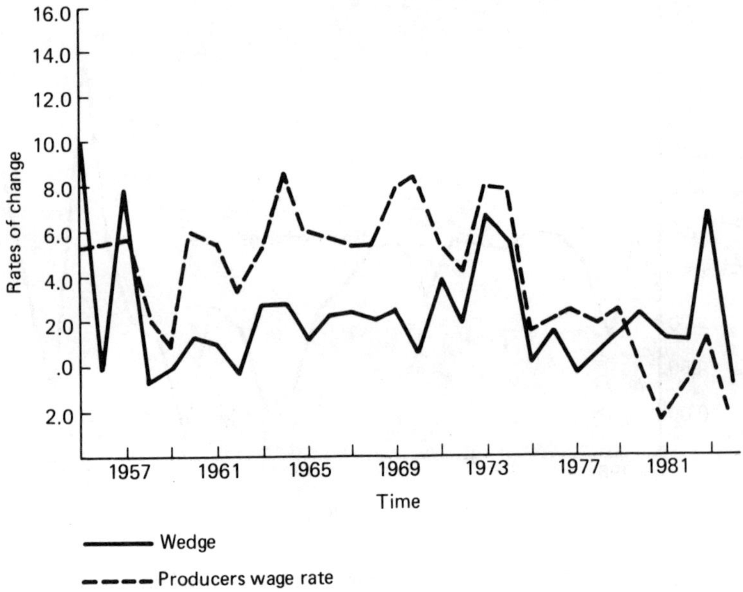


wage rates, but by a smaller percentage than the tax or social security contribution rate increase. This behaviour results in increased producer-wages, reduced levels of employment and increased unemployment.

Another major impact on the economy has come from the benefit-setting behaviour of the government. Benefits, $b^c$, have grown at an incredible pace up to 1979 (Figure 8.13). The effects on real wage costs (producer-wage-rates) of raising real benefit levels are rather large. In this way the government reduces the marginal costs to the union of raising the consumers' wage. The effects on wages were especially large since around 1970. Benefits were linked to the consumers' wage rates at that time, effectively reducing the marginal costs to the union of raising the consumers' wage rate even further.

The gradual enlargement of the number of civil servants, $l_g$ and the rapidly increasing number of beneficiaries of disabled 'pensions' (see Figure 8.2) will have had the same effect as increasing benefits had. By removing unemployed from the labour force, in particular the private-sector labour force, the government prevented the rapidly increasing labour force, $n$, from exerting a moderating influence on

*Figure* 8.13 Changes in real benefits in the Netherlands, 1965–84

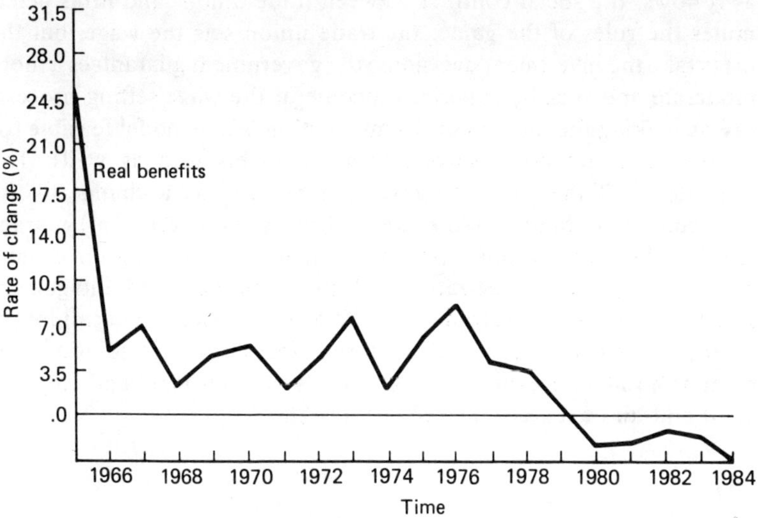


the consumers' wage rate by increasing the marginal costs to the trade union of raising the wage rate.

Another cause for the large drop in the employment growth rate coinciding with the drop in investment can be sought in the institutional relations between trade union(s) and firms. The post-war history of Holland was one of close cooperation between trade union(s), government and firms to rebuild the war-damaged Dutch economy. The ensuing cooperation led to wages below the free market level and the observation of 'black wages', illegal bonuses paid on top of the officially agreed wages (Windmuller, de Galan and van Zweeden, 1983). In the 1960s the wage-guide policy of the government was relaxed, though the government retained some instruments to influence the wage-setting process. The dispute about the new wage-guide act, 'de Loonwet 1968', indicates that even the reduced role of the government in wage-setting was no longer generally accepted.

One might say that the social contract between trade unions and firms broke down at the end of the 1960s and the beginning of the 1970s. The year 1971 saw a wild strike in the harbour, warning the trade-union leadership that a more aggressive attitude was wanted. In the labour party's political programme 'turnpoint '72', various proposals were launched by which the trade unions would be given, among other things, a say in the investment decision of firms.

In the terminology of our model we can describe these developments as follows; the social contract between trade unions and firms determines the rules of the game: the trade union sets the wage, but the firms take the investment decisions; the government guarantees a more moderate and socially superior outcome of the wage-setting process, say by making the time-inconsistent solution of the model feasible (of course there are other ways to formalise this idea as well). The breakdown of the social contract can be seen as a change to the time-consistent solution of the model. Without a (government) guarantee that the trade union(s) stick to their words (the announcements of future consumer-wage-rates) and given the increased antagonism and distrust between the trade union(s) on the one hand and employers on the other hand, the socially inferior time-consistent solution will be appropriate, implying decreased levels of investment and employment and an increased unemployment rate.

## 8 CONCLUDING REMARKS

In this chapter we have modelled a small open economy with strong trade unions. The supply side was well-developed, investment was explicitly treated as well as trade union behaviour, and a demand side was specified.

The results of our formal analysis were used to trace the consequences of demand side, supply side and institutional changes on the Dutch economy. The most striking facts are the historical increase in the wedge between the producers' and the consumers' real wage, the rise in real benefit levels and possibly, a regime switch from 'rules' to 'discretion'. They have all contributed significantly to the large drop in investment and the large rise of unemployment in the Netherlands.

## Appendix: Summary of Model

*Supply-model*

$$l = kh(t\bar{W}^c, \overset{+}{y}); \qquad y = kf(l, h(tW^c, y)) \tag{A.1}$$

$$\dot{k} = I\left(\frac{\lambda - (1-\sigma)}{1-\sigma}\right) - \delta k, \qquad k(0) = k_0 \tag{A.2}$$

$$\dot{\lambda} = (r^* + \delta)\lambda - g(t\bar{W}_c, \overset{+}{y}), \qquad \lim_{t\to\infty} e^{-r^* t}\lambda(t)k(t)] = 0 \tag{A.3}$$

*Demand-side*

$$r^* = r - \dot{P}/P = \text{exogenous} \tag{A.4}$$

$$y = Y\left(\overset{+}{\lambda}, \overset{+}{a}_p, \overset{-}{t}_1, \overset{-}{t}_2, \overset{-}{t}_3, \overset{-}{t}_4, \overset{+}{\sigma}, \overset{+}{g}\,\overset{+}{l}_g, \overset{-}{b^c}, \overset{-}{r}^*, \overset{+}{y}^*, \frac{\overset{+}{p}^* e}{P}, W^p\right) \tag{A.5}$$

$$\frac{(p^* e/P)^{-(1-\beta)}}{(1+t_3)}\frac{M}{P} = M/P^c = l(y \cdot \overset{+}{\dot{P}}/P_c, -r^* + \dot{P}/P, \overset{+}{a}_p) \tag{A.6}$$

$$\dot{a}_f = r^* a_f + f(k, l) - \phi(i) - c - g - i, \qquad a(0) = a_0 \tag{A.7}$$

*Union behaviour*

$$\underset{W^c}{\text{Max}} \int_0^\infty \left[\frac{l}{n-l_g} u(W^c) + \frac{(n-l-l_g)}{(n-l_g)} u(b)\right] e^{-r^* t}\, dt \tag{A.8}$$

*s.t.* (1) – (7)

## Notes

1 Note that $c = (c^d P + c^* p^* e)/P$ where $c^d$ is consumption of domestic goods and $c^*$ is consumption of foreign goods.
2 After inflation adjustment of the asset holdings.
3 From (8.16) $c^* p^* e = (1-\beta)(c^d P + c^* p^* e)$, so $m = c^* = (1-\beta)c(p^* e/P)$.
4 World-trade differs from world activity in the sense that it signals improved international division of labour as well as world activity. An improved international division of labour shifts the production frontier Holland may well have benefited to a large extent from such tendencies in the 1960s.

## References

BARRO, R. J. and GORDON, D. B. (1983) 'Rules, Discretion and Reputation in a Model of Monetary Policy', *Journal of Monetary Economics*, 12, pp. 101–21.

BEAN, C. R. (1983) 'Capital Formation and the Role of Long-term Labour Contracts', Centre for Labour Economics discussion paper no. 181, London School of Economics.

CALMFORS, L. (1982) 'Employment Policies, Wage Formation and Trade Union Behaviour in a Small Open Economy', *Skandinavian Journal of Economics*, 84, 2, pp. 345–73.

DRIFFILL, E. J. (1985) 'Macroeconomic Stabilisation Policy and Trade Union Behaviour as a Repeated Game', *Skandinavian Journal of Economics*, 85, 2, pp. 300–26.

DUNLOP, J. T. (1944), *Wage Determination under Trade Unions* (New York: Macmillan).

FRIEDMAN, M. (1968) 'The Role of Monetary Policy', *American Economic Review*, pp. 1–17.

GOULD, J. P. (1968) 'Adjustment Costs in the Theory of Investment of the Firm', *Review of Economic Studies*, 35, pp. 47–55.
GROUT, P. A. (1984) 'Investment and Wages in the Absence of Binding Contracts: A Nash Bargaining Approach', *Econometrica*, 52, 2, pp. 449–60.
GYLFASSON, T. and LINDBECK, A. (1986) 'Endogenous Unions, Cost Inflation and Capacity Utilization: A Game Theoretic Approach', *European Economic Review* 30, pp. 5–26.
HART, P. (1982) 'A Model of Imperfect Competition with Keynesian Features', *Quarterly Journal of Economics*, XCVIII, 2, pp. 109–38.
HERSOUG, T. (1985) 'Workers *versus* Government – Who Adjusts to Whom?, *Skandinavian Journal of Economics*, 87, 2, pp. 270–291.
HORN, H. and PERSSON, T. (1985) 'Exchange Rate Policy, Wage Formation and Credibility', mimeo, Institute for International Economic Studies, Stockholm.
IWAI, K. (1981) *Disequilibrium Dynamics: A Theoretical Analysis of Inflation and Unemployment*, (New Haven: Cowles Foundation Monograph) no. 27.
KYDLAND, F. and PRESCOTT, E. (1977) 'Rules rather than discretion: The Time Inconsistency of Optimal Plans', *Journal of Political Economy*, 3, pp. 473–92.
MCDONALD, I. M. and SOLOW, R. M. (1981) 'Wage Bargaining and Employment', *American Economic Review*, 71, 5, pp. 896–908.
MENIL, G. DE (1971) *Bargaining: Monopoly Power Versus Union Power* (Cambridge, Massachusetts: MIT Press).
MINFORD, P. (1983) 'Labour Market Equilibrium in an Open Economy', *Oxford Economic Papers*, 35, Supplement, pp. 207–44.
NICKELL, S. J. and ANDREWS, M. (1983) 'Unions Real Wages and Employment in Britain 1951–79', *Oxford Economic Papers*, 35, Supplement, pp. 183–206.
NICKELL, S. J. (1985) 'The Government's Policy for Jobs: An Analysis', discussion paper no. 222, Centre for Labour Economics, London School of Economics.
OSWALD, A. (1979) 'Wage Determination in an Economy with Many Trade Unions', *Oxford Economic Papers*, 31, 3, pp. 369–85.
OSWALD, A. (1985) 'The Economic Theory of Trade Unions: An Introductory Survey', *Skandinavian Journal of Economics*, 87, 2, pp. 160–93.
PENCAVEL, J. H. (1984) 'The Trade-off between Wages and Employment in Trade Union Objectives' *Quarterly Journal of Economics*, 99, pp. 213–32.
PLOEG, F. VAN DER (1982) 'Government Policy, Real Wage Resistance and the Resolution of Conflict', *European Economic Review*, 19, 3, pp. 181–212.
PLOEG, F. VAN DER (1987) 'Trade Unions, Investment and Employment: A Non-Cooperative Approach', *European Economic Review*, 31, 7, pp. 1465–92.
PLOEG, F. VAN DER (1986) 'Monopoly Unions, Investment and Employment: The Benefits of Contingent Wage Contracts, Centre for Labour Economics, working paper no. 834, London School of Economics.
RAAUM, D. (1986) 'Wage Formation in a Two-Sector Open Economy with Two Strong Unions', presented to a conference on Unemployment in Europe at Maastricht, in April. (Chapter 9 of this volume).

SVENSSON, L. E. O. (1986) 'Sticky Goods Prices, Flexible Asset Prices, Monopolistic Competition, and Monetary Policies', *Review of Economic Studies* (forthcoming).

WINDMULLER, J. P., GALAN, C. DE and VAN ZWEEDEN, A. F. (1983) *Arbeidsverhoudingen in Nederland* (Utrecht: Het Spectrum).

# 9 Wage Formation in a Two-sector Open Economy with Two Strong Unions

Oddbjørn Raaum*

ABSTRACT

This chapter focuses on a two-sector model describing a small open economy with trade unions able to set nominal wages. The wage formations are interdependent in the sense that the optimal wage for one union depends on the outcome of the other sector. This interdependence takes place through demand for labour, the overall price level and 'relative wage effects'.

Two different equilibria, the non-cooperative (Nash) equilibrium and a 'leader–follower' equilibrium, are studied and compared. The latter involves lower wages and higher employment compared with the non-cooperative equilibrium.

The importance of aggregate demand, traded sector prices and productivity are outlined. Comparative static predictions depend crucially on the unions' utility functions.

Implications of 'relative wage focusing' are discussed. The wage levels increase as unions attach more importance to relative wages. But the effect on wage changes, due to changing aggregate demand, prices and productivity is ambiguous.

## 1 INTRODUCTION

Observing wage formation, at least in Norway during recent years, you cannot miss the unions increased emphasis on *relative wages* in the wage negotiations. This focus might be motivated by tactical reasons. Relatively decreasing wages is often a good argument, at least

* I wish to thank Tor Hersoug, Michael Hoel and Eva Uddén-Jondal for helpful discussions and comments.

as far as support from the public opinion is concerned. On the other hand, people's appreciation of their situation (here wages) does often depend on the situation of 'groups with which we naturally compare ourselves'.

The economics of trade unions is a rapidly expanding area. Oswald (1985) and Pencavel (1985) have given surveys of the last years' literature. So far, little attention has been paid to the existence of different sectors and trade unions in the economy. A multisectoral framework may imply interdependence between the wage claims of the different unions. When the unions care about relative wages, there will be implications for the wage formation process. In an economy with more than one union there might exist links between wage claims of different trade unions. There are roughly three main ways in which the interdependence takes place. First, the wage claims of one union may affect the demand for workers who are members of the other unions. Secondly, (the members of) one union might well consider increased wages in other sectors as a deterioration of their situation. Thirdly, raising wages may influence the overall price level and subsequently real wages. These three sources of interdependency are present in the model in this chapter.

Oswald (1979) was the first to treat this kind of interdependence explicitly in a microeconomic framework. His article focuses on the existence and stability of a non-cooperative wage equilibrium in an economy with many powerful trade unions. He does not, however, look at the factors that may change this equilibrium and how for example stabilisation policy and world market prices affect the wages in this context. If the model should tell a more complete story about wage formation, it is natural to analyse how changes in exogenous variables affect the equilibrium solution.

Gylfason and Lindbeck (1984a) and (1984b) use the same framework as Oswald (1979), but the two articles differ as far as the description of the production and demand side of the economy is concerned. Gylfason and Lindbeck (1984a) emphasise wage rigidity as a consequence of rational union behaviour in an economy with many trade unions. They argue that less than full compensation for increased prices might well be rational, as long as expectations about other unions' wage levels are constant (and not influenced by the changes in the price level). In the long run though, when expectations catch up with reality, the nominal wages adjust fully to expected inflation. In Gylfason and Lindbeck (1984b) the model is extended and incorporates this microeconomic theory of labour union behaviour into a macroeconomic general equilibrium model with goods, money and bonds as well as two kinds of labour.

This chapter is influenced by these three articles but differs at important points. As opposed to Oswald (1979) and Gylfason and Lindbeck (1984a), our model is more general as it treats prices (in non-traded sector) as endogenous and affected by wage claims.

The two articles of Gylfason and Lindbeck have one important assumption in common. Both are only concerned with (simultaneous move) non-cooperative equilibria. While Gylfason and Lindbeck (1984a) point out that a Stackelberg solution is more plausible than the non-cooperative equilibrium, when the number of unions is quite small, we explicitly compare these two kinds of equilibria. Many models, both theoretical and empirical ones, assume that the traded sector is a wage leader and the other group(s) of workers get wage increases that maintain relative wages. The 'Scandinavian Model of Inflation' (see, e.g. Aukrust, 1978) is probably the best known. But the theoretical arguments for this constant relative wages assumption are often unsatisfactory. This chapter intends to investigate whether a theoretical model with two strong, rational unions that care about relative wages, implies a development with constant relative wages.

This chapter describes the wage formation in a small open economy consisting of one traded ($T$) and one non-traded ($N$) sector.[1] The distinction between the two sectors is important, at least with respect to price behaviour and the effects of stabilisation policy. We assume that producers in the $T$-sector are profit-maximising pricetakers and the $N$-sector follow a 'mark up' rule. The nominal wage is set by the trade union in each sector. In addition to their own employment and real wages, the unions are assumed to care about relative wages. Formally, this means that the wage rate in the other sector is an argument in the utility function (with negative partial derivative). This is often called an 'envy effect' or a 'jealousy effect' (see Oswald, 1979; Gylfason and Lindbeck, 1984a).

The chapter is organised as follows: The basic model is described in section 2. Non-cooperative equilibria are discussed in section 3. In section 4, a leader–follower model is introduced and the union in the $T$-sector is assumed to be the leader. The leader–follower solution is compared with the non-cooperative equilibrium. Comparative static predictions are derived in section 5. Section 6 discusses the possibilities of establishing, and the properties of cooperative solutions. The implications of 'relative wage focusing' are derived in section 7.

## 2 THE BASIC MODEL

The production of $T$-goods ($Y^T$) requires labour ($N^T$) and intermediate $N$-goods ($X$).

$$Y^T = A^T F(N^T, X) \qquad F_i > 0 \qquad F_{ij} < 0 \quad i = j$$
$$F_{ij} \gtreqless 0 \quad i \neq j$$
$$A^T (\text{constant}) > 0.$$

Producers are assumed to be profit-maximising pricetakers. This gives us demand for labour (and $N$-goods) from $T$-sector, where small letters denote the logarithm (ln).

$$n^T = \ln N^T = n^T(w^T - p^T - a^T, p^N - p^T - a^T) \tag{9.1}$$

where

$n^T$ = labour demand $T$-sector
$w^T$ = nominal wage $T$-sector
$p^T = p^{T*} + e$
$p^{T*}$ = price level $T$-sector (foreign currency)
$e$ = exchange rate (constant)
$a^T$ = constant
$p^N$ = price level $N$-sector

$$n_1^T = \frac{\partial n^T}{\partial(w^T - p^T - a^T)} < 0, \qquad n_2^T = \frac{\partial n^T}{\partial(p^N - p^T - a^T)} \lesseqgtr 0.$$

The labour demand elasticities are assumed to be constant, hence $n_{ij}^T = 0$ (for all $i, j$).
Production of $N$-goods ($Y^N$) requires labour ($N^N$) in constant proportion:

$$Y^N = A^N N^N. \tag{9.2}$$

The producers follow a 'mark-up rule' where prices are set to obtain a constant profit share.

$$\frac{P^N Y^N - W^N N^N}{P^N Y^N} = \alpha$$

where

$W^N$ = nominal wage $N$-sector
$\alpha$ = profit share (constant).

Thus,

$$P^N = \frac{1}{(1-\alpha)A^N} W^N. \tag{9.3}$$

No crucial difference appears, if the production function is strictly concave and the producers are price-takers. Market-clearing would in this case determine the prices on $N$-goods. The relationship between wages and prices in $N$-sector would be more complicated, but qualitatively the same.

The demand for $N$-goods consists of final ($C$) and intermediate ($X$) goods.

$$Y^N = C\left(\frac{P^N}{P^T}, D\right) + X\left(\frac{P^N}{A^T P^T}, \frac{W^T}{A^T P^T}\right).$$

$D$ is a parameter representing the level of aggregate demand. Hence,

$$\begin{aligned} y^N &= y^N(p^N, p^T, d, w^T, a^T) \\ &= \beta c(p^N - p^T, d) + (1-\beta)x(p^N - p^T - a^T, w^T - p^T - a^T) \end{aligned} \tag{9.4}$$

where

$$\beta = \frac{C}{Y^N}, (1-\beta) = \frac{X}{Y^N},$$

$$c_1 = \frac{\partial C}{\partial(p^N - p^T)} < 0, \quad c_2 > 0, \quad x_1 < 0, \quad x_2 \gtreqless 0, \quad x_1 + x_2 < 0.$$

We assume that $x_{ij} = c_{ij} = 0$. $i, j = 1, 2$.

$$y_1^N < 0, y_2^N = -y_1^N - (1-\beta)x_2 > 0,$$
$$y_3^N > 0, \quad y_4^N = (1-\beta)x_2 \gtreqless 0, \quad y_5^N > 0.$$

These elasticities of total demand for $N$-goods are not necessarily constant because $\beta = C/Y^N$ may vary. The properties of $y_1^N$ (the labour-demand elasticity with respect to wages in the $N$-sector) are especially important in our context.

If $c_1 = x_1$, then $y_{1i}^N = 0$ $(i = 1, \ldots 5)$.

If $c_1 \neq x_1$, then $y_{11}^N > 0$, $y_{12}^N \gtreqless 0$, sign $y_{13}^N = \text{sign}(c_1 - x_1)$, $y_{14}^N \gtreqless 0$,

sign $y_{15}^N = \text{sign}(c_1 - x_1)$.

(Details in Appendix 9.1.)

Aggregate demand is treated as exogenous, though influenced by stabilisation policy. This simplification means that the impact of wages on disposable income and consumption is left out. Policy variables are assumed to vary in order to keep $d$ constant as other variables, like wages, change (see Hoel (1981) for further discussion).

Combining (9.2)-(9.4) gives:

$$p^N = w^N - a^N - \ln(1-\alpha) \tag{9.5}$$

$$n^N = y^N(p^N, p^T, d, w^T, a^T) - a^N. \tag{9.6}$$

The price level is given by $P = (P^N)^\lambda \cdot (P^T)^{(1-\lambda)}$ which means

$$p = \lambda p^N + (1-\lambda)p^T. \tag{9.7}$$

The utility functions of the trade unions have three arguments: own real wage, employment and the real wage in the other sector:

$$U^T = U^T(r^T, n^T, r^N), \qquad U^N = U^N(r^N, n^N, r^T)$$

where

$$r^i = w^i - p, \qquad i = N, T.$$

The utility functions are assumed to fulfil the following conditions (where, of course, the second order assumptions are cardinal):

$$U_1^i = \frac{\partial U^i}{\partial r^i} > 0 \quad U_2^i > 0 \qquad U_3^i < 0$$

$$U_{11}^i < 0 \qquad\qquad U_{22}^i \leqslant 0$$

$$U_{21}^i \geqslant 0 \qquad U_{31}^i > 0 \qquad U_{23}^i = U_{33}^i = 0 \quad i = N, T.$$

The assumption, $U_{13}^i > 0$, is essential and means that the marginal utility of own wages increases when the other group is better paid. $U_{13}^i > 0$ and $U_3^i < 0$ is one way to formulate the fact that the unions are concerned with their relative wage rate (compared with other workers). (A situation where the union cared *only* about relative wages would be a special case.)

A common approach in trade union theory is to use an expected utility or utilitarian objective function to represent the union's preferences. These two functions have the same properties if all workers have identical utility functions and the membership is fixed. In the expected utility case, the probability of being unemployed is assumed not to vary between workers (see, e.g., Oswald, 1985). The union chooses the wage rate that maximises $N \cdot \tilde{U}(R, R^*, B)$ subject to relevant constraints. $\tilde{U}$ is the gain from employment ($N$) and this depends on the real wage ($R$), real wage rate in other sectors ($R^*$) and unemployment benefits ($B$). This formulation implies that the marginal utility of employment in our context ($U_2^i(r^i, n^i, r^i)$) is constant ($U_{22}^i = U_{21}^i = 0$), because the arguments in the utility function are measured in logs. The expected utility and the utilitarian approach have been heavily criticised in the literature. For example, the existence of non-fixed membership or any kind of seniority rules makes these objective functions inappropriate. (Oswald (1985) gives some of the arguments.) However, no consensus about how to represent the labour union objectives has yet been reached.

Therefore, a distinction is made between two classes of trade union utility functions throughout this chapter. First, the expected utility/utilitarian approach (*EUU*-case) and secondly a case with no such 'separability' ($U_{21}^i > 0$, $U_{22}^i < 0$). The latter is called the *G&L*-case for convenience. These assumptions are made in Gylfason and Lindbeck (1984a). This distinction turns out to be important. The comparative statics and the interdependency between the two sectors depend on the utility functions.

The wage concept in this model is before-tax real wage. Many authors argue that after-tax real wages are more relevant (see Hersoug (1983) for a discussion). We will not focus on the implications of tax changes on wage formation. Thus, taxes are kept constant and for simplicity left out. Properties of demand for labour and the utility functions are obviously not sufficient to determine our model. We need a description of the strategic position of the unions, according to the other groups of workers. The model represents a game situation where the unions control their own (nominal) wage rate. It is quite clear that the unions, to some extent, have divergent interests. Partial changes in the wage rate of one sector will certainly worsen the situation for the other union. An increased wage rate (given that the other sector is unaffected) will be beneficial as long as the negative employment effect does not dominate.

The interdependency between the wage claims has different causes. First, the wage rate in the other sector has a direct influence because of the 'envy' effect. Secondly, wages in one sector influence demand for labour in the other sector. Moreover, the wage rate in $N$-sector affects the price level and subsequently real wages. But it is easy to recognize that cooperation could represent a community of interests. The game is not a 'zero sum' game. Either side will, as we shall see, prefer a (binding) cooperative solution with wages.

There is no game-theoretic equilibrium which points out to be superior to others in this context. Nevertheless, among the non-cooperative ones we shall focus on the non-cooperative (Nash–Cournot) equilibrium and a solution where the $T$-sector is a Stackelberg leader and the $N$-sector a Stackelberg follower.

The non-cooperative equilibrium has many interpretations in the literature. Leif Johansen has often argued (see, e.g., Johansen (1982)) against the most common (?) 'Cournot-interpretation' where the participants take the others' actions as given. When each player knows the full range of possible decisions which can be taken by the other players, a 'thought' process will go on until each player has found predictions which will not be frustrated and a situation where his own decision will not be regretted. This is the characteristic of a non-cooperative equilibrium. On the other hand, when the unions do not have all relevant information available, the non-cooperative equilibrium can be interpreted as a 'long-run' equilibrium where a trial-and-error process has been brought to conclusion. Since the wage adjustment does not take place continuously, but by local or central negotiations once or twice a year, this process can go on for some time. Lack of information as far as preferences and uncertain exogenous events are concerned, may imply that this equilibrium is not easily established.

The Stackelberg solution represents another common non-cooperative solution. This model is based on the existence of one leader and a follower. The follower takes the other player's action as given and does his best according to a preference function. On the other hand, the leader knows the follower's decision rule and takes that as given when he decides what action maximises his objective function. The weak point of this solution is the determination of who is leading and who is following.[2]

The Stackelberg solution, where $T$-sector is the leader, does not represent a theoretical explanation of the existence of wage-leading and wage-following sectors. Still, it can tell us something about the implications of this strategic position in our model. In addition, it can count as contribution to the discussion of the 'Scandinavian model' assumption about constant relative wages.

Different kinds of cooperative solutions, where the unions coordinate their wage claims may be a good description of reality. Bargaining between a union and an employer is often described in the literature. (See, e.g., Oswald (1985).) Recent bargaining theory has shown that care must be taken when specifying utility functions and the disagreement points in a Nash bargaining solution, cf., Binmore, Rubinstein and Wolinsky (1985). In our model, unions would bargain with each other. The consequences of not reaching an agreement are far from obvious. The bargaining may break down or the consequences could be a costly delay of the outcome. Even a combination will in some cases be relevant. In the case of a breakdown, what would be the outcome? One could argue that the non-cooperative equilibrium represents the alternative to an agreement and subsequently the disagreement points. Moreover, it seems even harder to specify the costs if an agreement is delayed. Thus, modelling this bargaining game is too comprehensive a task for this paper. Nevertheless, some general remarks on efficient bargaining solutions are made below.

The fact that the game is repeated (at different intervals) should have brought us to the theory of supergames. A discussion of the structure in a supergame like ours, but between a union and a government, is given in Hersoug (1985).

## 3 NON-COOPERATIVE EQUILIBRIUM

The equilibrium implies that each part (here union) has done its best and does not regret when it recognises the action (here wage) taken by the other part. In equilibrium, the unions' expectations about the wages of other sectors catch up with reality. (See Oswald (1979) for a wage-equilibrium existence proof in a multi-sectorial model with utility-maximizing trade unions.)

However, it is not just the properties of the equilibrium that may be of interest. The expectations can be wrong and some time may be necessary to 'correct' the wage level according to the right expectations. The reaction functions of the unions will be of special interest. In other words, to what extent do changes in the other union's wage rate (*ceteris paribus*) influence the optimal wage rate? The slope of the reaction functions will indicate how strong the interdependence between the two sectors is.

One might argue that 'reaction function' is not an appropriate phrase in a simultaneous-move game. The 'union equilibrium locus' or 'best reply curve' would be better, but the tradition and advantage of brevity favours 'reaction function'.

On the other hand, the wages are influenced by several (for the unions) exogenous variables such as world market prices, the exchange rate, level of aggregate demand and growth in productivity due to (Hicks-neutral) technical progress.

The unions maximise their utility function subject to a labour-demand constraint. They are aware of the relationship between wages and prices in the $N$-sector. Moreover, the unions have perfect foresight about exogenous variables and are rational in the sense that they know the whole model describing the economy. An interior solution of:

$$\max_{w^T}\{U^T(r^T, n^T, r^N); (9.1)\} \text{ requires}$$

$$U_1^T + n_1^T U_2^T = 0 \tag{9.8}$$

and

$$U_{11}^T + 2n_1^T U_{21}^T + n_1^T n_2^T U_{22}^T < 0.$$

Similarly, for the $N$-sector;

$$\max_{w^N}\{U^N(r^N, n^N, r^T); (9.5), (9.6), (9.7)\} \text{ requires}$$

$$(1-\lambda)U_1^N + y_1^N U_2^N - \lambda U_3^N = 0 \tag{9.9}$$

and

$$(1-\lambda)^2 U_{11}^N + 2(1-\lambda)y_1^N U_{21}^N + (y_1^N)^2 U_{22}^N$$
$$-2\lambda(1-\lambda)U_{31}^N + U_2^N y_{11}^N < 0.$$

The interpretations of the first order conditions (9.8) and (9.9) are straightforward. The prices in the $T$-sector are given, so the 'marginal utility of wages' in this sector will consist of a real wage effect ($U_1^T > 0$)

and an employment effect $(n_1^T U_2^N < 0)$ which is negative because of the downward sloping demand for labour. In optimum, the increased wage level exactly compensates the reduced employment.

The wages in the $N$-sector influence the price level. Hence, the increasing wage rate will have two effects in addition to the negative employment effect $(y_1^N U_2^N < 0)$. Increased $w^N$ means higher prices reducing $r^T$. This is, from the $N$-union's point of view, positive $(-\lambda U_3^N > 0)$. A change of one percentage point in nominal wages turns out to be a change of $(1-\lambda)$ percentage in real wage because of the price formation in the $N$-sector. The positive real wage effect is then $(1-\lambda)U_1^N$.

(9.8) and (9.9) give us the non-cooperative equilibrium:

$$w^i = w^i(p^T, d, a^T, a^N), \qquad i = T, N. \tag{9.10}$$

The equilibrium wages are influenced by world market prices, the exchange rate, aggregate demand, a scale-neutral productivity parameter, and of course properties of labour demand in the two sectors. As we shall see, the unions' focus on relative wages (the 'envy-effect') also affects the wage level.

### The Reaction Functions

The wage-formations in the two sectors are interlinked in the sense that changes in the wage level in one sector will influence the other sector's optimal wage.

The reaction functions are implicitly defined by (9.8) and (9.9):

$$w^T = R^T(w^N; p^T, d, a^T, a^N) \text{ and } w^N = R^N(w^T; p^T, d, a^T, a^N).$$

The slope of the reaction function of sector $T$ is given by:[3]

$$\frac{\partial R^T}{\partial w^N} = \frac{\lambda(\overset{-}{U_{11}^T} + \overset{-}{n_1^T U_{21}^T}) - \overset{?}{n_2^T}(\overset{+}{U_{21}^T} + \overset{-}{n_1^T} \overset{-}{U_{22}^T}) - (1-\lambda)\overset{+}{U_{13}^T}}{\underset{-}{U_{11}^T} + \underset{-}{2n_1^T} \underset{+}{U_{12}^T} + \underset{-}{(n_1^T)^2} \underset{-}{U_{22}^T}}. \tag{9.11}$$

The denominator is negative. Thus, the slope depends on the numerator and we recognize the different effects that make the wages interdependent:

(i) $(1-\lambda)U_{13}^T$ is positive and represents the 'envy' or 'jealousy' effect. Increased wages in the $N$-sector imply that the union now prefers higher wage rate at the expense of employment. (The marginal utility of own wage-rate increases and the marginal utility of employment are unaffected, by assumption.)

(ii) $n_2^T(U_{21}^T + n_1^T U_{22}^T)$ represent the 'spillover effect' and may have any sign. Higher wages in the $N$-sector raise prices and influence the demand for labour in the $T$-sector. This 'shift' depends on $n_2^T$, whether the factors of production in the $T$-sector are gross complements ($n_2^T < 0$) or gross substitutes ($n_2^T > 0$). The 'spillover effect' is zero in the *EUU*-case. This reflects the general result that the real wage is independent of the level of labour demand as long as the labour-demand elasticity is constant.

(iii) $-\lambda(U_{11}^T + n_1^T U_{21}^T)$ is positive and appears because of the direct real wage decline in the $T$-sector caused by increased wage and price level in the $N$-sector.

The slope of the reaction function in the $T$-sector is assumed to be positive. (Hence, we exclude the possibility that a strong, negative 'spillover' effect dominates.)

The 'compensation' is normally not complete;

$$\frac{\partial R^T}{\partial w^N} < 1 \Leftrightarrow (1-\lambda)\underset{-}{U_{11}^T} + [\underset{-}{n_2^T} + (2-\lambda)n_1^T]\underset{+}{U_{21}^T} + \underset{-}{n_1^T}(\underset{-}{n_1^T} + n_2^T)\underset{-}{U_{22}^T} + (1-\lambda)\underset{+}{U_{13}^T} < 0 \tag{9.12}$$

which is fulfilled if the 'envy effect' is not too strong.

Given reasonable assumptions, the $T$-sector union compensates a higher wage level in thc $N$-sector, but not completely in the sense that relative wages are constant along the reaction function. Even without the envy effect, the compensation might be positive. The intuitive explanation of the partial 'compensation' could be that the union minimizes its loss by dividing it between a lower real (and relative) wage and reduced employment.

The reaction function of the $N$-sector is given by:

$$\frac{\partial R^N}{\partial w^T} = \frac{(1-\lambda)\overset{+}{U_{13}^N} + \overset{?}{y_4^N}((1-\lambda)\overset{+}{U_{12}^N} + \overset{-}{y_1^N} U_{22}^N) + \overset{+}{U_2^N}\overset{?}{y_{14}^N}}{-(1-\lambda)^2\underset{-}{U_{11}^N} - 2(1-\lambda)\underset{-}{y_1^N}\underset{+}{U_{12}^N} + 2\lambda(1-\lambda)\underset{+}{U_{13}^N} - (\underset{-}{y_1^N})^2\underset{-}{U_{22}^N} - \underset{+}{y_{11}^N}\underset{+}{U_2^N}} \tag{9.13}$$

The wage rate in the $T$-sector influences the optimal $N$-sector wage in three different ways:

(i) The 'envy'-effect $((1-\lambda)U_{13}^N)$ is positive.
(ii) The demand for intermediate $N$-goods from the $T$-sector shifts, but the direction is ambiguous. This 'spillover effect' $(y_4^N((1-\lambda)U_{12}^N+y_1^N U_{22}^N))$ is negative if the factors of production in the $T$-sectors are gross complements and positive in the case of gross substitutes. The 'spillover effect' is zero in the $EUU$-case.
(iii) The elasticity of labour demand with respect to wages is not generally constant in the $N$-sector. Therefore, higher wages in the $T$-sector may change this elasticity $(y_{14}^N \neq 0)$, and subsequently the optimal $w^N$. The sign of this effect depends on $y_{14}^N$ and it also occurs in the $EUU$-case.

However, the slope of the reaction function in the $N$-sector is generally ambiguous. The 'compensation' is not complete if

$$\frac{\partial R^N}{\partial w^T}<1 \Leftrightarrow (1-\lambda)^2 \underset{-}{U_{11}^N}+[(1-\lambda)\underset{-}{y_4^N}+2(1-\lambda)y_1^N]\underset{+}{U_{12}^N}$$

$$+\underset{-}{y_1^N}(\underset{-}{y_1^N}+y_4^N)\underset{-}{U_{22}^N}-(2\lambda\underset{?}{-}1)(1-\lambda)\underset{+}{U_{13}^N}+(\underset{?}{y_{14}^N}+\underset{+}{y_{11}^N})\underset{+}{U_2^N}<0.$$

The reaction function is assumed to be increasing with less than full 'compensation': $0<\partial R^N/\partial w^T<1$.

Figure 9.1 describes the reaction functions where $0<\partial R^i/\partial w_j<1$ $(i, j=T, N, i \neq j)$, and the non-cooperative equilibrium ($NCE$).

The arrows indicate that utility is increasing when moving towards each axis.

## 4 LEADER–FOLLOWER EQUILIBRIUM

Different theoretic and econometric models assume that the exposed sector, the sector producing traded goods, is a leader in the wage formation. We will now discuss the implications of this assumption within our framework and compare the results with the non-cooperative equilibrium. The decision rules of the two unions are quite different. The follower (here the union in the $N$-sector) considers the wage-rate of the other part as given or fixed. The leader, on the other

*Figure* 9.1 The non-cooperative equilibrium (*NCE*)

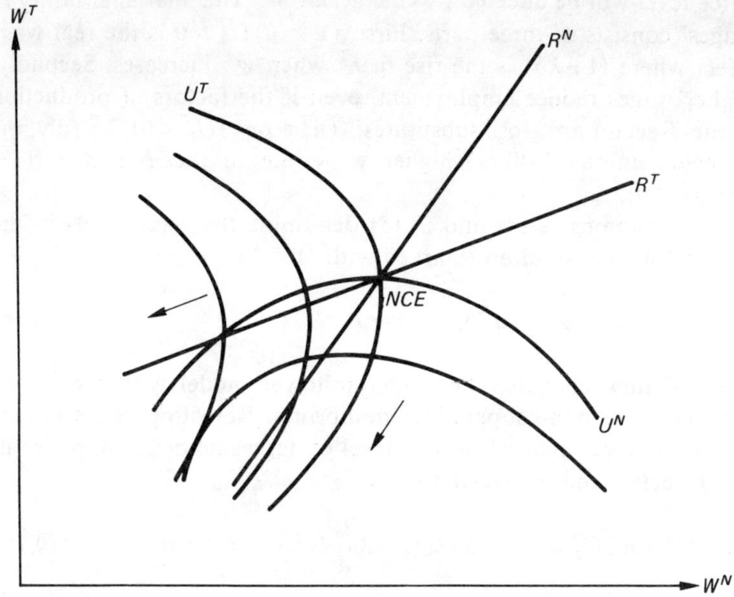


hand, takes the follower's reaction function into account, when he decides what would be the optimal wage level.

We shall assume that the reaction function of the $N$-sector is linear, which means that:

$$w^N = R^N(w^T; p^T, a^N, a^T, d), \qquad \frac{\partial R^N}{\partial w^T} = R_1^N = \delta. \tag{9.14}$$

An interior solution of

$$\max_{wT}\{U^T(r^T, n^T, r^N); (9.1), (9.5), (9.7) \text{ and } (9.14)\}$$

requires

$$(1-\lambda\delta)U_1^T + (n_1^T + \delta n_2^T)U_2^T + (1-\lambda)\delta U_3^T = 0. \tag{9.15}$$

The second-order condition is assumed to hold.

The interpretation of condition (9.15) is the following. The $T$-sector union knows that its wage level will influence the $N$-union according to the reaction function. Thus, the prices in $N$-sector and the overall price level will be affected by changes in $w^T$. The 'marginal utility of wages' consists of three parts. First, $(1-\lambda\delta)U_1^T>0$ is the real wage effect where $(1-\lambda\delta)$ is the rise in $r^T$ when $w^T$ increases. Secondly, higher wages reduce employment, even if the factors of production in the $T$-sector are gross substitutes: $((n_1^T+\delta n_2^T)U_2^T<0)$. Thirdly, the $T$-sector union 'dislikes' higher wage-rate in the $N$-sector $((1-\lambda)\delta U_3^T<0)$.

The equations (9.14) and (9.15) determine the wage levels in the leader–follower solution (marked with ˆ):

$$\hat{w}^i=\hat{w}^i(p^T, d, a^T, a^N), \qquad i=T, N. \tag{9.16}$$

We will now compare the leader–follower model with the simultaneous-move non-cooperative equilibrium. Rewriting (9.15) proves that $\hat{w}^i$ is lower than $w^i$ for any level of aggregate demand, prices in the $T$-sector, and 'productivity':

$$U_1^T+n_1^TU_2^T=-(1-\lambda)\delta U_3^T-\delta n_2^TU_2^T+\lambda\delta U_1^T>0. \tag{9.15$'$}$$

The left side of (9.15′), $U_1^T+n_1^TU_2^T$, is a decreasing function of $w^T$. The non-cooperative equilibrium implies $U_1^T+n_1^TU_2^T=0$. In the leader–follower solution this expression $(U_1^T+n_1^TU_2^T)$ will be positive, which implies that $w^T>\hat{w}^T$. The wage level in the $N$-sector is an increasing function of $w^T$ along the reaction function. Hence, $w^N>\hat{w}^N$. The two solutions are illustrated in Figure 9.2. Both groups are better off in the leader–follower situation ($LF$) than in the non-cooperative equilibrium ($NCE$). Moreover, the employers prefer the $LF$ to the $NCE$ solution because both wages are lower.

## 5 COMPARATIVE STATICS

The *non-cooperative equilibrium* wages are determined by (9.8) and (9.9), or the reaction functions (9.17):

$$w^i=R^i(w^j, p^T, a^N, a^T, d), \qquad i, j=T, N, \qquad i\neq j. \tag{9.17}$$

*Figure* 9.2 The non-cooperative equilibrium ($NCE$) and the leader–follower equilibrium ($LF$)

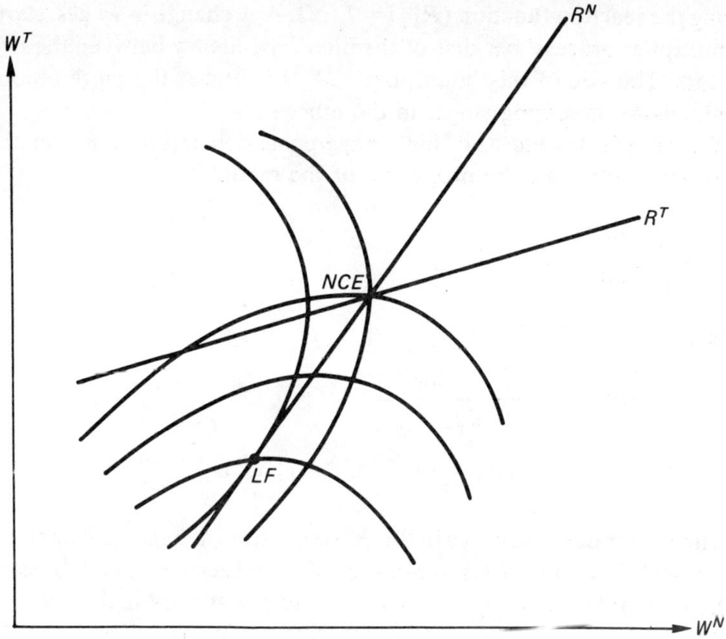


Implicit differentiation of (9.17) gives;

$$\begin{bmatrix} 1 & -R_1^T \\ -R_1^N & 1 \end{bmatrix} \begin{bmatrix} dw^T \\ dw^N \end{bmatrix} = \begin{bmatrix} 0 & R_2^T & R_3^T & R_4^T \\ R_5^N & R_2^N & R_3^N & R_4^N \end{bmatrix} \begin{bmatrix} dd \\ dp^T \\ da^N \\ da^T \end{bmatrix}$$

$$D = \begin{vmatrix} 1 & -R_1^T \\ -R_1^N & 1 \end{vmatrix} = 1 - R_1^T R_1^N, \qquad 0 < D < 1 \text{ if } 0 < R_1^i < 1$$

$(i = T, N)$.

(Detailed results in Appendix 9.2.)

The exogenous variables affect the optimal wage-rates in different ways. First, the labour-demand curve shifts and changes the desired wage (at least in the *G&L*-case). Secondly, exogenous changes (such as higher aggregate demand) may influence the elasticity of labour demand with respect to wages. In other words, some cases will represent both a twist and a shift in the labour-demand curve. The comparative static predictions do also depend on the 'compensation' along the reaction function ($R_1^i$, $i = T, N$). Any change in wages 'starts a multiplier process' because of the interdependency between the two sectors. The size of this 'multiplier' ($D^{-1}$) is higher the more unions compensate increasing wages in the other sector.

We describe the effects of higher aggregate demand in some details, in order to illustrate the properties of the model.

$$w_d^N = \frac{dw^N}{dd} = D^{-1}R_5^N,$$

where

$$\text{sign } R_5^N = \text{sign } \frac{dw^N}{dd_{|w^T\text{constant}}}$$
$$= \text{sign } \{(1-\lambda)\underset{+}{y_3^N}\underset{+}{U_{12}^N} + \underset{-}{y_1^N}\underset{+}{y_3^N}\underset{-}{U_{22}^N} + \underset{?}{y_{13}^N}U_2^N\}.$$

The labour demand curve in the $N$-sector shifts if aggregate demand increases. This 'shift-effect' is non-negative and zero in the $EUU$-case. (The level of labour demand does not influence the optimal wage-rate in the $EUU$-case as long as the elasticity is constant.) The elasticity of labour demand with respect to wages in the $N$-sector ($y_1^N$) may rise or fall as aggregate demand increases ($y_{13}^N \gtreqless 0$). Hence, the sign of the 'twist-effect' is ambiguous.

If the labour-demand elasticity is constant, more precise conclusions can be drawn. Wages are constant in the $EUU$-case and increase, if the unions maximise a '$G\&L$-utility function'.

Aggregate demand does not affect the wage-rate in the $N$-sector 'directly', but $w^T$ will change because of the interdependency;

$$w_d^T = R_1^T w_d^N.$$

If wages rise, the relative wages will change in favour of the $N$-sector union ($R_1^T < 1$).

Obviously, the employment implications depend crucially on what happens to the wage rate. If wages do not change, employment (in the $N$-sector) increases. The results are ambiguous if wages rise:

$$n_d^N = \underset{-}{y_1^N}\underset{+}{w_d^N} + \underset{+}{y_3^N} \gtreqless 0, \qquad n_d^T = \underset{-}{n_1^T}\underset{+}{w_d^T} + \underset{?}{n_2^T}\underset{+}{w_d^N} < 0 \quad \text{if } n_2^T < 0.$$

Real factor prices increase in the $T$-sector. Hence, employment falls in this sector if factors of production are gross complements. In the $N$-sector though, higher wages (and prices) counteract the positive demand effect.

Equilibrium wages change as *world market prices* or the exchange rate change; $w^i_{p^T} > 0$ $(i = N, T)$. In the $EUU$-case, prices in the $T$-sector (measured in domestic currency) have no real effects; $w^N_{p^T} = w^T_{p^T} = 1$. This result appears without tedious calculations since both labour demand and utility functions are homogeneous of degree zero in prices and wages. Thus, $w^T_{p^T} = w^N_{p^T} = 1$ represent a new equilibrium and both real and relative wages are constant. The demand for labour shifts in both sectors when $p^T$ increases, but for different reasons. Marginal revenue rises in the $T$-sector and makes it profitable to hire more workers at any wage level. The demand for labour in the $N$-sector increases because consumers substitute in favour of $N$-goods. Besides, demand for intermediate $N$-goods rises. In the $EUU$-case, higher nominal wages counteract exactly these effects and leave the employment unaffected. Real wages may change in any direction if the utility functions are of the *G&L*-type. Moreover, the implications for real factor prices $(w^T - p^T, p^N - p^T)$ and employment are ambiguous.

*Technical progress* in general affects equilibrium wages. A Hicks-neutral productivity improvement in the $T$-sector implies that both unions face a higher demand for labour. As in the discussion above, wages rise in the *G&L*-case, but remain constant in the $EUU$-case. However, technical progress in the $T$-sector may change the elasticity of labour demand with respect to wages in the $N$-sector (because demand for $N$-goods increase) and subsequently the desired wage rate. This 'twist-effect' would change the wage rate, even in the $EUU$-case. The implications of productivity improvements in the $N$-sector are even more complex, as the labour demand is changed in different ways. The need for labour at any production level, in the $N$-sector, declines. On the other hand, the $N$-sector prices fall because of lower unit costs and induce higher demand for $N$-goods. The $T$-sector union faces increased demand for labour, due to lower $p^N$. The total effects on wages, as productivity increases in the $N$-sector, are obviously indeterminate.

The comparative static predictions, in the non-cooperative equilibrium, depend on the utility function describing the preferences of the union. Moreover, exogenous changes may involve both a shift and a twist in the $N$-sector labour demand curve, and these two effects are possibly contrary.

We have shown that (nominal) wages rise if $T$-sector prices increase. Moreover, real wage rates and employment are independent of $p^T$ (world market prices and exchange rate) in the $EUU$-case.

Higher aggregate demand involves increased wages in the $G\&L$-case if $y_{13}^N \geq 0$ (the 'twist-effect' is either positive or zero). The wage changes in the $EUU$-case are totally dependent on this 'twist-effect'; sign $w_d^i = \text{sign } y_{13}^N = \text{sign}(c_1 - x_1)$.

The *leader–follower* solution is determined by

$$\hat{w}^T = S^T(w^N, p^T, a^N, a^T, d) \quad \text{(from (9.15))}$$
$$\hat{w}^N = R^N(w^T, p^T, a^N, a^T, d), \quad \text{where } R_1^N = \delta.$$

Total differentiation yields:

$$\begin{bmatrix} 1 & -S_1^T \\ -R_1^N & 1 \end{bmatrix} \begin{bmatrix} d\hat{w}^T \\ d\hat{w}^N \end{bmatrix} = \begin{bmatrix} 0 & S_2^T & S_3^T & S_4^T \\ R_5^N & R_2^N & R_3^N & R_4^N \end{bmatrix} \begin{bmatrix} dd \\ dp^T \\ da^N \\ da^T \end{bmatrix}$$

$$S = \begin{vmatrix} 1 & -S_1^T \\ -R_1^N & 1 \end{vmatrix} = 1 - S_1^T R_1^N > 0.$$

It can be shown that $S_1^T < 1$. Hence, $R_1^N < 1$ implies $S > 0$.

Most of the comparative static predictions are ambiguous and there are mainly two reasons for that. (Detailed results in Appendix 9.3.) First, the reaction function in the $N$-sector may shift in any direction as aggregate demand or 'productivity' changes (In some cases, the signs of $R_i^N (i = 2, \ldots, 5)$ are ambiguous.) Secondly, a shift in the $N$-sector reaction function influences $w^T$ in an ambiguous way ($S_1^T \gtreqless 0$). For example, a positive shift in $R^N$ (due to a higher aggregate demand) might well reduce $w^T$. This case is illustrated in Figure 9.3. (Labour demand and the contour lines of $U^T$ are constant.) The wage rate in the $T$-sector changes in any direction as exogenous variables change, because of this ambiguity.

Nevertheless, some precise conclusions can be drawn. *Aggregate demand* affects the $N$-sector wage rate in the same way (qualitatively) as in the non-cooperative equilibrium. The labour-demand curve shifts and the slope may change (if $y_{13}^N \neq 0$).

*Figure* 9.3 A positive shift in the $N$-sector reaction function ($R^N$) may reduce $T$-sector wages ($w^T$)

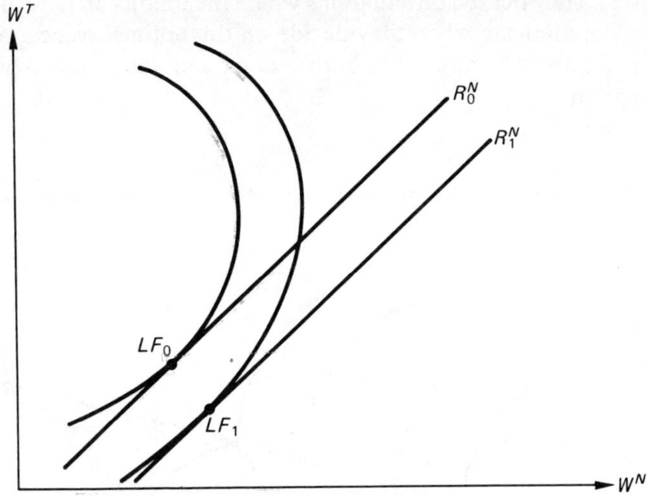


The neutrality of *prices in the T-sector*, if unions maximise expected utility or an utilitarian objective function, is still valid. The real wage and employment are constant ($\hat{w}^T_{p^T} = \hat{w}^N_{p^T} = 1$). The nominal wage rate in the $N$-sector increases as $p^T$ rises in the *G&L*-case, but the implications for $w^T$ are ambiguous.

Similar to the non-cooperative equilibrium, the implications of *technical progress* in the $N$-sector are indeterminate. Wages in the $N$-sector rise as 'productivity' in the $T$-sector increases (assumed that the shift dominates the 'twist' effect).

The comparative static predictions in the leader–follower solution are similar to those in the non-cooperative equilibrium, as far as the $N$-sector is concerned. The results for the $T$-sector may differ if a shift in the reaction function in the $N$-sector induces $w^T$ to fall.

Moreover, a comparison of the size of the comparative static predictions (between the leader–follower solution and the non-cooperative equilibrium) gives no precise conclusions. For example, we cannot say that an expansive fiscal policy (raising aggregate demand) has a larger impact on wages in the non-cooperative equilibrium than in the leader–follower solution.

## 6 COOPERATIVE SOLUTIONS

We have so far focused on situations where the unions do not collaborate or communicate when they decide on the optimal wages. A brief look at Figure 9.4 shows that both unions will gain from a binding cooperation.

*Figure* 9.4 Pareto optimal collusive solutions are on the contract curve *PP*

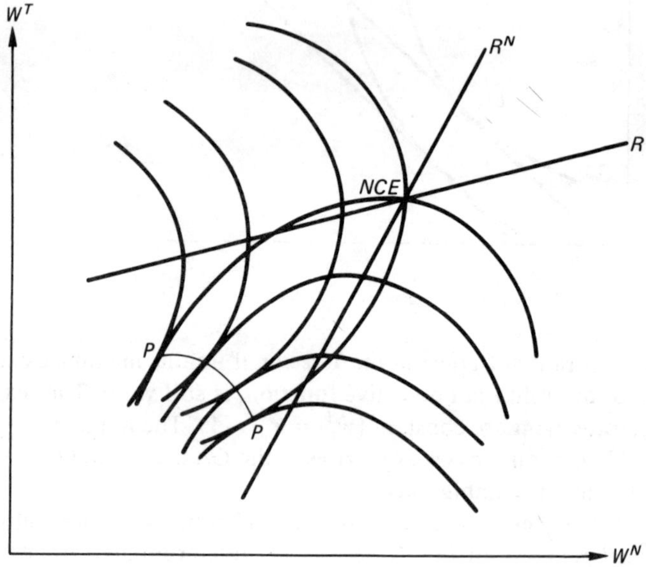


Efficient solutions, superior to the non-cooperative equilibrium are represented on the *PP*-line.

A Pareto-optimal solution implies that the wage levels are lower compared both to the leader–follower solution and to the non-cooperative equilibrium. Hence, the employment level is higher.

An important issue deals with the possibilities of establishing a cooperative solution. Leif Johansen (1977) emphasises that 'some sort of control and enforceability of agreements are required for the game to take a cooperative character'. The consequences of not following the agreement must be serious enough to prevent any from violating.

Thus we see there are problems of establishing a cooperative solution. The unions can hardly prevent local agreements implying higher wages (wage drift). A collaboration where all members abstain from higher wages due to local agreements can be difficult to implement.

There will obviously be gains from increasing one's own wage level if the other wages remain constant. This is a characteristic which makes the cooperative solution fragile. If one union expects the other not to change its wage level, there will be a temptation for the first union to increase its own wage rate. This would surely make the union better off. On the other hand, the fact that the wage negotiations are repeated makes the advantages of 'breaking out' quite brief. After some time the other union can compensate by adjusting its wages. And one might well end up in a non-cooperative equilibrium which, for both unions, represents a worse situation. This will probably discipline the unions in a cooperative solution, raising possibilities of establishing a lasting collaboration.

## 7 THE IMPLICATIONS OF 'RELATIVE WAGE FOCUSING'

The fact that unions care about relative wages may increase the interdependence between the different sectors as far as the wage determination is concerned.[4] For example, in the non-cooperative case, the 'envy' or 'jealousy effect' implies that changes in the $T$-sector wage will not leave the wages in the $N$-sector unchanged. In this section we study the implications of the 'relative wage focusing' more systematically. There are at least two important questions to be answered. Does the 'relative wage focusing' increase the nominal (and real) wage level? In other words, will higher wage level be a result of unions attaching more importance to relative wages? The other important question deals with the implications for changes in the equilibrium wages caused by changes in exogenous factors (i.e. comparative static predictions). For example, will changes in aggregate demand affect the equilibrium wage rates differently, depending on the weight the unions give to relative wages?

I think the first question can be answered within a rather general framework. The second will be discussed in terms of an example with separable utility functions.

It seems reasonable to argue that the 'relative wage focusing' affects the preferences in the sense that the indifference curves in a real wage–employment diagram change. For any given wage $(r)$ –

employment ($n$) point in Figure 9.5, the contour line through this point would be steeper the more concerned the union is about relative wages. As a consequence of more intensive relative wage focusing the union can accept a greater decline in employment for a higher real wage.

Hence, the optimal wage level increases if the union gives more weight to relative wages. This is illustrated in Figure 9.5 where the contour lines change from $U$ to $I$.

*Figure* 9.5 The indifference curves change if a union attaches more importance to relative wages

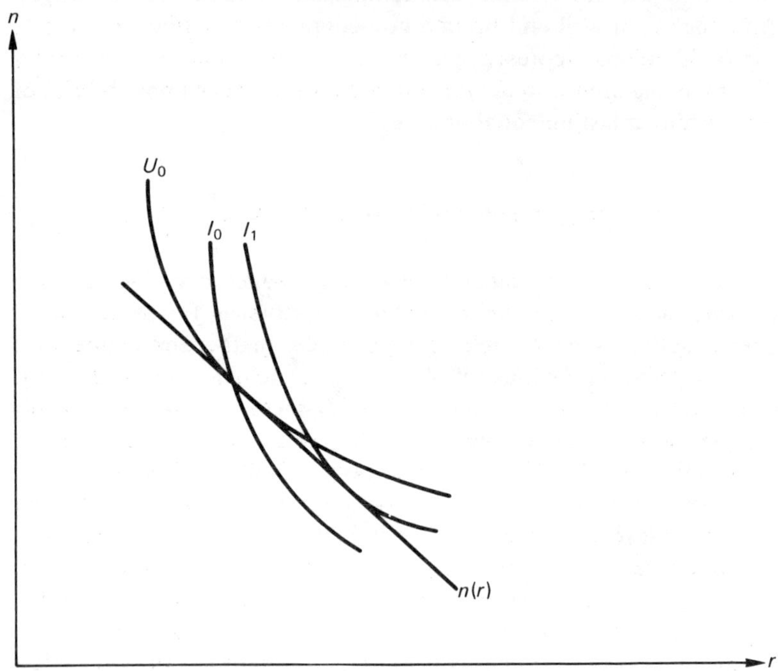


Until now we have implicitly assumed that the wage rate in the other sector is given.

Let us first look at the non-cooperative equilibrium. If the reaction functions have positive slopes in the $(w^T, w^N)$ diagram, both wage levels will increase, if one union (or both unions) 'get more concerned' about relative wages. The reaction function may shift as illustrated in Figure 9.6.

*Figure* 9.6 The non-cooperative wages increase if the *N*-sector union gives more weight to relative wages

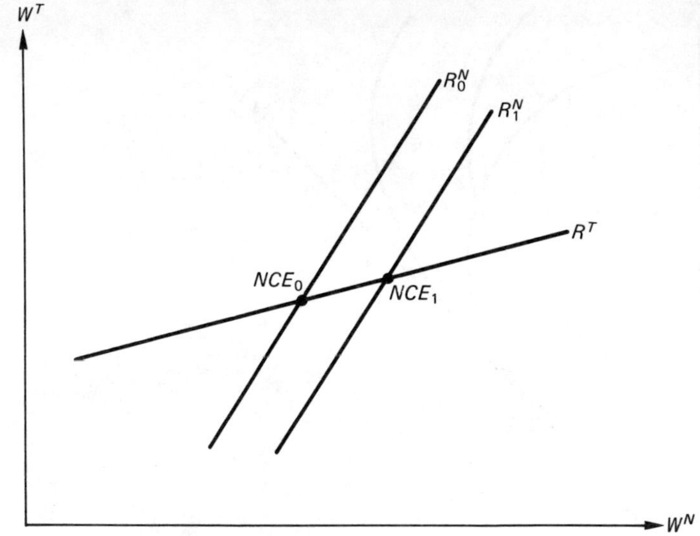


*Figure* 9.7 Wages may change in opposite directions in the *LF* equilibrium if the *N*-sector union gives more weight to relative wages

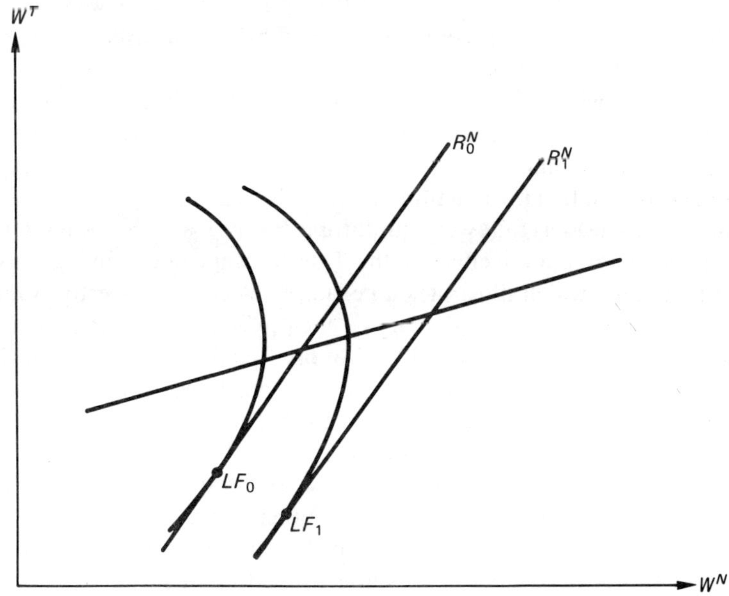

*Figure* 9.8 Wages in both sectors increase if the *T*-sector union attaches more importance to relative wages

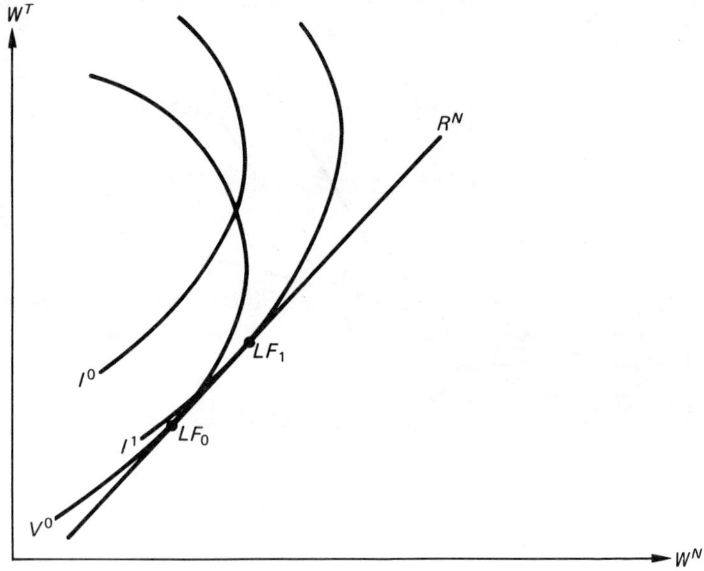


Given any wage in the $T$-sector, the optimal $N$-sector wage level is higher. The new non-cooperative equilibrium consists of higher wage rates in both sectors.

The results within the leader–follower model though, are ambiguous, at least as far as the effects on the $T$-sector wage level are concerned. If the $N$-sector union attaches more importance to relative wages, we have argued that the reaction function shifts positively. This means that the new leader–follower equilibrium involves a higher wage rate in the $N$-sector, but the effect on the $T$-sector wage rate is ambiguous. See Figure 9.7 which illustrates an example where the $T$-sector wage rate decreases. The results depend on the preferences and on how the $N$-sector reaction function shifts. A more 'relative wage concerned' union in the $T$-sector implies that the contour lines in the $(w^N, w^T)$ diagram in Figure 9.8 shift from $V$ to $I$. The new tangency point consists of higher wage rates in both sectors.

We now turn to a discussion of the 'relative wage focusing' and its implications for comparative statics. In other words, will the changes in equilibrium wage rates, caused by (model) exogenous changes, depend on the weight the unions give to relative wages?

Before we discuss this problem systematically, using a separable utility function, some comments must be made. In the non-cooperative equilibrium case we may split the effects of changes in aggregate demand and world market prices into two parts. First, exogenous changes may affect the optimal wage rate in one sector, given the other wage constant. We call this the direct effect. Second, one union will change its own optimal wage rate because of wage changes in the other sector. We may call this an indirect effect. The question is then if, and how, the direct and indirect effects would be influenced by the importance unions attach to relative wages. The direct effect occurs because changes in exogenous variables change the wage employment trade-off (the labour demand curve). It is possible that unions give higher preference to employment (for wages) when the labour-demand curve shifts (and other wages given), as a result of a more intensive 'relative wage focusing'. On the other hand, the indirect effect is stronger the more weight unions give to relative wages. Hence, the implications of the 'relative wage focusing' on wage changes are generally ambiguous, because the direct and indirect effect might well have an opposite sign.

Further discussion will be based on additive utility functions as:

$$U^T(r^T, n^T, r^N) = W^T(r^T, n^T) + \tilde{l}_T V^T(r^T - r^N)$$
$$U^N(r^N, n^N, r^T) = W^N(r^N, n^N) + \tilde{l}_N V^N(r^N - r^T)$$

where

$$\tilde{l}_i > 0 \text{ and } V_1^i = \frac{\partial V^i}{\partial (\ )} > 0$$
$$V_{11}^i < 0$$
$$U_1^i = W_1^i + \tilde{l}_i V_1^i > 0$$
$$U_{11}^i = W_{11}^i + \tilde{l}_i V_{11}^i < 0$$
$$U_{12}^i = W_{12}^i \geqslant 0$$
$$U_{13}^i = -\tilde{l}_i V_{11}^i > 0, \qquad i = T, N.$$

The $\tilde{l}$s are parameters expressing the weight unions give to relative wages. They are larger the more importance unions attach to relative wages. This means that the influence from the wage rate in the other sector on the marginal utility of one's own wage ($U_{13}^i$) increases. But within our specification of the utility function, increasing $\tilde{l}$s will also affect the slope of the marginal utility of wages: $U_{11}^{i}$ decreases.

*The non-cooperative equilibrium* is given by equations similar to (9.8) and (9.9):

$$W_1^T + \tilde{l}_T V_1^T + n_1^T W_2^T = 0 \tag{9.8'}$$

$$(1-\lambda) W_1^N + \tilde{l}_N V_1^N + y_1^N W_2^N = 0. \tag{9.9'}$$

(9.8′) and (9.9′) implicitly define the equilibrium wage rates

$$w^i = w^i(d, p^T, a^T, a^N, \tilde{l}_T, \tilde{l}_N), \qquad i = T, N. \tag{9.10'}$$

We have argued that $\partial w^i/\partial l_j > 0$ $(i, j, = T, N)$, real wages increase if unions give more weight to relative wages. The implications for comparative statics are given by the sign of the cross derivates, for example $\partial^2 w^i/\partial p^T \partial l_j$ $(i, j = T, N)$ in the case of $T$-sector prices. Tedious, but straightforward calculations, show that the comparative static predictions are influenced in different ways as unions attach more importance to relative wages. (Detailed result are given in Appendix 9.4.) The interdependency between the sectors, defined as the slope of the reaction functions, increases. Hence, the more unions focus on relative wages, the larger are the indirect effects of exogenous changes. But the direct effect of, for example, higher aggregate demand (given the wage rate in the other sector constant) may pull in the other direction. Our example has shown that the latter effect might well dominate.

## 7 CONCLUSIONS

The wage formation in a small open economy with strong rational unions would be characterised by interdependent wage claims. Wages and the employment level depend on the institutional framework in which the wage formation is taking place. This paper focuses and compares the non-cooperative equilibrium and a leader–follower solution. The latter involves lower wages and higher employment. Both unions prefer the leader–follower solution to the non-cooperative equilibrium. The comparative statics depend on the unions' objective function. Prices in the $T$-sector are 'neutral', real wages and employment are constant as world market-prices or the exchange rate change, if unions maximise an utilitarian or expected utility function. The implications of higher aggregate demand with respect to wages and employment are in general ambiguous. The fact that unions attach importance to relative wages implies higher wages levels. However it is not obvious that this 'relative wage focusing' is inflationary in the sense that given changes in exogenous variables (world market-prices or aggregate demand) have a larger influence on wages, the more unions attach importance to relative wages.

This chapter describes an economy with powerful unions able to set wages unilaterally. The interdependency between sectors would probably be present, if wages (and employment) in each sector were fixed by (efficient) bargaining. Moreover, unions have perfect information (knowledge) about relevant exogenous variables and relations in the economy. Obviously, unions make their decisions on the basis of expected labour demand and prices. Our model can be interpreted as a 'long-run' equilibrium when a trial-and-error progress has been brought to conclusion, and expectations catch up with reality. The properties of this model in the short run will surely depend on the way in which expectations are formed. Expectations play a more fundamental role, if currently employed members receive a higher weight than the unemployed in the trade-union objective function. This asymmetry implies that the union indifference curves (over wage and employment) have a 'kink' at the initial or existing level of employment. There is no tangency between an indifference curve and a labour-demand curve. Hence, a range of different wages and employment levels are consistent with the given labour demand. An unanticipated price change may alter the employment 'permanently', even though real wages are higher or lower than expected (see, e.g., Pemberton, 1984).

## Appendix 9.1: The Demand for Non-Traded Goods

$$Y^N = C\left(\frac{P^N}{P^T}, D\right) + X\left(\frac{P^N}{A^T P^T}, \frac{W^T}{A^T P^T}\right) \quad \text{implies}$$

$$\begin{aligned} y^N &= y^N(p^N, p^T, d, w^T, a^T) \\ &= \beta c(p^N - p^T, d) + (1-\beta)x(p^N - p^T - a^T, w^T - p^T - a^T) \end{aligned}$$

$$\beta = \frac{C}{Y^N}, \qquad (1-\beta) = \frac{X}{Y^N}$$

$$y_1^N = \beta \underset{-}{c_1} + (1-\beta)\underset{-}{x_1} < 0$$

$$y_2^N = -\underset{-}{y_1^N} - (1-\beta)\underset{?}{x_2} > 0$$

$$y_3^N = \beta c_2 > 0$$
$$y_4^N = (1-\beta)x_2 = -y_1^N - y_2^N \gtreqless 0 \Leftrightarrow x_2 \gtreqless 0$$
$$y_5^N = -(1-\beta)(x_1 + x_2) > 0$$
$$\frac{\partial \beta}{\partial d} = El_D\left(\frac{C}{Y^N}\right) = (1-\beta)c_2 > 0, \qquad \frac{\partial \beta}{\partial p^N} = (1-\beta)(c_1 - x_1),$$
$$\frac{\partial \beta}{\partial p^T} = -(1-\beta)(c_1 - x_1 - x_2).$$

Hence:

$$y_{11}^N = (c_1 - x_1)^2(1-\beta) > 0$$
$$y_{12}^N = (c_1 - x_1)\frac{\partial \beta}{\partial p^T} \gtreqless 0$$
$$y_{13}^N = (c_1 - x_1)c_2(1-\beta) \gtreqless 0 \Leftrightarrow c_1 - x_1 \gtreqless 0$$
$$y_{14}^N = -\frac{x_2}{c_2} y_{13}^N \gtreqless 0$$
$$y_{15}^N = (c_1 - x_1)(x_1 + x_2)(1-\beta) \gtreqless 0 \Leftrightarrow c_1 - x_1 \lesseqgtr 0$$

## Appendix 9.2: Non-Cooperative Equilibrium: Comparative Statics

(i) $w^T = R^T(w^N, p^T, a^N, a^T)$

(ii) $w^N = R^N(w^T, p^T, a^N, a^T, d)$.

Total differentiation yields;

$$\begin{bmatrix} 1 & -R_1^T \\ -R_1^N & 1 \end{bmatrix} \begin{bmatrix} dw^T \\ dw^N \end{bmatrix} = \begin{bmatrix} 0 & R_2^T & R_3^T & R_4^T \\ R_5^N & R_2^N & R_3^N & R_4^N \end{bmatrix} \begin{bmatrix} dd \\ dp^T \\ da^N \\ da^T \end{bmatrix}$$

$$D = \begin{vmatrix} 1 & -R_1^T \\ -R_1^N & 1 \end{vmatrix} = 1 - R_1^T R_1^N, \qquad 0 < D < 1 \text{ if } R_1^i < 1 \qquad (i = T, N).$$

Define,

$$U_{11}^T + 2n_1^T U_{12}^T + (n_{12}^T)^2 U_{22}^T = \Phi_T < 0$$
$$-(1-\lambda)^2 U_{11}^N - 2(1-\lambda)y_1^N U_{12}^N + 2\lambda(1-\lambda)U_{13}^N - (y_1^N)^2 U_{22}^N - y_{11}^N U_2^N = \Phi_N > 0$$

Hence;

$$R_2^T = \{(1-\lambda)U_{11}^T + (n_2^T + (2+\lambda)n_1^T)U_{12}^T + n_1^T(n_1^T + n_2^T)U_{22}^T + (1-\lambda)U_{13}^T\}\Phi_T^{-1} > 0$$

$$R_3^T = \{-2U_{11}^T + (n_2^T - \lambda n_1^T)U_{21}^T + n_1^T n_2^T U_{22}^T + \lambda U_{13}^T\}\Phi_T^{-1} \gtreqless 0$$

$$R_4^T = (n_1^T + n_2^T)(U_{12}^T + n_1^T U_{22}^T)\Phi_T^{-1} \geqq 0 \text{ (=0 in the } EUU\text{-case)}$$

$$R_2^N = \{-(1-\lambda)^2 U_{11}^N - (1-\lambda)(y_1^N - y_2^N)U_{21}^N + y_1^N y_2^N U_{22}^N - (1-\lambda)(2\lambda - 1)U_{13}^N + y_{12}^N U_2^N\}\Phi_N^{-1} > 0$$

$$R_3^N = \{\lambda(1-\lambda)U_{11}^N - (2\lambda - 1)y_1^N U_{21}^N - (y_1^N)^2 U_{22}^N + \lambda(1-2\lambda)U_{13}^N - y_{11}^N U_2^N\}\Phi_N^{-1} \gtreqless 0$$

$$R_4^N = \{(1-\lambda)y_5^N U_{12}^N - y_1^N y_5^N U_{22}^N + y_{15}^N U_2^N\}\Phi_N^{-1} > 0$$

$$R_5^N = \{(1-\lambda)y_3^N U_{12}^N + y_1^N y_3^N U_{22}^N + y_{13}^N U_2^N\}\Phi_N^{-1} \gtreqless 0$$

$$\frac{dw^N}{dd} = D^{-1}R_5^N$$

$$\frac{dw^T}{dd} = R_1^T \frac{dw^N}{dd}$$

$$\frac{dw^T}{dp^T} = D^{-1}(R_2^T + R_1^T R_2^N) > 0$$

$$\frac{dw^N}{dp^T} = D^{-1}(R_2^N + R_1^N R_2^T) > 0$$

$$\frac{dw^T}{da^N} = D^{-1}(R_3^T + R_1^T R_3^N) \gtreqless 0$$

$$\frac{dw^N}{da^N} = D^{-1}(R_3^N + R_1^N R_3^T) \gtreqless 0$$

$$\frac{dw^T}{da^T} = D^{-1}(R_4^T + R_1^T R_4^N) \geqslant 0$$

$$\frac{dw^N}{da^T} = D^{-1}(R_4^N + R_1^N R_4^T) \geqslant 0$$

## Appendix 9.3: Leader Follower: Comparative Statics

$$(1-\lambda\delta)U_1^T + (n_1^T + \delta n_2^T)U_2^T + (1-\lambda)\delta U_3^T = 0 \text{ and}$$

$$U_1^N + n_1^N U_2^N = 0 \text{ give}$$

(i) $w^T = S^T(w^N, p^T, a^N, a^T, d)$

(ii) $w^N = R^N(w^T, p^T, a^N, a^T, d)$; $R_1^N = \delta$.

Total differentiation of (i) and (ii) implies;

$$\begin{bmatrix} 1 & -S_1^T \\ -R_1^N & 1 \end{bmatrix} \begin{bmatrix} d\hat{w}^T \\ d\hat{w}^N \end{bmatrix} = \begin{bmatrix} 0 & S_2^T & S_3^T & S_4^T \\ R_5^N & R_2^N & R_3^N & R_4^N \end{bmatrix} \begin{bmatrix} dd \\ dp^T \\ da^N \\ da^T \end{bmatrix}$$

$$S = \begin{vmatrix} 1 & -S_1^T \\ -R_1^N & 1 \end{vmatrix} > 0.$$

It can be shown that $S_1^T < 1$. Hence, $S > 0$ if $R_1^N < 1$. Define

$$(1-\lambda\delta)U_{11}^T + (2n_1^T + \delta(1-\lambda))U_{12}^T + W_1^T(n_1^T + \delta n_2^T)U_{22}^T = K^T < 0$$

Hence;

$$S_1^T = \{(1-\lambda)(1-\lambda\delta)U_{11}^T - ((1-\delta)n_2^T - (1-\lambda)n_1^T)U_{12}^T + (1-\lambda)(1-2\lambda\delta+\delta)U_{13}^T\}K_T^{-1} \gtreqless 0$$

$$S_2^T = \{\lambda(1-\lambda\delta)U_{11}^T + [(1-\lambda)(n_1^T + \delta n_2^T) + (1-\lambda\delta)(n_1^T + n_2^T)]U_{12}^T + (n_1^T + \delta n_2^T)(n_1^T + n_2^T)U_{22}^T + (1-\lambda)(1-2\lambda\delta+\delta)U_{13}^T\} \cdot K_T^{-1} > 0$$

$$S_3^T = \{-\lambda(1-\lambda\delta)U_{11}^T + \lambda[(1-\delta)n_1^T - \delta\lambda n_2^T]U_{12}^T + (n_1^T + \delta n_2^T)n_2^T U_{22}^T - (1-\lambda)(1-2\lambda\delta+\delta)U_{13}^T\}K_T^{-1} \gtreqless 0$$

$$S_4^T = \{(1-\lambda\delta)(n_1^T + n_2^T)U_{12}^T + (n_1^T + n_2^T)(n_1^T + \delta n_2^T)U_{22}^T\}K_T^{-1} \geq 0$$

(=0 in the *EUU*-case).

$$\frac{d\hat{w}^T}{dd} = S^{-1}S_1^T R_5^N \gtreqless 0$$

$$\frac{d\hat{w}^N}{dd} = S^{-1}R_5^N \gtreqless 0$$

$$\frac{d\hat{w}^T}{dp^T} = S^{-1}(S_2^T + R_2^N S_1^T) \gtreqless 0$$

$$\frac{d\hat{w}^N}{dp^T} = S^{-1}(R_2^N + R_1^N S_2^T) > 0$$

$$\frac{d\hat{w}^T}{da^N} = S^{-1}(S_3^T + R_3^N S_1^T) \gtreqless 0$$

$$\frac{d\hat{w}^N}{da^N} = S^{-1}(R_3^N + R_1^N S_3^T) \gtreqless 0$$

$$\frac{d\hat{w}^T}{da^T} = S^{-1}(S_4^T + S_1^T R_4^N) \gtreqless 0$$

$$\frac{d\hat{w}^N}{da^T} = S^{-1}(R_4^N + R_1^N S_4^T) \gtreqless 0.$$

## Appendix 9.4: The Implications of 'Relative Wage Focusing'

The slopes of the reaction functions increase if unions give more weight to relative wages:

$$\frac{\partial R_1^N}{\partial l_N} = -(1-\lambda)\frac{V_{11}^N}{\Phi_N}(1-R_1^N) > 0, \qquad \frac{\partial R_1^T}{\partial l_T} = \frac{V_{11}^T}{\Phi_T}(1-R_1^T) > 0.$$

The comparative static predictions depend on the parameters, expressing the importance unions attach to relative wages.

$$w_{dl_N}^N = \frac{\partial w_d^N}{\partial l_N} = -(1-\lambda)D^{-2}\frac{V_{11}^N}{\Phi_N} R_5^N(1 + R_1^T - 2R_1^T R_1^N) \gtreqless 0 \Leftrightarrow R_5^N \gtreqless 0$$

$$w_{dl_N}^T = R_1^T w_{dl_N}^N \gtreqless 0 \Leftrightarrow R_5^N \lesseqgtr 0$$

$$w_{dl_T}^N = D^{-2}\frac{V_{11}^T}{\Phi_T} R_5^N(1-R_1^T) \gtreqless 0 \Leftrightarrow R_5^N \gtreqless 0$$

$$w_{dl_T}^T = D^{-2}\frac{V_{11}^T}{\Phi_T} R_5^N(1-R_1^T)(R_1^T + D) \gtreqless 0 \Leftrightarrow R_5^N \gtreqless 0$$

$$w_{p^T l_T}^N = D^{-2}\frac{V_{11}^T}{\Phi_T} R_1^N(R_2^N + R_1^N R_2^T(1-R_1^T) + DR_2^T) > 0$$

$$w_{p^T l_T}^T = D^{-2}\left\{\frac{\partial R_1^T}{\partial l_T}(R_2^N + R_2^T R_1^N + R_2^N R_1^T R_1^N) - D\frac{V_{11}^T}{\Phi_T}\right\} > 0$$

$$w_{p^T l_N}^N = D^{-1}\left\{\frac{(1-\lambda)V_{11}^N}{\Phi_N}(1-R_1^N)(w_{p^T}^N R_1^T - R_2^T) + \frac{\partial R_2^N}{\partial l_N}\right\} \gtreqless 0$$

$$w_{p^T l_N}^T = D^{-1}R_1^T\left\{\frac{(1-\lambda)V_{11}^N}{\Phi_N}(1-R_1^N)w_{p^T}^T + \frac{\partial R_2^N}{\partial l_N}\right\} \gtreqless 0.$$

Thus, the size of comparative static predictions may change in any direction as unions get more concerned about relative wages.

## Notes

1. Calmfors (1982) discusses wage formation and employment policies in a small open economy with *one*, central trade union which sets the wage rate unilaterally. The wage is the same in both sectors.
2. Although the institutional aspects of wage determination can justify this approach. In Norway (parts of) the *T*-sector usually is the first to negotiate about wages. The results of these negotiations are known when other groups are supposed to adjust their wages. Such a system has many characteristics in common with a Stackelberg where the leader–follower question is institutionally determined. On the other hand, a large part of the wage increases in Norway during the past decades have been caused by wage drift.
3. '+' means that expressions are non-negative and '−' means that expressions are non-positive.
4. See also Oswald (1979) p. 375.

## References

AUKRUST, O. (1978) *Inflation in the Open Economy: A Norwegian Model*, Artikler nr. 96, Central Bureau of Statistics, Oslo 1977.

BINMORE, K., RUBINSTEIN, A. and WOLINSKY, A. (1985) *The Nash Bargaining Solution in Economic Modelling*, ICERD Discussion paper 85/112, London School of Economics.

GYLFASON, T. and LINDBECK, A. (1984a) 'Union Rivalry and Wages: An Oligopolistic Approach', *Economica*, 51, no 202, May 1984.

GYLFASON, T. and LINDBECK, A. (1984b) 'Competing Wage Claims, Cost Inflation and Capacity Utilization', *European Economic Review*, no. 24, pp. 1–21.

HERSOUG, T. (1983) 'Union Wage Responses to Tax Changes', *Oxford Economic Papers*, 36, pp. 37–51.

HERSOUG, T. (1985) 'Workers *versus* Government? Who Adjusts to Whom?', *Scandinavian Journal of Economics*, 87 (2) pp. 270–91.

JOHANSEN, L. (1977), *Lectures on Macroeconomic Planning, Part* 1. *General Aspects* (Amsterdam: North Holland).

JOHANSEN, L. (1982) 'On the Status of the Nash Type of an Non-Cooperative Equilibrium in Economic Theory', *Scandinavian Journal of Economics*, 1982.

HOEL, M. (1981) 'The Domestic Demand Compensated Effects of Changes in the Exchange Rate, Foreign Prices, Tariffs and Foreign Demand', *Scandinavian Journal of Economics*, 1981, pp. 508–21.

OSWALD, A. (1979) 'Wage Determination in an Economy with many Trade Unions', *Oxford Economic Papers*, 31, no 3.

OSWALD, A. (1985) 'The Economic Theory of Trade Unions: An Introductory Survey', *Scandinavian Journal of Economics*, 87 (2) pp. 160–93.

PEMBERTON, J. (1984) 'Wage Bargaining and the Microeconomic Theory of the Trade Union', mimeo, Reading University, 1984.

PENCAVEL, J. (1985) 'Wages and Employment, under Trade Unionism: Microeconomic Models and Macroeconomic Applications', *Scandinavian Journal of Economics*, 2, pp. 197–225.

## COMMENT ON CHAPTERS 8 AND 9

**P. Keizer**

The analysis of Mulder and van der Ploeg is about a small open economy with so-called dominant unions. The supply side as well as the demand side of the economy is well developed. Firms are operating on goods markets characterised by monopolistic competition and are striving for a maximisation of the discounted value of the profits. On the labour market, there is one monopoly union, which chooses the consumers' real wage to maximise a utility function, containing net wage income, employment and unemployment benefits. The union is dominant in the sense that it has the power to set nominal wages unilaterally. The central theme of this contribution is the union's problem of maintaining credibility with the firms when setting the wage rate rather low. The problem is especially relevant when long-term contracting is not possible. The motive of the union in setting the wage rate rather low, is to induce a rather high level of investments. But in the absence of a binding contract the union has the possibility of raising the wage level, when the desired and expected investments are realised. In that way the union squeezes the quasi capital rent. Firms who are afraid of this kind of reneging of the contracts, are not prepared to realise a high investment level. To take away that fear the union must build up a reputation 'not to renege' contracts.

On the other hand firms must build up a reputation of good investors in case of a low wage level. The authors build a macro model for an open economy and compare the results in a situation of absence of mutual credibility with the results in a situation of mutual thrust. The low-wage-high-investment scenario leads to more economic growth and employment than in the high-wage-low-investment scenario.

Another important feature of the model is the role of the so-called 'wedge', that is the difference between the wage level paid by the employers and the wage level received by the employees. The collective burden especially is responsible for this difference.

With the help of this model the authors try to explain the development of employment in the Dutch economy over the last twenty years. The most important variable in their explanation is the real wage level. The strong increases during the 1960s and 1970s meant a breakdown of the favourable competitive position of the Netherlands in the world economy achieved during the 1950s and early 1960s. Three main causes of the real-wage rise play a role. First of all the growing government budget implied a heavy and increasing collective burden leading to an ever-growing wedge between wages paid by employers and wages received by employees. This collective burden is partly shifted by the employees leading to an increase in the gross wages. A second way the Dutch wage level increased, was the rise in unemployment benefits leading to lower marginal costs to the unions in case of unemployment. The third and most typical factor for the analysis of Mulder and van der Ploeg is the assumed change in regime from rules to discretion. Labour relations can be characterised by the degree of consensus about distribution rules. In the 1950s and early 1960s the Dutch labour relations were characterised by a high degree of consensus. During the 1960s and 1970s this consensus broke down. In terms of the analysis of Mulder and van der Ploeg: the Dutch economy moved from a regime characterised by rules and a high level of credibility in which the Pareto-superior low-wage–high-investment–high-employment strategy was possible, to a regime of discretion and absence of consensus and credibility, in which the Pareto-inferior high-wage–low-investment–low-employment strategy only was possible.

This analysis leads to the following comments:

1. The strong rise in the real-wage level as a main cause of the high Dutch unemployment figures is a view accepted by most Dutch economists. About the way we can explain this wage-level development economists have a lesser degree of consensus. Most people stress the growth of the collective burden and the subsequent shift in the wage level paid by employers. Some other people add to this explanation the phenomenon of the change in ideology and/or militancy of the unions. The first stand is especially popular in circles of theoreticians and model-builders. The second view is only popular in circles of scientists with a more literal style. Because the model of Mulder and van der Ploeg must be considered as a mathematical illlustration of the second view, their contribution is an important step forward.
2. As already said the analysis stresses the move from a 'rule regime' to a situation of discretion. But for a proper valuation of such a proposition, we need a careful description of both regimes. Thereafter, we need a careful description of the Dutch labour relations system in terms of regimes. Only in this way can adherents of the second view convince the adherents of the first view.

3. In a paper van der Ploeg sent to the conference, which differed from the chapter he actually presented, he discusses several regimes. First, it is possible that a social planner weights the interests of firms and unions and decides about the optimal wage, profit, capital stock and employment levels. The second possibility is the existence of consensus about the use of an equity rule. The third regime which is to be distinguished is a situation in which all parties have build up so-called reputation assets, making possible Pareto-superior solutions without binding contracts. A fourth regime is a situation of bargaining, in which the relative power of the parties determines the results. In the contribution of Mulder and van der Ploeg, as actually presented to the conference, however, the discussion of the regimes disappeared. I consider this as a step backwards. What we need is a more careful analysis of the regimes mentioned, as an evaluation of Dutch labour relations in terms of those regimes. Maybe one of the results of this careful examination would be a change in the set of goals for which some parties are striving.
4. I wonder about the conclusion that the high-employment-low-wage strategy is Pareto-superior with respect to the low-employment-high-wage strategy, while the utility function of the union is not specified. One element leads to a higher utility level (wages), another to a lower utility level (employment). As long as the weights of both elements in the utility function are unknown, we do not know which situation is to be considered as superior in the sense of Pareto.
5. The analysis is also of high importance, because it can contribute to the introduction of social and political factors in economic analyses. Integration of sociology and economic science is, as I see it, one of the most important developments of today. The marginal utility of further specialisation nowadays is lower than the marginal utility of one extra unit of integration between the various behavioural sciences. But if we judge Mulder's and van der Ploeg's work from that point of view, other kind of criticisms are possible. The accessibility of the text leaves much to be desired. For example, not all symbols are defined. Sometimes the meaning of a symbol changes during the analysis. The precise difference between concepts as 'shadow-price of capital', 'user-cost of capital', 'capital gains' and 'the price of investment goods' is not explained and many effects and results from changes in the exogenous variables are only mentioned but not explained.

Summarising my comment, Mulder and van der Ploeg present an analysis which is very interesting and important. The analysis needs further extension in sociological direction and a better presentation.

The institutional context in the paper by Raaum is a small, open economy consisting of two sectors. One sector, the so-called $T$ (traded)-sector has strong connections with other economies and the firms within this sector must be considered as price-takers. The other sector, the so-called $N$ (non-traded)-sector has no connections with foreign economies and the firms within this sector must be considered as price-setters. In both sectors there are strong unions - strong in the sense that they are able to set the nominal value of the wages. The author develops a model with production and employment functions for both sectors, a price-level function and for the $N$-sector a demand-for-goods- and a profit-share-function.

The unions are assumed to be interdependent in a very direct way in their wage claims. The direct relationship between both wage levels is called the envy-effect. Moreover, there is an interdependency via the general price level. If wages in the one sector are raising, this leads to price increases, which affects the real value of the wages. Via price-compensation clauses unions can try to mitigate this effect. Third, the author says that a wage increase in the $N$-sector leads to a decrease of the demand for labour in the $T$-sector.

Both unions are assumed to derive utility from the real value of their own wage level (+), the real value of the wage level of the other union (−) and the employment level in the own sector (+). The main problem of the paper is to analyse the relationship between the wage interdependency and the utility level of the unions under different regimes of (non)-cooperation.

In the first instance Raaum analyses the relationship in a non-cooperation setting. A Nash–Cournot equilibrium is assumed. Wage reaction functions are developed and confronted with the utility functions. The intersection-point of both reaction functions determines the so-called non-cooperative equilibrium (NCE).

In the second instance Raaum analyses the relationship in a 'leader–follower' setting. A leader is defined as the union which takes the followers' reaction function into account, when deciding what would be the optimal wage level. A follower is defined as the union for which the wage rate of the leader is given. The $T$-sector union is considered to be the leader. In comparison with the first (non-cooperation) situation the reaction function of the $N$-union remains the same, whereas the reaction function of the $T$-union disappears: it derives an optimal wage by maximising its utility. Raaum's analysis indicates that in the new leader–follower equilibrium (LFE) both parties are better off.

In the third instance other forms of cooperation are researched, leading to the conclusion that there is a whole range of cooperative equilibria which are all Pareto-improvements if compared with LFE and NCE.

With respect to the implications of relative wage focusing (RWF) for the economy Raaum comes to the following conclusions: a stronger RWF leads to a higher wage level in the NC- as well as in the LF-model. It is not obvious whether a stronger RSF does make the wages more sensitive for exogenous shocks or not.

My comments on this paper are as follows:

- The paper deals with interesting problems in a sophisticated way. Alas, the presentation of relations and of the model as a whole is not clear enough. The paper needs a list of symbols and a careful exposition of assumptions and relations.
- A strong union is defined as a union, which is able to set nominal wages. But it seems to be that this definition is suggested by the necessity of having assumptions which are easily used from an analytic–technical point of view. But in reality, it is difficult to imagine a union so strong as to determine nominal wages completely and yet have to wait passively what the results in real terms will be. A union is strong if it is able to influence real wages considerably and a union is weak when it is not able to have an important influence on the real wage;
- The difference between NC and LF appear to be gradual. In both cases both sectors depend on each other. Also in the LF-case the leader have a reaction function. At least, the wage rate of the $T$-sector changes in reaction on a change in the wage rate of the $N$-sector. In the Scandinavian model of Edgren, Faxèn and Odhner (the so-called EFO-model), the wages in the leading sector depends only on the world market prices and there is no influence of the wage rate in the $N$-sector on the wage-rate in the $T$-sector. That implies that only in the EFO-model there is a pure LF-relation;
- Raaum concludes that both parties are better off in an LF-situation but I cannot imagine that being so in a situation in which both wage levels are lower. As long as the utility functions are not specified the conclusion 'better off' cannot be drawn.

My main problem with the paper is the difficulty of understanding the model. The conclusions are, however, in line with my intuition. An improvement of the presentation is important, because the subject and the conclusions are of high relevance.

# 10 Unemployment in the European Community: Counting the Costs*

P. N. Junankar

## 10.1 INTRODUCTION

In the past few years unemployment has grown rapidly and reached post-war record levels in the European Community (EC). The total registered unemployment in the EC in February 1988 was 16.6 million while the total in the 'big four' (France, Germany, Italy and the United Kingdom) was 11.5 million. An especially worrying feature has been the growth of youth unemployment as well as the increase in long-term unemployment. Table 10.1 gives a summary picture of these trends:

These high levels of unemployment have imposed significant costs on individuals (both unemployed and employed), on their families, on social classes, on the Government, and on society in general. The costs of unemployment are not only economic but also social and political. The aim of this paper is to discuss these costs of unemployment and to provide some estimates for the economic costs. The chapter is structured as follows: Section 10.2 discusses the problem of assessing the costs of unemployment, Section 10.3 provides some estimates for the output loss costs of unemployment, and Section 10.4 concludes the chapter.

## 10.2 ASSESSING THE COSTS[1]

In this section we shall discuss some of the analytical problems involved in evaluating the costs of unemployment. The costs of unemployment are economic, social and political. These costs are borne (to differing extents) by individuals (both unemployed and employed), by their families, by social groups or classes, by the Government and,

* Acknowledgements: I should like to thank Sue Bowden and Mark Conaty for research assistance.

*Table* 10.1 Growth of unemployment in the EC

| | 1979 | | | 1986 | | |
|---|---|---|---|---|---|---|
| | *Unemployment rate*[1] | *Long-term unemployment*[2] | *Youth unemployment*[3] | *Unemployment rate*[1] | *Long-term unemployment*[2] | *Youth unemployment*[3] |
| Federal Republic of Germany | 3.2 | 19.9 | 3.4 | 8.0 | 32.0 | 8.4 |
| France | 9.9 | 30.3 | 13.4 | 10.5 | 47.8 | 23.4 |
| Italy | 7.6 | n.a. | 25.6 | 10.9 | n.a. | 39.3 |
| United Kingdom | 5.6 | 24.5 | 10.6 | 11.8 | 41.1 | 20.7 |

*Source*: OECD, *Employment Outlook*, 1984, 1985, 1986.

*Notes*:

1. Standardised unemployment rates.
2. Percentage of unemployed with duration of 12 months and over.
3. Percentage of total youth labour force (less than 25 years) unemployed.

n.a. = not available.

of course, society in general. The economic costs faced by the individual depend on whether (s)he is employed or unemployed. If the individual is employed, the overall level of unemployment may affect the increases in (real) earnings as well as decreasing the probability of moving to better paid or more satisfying employment. For the unemployed person the economic costs are obviously the loss of income (less any social security benefits and the value of leisure). The economic costs to society are the loss of potential output both in the current period (static costs) and in the future (dynamic costs). The economic costs to the Government involve the extra social security payments plus the loss of tax revenue due to lower incomes and expenditure. However, except for the administrative costs, these are transfer payments and hence not a cost to society. The social (psychological) costs to the individual are the loss of status and esteem for the unemployed person while the social costs to society are due to increased social tension, civil strife, increased crime, morbidity and mortality. The social, and political costs to groups (classes) are in altering the balance of power (both in industrial relations and in the political process) away from workers towards the employers (capitalists). Governments may find that their political base is eroded by growing unemployment and may be forced to alter course. There are also signs of a growth of racism and an attack on ethnic minorities by the extreme right.

In evaluating the costs of unemployment, we need to aggregate the various costs and benefits of running an economy with a certain level of unemployment. In fact many of the costs and benefits are difficult (if not impossible) to quantify. However, even if we could obtain a numerical estimate for the different costs and benefits, it is not clear how these should be 'weighted' to obtain some aggregate measure of the costs of unemployment. Let us enumerate the different costs and benefits:

(a) current output loss (static costs);
(b) future output loss (dynamic costs);
(c) costs to the unemployed individual (loss of income minus social security benefits, loss of future income because of decreased probability of obtaining a future job);
(d) costs to the unemployed individual (increased morbidity, increased probability of mortality, psychological costs);
(e) costs to the employed individual (lower rate of increase of wages/earnings);

(f) costs to the employed individual (increased amount of labour services extracted because of the threat of losing one's job, decreased job mobility leading to dissatisfaction);
(g) costs to the family of unemployed individuals (both monetary and social - psychological stress, arguments, separation/divorce);
(h) costs to the Government Revenue Department (Exchequer) (higher social security payments, less taxes collected from lower incomes and lower expenditure);
(i) costs for society (greater social tension, strife, crime, etc.);
(j) costs (benefits?) to society in terms of changed balance of power between workers and capitalists (weakening of trade union power);
(k) benefits of lower rates of inflation;
(l) benefits of leisure to an unemployed individual[2];
(m) benefits of a revitalised capitalist economy by weeding out of inefficient firms and helping the concentration of economic power;
(n) macroeconomic effects on saving and investment of large Government expenditures on social security and declining tax revenues.

Clearly this is a wide range of costs and benefits to try to estimate and in many cases, they would be impossible to quantify. Even if we could quantify each of them we would have to avoid an element of double counting. For example, we cannot add together the output loss costs and the fiscal (Exchequer) costs. In an ideal world we would aggregate all these costs and benefits by attaching weights to the costs and benefits obtained by different individuals or groups (classes). However, this would require making a series of value judgements which would very likely be questioned. In this chapter we shall simply provide some estimates of the output loss costs of unemployment.

To be able to properly evaluate the costs and benefits of unemployment we need to specify:

(i) what caused unemployment to rise;
(ii) what lower level of unemployment we consider;
(iii) how is this lower level of unemployment to be achieved, i.e. what specific policies generate the lower unemployment level.

The implicit assumption in this chapter is that unemployment is avoidable, i.e. an alternative set of policies would lead to a lower unemployment rate. The view taken by this author is that the main reason for the growth in unemployment is a lack of effective demand. Some authors have argued that high real-wage rates, high social-security benefits, or increased power of trade unions, etc., have caused the growth of unemployment. Clearly one's view of the causes of unemployment affects the evaluation of the costs of unemployment. For example, if higher unemployment were caused by increased social security benefits, the unemployment is voluntary and therefore has no costs, if we ignore externalities in the search process (congestion costs).

## 10.3 THE REAL COSTS OF UNEMPLOYMENT: OUTPUT LOSS

The real economic cost to society of the high levels of unemployment lies in the loss of current and future potential output. If all (or perhaps, more accurately, many) of the unemployed found work today, they would be producing more goods and services and national income would be higher today. Clearly an interesting question is how much higher would national income have been if the unemployment levels in the EC were at a lower level (say that before the oil-price shock). If the answer to this question is that the order of magnitude is in excess of 10 per cent of national income, then society is paying a very high price for this unemployment. If the answer were less than 1 per cent, perhaps we would be justified in saying that it is not worth making such a fuss about unemployment. In addition, an interesting (but difficult) question is to what extent *future* output is affected by current high levels of unemployment. A slack economy lowers the rate of real investment in new capital goods and new technology. In addition, skills of unemployed workers deteriorate and they would be less productive in the future. However, quantitative estimates to this future loss are difficult to obtain. Implicit in our approach is that the unemployment levels of the past decade are not 'natural' or 'God-given' – society and governments can lower the unemployment level by alternative social and economic policies.

Having emphasised the importance of measuring the output loss costs of unemployment, we enter the problematic area of estimating this cost. Ideally, we would like to estimate the potential output (that level of output which would have been produced) if the unemployment level was at some lower level. Two problems appear immediately: first, which particular lower rate of unemployment do we assume?

and second, how do we estimate the increased output from the increased employment (decreased unemployment)? One possibility is to use estimates of the so-called natural rate of unemployment. However, there are analytical problems in defining it, and there are several different estimates (or for some countries, none) of this rate and hence there is no obvious rate to choose. In our view, the concept of a natural rate is very unhelpful, especially when the natural rate seems to increase, *pari passu* with the actual rate of unemployment.[3] An alternative to using the natural rate concept is to use an *ad hoc* procedure: what would national income have been if unemployment levels were those experienced in (say) 1968–73 (prior to the first oil shock) or 1974–9 (prior to the recent international recession). In our discussion we shall use these alternative definitions.

As mentioned earlier, there are short-run (static) and long-run (dynamic) costs of unemployment. The static costs of unemployment are the opportunity costs of unemployment: what is the alternative level of national income (gross domestic product - GDP) is the unemployment level were lower? To answer this question completely correctly we need to know how this alternative level of unemployment would be achieved (i.e. what alternative policies or alternative values of exogenous variables would lead to this outcome) since this would provide us with information about which sectors' employment would increase (and with knowledge of the sectoral output response or elasticity) we could then evaluate and aggregate the increased national income. For example, if the current level of unemployment is 3 million and we want to know the loss of output due to this, we can ask how much extra output would be produced if unemployment were reduced to (say) 1 million. The extra output produced would depend on whether the policies were stimulating labour-intensive but low-valued products (say hand-crafted toys) or capital-intensive but high-valued products (say radio-telescopes). Again, if the unemployment were to be reduced by assuming alternative values of exogenous variables, we would get different estimates of lost output depending on the different assumptions, for example, a faster rate of growth of GDP (or higher rates of inflation) in America would stimulate exports and hence decrease unemployment. This sectoral information is particularly relevant since the recent growth of employment has been mainly in the services sector while the decline has been mainly in the industrial sector. However, this would require multisectoral econometric models of the economy with an amount of information and data which were not available to us. To reiterate, to get precise estimates, we need a well-specified multisectoral model and a well-specified alternative 'scenario': for each different scenario, we would get a different estimate.

In fact, what we have done (in line with previous investigators) is to assume that by some unspecified method, unemployment is lower and the previously unemployed are employed in different industries in the same proportions as the existing stock of employment. In some cases we have assumed that the unemployed would find work in the industries *from which they had lost their jobs.* We know that both these assumptions are approximations to reality and the longer the period over which we calculate these losses, the less precise the estimates become. This is because over the years the structure of the economy has changed enormously.

The dynamic costs of unemployment may be far greater than the static costs. However, they are difficult to estimate. As mentioned earlier, the dynamic costs of unemployment are the *future* output losses due to current high levels of unemployment. A high level of unemployment, a low level of capacity utilisation, depressed expectations of aggregate demand and profitability lead to lower levels of investment in real capital goods and slow down the introduction of new technology (via the new capital goods). This lower investment implies lower levels of future output and hence much greater economic losses. However, opposed to this view is the one put across by the UK government that the high unemployment is leading to a weeding-out of inefficient firms and industries and *increasing* productivity of workers due to a 'new realism in industrial relations'.

Perhaps an equally important dynamic (long-term) cost of unemployment is the *deterioration of human capital* due (especially) to long duration of unemployment. People who have been unemployed for long periods would lose their skills and, in some cases due to technological change, their previous skills would be obsolete. Of course, there is a high proportion of the unemployed who are unskilled workers without any formal training. But even so-called unskilled workers learn on the job and are more efficient than complete newcomers. The recent recession has seen a big increase in unemployment of older (presumably more skilled) workers and an increase in early retirement schemes. These schemes are equivalent to 'early-scrapping' schemes for physical capital goods. In addition, because of the growing problem of youth unemployment, investment in human capital has declined (at least in work-experience-related human capital). This means that future levels of production would be lower if and when the young of today find work.

There are several reasons why an estimate of the output loss costs is subject to measurement error.[4] Some of these factors might lead to an underestimate and some to an overestimate or, with some small probability, these two biases might just cancel out.

The factors that might lead to estimate of output loss being an underestimate are:

(a) Because the measured unemployment rates excludes certain categories of potential workers, for example, married women, young people who have never had jobs, early retirement of workers and, in Italy, those covered by the Cassa Integrazione Guadagni (CIG). In this paper we have relied on published statistics on unemployed so that, in general, we have made no allowance for these 'hidden unemployed'. Some of the methods of estimating output loss make no allowance for the fall in average hours worked, decreases in participation rate and lower rate of utilisation, which usually accompany the increase in unemployment.

(b) A particular problem, especially for West Germany, is that the unemployment figures do not take account of returned migrants.

(c) In general, the dynamic output loss costs are not quantified.

The factors that might lead to an *overestimate* of output loss are:

(a) The measured unemployment rate which includes the voluntarily unemployed (which for the New Classical school includes *all* the unemployed). In addition, a large proportion, so it is argued, of the unemployment rate is a 'natural rate' and hence should be deducted from the measured unemployment rate. The 'benefits' of leisure should be subtracted from the measured output loss costs.

(b) It is argued that a proportion (for some economists a very high one) of the unemployed is engaged in the 'informal sector' (or the 'underground economy') so that, if unemployment is reduced via growth in the formal sector, the informal sector would decline. Hence the net increase in real GDP (as opposed to measured GDP) would be small. Work done on the informal sector by some sociologists, however, suggests that participants in the informal sector are more likely to have formal-sector employment as well. Employment in the formal sector provides the workers with a network of contacts as customers as well as intermediate producers. In addition, employees in the formal sector (for example, garage mechanics) have access to tools and equipment for use in the evenings or at weekends.

(c) Unemployed people are usually less skilled and often work in industries (occupations) with low productivity. To ascribe to the unemployed average productivity in the economy would lead to an upward bias. Some of the methods listed below attempt to make some correction for this bias.

(d) The high level of unemployment may lead to increased productivity of the employed labour force due to the threat of being fired (made redundant). Hence, if unemployment were decreased, productivity would then be biased upwards.

Thus we see that there are some conceptual problems as well as several measurement problems involved in estimating the output loss costs of unemployment. In other words, the numerical estimates we provide give a rough indication of the magnitudes of the costs. For purposes of comparability we have used annual OECD time-series data on employment, unemployment and GDP.

In this chapter we provide estimates for output loss using Okun's Law method which is a relationship between the percentage unemployment rate and the percentage output 'gap'. This output gap is defined as the deviation of actual output (GDP) from 'potential output' (GDP) expressed as a percentage of potential output (GDP). To obtain potential GDP we fitted simple exponential time-trends to GDP allowing for a break as a result of the oil shock in 1974. The time-trends were fitted up to 1980 and then extrapolated up to 1984. We then iterated around the estimated growth rate and constructed alternative series for 'Gap'. We then estimated (by ordinary least squares) an equation:

$$UR = a_0 + a_1 \, \text{Gap}(i) + \varepsilon$$

where $UR$ is the percentage rate of unemployment, Gap($i$) is the $i$th series on which we iterated and $\varepsilon$ is a random error. We then chose that equation which gave the best fit in terms of $R^2$s. If we find $a_1$ is 0.5 it means that each percentage point of unemployment implies an output loss of 2 per cent.

Table 10.2 provides estimates of the static output loss using this method. We estimated these costs assuming that unemployment is brought down (by unspecified policy measures) to the average levels of either 1968–73 or to that of 1974–9. The former period had lower

*Table* 10.2 Static output loss costs of unemployment (Okun's Law estimates)

| | *1980* | | *1981* | | *1982* | | *1983* | |
|---|---|---|---|---|---|---|---|---|
| | *Low* | *High* | *Low* | *High* | *Low* | *High* | *Low* | *High* |
| Federal Republic of Germany | — | 6.69 | 3.00 | 10.25 | 8.74 | 15.98 | 13.38 | 20.63 |
| France | 6.14 | 13.27 | 9.59 | 16.72 | 12.00 | 19.14 | 14.06 | 21.20 |
| Italy | 3.43 | 6.77 | 7.06 | 10.40 | 9.48 | 12.82 | 13.51 | 16.85 |
| United Kingdom | 3.01 | 6.53 | 9.54 | 13.07 | 12.32 | 15.84 | 13.70 | 17.23 |

*Notes*: 'Low' estimates are when unemployment is brought down to the unemployment levels of 1974–9, while 'high' estimates are for 1968–73 levels.

levels of unemployment and hence implies a higher output loss, while the latter period had higher unemployment and, hence, lower output loss.

Even ignoring the dynamic output loss costs, we find that the real costs of unemployment in terms of output loss have increased dramatically and, even allowing for measurement error, are massive.

To end this section, let me quote Okun: 'It is striking that a corrected estimate of social costs does not appear to be significantly smaller than output loss. . . . The loss of output is thus a good first approximation in assessing the social costs of recession and slack' (Okun, 1981, p. 272).

## 10.4 SUMMARY AND CONCLUSIONS

I began this chapter by outlining the problem of growing unemployment in the European Community and then discussed the problems of evaluating the costs and benefits of unemployment. I then provided some estimates for the (static) output loss due to unemployment: these estimates were all over 10 per cent of GDP which is a staggering cost to pay for a lower rate of inflation. Milton Friedman in evidence to the (British) House of Commons Treasury and Civil Service Committee (1980) argued:

> The best evidence is from the prior experience of the UK and other countries. As I read that experience . . . I conclude that . . . only a modest reduction in output and employment will be a side effect of reducing inflation to single figures by 1982 (House of Commons, 1980, p. 61).

In fact, what we see is that Friedman was clearly wrong - the output loss costs have been enormous and persistent. In our view the costs of unemployment are not only these output loss costs, but more long-term effects on individuals and society in terms of morbidity (physical and mental) and social tension. We do not really know what problems we are storing up for the future when we have millions of people who have experienced long-term unemployment. We are observing increasing social tensions in terms of civil riots as well as the growth of neo-Nazi movements in the EC. How long will it be before governments decide to engage in reflationary policies? To propitiate (appease) the gods of inflation do we have to sacrifice the lives of millions of unemployed people?

## Notes

1. For a detailed discussion see Junankar (1985).
2. See Feldstein (1978).
3. See Solow (1985) and Hargreaves-Heap (1980).
4. Some of these issues are discussed in OECD (1982).

## References

EUROPEAN TRADE UNION INSTITUTE (1984) *The Economic Costs of Unemployment in Western Europe* (Brussels: ETUI).

FELDSTEIN, M. (1978) 'The Private and Social Costs of Unemployment', *American Economic Review*, 68, no. 2, May, pp. 155–8.

HARRISON, R. (1976) 'The Demoralising Experience of Prolonged Unemployment', *Dept. of Employment Gazette*, pp. 339–48.

HARGREAVES-HEAP, S. (1980) 'Choosing the Wrong 'Natural' Rate: Accelerating Inflation or Decelerating Employment and Growth', *Economic Journal*, 90, September 1980, pp. 611–20.

HOUSE OF COMMONS (1980) 'Treasury and Civil Service Committee Session 1979–80, *Memoranda on Monetary Policy* (London: HMSO).

HOUSE OF LORDS (1982) *Report of Select Committee on Unemployment*, vol. 1, 10 May 1982 (London: HMSO).

JUNANKAR, P. N. (1985) 'The Political Economy of Unemployment: Causes and Consequences', *Political Quarterly*, 56, no. 1 January–March 1985, pp. 56–67.

JUNANKAR, P. N. (1986) *Costs of Unemployment, Main Report* (Luxembourg: Office for the Official Publications of the European Communities).

OECD (1982) *The Challenge of Unemployment: A Report to Labour Ministers* (Paris: OECD 1982).

OECD (1984) *High Unemployment: A Challenge for Income Support Policies* (Paris: OECD 1984).

OKUN, A. (1981) *Prices and Quantities* (Oxford: Blackwell).
SINFIELD, A. and FRASER, N. (1985) 'The Real Cost of Unemployment' March 1985, Dept. of Social Administration, University of Edinburgh.
SOLOW, R. M. (1986) 'Unemployment: Getting the Questions Right', *Economica*, 53, no. 2105, Supplement, pp. 523-34.

# 11 Job Creation Programmes in an International Comparison

Marcia de Wachter and Yolanda Somers

This article contains a comparative analysis of job-creation policies pursued in France, Belgium, W. Germany, Great Britain and the Netherlands.[1] Striking conclusions are the high degree of congruency in the various policies and the low quality of research material available on this matter. Nevertheless an attempt is made to deduce some proposals that can be useful when tracing out an employment strategy for the future.

## 11.1 INTRODUCTION

With an election year in France and in the Netherlands, a national collective convention in Belgium and high unemployment rates in most European countries, an economic reflection on the effectiveness and efficiency of the job-creation policies pursued is certainly meaningful. The main purpose of the job-creation policies, as conceived in most European countries, is the promotion of an effective and fair fine-tuning of supply and demand of labour.

The instruments traditionally used, can be divided into five categories, namely:

1. wage-cost subsidies;
2. educational and vocational measures;
3. direct job-creation measures;
4. reduction of labour supply;
5. promotion of entrepreneurship.

In the report 'Evaluation of measures, 1980' of the Directorate General for Job Creation Policy (The Netherlands), these measures are further described as follows:

Wage-cost subsidies aim for the (re)admission of categories of unemployed people with a weak labour market position. The target group of this policy consists then of categories of unemployed people that experience great difficulty in acquiring a permanent place in the labour market without such measures.

Through temporary reduction of the wage-costs (mostly reductions of employer contributions in social security funds) this group of measures tries to neutralise the crowding-out of lower skilled by higher skilled as a result of regulations and rigidities in the labour market (combined with the negative energy shocks of 1973 and 1979).

A variant of this measure is a supplementary payment to unemployed people who are willing to accept work at a lower average than that of their previous job.

*Educational and vocational measures* are created to stimulate the functional job mobility and to improve the match of supply and demand in the labour market. In other words, these measures try to fill the gap between the general knowledge of school leavers, young unemployed people and employees in unstable jobs and the need for 'highly technical' skills of the private sector.

*Direct job creation measures* create – temporarily – new jobs in the public sector for unemployed people who have not been helped by the policy instruments mentioned above. These jobs are explicitly directed to improve the possibilities for acquiring a permanent job in the labour market. These measures not only strive for more justice by the division of the available work but also for upgrading the labour skills of the unemployed.

*Reduction of labour supply* involves a package of measures oriented towards the rearrangement of the number of available jobs through early retirement paired with replacement by younger workers.

Finally, in the job-creation policy attention is also paid to *the promotion of entrepreneurship.* This group of measures encourages unemployed people to start their own company through subsidies and long-term loans.

The description of those five groups of labour policy instruments as found in public documents remains rather vague and general. In order to evaluate whether these measures have indeed reached their targets and to what extent this happened in an 'effective' and 'efficient' way, we opted for an economic analysis of the existing evaluation studies that have been made by scholars in the selected countries. This process is summarised in the following pages.

Section 11.1 implied the construction of a list of criteria the evaluation studies could have used to evaluate whether a job creation measure was effective or not. This is discussed in the next paragraph. Section 11.2 involves a chronological overview of the size and the number of measures that have actually been implemented in the selected countries. The highlights of this evolution are described in paragraph three. Section 11.3 consists of a check-up of each measure with the criteria put forward in section 11.1. This work was described elsewhere in an extensive way.[2]

However the main results are synthesised in the last part of this article and give some insights into what measures seem to function better than others to realise the above-mentioned targets of the job creation policies.

## 11.2 EVALUATION CRITERIA OF JOB CREATION MEASURES

In order to compare the results of the evaluation studies a check-list of criteria (Table 11.1) which these job-creation instruments should satisfy, was set up. The check-list contains four parts: (1) the profile of the participants; (2) criteria of labour-market effectiveness; (3) criteria of financial and economic effectiveness; (4) organisational effectiveness.

### The Profile of the Participants

Before these measures can be tested upon their effectiveness, it is necessary to obtain a detailed picture of the profile of the participants (and control group if possible). Therefore a statistical survey of labour-supply determinants such as age, level of education, sex, labour antecedents and nationality of the participants is necessary. Also important is to know through what channels the participants are placed in a programme. The ideal would be to construct a control group with identical characteristics to the participating group. Based on this information the volume of placements which were part of the target group and the real number of placings can be calculated.

*Table* 11.1 Evaluation criteria of job-creation measures

**1 Profile of the participants**

(i) Number of males versus females
(ii) Level of education
(iii) Division of age
(iv) Difficult-to-place unemployed
(labour-antecedent, unemployed duration)
(v) Sector division

**2 Labour-market effectiveness**

(i) Volume effectiveness
- Labour-market position in the short run (percentage and profile of participants who have a given labour-market position, percentage of participants hired by the employer that took part in the program.)
- Premature leavers (percentage and profile)

(ii) Quality effectiveness
- Long-run effects of the job-creation policy

(iii) Quality evaluation
- Percentage of participants who claim an improvement of their labour market position
- Other qualitative aspects: content of obtained training, stigmatisation, etc.

**3 Financial and economic effectiveness**

(i) Windfall, substitution and anticipation effects, unfair competition, etc.
(ii) Macroeconomic implications of the measures
(iii) Social cost-benefit analysis

**4 Organisational effectiveness**

(i) Organisation of the measure
- number of employees involved in a project and number of officials concerned
- selection and motivation techniques of the employers
- selection and motivation techniques of the participants

(ii) Implementation of the measure
- effectiveness/competency of the personnel of the mediatory service
- the speed of the placements/contacts with the employers
- the quality of the mediation

(iii) Control
- Evaluation of the participants/personnel/the project
- Control of the target/the target group/the employers
- Control of the accountancy/the budget

## Labour-Market Effectiveness

The labour-market effectiveness can be divided into two parts: volume and quality.

In order to evaluate the volume effectiveness, it should be calculated to what extent the number of effective placements form part of a specified target group. This is also called 'the effectiveness', the extent to which the target group is reached. Under this heading also belong the percentages of participants who either have or have not finished the job-creation measure (with an analysis of their personal and labour-market characteristics) and the percentage of placements by the employers who participate in the measure.

The quality effectiveness measures the durability of the job-creation measure. It indicates to what extent the participants in the job-creation programmes remain in the labour market in the short and in the long run. In the case of schooling, the impact of the received education on a durable participation in the labour market is evaluated. Finally the participants are asked to give an appreciation of the quality of the received training; whether they are being stigmatised, etc.

## Financial and Economic Effectiveness

The financial and economic effectiveness is important on three levels, namely, the level of the participant, that of the government budget and that of the economy as a whole.

For an individual the cost of participation in the programme is the budget he foregoes in terms of time and money, for example, in case of an education programme its cost is mainly the income the participants could have gained if they had worked.

The individual benefits are measured through the nett discounted future income increased over the life-cycle as result of the participation in the measure (in comparison with the nett discounted income of a control group with analogous personal and labour-market characteristics). The individual return of a measure can be calculated on that basis.

To know the overall cost effect on the government budget, the average cost price per application has to be calculated. Possible refinements are, for example, the average cost price per effective application, i.e. inclusive of the costs of non-effective applications. This can be a relevant concept in comparison with analogous programmes or with an alternative job-creation policy. To these costs should be added the operational costs of the mediation agencies.

At the same time, the returns can be calculated in terms of savings in social payments and increments in tax income and social security payments. Finally, goods and services specially produced by the job-creation measures can be added on the side of the benefits.

On the macro economic level, the positive effect on the employment has to be quantified. What is the number of employees that can participate in the labour process through job-creation measures? Do the job-creation measures induce additional hirings beyond the number of applications registered? On the cost side is there a substitution effect through which employees are gradually replaced by subsidised persons or is there employment in NET terms? Do capital-intensive sectors experience damage of subsidisation of the labour-intensive sectors? Is there a windfall effect, etc.?

**Organisational Effectiveness**

Finally, in the evaluation process of the job-creation programmes, an appreciation of the organisational effectiveness has to be made. Five rules of thumb are in force for the job-creation measures on the whole as well as for labour projects in particular. First, the organisational effectiveness will depend strongly on the organisation talent of the officials concerned with the local project, in connection with, for example, the timing and the preparation of the projects. Second, the support of established pressure groups (particularly employers' and employees' organisations) is indispensable for the success of the labour projects. Third, the attitude and the motivation of the participants on the measures; fourth, the effectiveness of the supporting services, and fifth, the economic climate are of decisive importance for the success of the job-creation policy.

## 11.3 EVOLUTION OF THE JOB-CREATION POLICIES IN FIVE EUROPEAN COUNTRIES

In the past decade, the European countries have been confronted with increased competition on the foreign markets, with a rise of energy prices and a wave of new technologies. Whatever the design of their employment policy, no country escaped the necessity to formulate solutions to the exploding unemployment rates. As a result, Europe during the second half of the 1970s became the laboratory for all kinds of experiments in job-creation measures.

The great diversity in the job-creation policies of the countries studied makes every systematisation a bit laborious and defective. Nevertheless the tendencies in the policy can be called syncretic and even in countries with an opposite socioeconomic frame of reference, the similarities among the different measures are clear.

Three periods can be distinguished:

1. After the first oil shock in 1973, the policy-makers made use of the traditional business-cycle instruments to stimulate the economy. More particularly, wage-cost subsidies were used to upgrade the employment rate.
2. Nevertheless, as the economic growth kept stagnating and structural changes came about, questions were asked about the priority of economic issues in the labour market *versus* social ones. Since 1977 the job-creation policy tried to offer additional socioeconomic security on the basis of the so-called social innovation. New solutions were worked out in the form of education and direct job-creation measures, reduction of labour supply and of working time. To the existing schooling programmes, alternative schooling formulas were added. Direct creation of jobs occurred through the establishment of labour circuits in the public sector in order to fulfil unrealised and non-competitive social needs. The reduction of labour supply and of working-time rested on the solidarity principle.
3. A third tendency that started in the beginning of the 1980s brought about a shift in the job-creation policy from social innovation into more economic considerations. The social innovation had not fulfilled the large expectations that had been reposed in it. As a consequence they were no longer the central source of inspiration of the employment policies in the selected countries. The centre of gravity of the government policy even shifted to some extent from job creation to industrial policy.

In relation to the job-creation policy more attention is paid to:

1. Education programmes that are better adapted to the needs of the private sector.
2. A shift from public financing to private or autofinancing of the programmes and a reallocation of the public finances to investments on behalf of new technologies.
3. Job-creation programmes set up in a decentralised way and in time with local developments in the labour market.

4. Introduction of more flexible working time.

These tendencies are being reviewed in detail.

**Phase I (1973–7)**

Most European countries replied to the increase in unemployment after the oil shock of 1973 with already-tested instruments. Business-cycle instruments such as '*Préretraite*' (F), '*Conventioneel Brugpensioen*' (B), '*Tewerkgestelde Werklozen*' (B), '*Regeling Tijdelijke Arbeidsplaatsen en Aanvullende Werken*' (NL) and '*Kurzarbeit*' (BRD) gained importance. They were introduced in a period when policy-makers were convinced that economic growth was temporarily restrained, but that the disequilibrium between supply and demand of labour was not structural. As unemployment seemed to be more obstinate, a plea was made for more concentrated action in the form of wage-cost subsidies. France had its *Embauches avec exonération de charges sociales*, Belgium the *Regeling Tijdelijke Ontlasting Sociale Lasten* and the BRD *Eingliederungsbeihilfe* and *Zuschüsse zu den Lohnkosten älterer Arbeitnehmer*, the Netherlands the 30% *Loonkostenregeling* and the *Loonsuppletieregeling*. The most important form of wage-cost subsidies was the British 'Temporary Employment Subsidy'. This measure was so successful that it came under pressure by the other EEC countries because of unfair competition. It was abolished in 1978.

Most of these interventions were not generalised or prolonged. Sometimes they were reformulated within the framework of other measures, directed towards small and medium-sized entreprises or vocational training, or placed within a wider framework of reduction or fiscalisation of social charges.

**Phase II (1978–81)**

Social innovation was the answer to the structural unemployment announced in the course of the 1970s. First the traditional schooling programmes were extended with alternating schooling variants with education and/or labour contracts: for example *Bijdrageregeling Vakopleiding Jeugdigen* (NL) and *Stages pratiques et entreprises* (F), *Stages de Formation Professionnelle* (F), *Stages voor Jongeren* (B) and *Youth Opportunities Programme* (GB). All these measures were negotiated on a sector or industrial level and offered the youth an indenture.

*Contrats Emploi-Formation* (F) and *L'Apprentissage* (F), *Schwerpunkt* 1 *of the Sondernprogram* 1979 (BRD) offered the employees the opportunity of retraining within the framework of their job.

Second through new labour circuits and existing direct job-creation measures an attempt was made to create new jobs in the non-commercial sphere. The programmes were also meant to couple economic to social considerations and involved activities considered before as non-profitable. There are three types of programmes, namely:

1. Programmes that try to improve the match of labour supply and demand, for example the German '*Arbeitsbeschaffungsmassnahmen.* This measure creates a permanent job for long-term unemployed and older hard-to-place employees (strengthened in 1979 with *Schwerpunkt* 3).
2. Programmes that create new jobs in the short run, for example, *Interim Maatregel Jeugdige Werklozen,* and *het Aanvullende Werkgelegenheidsbeleid* in the Netherlands, afterwards developed to the *Werkgelegenheidsverruimende Maatregelen* 1979 and the *Experimenten Arbeidsprojecten Jeugdige Werklozen.* These measures were all temporary and attempted to absorb the effects of the downturns of the business cycle. The *Job Creation Programme* (GB) converted into *Special Temporary Employment Programmes* aim to stop the creeping unemployment without being an instrument in the long run.
3. Programmes that pursue quantitative as well as qualitative employment purposes such as, for example *L'Emploi d'Utilité Collective* (F) and *Het Bijzonder Tijdelijk Kader* (B) in which temporary jobs in the collective sector were created for general purposes.

Third, Belgium, France and Great Britain experimented with measures to reduce the labor supply. Therefore, early retirement contracts were coupled to the recruitment of young unemployed. Originally, these early pensions were entirely financed by the government.

Of all the measures that tried to solve the unemployment problem by means of social innovation, the various forms of redistribution of working-time are the most progressive. However, reduction of labour-time of all employees in order to get more jobs, implies a certain degree of solidarity among the employees and a certain degree of flexibility in work organisation that does not always correspond with reality. Therefore, this measure loses its importance during Phase III.

**Phase III (1982–5)**

Since 1981–2 the centre of gravity of the job-creation policies in the selected countries has shifted from social innovation to more financial and economic aspects of employment. The reasoning was that in open economies additional employment can in the end only be generated through additional investments and a labour-demand-oriented job-creation policy.

Hence, existing schooling programmes and alternating education were reoriented towards the needs of the private sector. In new programmes such as *Contrats de qualifications et d'adaption de la formation en alternance, Formations réservées aux jeunes de* 16 *à* 18 *ans* and *La préparation à la vie professionnelle* (F) and *Youth Training Scheme* (GB) the accent lies on the quality of the education and on the technological update of the students.

Second, job-creation programmes switched over from public financing to private or autofinancing. By moulding the new measures into form, more attention is paid to the market logic. This tendency implies a shift to the relative cheaper schooling measures and a reduction of expensive short-run direct job-creation measures. For those who have been unemployed for a prolonged period, permanent solutions such as the Belgian *Derde Arbeidscircuit* are sought. The very expensive experiments of reduction of labour supply were stopped or replaced by early-retirement formulas financed by the trade and industry. Measures such as entrepreneurship were preferred because the funds are allocated to productive rather than to consumptive projects.

Moreover new programmes under which decentralisation and local development come into prominence, got more attention. They aimed for a better functioning of local unions and employer organisations and for a more flexible response to changes in the local labour-market situation. This also implied more attention to small and medium-sized business, as for examples, *Plus Eén Plan* (B), *Indienstneming Werklozen in KMOs* (B).

Finally, there is also a shift from the reduction of labour time to a more flexible labour time with an extension of the production time. The possibilities of working-time reduction are strongly limited by inherent restrictions of profitability of the enterprises. Therefore, combination measures, that stipulate reduction of working time with wage moderation, wage subsidisation and additional hirings were created – for example, *Compenserende Indienstnemingen* (B) or *Experimenten inzake flexibilisering van de arbeid* (B) (working-time reduction with prolongation of production time and 2×12 hours labour per week).

## 11.4 EVALUATION OF THE JOB CREATION MEASURES[3]

Despite the wide variety of the socioeconomic framework of the countries under study, a great similarity can be observed in the job-creation policies of Belgium, the Netherlands, BRD, Great Britain and France. This becomes clear when the evolution of the costs of those countries on the 'pure' job-creation policy per unemployed person (see Figure 11.1) and the evolution of the percentage of unemployed persons reached through the measures (see Figure 11.2) are traced out. Belgium and France have applied a very large job-creation policy and have also covered the greatest number of unemployed persons, but against very high costs. The bankruptcy of the

*Figure* 11.1 Cost of the 'pure' job-creation policy per unemployed, 1975–83, in guilder of 1983

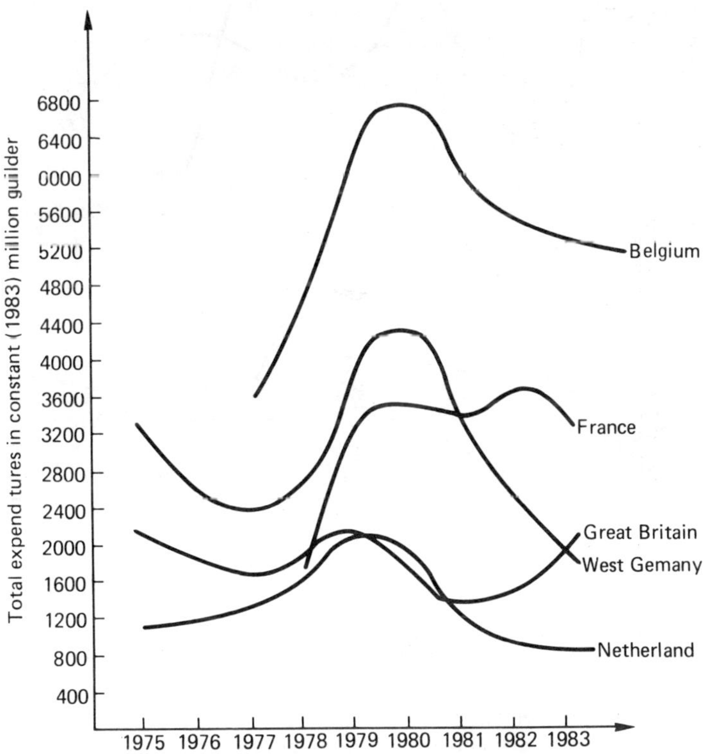


* Total expenses in million guilder in 1983.
\# unemployed + participants job creation policy.

*Figure* 11.2 Percentage of unemployed* persons reached through the measures 1975–83

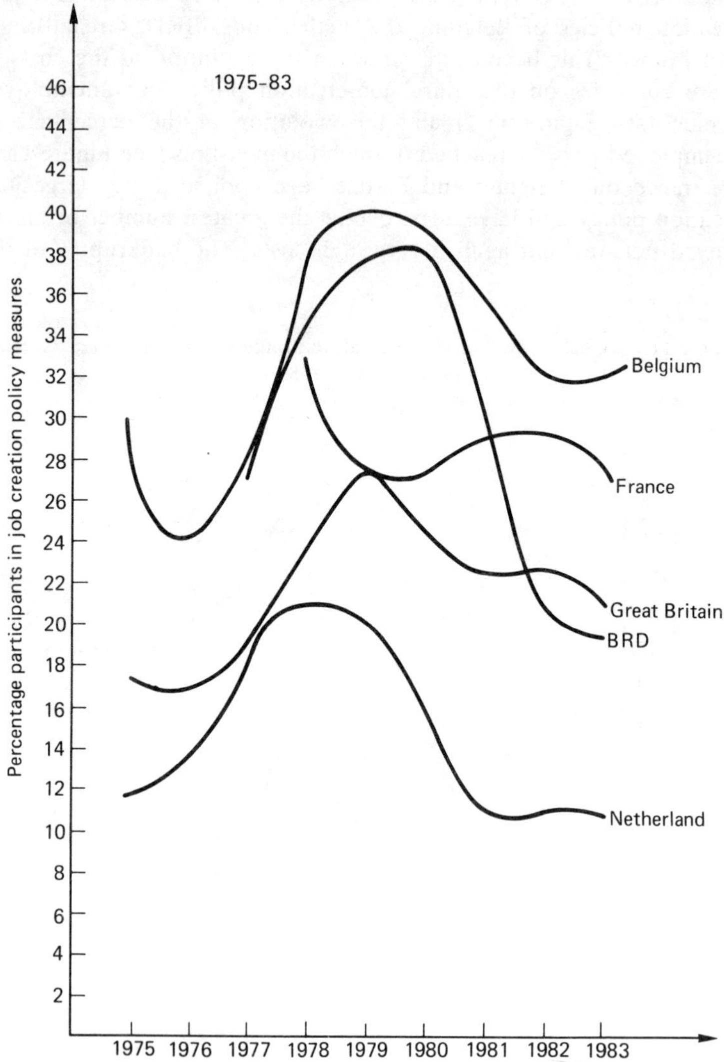


* Participants job creation policy.
\# unemployed + participants job creation policy.

publicly financed early retirement is the first reason for the decline in the figures since 1981. The second reason, namely the restriction of direct job-creation measures, is valid for all countries. This tendency is strongest in West Germany. West Germany is the country where the job-creation policy was relatively the most demand-directed. Finally, it can be kept in mind, that the job-creation policy of the Netherlands was very limited over the whole line, namely, it had very little reach and has required little financing.

After these general remarks we give now a more detailed evaluation of the different measures:

1. The *wage-cost subsidy* policy conducted in the countries studied, did not result in an improvement of the labour-market position of the participants. France and Belgium have strongly reduced the importance of the package of measures *Loonkostensubsidies* in case it was applied without conditions to engage personnel and/or working-time reduction. Also in the BRD and in Great Britain the wage-cost subsidies, with a view to placing difficult-to-place unemployed are respectively abolished. Only the German wage-cost subsidy *Kurzarbeit* can be called successful because it offers enough flexibility to reduce the working-time during the downturns of the business cycle and to increase labour-time. About the *Regeling Werktijdverkorting* (NL) no evaluation material is available. Since this measure closely corresponds with the successful German *Kurzarbeit*, it is presumably effective.
2. The *schooling policy* is the most uniform and overall the most successful measure of all categories of instruments. Only the organisation and the relative number of participants differ in the various schooling measures. The schooling measures can be divided into three categories, namely traditional training programmes, schooling measures that provide an indenture and schooling measures that provide a labour contract.

- The *traditional training programmes* are the oldest schooling measures and are generally positively evaluated. However for unemployed youngsters these measures seem to be unattractive. The regular participants (unemployed with work experience, and employers who desire to retrain) perceive these programmes as an improvement of the labour-market position.
- In the Netherlands, France, Belgium and Great Britain, the alternative schooling measures with an indenture aim for low-skilled and

for unemployed youngsters. In the Netherlands, this measure has not been evaluated. In the other countries the measure is evaluated as being positive. The French schooling measures *Formations professionnelles avec un statut de stagiaire* consist of training programmes with various training levels for youngsters. The most important training programme is *Les Formations réservées aux jeunes de 16 à 18 ans.* This measure gives an additional training to poorly qualified young people by means of three types of training programmes (an orientation, an introductory and an advanced-training programme). This measure reaches a great number of people from the target group and is very effective.

In Belgium, companies with more than fifty employees are forced to recruit full-time an additional 3 per cent of youngsters in the measure *Stages voor Jongeren.* This is the most important reason for the vocational-training size of this measure. In a period of six years, almost 20 000 young people were temporarily employed through the training system.

Besides the reorganisation and the simplification of the package of schooling measures, in Great Britain there are two other measures – one for the youngsters and one for the adults. At the moment, the measure for the youngsters is the most-important job-creation instrument. In Great Britain, all unemployed school-leavers are taken up in the *Youth Training Scheme*; this scheme offers a training of high quality to the youth for one year.

The non-evaluated measure of the Netherlands *Bijdrageregeling, Vakopleiding Jeugdigen* is unique in its framework. The Directorate-General for the job-creation policy does not interfere with the content of the training places, but contributes a particular amount (f. 4000) per indenture in a special training fund. On the sectorial level, the social partners decide on the number and the content of the training places.

- The schooling measures that provide a labour contract to the participants evidently offer the greatest chance of a permanent job when the training is finished. In the Netherlands (*Scholing in samenwerking tussen overheid en bedrijfsleven*) and the BRD (*Einarbeitungszuschüsse* and *Schwerpunkt*) these measures aim for adults. They are very successful. Problems arise in times of high unemployment, when it becomes harder to capture the interest of the employers for these measures. The successful French measure *Contrats Emploi-Formation* is targeted on the youth.

The disadvantage of these measures remains however, that difficult-to-place unemployed are hardly reached.

3. The experiences with the *traditional job-creation measures* in almost all countries are negative. The measures are too expensive, too short, offer no improvement of the labour-market position of the difficult-to-place unemployed and they tempt the youth to suspend their formal schooling. Only the formula *Derde Arbeidscircuit* (B) offers a permanent solution to very specific target groups (namely unemployed persons over 45 and/or people unemployed for a long time (minimum two years)). Nevertheless, this measure is also expensive and the chances of a transition to the regular labour-market are slim. Overall direct job-creation measures, connected with special conditions are very promising. The *Compenserende Indienstnemingen* and the *Experimenten tot Aanpassing van de Arbeidstijd* are evaluated 'positive by' both employers and employees. However, two major shortcomings are:

   (i) companies are forced to hire new people in return for labour-time reduction and a wage-cost subsidy or else must deposit a contribution in a national fund;
   (ii) the cost of this form of job-creation is placed on the production factor, labour.

   The enterprises are forced to enlarge their personnel base with 3 per cent relative to the previous year after 5 per cent working-time reduction and 3 per cent wage moderation. This means that labour-intensive companies have to make a greater effort than capital-intensive companies to create new jobs. In a number of cases, these are companies which have an obsolete production structure and which need rationalisation.

4. The system of *early retirement* combined with hiring young unemployed people was the most important form of new employment. In France, for example, a quarter of the employees between 60 and 65 years took advantage of this measure. The employers and the employees were very satisfied with the measure, for the employers could improve the promotion chances of the young employees and reduce the overall wage sum. In some cases the measure also allowed for the reorganisation of the production process. On the side of the employees the inability to follow the new technologies and the attractive financial status of an early-retiring employee motivated many to leave the labour market.

Financing this scheme however posed insurmountable problems. Given the large effect on the total number of new jobs and the positive appreciation by employers and employees of this measure, it seems useful to look for adequate forms of financing.

5. Entrepreneurship produced positive results in all countries, which have taken up the measure in their job creation policy.

*–*–*

As stated in the extensive analysis none of the examined measures can be scientifically proven to be effective due to the important lack of data and information about control-groups. Nevertheless recommendations with respect to a new job-creation policy in the short run should go in the direction of large-scale alternating schooling programmes.

## Appendix 11.1

*Scheme* 1 Development job creation policy – the Netherlands 1975–85

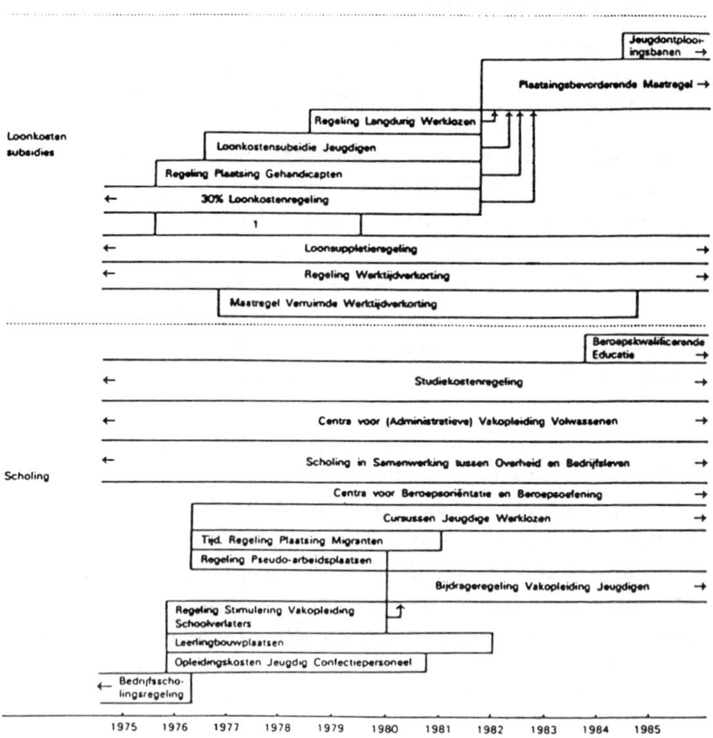

*Scheme 1 (continued)*

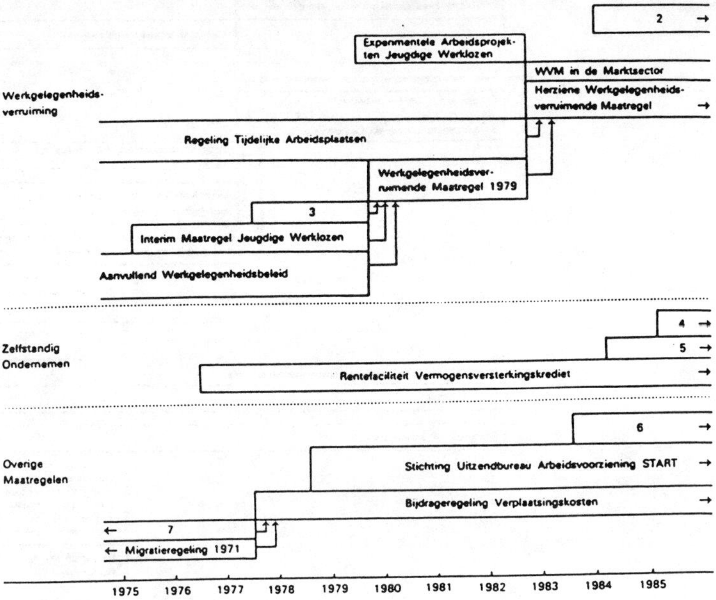


Noten bij schema 4.1

1. Besluit Stimuleringspremie Partiële Leerplicht.
2. Terugploegexperiment in de bouw.
3. Experimentele Werkgelegenheidsprojekten Vrouwen.
4. Rijksgroepsregeling (startende) Zelfstandigen.
5. Experimentele Regeling Startfaciliteiten Vrouwenbedrijven.
6. Onbeloonde arbeid uitkeringsgerechtigden.
7. Migratieregeling Noorden des Lands.

*Scheme* 2 Development job creation policy – France 1975–85

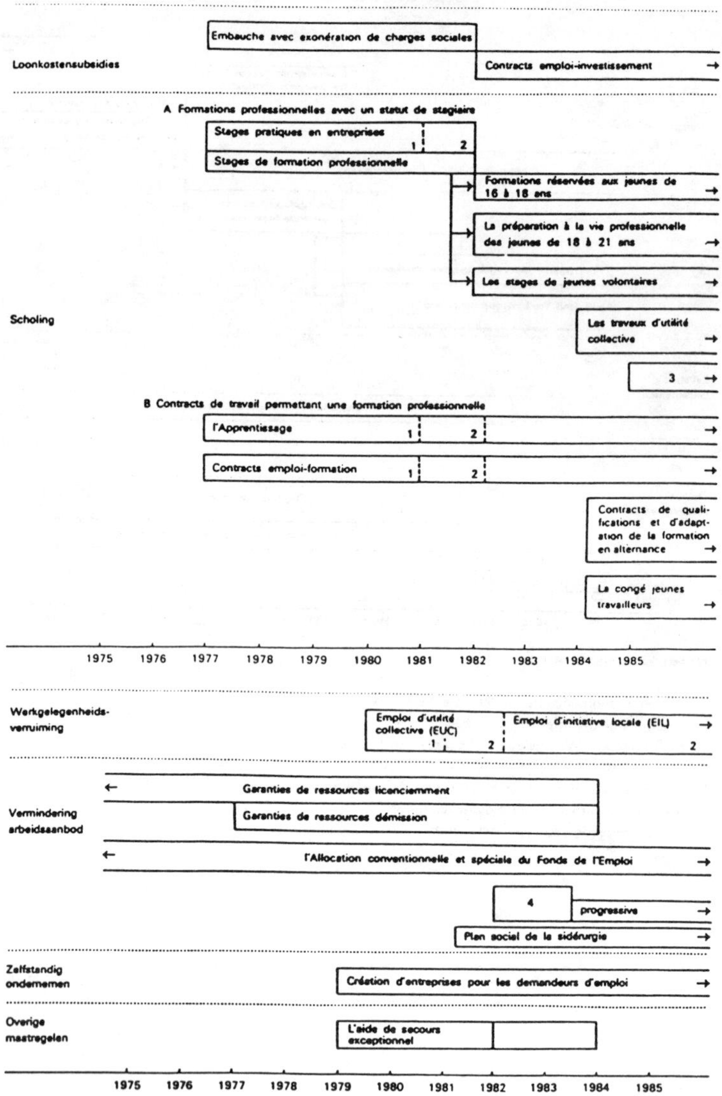


**Noten bij schema 4.2**

1. Pactes Nationaux pour l'emploi des jeunes
2. Plan Avenir Jeunes
3. Les stages d'initiation à la vie professionelle de la formation en alternance
4. Contracts de solidarité de préretraite demission
5. Campagne pour les chômeurs de longue durée

*Scheme* 3 Development job creation policy - Belgium 1975-85

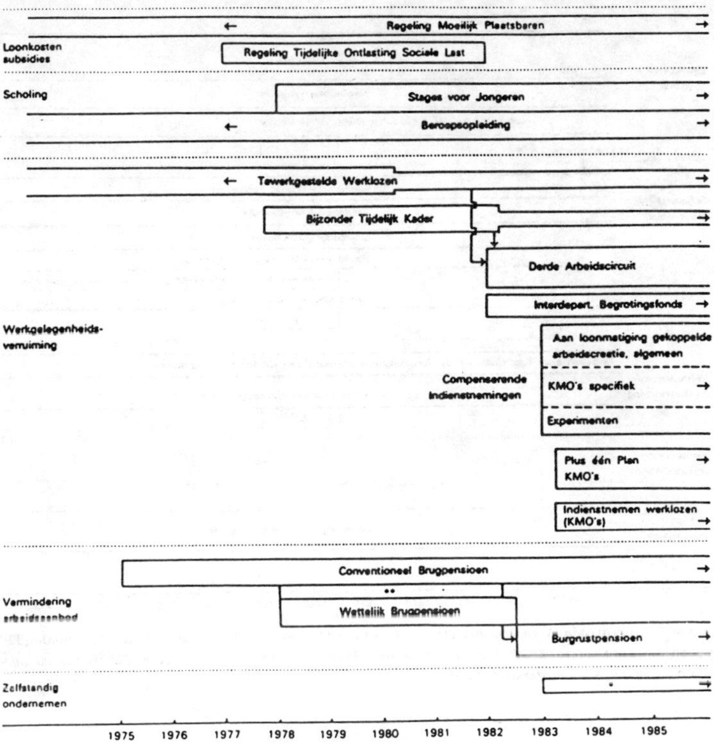


* Hulp aan werklozen die eigen onderneming willen oprichten.

** Bijzondere stelsels van brugpensioen.

*Scheme* 4 Development job creation policy – the BRD 1975–85

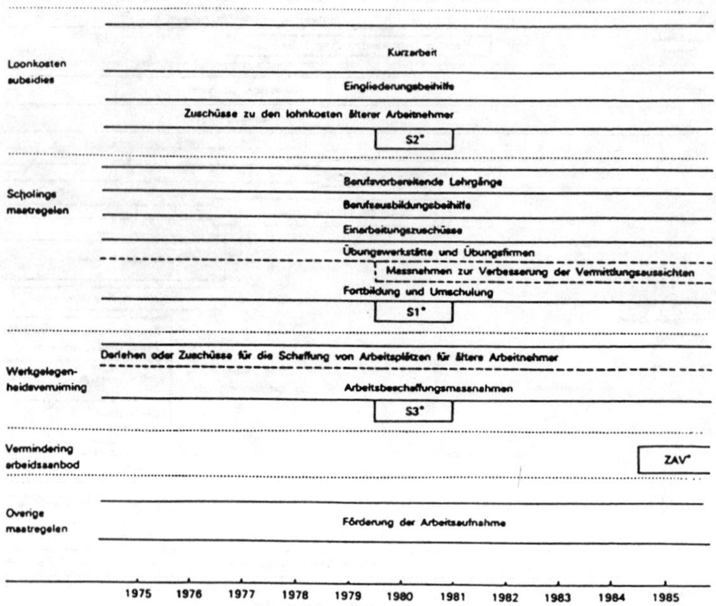


* S1, S2 en S3 zijn de drie Schwerpunkte van het Arbeitsmarkt-politische Programm der Bundesregierung für Regionen mit besonderen Beschäftigungsproblemen (Sonderprogramm 1979); ZAV = Zuschüsse zu den Aufwendungen für Vorruhestandsleistungen.

*Scheme* 5 Development job creation policy - Great Britain 1975-85

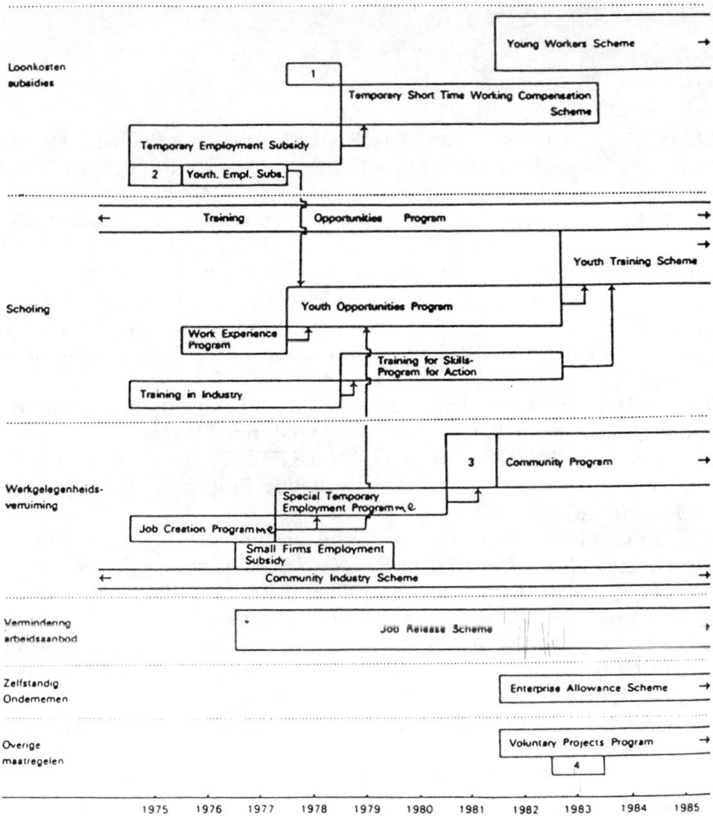


## Notes

1. This chapter is based upon an extensive comparison of job creation policies, sponsored by the SER/COB. For detailed information see: de Wachter, M. and E. Visser (1986), Doelmatigheid intredingbevorderende arbeidsmarktinstrumenten, SER/COB.
2. This is covered in detail and country by country in de Wachter, M. and Visser, E. (1986) Arbeidsvoorzieningbeleid in Nederland, SER/COB; de Wachter, M. and Visser, E. (1986) Arbeidsvoorzieningsbeleid in België, SER/COB; de Wachter, M. and Visser, E. (1986) Arbeidsvoorzieningsbeleid in West-Duitsland, SER/COB; de Wachter, M. and Visser, E. (1986) Arbeidsvoorzieningsbeleid in Frankrijk, SER/COB; de Wachter, M. and Visser, E. (1986) Arbeidsvoorzieningsbeleid in Groot-Brittannië, SER/COB.

3. See appendix for schemes of the development of the labour job-creation policies in the Netherlands, France, Belgium, BRD and Great Britain.

**References**

ADAMS, C. (jr), COOK R. and MAURICE, A. (1983) 'A Pooled Time-series Analysis of the Job Creation Impact of Public Service Employment Grants to Large Cities', *Journal of Human Resources,* XVII, no 2, pp. 283–94.

AISLABIE, C. J. (1980) 'Temporary Employment Subsidies in Industrialised Market Economies', *International Labour Review,* 119, no 6, pp. 775–92.

ASHENFELTER, O. C. (1978) 'Estimating the Effect of Training Programs on Earnings', *Review of Economics and Statistics,* 60, no 1, pp. 47–57.

ASHENFELTER, O. (1978) 'Evaluating the Effects of the Employment Tax Credit', *US Conference Report on Evaluating the* 1977 *Economic Stimulus Package.*

BALKENHOL, B. (1981) 'Direct Job Creation in Industrialised Countries', *International Labour Review,* 120, 1981, no 4, pp. 425–38.

BAROCCI, T. A., HARRISON, B. and JERRETT, R. (1978) 'Structure, Cost and Performance of the Job Opportunities Program', *Monthly Labour Review,* 101 (8) pp. 40–5.

BASSI, L. G. (1983) 'The Effect of CETA on the Postprogram Earnings of Participants', *Journal of Human Resources,* XVIII, no 4, pp. 539–56.

BASSI, L. J. (1984) 'Estimating the Effect of Training Programs with non-random Selection', *Review of Economics and Statistics,* vol. LXVI, pp. 36–43.

BAUMEN, D. C., VAN HORN, C. E. and MARVEL, M. (1979) Explaining Benefit Distribution in CETA Programs', *Journal of Human Resources,* 14 (2) pp. 171–96.

BEKEMANS, L. (ed.) (1983) *Employment Generation in Europe* (Maastricht: European Centre for Work and Society).

BISHOP, J. H. (1979) *Employment in Construction and Distribution Industries* (*Impact of the New Jobs Tax Credit*), Institute for Research on Poverty Discussion Papers (Madison: Univ. of Wisconsin).

BISHOP, J. and HAVEMAN, R. (1979) 'Selective Employment Subsidies: Can Okun's Law be Repealed?' *American Economic Review,* 69, no 2, pp. 124–130.

BOLLE, M., FIEDLER, A. *et al.* (1982) *Efficiency of Labour Market and Employment Policy Measures,* (*Study no.* 82/6) (Brussels: EC).

BORUS, M. E. *et al.* (1970) 'A Benefit-Cost analysis of the NYC: The Out-of-School Program in Indiana', *Journal of Human Resources,* 2, pp. 147–59.

BORUS, M. E. (1978) 'Indicators of CETA Performance', *Industrial and Labour Relations Review,* 32, (1) pp. 3–14.

BORUS, M. E. and HAMERMESH, D. S. (1978) 'Estimating Fiscal Substitution by Public Service Employment Programs', *Journal of Human Resources,* 13, (4) pp. 561–5.

BOVARD, J. (1983) 'Busy Doing Nothing: The Story of Government Job Creation', *Policy Review,* 24, pp. 87–102.

BURNIM, M. L. and COBBE, J. H. (1982) 'Benefits and Costs of a CETA Public Service Employment Program', *Growth Change*, 13 (1) pp. 9–18.

BUTT-PHILIP, A. (1978) *Creating New Jobs: A Report on Long-term Job Creation in Britain and Sweden* (Sheffield: Policy Studies Institute).

CISCEL, D. H. and TUCKMAN, B. H. (1981) 'The Peripheral Worker: CETA Training as Imperfect Job Socialization', *Journal of Economic Issues*, 15 (2) pp. 489–500.

DAMME, F. VAN (1975) 'De plaats van de minst bedeelden binnen de huidige programma's en activiteiten van de EEG', *Belgisch tijdschrift voor sociale zekerheid* 25, nr. 3, blz. 505–22.

DANZIGER, S. K. (1981) 'Postprogram changes in the Lives of AFCD Supported Work Participants: A Qualitative Assessment', *Journal of Human Resources*, 16 (4)pp. 637–48.

DEPARTMENT OF LABOR, *Employment and Training Report of the President* 1976–1980–1982 (Washington: US Government Printing Office).

ECONOMISTS ADVISORY GROUP S. A. (1978) *Swedish and Swiss Manpower Policy - Its Relevance for the EEC* (Brussels: EC).

FARKAS, G., SMITH, D. A. and STROMSDORFER E. W. (1983) 'The Youth Entitlement Demonstration: Subsidized Employment With a Scholling Requirement, *Journal of Human Resources*, XVIII, no. 4, pp. 557–73.

FAULKNER, M. J. (1978) *Direct Job Creation - A Comparative Study* (Brussels: EC).

FOTTLER, H. D. (1977) 'Management Commitment and Manpower Program Success', *California Management Review*, vol. XIX, no. 3, pp. 71–7.

GAY, R. S. and BORUS, M. E. (1980) 'Validating Performance Indicators for Employment and Training Programs', *Journal of Human Resources*, 15 (1) pp. 29–48.

GRAMLICH, E. M. (1979) 'Simulating the Macro Economy through State and Local Governments', *American Economic Review, Papers and Proceedings*, pp. 180–5.

HARRIS, R. (1979) 'Job "Creation" - or Destruction', *Six Essays on the Effects of Government Intervention in the Labour Market* (London: The Institute of Economic Affairs).

HAVEMAN, R. H. and CHRISTIANSEN G. B. (1978) 'Public Employment and Wage Subsidies in Western Europe and the United States: What We're Doing and What We Know', *European Labor Market Policies*, special report 27 (National Commission for Manpower Policy) pp. 259–345.

HAVEMAN, R. H. and PALMER, J. L. (eds) (1982) *Jobs for Disadvantaged Workers*, (Washington, DC, The Brookings Institution).

HORN, C. E. VAN (1978) 'Implementing CETA: The Federal Role', *Policy Analysis*, 4(2) pp. 159–83.

JAIN, H. C. (1979) *Disadvantaged Groups on the Labour Market, and Measures to Assist Them* (Paris: OECD).

JOHNSON, G. and TOMOLA, J. (1977) 'The Fiscal Substitution Effect of Alternative Approaches to Public Service Employment Policy', *Journal of Human Resources*, 12, pp. 3–26.

KARSTEN, D. (1981) *Job Creation Schemes in the European Community* (Brussels: EC).

KIEFER, N. M. (1978) 'Federally Subsidized Occupational Training and the Employment and Earnings of Male Trainees', *Journal of Econometrics*, 8 (1) pp. 111-25.

LEVITAN, S. and TAGGART, R. (1973) '*Evaluation of the First* 18 *months of the Public Employment Program*, US Congress, Senate Committee on Labor and public welfare (Washington: US Government Printing Office).

LONG, D. A., MALLON, C. D. and THORNTON, C. V. D. (1981) 'Evaluating the Benefits and Costs of the Job Corps', *Journal of Policy Analysis and Management*, 1 (1) pp. 55-76.

MANPOWER DEMONSTRATION RESEARCH CORPORATION (1980) *The Youth Entitlement Demonstration: Second Interim Report on Program Implementation.*

MASTERS, S. H. (1981) 'The Effects of Supported work on the Earnings and Transfer Payments of its AFDC Target Group', *Journal of Human Resources*, 16 (4) pp. 600-36.

MCKEWITT, J. D. (1978) *Testimony on Jobs Tax Credit* (US Congress Print) 26 July 1978.

MUELLER, D. C., (1979) *Public Choice* (Cambridge, Cambridge University Press).

NATHAN, R., COOK, R. F. RAWLINS, V. L. (1981) *Public Service Employment: A Field Evaluation* (Washington, Brookings Institution).

NATIONAL COMMISSION FOR MANPOWER PLANNING (1978) *Job Creation Through Public Service Employment*, vols I, II and III (Washington: US GPO).

OECD (1978) *Youth Unemployment, Inventory of Measures Concerning the Employment and Unemployment of Young People* (Paris: OECD).

OECD (1979) *Unemployment Compensation and Related Employment Policy Measures General Report and Country Studies: Canada, France, Germany, Sweden, UK, USA* (Paris: OECD).

OECD (1980a) *Direct Job Creation in the Public Sector* (Paris: OECD).

OECD (1980b) 'Experts' Meeting on Incremental Employment Subsidies', *National Report: United States* (Paris: SME/MP (80) 6).

OECD (1982) *Marginal Employment Subsidies* (Paris: OECD).

O'NEILL, D. (1979) 'Evaluation of Job Creation Programs', *Paper for General Accounting Office* (Washington, DC: USGPO).

O'NEILL, D. M. (1982) 'Employment Tax Credit Programs: The Effects of Socioeconomic Targeting Provisions', *Journal of Human Resources*, 17 (3) pp. 449-59.

PALMER, J. L. (ed.) (1978) *Creating Jobs, Public Employment Programs and Wage Subsidies* (Washington, DC: The Brookings Institution).

PERLOFF, J. M. and WACHTER, M. L. (1979) 'The New Jobs Tax Credit: An evaluation of the 1977-78 Wage Subsidy Program', *American Economic Review*, 69, pp. 173-79.

REHN, G. (1980) *Employment Premiums in Economic Policy* (Paris, OECD).

ROSENBERG, S. (1983) 'Reagan Social Policy and Labour Force Restructuring', *Cambridge Journal of Economics*, 7, pp. 179-96.

SAWHNEY, P. K., JANTZEN, R. H. and HERZNSTADT, I. L. (1982) 'The Differential Impact of CETA Training', *Industrial and Labour Relations Review*, 35 (2) pp. 243-51.

SCHILLER, B. R. (1978) 'Lessons from WIN: A Manpower Evaluation', *Journal of Human Resources*, 13 (4) pp. 502–23.

TAMMENWALD, R. (1982) 'Are Wage and Training Subsidies Cost-Effective? - Some Evidence from the New Jobs Tax Credit', *New England Economic Review*, pp. 25–34.

US CONGRESS (1977) *Employment Subsidies and Employment Tax Credits, Background Paper* (Washington: Congressional Budget Office).

WERNEKE, D. (1976) 'Job Creation Programmes: The United States Experience', *International Labour Review*, vol. 114, no 1, pp. 43–59.

WILLIAMS, S. *et al.* (1981) *Youth Without Work, Three Countries Approach the Problem* (Paris: OECD).

WISSEN, K. VAN (1982) *Jeugdwerkloosheid en overheidsbeleid* (Rotterdam: EUR) (scriptie).

WONG, R.A., KROFT, H. P. A., DIJKHUIS-POTGIESER, H. I. E. (1984) Hoe werken maatregelen voor werklozen? *Een literatuurstudie naar evaluatie van maatregelen ten behoeve van werklozen in zeven Europese landen*, in opdracht van het Ministerie van Welzijn, Volksgezondheid en Cultuur, Werkgroep Arbeidsvraag-stukken en Welzijn, Faculteit der Sociale Wetenschappen, Rijksuniversiteit Leiden.

# COMMENT ON CHAPTERS 10 AND 11

**J. A. H. Maks**

## CHAPTER 10 COUNTING THE COSTS

### Section 10.1 Introduction

In the economic science there has been a clear development away from an objective economic motive towards subjective motives driving economic behaviour. The emphasis shifted to the economic principle, i.e. goal-directed behaviour. Moreover this principle was also considered to be subjective, because it was acknowledged that efficient behaviour is determined by subjective expectations and subjective information. These developments were not without influence on the cost concepts. 'Opportunity costs' are by definition subjective and even the 'minimum-outlay'-cost concept is acknowledged to be subjective because it is determined by subjective expectations on, for example, future prices and technologies. Moreover expressions such as 'economic costs', 'economic welfare' became tautological. Recognising the subjective character of costs and benefits there was an intensive compensation debate related to the Pareto principle. Moreover there was a substantial development in the theory of (quasi-)collective goods, in the theory of external effects, in the theory of aggregating individual preferences and in economic index theory.

These developments are, to a large extent, ignored by Junankar in the first two sections of his paper 'Unemployment in the European Community: Counting the Costs'. He proposes the following typology of costs:

*Table* C.1 Summary of Junankar's typology of costs

| | *Individual* | *Family* | *Social groups* | *Government* | *Society* |
|---|---|---|---|---|---|
| Economic | c, e, l | g | | h | a, b, k, m, n |
| Social | d, f | g | | | i |
| Political | | | j | * | j |

In Table C.1 we have classified Junankar's enumeration (a) until (n) (see section 10.2) of the different costs, according to his own indication, to bearer and to nature. The * in the table indicates that this enumeration was not quite effective in summarising his section 2. We note that there are several blanks in the table. There may exist very good reasons for these blanks, but Junankar does not elaborate them in this paper. Moreover, although Junanker is aware of the double-counting problem and the aggregation problem with questionable value judgements, it is nevertheless most obvious that choosing for estimation of (a) (current output loss to society), as he does, involves aggregation and questionable value-judgements. It implicitly attaches values to the utility change of individuals, it focuses on some variables of the utility function (mainly real income) and neglects leisure. With regard to the types of cost distinguished the following is to be noted: psychological costs to the family are classified as social. (Why is this not a fourth entry with the heading 'psychological' in Junankar's typology of costs?) This social-cost item can be expressed in *economic* terms: an increased disutility of offering labour services, thus a change in the utility function. Political costs in terms of a loss of voters are already a fairly established research item for economists analysing the relation between government behaviour and voter behaviour. Obviously voters expect to gain (increase in their utility) by voting for or against a government.

Reviewing the first two sections one is tempted to conclude that they do not constitute an adequate justification for the main point of the paper: estimating the aggregated output loss as costs of unemployment.

## Section 10.2 Immanent Evaluation of the Estimation of the Aggregated Output Costs of Unemployment

In this section we will take Junankar's theoretical point of view for granted. He identifies the lack of effective demand as cause for unemployment. Moreover he rejects the concept of the natural rate of unemployment and ignores differences in production technology and in excess capacity in the various sections of the economy. In the next section we will evaluate his results outside this narrow theoretical scope.

To estimate the output loss Junankar uses a very simple equation introduced by Okun. Junankar does not sufficiently specify his data-set and he does not precisely explain how he estimates the gap between potential and actual output. He obviously employs a kind of data-mining procedure without informing us about quantity measures of any statistical quality indication. Hence, it is impossible to reconstruct his estimation results. Moreover he does not present the estimated values of the parameters $a_0$ and $a_1$, of the Okun equation. On the basis of the (limited) information given in Tables 10.1 and 10.2 in Junankar's paper I have guestimated these values. They are given in Table C.2.

*Table* C.2 Guestimate of the Okun parameters

| | $a_0^*$ % | $a_1$ % |
|---|---|---|
| Germany (FRG) | 1-3 | 2.5 |
| Italy | 5.5-6.5 | 3 |
| France | 9.7 | 0 |
| United Kingdom | 3-4.6 | 3 |

* Low guestimate corresponds with Junankar's high estimate of output loss and v.v.

The values of the parameters of France show us, that given Junankar's theoretical point of view the Okun equation is probably highly misspecified: a reduction of the gap does *not* have any influence at all on unemployment. There seems to be a considerable influence in the cases of the FRG, Italy and the UK. But we note substantially differing values of $a_0$. This parameter indicates the rate of unemployment if the gap equals zero. So its value may be interpreted as the 'natural rate' of unemployment. Only the FRG seems to have an acceptable 'natural rate' of 1–3 per cent. In the UK, Italy and France these rates are higher and *differ.* This again may indicate misspecification of Okun's equation. On the other hand one might have estimated this equation under the restriction of $a_0$, say, equal 2 and test this result against a free estimation. Whatever the results may be of such a test, it seems that just estimating Okun's equation and leaving scope for high and differing rates of natural unemployment, as Junankar did, is not consistent with his own theoretical point of view that rejects the concept of a natural rate of unemployment.

## Section 10.3 Transcendental Evaluation

The guestimated values of $a_0$, may already indicate that Junankar's theoretical point of view is too narrow. The problem is that the market participants, given their expectations, decided not to engage in the production of this output. Government may try to persuade and stimulate *private* expenditures or raise the government expenditures. The essential questions then are: is the government sufficiently informed to do this in an adequate way, i.e. without sustaining or creating a production and capital structure that is not maintainable by pure market forces, without creating excess demand on various markets with binding capacity constraints, leading to inflation,[1] without a stimulating influence on the natural rate of unemployment,[2] and in relation with this rate, without increasing the malfunctioning of the labour markets?[3] If one accepts serious doubt about the ability of the government to perform such an adequate demand stimulating policy, one should also doubt the value of Janankar's estimation results. If e.g. we accept that an inflexible labour market is one of the substantial causes of unemployment, then both employed and unemployed had in some sectors of the labour market a too *high* income.

### Section 10.4 Friedman

Friedman stated that reducing inflation would lead only to 'a modest reduction in output and employment'. Junankar denies the validity of this statement. In fact however the economies he deals with did not even stop *growing*, measured in national production and in employment. Of course one has to admit that employment in the market sector decreased over the past two and half decades in the EC and that in the same period this employment increased considerably in the USA (approximately 50 per cent) and Japan (ca. 20 per cent). So this might be a good reason to *not* reject Friedman's natural rate of unemployment, that connects the height of this rate with the extent to which governments impede the flexible functioning of the market economy. Indeed one may very well argue that these restrictions in and between the EC-countries is an important course of the inability to react quickly and flexibly, and to discover with success changing market conditions.

## CHAPTER 11 MARKET SECTOR EMPLOYMENT

### Section 11.1 Introduction

During the past few decades the Western European countries have faced structural problems with the creation of employment in their market sector. The situation is much worse than in the USA and Japan. This is clearly illustrated in Table C.3. The first column gives the change in percentage of the labour force ($\Delta LF$) in the period 1962–79.

*Table* C.3 The development of the labour force and employment in the market sectors of various countries, 1962–79

| | $\Delta LF$ *1962–79* | $\Delta EMS$ *1962–79* |
|---|---|---|
| Sweden | 15 | −10 |
| Netherlands | 13.4 | −10† |
| United Kingdom | 5.7 | −5.5 |
| FRG | −1.5 | −9.9 |
| France | 16.2 | 8.6* |
| USA | 43 | 42.4 |
| Japan | 21 | 17 |

*Source*: *change in %· of the labour force* ($\Delta LF$): OECD, *Labour Force Statistics*, 1964–1975 and 1968–1979.
*Change in % of the employment in the market sector* ($\Delta EMS$): *idem* but also OECD, *National Accounts*, 1982–79. Results derived by subtracting from total employment the employment in sector B, i.e. producers of government services.
* *Idem*, and Frey and Weck Hanneman (1984) 'The Hidden Economy as an "Unobserved" Variable', *European Economic Review*, 26, pp. 33–53.
† This figure is obtained by extrapolating the decrease in the market sector over the period 1970–1980 back to 1960, using data from Jaarverslag 1981, De Nederlandsche Bank, p. 38. The figure is corrected for the growth of the Dutch semi-collective sector, although it still does not include heavily subsidised sectors as public transport. The OECD figure overestimates the employment in the market sector because the OECD does *not* take the corrections of de Nederlandsche Bank into account.

The second column indicates the change in percentage of employment in the market sector ($\Delta EMS$). These data reveal that the listed Western European economies were not able to create sufficient employment in their market sector to match their increase in labour force. On the contrary, we see in all but one case a notable decrease of the employment in the market sector. Only France is an exception, but even there the 'increase' is very insufficient. Although not indicated in the table, it is a fact that the Western European countries, if taken together, were not able to increase their employment at all in the period under consideration, even including government-sector employment, despite a considerable increase in labour force. The achievements of the

Western European economies in the creation of market-sector employment differ markedly from the US and Japanese results, as the table shows. In the USA especially we see that despite the really tremendous increase (two or three times that of the Western European countries) in the labour force the increase in employment in the market sector almost perfectly matches.

From these observations we might be able to place the 'evaluation of the job-creation measures' in Belgium, the Netherlands, the FRG and the UK, as shown in the paper of Somers and De Wachter in an effective perspective. This perspective indicates that the policies to increase employment in the market-sector they evaluate can hardly be seen as differing from 'swabbing with the taps running'. This may explain their conclusion that none of the policies they evaluate can be scientifically proved to be effective.

## Section 11.2 Structural Causes of the Incapability of the Western European Economies to Generate Employment in the Market Sector

Important basic causes underlying the bad performance of the Western European economies with respect to the creation of employment in the market sector are:

1. the inflexible labour markets; see, for example, Klau and Mittelstädt (1986);
2. the mere existence of a great number of Western European national states with, despite the EC, a lot of nation-law-based barriers of market entry; see, for example, Witboek ECC (1985), Costs and Benefits of Protection, O.E.C.D. (1985);
3. a relatively hostile political climate towards entrepreneurial activities.

Without elaborating these points to a great extent in this comment we just mention that:

*ad 1* Especially in the labour markets the various Western European governments went far in law-enforcing and law-privileging of the position of the labour unions on the labour markets, i.e. too far to conserve sufficiently flexible labour markets. The trade unions obtained something close to legal monopolies. We may point at, for example, the Trade Dispute Act in the UK and the law that enforces collective labour agreements to hold also for non-union members in the Netherlands. These legal arrangements effectively prevent a lot of competitive actions on the labour markets and give the unions an exclusive bargaining right. Indicators of the extent of the labour market inflexibility are the rate of wage rigidity and the extent of wage differentials. An impression of these latter phenomena is given in Table C.4.

From the indicators in this table we may conclude that the USA and Japan have relatively flexible labour markets and France and the UK relatively inflexible labour markets. The development of market-sector employment in the USA might also be revealing if distinguished in a unionised and a non-unionised sector. In 1956 unionised jobs were 39 per cent and in 1984 15 per cent of the total employed in the market sector, see Bellante (1988). The increase in total non-unionised market-sector employment was 244 per cent (from 27 million to 66 million jobs). The *de*crease of unionised market-sector employment was 70 per cent in this period (from 17 million to 12 million).

In various Western European countries we also have a relatively high minimum-wage system, a relatively ineffective unemployment-security system, with premiums not all related to the risks they cover, and progressive income-tax systems. Regarding minimum-wage laws a survey of empirical studies is provided in Brown, Gilroy and Koken (1982). These studies generally indicate a loss of employment especially for the youth, women and racial minority groups. Again one may refer to the USA where the relative flexibility of youth wages, manifested in the decrease in youth's relative wage, did result in an improvement of its labour-market position (see OECD, *Economic Outlook*, September 1984). The Western European government policies:

(a) made labour an expensive production factor and introduced labour-saving techniques very strongly, leading to the decline of employment in the market sector in Western Europe, as shown in Table 3.
(b) created a weak competition situation for labour-intensive products (for example, the service sector);
(c) caused a lack of information upon which labour supply has to take its allocative decisions. To a large extent the wage-differentials are too low and do not signal any more in what activities labour is most urgently needed, see the second row in Table 4.

It is to be noted that the employment in the USA increased strongly in the service sectors in the southern and western part of the country, thus, in those sectors and states in which the trade unions have a weak and unprivileged position.

*Table* C.4 Indicators of labour market flexibility (1970s and early 1980s)

| | *Sweden* | *Netherlands* | *United Kingdom* | *FRG* | *France* | *USA* | *Japan* |
|---|---|---|---|---|---|---|---|
| 1. Short-run real wage rigidity | n.i. | high | high | low | high | low | low |
| 2. Inter-industry wage-differentials | low | n.i. | low and falling | low and rising | low and falling | high and rising | high and rising |

*Source*: Adapted from Klau and Mittelstädt (1986) p. 41, table 11.
'n.i.' means that *no* indication was given in this table.

*ad 3* The left-wing parties are bigger in Western European Countries and were able to induce a lot of laws and policies distracting the entrepreneurial activities from what they should do: competing in the market. Instead the entrepreneurial energy and inventive potential was to be devoted, to too large an extent, to dealing with the bureaucracy to obtain subsidies or other favours, to evade taxes, etc. (see, for example, Appels (1986)). A rough indicator, with certain shortcomings, of the extent of political interference with the market sector is the share of taxes and social-security contributions in the gross domestic product. For Sweden and the Netherlands this share rose considerably in the 1960s and 1970s (1978, ca. 53 and 57 per cent respectively). In the USA and Japan this share hardly increased and the level is considerably lower (1978, 31.1 and 22.2 per cent respectively).

Given these basic causes underlying the bad performance of the Western European economies regarding the creation of employment in the market sector the best job-creation policy would be a gradual, firm, consistent and long-term movement towards making the labour markets more flexible, a decrease of the nation-law-based barriers of market entry and an improvement of the political climate towards market entrepreneurial activities. Several EC countries and the EC nowadays attempt to design policies of this kind. The road into this direction however is long and heavy, and it will take some time before the fruits will be visible. So it is not certain at all that the politicians will be sufficiently patient. If they turn out to be too impatient the structural weakness of the EC economies in the creation of market-sector employment will remain.

### Section 11.3 Evaluation of the Policy Recommendations

The facts revealed and the analysis given in sections 11.1 and 11.2 lead to the evaluation that the five measures of job creation discussed by Somers and De Wachter can indeed hardly be seen as differing from 'swabbing with the taps running'. So it is not very surprising that they find that none of the five measures examined can be scientifically proved to be effective. Nevertheless they recommend the training instrument as most promising. However, this instrument does *not* lead to the desired results in an inflexible labour market. For, in what direction should there be training? Neither the individual nor the planner receives an adequate signal about the present and past scarcity relations in the labour markets. Expectations on future scarcity relations cannot be made by the individual and the planner with due care and are not reflected in current wage differentials.

Furthermore Somers and de Wachter conclude that the promotion of entrepreneurship through subsidies and long-term loans was productive. Again, if this takes place in the context of the typical Western European situation, we can see such a measure as a well-known Casino policy to give the player some free money with his entrance but at the same time to take back a substantial part of the profit if he wins and/or to let him play with diminished chances of winning.

## Notes

1. See J. Taylor's contribution to this volume.
2. See Minford's and J. Davis' chapter in this book.
3. See the chapter by B. Compaijen and K. Springer.

## References


APPELS, A. C. W. (1986). 'Political Economy and Enterprise Subsidies', Dissertation, University of Brabant, The Netherlands.

BELLANTE, D. (1988) 'Labor Markets in the Welfare State', in K. Groenveld, J. A. H. Maks, J. Muysken (eds.), *Economic Policy in the Market Process: Success or Failure?*, North-Holland, Amsterdam, forthcoming.

BROWN, C., GILROY, C. and KOKEN, A. (1982) 'The Effect of the Minimum Wage on Employment and Unemployment', *Journal of Economic Literature*, 20, pp. 487–528.

KLAU, F. and MITTELSTÄDT, A. (1986) 'Labour Market Flexibility' OECD, *Economic Studies*, no 6, Spring.

*De voltooiing van de interne markt* (1985) Witboek van de Commissie voor de Europese Raad, Commissie van de Europese Gemeenschappen, Brussels.

OECD (1985) *Costs and Benefits of Protection*, OECD Economic Studies, Paris.

# 12 Germany and the European Disease[1]

John Davis and Patrick Minford

This chapter is concerned with the growth of unemployment in Europe in the late 1970s and early 1980s. Unemployment has risen to double digit rates in many countries, rates which are not considered likely to fall much in the rest of the 1980s. A theory - 'the disease' - is expounded, with empirical evidence from the Federal Republic of Germany. The disease is characterised by high unemployment and low output growth, these being systematic rather than the consequence of some temporary phenomenon such as the downphase of the business cycle. Consequently we present a 'natural rate' explanation as an underlying determinant of unemployment with consideration given to the role of the business cycle in recent German unemployment. The latter role is examined with the use of a full macroeconomic model of the Federal Republic. The model is new-classical with two of its most distinguishing features being the assumption of rational expectations throughout and the endogenous determination of natural rates. We find that the natural rate of unemployment in Germany more than trebled its 1973 level by the end of the 1970s, reaching 1.21 million by 1982 before falling to 1.16 million in 1983. We suggest that Germany may have caught the now familiar 'British disease' - that is, the prevention, by way of unemployment benefits and social aid, of real wage adjustment.

## 12.1 INTRODUCTION

Unemployment in Europe has risen during the 1970s and early 1980s to double digit rates, rates which are not considered likely to fall much in the remaining years of the 1980s. This is so in enough countries to encourage some to speak of a 'European disease'. Those of us who live in Britain have long been familiar with the 'British disease', as have the Dutch with their 'Dutch disease' (supposedly related to North Sea energy resources). This chapter suggests that these earlier national ailments are precursors of the general European one to which attention has more recently been drawn – notably by Professor Giersch who has spoken of a 'market sclerosis' in Europe, especially in the labour market (Giersch, 1985). (Also see OECD (1985, p. 38)).

However, in spite of this provocative general opening we wish to focus on West Germany, and thus to highlight a specific case of what may well be a general phenomenon.[2] Our motivation is fourfold: to widen the analysis of the possible disease to a country in which there is wide interest; to stimulate other European researchers to work along the lines of analysis portrayed here; to follow up the echoes sounded in the comments of authoritative national students (e.g. Giersch, 1985; and de Grauwe, Fratianni and Nabli, 1985), and finally, to utilise a full macroeconomic model of the Federal Republic of Germany in this direction of research.

In the next section the theory behind the 'disease' is expounded. This is followed by some empirical work on the natural rate of unemployment in Germany. Section 12.4 presents a cross-country comparison of the disease. We then use a full macroeconomic model of the FRG to analyse the role of the business cycle in recent German unemployment, before concluding in the final section.

## 12.2 A THEORY OF 'THE DISEASE'

The disease under discussion is characterised by high unemployment and low output growth, these being systematic rather than the consequence of some temporary phenomenon such as the downphase of the business cycle. This suggests we must look for a 'natural rate' explanation. This is not to deny that the recent world recession has had a part to play; in a later section we will discuss the role of the business cycle, once we have isolated the underlying natural rate phenomenon.

We begin with an outline of the basic open economy model in so far as it relates to the natural rate of unemployment.[3] It is assumed that industry is competitive and distributed into two sectors, unionised and non-unionised (or 'competitive') in a way that is outside firms' control. Firms are able to buy capital goods on an international market at a world real rental cost which is enforced domestically by perfect capital mobility. Each firm enjoys constant returns to scale but is limited by a fixed factor ('entrepreneurship') so that marginal product declines as the industry expands. It buys imported inputs at a given world price.

Accordingly, we write the demand for labour in each sector by profit-maximising firms as:

$$L_u^d = (\overset{-}{w}_u, \overset{-}{T}_F, \overset{+}{e}, \overset{+}{k}) \tag{12.1}$$

$$L_c^d = (\overset{-}{w}_c, \overset{-}{T}_F, \overset{+}{e}, \overset{+}{k}) \tag{12.2}$$

where $u$, $c$ subscripts stand for union and competitive sectors respectively, $L^d$ = labour demand, $w$ = real wage, $T_F$ = labour tax rate (as fraction of wage) paid by employer, $e$ = real exchange rate (price of domestic goods relative to price of imported goods, in common currency, rise = appreciation), $k$ = aggregate (positive) effect of technological progress, real rental on capital, and fixed factor supplies. The expected signs are indicated over the variables.

We complete the description of firms' activities by writing down their production function (we only need the economy's aggregate) as a supply of output equation:

$$y = (\overset{+}{L}_u^d + \overset{+}{L}_c^d, \overset{+}{k}) \tag{12.3}$$

where $y$ = total output of the economy. To avoid aggregation problems we assume the production functions of union and non-unionised industry are identical.[4]

We now turn to the behaviour of workers and unions. Unions maximise the present value of their potential members' aggregated real incomes by setting the union wage. This gives rise to a variable mark-up equation of the form:

$$w_u = m(\overset{+}{UNR}, \overset{-}{P}^{ue}, \overset{+}{k})w_c \tag{12.4}$$

where $m$(=one plus the mark-up) is a function of $UNR$ (=the unionisation rate), $k$, and $P^{ue}$ (=unanticipated inflation). $UNR$ enters as a proxy for the elasticity of demand for union labour, it being argued that the more unionised an industry, the greater the difficulty of substitution of non-union for union labour in that industry, whether in union firms or by the expansion of non-union firms. $P^{ue}$ enters because unions find it convenient - in order to minimise the transactions costs of controlling work conditions - to draw up nominal wage contracts with only partially contingent price clauses; hence a surprise rise in prices will reduce the real union wage.

It is assumed that firms choose workers' hours given the union-set wage rates. Therefore unionised workers are rationed in their labour supply. We assume that total labour supply of hours in the economy is such that the marginal rate of substitution of leisure for goods equals the *marginal* net real wage available. This is, for union and non-union workers alike, the real wage in the competitive market (which is assumed to be continuously cleared), minus benefits lost and taxes paid through working extra. Because of the wide differences in individual tax/benefit circumstances, tight restrictions across the parameters of benefit, tax, and real wage variables are unlikely to hold and we write labour supply, $L^s$, generally as:

$$L^s = (\overset{+}{w}_c, \overset{-}{b}, \overset{-}{T}_L, POP) \tag{12.5}$$

where $b$ = real unemployment benefit, $T_L$ = tax rate (fraction of wage) paid by employee, $POP$ = size of (registered) working age population (because this also acts as a proxy for demographic trends, the sign is left ambiguous).

The labour-market equations are completed by the equilibrium condition in the competitive sector:

$$L^s - L_u^d = L_c^d \tag{12.6}$$

and by the unemployment relation:

$$U = POP - L^s \tag{12.7}$$

where $U$ = unemployment. (12.7) states that those registered as potential workers will draw unemployment benefits if not working and still therefore under normal European practice be counted as unemployed (this is of course an oversimplification).

(12.6) taken with (12.1), (12.2), (12.4) and (12.5) yields a solution for $w_c$, $w_u$, $L_u^d$, $L_c^d$, $L^s$, in terms of $e$, $T_F$, $b$, $P^{ue}$, $T_L$, $UNR$, $k$, and $POP$. Using (12.3) we can then solve for $y$, and from (12.7) for $U$. The set-up, the economy's 'supply side', is illustrated in Figure 12.1.

Quadrant (a) in Figure 12.1 shows the equation of the production function (12.3); quadrant (b) shows $SS$, the equation of labour supply (12.5), and $DD$, total labour demand $L_u^d + L_c^d$ in terms of $w_c$ from (12.1), (12.2), and (12.4) the mark-up relation.

We may now conveniently extract from this an open economy supply curve, relating output supply to the real exchange rate, holding the other variables constant. Thus as we lower $e$, shifting $DD$ to the left, we trace out a falling output path along the $PF$ curve corresponding

*Figure* 12.1

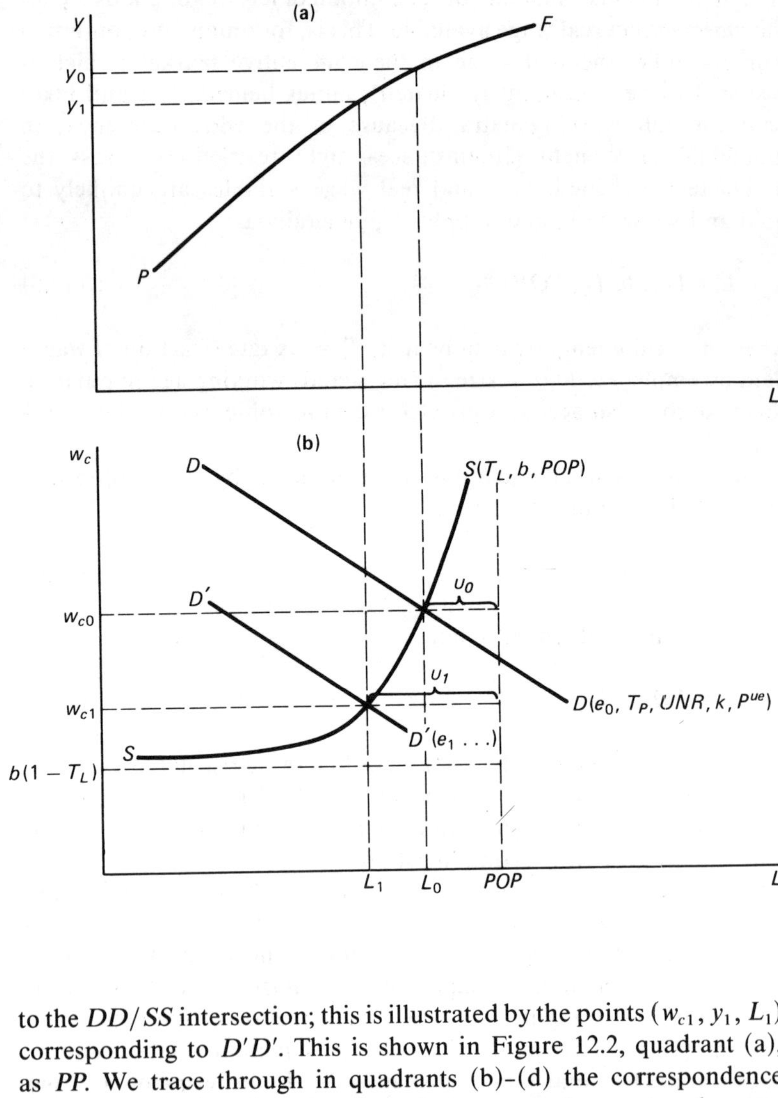


to the $DD/SS$ intersection; this is illustrated by the points $(w_{c1}, y_1, L_1)$ corresponding to $D'D'$. This is shown in Figure 12.2, quadrant (a), as *PP*. We trace through in quadrants (b)–(d) the correspondence between the real exchange rate, real wages, employment and unemployment, for other given variables. (Note that changes in all these other variables will shift both the *PP* and *EW* curves, and changes in $T_L$, *b*, *POP* will shift the *SS* curve. Also note that the shift in *PP* due to $P^{ue}$ is the 'Phillips curve' effect.)

Figure 12.2

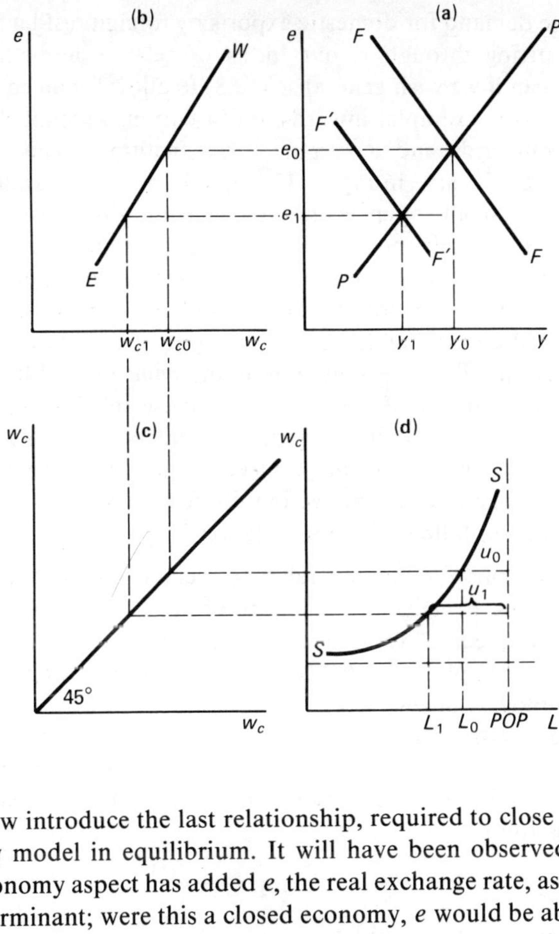


We now introduce the last relationship, required to close the open-economy model in equilibrium. It will have been observed that the open-economy aspect has added *e*, the real exchange rate, as a supply-side determinant; were this a closed economy, *e* would be absent, and there would be a unique equilibrium supply, corresponding to that which can be produced given labour market equilibrium. This is the usual vertical aggregate supply curve set-up. However the addition of *e* has produced an upward-sloping supply curve; the reason being that as *e* rises, the terms of trade improve and with them profits, enabling firms to induce a higher labour-supply profitably.

To close the model we specify a current account balance ($x$) equation and set it to equilibrium:

$$0 = x = (\overset{+}{WT}, \bar{e}, \bar{y}) \tag{12.8}$$

where $WT$ = the volume of world trade (or output). (12.8) simply states that the demand for imports by domestic residents must be equal to the demand for domestic exports by foreign residents, equilibrium occurring through $e$, our index of relative home-to-foreign prices. We can if we wish generalise (12.8) to allow for an equilibrium net transfer (for example, inwards and a current account deficit for an *LDC*, outwards and a surplus for a mature capital exporting country). The *FF* curve in Figure 12.2, quadrant (a), illustrates (12.8). If this was a 'small' open economy, then the *FF* curve would be horizontal. But in this model this is not an appropriate assumption. Full equilibrium of the economy - with corresponding 'natural rates' - occurs at the intersection of the *FF* and *PP* curves. So one may think of *PP* as describing the short-run supply *curve* of the economy, the intersection *FF*/*PP* as determining the *point* of equilibrium.

There are a number of ways in which these relationships can be grouped for econometric investigation. In practice we wish to determine aggregate unemployment ($U$), real wages ($w$), output ($y$), and the real exchange rate ($e$). So we require four relationships.

We choose the following representation:

1. a 'supply curve' of labour relating average wages to unemployment, taxes, benefits and union power.
2. a 'demand curve' for labour, conditional on planned output, relating unemployment to real wage costs (=real wages adjusted for employers' taxes).
3. a price = marginal cost function; price depends on real wage costs, other costs, and output. This function can be simply transformed into a relation between the real exchange rate, real wage costs, etc., as follows: if

$$\log P = \alpha \log W + (1-\alpha) \log P_F + \cdots,$$

(where $P$ = price level, $P_F$ = foreign price level converted into domestic currency, $W$ = nominal wage) then

$$e = \log P - \log P_F = \left(\frac{\alpha}{1-\alpha}\right)(\log W - \log P) + \cdots$$

$$= \frac{\alpha}{1-\alpha} \log w + \cdots$$

((2) and (3) are our analogue of the marginal product of labour curve and the production function.)

4. is an external current-balance condition which relates output to the real exchange-rate and to world-trade volume; this can be thought of as a 'demand curve' for domestic output under the restriction of current balance.

This formal outline has not discussed the substantive issue of what determines the shape of the supply curve of labour. The theory so far has been relatively standard, including the impact of benefits on *search* time of the unemployed, the empirical evidence indicating a fairly modest effect on duration of search and thus on labour supply.[5]

However, our theory departs from standard search theory in respect of a crucial category of unemployed whom we will call 'long-term unemployed'. If a person's benefits are 'high' enough and last indefinitely, then he or she may have very little chance of finding a job whose pay matches those benefits in terms of utility. 'High' here is to be related to this person's marginal value product. This person may search in some sense, but the search will be degenerate.

The situation can be depicted in Figure 12.3, which shows the distribution of population by their potential wages (their expected marginal value product).

Suppose there are two systems of benefit – a 'flat rate' benefit based on *need* ('social aid' as it is called on the Continent, 'supplementary benefit' in the UK), and a benefit based on previous income designed

*Figure* 12.3

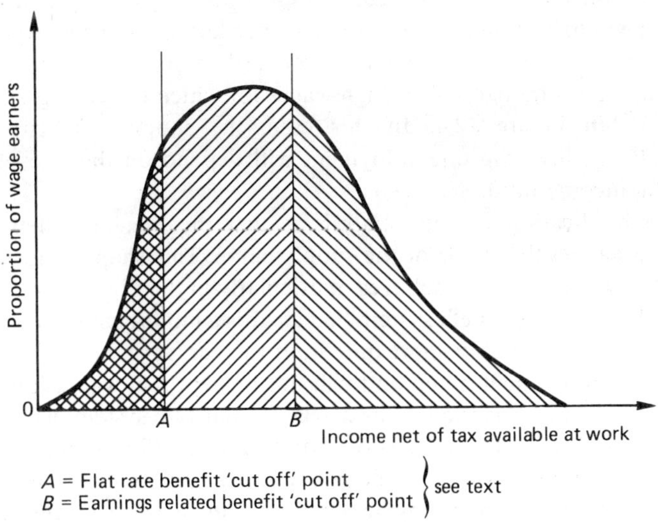

to assist those searching for new jobs (usually this will award some benefit/income ratio which may decline over time spent unemployed subject to some ceiling above which benefits do not rise). Let *A* represent the gross wage equivalent (in utility) of the flat rate benefit; let *B* represent the gross wage equivalent for the ratio benefit system.

In Figure 12.3, there are correspondingly two types of person. First there are those whose marginal product is more than *A* who will want a job but who if unemployed will search for a duration affected by the benefit/income ratio schedule; these people are the people of normal search theory. Second, there are those whose productivity is less than *A*. If, as seems likely for such unskilled workers, their distribution of wage offers is highly concentrated, then these workers will not desire work; they will be long-term unemployed.

Consider now what the supply curve of labour with respect to average wages would resemble with only a flat-rate benefit system. As average wages dropped, the wage distribution would shift leftwards, including more and more people in the area below *A*. As average wages tended to *A*, labour supply would of course tend to zero. By contrast, as average wages rose, wage distribution would eventually shift to the right of *A* altogether; labour supply would then tend to the total 'labour force', excluding some frictional unemployed (searching for the minimal duration). This supply curve is shown as $S^F S^F$ in Figure 12.4. Notice how the elasticity of supply varies along it, reaching an 'infinite elasticity' at low wages ('real wage rigidity').

Next consider the supply curve with a benefit-ratio system only. Search would be higher for all workers when laid-off and consequently labour supply would be displaced leftwards more or less equally at all wage levels though less at high wages for which the ceiling applies – $S^R S^R$ in Figure 12.4. In this case, the supply elasticity will typically be low; the unemployment will depend on the size of the benefit/income ratio.

The implication of this analysis is that the benefit system will crucially affect the shape of the supply curve. This shape in turn will affect how the economy behaves, particularly in the dimension of real wage flexibility. A benefit system that awards a modest benefit/income ratio with a reasonably short time limit (a year, say), is not likely to affect unemployment much and will not prevent real wages falling if a negative shock hits the labour market. A flat-rate system, where the flat rate is high relative to productivity for significant numbers of low-paid workers, will set a floor below real wages and a negative shock will induce unemployment rather than real wage adjustment.

*Figure* 12.4 Supply curves with flat rate ($S^FS^F$) and benefit ratio ($S^RS^R$) system of unemployment support

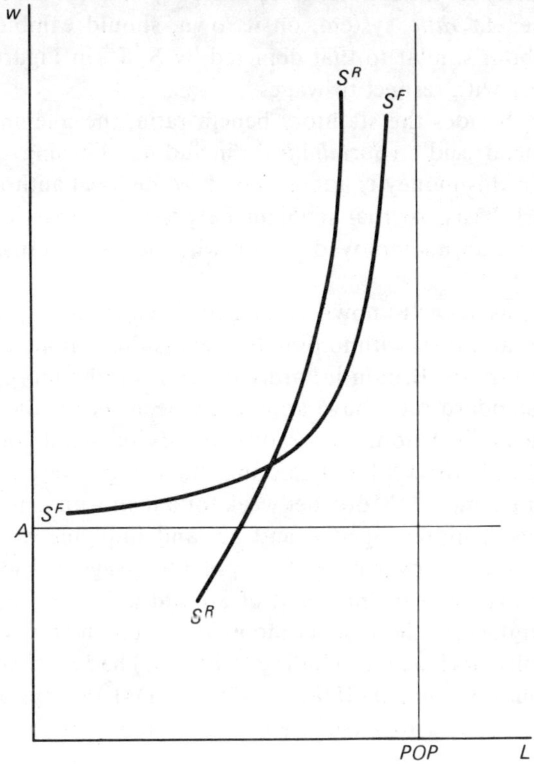


## 12.3 SOME EMPIRICAL WORK ON THE NATURAL RATE FOR GERMANY, 1961–83

We have identified four key equations required to solve for the 'natural rate' of unemployment, real wages, output, and the real exchange rate. To recapitulate, they are: a supply curve of labour; a demand curve for labour; a price-cost function; and an external balance condition.

Before we present some empirical findings we first briefly explain the German system of unemployment benefits/social aid in relation to our earlier theory. During the first year of unemployment the recipient is entitled to 63 per cent of his previous net wage or salary (*Arbeitlosengeld*).[6] Beyond a year, the unemployed person may receive

*Arbeitslosenhilfe* - a ratio of 53 per cent of previous net pay. A ceiling occurs with the previous income basis being DM 1305 a week[7] (approximately 1.7 times average earnings (Minford *et al.*, 1985). This statutory benefit *ratio* system, on its own, should exhibit a supply curve of labour similar to that depicted by $S^RS^R$ in Figure 12.4, i.e. low elasticity with respect to wages.

However, besides the statutory benefit ratio, the unemployed can receive 'social aid' (*Sozialhilfe*)[8] including housing assistance (*Wohngeld*); this money is administered by the local authorities on a discretionary basis, so that it might be presumed that it would be withheld from an unemployed person who was, say, refusing a low-paid job.

However, as is well-known from British experience, establishing such refusal and then withholding benefits is difficult and, therefore, likely to be rare (in Britain it hardly occurs). Furthermore, since the late 1970s standard rates have apparently been set for these benefits to 'guide' local discretion; 'illustrative' figures informally provided by German officials for 1981 indicate that these rates were substantial, totalling for example DM 365 per week for a man with a non-working wife and two children aged 8 and 12, and implying an indefinite replacement ratio of over unity if his potential wage was less than 80 per cent of average earnings, and of around 0.75 if he can achieve average earnings (in the first six months only this man's ratio would be higher still). Social aid (including *Wohngeld*) had reached DM 12.5 billion (about 1 per cent of GDP) by 1978, and DM 16.5 billion by 1982.

Indeed it appears to have been an aim of the Social Democrat Government of this time to turn the social aid system into a national system of 'decent' minimum living standards much as was aimed for by the UK supplementary benefit system. To our knowledge this philosophy has not changed in Germany since the accession of the Christian Democrats,[9] just as it has not changed in Britain under Mrs Thatcher's government.

This situation is therefore similar to that in Britain, and would imply a UK-style model; however, it would be emerging late in the sample period. This would suggest, in terms of Figure 12.4, that the German benefit system results in the supply curve of labour flattening at the lower end of $S^RS^R$ moving some way to that shown by $S^FS^F$. This in turn could produce a large rise in unemployment among workers whose marginal product lay below average earnings. (This may reflect the fact that the proportion of registered unemployed out of work for more than one year has risen to 28.5 per cent (May 1983) from 7.0

per cent (May 1975) - made up largely by young unskilled workers (see Hallett, 1985, p. 182) and Ginneken and Garzuel (1983, p. 116)).

Table 12.1 shows the results of estimation of the four equations, together with the implied long-run coefficients. The results in Table

*Table* 12.1 The German equations*

Estimated equations (instrumental variable estimation (*ARl* transformed where $\rho_1$ is significant), $\rho_1$ not reported were insignificant, *t*-statistic bracketed, $s$ = standard error of the regression, $DW$ = Durbin–Watson statistic).

---

(1) *Supply of Labour*:

$$\log w_t = \underset{(7.25)}{0.80} \log w_{t-1} + \underset{(2.76)}{2.22}\, UNR_t$$

$$\underset{(-4.14)}{-0.089} \log U_t + \underset{(2.32)}{0.17} \log(b_t(1+T_{Lt}))$$

$$\underset{(-0.62)}{-0.47}(INFL_t - E_{t-1}INFL_t) \underset{(-1.89)}{-0.88} \log POP_t + \underset{(1.44)}{7.07}$$

$\bar{R}^2 = 0.99$

$\bar{S} = 0.02$

annual, 1962–83

(2) *Demand for Labour*:

$$\log U_t = \underset{(2.32)}{0.41} \log U_{t-1} \underset{(-4.86)}{-9.64} \log y_t$$

$$+ \underset{(2.61)}{5.05} \log(w_{t-1}(1+T_{Ft-1})(1+VAT_{t-1})) + \underset{(1.87)}{0.16}t + \underset{(4.31)}{56.18}$$

$\rho_1 = \underset{(2.17)}{0.45}$ $\bar{R}^2 = 0.97$, $s = 0.208$

annual, 1962–83

(3) *Real exchange rate* (price–cost function):

$$e_t = \underset{(3.53)}{0.81} \log(w_t(1+T_{Ft})) + \log(1+VAT_t)$$

$$\underset{(-2.67)}{-0.026}t + \underset{(2.26)}{1.47}$$

$\rho_1 = \underset{(3.67)}{0.616}$ $\bar{R}^2 = 0.77$, $s = 0.038$, $DW = 1.40$

annual, 1962–83

*Table* 12.1 (*continued*)

(4) *External balance condition*

$$\frac{XVOL}{0.24y_t^*} = \underset{(2.87)}{1.72} \log WT_t \underset{(-2.76)}{-3.07} \log y_t$$

$$\underset{(-3.04)}{-0.67}(e_t - \log(1+VAT_t)) + \underset{(2.77)}{21.69}$$

$DW = 1.28$ $\bar{R}^2 = 0.47$
$s = 0.037$

annual, 1961-83

*Implied long-run coefficients*

$$\log w_t = 10.85\, UNR_t - 0.43 \log U_t + 0.85 \log(b_t(1+T_{Lt})) - 4.32 \log POP_t$$

$$\log U_t = -16.41 \log y_t + 8.597 \log(w_t(1+T_{Ft})(1+VAT_t)) + 0.28t$$

$$e_t = 0.81 \log(w_t(1+T_{Ft})) + \log(1+VAT_t) - 0.026t$$

$$\log y_t = 0.56 \log WT_t - 0.22[e_t - \log(1+VAT_t)]$$

*where*:

* denotes equilibrium value of variable
log = natural logarithm
$E_t$ = expectation formed in time $t$
$w$ = gross average weekly earnings of employees in industry (deflated by the consumer price index)
$UNR$ = unionisation rate, proportion of union membership to employees
$U$ = unemployment
$b$ = real average net benefits, including *Sozialhilfe*
$T_L$ = employees' national insurance and tax deductions - fraction of employees' gross wages and salaries
$INFL$ = rate of inflation (consumer price index)
$y$ = real gross national product
$T_F$ = employers' costs (other than $w$), indirect costs expressed as a fraction of direct costs
$VAT$ = value added tax rate, net indirect taxes expressed as a fraction of nominal income
$POP$ = working population
$XVOL$ = real trade balance (excluding terms of trade effects)
$WT$ = index of world trade
$e$ = real exchange rate (rise = appreciation)

The 0.24 in the $XVOL$ equation is the mean proportion of exports in $y^*$, thus

Table 12.1 (continued)

the right-hand-side coefficients can be interpreted as long-run elasticities (source of variables in Appendix 12.1).
* *Note*: In the supply of labour equation we normalise on real wages giving a supply price of labour equation. This has a relevant practical advantage. If the economy has been operating over the sample period in the elastic portion of the supply curve shown in Figure 12.4 (high 'real-wage rigidity'), then normalising on real wages will give better determined results than normalising on unemployment. (This is the same argument as used under conditions of high capital mobility for estimating interest rate rather than capital flows equations.) Also see Minford (1983). We choose to enter log $U$ rather than $U$ into this supply equation because our theory suggests that at high unemployment levels a 1% change in benefits will have a larger absolute effect on unemployment than at low unemployment levels because the slope of the supply curve will be flatter. We choose (the log of) unemployment as the dependent variable in the demand for labour equation for empirical convenience, to match up with the supply price equation.

12.1 are encouraging. All the variables in the model are signed as expected. Both *UNR* and grossed-up benefits are reasonably well determined, especially so when we expect a *strong* impact to be felt only after the mid-1970s (see Figure 12.7 in the case of *UNR*). Although the coefficient on unanticipated inflation is statistically insignificant the variable is retained since theoretically we would expect a zero effect only in the case of full indexation of wages, which did not occur in Germany following the Monetary Law of 1948 (see Bruno and Sachs, 1985, p. 244). The important variables in the demand-for-labour equation – real income and the product wage – are both well determined. The product wage enters with a one-period lag which reflects costs of adjustment.

When the equations in Table 12.1 are solved simultaneously for the natural rate of unemployment they indicate that for some twelve years the natural rate in Germany did not rise significantly from its 1961 level of 230 000. The rise in the natural rate occurred after 1974 – about the same time as the possible regime change discussed above. Also, the analysis is consistent with explaining the three major recessions in Germany – those of 1967, 1975 and 1981/3. In each of these periods actual unemployment rose above the natural rate as a result of negative shocks to the economy. However, after 1967/8 and 1975/6, unemployment returned to its natural level (rising after 1974) as the effect of these shocks died away. This can be seen from Figure 12.5. We consider recent German unemployment in section 12.5.

*Figure* 12.5 West Germany: unemployment ($U$) and equilibrium unemployment ($U^*$)

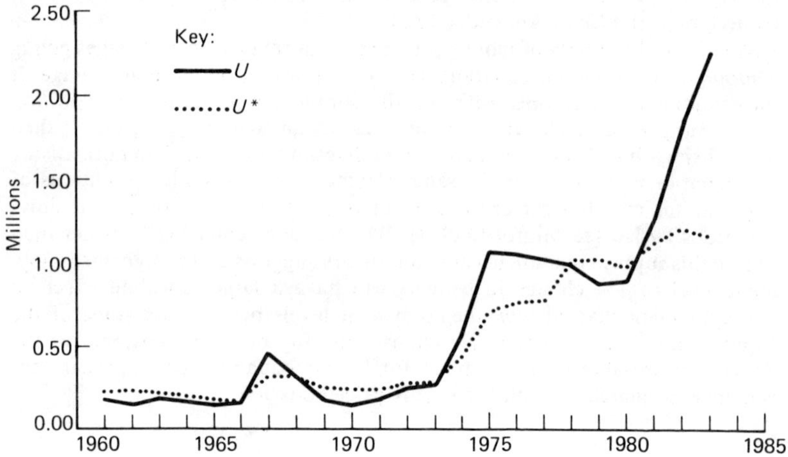


## 12.4 CROSS-COUNTRY COMPARISON: THE EUROPEAN DISEASE RECAPITULATED

Figure 12.5 shows what this model suggests is the 'natural' rate of unemployment for West Germany – alongside the actual rate. The key feature that stands out is that there has been a sharp upward tendency in the *underlying forces* creating unemployment.[10]

The contributory causes are charted in Figures 12.6 (real benefits), 12.7 (unionisation rate), 12.8 (tax and other non-wage costs on employers), and 12.9 (employees' tax and national insurance deductions). The charts we have just discussed depict an example of the

*Figure* 12.6 Logarithm of real unemployment benefits, including *sozialhilfe* ($b$).

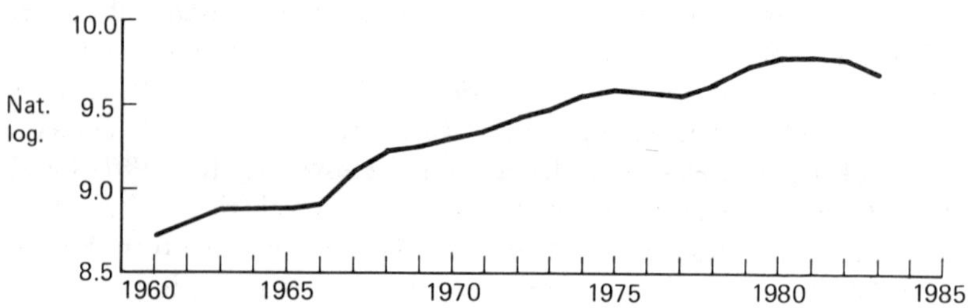

*Figure* 12.7 Unionisation rate (*UNR*): percentage of employees in unions.

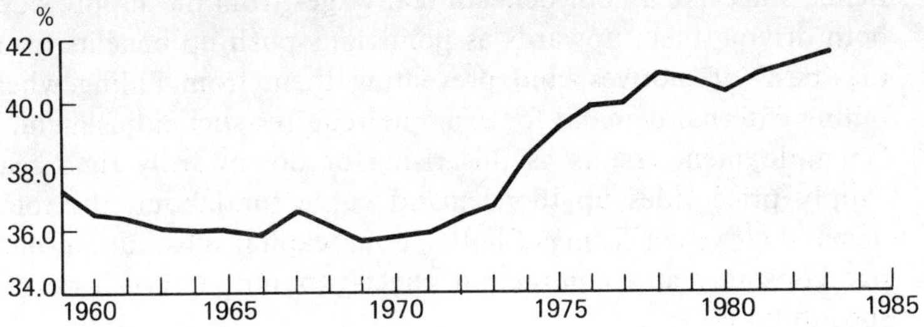


*Figure* 12.8 Employers' national insurance contributions and non-wage costs ($T_F$): indirect costs as a proportion of gross wages.

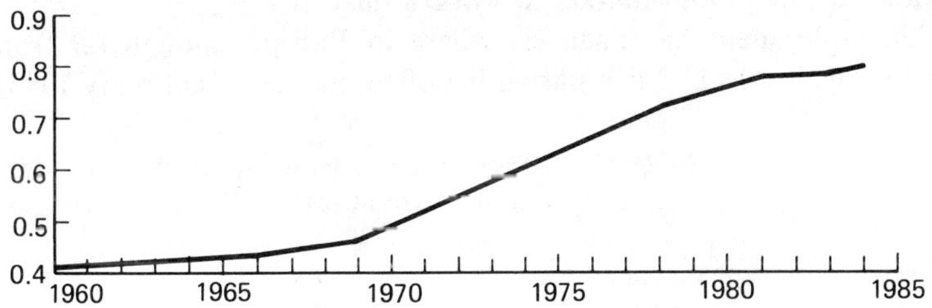


*Figure* 12.9 Employees' direct tax and national insurance contributions as a percentage of employees' gross income ($T_I$).

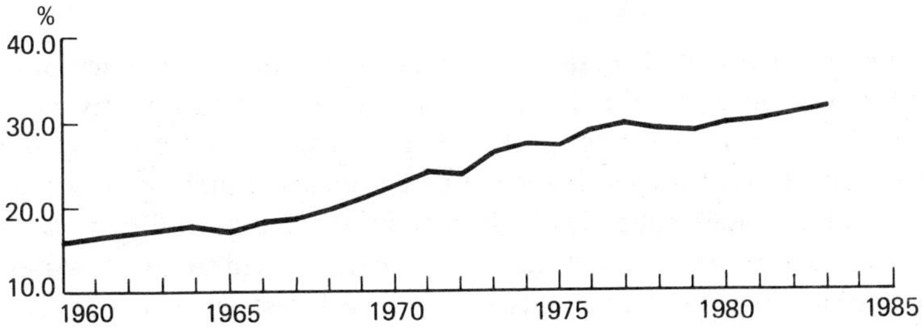

European disease. This disease has the following characteristics:

1. Benefits act like a floor beneath real wages from the supply side, both driving them upwards as politicians push up benefits from the 'best' of motives, and preventing them from falling when falling external demand for example requires such adjustment.
2. Unemployment results as this rising or downwardly rigid real supply price rides up the demand curve for labour, the total demand curve consisting of both labour/capital substitution (output constant) and contraction effects on output (via external substitution).
3. This falling employment (rising unemployment) is mirrored, via the production function, in reduced output; hence high unemployment and low output growth are two sides of the same coin.

Thus (3) – the European disease – is produced by (1) and (2) – the causal mechanism. It must be clear how the latter can give rise to such descriptive phrases as 'real-wage rigidity', 'labour-market sclerosis', 'failure of the labour market to work/adjust'.

Unemployment has risen elsewhere in Europe, though far from uniformly. Table 12.2 is a partial list of recent rates (February 1985).

*Table* 12.2 Unemployment rates in major European countries

| | |
|---|---|
| Belgium | 14.5 |
| France | 10.9 |
| West Germany | 9.2 |
| Holland | 16.1 |
| Italy | 14.1 |
| Sweden | 3.0 |
| Switzerland | 1.2 |
| UK | 13.0 |
| (Memorandum) | |
| USA | 7.3 |

The suggestion made in this chapter is that to understand unemployment one should examine the *mechanism* of government intervention through unemployment support and specifically how far it acts as a floor beneath real wages. It should be emphasised that one can have both high replacement ratios and substantial wage flexibility, if 'work tests' are rigorously applied (i.e. if people are forced to take low-paid jobs rather than stay on benefits). Tough work-tests may well account for the low unemployment in Sweden and Switzerland, both of which award generous benefit ratios; in the former the unions administer and partly finance the benefits, while in the latter local authorities (cantons) provide both administration and finance.

In France and Italy, systems of unemployment support are extraordinarily complex, comprising formal benefit ratios, social aid, family allowances, and (in Italy) special lay-off compensation. French replacement ratios range, depending on work income, from 0.96 to 1.32 for those unemployed for up to a year; they fall to 0.77 to 1.10 in the second year of unemployment; and then supposedly fall dramatically in the third year (to 0.25 to 0.57). However, to renew early-year entitlements a person needs only to get another job for a short time; and this cycle can keep someone in quite good circumstances on the dole for long periods. In Italy, the ratios range, depending on work income, from 0.73 to 0.9 from one year indefinitely. The shadow economy also is very large (estimates of over 25 per cent of GDP are dominant) and presumably raise the effective ratios substantially.[11] It seems reasonable to assume that these expensive systems of support create substantial real-wage rigidity.[12]

In Holland, the income from North Sea energy appears to have been spent in a large increase in government expenditure,[13] and welfare benefits in particular. Replacement ratios there appear to have been even higher than elsewhere in Europe (in 1979, the statutory benefit ratio was 80 per cent in the first year of unemployment, 75 per cent for the succeeding two years; but there was a minimum flat rate benefit of Fl 424 - £105 - per week). The 'Dutch disease' is supposedly produced by the resource windfall itself. Yet inspection of Figure 12.2 indicates clearly that this cannot be so; such a windfall loosens the external balance condition, permitting *higher* employment and output - the commonsense conclusion (it requires extraordinary perversity to believe a country must be damaged by an income windfall!)

The suggestion of this chapter is that the Dutch disease arose from the way in which the income was spent. By raising benefits, labour *supply* was reduced, shifting the supply curve by more than could be absorbed by the higher external-earning capacity of the economy - i.e. in Figure 12.2, the *PP* curve shifts *left* by more than the *FF* curve shifts *right*. (Similar comments apply to the British version of the Dutch disease.)

The principal non-European country with which all this can be contrasted is the USA, where unemployment support is limited to one year or less depending on the state and 'supplementary benefit' consists of food stamps and some other discretionary vouchers. Because of the size of the country and high mobility, one would expect search time to be higher than in a European country, with a higher frictional unemployment rate; the US evidence suggests that the natural rate has not risen significantly from a region of 6–7 per cent (see Figure 12.10).

*Figure* 12.10 Changes in prices and unemployment rates, 1954–79, and Phillips curves for USA

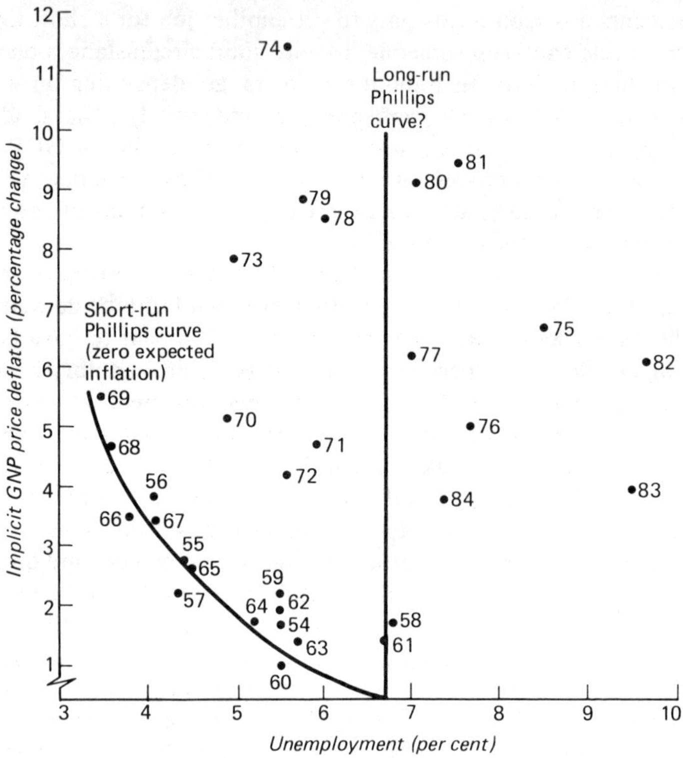


Real wages in the USA have not risen at all on average for the last ten years, indicating a considerable flexibility; real wages appear to have fallen at the bottom end of the pay spectrum to absorb a rapid growth in the labour force in mainly service industries.

## 12.5 THE ROLE OF THE BUSINESS CYCLE IN RECENT GERMAN UNEMPLOYMENT

Implicitly, the estimate of the cyclical component of unemployment falls out of our earlier estimate of the natural rate, as the difference between actual and natural rates. The implicit estimate is shown in Figure 12.11.

*Figure* 12.11 Actual unemployment – equilibrium unemployment as a percentage of the working population

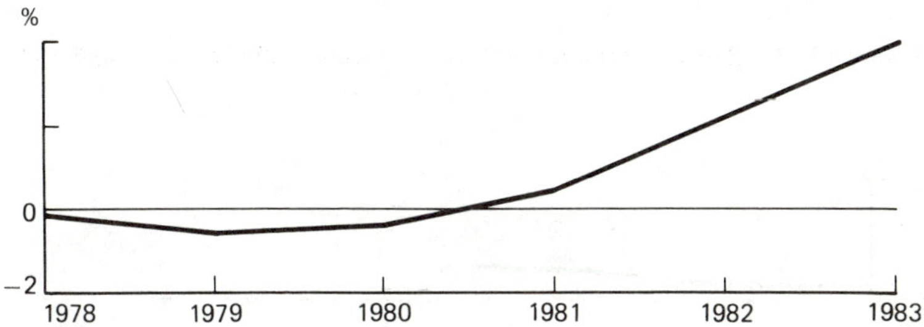


In this section we attempt to identify the main shocks that have produced this cyclical experience. This is done with the use of an annual macroeconomic model of the Federal Republic. The model is new-classical with two of its most distinguishing features being the assumption of rational expectations throughout (with terminal conditions being used to solve for forward rational expectations) and the endogenous determination of natural rates. The model has thirty-one endogenous variables, including seven behavioural equations. It accommodates both stock and flow equilibrium and the balance sheets of the external, government and private domestic sectors. Accordingly, with fully flexible prices, real wealth effects are integrated into both the domestic and overseas sectors. The model allows for an open economy with trade and capital flows and at the same time integrates the private sector's portfolio balance. Capital flows implicitly underlie the determination of exchange rates and interest rates with financial markets assumed to be efficient.[14]

It is natural to look for three main sources of shocks; those from German monetary and fiscal policy, and from external effects (for example, world trade). Figures 12.12–12.14 show measures of German monetary and fiscal expansion and the growth of world trade in the late 1970s and early 1980s. It can be seen that over the period 1980–2

*Figure* 12.12 Recent German monetary shocks (% p.a. change in real M1).

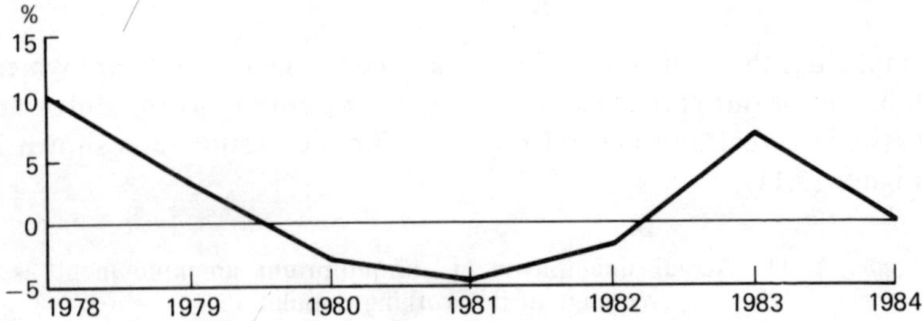


*Figure* 12.13 Recent German fiscal shocks (change in the real budget deficit as a % of real GNP)

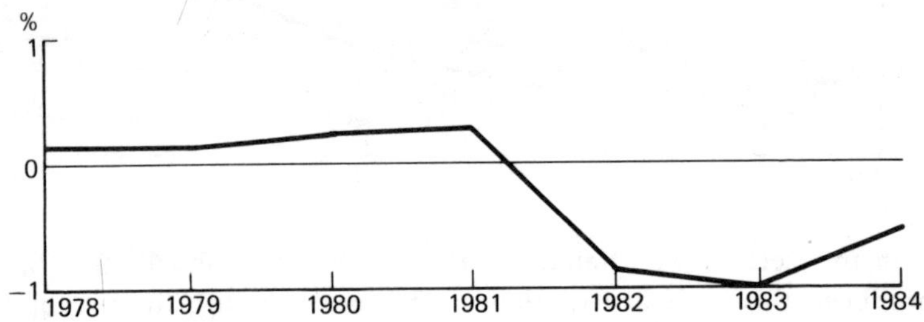


*Figure* 12.14 Recent world trade shocks (% p.a. change in world trade)

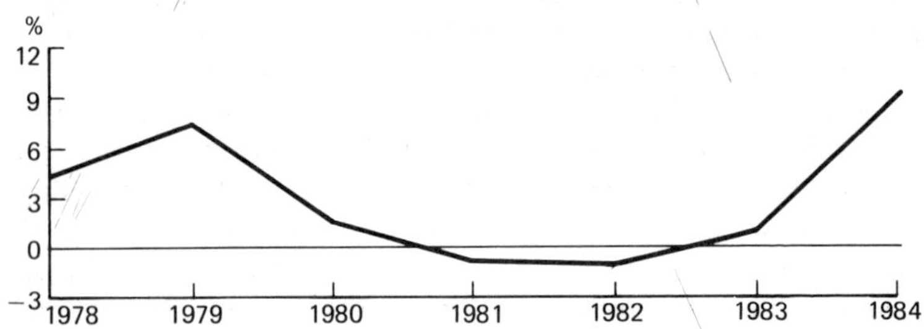


the real money stock fell, particularly in 1981. With regard to fiscal policy, the real budget deficit[15] steadily grew over the period 1978–81, before falling sharply in 1982. This fall continued into 1983 and 1984. Finally, the growth of world trade began to slow down as the 1970s ended, and in fact was negative in 1981 and 1982.

Thus we expect the cyclical component of unemployment to be affected by these three negative shocks to the German economy. Table

*Table* 12.3 Shocks (unanticipated) simulated by the model

| *Year* | *MP* % | *FP* % | *WT* % |
|---|---|---|---|
| 1981 | −7 | 0 | −5 |
| 1982 | −5 | −1 | −5 |
| 1983 | 0 | −1 | −5 |
| 1984 | −5 | −1 | 0 |

where:

*MP* = Monetary policy - change in inflation through change in *nominal* money supply;
*FP* = Fiscal policy - change in real government expenditure as a proportion of real GNP;
*WT* = world trade - change in growth rate of total volume of world trade;
− = reduction.

12.3 shows the shocks (unanticipated) that were simulated by the model, these shocks being representative of the patterns shown in Figures 12.12–12.14.

Figure 12.15 shows the accumulated effect on unemployment (differences from base) of each of these three simulations, together with the total effects on cyclical unemployment ($U-U^*$) of the three simulations combined. Figure 12.15 suggests that we may have captured some of the recent business cycle. It is also interesting to note that the cyclical component we are seeking to identify here (i.e. for 1981–3) is somewhat larger than that of the two previous recessions in Germany referred to in Section 12.3. This may be due to the fact that in these other two periods Germany did not experience three shocks as severe as those described above simultaneously. For example, the growth in world trade continued to be positive for every year except 1975, whilst the growth in real $M1$ was negative only in 1973 and 1974. True, the real budget deficit fell around both these times, but in no one year did all these three variables actually fall (unlike in 1982).[16] Of course, a full analysis of these other periods utilising our model would be necessary before definitive conclusions could be made, but this section suggests that we have gone a good way towards explaining the behaviour of recent unemployment in Germany, over and above that of the natural rate. Finally, the simula-

*Figure* 12.15 Effect of recent shocks on unemployment (see Table 12.3), differences from base

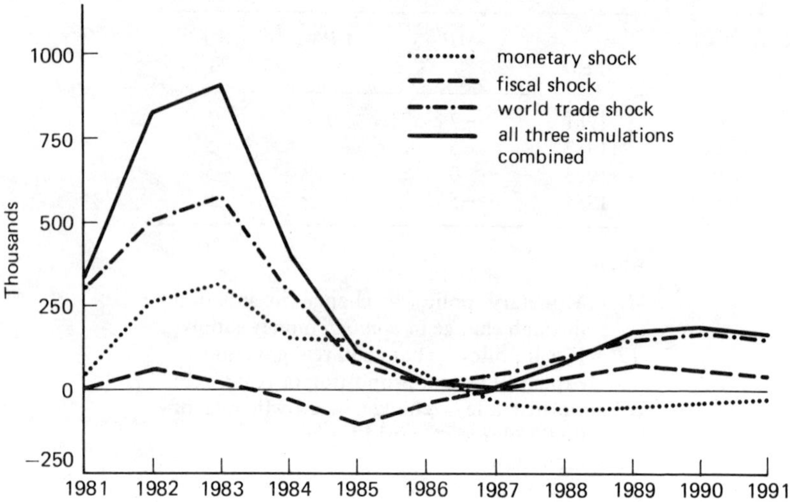


tions shown here are consistent with the slowdown in the growth of unemployment since 1983,[17] with the actual level expected to return to its natural level in the absence of further unanticipated shocks.

## 12.6 CONCLUSION

Germany may have caught the British disease, which has apparently become general in Europe. The disease is the prevention – by way of unemployment benefits – of real wage adjustment, and its manifestation is high unemployment and low growth. The natural rate of unemployment in Germany rose from only 282 000 in 1973 to 1.21 million by 1982, before falling back to 1.16 million in 1983. Actual unemployment in excess of this is cyclical, the result of macroeconomic shocks, but while substantial, it should decline steadily as the business cycle continues its recovery, in spite of 'conservative' macro-policies. The clear implication of this chapter is that if we want a lasting reduction in unemployment in many European countries, then action to remove labour-market distortions and, in particular, action to increase real-wage flexibility needs a high priority. We have not argued that demand factors do not matter – indeed we have shown that they do through shocks to the economy - rather, we have sought to demonstrate that supply factors are also important in analysing unemployment in Europe today.

## Appendix 12.1

*Table* 12.A.1 Source of variables used in German equations

| *Variable* | *Definition and Source* |
|---|---|
| $w$ | Gross average weekly earnings of employees in industry. Statistisches Taschenbuch 1984, Arbeit und Sozialstatistik, 5.3, deflated by $P$ (see *INFL* below). |
| *UNR* | Proportion of union membership to employees. 1. Statistisches Jahrbuch für die Bundesrepublick Deutschland, editions from 1962–84. 2. Sachverständigenrat zur Begutachtung Gesamtwirtschaftlichen Entwicklung, Gegen Pessimismus, Jahresgutenachten 1982/3, p. 268 (updated from Bevölkerung Erwerbstatistigkeit, Sachverständigenrat, 1984/5). |
| $U$ | Unemployment. Source as in 2. for *UNR* above. |
| $b$ | Real average net benefits, including Sozialhilfe. Net benefits from Ramb (1985, p. 19 - benefits per recipient, adjusted for the composition of unemployment in 1982 and 1983). Sozialhilfe data from various issues of Landesamt für Datenverarbeitung und statistik Nordrhein-Westfalen, Statistische Berichte, Die Sozialhilfe in Nordrhein-Westfalen: Teil 1 Ausgaben und Einnahmen, seite 6, und Teil 2, Empfänger von Sozialhilfe, seite 4. |
| $T_L$ | Employees' national insurance and tax deductions - fraction of employee gross wages and salaries. Volkswirtschaftlichen Gesamtrechnungen (Statistisches Bundesamt) Fachserie 18, Reihe 1, Konten und standardtabellen 1983, 2.12 Einkommen aus unselbständiger Arbeit. |
| *INFL* | Rate of inflation. $INFL = \Delta \log P$. $P$ from: Preise, Fachserie 17, Reihe 7, Preise und Preisindizes für die Lebenshaltung, März 1984, seite 3, Gesamtlebenshaltung Eilbericht. |
| $y$ | Real gross national product. Volkswirtschaflliche Gesamtrechnungen, Fachserie 18, Reihe 5.5, Revidierte Ergebnisse 1960 bis 1981, 2.5 Verwendung des sozialprodukts. Updated by the Deutsche Bundesbank. |
| $T_F$ | Employers' costs other than wage costs, indirect costs expressed as a fraction of gross wages. From: Argumente zu Unternehmenfragen, Institut der Deutschen Wirtschaft (material supplied by Professor Fels). |
| *VAT* | Value added tax. Net indirect taxes (supplied by the Deutsche Bundesbank) expressed as a fraction of nominal income. |
| *POP* | Working population. As in 2. for *UNR* above. |
| *XVOL* | Real trade balance (excluding terms of trade effects). As in $y$ above. |

Table 12.A.1 (*continued*)

| *Variable* | *Definition and Source* |
|---|---|
| $WT$ | Index of world trade. National Institute of Economic and Social Research (Quarterly Bulletin) and OECD (Main Economic Indicators). |
| $e$ | Real exchange rate. $e = \log S + \log P - \log P_F$, where $S$ = nominal exchange rate of the DM, $P$ is as above ($INFL$) and $P_F$ is foreign price level. $S$ and $P_F$ constructed from International Financial Statistics, using series *amx*, *MERM*, and 64 (a weighted average for Germany's principle trading partners). |

## Notes

1. Paper presented at the Conference 'Unemployment in Europe', The European Production Study Group, Maastricht, April 1986. Useful comments were received from participants in this Conference and in a seminar at International Finance Division, Federal Division, Federal Reserve Board; thanks are due especially to Victoria Chick, Neil Ericsson, Michael Gavin, David Germany and Karen Johnson. We are grateful to S. Blackman and J. Riley for computational assistance with the German model, and for production of the graphs. We also thank the ESRC for their financial support of this research. We alone of course remain responsible.
2. For work on the United Kingdom see Minford (1983), Minford *et al.* (1985). The latter also contains preliminary work on some other European countries. See also section 12.4.
3. The analytical approach and the empirical work on the UK is set out in detail in Minford (1983).
4. (12.3) is derived from a production function of the form

   $$y_i(1-u) = f(k_i, L_i, \bar{T}_i)$$

   where $u$ is the (assumed inflexible) share of imports in production and $\bar{T}$ is the stock of the exogenous factor ('entrepreneurship') which is assumed to be growing steadily over time. To obtain (12.3) we substitute for capital (from the marginal productivity condition for capital) in terms of the cost of capital, labour, and the fixed factor.
5. For example Franz (1982) concludes that there is a positive effect (although small) of the entitlement to unemployment compensation on the reservation wage and hence on the duration of unemployment.
6. Given that he/she has contributed to the social insurance scheme for six months sometime within the last three years. This figure was increased from 62.5 per cent to 68 per cent in 1975 and then reduced to its present level in 1983.

7. This is in 1986, from table supplied by the Bundesanstalt für Arbeit.
8. In 1983 33 per cent of the registered unemployed were supported by *Sozialhilfe*, 45 per cent by *Arbeitslosengeld* and 22 per cent by *Arbeitslosenhilfe* (Hallett, 1985).
9. This is consistent with comments made in Hallett (1985).
10. This is similar to findings in the UK (see Minford, 1983; Minford *et al.*, 1985) and Belgium (work in progress at Liverpool).
11. The figures from France and Italy are from Minford *et al.* (1985).
12. In Italy this is often blamed on full indexation, the *Scala Mobile*; yet indexation as such implies nothing for the real wage.
13. Up to 1983 Government expenditure had grown at 5.8 per cent per annum in real terms since 1970, 2.6 per cent faster than GDP. Its share of GDP rose from 27 per cent to 41 per cent.
14. A fuller description, including a stylised version, of the model is available from the authors.
15. This is equal to total public-sector debt minus interest payments on outstanding debt.
16. We should also note that the effect on unemployment of the 1975 recession was to some extent reduced by the expulsion of foreign workers - 726 000 between 1973 and 1978 (see Valli, 1983).
17. Unemployment growth in 1984 and 1985 was basically zero.

## References


BRUNO, M. and SACHS, J. D. (1985) *Economics of Worldwide Stagflation* (Oxford: Basil Blackwell).

DE GRAUWE, P., FRATIANNI, M. and NABLI, M. K. (1985) *Exchange Rates, Money and Output - the European Experience* (London: Macmillan).

FRANZ, W. (1982) 'The Reservation Wage of Unemployed Persons in the Federal Republic of Germany: Theory and Empirical Tests', *Zeitschrift für Wirtschaft und Sozialwissenschaft*, 2, pp. 29-51.

GIERSCH, H. (1985) 'Euro-Sclerosis: The Malaise that Flattens Prosperity', *Financial Times*, 2 January.

GINNEKEN, W. VAN and GARZUEL, M. (1983), '*Unemployment in France, the Federal Republic of Germany and the Netherlands. A Survey of Trends, Causes and Policy Options*', International Labour Office, Geneva, 2nd impression.

HALLETT, G. (1985) 'Unemployment and Labour Market Policies: Some Lessons from West Germany', *Social Policy and Administration*, 19, pp. 180-90.

MINFORD, P. (1983), 'Labour Market Equilibrium in an Open Economy', *Oxford Economic Papers*, November Supplement on Unemployment, vol. 35(4), reprinted in C. A. Greenhalgh, P. R. G. Layard and A. J. Oswald (eds) *The Causes of Unemployment* (Oxford: Oxford University Press, 1983, pp. 207-44.

MINFORD, P., ASHTON, P., PEEL, M., DAVIES, D. and SPRAGUE, A. (1985) *Unemployment - Cause and Cure* (Oxford: Basil Blackwell) 2nd edn.

OECD (1985) *OECD Economic Surveys 1984/85*, Germany, June.

RAMB, B. T. (1985) 'Effects of Unemployment Benefits on the Inflation Rate: The Horizontal Phillips Curve', mimeo, University of Siegen.

VALLI, V. (1983) 'The Rise of Unemployment and Employment Adjustment Policies in Japan, Italy and West Germany', *Revista Internazionale di Scienze Economiche e Commercial*, August, pp. 716–34.

**Further Reading**

ADDISON, J., *et al.* (1979), '*Job Creation or Destruction, Six Essays on the Effect of Government Intervention in the Labour Market*', The Institute of Economic Affairs.

BEENSTOCK, M. and MINFORD, P. (1976) 'A Quarterly Econometric Model of World Trade and Prices, 1955-71', in M. Parkin and G. Zis, (eds) *Inflation in Open Economies* (Manchester: Manchester University Press).

HENRY, S. G., PAYNE, J. M. and TRINDER, C. (1985) 'Unemployment and Real Wages: The Role of Unemployment, Social Security Benefits and Unionisation' *Oxford Economic Papers*, 37, pp. 344–5.

MINFORD, P. (1984) 'Response to Nickell', *Economic Journal*, 94, pp. 954–9.

MINFORD, P. (1985a) 'The Effects of American Policies – a New Classical Interpretation', in W. H. Buiter and R. C. Marston (eds) *International Economic Policy Coordination* (Cambridge: Cambridge University Press) pp. 84–138.

MINFORD, P. (1985b) 'Reply to Henry, Payne and Trinder', *Oxford Economic Papers*, 37, pp. 339–43.

NICKELL, S. J. (1984) 'A Review of Unemployment Cause and Cure by Patrick Minford (*et al.*)' *Economic Journal*, 94, pp. 946–53.

# 13 Keynesian Policies for Voluntary Unemployment*

William Peterson

This chapter represents an attempt to construct a simple classical model of the aggregate labour market from which it is nevertheless possible to draw certain Keynesian conclusions about the desirability of intervention, in the form of a conventional counter-cyclical fiscal policy, in order to maintain full employment. The starting-point of the paper is the observation - based on recent studies of the simulation properties of two macroeconomic models of the United Kingdom (Brooks *et al.* 1983; Peterson, 1984) - that it appears to be possible to devise policies which start from current levels of output, employment and inflation and which represent an unambiguous improvement in all welfare indicators. Such policies have become known as 'free lunches', apparently after the habit of nineteenth-century American bar-keepers in providing their customers with free, but thirst-provoking, food in order to stimulate sales of drink: similar incentives are offered by Nevada casino proprietors. In these contexts the catch is obvious, but in the case of expansionary macroeconomic policies there is scope for more controversy.

The presence of a free lunch, or more specifically of a Pareto-improving strategy which is not acted on by private agents operating in decentralised markets, is strenuously denied by most macroeconomists of the new classical school. If agents are perfectly informed, or if their expectations are rational, they will always be at a position at which the marginal product of labour is equated to the real cost of employing labour. An expansion in output, by a conventional diminishing returns argument, can only be achieved at the expense of a decline in this marginal product and hence in the real

* An earlier version of this chapter was presented to the European Production Study Group Conference on 'Unemployment in Europe', Maastricht, Netherlands, 17–19 April, 1986. I am grateful to participants at the conference for their comments: responsibility for errors remains mine. The research of the Cambridge Growth Project is financed by the UK ESRC, and their financial support is gratefully acknowledged.

wage. But rationality on the part of workers, who are always assumed to be on their supply curve, ensures that such a reduction cannot be achieved. Hence unemployment is on average at the 'natural rate', although stochastic disturbances can cause it to deviate from this in the short run, and the only way to reduce unemployment permanently is to remove the labour-market distortions (union power, unemployment benefits) which have reduced the supply of labour forthcoming at the real wage which technology and the existing capital stock make feasible. Simulation results such as those cited above, which lack the backing of a theoretical analysis based on the methodologically essential assumption of rational maximising behaviour, are treated with contempt as indicating that the models concerned are fundamentally misspecified, and thus do little to advance the adoption of Keynesian policies.

The analysis of 'free lunch' policies set out in this chapter differs from that given by Corden (1981) in several respects. First, in order to simplify the exposition while remaining as classical as the most devout new classical macroeconomist, the analysis focuses exclusively on the labour market and the supply side of the economy. Firms are assumed to operate in perfectly competitive markets, and can therefore sell as much output as they find it profitable to produce: there is no problem of effective demand. The approach which we have adopted is nonetheless Keynesian, in that the analysis can be related to that adopted by Keynes before the publication of the General Theory in 'The Means to Prosperity' (Keynes, 1933). Second, and again for simplicity, we neglect all the complications which arise as a result of foreign trade by assuming that the economy in question is closed, and thus simplify the analysis considerably. As Keynes was well aware, one of the most powerful classical arguments why supply-side labour-market policies, aimed at reducing labour costs, can help to cure unemployment under fixed exchange rates is that they also reduce the real exchange rate and increase competitiveness. However such an argument is essentially mercantilist, as well as being much less credible under floating exchange rates, and we shall therefore deliberately ignore it.

Instead we concentrate on the relation between the fiscal regime operated by the government and the possibility of a 'free lunch'. The realisation that optimal discretionary policy will usually be time-inconsistent (Kydland and Prescott, 1977) has led to a revival of intellectual support for policies based on unconditional adherence to a fixed rule, either in the form of target growth rates for particular monetary aggregates or target ratios for the budget deficit relative to GDP. The medium-term financial strategy adopted by the Conservative Government in the UK is an example of this approach. It can be argued that this attempt to reduce or eliminate what had previously been seen by Keynesians as a valuable automatic stabiliser represents a more fundamental change in policy stance than the switch from unemployment to inflation as the main policy target which accompanied it. However, as we will show, adherence to unconditional fiscal targets makes the 'free lunch' possibility more relevant.

An additional feature of this chapter is that we attempt to assess, on the basis of a number of stylised facts about labour supply and demand and the tax system, whether at the time of writing (early 1986) a 'free lunch' is in fact possible for the UK. Clearly such an analysis is no substitute for a full attempt to model the necessary behavioural relationships, although it should be noted that an analysis based on results from a particular macroeconomic forecasting model could be equally misleading. Thus if the model concerned specifies that wages respond in an asymmetric way to changes in direct and indirect taxes it is easy to see how simulation results might indicate the possibility of a 'free lunch' which was unlikely in practice to be available. Nevertheless one purpose of the analysis presented here is to provide some support for those who have based their policy recommendations on simulation results derived from Keynesian macroeconomic models.

Figure 13.1 is the conventional classical diagrammatic exposition of the labour market, with the only departure from tradition being that we have used a logarithmic scale on both axes: since we shall work later with constant elasticity functions this is a useful device. Because the analysis is in real terms, the vertical axis is the logarithm of the real wage: this is defined as the consumption wage, net of all taxes (including indirect taxes) which fall on labour. The *Ns* and *Nd* curves should be interpreted as indicating the demand price and supply price of labour corresponding to a given level of employment, so that the downward slope of the *Nd* curve arises purely because of diminishing returns to employment with a given capital stock, rather than because of capital–labour substitution in producing a given output. For this reason it seems plausible to argue that the slope of *Nd* is unlikely to be very steep. *Ns* slopes upwards, basically because of disutility of effort, although some economists (notably Minford, 1983) would add the disincentive effects of unemployment benefits.

Suppose now that there exists a government which levies taxes to pay for public goods, and to provide unemployment benefit. To do

*Figure* 13.1

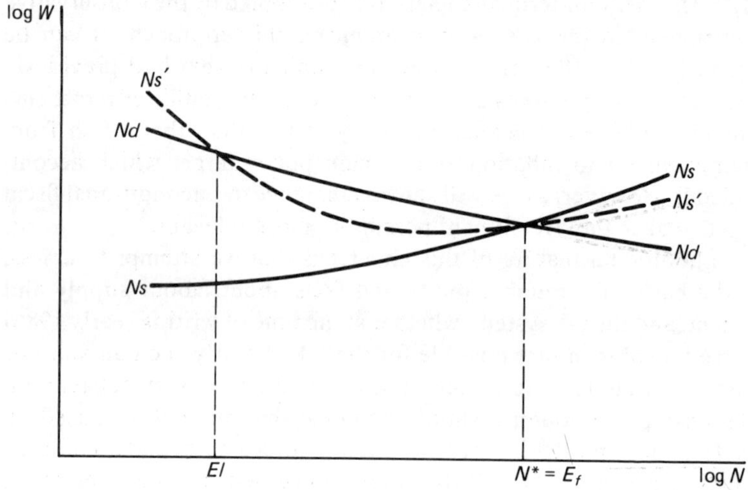


this it imposes taxes on labour and on wage-goods to supplement any revenue it may be able to raise from lump-sum taxes and mineral royalties. Without loss of generality we can assume that the *Ns* curve in Figure 13.1 has been drawn after allowing for the effects of such taxes levied at rates sufficient to balance the budget at the 'natural' rate of unemployment $N^*$. The distortions (including voluntary unemployment) which are caused by taxes levied at these rates are unavoidable given society's decision about the optimal provision of public goods and income maintenance. However it should be noted that, by affecting the 'baseline' tax burden on workers, they may also affect the elasticity of supply of labour in the neighbourhood of the natural rate and thus help to determine whether a free lunch is available.

Consider the response of this economy to an exogenous shock which temporarily causes unemployment to rise above the natural rate. If the Government is committed to maintaining budget balance (or indeed any unconditional path for the stock of public debt) it must raise taxes. As a result the supply price of labour to the employer, which is the product wage variable relevant to the employment decision, will rise further above the consumption wage actually received by the worker (the variable which defines *Ns*), with the difference representing the worker's *per capita* contribution to providing income support for the unemployed and paying part of their share of the public good. Obviously the magnitude of this difference will depend on the level of unemployment benefit and whether this is taxed, the extent of collective consumption, and the balance between direct, indirect and payroll taxes.

The dotted line $Ns'$ in Figure 13.1 shows the resulting supply curve of labour in terms of this product wage. In order to analyse the relationship between the two supply curves $Ns$ and $Ns'$ it is convenient to work in terms of a very simple tax system which can be characterised by two parameters: $Tw$, the positive net tax payments of an employed worker, and $Tu$, the negative net tax payments (i.e. positive benefits) of an unemployed worker. $Tu$ is defined to allow for indirect taxes on consumption and any direct taxes on unemployment benefits. Both $Tw$ and $Tu$ are measured as proportions of the product wage $Wp$. Total tax revenue, net of unemployment benefit, is:

$$R = Wp(TwN + TuU), \qquad Tw > 0,\ Tu < 0 \tag{13.1}$$

and the maintenance of an unconditional target for public borrowing requires:

$$\begin{aligned} dR = Wp[&(NdTw + TwdN + (L-N)dTu - TudN) \\ &+ Wp^{-1}(TwN + TuU)dWp] = 0 \end{aligned} \tag{13.2}$$

where $L$ is the full employment labour force. If we assume that institutional constraints such as a legal commitment to the indexation of welfare benefits preclude any effective increase in $Tu$ we can derive the result that

$$\frac{d\log(1-Tw)}{d\log N} = \frac{(Tw-Tu)}{(1-Tw)}\left(1+\frac{1}{\eta_D}\right) + \frac{Tu(1+U/N)}{(1-Tw)\eta_D} \tag{13.3}$$

where $\eta_D$ is the elasticity of demand for labour with respect to the product wage. This expression is positive provided $|\eta_D| > 1$, although since the second term is certainly positive this is a sufficient rather than a necessary condition. Under these conditions the retention ratio $(1-Tw)$ which is consistent with budget balance will be a decreasing function of the level of unemployment.

As a result there is a distinct possibility that for certain values of the tax parameters and labour-market elasticities there will be two distinct 'equilibrium' unemployment levels at which workers are on their supply curve and receiving the consumption wage $Wc$ while firms are on their demand curve and paying the product wage *Wp*. One of these is the natural rate of unemployment, at which the two definitions of the wage coincide because of our assumption that 'full-employment' taxes are incorporated in the definition of *Ns*. The other is an unemployment equilibrium at which the high effective rate of taxation on labour is distorting the choice of both workers and employers. These two equilibria are shown as *Ef* and *El* in Figure 1. Clearly for an economy which is trapped at *El* there is a Pareto-improving move to *Ef*, but since *El* is a Nash equilibrium for the three players (workers, employers and government) it is not clear how such a move could be achieved by decentralised market action. In particular since both workers and employers take tax rates as given it is not possible for the private sector acting as a coalition to improve on *El*. The supply curve of labour to the firm, conditional on constant tax rates, is a vertical displacement of *Ns* and therefore slopes upwards, so that at *El* firms appear to be constrained by labour shortages at the current pre-tax wage, while some workers are voluntarily unemployed, either through reduced hours of work or 'true' unemployment.

The possibility of a 'free lunch' arises for an economy which is trapped at *El* because a reduction in the taxes paid by workers shifts the labour supply curve *Ns'* in such a way as to expand the level of employment, and this in turn generates enough tax revenue to maintain budget balance. A general reduction in indirect taxes could have the same effect, but would be proportionately more expensive because it increases the net cost of the unemployed as well. On the other hand an economy which is trapped at *El* is potentially extremely vulnerable to any adverse external shock, because the resulting fall in employment will unbalance the budget and push the economy into an unstable region below *El*. In this region fiscal austerity is impossible, because the burden on the work-force of supporting the unemployed is too high: the attempt to maintain borrowing targets will merely lead to a further increase in unemployment. The classical response to such a dilemma is to cut the level of benefits and expenditure, and such a policy may succeed if the adverse shock was not too violent. However a Keynesian policy of expansion stimulated by tax cuts will be equally effective and Pareto-superior.

The failure of decentralised market behaviour to attain a Pareto-efficient outcome in this simple model arises because once the economy is shocked away from the natural rate of unemployment fiscal policy aimed at unconditional borrowing targets creates an externality: any worker taking a job has a social marginal product which exceeds the private marginal product (the consumption wage) by his net contribution to reducing the *per capita* cost of public goods and unemployment benefit. It is easy to analyse the extent of this externality: the private marginal product is defined by:

$$Wc = Wp(1 - Tw) \tag{13.4}$$

while the social marginal product is defined by:

$$Ws = Wc\left(1 + \frac{d\log(1 - Tw)}{d\log N}\right). \tag{13.5}$$

An additional feature of this model is that the social marginal product of employing someone who was previously unemployed exceeds the product wage, which is the social marginal product of a new entrant to the labour force. The easiest way to illustrate this result is to assume that total employment remains unchanged, presumably because the new worker is replacing an older worker who has retired. Then the second term in equation (13.2) and all terms involving $\eta_D$ in equation (13.3), which arise from variations in *Wp*, drop out, and the expression for *Ws* which is relevant to the employment of an unemployed worker becomes:

$$Ws' = Wc\left(1 + \frac{(Tw - Tu)}{(1 - Tw)}\right) = Wp(1 - Tu) \tag{13.6}$$

which, since *Tu* is negative, exceeds *Wp*. This difference arises because it is no longer necessary to pay the individual concerned unemployment benefit, so that once full employment is attained the difference disappears. Since the distortions caused by taxes levied to ensure full-employment budget balance are unavoidable, any attempt to compute a shadow wage (for example, to evaluate public expenditure projects along the lines suggested below) should not correct for them, but only for the excess distortion caused by unemployment.

The type of market failure considered here is similar to that analysed by Startz (1984). In Startz's paper the externality arises because firms are unable to observe the worker's marginal product exactly. As a result the wage offer facing workers can be written as a linear combination of the individual effort 'signal', which is specific to the worker, and the mean level of aggregate labour supply. Since in making employment decisions both firms and workers regard aggregate labour supply as fixed, individual workers receive only a fraction of the additional output that they produce. This distortion generates unemployment which is voluntary from the point of view of the worker, since he is maximising a utility function defined over leisure and goods, but Pareto-inefficient in the sense that there is a feasible increase in aggregate labour supply (and hence real wages) which would make all better off. Although the cause of the externality in our case is different, the end result is the same. The wage offer function facing the worker can be written as

$$Wc = W(Wp, N), \qquad W1 > 0, \qquad W2 > 0 \tag{13.7}$$

so that the consumption wage is an increasing function of the aggregate level of employment, as well as of the product wage.

The simple model which we have employed makes it comparatively easy to assess whether or not the possibility of a 'free lunch' exists for the UK. If an expansion of employment would, after taking account of the induced reduction in unemployment, lead to a rise in the real consumption wage greater than that required to induce the necessary increase in the labour supply, then a 'free lunch' is available. This requirement implies:

$$\frac{d \log Wc}{d \log N} = \frac{d \log Wp}{d \log N} + \frac{d \log(1 - Tw)}{d \log N} > \frac{d \log Wd}{d \log N} \tag{13.8}$$

or

$$\frac{1}{\eta_D} > \frac{1}{\eta_s} - \frac{(Tw - Tu)}{(1 - Tw)}\left(1 + \frac{1}{\eta_D}\right) - \frac{Tu(1 + U/N)}{(1 - Tw)\eta_D}$$

where $\eta_D$ and $\eta_s$ are measures of the elasticity of demand and supply for labour with respect to the appropriate definition of the real wage. Since $\eta_D$ is measured allowing output to vary, rather than along a particular isoquant, it is likely to be low (implying a significantly negative slope to the labour demand curve) only if there are serious capacity limitations because the economy is close to full employment or because the existing capital stock is obsolete. Similarly at high levels of unemployment it is unlikely that a large increase in the consumption wage will be needed to induce additional employment: indeed a strictly Keynesian definition of involuntary unemployment suggests that additional workers should be available with no increase at all.

The condition expressed by equation (13.8) indicates clearly one set of circumstances in which the externality which is the topic of this chapter is likely to be of considerable practical importance. In states where a substantial proportion of public expenditure, possibly including unemployment insurance, is financed by local governments with limited borrowing powers, some local authorities may well experience peculiarly large adverse shocks. Unless there is some mechanism for redistributing tax revenues between authorities, the unfortunate local governments will be forced to raise taxes to maintain budget balance while the fortunate ones will be able to lower them. But the comparative ease of intranational migration for both jobs and workers will mean that the absolute value of both supply and demand elasticities in equation (13.8) will be large, so that the third, tax-related, term will dominate. Thus it is likely that some individual authorities will either be trapped at the low-level equilibrium *El*, or will be in the unstable region where raising taxes to balance the budget causes a further atrophy of the tax base.

In order to judge whether the condition expressed in equation (13.8) might be satisfied for the UK in early 1986, we need estimates of the relevant demand and supply elasticities and of the tax parameters *Tw* and *Tu*. A recent survey of research on the relation between employment and wages in the UK, undertaken by Treasury officials (Treasury, 1985), sets out a number of estimates for the demand elasticity $\eta_D$: these range from a figure of −1.75 for the manufacturing sector (Symons, 1985) to −0.5 for the economy as a whole (Nickell and Andrews, 1983). These estimates are conditioned on the actual value of the capital stock, and cover a period during which output was probably capacity-constrained on a number of occasions, so that in current circumstances the relevant value may be towards the upper end of the range. Estimates of the inverse of the labour supply elasticity $1/\eta_s$ can be derived from an analysis of the measured effect of unemployment in real wage equations. The estimates of Layard and Nickell (1985) suggest that an increase of 1 per cent (**not** 1 percentage point) in unemployment leads in the long-run to a fall of 0.07 per cent in the real wage. This implies, at the level of unemployment currently prevailing in the UK, a figure for $1/\eta_s$ which is slightly less than 1: this estimate is close to that cited by Minford (1983). However the existence of a **long-run** effect of unemployment on wages in the UK is a controversial issue, with some authors (i.e. Lawson, 1987) arguing that increases in unemployment, rather than a particularly high sustained level, are necessary to reduce real wages. In this case the appropriate value of $1/\eta_s$ is zero, corresponding to the pure case of Keynesian involuntary unemployment discussed above.

Although the actual UK tax system is very much more complex than the simple two-parameter model of this paper, the fact that the marginal income tax rate (including social security contributions) is constant over a wide range of incomes makes it possible to obtain plausible values for *Tw* and *Tu* without too much difficulty. In 1984 income from employment per employed worker (a measure of *Wp*) was approximately £8500. Allowing for the proportion of income tax which fell on income from property and other sources, income taxes and social security contributions amounted to 29 per cent of this. If we assume that no saving was done by the unemployed, the average employed worker also contributed 11.5 per cent of his product wage in the form of indirect taxes on consumption. Thus an approximate figure for *Tw* is 0.405.

It is slightly harder to obtain an adequate estimate of *Tu*. This is because the unemployed in the UK receive either unemployment benefit, which is a contributory benefit not subject to a means test, but of limited duration, or supplementary benefit, which is part of the general means-tested welfare benefit system. The long spells of unemployment which have been experienced during the current recession mean that supplementary benefit has become the main source of income support for the unemployed. The *Digest of Social Security Statistics* (DHSS, 1986) can be used to distinguish supplementary benefit payments associated with unemployment, and if this is done it appears that the average payment to an unemployed worker was approximately £1550 per year, or 18 per cent of the product wage. Since 1982 unemployment benefit has been subject to income tax, but this measure was designed to reduce the incentive to finance short spells of unemployment by exploiting tax rebates, and is unlikely to be relevant for the long-term unemployed. However, on the assumption that all unemployment benefit is spent on consumption, approximately 3 per cent of the product wage returns to the government in the form of indirect taxes, so that *Tu* is approximately −0.15.

The calculations in the previous paragraph exclude the costs of a substantial number of benefits, in cash and kind, which are conditional on low income rather than employment status. Whether or not a reduction in unemployment would lead to savings in these areas would obviously depend on the wages paid in the newly created jobs. In general we would expect our calculations, which implicitly assume labour to be homogeneous, to overstate the beneficial revenue effects from an expansion of employment because the unemployed are likely to have relatively few skills and their marginal product, and tax payments in work, will therefore be below the average value for the economy as a whole. However this factor may to a considerable extent be balanced by the savings in those income-related benefits which we have ignored.

Taking the values of 0.405 and −0.15 for *Tw* and *Tu* respectively, the critical tax-related term $(Tw - Tu)/(1 - Tw)$ in equation (13.8) has the value 0.933. This calculation indicates that the UK is almost certainly not at present in a position where a 'free lunch' is available. If we take the most favourable combination of elasticity estimates (a demand elasticity of −1.75, and an infinite supply elasticity, implying true Keynesian involuntary unemployment) the condition for a 'free lunch' to be available is that $U/N$ should be greater than 18.7 per cent: the actual value of $U/N$ in early 1986 was 13.7 per cent. If we drop the assumption of an infinitely elastic labour supply, and assume instead a value for $\eta_s$ of 2, which is higher than most empirical estimates, the critical value of $U/N$ exceeds unity, implying that no low-level equilibrium *El* for the UK economy exists which is consistent with constant elasticity labour demand and supply functions. Nevertheless the analysis presented here does suggest that if labour market elasticities are sufficiently high, as they may well be at high levels of unemployment where there is substantial excess capacity and little scope for real wage increases, the possibility of a 'free lunch' may become relevant to policy-makers in the UK and other European countries.

The model which we have set out suggests that the combination of distortionary taxes on labour income and unconditional budgetary targets is sufficient to generate a significant externality. Under certain circumstances this externality will limit the ability of private firms and workers to find a Pareto-improving move towards full employment. However even if it were true that such circumstances prevailed currently in the UK or other major industrialised countries, a condition on which our simple-minded calculations throw some doubt, it can be argued that there may be little scope for conventional Keynesian policies, defined as a higher level of public expenditure or lower taxation, to remedy this market failure. In principle the government could internalise the externality by instructing any of its agencies which was producing marketed output to hire additional workers if their social marginal product, defined by *Ws* in equation (13.5), exceeded the wage necessary to induce them to work by more than the full-employment tax revenue per worker. Such a policy, which has sometimes been advocated by Keynesian economists (e.g. Rowthorn and Ward, 1979), would imply an operating loss for the agency concerned, although the overall effect on the budgetary position would be favourable. However if the agencies concerned were in direct competition with private-sector firms this would violate the efficiency condition of a uniform shadow wage rate for employment decisions throughout the economy. A similar argument can be used against any proposal for selective wage subsidies to the private sector. Nor is it sensible to think of introducing a general system of wage subsidies, as advocated in the 1930s by Kaldor (1935), given the impossibility of lump-sum taxation which is the prime cause of the market failure. In our simple model all taxes are essentially equivalent in their effects on labour supply, and there is no balanced-budget multiplier.

One possibility would be for the government to instruct its commercial agencies to operate as profit-maximising firms, hiring labour only if the private marginal product exceeded the wage, but to use the formula for the social marginal product given in equation (13.5) to determine the implicit value and optimal level of output for the non-market sector of the economy. However, under a regime of unconditional budgetary targets any expansion of such services can only be achieved by increasing the distortionary tax rate *Tw*, although the required increase will of course be lower than that required to pay the full cost of the additional resources. Hence such a policy would merely lead to higher 'voluntary' unemployment unless the public services concerned were regarded by workers as a valuable component of the social wage. This is not necessarily an idealistic point of view: most economists who have supported moves to shift the provision of such services in the UK to the market sector have also recognised that voucher schemes or substantial cuts in taxation will be needed if their schemes are not to be perceived as equivalent to a general reduction in real wages. Such an attitude suggests that the implications for labour supply of a tax-financed expansion of 'desirable' social services may be more favourable than those of raising the equivalent revenue in order to dissipate it on lump-sum payments to the unemployed.

Higher expenditure on public services, financed through an implicit or explicit agreement to accept lower consumption wages as a consequence, represents one Keynesian route towards a cooperative equilibrium which is superior to *El* in Figure 13.1. The alternative is a reduction in the distortionary tax rate *Tw* in order to stimulate employment. In our simple model the assumption that firms are perfect competitors facing infinitely elastic demand curves is sufficient to ensure that the economy moves rapidly to *Ef*, so that there is no increase in the budget deficit to be financed and to destroy agents' belief in the fundamental rectitude of the government's financial strategy. In practice it is unlikely that any free lunch attainable at *El* could be achieved so easily, since imperfectly competitive firms would require some evidence that their demand curve had shifted outward before being prepared to undertake the full expansion of employment necessary to ensure that the cut in tax rates did not lead to a drop in revenue net of unemployment benefit.

It is this lag in the response of employment which means that a government which has committed itself to short-run and unconditional targets for the budget deficit, and which has founded its counter-inflationary reputation on the fulfilment of such targets, will find itself unable to accept a 'free lunch' even if one is offered. In the course of an analysis very similar to that conducted here, Keynes could advocate (Keynes, 1933) a variety of ingenious accounting devices, such as the suspension of the Sinking Fund, to eliminate the short-run budgetary strait-jacket which appeared to frustrate policy-makers. Such proposals could be highly effective in an era when the fiscal rules of the game required governments to balance the budget on current account, but allowed (subject to certain safeguards) some capital expenditure to be loan-financed. Furthermore in the 1930s investment by public corporations was proportionately less significant: attention was therefore focused on general government rather than the public sector as a whole, and commercially viable projects were not held back by limits on public borrowing. Fortunately for the inhabitants of the UK, the peculiar accounting treatment of public-sector asset sales, and the deaf ear turned to those who have with impeccable economic logic advocated treating the tax receipts from North Sea oil on a permanent income basis, have provided a fresh set of bookkeeping devices and limited the damage which might otherwise have been caused by unconditional targeting.

Nevertheless in the last resort the successful adoption of Keynesian policies to reduce unemployment is likely to involve a temporary abandonment of fiscal rectitude. In the 1930s such actions did not immediately lead to higher inflation, and provided that agents can free themselves from the pre-Keynesian dogma, revived by the monetarist and new classical economists, that the economy always attains a unique market-clearing equilibrium, there is no reason why it should do so now. Unfortunately, as Hahn (1983) has noted, the 'monetarists have done us the disservice of inducing agents to hold the least helpful rational expectations'.

## References


BROOKS, S. *et al.* (1983) 'Policy Trade-offs in the NIESR Model: Exercises Using Optimal Control', *National Institute Economic Review*, August 1983.

CORDEN, W. M. (1981) 'Taxation, Real Wages and Employment', *Economic Journal*, June 1981.

DHSS (1986) *Social Security Statistics 1985.*

HAHN, F. H. (1983) 'Comment on A. H. Meltzer, "On Keynes and Monetarism"', in G. D. N. Worswick and J. A. Trevithick (eds) *Keynes and the Modern World* (Cambridge: Cambridge University Press, 1983).

KALDOR, N. (1935) 'Wage Subsidies as a Remedy for Unemployment', reprinted in N. Kaldor, *Essays on Economic Policy, I* (London: Duckworth, 1964).

KEYNES, J. M. (1933) 'The Means to Prosperity', reprinted in J. M. Keynes, *Essays in Persuasion* (*Collected Works IX*) (London: Macmillan, 1972).

KYDLAND, F. W. and PRESCOTT, E. C. (1977) 'Rules Rather than Discretion: The Inconsistency of Optimal Plans', *Journal of Political Economy*, June 1977.

LAWSON, A. (1987) 'Incomes Policy and Earnings', in T. Barker and W. Peterson (eds) *The Cambridge Multisectoral Dynamic Model* (Cambridge: Cambridge University Press, forthcoming).

LAYARD, R. and NICKELL S. (1985) 'The Causes of British Unemployment', *National Institute Economic Review*, February 1985.

MINFORD, A. P. L. (1983) *Unemployment - Cause and Cure* (Oxford: Martin Robertson, 1983).

NICKELL, S. and ANDREWS, M. A. (1983) 'Unions, Real Wages and Employment in Britain 1951–79', *Oxford Economic Papers*, November 1983.

PETERSON, W. (1984) 'Policy Analysis Using a Large Econometric Model', *Growth Project Paper 554*, Department of Applied Economics, Cambridge.

ROWTHORN, R. E. and WARD, T. S. (1979) 'How to Run a Company and Run Down an Economy: The Effects of Closing Down Steel-making in Corby', *Cambridge Journal of Economics*, December 1979.

STARTZ, R. (1984) 'Prelude to Macroeconomics', *American Economic Review*, December 1984.

SYMONS, J. S. V. (1985) 'Relative Prices and the Demand for Labour in British Manufacturing', *Economica*, February 1985.

TREASURY (1985) 'The Relationship between Employment and Wages: Empirical Evidence for the United Kingdom', Review by officials, April 1985.

# COMMENT ON CHAPTERS 12 AND 13

**Victoria Chick**

Both these papers are concerned, in very different ways, with the effects of government intervention in the labour market on employment. The first applies the model proposed by Patrick Minford (1983) to Germany. The second examines some perverse effects of the tax wedge.

## I

Patrick Minford is often represented as saying that unemployment benefits encourage voluntary withdrawal from the labour force, therefore the level of benefit should be reduced to increase employment. When pressed, what he says is that for those of low earning-capacity the fixed-rate component of benefits is higher than their productivity and their expected real wage. Hence, rationally, those people cease to search for work. And those on earnings-related benefits can afford longer search. Reducing the disincentive effect of benefits would encourage the unemployed into jobs; society would have the benefit of their output, and their incomes could be 'topped up' later.

Allowing for the fact that for psychological and social reasons some people will accept a wage below benefit level, this seems to me not entirely an unfair point, though it says something devastating about either the ability of some people to earn a minimum standard of living or the ability or willingness of firms to pay it. As a microeconomic proposition the model of Figures 12.3 and 12.4 deserves to be tested on a disaggregated basis. Mr Davis avers that data are not available.

In any event, Davis and Minford are looking for macroeconomic results: the thesis of the paper before us is that the cause of unemployment is to be found in 'the prevention – by way of unemployment benefits and social aid' – of real wage adjustment. Such a thesis supposes that all unemployment is voluntary (in the technical sense used by Keynes, which includes, *inter alia*, the effects of trade-union pushfulness). Not only does the model assume that we know the 'labour force' which serves as a benchmark, thus ignoring those who are ineligible for benefit because not registered (for example – and these must be numerous now – discouraged workers). But more important, demand-deficient unemployment is ruled out, despite what they say in their last paragraph.

I shall have to make that charge stick, but since the treatment of demand is a problem in both papers I shall deal with some other matters, theoretical and empirical, first.

On the theoretical side I point out two puzzles which occur throughout Minford's work on unemployment. One is why, if unionised labour always sells at a premium, firms buy it at all. Another is that unions seem to be the only agents in the economy which make price or inflation expectations, although this seems not to matter empirically in the German case. This specification problem is related to the demand issue.

When we come to the empirical work (section 12.3) we face the usual problem of the correspondence between the theory and the empirical investigation. A theory of the effects of benefits is transformed into a four-equation model of the German economy, from which a 'natural rate of unemployment' can be extracted. Little can be said about the effects of benefits as such, apart from noting the size and significance of the actual coefficients on $T_L$ and $T_F$.

It is concluded that the 'natural rate of unemployment' rose significantly after 1974 (we are to infer this fact from Figure 12.5) at '*about* the same time as the *possible* regime change' (italics added) toward a greater reliance on fixed-rate benefit. A somewhat less equivocal statement of what actually did happen to German benefit policy, and when, is required to make Davis's and Minford's case convincing even if one has no doubts about their econometric evidence. There is no formal test for a change of regime.

The evidence is also subject to Nickell's (1984) criticisms of Minford's earlier work, not, in my view, adequately answered by Minford (1984). The point I have in mind concerns the importance of the lagged values of the dependent variable in the 'short-run' equations. These generate spuriously large long-run effects for the other regressors.

The authors conclude that unemployment benefits, unionisation, and employers' taxes have resulted in real-wage rigidity, thus confirming and reinforcing their prediction that benefits cause demand shocks to result in unemployment rather than wage adjustment. As a Keynesian I should expect negative demand shocks to result in unemployment anyway, and not to be much alleviated even if wages were to fall.

## II

William Peterson's paper demonstrates that the tax wedge between the consumption and the product wage may give rise to multiple equilibria, such that private-sector employment might be capable of an improvement which the participants 'cannot see'. It is even possible that an expansionary policy on the part of government could move the private sector out of its 'low-level employment trap' at no net cost, as a reduction in workers' tax rates may be balanced by an increased tax-take as employment expands. This is the 'free lunch'.

This is an important demonstration. It refutes the neoclassical maintained hypothesis that decentralised agents are always capable of achieving their most favourable outcomes. And even a neoclassical economist may be attracted by a 'free lunch'. Sadly, a truly free lunch seems unlikely in the light of reasonable parameter values, though a lunch which promises good value (which is all a Keynesian requires before ordering) looks a distinct possibility.

From a Keynesian perspective there are two points to be made about Peterson's paper. The first concerns what happens to the tax proceeds. Surely in a period of unemployment even a government dedicated to 'fiscal probity' will not run surpluses: the marginal propensity to spend taxes should be at least one. Similarly the marginal propensity to spend unemployment benefits ought to be well above average, probably one. These factors contribute to the reduction of the 'lunch bill'.

## III

The above is a complaint about ignoring demand factors, which I have saved to the end. Both papers have accepted the neoclassical convention of making propositions about the labour market in terms of real wages and assuming that in so doing they are modelling independently of aggregate demand. But logically there are only two ways of looking at real wages. Either we are talking about wages received in terms of output, direct - a corn wage - or (more likely I should have thought) the authors have in mind money wages deflated by some price index. But *prices are an indication of the level of demand.*

Peterson explicitly assumes perfect competition, stating that firms produce as much as they find profitable. But what does this mean? It means they produce given a price established by the interaction of their and other firms' supply decisions and market (or aggregate) demand. The price indicates what that level of demand is; if the level of demand were different the price would be different. (If you think about it, once the distribution of market demand is established by the configuration of cost curves in the industry, the demand curve each firm faces, viewed objectively, becomes downward-sloping. It is only in the producer's subjective view, which is not fully informed, that his demand curve is flat.) This point may be generalised to allow for any degree of monopoly as long as the size of the mark-up is relatively stable.

The point I wish to press is this: that once one elects to analyse the labour market using prices at all - and it is difficult to know how, in a modern economy, one can escape doing that - one is embodying information about aggregate demand. That is at least part of the reason why the Minford–Davis model does not rule out Keynesian conclusions if one chooses to draw them, and why Peterson's Keynesian policy recommendations can be strengthened.

**References**

MINFORD, P. (1983) 'Labour Market Equilibrium in an Open Economy' *Oxford Economic Papers*, 35, November (Supplement on Unemployment).

MINFORD, P. (1984) 'Response to Nickell', *Economic Journal*, 94, pp. 954–9.

NICKELL, S. J. (1984) 'Unemployment: Cause and Cure: A Review', *Economic Journal*, 94, pp. 946–53.

# 14 Unemployment and Fiscal Activism in a Small Open Economy*

John Bradley

## 14.1 INTRODUCTION

An endemically high rate of unemployment has always been one of the most pressing problems facing policy-makers in Ireland. Since 1980 the unemployment rate has risen inexorably, as illustrated in Figure 14.1. Furthermore, on the basis of the most recent medium-term projections to 1990 (Bacon, 1986) the unemployment rate is set to continue to rise, albeit at a much slower rate, to over 18 per cent of the labour force. This more recent rise in unemployment is, of course, a phenomenon not confined to Ireland, but shared, in one form or another, by many other European economies.

All political groups in Ireland place great emphasis on their policies to alleviate unemployment. The extent of direct state intervention in the Irish labour market can be seen clearly from Figure 14.2. Employment in the sheltered marketed services sector grew over the period 1973–83 by 18.4 per cent (56 900), while employment in the non-market sector (public administration and other non-marketed services) grew by 40.2 per cent (68 700). While industrial employment remained relatively stagnant, displaying cyclical highs in 1974 and 1980, agricultural employment declined steadily. Over the same period, the labour force grew by 17.7 per cent (196 900) and migration abroad, having declined from a net out-flow of about 60 000 per annum in 1959 to a zero net flow by 1970, became a net in-flow during the years of 1973–8, but has returned to a net outflow since 1983 (Figure 14.3).

The costs of total state activity (direct employment, consumption, investment, subsidies and transfers) were paid in part by increased taxation (Figure 14.4), although the years 1977–79 were characterised by net cuts in a wide range of indirect taxes. However, the total public

* The Economic & Social Research Institute. I am indebted to my ESRI colleague, John Fitzgerald, for collaboration on some of the work described in this paper.

*Figure* 14.1 Unemployment rate (%)

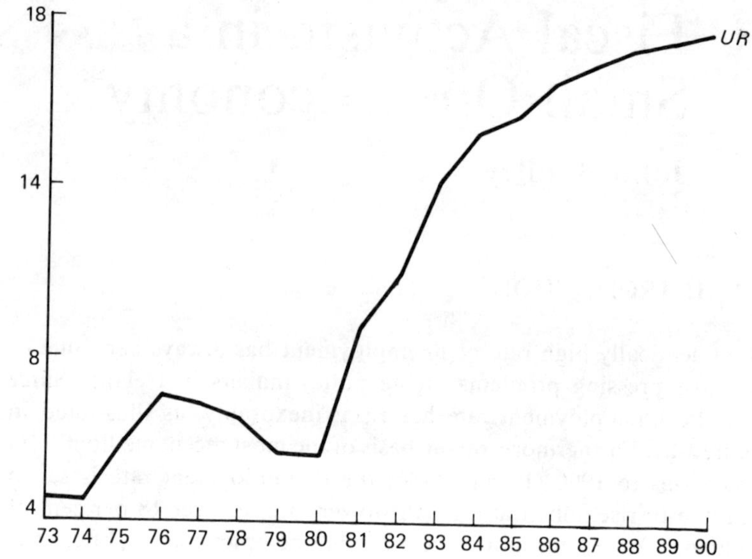


*Figure* 14.2 Sectoral employment (thousands)

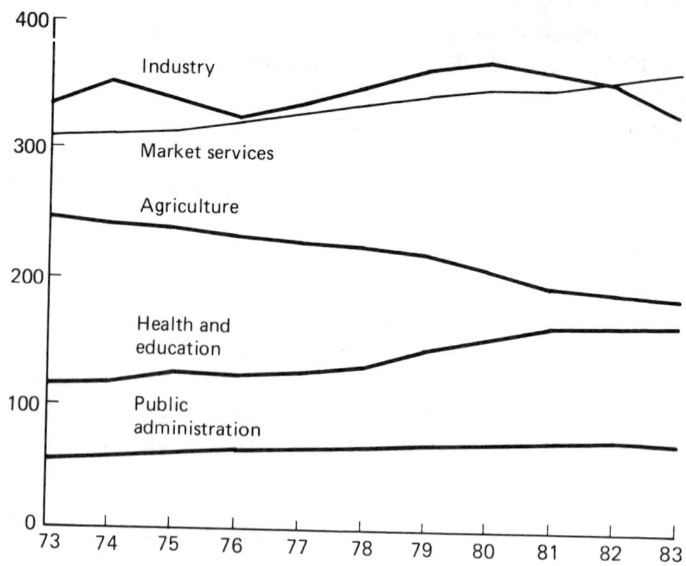

*Figure* 14.3 Labour force change and net migration abroad (thousands)

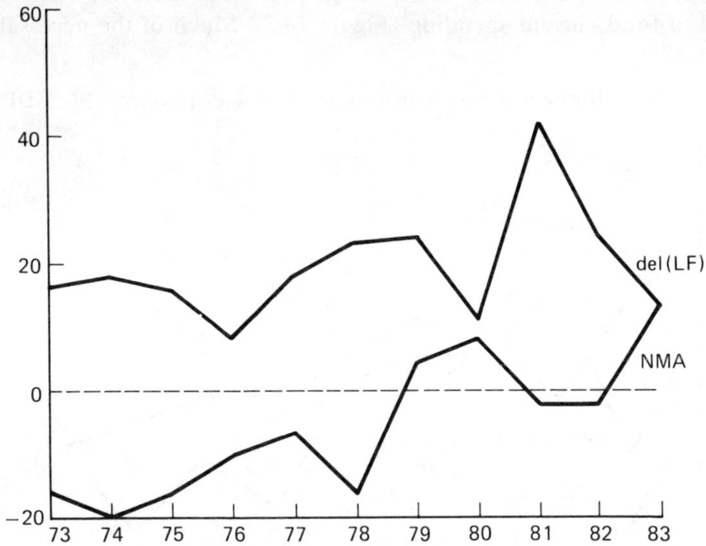


*Figure* 14.4 Tax rates (indirect, direct, payroll, corporate)

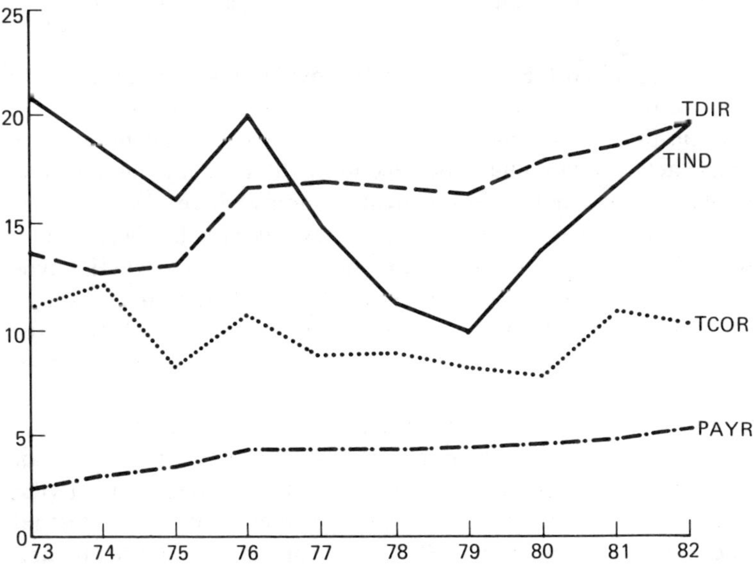

authorities' borrowing requirement as a percentage of GDP grew rapidly and, from the year 1974, a large portion of the borrowing was used to fund current spending (Figure 14.5). Much of the necessary

*Figure* 14.5 Borrowing requirements and balance of payments (% GDP)

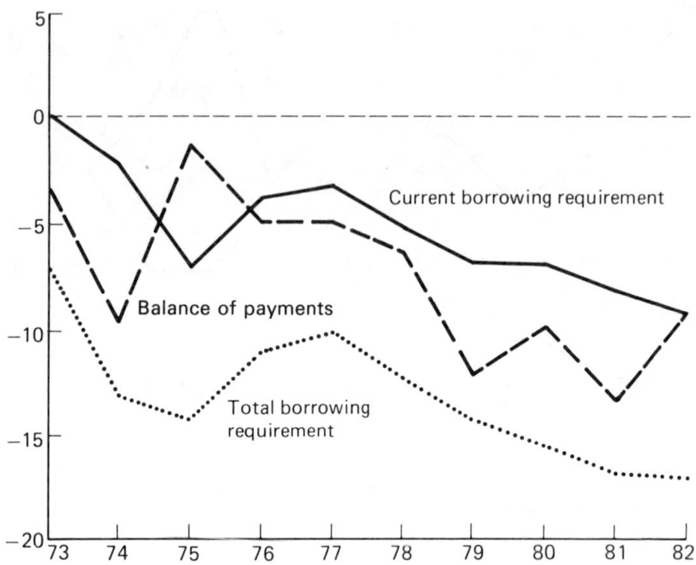


finance was raised through foreign borrowing, resulting in a greatly increased outflow of debt-interest payments abroad (Figure 14.6).

Our purpose in this chapter is to examine some of the consequences of fiscal activism in a small open economy (SOE). Although the State has played a major role in the Irish economy, there has been little systematic formal analysis of this role. Previous work has been carried out within the context of macroeconomic models of a Keynesian type and focused on the low Keynesian fiscal multipliers characteristic of small open economies. A more complete framework for the examination of fiscal activism and its employment consequences requires three separate, but interrelated, elements. First, in Section 14.2 we look at the way the labour market has been studied in Ireland. Second, while looking at labour-market studies within the context of the entire economy some important issues arise which, while of vital concern to the labour market, relate to the determination of industrial capacity and investment in an SOE. These are issues not often treated

*Figure* 14.6 Domestic and foreign debt interest (% GDP)

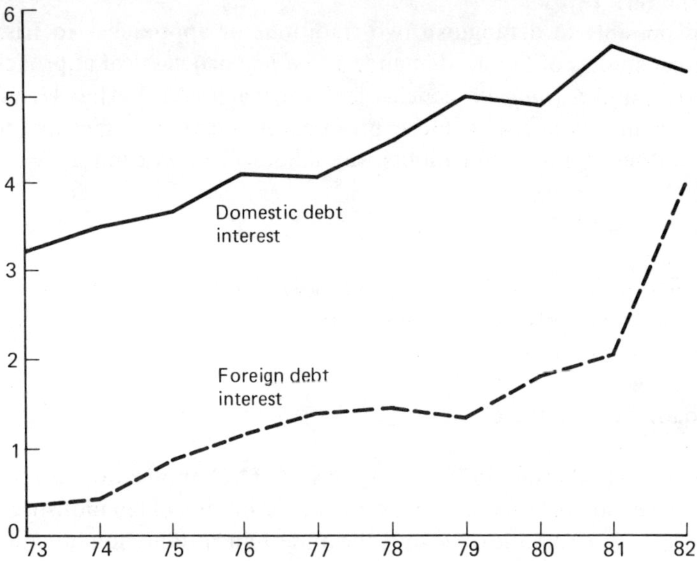


in separate 'stand alone' labour-market models. Our conclusion is that the isolated study of the labour market is at best unnecessarily limiting and, at worst, can be very misleading. We illustrate this for one particularly important case, the policy implications of the association between real wages and employment. Third, in Section 14.3 we look at some of the features of a model which attempts to encapsulate these ideas and illustrate, in Section 14.4, its use in examining the consequences of fiscal activism.

## 14.2 EMPIRICAL LABOUR-MARKET RESEARCH IN A SMALL OPEN ECONOMY

An examination of the Irish empirical labour-market literature shows, broadly, that whereas the separate demand and supply aspects have been moderately well covered, the market-closure aspect has not. We use the term 'market closure' to denote the process whereby the market price and quantity traded is determined. This is not a uniquely Irish lacuna, and is understandable in the light of the Keynesian empirical legacy which dominated applied economic work in macroeconomics until the late 1970s.

It is possible to distinguish two traditions or approaches to Irish empirical studies of labour demand: an *ad hoc* neoclassical approach (*AHNC*), and a *complete* neoclassical approach (*NC*). The *AHNC* approach makes use of a loose production function framework to relate output ($Q$) to factor inputs, say labour ($L$) and capital ($K$):

$$Q = f(K, L).$$

This relationship is usually inverted, solved for $L$, and the capital stock usually substituted by a time trend, yielding, in a Cobb-Douglas log-linear approximation:

$$\log L = a_0 + a_1 \log Q + a_z t.$$

Smyth and McMahon (1975) in a typical *AHNC* application, used a dynamic version of the above in a study of a grouping of ten industries. It is normally impossible to recover the underlying production function parameters from this method, so one can only investigate the goodness of statistical fit and the dynamics of adjustment.

The *NC* approach attempts to implement the full neoclassical theory of the firm, and is characterised by a high degree of technical sophistication in the use of complex production and/or cost functions and estimation techniques. It is important to realise that what is going on in this approach is is not just the derivation of labour or, more generally, factor-demand relations, but the testing, at least to some degree, of many aspects of the neoclassical theory of the firm such as:

(i) assumptions about the motivation of the firm (e.g. profit-maximisation, cost-minimisation);
(ii) the market structure within which the firm operates (often assumed to be perfectly competitive, but allowing imperfect competition);
(iii) the allowance of a certain degree of factor substitution, and the choice of different models of the capital stock (e.g. vintage, non-vintage).

Studies which implement this approach empirically differ mainly in the 'technical' choices which must be made. For example, choices must be made as to the number and type of the factor inputs appropriate; whether to use a vintage capital model or a non-vintage model and the exact nature of the vintage model; which of the many different production and cost functions should be used to characterise the technological possibilities of firms. These 'technical' choices are heavily circumscribed by data availability and by one's ability to handle complex non-linear estimation problems and they provide a rich systematic agenda for work on labour demand. For references to published Irish work in this area, refer to Bradley and Fanning (1984) and Bradley *et al.* (1985). A significant finding emerging from most Irish studies is that the own-elasticity of demand for labour is small, an estimate in the region of −0.3 being typical. We return to this point later.

Two strands dominate the empirical work on the macroeconomics of labour supply: the study of labour-force participation and the study of migration abroad. The former is a feature of all economies; the latter is of importance only to economies with 'open' labour markets, such as Ireland. Basically all models of the migration process use a measure of the relative attractiveness of the Irish labour market to that of the destination of most migrants, mainly the United Kingdom (Keenan, 1981). Various combinations of relative unemployment rates and relative wages are used to measure this attractiveness. The policy implications of the migration process thus modelled are important (McCarthy, 1979) and the migration equation, although often of poor quality due to suspect data, forms a vital link in the modelling of Irish labour-supply responses to policies aimed at the labour market.

Turning to the determination of labour-force participation, the theory of rational household behaviour leads to a decision model, involving the unemployment rate, real wages, taxation, unemployment compensation, etc. That few macro studies have been published in Ireland in this area is probably accounted for by the 'bad' empirical results obtained from such models. Only degenerate forms of the participation model tend to survive, involving, say, unemployment, policy dummy variables and a time trend to pick up slowly changing demographic factors (Bradley *et al.*, 1985, pp. 28 and 184). This is probably an area where detailed sociological and micro studies will throw more light (Blundell *et al.*, 1986) and where the imperative to obtain simple macro-aggregate models will always be unsatisfactory.

Empirical work on methods of 'closing' the labour market has taken place almost entirely within large macroeconomic models. Such models usually have a labour-demand function (more often than not drawn from the *AHNC* tradition) and a wage equation (usually embodying a form of indexation and sometimes incorporating a

Phillips-curve effect). Leaving aside any econometric criticisms (Nickell, 1984), such an arrangement is unsatisfactory unless it can be interpreted within a market perspective. More recent work, particularly in the UK (Nickell and Andrews, 1983; Andrews *et al.*, 1985) has provided such a perspective, and has highlighted the crucial importance of the wage equation in 'closing' the labour market. Some recent Irish studies provide explicit models of the labour market and its closure (Hughes, 1985; Geary and Murphy, 1985; Bradley and Prendergast, 1986). This work confirms that the wage bargain is influenced by the 'wedge' driven by taxation between the firm's real labour costs and the real wage received by the suppliers of labour, and by unemployment. In addition, it was found that labour-market disequilibrium can persist for long periods. The policy implications of these findings are important in that an increase in public spending financed by raising taxes will have a low 'balanced budget' multiplier, which could be negative (van de Klundert, 1982). We examine this further in Section 14.4 with the complete model.

We have looked at the functioning of the labour market in isolation. However, the Irish industrial (traded-goods) sector is particularly open to influences from the outside world, with a high proportion of new industrial investments over the past thirty years being undertaken by foreign transnational corporations (O'Malley, 1986). The single largest source of this new foreign investment has been the USA, other major sources being German, Japanese and United Kingdom firms. In Bradley and Fitzgerald (1986), we look at some of the ways in which the study of the problem of determining 'world' output and factor demands can be decomposed into a series of simpler problems which are useful when examining these issues from the point of view of a policy model of a small open economy. One such case is when restrictions are placed on the manner in which factor inputs in the SOE can be combined with factor inputs in other countries, for a production location in the SOE (more technically, weak separability) and where the production function displays constant returns to scale (more correctly, is homothetic in each of the countries' outputs). This permits one to examine the 'technology' or factor-mix of the individual country separately, conditional on the scale of operation being given, i.e. for exogeneous country output. This is the normal formulation used in 'stand-alone' labour-demand studies.

For simplicity, consider a two-country world, consisting of Ireland and the rest of the world (*ROW*). We also assume that world output, $Q_w$, is a *CES* function of Irish output, $Q_I$, and rest of world output,

$Q_R$.[1] Both Irish and rest of world output are *CES* functions of their factor inputs, capital and labour. Within this simple framework of nested *CES* functions, we can test the validity of the traditional 'closed economy' approach to determining factor demands. In estimating the model, the factor-demand equations are first estimated for Ireland alone in the usual way, assuming that the necessary factor price data for the *ROW* are unavailable, and the estimated parameters are used to determine an index of Irish optimal unit costs. This unit cost index, given unit costs for the *ROW*, is then used to determine Ireland's share of world output. A simpler, but less rigorous, alternative would be to use actual unit labour costs for Ireland and the *ROW*. In the traditional approach to estimating factor-demand equations, the elasticities of demand for each factor are derived conditional on a fixed level of output. Using the terminology of Berndt and Wood (1979) these are **gross** elasticities. However, as outlined above, domestic output itself must be considered variable in the international context. When it is allowed to vary, the resulting elasticities of demand for factors will also change. Such elasticities, calculated allowing output to vary, are termed **net** elasticities.

Set out in Table 14.1 are the estimates of both the **gross** and **net** elasticities of demand derived from an estimated model for the Irish industrial sector. As can be seen from this table, the **gross** own-price elasticities of demand for both capital and labour are extremely small. However, when output is treated as endogenous, the **net** elasticities are greatly increased in absolute magnitude. In the case of the own-price elasticity for labour, the difference is quite remarkable, rising

*Table* 14.1 Price elasticities of demand for Irish factors of production in the industrial sector

| | *Gross* 1970 | *Gross* 1975 | *Gross* 1980 | *Net* 1970 | *Net* 1975 | *Net* 1980 |
|---|---|---|---|---|---|---|
| Own price elasticities | | | | | | |
| Labour | −0.058 | −0.066 | −0.073 | −0.754 | −0.762 | −0.748 |
| Capital | −0.262 | −0.254 | −0.247 | −0.426 | −0.417 | −0.426 |
| Irish output | | | | −0.861 | −0.858 | −0.854 |
| Cross price elasticities | | | | | | |
| Labour | 0.058 | 0.066 | 0.073 | −0.106 | −0.097 | −0.106 |
| Capital | 0.262 | 0.254 | 0.247 | −0.435 | −0.442 | −0.428 |

*Source*: Bradley and FitzGerald (1986).

from close to zero to between −0.85 and −0.9. In the case of the cross-elasticities of demand the results of the model indicate that Irish capital and labour are **gross** substitutes at the national level but **net** complements in a global context.

What we have illustrated with this simple model is that, viewed as a closed economy, the Irish industrial sector may indeed approximate a Leontief or fixed coefficients production technology with low **gross** own-price elasticities. However, viewed in the context of a world model, the **net** own-price elasticities of demand for the Irish factors of production are much higher, and the question of the competitiveness of the Irish industrial sector must be a major policy issue. Substitution of capital for labour, in the vintage model used in the study quoted, normally takes place through the installation of new plant. Such installation of new plant itself often involves the possibility of a physical change in the location of production. The smaller the economy, the more likely that the substitution of capital for labour (or *vice versa*) will involve a shift in productive capacity across national boundaries. On the other hand, in larger economies it is more likely that relocation may take place **within** the country, leaving national output capacity unchanged. As a result, the manner in which domestic industrial output is treated in the model is likely to be more crucial for the smaller economy. The supply sides of small open economies, such as Ireland, are closely integrated into the wider OECD economy and the movement of investment, and the choice of location where output prospers, is a further important channel for transmitting international shocks. A consequence of these findings is that the role of the domestic wage equation in determining Irish international competitiveness is of much greater importance than 'closed-economy'-type labour-demand studies would seem to imply. For example, the use of **gross** own-price elasticities in the range −0.2 to −0.5, typical of 'stand-alone' labour-demand studies, would seem to be low by a factor of between two and five for any realistic policy analysis.

## 14.3 AN EMPIRICAL SOE MODELLING FRAMEWORK

A full description of the macro model would exceed the space available. However, any model, no matter how 'large', always has a simple theoretical core and only a limited number of key sectors and equations.[2] The stylised block structure of the model is illustrated in Table 14.2. The first major methodological issue which one faces in

*Table* 14.2 Block structure of model

| Block | Components |
|---|---|
| Supply block | • Industry<br>• Agriculture, forestry and fishing<br>• Services<br>• Imports<br>• Labour supply<br>• National aggregates: supply and income |
| Absorption block | • Consumption<br>• Investment<br>• Exports and the balance of payments<br>• Inventory changes<br>• National aggregates: demand |
| Income distribution block | • Producer prices<br>• Expenditure prices<br>• Wages<br>• Fiscal activities<br>• National Debt interest payments<br>• Monetary activities |

constructing an economy model concerns the level of sectoral disaggregation to be used and in order to analyse the behaviour of an economy like Ireland over the period 1960 to 1982, a division into resource-based traded ($R$), 'footloose' traded ($M$) and non-traded ($NT$) sectors was felt to be an irreducible minimum. This suggests the following empirical categories:

| | |
|---|---|
| *R* | agriculture, mining, some food-processing |
| *M* | remainder of manufacturing |
| *NT* | services, building and construction, public utilities, public administration |

Unfortunately, since there are some difficulties in splitting down even this simple empirical categorisation, we have adopted a less satisfactory classification as follows:

| | |
|---|---|
| *AFF* | agriculture (including forestry and fishing) |
| *I* | industry (manufacturing, building and construction, utilities and mining) |
| *MS, NMS, PA* | Services (marketed, non-marketed and public administration) |

Although we continue to regard industry as broadly 'tradable' for the purposes of stylisation, this is not completely satisfactory.

A second major empirical issue concerns the manner in which the theoretical SOE model framework is actually to be implemented. We adopt the Scandinavian version of the SOE model, which assumes perfect commodity arbitrage for the homogeneous aggregate tradable commodity (i.e. the domestic price of tradables is a function of the world price and the exchange rate); wage inflation in the tradable sector tends to adjust to the 'room' for wage increases (i.e. factor income shares remain on average at 'normal' levels); the economy-wide labour market is assumed to be homogeneous (wage inflation in the tradable and non-tradable sectors is the same); non-tradable prices are determined as a mark-up on costs; and the overall domestic inflation rate is a weighted average of tradable and non-tradable inflation. In most presentations of the Scandinavian model, the rate of productivity increase in the tradable sector is assumed to be higher than in the non-tradable sector, both being exogenous to the model, with a cost-accommodating demand side in the domestic economy (Lindbeck, 1979). In our model we interpret the Scandinavian model broadly as follows:

(i) The tradable price is the price of industrial output (*POI*) and we set

$$P\hat{O}I = f(PW\hat{O}RLD)$$

where *PWORLD* denotes a representative 'world' price and the '$\hat{\ }$' denotes proportional rate of change.

(ii) The implementation of the bargaining process underlying the Scandinavian model wage equation is a more controversial matter. If one drives the real product wage by productivity growth, i.e.:

$$W\hat{I} = P\hat{O}I + O\hat{P}RI$$

(where *WI*, *POI* and *OPRI* are the industrial average annual earnings, price and labour productivity respectively); as in Lindbeck (1979) this implies that the bargaining process is denominated in terms of the employers' 'price' and workers are indifferent to any wedge driven between the consumption price (*PCPER*) and the producer's price (*POI*), i.e. no distinction is made between gross pay and net-of-tax pay. In reality, the bargaining for factor-income shares is a more complex process and our implementation introduces a price 'wedge' as well as a proxy for labour bargaining power (i.e. a structural Phillips curve).

(iii) Homogeneity in the labour market is a strong assumption. It implies that if wage inflation initiates in the tradable sector, it then spreads to the non-tradable sector. Depending on the price used in denominating the wage, this process may become circular rather than remain unidirectional.

A third major issue concerns the manner of endogenising output, or, more correctly, output capacity of the industrial sector. In most macromodels this is done by setting output equal to demand. For an SOE model, this means that 'world' influences work through the demand side, which focuses attention on the trade equations. However, as discussed in section 14.2, the close integration of the supply sides of SOEs like Ireland into the wider OECD economy suggests a more direct supply-side linkage where Irish industrial capacity is determined as a share of 'world' capacity and is influenced by the competitiveness of Irish factors of production. This latter approach has been implemented in the model.

Having highlighted three major methodological issues, i.e. sectoral disaggregation, the SOE wage-price mechanism, and industrial output determination, we now turn now to the block structure of the model and examine briefly some important features of the supply block, the absorption block and the income-distribution block. Selected results are given in Appendix 14.1.

## The Supply Block

The core of the industry sub-model involves the determination of industrial capacity output and the related long-run factor demands for labour and capital. In the highly stylised treatment used in the model the world is divided into two components - Ireland and the 'rest of the world', henceforth *ROW*. Firms making a choice between locating production activities in Ireland or in the *ROW* do so on the basis of relative unit labour costs, and Ireland's capacity output share is a function of its competitiveness, thus measured. The technology describing this decision is assumed to be of *CES*-type. Given this capacity output share, and assuming constant returns to scale, the 'technology' used to produce in Ireland - i.e. the optimal capital/labour ratio - is arrived at by a process of cost-minimisation. Once again the production function is assumed to be of *CES*-type, bearing in mind that we are restricting ourselves to an added-value treatment. This second stage is modelled using a simple vintage 'putty-clay' approach, and the results from Appendix 14.1 show it to be characterised by a low elasticity of substitution (0.32), and technical progress which is labour-augmenting and capital-using.[3]

Thus, our interpretation of the technology of the industry sector is along standard neoclassical lines. Capacity output together with measures of expected relative factor prices are used to determine the cost-minimising long-run demands for labour and capital. Since we impose a specific technology on the relationship between capacity output and long-run marginal factor inputs (i.e. a *CES* technology) the labour and capital requirements cannot become inconsistent with the underlying technology of the model, a very desirable property for medium-term analysis. The translation of the long-run to the actual labour demand is by means of an adjustment mechanism which attempts to capture the processes which prevent instant adjustment. Hence, in the short run the national industrial 'firm' need not be on its long-run production function. Finally, capacity utilisation in industry is determined by abnormal changes in final sales of industrial goods and by the profitability of production (Helliwell and Chung, 1985).

In the case of agriculture, forestry and fishing (*AFF*), we recognised that employment and investment decisions were unlikely to derive from neoclassical optimising paradigms which are more appropriate to an industrial sector exposed to international competitive forces and relatively capital-intensive. In Irish agriculture, institutional, government and demographic forces become dominant and any realistic model must recognise this. We model gross agricultural output by means of a simple supply function making output sensitive to the relative prices of output and inputs, and weather conditions. Output prices are exogenous, being determined largely within the Common Agricultural Policy (CAP). Employment in *AFF* is modelled as a labour-release or migration-out process in that agents who do not leave are employed. The long-term factors permitting and encouraging the release of labour from *AFF* are the growth of labour productivity, the relative earnings differential *vis-à-vis* the non-agricultural sector and the availability of work elsewhere in the economy. We consider only a subset of the investment process - machinery and buildings - and use a simple flexible accelerator model which links the capital stock to output and the real cost of capital. Agricultural stock changes are left exogenous.

The complex heterogeneity of the service sector makes it difficult to justify implementation of a comprehensive decision-based factor-demand system. For example, the inclusion of large non-commercial and self-employment components is likely to affect the sensitivity of employment and investment to a relative factor-price measure. Also, the distinction between capacity output and actual output is less clear since there are shorter production processes involved, a more simplified technology and a less structured labour force. We have attempted to 'purge' the total services sector of the non-marketed element. Public administration and defence are isolated clearly in the nations accounts and thus provide little trouble (ignoring, of course, the underlying difficult measurement problems and the somewhat suspect national accounting conventions involved). The isolation of other non-marketed services is a more difficult problem and our attempts represent a very crude first effort. Output in the marketed services sector (*MS*) is determined by a weighted measure of final demand and by profitability. The factor-demand system for capital and labour is derived by cost-minimisation subject to a flexible functional form technology (a generalised Leontief cost-function). This imposes a certain consistency of behaviour (perhaps unwarranted) on the *MS* sector and while such assumptions are undoubtedly unrealistic, they seem preferable to an approach based on unrelated employment and investment equations. They also permit us to make stylised comparisons between industry and marketed services.

In the case of public administration and much of other non-marketed services, output is actually **measured** in the national accounts by labour inputs with essentially no productivity or capital stock corrections. Employment and investment decisions are regarded as discretionary policy instruments.

In modelling imports we distinguish five broad economic categories: imports of investment goods (related to total investment); consumption goods (related to total private consumption); materials for further production in agriculture (related to agricultural output); services (related to a broad measure of total activity in the economy); and imports of intermediate industrial goods, which constitute some 65 per cent of total imports (determined residually from the output-expenditure identity). The residual determination of industrial intermediate imports implies that capacity utilisation and intermediate imports act as buffers between variable final demand and quasi-fixed factors.[4]

Finally, labour supply is determined in an integrated schema involving population growth, education participation, labour-force participation and migration abroad. The labour-force participation rate is determined by the unemployment rate and implements an 'encouraged worker' hypothesis.[5] Migration flows are dependent on the population exposed to migration and on the relative attractiveness of Irish and UK labour markets. Unemployment is determined as the difference between labour supply and employment, the latter determined by the interaction between the labour demand and wage-bargaining schedules.

**The Absorption Block**

Our treatment of the absorption block of the model involves the determination of domestic and foreign absorption. Domestic absorption is treated in a quite conventional fashion. The consumption function is an aggregate one and is of the conventional permanent income type. Government consumption is treated as a policy instrument, the components of which are employment in public administration and other purchases from the non-marketed service sector. Our approach to modelling private housing investment uses an expenditure-type relation driven by real personal disposable income, but influenced by government housing transfers, interest rates and inflation. Government housing investment is treated as a discretionary policy instrument. The remaining investment categories have already been treated in the supply block, namely fixed investment by industry, agriculture and services. Agricultural inventory changes are left exogenous. Non-agricultural inventory changes are determined in a simple stock-adjustment model.

Concerning exports, the component of gross agricultural output which is exported abroad is determined in the supply block as the residual when domestic absorption, a rather stable function of output, is subtracted from total output. The determination of industrial exports has been the subject of much controversy in Ireland and in the international literature (Goldstein and Khan, 1978; Browne, 1982). The choice of approach lies between supply-driven, demand-driven or hybrid models. However, choice in this area is circumscribed by other assumptions made in the model. In particular, we have made the small-country assumption that domestic industrial firms have no market power on world markets, i.e. that they behave as price-takers. While this may not apply to all Irish exporters (Honohan, 1982), it is a legitimate assumption to make and may indeed be reasonable at our level of aggregation. Hence, the level of industrial exports is determined by what domestic firms produce to sell at the given world-market price. Thus, an export supply function is used to close the model, the appropriate relative price variable being the competitiveness of production in Ireland *vis-à-vis* the *ROW*. In such a specification, a devaluation affects exports by increasing the competitiveness of Irish production in the industrial supply block through lowering relative labour costs. The dynamics of the devaluation work through the domestic wage-bargaining system and will eventually return competitiveness to its original level. Our approach can be thought of as a structural model of the export process so that within the overall model system the controversy over export determination becomes less important than the key issue of the determination of industrial output.

### The Income Distribution Block

The income-distribution block of the model deals with price- and wage-formation and with fiscal and monetary activities. The basic inspiration for the determination of prices and wages comes from the Scandinavian model (Lindbeck, 1979), where we identify our industry sector with the 'tradables' sector and the services sector with the 'non-tradables' sector.

The number of expenditure categories distinguished in the model is quite large and each of these categories requires its separate price. The basic approach to modelling the expenditure deflators is quite uniform in that they are 'explained' in terms of their component prices, i.e. any such deflator simply incorporates the prices of all goods and services which go to make them up, and includes any tax effects. The weights, which are assumed constant, can be obtained by statistical estimation – the approach we have used – or from input–output tables.

The fiscal and monetary aspects of the model are concerned with three issues:

(i) income redistribution via taxes and expenditures;
(ii) derivation of the government's budget constraint;
(iii) monetary consequences of financing the borrowing requirement.

Consequently, the fiscal sector determines, in a conventional way, direct and indirect tax revenues, subsidies, personal transfers, interest payments on national debt, etc., and isolates the instruments of fiscal policy. The monetary environment is modelled using a conventional SOE fixed-exchange approach.

*Wages*

Wages are determined in a bargaining model where employers and employees in industry are in contention for a share of added-value. The price of tradables (industrial output prices in our model) is determined in world markets. Wage inflation in the tradables sector adjusts to the 'room' for wage increases - i.e. an increase which is consistent with a 'normal' profit share. One can define a 'wedge' which is driven between the firm's real labour costs ($W/P^*$) and the real wage received by the suppliers of labour ($W/PC$) as follows.

$$WEDGE = (W/P^*)/(W/PC)$$

where

$$PC = PCNT^*(1+t_i)/(1-t_d),$$

*PCNT* being the deflator of consumption expenditure net of indirect taxes, and $t_d$ being the average rate of direct taxation on wages (i.e. income tax and employee's *PRSI* contributions). Also, we can write:

$$P^* = P/(1+t_e)$$

where $P$ is the deflator of industrial added value and $t_e$ is the average rate of employer's *PRSI.* Hence, we can write the wedge as:

$$WEDGE = (PCNT/P)^*(1+t_e)^*(1+t_i)/(1-t_d).$$

Figure 14.7 shows the evolution of the 'wedge' variable over the period 1973–82. It is seen that it increased in size in all years other than 1974 and 1977/8.

We determine labour's share of added value in industry (*LSVAI*) as a function of this wedge variable and of labour's bargaining power (proxied by deviations of the unemployment rate from its trend), with a dynamic adjustment, i.e.

$$\log LSVAI = a_1 + a_2 \log WEDGE + a_3(UR\text{-}URNAT)_{-1} + a_4 \log LSVAI_{-1}$$

Figure 14.7 Tax wedge

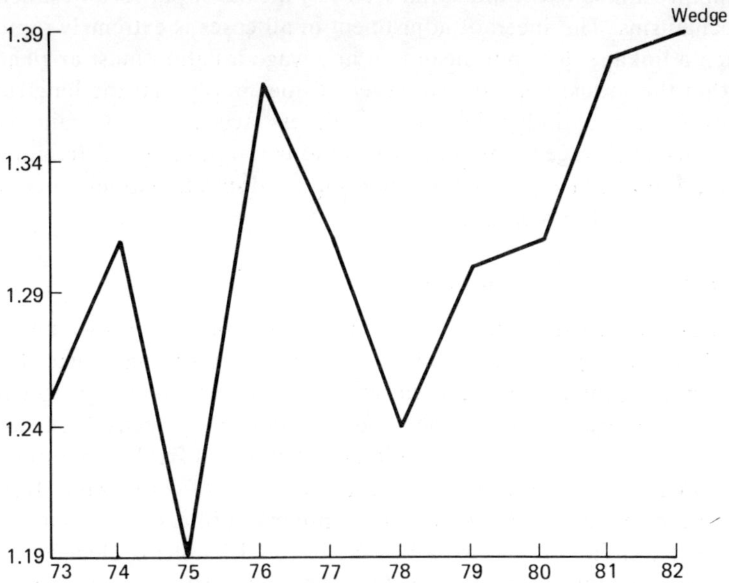


where labour's share of added value (*LSVAI*) is defined as

$$LSVAI = (W \cdot L)/(P \cdot O),$$

*W* being the wage rate in industry, *L* employment, *P* the output deflator, *O* real added value and *UR* the unemployment rate (*URNAT* being its trend).

In the model, six versions of the industrial wage equation are available, and differ in the manner of including the wedge (i.e. either level or first difference forms), in the treatment of productivity and in the dynamics of the equation. The fact that we have felt obliged to include choices in the wage equation should serve as a measure of our relative ignorance of this area and may be preferable to 'pumping' for a particular single formulation. Indeed, the frequent absence of direct taxation effects in wage equations is one of the more curious features of many operational macroeconometric models (Brittain, 1983, on the *NIESR* model of the United Kingdom is a recent example) and serves to introduce a serious asymmetry between, say, the employment effects of direct and indirect taxation policy changes.

Wage inflation in the marketed and non-marketed services sectors is simply linked to the industrial sector by means of partial adjustment mechanisms. The speed of adjustment in all cases is extremely rapid. Such a linkage does not mean that any wage inflation must **originate** within the industry sector. However, it does imply that the long-run maintenance of industrial competitiveness acts as a constraint on inter-sectoral wage differentials when industrial prices are determined abroad but service prices are a mark-up on domestic labour costs, as is the case in the present model.

*National debt interest payments*

Identities are used to build up total current expenditure by government, total capital expenditure, total revenue and the resulting deficit, thus determining the borrowing requirement. This borrowing requirement can be financed by either monetary or non-monetary means. Monetary financing consists of money creation by the Central Bank or of foreign borrowing. Non-monetary financing consists of borrowing from domestic commercial banks and the non-bank public. Foreign borrowing is determined in the model as the residual financing element.

National debt is considered in two parts: debt denominated in Irish pounds and debt denominated in foreign currency. Interest payments on the first component are explained in terms of a rate of interest and changes in National Loans outstanding. The actual stock of debt outstanding is exogenous. We determine interest payments on foreign debt as if all foreign debt was of infinite maturity and also permit a simple revaluation option for the stock of foreign debt outstanding when exchange rates change. The details of this area are probably best handled in satellite sub-models by analysts with particular concern for the composition of the foreign debt and the debt maturity structure.

## 14.4 FISCAL ACTIVISM AND THE LABOUR MARKET IN A SMALL OPEN ECONOMY

It should be clear that there are four main prerequisites to any formal analysis of the influences of fiscal activism on the labour market; a clearly specified labour-demand schedule, based on the neoclassical theory of the firm; a model of labour supply, incorporating the separate elements of migration abroad, labour-force participation and population growth; a method of 'closing' the labour market, probably involving a wage-bargaining model and preferably estimated jointly with the demand schedule; and an economy-wide macro framework which reflects the characteristics of the economy being studied, within which to place the above three elements of the labour market.

If any one or more of these four components is ignored, there is a risk of serious misspecification, with resulting policy errors. The fact that previous Irish (and other) macro models may have had serious theoretical and econometric flaws should not colour one's attitude too much to the above scheme. The final stage need not always involve a complex or large model. In fact, the simpler the better, once it is adequate for the task in hand.

Since economic models are unstable experimental tools, and in a state of constant evolution, the methods of calculation used with them should be kept as simple as possible. Hence, the use of sophisticated optimal-control-type calculations should probably be avoided. In stylised form, a model may be expressed as a vector equation relating endogenous variables ($Y_t$) to exogenous policy variables ($X_t$) and other exogenous variables ($Z_t$), i.e.

$$Y_t = f(X_t, Z_t, Y_{t-1}).$$

The vector of endogenous variables, $Y_t$, can be further subdivided into ($YT_t$, $YO_t$), where $YT_t$ represents target endogenous variables and $YO_t$ represents other endogenous variables.

For example, the vector of targets would typically include the unemployment rate, the borrowing requirement, the balance-of-payments deficit, real personal disposable income, inflation rates, etc. Typical policy instruments would be public-sector employment, direct and indirect tax rates, *PRSI* rates for employers and employees, public-sector direct investment and transfers to persons and companies.

The comparison of the results of any one macro policy configuration with an alternative usually consists in evaluating the two separate outcomes in terms of selected target variables, and deciding which is preferred.[6] For a unidimensional criterion, say unemployment, this is a simple task. For a multidimensional criterion it becomes more difficult, for example, one may have to decide how much of a change in the borrowing requirement can be traded off against a specific change in unemployment. The fact that trade-offs must usually be evaluated reinforces the requirement to operate within a complete economy-model structure, particularly one which permits taxation and expenditure to feed back to the rest of the economy.

We illustrate these concepts for the Irish case by looking at a policy experiment where, in 1974, 1000 extra public-administration employees were hired and retained in all subsequent years. We examine the following fiscal policy stances:

(i) marginal borrowing to fund the extra wage bill is made abroad, thus increasing foreign borrowing and debt-interest payments, but all tax rates are unchanged;
(ii) as for (i), but the marginal foreign debt **interest** payments are funded by an (increased) direct tax rate, endogenously determined;
(iii) the *ex ante* cost of the extra wage bill is funded in its entirety by an *ex ante* increased direct-tax rate
(iv) as for (iii), but with wage rates in the non-marketed-service sector kept fixed at their historical levels.

A more interesting case than (iii) would be to fund the extra wage bill by endogenising the direct tax rate to offset any change in the borrowing requirement completely, but it proved difficult to simulate the model in this mode. Smith (1986) examines conditions under which it may be impossible to balance the budget if expenditures are too large, although in the present model it is not known if the necessary 'adverse selection' problems apply to the labour markets.

In Figure 14.8 we show how total numbers employed change, relative to the historical out-turn, under the public-sector employment increase. In case (i) there is a net increase of 1170 jobs initially, but an instability of response over time is apparent. In cases (iii) and (iv) this cycle is partially damped, but cycles of long duration persist.

In Figure 14.9 we show how numbers employed in the market sector (comprising industry, agriculture and marketed services) change under the policy shock. For cases (i) and (ii) a net increase is registered in the first year, although this vanishes by year 3. For cases (iii) and (iv), a net loss of jobs is registered from the initial year, with a long cycle.

Figure 14.10 and 14.11 decompose the above into its separate components. From Figure 14.10 we see that even for the 'benign' scenario (i), a net loss in industrial employment is registered by year 4. From Figure 14.11 we see that under the severe financing case (iii), the market services sector registers a fall in numbers employed from year 1. This phenomenon is well-known theoretically and could be termed 'supply-crowding-out'. For cases (ii), (iii) and (iv), the higher public

*Figure* 14.8 Total employment effect (nos)

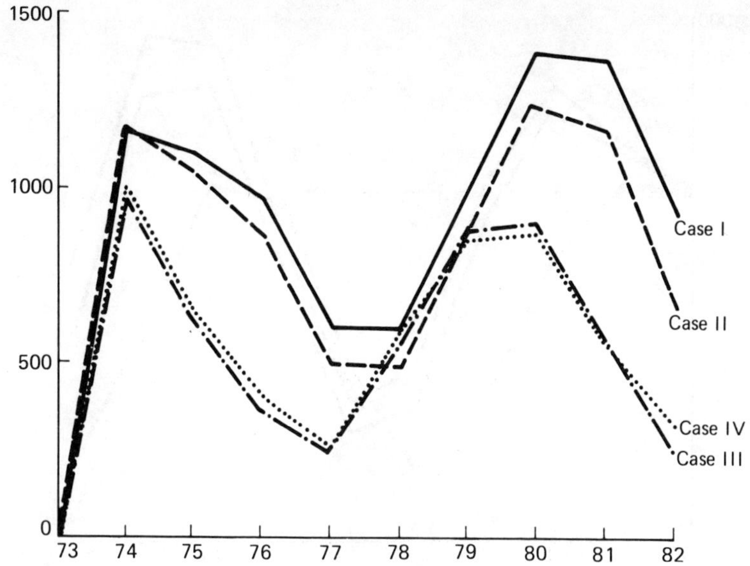


*Figure* 14.9 Market sector employment effect (nos)

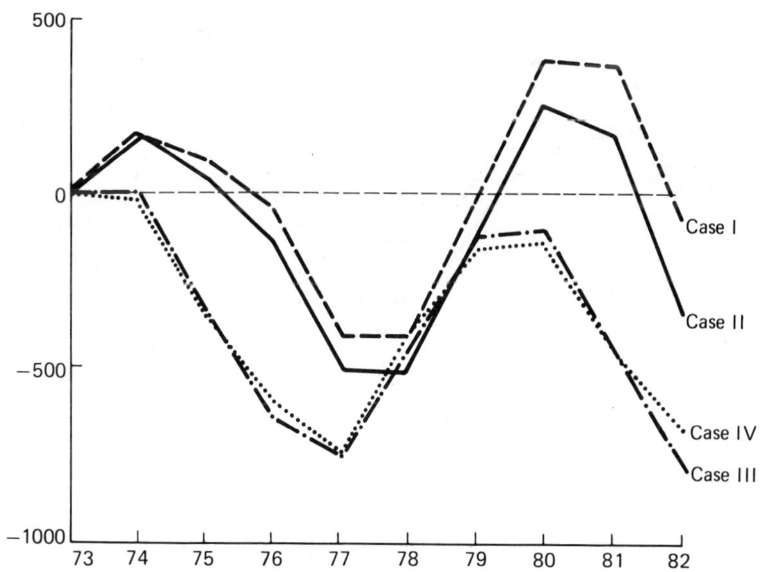

*Figure* 14.10 Industrial employment effect (nos)

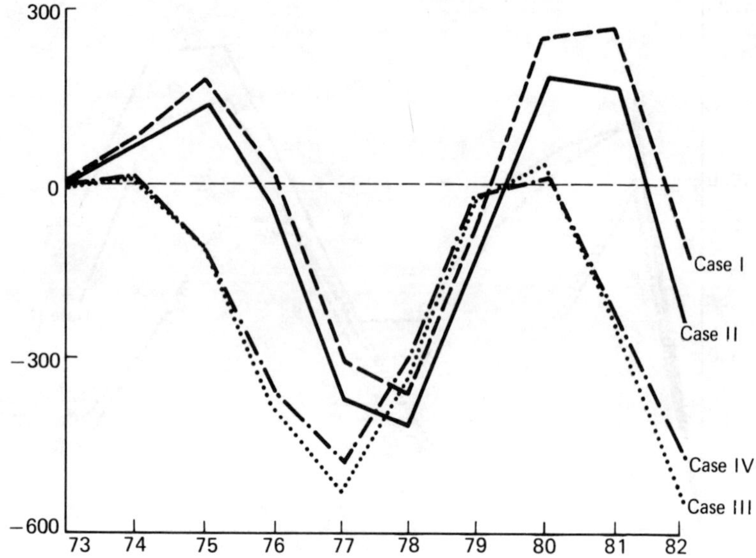


*Figure* 14.11 Market services employment effect (nos)

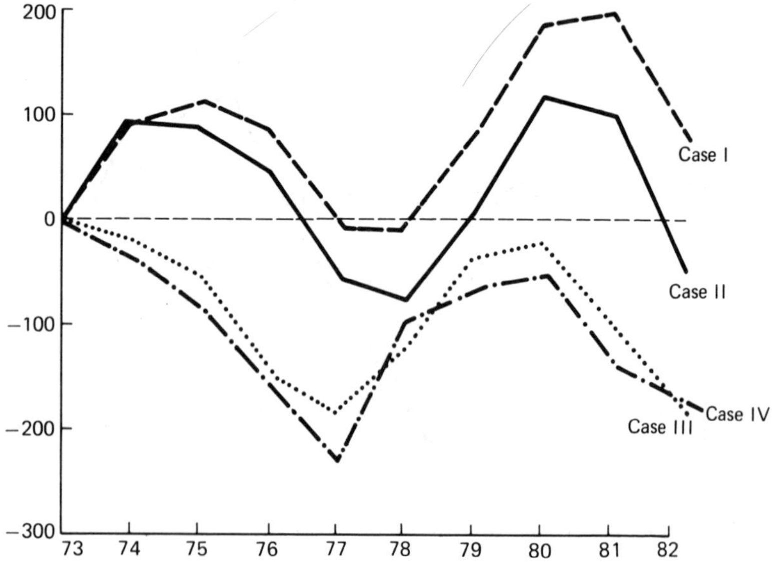

expenditure is financed by a rise in the direct tax rate. This drives up wages as labour attempts to bargain in net-of-tax terms and partially succeeds. Indeed, for certain policy actions a balanced-budget GDP multiplier could become negative.

Turning to the effects on unemployment, Figure 14.12 shows that, by year 9, all cases still register a decrease in numbers unemployed.

*Figure* 14.12 Unemployment effect (nos)

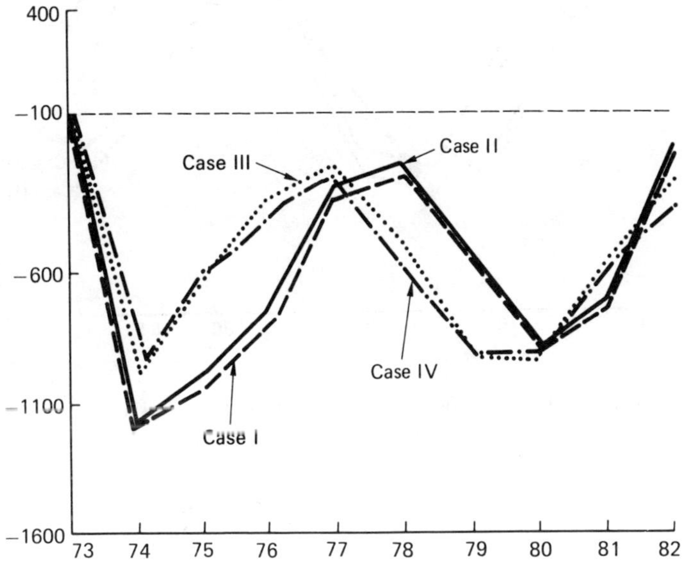


For case (iii), the initial fall in unemployment is lower than for cases (i) and (ii) as the effects of the large rise in direct taxation feeds through the economy and drive up wages.

The effects on real industrial exports are shown in Figure 14.13. Exports are determined in the model mainly by industrial capacity, as appropriate to a price-taking sector. Capacity is determined by world capacity and competitiveness, measured in terms of relative unit labour costs. Hence, we see for case (iii) a strong initial negative effect on exports arising from a loss in competitiveness.

In Figure 14.14 we show the effects on the borrowing requirement expressed as a percentage of GDP. The unsatisfactory nature of the *ex ante* budget balance of cases (iii) and (iv) is apparent since the borrowing requirement falls relative to the historical out-turn.

*Figure* 14.13 Industrial exports effect (#m, 75)

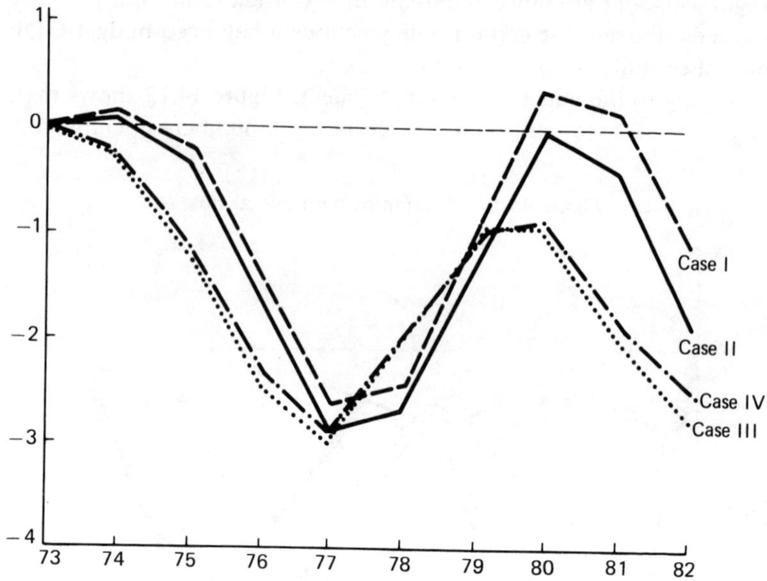


*Figure* 14.14 Borrowing requirement effect (% GDP)

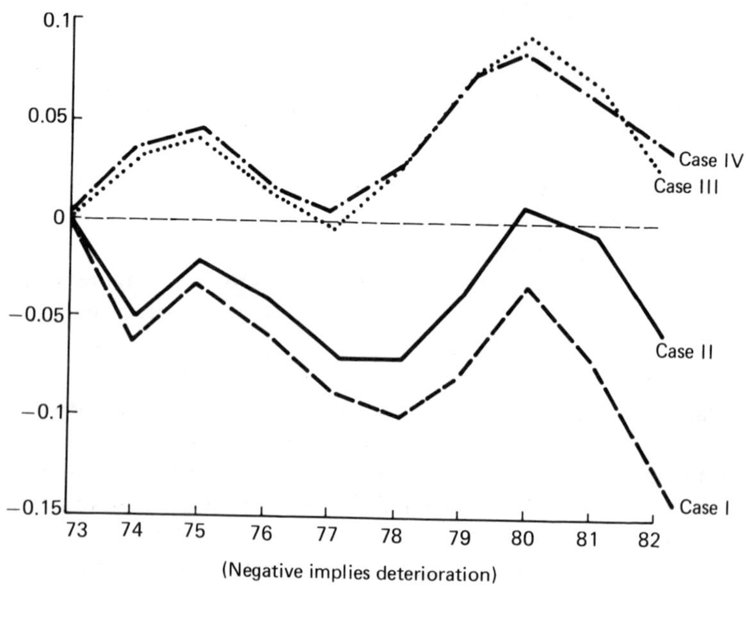

*Figure* 14.15 Balance of payments effect (% GDP)

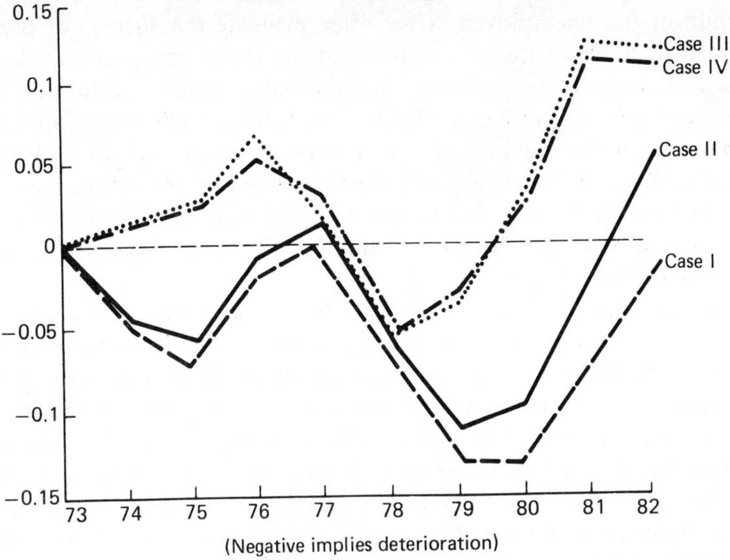


Finally, in Figure 14.15 we show the effects on the balance of payments, expressed as a percentage of GDP. Cases (iii) and (iv), the full tax-financing of the job-creation, results in a balance -of-payments surplus relative to the historical out-turn, compared with a relative deficit in cases (i) and (ii).

These results are presented merely as illustrations of the complexity of interactions that can arise out of a relatively simple policy action, i.e. raising direct public employment. They should warn one about making simplistic *ceteris paribus* calculations on the effects of public expenditure and employment creation on the rest of the economy where such expenditures are partially or wholly financed by taxation, and reinforce the need to understand the functioning of the various labour markets and their interaction with the rest of the economy.

## 14.5 CONCLUSION

The problem of designing, implementing and evaluating policies which affect the labour market requires a detailed quantitative knowledge of how the labour-market functions, and how it is integrated into the rest of the economy. Organisations given responsibility for this task normally work from a microeconomic point of view involving, say, a specific employment, training or support scheme targeted at a specific group of the unemployed. They often evaluate the success of their efforts in terms of the performance of the target group and seldom have to evaluate the feedback effects of their activities on the rest of the economy. In particular, the adverse feedback effects due to tax-financing of the funding of job-creation or other activities on the marketed sectors, especially the exposed industrial sector, are seldom studied. Furthermore, job-creation normally increases labour's power to bargain and can lead to a further loss in competitiveness in the exposed sector.

In this chapter we have taken a purely macroeconomic point of view and have sought to establish a suitable framework within which to evaluate the macroeconomic consequences of employment-creating policies. In reviewing empirical work on the functioning of the Irish labour market we have tried to identify what are the most fruitful and profitable ways to build on existing knowledge. Any such process will involve greater quantification within well-designed and flexible simulation models whose properties are understood and whose theoretical structure commands at least some support within the circle of policy-makers, their advisors and their critics.

In its present form the macro model is not completely satisfactory. The need to use 'derived' data (for example, measures of capacity output, capacity manning levels, vintage data, extrapolative expectations) makes it difficult to evaluate econometric tests. The added-value model of the industrial sector should be generalised to a full *KLEM* approach. Indeed, the further disaggregation of industry into 'traditional' (or 'indigenous') and 'advanced' would allow greater precision with the modelling of transnational investment activity in Ireland. A better understanding of the important issues on the supply side of the labour market certainly require disaggregation of the labour force into males and single and married females, together with an age breakdown. Finally, the long cyclical reactions of the model to shocks should alert one to the possibility that the model may not be stable unless 'closed' by an appropriate fiscal rule.[7]

## Appendix 14.1: Listing of Selected Model Equations

For selected equations we present the estimated coefficients and a variety of diagnostic statistics. In all cases the estimation technique used was OLS except in the case of the joint factor demand system for industry and for marketed services, where FIML was used. The estimation period was 1964–82. In presenting the statistical results, the following notation is used: *RSQ* denotes the multiple correlation coefficient, corrected for degrees of freedom; *DW* denotes the first-order Durbin–Watson statistic; *RHO* gives the first-order autoregressive parameter; the *t*-statistics are indicated in brackets beside, or under, the coefficients. A full listing of an earlier version of the model is given in Bradley *et al.* (1985), and an up-to-date listing is available from the author on request.

### *The Supply Block*

*Industry* The Irish share of marginal industrial capacity output (*MQCII*) relative to that of the rest of the world (*MQCIW*) is determined by Irish unit labour costs relative to those of the ROW (ECOMP), and a time trend:

$$\log MQCII/MQCIW = \underset{(8.8)}{-1.079} + \underset{(3.2)}{0.843} \log ECOMP + \underset{(10.5)}{0.055t}$$

$$RSQ = 0.95 \qquad DW = 1.00 \qquad RHO = 0.426\ (3.6).$$

The assumption that the technology of the industry sector is of vintage, putty–clay, *CES*-type gives long-run marginal factor/output ratios for capital (*MKQRI*) and labour (*MLQRI*) as functions of the expected relative factor price of labour to capital (*ERFPI*):

$$\begin{aligned}\log MKQRI = {} & s/(1-s)[\log(1-d) - \log A] - t\log(1+lmk) \\ & + s/(1-s)\log[1 + (d/(1-d))^s ERFPI^{1-s} \\ & \times \{(1+lml)/(1+lmk)\}^{t(s-1)}] \\ \log MLQRI = {} & s/(1-s)[\log d - \log A] - t\log(1+lmk) \\ & + s/(1-s)\log[1 + ((1-d)/d^s ERFPI^{s-1} \\ & \times \{(1+lml)/(1+lmk)\}^{t(1-s)}].\end{aligned}$$

Estimation by FIML yielded the following production functions parameters:

| *Parameter* | *Interpretation* | *Value* |
|---|---|---|
| *A* | Scale/efficiency parameter | 3.69 |
| *s* | Elasticity of substitution | 0.320 |
| *d* | Labour intensity parameter | 0.591 |
| *lmk* | Capital saving rate of technical change | −0.038 |
| *lml* | Labour saving rate of technical change | 0.033 |

Fixed industrial investment (*IFI*) and optimal marginal labour demand (*MLCI*) are obtained as the products of the marginal capacity (*MQCII*) and the optimal marginal capital/output ratio (*MKQRI*) and optimal marginal labour/output ratio (*MLORI*):

$$IFI = MQCII^{*}MKQRI \quad \text{and} \quad MLCI = MQCII^{*}MLORI.$$

Aggregate capacity labour demand, *LCI*, is determined as:

$$LCI = MLCI + (1 - 0.084857)LCI_{-1}$$

and the capacity labour demand (*LCI*) is translated into actual labour demand (*LI*) by means of an error-correction mechanism (*ECM*):

$$\begin{aligned} d \log LI = \; & \underset{(2.4)}{0.443} del \log LCI + \underset{(4.2)}{0.826} \log LCI_{-1}/LI_{-1} \\ & + \underset{(7.2)}{0.675}(0.443 \log CURI + (0.826 - 0.443) \log CURI_{-1}) \end{aligned}$$

$RSQ = 0.62 \qquad DW = 1.35.$

Industrial capacity utilisation (*CURI*) is determined as a function of sales-capacity disequilibrium (*GSOI*/*QCII*) and of short-run profitability (*COIL*). Two versions are provided:

$$\log CURI = a_1 + a_2 \log GSOI/QCII + a_3 \log COIL_{-1} \qquad \text{(A.1)}$$

$$\log CURI = a_1 + a_2 \log GSOI/QCII \qquad \text{(A.2)}$$

| *Eqn. no.* | $a_1$ | $a_2$ | $a_3$ | *RSQ* | *DW* | *RHO* |
|---|---|---|---|---|---|---|
| (A.1) | −5.56 (4.4) | 0.766 (4.1) | 0.291 (1.7) | 0.76 | 1.55 | 0.767 (4.2) |
| (A.2) | −6.75 (6.1) | 0.949 (6.0) | — | 0.72 | 1.90 | 0.691 (3.6) |

Actual output (*QII*) is the product of the rate of capacity utilisation (*CURI*) and capacity output (*QCII*), i.e. $QII = CURI^{*}QCII$.

*Agriculture, Forestry and Fishing* Agricultural output (*QA*) is determined by capacity output (*QCA*, a five-year moving average), but is modified by profitability (*PQA*/*PMAT*) and the weather conditions (*WEATH*):

$$QA = \underset{(3.1)}{177.4} + [\underset{(4.7)}{0.000249}\, WEATH + \underset{(4.1)}{0.311}\,(PQA/PMAT)_{-1}]QCA$$

$RSQ = 0.88 \qquad DW = 2.44.$

Employment in agriculture (*LAFF*) is a function of the relative agriculture/non-agriculture earnings (*ERAW*), the overall national unemployment rate (*UR*) and a time trend (acting as a proxy for labour productivity or technical change):

$$\log LAFF = \underset{(89.9)}{6.08} - \underset{(9.4)}{0.28}t + \underset{(2.1)}{0.115} \log ERAW + \underset{(1.8)}{0.034} \log UR_{-1}$$

$RSQ = 0.99 \qquad DW = 1.67 \qquad RHO = 0.784\ (7.3).$

The agricultural capital stock ($KFAFF$) is a function of output (added-value, $OAFF$) and the real cost of capital ($UCCAFF/POAFF$):

$$\log KFAFF = \underset{(2.1)}{-0.639} + \underset{(2.6)}{0.183} \log(OAFF_{-1} + OAFF_{-2})/2 \underset{(2.5)}{-0.062} \log(UCCAFF/POAFF) + \underset{(24.6)}{0.914} \log KFAFF_{-1}$$

$RSQ = 0.99 \quad DW = 1.41 \quad RHO = 0.671\ (3.8).$

*Services Sector*: Marketed services output ($OSM$) is determined by a weighted measure of gross sales ($EGSOSM$), where the weights reflect the services output content of each component of sales and short-run profitability ($COSML$):

$$\log OSM = \underset{(3.6)}{1.52} + \underset{(12.7)}{0.764} \log EGSOSM + 0.386 \log COSML$$

$RSQ = 0.99 \quad DW = 2.79 \quad RHO = 0.848\ (16.0).$

The technology of the marketed services sector is of generalised Leontief form, with the factor demand equations estimated using FIML. In the following, $KFSM$ represents the (non-vintage) capital stock, $LSM$ numbers employed, $OSM$ output and $ERFPSM$ the relative price of labour to capital:

$$KFSM/OSM = d_0 + c_1 ERFPSM^{0.5} + d_3 t$$

$d_0 = -1.86(6.2) \quad d_3 = -0.041(3.3) \quad RSO = 0.94 \quad DW = 0.70$

$$LSM/OSM = c_0 + c_1 ERFPSM^{0.5} + c_3 t$$

$c_0 = 0.231(6.6) \quad c_1 = 0.808(7.3) \quad c_3 = -0.0049(6.8)$

$RSQ = 0.97 \quad DW = 0.85.$

*Labour Supply and Demography* The labour-force participation rate ($LFPR$) is a function of deviations of the unemployment rate from its trend ($UR - URNAT$):

$$\log LFPR = \underset{(2.0)}{2.04} + \underset{(1.9)}{0.0197} \log UR/URNAT + \underset{(2.2)}{0.517} \log LFPR_{-1}$$

$RSQ = 0.63 \quad DW = 1.86 \quad RHO = 0.624\ (3.1).$

Net migration abroad ($NMA$) is a function of the relative attractiveness of the UK labour market and the domestic market. Relative attractiveness is measured as the product of the relative employment rates in the two countries ($RE$) and the relative real earnings rate ($RE$):

$$NMA = \underset{(1.8)}{-155.8} + (\underset{(1.7)}{0.137} + \underset{(1.6)}{0.0466} RE_{-1} * RW_{-1}) * (N1564A + N1564A_{-1})/2.0$$

$RSQ = 0.68 \quad DW = 2.41.$

*The Income Distribution Block*

*Price Determination* Two variants of the industrial added-value producer price equation are provided: the first relates industrial prices to world prices with a disequilibrium term in domestic labour costs; the second determines industrial prices simply as a function of world prices:

$$\log POI = \underset{(2.9)}{-0.039} + \underset{(49.0)}{1.068} \log PWORLD + \underset{(1.8)}{0.454} \, \mathrm{d} \log(UCLIRL/EUCLIRL) \qquad (A)$$

$RSQ = 0.99 \qquad DW = 1.58$

$$\log POI = -0.046 + \underset{(2.8)}{1.000} \log PWORLD \qquad (B)$$

$RSQ = 0.95 \qquad DW = 1.17.$

The service sector output price ($POS$) is a simple mark-up on domestic labour costs ($WS/EOPRS$):

$$\log POS = \underset{(16.0)}{0.485} + \underset{(4.1)}{0.562} \log(WS/EOPRS) + (1 - 0.562) \log(WS/EOPRS)_{-1}$$

$RSQ = 0.70 \qquad DW = 1.86 \qquad RHO = 0.779(4.5).$

The common format for the main expenditure deflators is as follows:

$$\log PEX = a_1 + a_2 \log PGDPFC + (1 - a_2) \log PMGS$$

where $PEX$ is a specific expenditure deflator, $PGDPFC$ is the $GDP$ deflator and $PMGS$ is the deflator of total imports. The main results are as follows, where $TINC$ is the net indirect tax rate:

Table A.14.1

| *Deflator* | $a_1$ | $a_2$ | *RSQ* | *DW* | *RHO* | *Description* |
|---|---|---|---|---|---|---|
| *PCPER*/ | −0.146 | 0.685 | 0.95 | 1.78 | 0.868 | Consumption |
| (1+TINC) | (5.2) | (14.5) | | | (10.7) | |
| *PIFI* | − 0.039 | 0.506 | 0.86 | 1.31 | 0.935 | Investment |
| | (0.4) | (6.8) | | | (15.4) | (industry) |
| *PIFS* | 0.016 | 0.505 | 0.83 | 1.75 | 0.791 | Investment |
| | (0.6) | (6.8) | | | (4.3) | (services) |
| *PIFAFF* | 0.063 | 0.501 | 0.976 | 1.80 | 0.902 | Investment |
| | (1.3) | (8.6) | | | (20.6) | (agriculture) |
| *PIH* | 0.257 | 0.562 | 0.904 | 1.45 | 0.952 | Investment |
| | (1.3) | (4.8) | | | (22.8) | (housing) |

The export deflator used in the model (*PXNA*) is determined by world prices:

$$\log PXNA = \underset{(1.7)}{0.020} + \underset{(11.5)}{0.840} \log PWORLD + (1-0.840) \log PWORLD_{-1}$$

$RSQ = 0.94$ $DW = 2.02$ $RHO = 0.572\ (2.8)$.

*Wage Determination* Six variants of the industrial wage equation are provided. In the first four, labour's share of added value (*LSVAI*) is determined as a function of a tax wedge (*WEDGE*), deviations of the unemployment rate from its trend (*UR-URNAT*), and a dynamic adjustment:

$$\log LSVAI = a_1 + a_2 \text{ d} \log WEDGE + a_3(UR_{-1} - URNAT_{-1}) + a_4 \log LSVAI_{-1}$$

| *No.* | $a_1$ | $a_2$ | $a_3$ | $a_4$ | *RSQ* | *DW* | *RHO* |
|---|---|---|---|---|---|---|---|
| 1 | −0.342 (28) | 0.272 (3.4) | −0.0116 (1.8) | — | 0.43 | 1.68 | 0.496 (2.3) |
| 2 | −0.168 (2.7) | 0.381 (3.7) | −0.014 (2.3) | 0.511 (2.9) | 0.52 | 1.67 | |

$$\log LSVAI = a_1 + a_2 \log WEDGE + a_3(UR_{-1} - URNAT_{-1}) + a_4 \log LSVAI_{-1}$$

| *No.* | $a_1$ | $a_2$ | $a_3$ | $a_4$ | *RSQ* | *DW* | *RHO* |
|---|---|---|---|---|---|---|---|
| 3 | −0.469 (13) | 0.509 (4.2) | −0.0182 (2.9) | — | 0.48 | 1.55 | 0.672 (3.6) |
| 4 | −0.452 (6.9) | 0.517 (3.9) | −0.0183 (2.8) | 0.0560 (0.3) | 0.45 | 1.61 | 0.655 (3.5) |

In the final two variants, the product wage (*WI/POI*) is determined by the tax wedge, the deviation of unemployment from its trend (*UR-URNAT*), labour productivity (*OPRI*) and lagged real wages.

$$\log WI/POI = \underset{(5.9)}{-0.178} + \underset{(7.4)}{0.488} \text{ d} \log WEDGE$$

$$= + \underset{(2.7)}{-0.0107}(UR_{-1} - URNAT_{-1})$$

$$+ \underset{(7.0)}{0.588} \log OPRI + (1-0.588) \log WI/POI_{-1}$$

$RSQ = 0.91$ $DW = 1.81$ $RHO = 0.250\ (1.1)$

$$\log WI/POI = \underset{(11.1)}{-0.431} + \underset{(5.1)}{0.624} \log WEDGE + \underset{(3.4)}{-0.019}(UR_{-1} - URNAT_{-1})$$

$$+ \underset{(9.0)}{0.820} \log OPRI + (1-0.820) \log WI/POI_{-1}$$

$RSQ = 0.81$ $DW = 1.67$ $RHO = 0.721(4.0)$.

The wage rate in marketed services is determined by the industrial wage rate:

$$\text{d} \log WSM = 0.916 \text{ d} \log WI + (1-0.916) \text{ d} \log WI_{-1}$$

$RSQ = 0.61$ $DW = 1.70$.

The wage rate in public administration is determined by the industrial wage rate. The dummy variables deal with the 'bunching' of public sector pay awards.

$$\mathrm{d}\log WPA = 1.0\,\mathrm{d}\log WI + \underset{(5.2)}{0.0534}\,WPADU - \underset{(7.9)}{0.0658}\,WPADD$$

$RSQ = 0.84 \qquad DW = 0.84.$

## Notes

1. If the world production function, $Q_w = f(Q_I, Q_R)$, were simply additive, then the world firm would, under *CRS*, tend to plump for one or other location since the marginal rate of substitution between Irish and *ROW* output is constant. It seems more plausible to rule out corner solutions by assuming **strict** concavity of the world production function, thus implying a strictly diminishing marginal rate of substitution between the higher level inputs $Q_I$ and $Q_R$.
2. The choice of theoretical core for the model can range over pure Keynesian (or demand-determined) models, a 'new classical' (or pure supply-determined) approach, or a switching regime model involving distinct supply-constrained and demand-constrained regimes. Our approach focuses attention on the disequilibrium adjustment processes called into play when demand and supply imbalances arise, and permits the simultaneous operation of demand and supply forces (Helliwell *et al.*, 1985).
3. The *CES* putty–clay technology results are broadly similar to those found for the Dutch economy (den Hartog, 1984). However, we feel that the debate in the Netherlands concerning putty–clay versus clay–clay specifications is less relevant than the issues which arise when industrial output (or investment) and wage bargaining are endogenised, particularly in the light of the very low elasticities of substitution.
4. Refer Helliwell *et al.* (1982) for an approach using inventory buffering.
5. More recent disaggregated work showed the male participation rate to be in secular decline, while the female participation was found to be of an added-worker kind. In the model simulations reported, the aggregate participation rate was fixed at its historical value.
6. The rational expectations critique applies, and should warn one against using the approach to examine large shocks which are untypical of the historical data sample.
7. Similar cycles were found in the numerical solutions reported by van de Klundert (1982) when the Phillips-curve term was introduced into the wage equation. The wide range of real and nominal fiscal instruments complicates the study of stability. Rose and Selody (1985) is an example of an empirical model where an equilibrium path is pre-specified and where all markets are forced to clear in the long-run.

## References

ANDREWS, M. J. *et al.* (1985) 'Models of the UK Economy and the Real Wage Employment Debate', *National Institute Economic Review*, May, pp. 41–52.

BACON, P. (1986) *Medium-Term Outlook*: 1986–1990 (Dublin: Economic and Social Research Institute).

BERNDT, E. and WOOD, D. O. (1979) 'Technology, Prices and the Derived Demand for Energy', *Review of Economics and Statistics*, 52, pp. 259–68.

BLUNDELL, R. *et al.* (1986) 'Unemployment and Female Labour Supply', paper presented at European Production Study Group, Conference on *Unemployment in Europe*, Maastricht, 17–19 April.

BRADLEY, J. and FANNING, C. (1984) *Aggregate Supply, Aggregate Demand and Income Distribution in Ireland: A Macrosectoral Analysis* (Dublin: Economic and Social Research Institute, paper no. 115).

BRADLEY, J. and FITZGERALD J. D. (1986) 'Industrial Output and Factor Input Determination in an Econometric Model of a Small Open Economy', paper presented at International Conference on *Economic Modelling in the OECD Economies*, London, 24–7 March, forthcoming, *European Economic Review*.

BRADLEY, J. and PRENDERGAST, C. (1986) 'Real Wages and Employment in Ireland in the 1970s', mimeo, Economic and Social Research Institute.

BRADLEY, J. *et al.* (1985) *Medium-Term Analysis of Fiscal Policy in Ireland: A Macroeconometric Study of the Period* 1967–1980 (Dublin: Economic and Social Research Institute, Paper No. 122).

BRITTAIN, A. (ed.) (1983) *Employment, Output and Inflation: The National Institute Model of the British Economy* (New Hampshire: Heinemann).

BROWNE, F. X. (1982) 'Modelling Export Prices and Quantities in a Small Open Economy', *Review of Economics and Statistics*, 64, pp. 346–7.

DEN HARTOG, H. (1984) 'Empirical Vintage Models for the Netherlands: A Review in Outline', *De Economist*, 132, no. 3, pp. 326–49.

GEARY, P. T. and MURPHY, A. (1985) 'Real Wages and Employment: Equilibrium and Disequilibrium Approaches to the Irish Labour Market', paper presented to the *Annual Conference of the IAUTE*, Renvyle.

GOLDSTEIN, M. and KHAN, M. S. (1978) 'The Supply and Demand for Exports: A Simultaneous Approach', *Review of Economics and Statistics*, 60, pp. 275–86.

HELLIWELL, J. F. and CHUNG, A. (1985) 'Aggregate Output with Operating Rates and Inventories as Buffers between Variable Final Demand and Quasi-Fixed Factors', National Bureau of Economic Research, Working Paper no. 1623.

HELLIWELL, J. *et al.* (1982) 'Stabilization, Allocation and the 1970's Oil Price Shocks', *Scandanavian Journal of Economics*, 84, no. 2, pp. 259–88.

HELLIWELL, J. *et al.* (1985) 'Aggregate Supply in INTERLINK: Model Specification and Empirical Results', Working Paper no. 26, Department of Economics and Statistics, OECD, Paris.

HONOHAN, P. (1982) 'Is Ireland a Small Open Economy?', *Administration*, 29, no. 4, pp. 356–75.

HUGHES, G. (1985) *Payroll Tax Incidence, the Direct Tax Burden and the Rate of Return on State Pension Contributions in Ireland*, (Dublin: Economic and Social Research Institute, paper no. 120).

KEENAN, G. (1981) 'Irish Migration: All or Nothing Resolved?', *The Economic and Social Review*, 12, no. 3, pp. 169–86.

LINDBECK, A. (1979) 'Imported and Structural Inflation and Aggregate Demand: The Scandinavian Model Reconstructed', in A. Lindbeck (ed.) *Inflation and Employment in Open Economies* (Amsterdam: North-Holland).

McCARTHY, C. (1979) 'The Impact of Job Creation on Unemployment and Emigration', *Quarterly Bulletin*, Central Bank of Ireland, no. 2, Summer.

NICKELL, S. J. (1984) 'The Modelling of Wages and Employment', Centre for Labour Economics, London School of Economics, Discussion Paper no. 187.

NICKELL, S. J. and ANDREWS, M. (1983) 'Unions, Real Wages and Employment in Britain 1951–79', *Oxford Economic Papers*, 35 (Supplement) pp. 183–206.

O'MALLEY, E. (1986) 'Foreign-Owned Industry in Ireland: Performance and Prospects', in P. Bacon (ed.) *Medium-Term Outlook* (Dublin: Economic and Social Research Institute).

ROSE, D. E. and SELODY, J. G. (1985) *The Structure of the Small Annual Model*, (Ottawa: Bank of Canada, Technical Report no. 40).

SMITH, B. D. (1986) 'Government Expenditures, Deficits, and Inflation: On the Impossibility of a Balanced Budget', *Quarterly Journal of Economics*, 100, pp. 715–45.

SMYTH, D. J. and McMAHON, P. C. (1975) 'Short-Run Employment Functions for Irish Manufacturing', *Economic and Social Review*, 6, no. 4, pp. 531–41.

VAN DE KLUNDERT, T. (1982) 'Distribution, Taxation and Employment in an Open Economy', *De Economist*, 130, no. 1, pp. 9–37.

# 15 Labour Market Flexibility: An Analysis with the DMS Model

Laurence Bloch

This chapter presents an analysis of labour market flexibility with the DMS model which is a dynamic macroeconomic multisectoral model of the French economy.[1]

This exercise is difficult, because the effects of a greater flexibility on the economy depend on mechanisms which are not all included in the current version of the model. It is sometimes necessary, therefore, to make additional assumptions on firms' behaviour. These assumptions may have no econometric justification but may be suggested by the economic analysis. Consequently, the results must be interpreted very carefully since they do not have the same robustness as those given by simulations where only exogenous variables are manipulated in the model. However, the exercise is of interest to demonstrate different ways in which greater flexibility of the labour market may affect macroeconomic aggregates, and give magnitudes and temporal profiles.

The focus is on only one aspect of labour-market flexibility: that being the adjustment of real wages to labour-market disequilibrium. There are many other examples both of flexibility, and of the labour market in existence. R. Boyer (1985), in a recent paper, notes five of them:

- insufficient adjustment of real wages to economic situation (this will be discussed later);
- insufficient adaptation of productive organisation (such as capacity utilisation);
- magnitude of juridical constraints on labour contracts;
- workers' inability to change work-station;
- importance of unfavourable social and fiscal contributions for business.

Adjustment of real wage rate and thence its decrease, in face of excess of supply in the labour market, can be justified in order to restore equilibrium in the two cases:

- within the framework of partial equilibrium; the restoration would be easier if the labour supply was sensitive to real wage and if the production function included substitutability of the factors;
- in the framework of general equilibrium, in a classical regime.

The DMS model has different options:

- the production function assumes complementarity of factors;
- the labour supply is not sensitive to real wage;
- in the short term the assumed regime is Keynesian: the production is determined by the demand and not by profitability.

However, it will be seen later:

- substitution between factors can be introduced by means of scrapping behaviour;
- furthermore, in the medium term, the regime is rather classical, being the result of the presence of supply effects in the model (for example, tensions on productive capacity in import and export functions) (see Figure 15.1).

Thus, the effects of a uniform decrease (1 per cent) of the *per capita* real gross wage depends on two crucial hypotheses concerning *exchange rate manipulation and firms' scrapping behaviour.* On one hand the exchange rate is assumed to be fixed (except when indicated to the contrary) in order to point out macroeconomic effects resulting from competitiveness. This assumption is supported by the fact that, between two monetary adjustments in the EMS, the country which is the less inflationary, benefits from competitive gains and is rather realistic at a time when price movements are not too large. On the other hand firms' scrapping is assumed to be sensitive to real wages (except when specified otherwise).

This behaviour which cannot be empirically observed, can be justified on theoretical grounds, however. Firms must have a scrapping behaviour so that only profitable equipment (i.e. that which has an hourly labour productivity superior to real hourly wage rate) is retained. Thus, the capacity margin (i.e. the age of the oldest installed equipment) is assumed to vary with the profitability margin (i.e. the age of the oldest profitable equipment) (Appendix no 1). As a result of this hypothesis some substitution between labour and capital may be introduced in the DMS model. Indeed the decrease in wage rate induces a slowing-down of the scrapping process and a consequent

*Figure* 15.1 Scheme of supply effects in the DMS model, induced by a decrease in the real wage

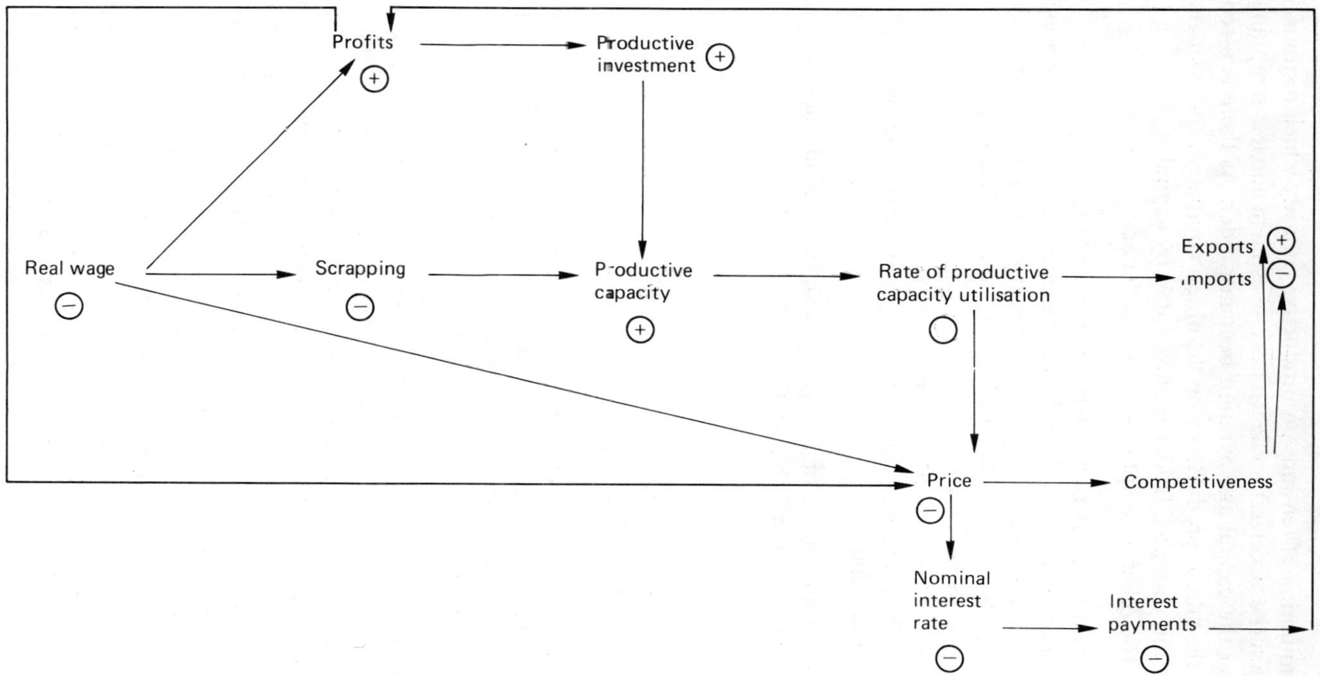

diminution of tensions on productive capacity which restrains investment (i.e. accelerator effect). Less investment and less scrapping imply that the capital age pyramid becomes older. As there is a reduction in the labour productivity on the oldest equipment and is smaller than on the youngest, labour is substituted by capital.

The other assumptions of the model are:

- real wages per employee are exogenous;
- *per capita* social benefits at constant prices are exogenous;
- potential deficits of Social Security are financed by additional employers' social contributions, additional workers' social contributions and income taxes;
- real monetary interest rate is exogenous;
- public deficit is financed half by monetary expansion and half by borrowing.

The results of the first variant which includes all these assumptions are presented in Table 15.1.

## FOR THE ENTERPRISES: EFFECTS ARE ALL FAVOURABLE

Decrease of real wage has positive supply effects coming from three directions (see Figure 15.1): slowing-down of the scrapping process, amelioration of profits, lowering of unit labour costs.

Decrease of real wage slows the scrapping process and in this way increases productive capacity. Thus, the first-year tensions in productive capacity diminish (−0.08 point in manufacturing industry). This increase of supply capacity has direct benefit effects to the external market. Moreover, it lowers domestic prices (added value price determination)[2] thereby increasing competitiveness and so improving external trade. However, in future years a larger demand, mainly in intermediate and investment goods, leads to the reappearance of tensions in spite of delayed scrapping.

Decrease of real wages induces a modification of the added value share in favour of profits and so increases investment with a delay of one year (profit effect). This investment then induces a rise in productive capacity and brings the supply mechanism of the DMS model into play. Moreover, the profit rate amelioration implies, with a delay of one year, a reduction in domestic prices (added value price determination).[3]

Decrease of real wages reduces unit labour costs and, therefore domestic prices (added value price determination).[4] Finally, price of GDP will be 0.9 per cent inferior to its reference, the first year, and 3.3 per cent inferior to the sixth year.

Finally (for the second time and indirectly) deflation permits the supply scheme to work. The lowering of prices induces a fall in nominal interest rates (hypothesis of real interest rate exogeneity); so enterprises' interest payments also reduce, causing profits to grow, and the supply mechanism is thereby amplified.

The decrease in domestic prices implies competitive gains in external markets, which, joined with the increase of supply capacity, allow a rise in the volume of exports particularly in intermediate and investment goods. During the following years the revival in exports continues to gain advantage from the competitive gains. Exports are 0.3 per cent superior to their reference the first year and 1.8 per cent superior to the sixth year.

The increase of the external demand, in industrial goods, and the improvement in firms' rentability, imply a growth in their investment (accelerator and profit effects) (it is 0.2 per cent superior to its reference the first year and 2 per cent in the sixth year).

## FOR HOUSEHOLDS: ALL THE EFFECTS ARE UNFAVOURABLE BUT THIS IS NOT THE CASE FOR THE NEWLY EMPLOYED

The 1 per cent decline in real wage for the employee implies a 0.8 per cent reduction in gross disposable income during the first year. Owing to a net rise in employment from the second year, this decrease would progressively reduce to 0.3 per cent at the end of the period. This reduction of households' purchasing power induces a lowering in residential construction investment and in consumption (−0.4 per cent the first year, −0.3 per cent the sixth year). It should be noted that the reduction in consumption would have been greater if households had not taken advantage of the increase in their real liquid assets (effect of inflation reduction).

## FOR THE NATIONAL ECONOMY: RESULTS ARE RATHER FAVOURABLE

In the first year, exports replace the household demand. Combined with firms' investment, they generate an increase of net final demand,

*Table* 15.1 Variant 1 Decrease of real wage – real-wage-sensitive scrapping behaviour – fixed exchange rate'

| | | *First year* | *Second year* | *Third year* | *Fourth year* | *Fifth year* | *Sixth year* | |
|---|---|---|---|---|---|---|---|---|
| $10^6$F | GDP | −45 592 | −77 836 | −101 161 | −126 876 | −154 273 | −183 065 | deviation |
| $10^6$F70 | GDPZ | −764 | −485 | 1 297 | 3 018 | 4 733 | 6 835 | deviation |
| $10^6$F70 | GDPMZ | −0.084 | −0.058 | 0.102 | 0.248 | 0.384 | 0.542 | relative deviation in % |
| $10^6$F70 | IMPOZT | −0.357 | −0.139 | 0.200 | 0.317 | 0.438 | 0.560 | relative deviation in % |
| $10^6$F70 | CMZPT | −0.356 | −0.575 | −0.483 | −0.410 | −0.340 | −0.274 | relative deviation in % |
| $10^6$F70 | IVEZPT | 0.159 | 0.868 | 1.370 | 1.641 | 1.848 | 2.038 | relative deviation in % |
| $10^6$F70 | EXPOZT | 0.338 | 0.687 | 0.974 | 1.260 | 1.494 | 1.703 | relative deviation in % |
| $10^6$F70 | STOTZT | −172 | 482 | 899 | 821 | 826 | 879 | deviation |
| | PCOM | −0.73 | −1.28 | −1.72 | −2.11 | −2.44 | −2.75 | relative deviation in % |
| | PGDP | −0.93 | −1.57 | −2.07 | −2.52 | −2.90 | −3.25 | relative deviation in % |
| | PSS | −0.08 | −0.07 | −0.07 | −0.08 | −0.09 | −0.11 | relative deviation in % |
| | SBR | −0.98 | −0.96 | −0.95 | −0.94 | −0.93 | −0.93 | relative deviation in % |
| | RDM | −0.82 | −0.68 | −0.59 | −0.50 | −0.42 | −0.32 | relative deviation in % |
| Thousand | PDRE | −0.8 | −6.2 | −15.1 | −24.5 | −33.8 | −44.1 | deviation |
| Thousand | EMPTBT | −1.5 | 2.5 | 13.1 | 25.8 | 39.4 | 55.2 | deviation |
| Thousand | EMPTBI | 4.9 | 15.4 | 27.4 | 38.5 | 48.7 | 57.8 | deviation |
| Point | TUI | −0.079 | 0.033 | 0.102 | 0.098 | 0.120 | 0.130 | deviation |

| | | | | | | | | |
|---|---|---|---|---|---|---|---|---|
| Point of GDP | BFE | −0.28 | −0.12 | −0.08 | −0.03 | 0.00 | 0.03 | deviation |
| | BFN | −0.04 | −0.03 | −0.03 | −0.04 | −0.04 | −0.05 | |
| | BFF | 0.06 | 0.12 | 0.14 | 0.17 | 0.18 | 0.21 | |
| | BFG | −0.14 | −0.09 | −0.10 | −0.15 | −0.17 | −0.19 | |
| | BFM | 0.31 | 0.05 | 0.04 | 0.03 | 0.03 | 0.04 | |
| | BFX | −0.09 | −0.08 | −0.02 | −0.01 | 0.01 | 0.03 | |
| | BALANS | 4.0 | 3.4 | 0.5 | −0.0 | −0.9 | −2.2 | |
| Billions of Francs | DOL | 0.0 | 0.0 | 0.0 | 0.0 | 0.0 | 0.0 | relative deviation in % |
| | MAR | 0.0 | 0.0 | 0.0 | 0.0 | 0.0 | 0.0 | |
| Point of GDP | PRE | 0.102 | 0.040 | 0.009 | 0.018 | −0.004 | −0.019 | deviation |

*Glossary of variables*

| | |
|---|---|
| Z | means in 'volume' (or in F 70) |
| GDPZ | Gross Domestic Product |
| GDPMZ | Market Gross Domestic Product |
| IMPOZT | Imports |
| CMZPT | Households' consumption |
| IVEZPT | Enterprises' investment |
| EXPOZT | Exports |
| STOTZT | Change of inventories |
| PCOM | Consumption price |
| PGDP | GDP price |
| PSS | Purchasing power of social benefits |
| SBR | Purchasing power of *per capita* gross wage |
| RDM | Purchasing power of households |
| PDRE | Unemployment (International Labour Bureau definition) |
| EMPTBT | Total employment |
| EMPTBI | Employment in manufacturing industry |
| TUI | Rate of capacity utilisation in manufacturing industry |
| BFE | Net financing capacity requirement of enterprises (minus public sector) |
| BFN | Net financing capacity requirement of public sector |
| BFG | Net financing capacity requirement of administrations |
| BFM | Net financing capacity requirement of households |
| BFX | Net financing capacity requirement of nation |
| BALANS | Goods and services balance |
| DOL | Value of $ in francs |
| MAR | Value of mark in francs |
| PRE | Compulsory taxes |

particularly in intermediate and consumption goods. Finally after a 0.08 per cent decrease the first year, the market GDP (in volume) rises to a higher level than that of its reference (from the third year), and is still 0.5 per cent superior in the sixth year (see Table 15.1 and Figure 15.2.)

*Figure* 15.2 Variant 1: 'Decrease of 1 per cent of the *per capita* real gross wage - fixed exchange rate - rate-wage-sensitive scrapping behaviour'

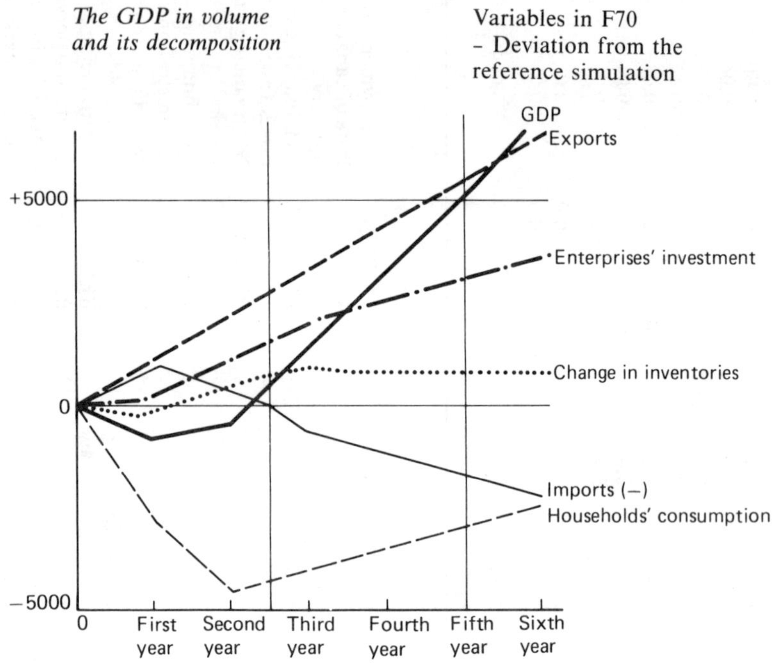


Finally and in spite of the adjustment delays, employment in manufacturing industry increases from the first year, due to utilisation of relatively older capital. However, in total, it diminishes by 1500 in the first year, and is 55 000 above its reference in the sixth year. Thus it corresponds to an *ex post* medium-term elasticity to real wage rate of −0.27. This result induces 0.03 per cent reduction of unemployment in the first year and a 1.5 per cent reduction by the sixth year (see Table 15.2). Indeed, new jobs in industry are mainly responsible for the decrease of unemployment because for such jobs 'the discouraged worker effect' is rather small (see Appendix no. 5).

*Table* 15.2 Employment and unemployment

| *Deviation (in thousands) from the reference* | *First year* | *Second year* | *Third year* | *Fourth year* | *Fifth year* | *Sixth year* |
|---|---|---|---|---|---|---|
| Total employment | −2 | 3 | 13 | 26 | 39 | 55 |
| Employment in the manufacturing industry | 5 | 15 | 27 | 39 | 49 | 58 |
| *Ex post* elasticity of employment to real wage rate | +0.01 | −0.01 | −0.06 | −0.13 | −0.19 | −0.27 |
| Unemployment | −1 | −6 | −15 | −25 | −34 | −44 |
| (∗) | −0.03% | −0.23% | −0.55% | −0.87% | −1.18% | −1.52% |

(∗) relative deviation in percent.

## OTHER LESS FAVOURABLE CONDITIONS

If it is assumed that scrapping behaviour from enterprises is invariant with profitability various simulations can be performed. A new path in the supply diagram of Figure 15.1 can be selected. In comparison with variant 1 (cf. Figure 15.2) the new path differs in the following respects:

- less supply capacity
- less competitive gains.[5,6]

Exports and enterprises' investment take a longer time than in the first variant to offset the reduction of households' consumption in order to assure the revival of growth. Moreover, invariant scrapping behaviour implies no substitution between the two factors.

If it is assumed that exchange rate is flexible,[7] an assumption which *a priori* seems to be in accordance with periodical monetary adjustments in the EMS, the gains in terms of reduction of inflation can be used to re-evaluate the franc rather than to obtain competitive gains. Only the rise in capacity supply may permit an increase in exports and a decrease in imports.

*Table* 15.3 Main macroeconomic effects of a 1 per cent decrease in real wage rate

| | *Sensitive to real wage scrapping behaviour* | | *Invariant scrapping behaviour* | |
|---|---|---|---|---|
| *At the sixth year in deviation from the reference* | *Fixed exchange rate* | *Flexible exchange rate* | *Fixed exchange rate* | *Flexible exchange rate* |
| Market GDP (in volume) | 0.54% | 0.17% | 0.17% | <0 |
| Ex post elasticity of employment to real wage rate | −0.27 | −0.04 | −0.03 | >0 |
| Unemployment | −44 thousands (−1.53%) | −14 thousands (−0.47%) | −15 thousands (−0.53%) | >0 |

Finally, Table 15.3 summarises the macroeconomic effects of a 1 per cent decrease in the real wage rate.

## CONCLUSION

Some conclusions can now be drawn from this exercise. In spite of the apparently unfavourable structure of the model (Keynesian model, insensitivity to real wage of labour supply, complementarity of production factors) it appears that a larger flexibility in labour market concerning real wage adjustment may, in the medium term, have favourable but limited effects on unemployment, compared with its reference level. However, these relatively good effects can only be obtained if a decrease in wages is combined with an increase in capacity, and if they are amplified by supply mechanisms. Thus they are extremely dependent on hypotheses or evaluations such as those concerning:

- firms' scrapping behaviour;
- firms' price-setting behaviour (repercussion of the decrease of wage costs on prices);
- profit effect in the investment function;
- tensions on productive capacity in export and import functions.

Finally supply effects might be larger if wages adjust to the individual situation of each firm, instead of to the labour market situation.

## Appendix 15.1 General Characteristics of the DMS (Dynamic Multi-Sectoral) Model (see Fouquet *et al.*, 1978, DMS4)

The principal characteristics of the DMS model are:

- field: general macroeconomic model of the French economy;
- model: dynamic;
- periodicity: annual;
- term: medium-term;
- way of utilisation: simulation;
- scale: about 3000 equations, 2600 being behavioural equations;
- exogenous variables: about 500 exogenous variables; they concern international environment, monetary fiscal and budget policy, demographic variables and some elements of the agriculture account and input–output matrix;
- way of determination of behavioural relations: econometric model, estimated mainly by ordinary least squares using annual series covering the period 1959–83 or 1959–84;
- statistical sources: generally National Accounts Series (base 1971).

The DMS Model distinguishes six institutional sectors:

- non-financial enterprises (less GEN);
- great national enterprises (GEN: Public sector);
- households;
- administrations;
- financial and insurance institutions;
- rest of the world.

Only the two first institutional sectors are disaggregated. The productive system is decomposed into twelve products and thirteen branches:

1 agriculture;
2 food industries;
3 energy;
4 manufacturing: intermediate goods;
5 manufacturing: investment goods;
6 manufacturing: consumer goods;
7 construction;
8 transport and communication;
9 housing services;
10 other non-financial services;
11 trade;
12 financial and insurances;
13 non-market services.

## Appendix 15.2 General Structure of the Model (see Fouquet *et al.*, 1978, DMS4)

Given the demand by commodities, gross output by branch is determined through an input–output table. Then employment + capital are obtained through actual production. The capacity utilisation is obtained through actual production and capacity – which is reliant on past investments and capacity margin. Then wage rates and prices are derived from unit labour costs and capacity utilisation. The calculation of complete accounts for institutional sectors and subsectors determines households' disposable income and business profits which together with prices are the main explanatory variables of demand determination.

The DMS describes financial accounts of the different sectors. The principal financial variables (for example, monetary rate) determine interest payments and receipts but at the present moment, has no direct influence on the main behavioural equations (investment, consumption, etc.).

### *An important economic mechanism: capital accumulation dynamics*

DMS, being a medium-term model, is crucially concerned with the process of capital accumulation (particularly in the areas of industry and construction) which determines the evolution of supply capacity and therefore has a strong influence on medium-term growth (and even on the short-term equilibrium, through the external trade relations and the mechanisms of market-sharing between French and foreign producers).

Although it neglects important features of the model (such as the productivity cycle, foreign trade, etc.) and only describes the behaviour in industrial and construction enterprises, Figure 15.A.1 is useful for an understanding of the mechanisms of the model.

Figure 15.A.1 is based upon the twofold nature of capital, which is both an investment and a factor of production. Two important endogenous variables of DMS, that of the profit rate and the capacity utilisation, correspond to these two aspects. The two relations determining capital accumulation and prices reflect the dual role of capital as they both include as explanatory variables the profit rate and the capacity utilisation.

The influence of the profit rate (which is almost always lagged in the reactions so far discussed) can be summarised as follows: a decrease of profit rates, and therefore of self-financing capacities, entails a decrease of investment and an increase in prices, which are the two main ways for firms to restore profitability (price increases of course being much more efficient in the short run). Both have a deflationary impact on real output.

Similarly, the capacity utilisation influences both investment and prices. Excess capacity tends to reduce investment, through a flexible accelerator mechanism, and reduces the rate of growth of prices. The two effects have stabilising consequences on capacity utilisation.

## **Appendix 15.3 Production Functions and Scrapping Behaviour in DMS** (see Fouquet *et al.*, 1978, DMS4)

### *The production function*

In each of the industrial branches (Appendix 15.1, nos 2, 4, 5, 6) and in the construction branch no. 7, the production functions are derived from a clay-clay vintage model including a formalisation of the productivity cycle.

*Figure* 15.A.1 Real and nominal dynamics of accumulation in industry and construction

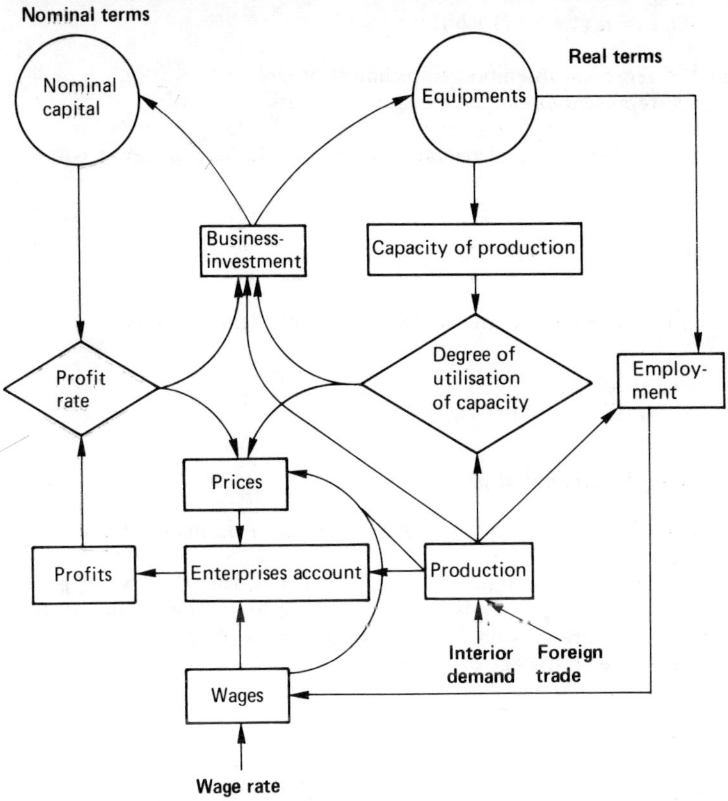


- $C(t, v)$ capacity of production at the date $t$ of installed equipment at the date $v$
- $\lambda(t, v)\mu(t, v)$ hourly productivity of the equipment at the date $v$
- $E(t, v)$ installed equipment at the date $v$, in life at the date $t$
- $N(t, v)$ employment at the date $t$ on installed equipment at the date $v$
- $DHC_t$ $DH_t$ average duration of utilisation of equipment and weekly duration of labour at the year $t$

The hypothesis of *ex post* complementarity for each generation can be written:

$$C(t, v) = \lambda(t, v) DHC_t E(t, v) = \mu(t, v) DH_t N(t, v).$$

It can be assumed that:

$$\lambda(t, v) = \alpha(1+a)^t(1+b)^v$$

$$\mu(t, v) = \alpha'(1+a')^t(1+b')^v$$

$a$ and $a'$ represent disembodied technical progress
$b$ and $b'$ represent embodied technical progress

The satisfaction of actual demand $Q_t$ implies the use of newer equipment than $me_t$:

$$Q_t = \sum_{v=t-me_t}^{t-1} \lambda(t, v)DHC_t E(t, v).$$

The desired employment in order to satisfy this demand $Q_t$ is:

$$N_t^* = \sum_{v=t-me_t}^{t-1} \frac{\lambda(t, v)DHC_t}{\mu(t, v)DH_t} E(t, v).$$

### *Scrapping behaviour of firms*

The hourly productivity of labour at the date $t$ on installed equipment at the date $t-v$ is $\mu(t, t-v)$.

The wage-earning sum (at constant prices) is measured by $N \cdot (w/p)$ where $w$ is the hourly wage and $p$ is the price of the output. The quasi-rents for the capital owners are measured by the superior part of the shaded rectangles. They decline with the age of equipment.

*Figure* 15.A.2 Scrapping behaviour of firms

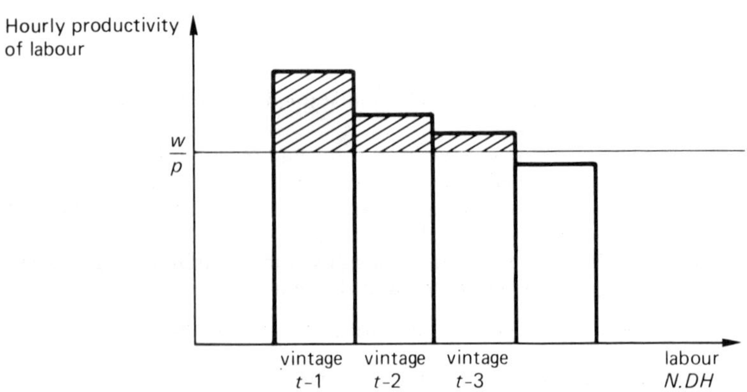

The profitability margin *mr* is the age of the oldest profitable machine:

$\mu(t, t-mr)=\frac{w}{p}$ (the rate of rentability is equal to 1).

Then three notions of capital appear:

- the profitable capital: it is all the equipment, having positive or zero quasi-rents; the margin (profitability margin) is the age of the oldest equipment which is profitable *mr*;
- the capital physically in existence: the margin (capacity margin) is the age of the oldest equipment which is physically in existence *mc*;
- the capital which is actually in use in order to produce $Q_t$; the margin (effective margin) is the age of the oldest equipment in use *me*.

For the present study two alternative hypotheses have been chosen:

1. each year the capacity margin varies with the profitability margin

$$mc_t=\tfrac{2}{3}mc_{t-1}+\tfrac{1}{2}mr_t.$$

The adjustment of the capacity margin to the profitability margin is progressive.

2. the capacity margin is exogenous and $mc_t \leqslant mr_t$. A marginal variation of *mr* has no influence on *mc*.

## Appendix 15.4 Productivity Cycle and Adjustment Mean Lag

The productivity cycle can be written:

$$\frac{N_t}{N_{t-1}}=\left(\frac{N_t^*}{N_{t-1}}\right)^{\lambda} \qquad 0<\lambda<1.$$

The justification for the productivity cycle is as follows. The firm does not instantaneously achieve the desired variation of its employments because of:

- administrative constraints
- formation costs, lay-off or hiring costs
- a kind of rigidity of labour market or mismatch between engaged employees and desired qualifications

The mean lag of adjustment is equal to $(1-\lambda)/\lambda$

## Appendix 15.5 The Determination of Unemployment in DMS (see Fouquet *et al.*, 1978, DMS4)

Unemployment derives from the confrontation between the labour demand of firms and the labour supply of households. The labour supply is calculated from the demographic evolution by age group and from the determination of labour-force participation rates by age group. The changes in labour-force participation rates depend partly on long-term trends (development of education, changes in women's labour participation, change in the age of retirement), and partly on the short-run business cycle. During a period of employment growth, a potential labour force enters the labour market, thus increasing labour-force participation (discouraged-worker effect).

The specification in the DMS model is:*

$$\Delta(PDRE - PDREO) = 0.57\Delta(POPACO - PDREO - EMP1) \\ -0.79\Delta EMPI \\ -0.42\Delta EMPTER$$

| | |
|---|---|
| *PDRE*: | unemployment |
| *PDREO*: | reference (in a normal cycle) unemployment |
| *POPACO*: | tendencial labour participating population |
| *EMP*1: | agricultural employment |
| *EMPI*: | secondary employment (Appendix 15.1, branches no. 2, 3, 4, 5, 6, 7) |
| *EMPTER*: | tertiary employment (Appendix 15.1, branches no. 8, 9, 10, 12, 13) |

Every 100 new occupations in the secondary sector will reduce unemployment by 79 people; every 100 new occupations in the tertiary sector will reduce the unemployment by only 42 people. A part of the new occupations are given to people entering the labour market at this time.

* $\Delta X_t = X_t - X_{t-1}$

## Appendix 15.6 The Determination of Prices in DMS (see Fouquet *et al.*, 1978, DMS4)

### *Added value prices*

Added-value price equations are theoretically derived by firms' profit maximisation in monopolistic situations. For given demand and production functions, prices will depend on marginal cost.

Thus the retained-price equations in the model explain the growth rate of added-value price by:

- growth rate of unit labour cost: firms will recover their wage costs through their prices;
- pressure of demand on supply;
- the time delay in profit rate; if profit rate is low, enterprises will increase their prices in order to restore their profit.

### *Export or import prices*

The growth rate of external price is determined by both the growth rate of production price on the national market and the growth rate of production price of the foreign competitors.

## Appendix 15.7

*Table* 15.A.1 Variant 2 'Decrease in real wage – invariant scrapping behaviour – fixed exchange rate' (see glossary of variables)

| | | *First year* | *Second year* | *Third year* | *Fourth year* | *Fifth year* | *Sixth year* | |
|---|---|---|---|---|---|---|---|---|
| $10^6$F | GDP | −42 240 | −68 915 | −86 050 | −105 496 | −126 633 | −149 529 | deviation |
| $10^6$F70 | GDPZ | −1 571 | −2 252 | −1 326 | −463 | 655 | 2 239 | deviation |
| $10^6$F70 | GDPMZ | −0.159 | −0.219 | −0.131 | −0.053 | 0.042 | 0.169 | relative deviation in % |
| $10^6$F70 | IMPOZT | −0.326 | −0.217 | 0.053 | 0.124 | 0.229 | 0.367 | relative deviation in % |
| $10^6$F70 | CMZPT | −0.376 | −0.632 | −0.580 | −0.547 | −0.509 | −0.470 | relative deviation in % |
| $10^6$F70 | IVEZPT | 0.185 | 0.683 | 1.059 | 1.264 | 1.445 | 1.670 | relative deviation in % |
| $10^6$F70 | EXPOZT | 0.196 | 0.392 | 0.554 | 0.723 | 0.899 | 1.078 | relative deviation in % |
| $10^6$F70 | STOTZT | −306 | 202 | 581 | 486 | 564 | 666 | deviation |
| | PCOM | −0.62 | −1.02 | −1.31 | −1.57 | −1.81 | −2.05 | relative deviation in % |
| | PPIB | −0.79 | −1.24 | −1.57 | −1.87 | −2.14 | −2.41 | relative deviation in % |
| | PSS | −0.08 | −0.07 | −0.07 | −0.07 | −0.08 | −0.09 | relative deviation in % |
| | SBR | −0.98 | −0.97 | −0.96 | −0.96 | −0.95 | −0.95 | relative deviation in % |
| | RDM | −0.82 | −0.71 | −0.67 | −0.63 | −0.59 | −0.52 | relative deviation in % |

**Appendix 15.7** – *Table* 15.A.1 (*continued*)

| | | *First year* | *Second year* | *Third year* | *Fourth year* | *Fifth year* | *Sixth year* | |
|---|---|---|---|---|---|---|---|---|
| Thousand | PDRE | 2.3 | 2.3 | −0.7 | −4.2 | −8.6 | −15.2 | deviation |
| | EMPTBT | −6.3 | −10.8 | −9.8 | −7.3 | −2.6 | 6.0 | |
| | EMPTBI | 1.2 | 5.7 | 11.5 | 16.6 | 21.9 | 27.4 | |
| Point | TUI | 0.059 | 0.195 | 0.258 | 0.254 | 0.249 | 0.248 | |
| Point of GDP | BFE | −0.26 | −0.12 | −0.09 | −0.05 | −0.04 | −0.02 | |
| | BFN | −0.04 | −0.03 | −0.02 | −0.02 | −0.03 | −0.03 | |
| | BFF | 0.05 | 0.09 | 0.10 | 0.12 | 0.14 | 0.16 | |
| | BFG | −0.12 | −0.06 | −0.05 | −0.08 | −0.10 | −0.12 | |
| | BFM | 0.30 | 0.04 | 0.03 | 0.02 | 0.02 | 0.03 | |
| | BFX | −0.08 | −0.08 | −0.03 | −0.02 | −0.01 | 0.02 | |
| | BALANS | 3.4 | 3.3 | 0.8 | 0.5 | −0.3 | −1.7 | |
| Billions of Francs | DOL | 0.0 | 0.0 | 0.0 | 0.0 | 0.0 | 0.0 | relative deviation in % |
| | MAR | 0.0 | 0.0 | 0.0 | 0.0 | 0.0 | 0.0 | |
| Point of GDP | PRE | 0.110 | 0.068 | 0.049 | 0.066 | 0.048 | 0.036 | deviation |

*Table* 15.A.2 Variant 3 'Decrease in real wage – real-wage-sensitive scrapping behaviour – flexible exchange rate' (see glossary of variables)

| | | *First year* | *Second year* | *Third year* | *Fourth year* | *Fifth year* | *Sixth year* | |
|---|---|---|---|---|---|---|---|---|
| $10^6$F | GDP | −56 782 | −110 912 | −165 878 | −235 173 | −320 422 | −425 244 | deviation |
| $10^6$F70 | GDPZ | −1 747 | −2 440 | −1 390 | −428 | 614 | 2 304 | deviation |
| | GDPMZ | −0.176 | −0.237 | −0.139 | −0.053 | 0.034 | 0.168 | relative deviation in % |
| | IMPOZT | −0.636 | −0.580 | −0.261 | −0.166 | −0.055 | 0.095 | relative deviation in % |
| $10^6$F70 | CMZPT | −0.351 | −0.556 | −0.445 | −0.341 | −0.232 | −0.102 | relative deviation in % |
| | IVEZPT | −0.149 | 0.221 | 0.631 | 0.870 | 1.073 | 1.301 | relative deviation in % |
| | EXPOZT | 0.057 | 0.127 | 0.174 | 0.211 | 0.227 | 0.242 | relative deviation in % |
| | STOTZT | −693 | −172 | 319 | 222 | 217 | 293 | deviation |
| | PCOM | −0.95 | −1.93 | −2.93 | −4.01 | −5.12 | −6.35 | relative deviation in % |
| | PGDP | −1.10 | −2.09 | −3.11 | −4.21 | −5.34 | −4.57 | relative deviation in % |
| | PSS | −0.06 | −0.03 | −0.00 | 0.01 | 0.03 | 0.03 | relative deviation in % |
| | SBR | −0.98 | −0.97 | −0.96 | −0.95 | −0.94 | −0.93 | relative deviation in % |
| | RDM | −0.85 | −0.74 | −0.66 | −0.57 | −0.48 | −0.33 | relative deviation in % |

**Appendix 15.7** – *Table* 15.A.2 (*continued*)

| | | *First year* | *Second year* | *Third year* | *Fourth year* | *Fifth year* | *Sixth year* | |
|---|---|---|---|---|---|---|---|---|
| Thousand | PDRE | 3.6 | 4.5 | 1.5 | −2.5 | −6.9 | −13.6 | deviation |
| | EMPTBT | −8.0 | −13.5 | −11.9 | −7.8 | −1.9 | 8.2 | |
| | EMPTBI | −0.2 | 2.9 | 8.2 | 12.8 | 16.7 | 20.6 | |
| Point | TUI | −0.298 | −0.335 | −0.310 | −0.349 | −0.344 | −0.349 | |
| Point of GDP | BFE | −0.32 | −0.24 | −0.22 | −0.18 | −0.17 | −0.16 | |
| | BFN | −0.05 | −0.06 | −0.07 | −0.09 | −0.11 | −0.14 | |
| | BFF | 0.05 | 0.12 | 0.19 | 0.26 | 0.34 | 0.44 | |
| | BFG | −0.16 | −0.10 | −0.11 | −0.17 | −0.20 | −0.24 | |
| | BFM | 0.33 | 0.09 | 0.10 | 0.10 | 0.11 | 0.13 | |
| | BFX | −0.15 | −0.18 | −0.12 | −0.08 | −0.04 | 0.02 | |
| | BALANS | 6.3 | 6.9 | 3.8 | 3.1 | 1.6 | −0.8 | |
| Billions of Francs | DOL | −0.89 | −1.91 | −2.92 | −4.03 | −5.17 | −6.39 | relative deviation in % |
| | MAR | −0.89 | −1.91 | −2.92 | −4.03 | −5.17 | −6.39 | |
| Point of GDP | PRE | 0.121 | 0.041 | 0.001 | 0.010 | −0.019 | −0.039 | deviation |

## Notes

1. See Appendixes for the description of the DMS model.
2. See Appendix 15.6.
3. Ibid.
4. Ibid.
5. See Appendix 15.1.
6. See Appendix 15.7.
7. Ibid.

## References

BOYER, R. (1985) 'Flexibilité des marchés du travail . . . et/ou recherche d'un nouveau rapport salarial', *Cahiers du CEPREMAP*, September, 1985.

CETTE, G., DURAND, B. and TYL, T. (1986) 'Réorganiser le travail: une solution pour l'emploi?', *Economie et Statistique*, no 184, January, 1986.

CEZARD, M. and RAULT, D. (1986) 'La crise a freiné la mobilité sectorielle', *Economie et Statistique*, no 184, January, 1986.

FOUQUET, D., CHARPIN, J. M., GUILLAUME, H., MUET, P. A. and VALLET, D. (1978) 'DMS, modèle dynamique multisectoriel', *Les Collections de l'INSEE*, no C 64–65.

OFCE (1986) 'La suppression de l'autorisation administrative de licenciement: des emplois ou des chômeurs', *Lettre de l'OFCE*, no 31, 22 January 1986.

Service des Programmes (1987) 'DMS 4, modèle dynamique multisectoriel', *Les Collections de l'INSEE*, Série C, No. 139, Juillet 1987.

# COMMENT ON CHAPTERS 14 AND 15

**F. C. Palm**

It is a pleasure for me to act as a discussant of the papers by L. Bloch and by J. Bradley. I read their papers with much interest. The authors present the results of simulations using respectively a large and a medium size model. They analyse the impact of various policy measures aimed at reducing unemployment. The size and structure of the models are different but more interestingly, the policy measures considered are distinct in spirit and nature. Laurence Bloch's model of the French economy consists of some 3000 equations and includes theirteen sectors. The policy measures considered in her paper are concerned with enlarging the flexibility of the labour market by adjusting real wages to reduce unemployment. I like to characterise this as a classical policy applied to a Keynesian regime. John Bradley analyses the effects for the Irish economy of an increase of employment in the public sector financed either by foreign borrowing or by increases in taxes. This policy is Keynesian in spirit. His model is rather small and includes only three production sectors: industry, agriculture and services.

Both models are annual and cover the period from 1959/60 to 1983. Although the model for Ireland is highly aggregated, it is more sophisticated in some respects than the model for the French economy. For instance the technology of the industry sector is of vintage putty-clay CES-type whereas in the model for France most sectors are assumed to have a clay–clay vintage production function. For Ireland, wages are endogenous. In the DMS-model, wages are treated as a policy instrument.

Although the models are not completely listed in the papers, the most important causal links can be inferred from the information provided by the authors. I shall comment on some of the assumptions underlying the models and briefly discuss the significance of the outcome of the simulations.

Let me begin with the DMS-model for the French economy. Bloch assumes a regime of Keynesian unemployment. This means that production is determined by demand and that firms are rationed on the goods market. This assumption is probably plausible at least for most of the estimation period. Evidence on this point is given by, for example, Artus, Laroque and Michel (1984) who show that from 1974 on the French economy is in a regime of Keynesian unemployment with probability larger than 0.8. It is not clear what is meant by this assumption in a multisector model. Are firms of all sectors rationed on the commodity market? More importantly, the behaviour of the model seems to be in contradiction with the implications of a Keynesian regime. If firms are rationed on the commodity market, a decrease of real wages administered by the policy-maker will lead to higher profits. According to the model, increased profits imply investment and additional supply. But which incentive do firms have to react in this way as long as there is idle capacity, a characteristic of a Keynesian regime? The wage policy leads to a contraction of domestic consumption. It is not obvious that the increase of exports as a result of the improved competitiveness will be sufficient to compensate for the decrease of domestic demand. In fact, Figure 15.2 indicates that the expansion of exports is insufficient to compensate for the decrease of household consumption in the first and second year. Inventories increase as a result of the decrease of wages. One is naturally led to ask what the incentives are for business firms to expand production capacity - at least in the short-run - and to increase their inventories when the domestic demand by consumers decreases and the size of foreign demand appears to be uncertain as it is very sensitive to the behavior of importing countries (terms of trade, exchange rate).

One can also raise the question of what happens to the effects of a wage policy if there is a regime switch. Does the model allow for this? Of course, one may answer that a decrease of real wages is not likely to lead into classical unemployment. The economy, however, may end up in a regime of repressed inflation as consumer prices and nominal wages (see Table 15.1) decrease. I realise that it is difficult to model regime switches appropriately in a multisector model. Some further qualification of the simulation results however would be useful to the reader. Finally one may question the extent to which the real wage is a policy variable.

Concerning the simulation results, I would like to make the following comments. On the whole, the results are plausible. Unfortunately no information is given about the impact of the wage policy on employment at a sectoral level. The numerical value of the elasticity of employment with respect to real wages under a regime of fixed exchange rates −0.3 is in line with empirical findings for other countries. For the Netherlands, Magnus (1979) finds an elasticity for the labour demand of −0.3 for a translog cost function and Driehuis

(1979) finds a value of −0.33. The assessment of the employment elasticity for Belgium by Drèze and Modigliani (1981) is −0.2. Bradley finds a value of approximately −0.85 for the elasticity of labour demand in Ireland, which is quite high in absolute terms compared with the figures just mentioned.

It is also not surprising that the precision of the estimated elasticity is low. The value of the elasticity is highly sensitive to changes in the exchange-rate regime or in the scrapping behaviour. The lack of robustness with respect to these key assumptions underlying the model, for which there is an obvious economic explanation should warn the reader from drawing strong conclusions about the exact impact of a wage policy on the employment level. It also illustrates that the success of an employment policy very much depends on the broader economic context, in particular on the economic autonomy of a country with respect to its trading partners. Bradley is probably right in concluding 'that the isolated study of the labour market is at best unnecessarily limiting and, at worst, can be very misleading'.

An interesting feature of his model is that decisions on plant location and therefore on production capacity directly depend on the competitiveness of the Irish economy compared with the 'rest of the world'. In addition, price arbitrage modelled along the lines of the so-called Scandinavian model takes place in the tradeable sector. The large absolute value of the labour-demand elasticity for Ireland results from the high dependence of the Irish economy on the economic conditions in the rest of the world. The presence of a time-trend in the Irish share of marginal industrial-capacity output relative to that of the rest of the world, in my opinion, can be interpreted only as a local approximation. An extrapolation of the model over a longer time-horizon is expected to lead to nonsensical results. A similar remark applies to the employment equation in agriculture where a negative time-trend is included.

The assumption that the component of gross agricultural output which is exported abroad is determined in the supply block as the residual when domestic absorption is subtracted from total output, is not proof against strategic optimising behaviour, given that output prices are assumed to be exogenous. It is not likely that, independently of relative prices (domestic relative to foreign prices), it is always profitable to export the residual (and not less than that leading to inventory formation or more than that by increasing production). The size of this residual ought to depend on relative prices. The level of aggregation of the model is at a maximum given the differences in the behaviour of employment in the various sectors as illustrated in Figure 14.2.

The fixed exchange approach is somewhat questionable. As the balance of payments is negative (Figure 14.15) under any policy and in the light of the monetary financing of the part of the additional employment in the public sector, a change of the exchange rate might become necessary after some time.

The simulation results of the employment policy are fairly plausible. Basically there is a shift of jobs from the private to the public sector. The instability of the response over time is apparent but not very plausible. It is probably the result of a misspecification of the model. Unfortunately, Bradley does not give a rationale for this change in the pattern of the dynamics of the model.

To summarise, both authors are mainly concerned with the macroeconomic effects of the employment policies simulated in their papers. On the whole, the simulation results are plausible and in line with findings by other authors. The models themselves do not seem to be entirely proof against strategic behaviour and should therefore be interpreted as approximations that can be improved by refining their microeconomic foundations.

**References**

ARTUS, P., LAROQUE, G. and MICHEL, G. (1984) 'Estimation of a Quarterly Macroeconomic Model with Quantity Rationing', *Econometrica*, 52, pp. 1387–1413.

DRÈZE, J. and MODIGLIANI, F. (1981) 'The Trade-off between Real Wages and Employment in an Open Economy (Belgium)', *European Economic Review*, 15, pp. 1–40.

DRIEHUIS, W. (1979) 'An Analysis of Demand and Cost Factors on Employment', *De Economist*, 127, pp. 225–86.

MAGNUS, J. R. (1979) 'Substitution between Energy and Non-energy Inputs in the Netherlands 1950–1976', *International Economic Review*, 20, pp. 465–84.

# 16 Wage Flexibility and Labour Market*

Bernard Compaijen and Klaas A. Springer

## 16.1 INTRODUCTION

It is a well-documented fact that the OECD-area can be dichotomised as far as employment trends and unemployment figures in the last fifteen years are concerned. On the one hand we have the USA and Japan, both countries with increasing employment and relatively contained unemployment rates. On the other we have the European countries, many of them with a stagnating employment development and mounting unemployment rates, sometimes into two digits. There is lack of consent on the causes of this malfunctioning of the labour market. In principle, two main weaknesses of the labour-market mechanism can be mentioned. Starting from labour-market equilibrium, we can imagine the occurrence of an exogenous shock, disturbing the initial equilibrium position. The adjustment to a new equilibrium may be hindered or retarded by imperfect quantity flexibility and/or imperfect price (i.e. wage) flexibility.

The first cause of labour-market failure, fast wage adjustment with slow quantity adjustment, is stressed by equilibrium economists. Reduced quantity flexibility is presumably a main cause of the increase in the so-called natural rate of unemployment. But why not switch emphasis from the one cause to the other? Perhaps the problem does not lie so much with quantity, as with price adjustment. Rigidity of wages may prevent the labour market from clearing. This line of research is proposed by economists as Malinvaud (1977, 1984) and Okun (1981).

We do not deny that there may be some room for improving quantity flexibility of the labour market, but in this chapter we shall concentrate upon wage flexibility, or its inverse, wage rigidity. We shall begin (in section 16.2) with a survey of several measures of wage flexibility. In

* *Acknowledgement.* This paper contains some of the results of a research project financed by the Organisation for Strategic Labour Market Research (Organisatie voor Strategisch Arbeidsmarktonderzoek (OSA)) in The Hague. The authors wish to thank the OSA for its financial support.

section 16.3 we shall present computations and estimations in order to make rankings of different OECD-countries (the various comparisons always include the Netherlands) as to several measures of wage flexibility. Moreover, we shall investigate if there is a relationship between wage flexibility and recorded employment or unemployment development. In section 16.4 we shall introduce our preferred concept of wage flexibility, which can be regarded as a logical extension of the existing measures. The chapter ends with a summarising and concluding section.

## 16.2 A SURVEY OF VARIOUS MEASURES OF WAGE FLEXIBILITY PROPOSED

### Standard Deviation of Wage Changes *versus* Employment Changes

Gordon (1982) argues that the hypothesis of market-clearing as opposed to disequilibrium requires a large variability of wages relative to the variability of employment. He presents as a measure of wage flexibility, the standard deviation of the percentage change of nominal-wage rates divided by the standard deviation of the percentage change of employment. Employment is measured in either man-weeks or total hours worked. The ratios show us, certainly in international comparison, whether the one country relies more heavily on the price mechanism and the other on the quantity mechanism.

### Real Wage Gap

A second measure of wage flexibility is Sachs's real wage gap (Sachs, 1983; also Bruno and Sachs, 1985). The real wage gap is intended to measure the percentage deviation of the actual wage level from its equilibrium level. To overcome the lack of statistical data on equilibrium wage rates Sachs proceeds as follows:

Calculate the real product wage $W/P_v$. Also calculate average labour productivity $(V/L)^f$, adjusted for cyclical variation. This can be done by assuming constant exponential growth between certain peak years (1960, 1973, 1979). The ratio of the two is a measure of the wage share of income.

The next step is to find an expression for the 'equilibrium' wage share. Sachs takes the period 1965–9 as being on the average representative for equilibrium, i.e. full employment. Call $\alpha^*$ the equilibrium wage share. Assuming a Cobb–Douglas technology and the usual profit-maximising behaviour, the ratio of the actual wage share and its equilibrium value ($[W/P_v]/[\alpha^*(V/L)^f]$) can be interpreted as the real product wage relative to the equilibrium wage rate. This ratio minus 1 is the real wage gap.[1] When the percentage change of the real product wage exceeds the growth of (full-employment) labour-productivity the real wage gap widens and vice versa.

## Labour Market Influences: the Phillips-Curve

Suppose there is a real wage gap. We can then ask if there is a mechanism that brings the wage rate back to its equilibrium level. The self-regulating power of the labour market is a phenomenon that is incorporated in the traditional Phillips-curve and its expectations-augmented variant. With excess capacity on the labour market being represented by the unemployment rate, one only needs to measure the strength of the influence of the labour-market disequilibrium on wage formation. Grubb, Jackman and Layard (GJL) argue in their 1983 article that $\beta$, the coefficient of the unemployment rate in a linear Phillips-curve, can be used as a measure of *real wage flexibility* and its inverse $1/\beta$ as a measure of *real wage rigidity.*

Apart from a measure of real wage rigidity GJL also construct a measure of *nominal* wage rigidity. With this measure account is taken of lags in the process of wage formation and/or price formation. Nominal wage rigidity is defined as real wage rigidity multiplied by the (total) average lag in the wage and price equations. Thus nominal wage rigidity is an expression of nominal inertia.

Real wage rigidity and nominal wage rigidity can go together, but do not need to. An attractive property of GJL's distinction is that it enables us to measure wage rigidity in two dimensions, the one referring to the labour-market mechanism and the other one also taking into account the amount of nominal inertia in the system. Nevertheless, it is at the same time somewhat misleading. With wages lagging behind prices the inflationary consequences of a real shock make for an adjustment of real wages towards their equilibrium level. Thus, a high nominal wage rigidity may entail real wage **flexibility** even without the labour market functioning as a servo mechanism i.e. $\beta = 0$. As a matter of fact, there are two correction mechanisms. The (partial) response of wages to the labour-market situation and the retarded or limited response of wages to inflation. Both mechanisms influence real wages.

**Sectoral Wage Dispersion**

Until now we have concentrated on macroeconomic wage flexibility. We can also have a look at mesoeconomic wage flexibility. The main tool of analysis is the coefficient of variation of sectoral wage rates. Compare OECD (1985). This tool enables us to compare the extent and development of sectoral wage differences for a number of countries. To the international comparison of macroeconomic and mesoeconomic flexibility we turn in the next section.

## 16.3 INTERNATIONAL COMPARISON OF WAGE FLEXIBILITY: ECONOMETRIC RESULTS

A number of possible measures of wage flexibility were discussed in section 16.2. Below we shall present some computational results for these measures in order to attain insight into the relative positions of the national labour markets with respect to their degree of wage flexibility. This analysis is restricted to annual data for a number of OECD member countries which can reasonably be compared with the Netherlands.

In Table 16.1 **coefficients of variation** of percentage annual rates of change of average hourly earnings in the manufacturing sector, of real hourly earnings and of annual unemployment rates are given for two periods. The coefficient of variation is used instead of the standard deviation, because with percentage changes (or rates) the mean and the standard deviation may be positively correlated.

The ratios in columns 4 and 5 of this table can be interpreted as crude measures of nominal and real wage flexibility respectively. For if wages vary strongly relative to the unemployment rate, this intuitively points to flexibility. However, because there is no reference to an equilibrium position these ratios could be more properly considered as measures of wage variability. Looking at the results in Table 16.1, the high nominal and real wage variability in Japan for both periods is striking. The ratios for the Netherlands do not deviate much from those for Belgium, France and Germany. Apparently Sweden, the UK and the USA differ rather strongly from the remaining countries regarding their degree of real wage variability. The very low average rate of growth of real hourly earnings in these countries (US: a decline of 0.3 per cent annually) in the period 1973–83 accounts for this result.

*Table* 16.1 Coefficients of variation for two periods

| | (1) $\sigma_{\dot{w}}/\bar{\dot{w}}$ | | (2) $\sigma_{\dot{w}-\dot{p}}/\overline{\dot{w}-\dot{p}}$ | | (3) $\sigma_U/\bar{U}$ | | (4) (1)/(3) | | (5) (2)/(3) | |
|---|---|---|---|---|---|---|---|---|---|---|
| | *1960–73* | *1973–83* | *1960–73* | *1973–83* | *1960–73* | *1973–83* | *1960–73* | *1973–83* | *1960–73* | *1973–83* |
| Austria | 0.3 | 0.5 | 0.4 | 1.1 | 0.2 | 0.4 | 1.5 | 1.3 | 2.0 | 2.8 |
| Belgium | 0.4 | 0.5 | 0.4 | 1.5 | 0.2 | 0.4 | 2.0 | 1.3 | 2.0 | 3.8 |
| France | 0.3 | 0.2 | 0.3 | 0.4 | 0.4 | 0.3 | 0.8 | 0.7 | 0.8 | 1.3 |
| Germany | 0.3 | 0.3 | 0.5 | 1.1 | 0.5 | 0.4 | 0.6 | 0.8 | 1.0 | 2.8 |
| Japan | 0.3 | 0.8 | 0.4 | 1.3 | 0.1 | 0.1 | 3.0 | 8.0 | 4.0 | 13.0 |
| Netherlands | 0.3 | 0.6 | 0.5 | 1.9 | 0.4 | 0.6 | 0.8 | 1.0 | 1.3 | 3.2 |
| UK | 0.4 | 0.4 | 0.7 | 13.3 | 0.3 | 0.5 | 1.3 | 0.8 | 2.1 | 26.6 |
| USA | 0.4 | 0.2 | 0.7 | −7.0 | 0.2 | 0.2 | 2.0 | 1.0 | 3.5 | −35.0 |
| Sweden | 0.2 | 0.3 | 0.3 | 16.5 | 0.3 | 0.3 | 0.7 | 1.0 | 1.0 | 55.0 |
| Switzerland | 0.3 | 0.6 | 0.8 | 1.3 | 1.0 | 2.0 | 0.3 | 0.3 | 0.8 | 0.7 |

*Variables*:

$\sigma_x$ standard deviation of series $x$;
$\bar{x}$ arithmetical average of series $x$;
$\dot{w}$ percentage annual rate of change of average hourly earnings in manufacturing;
$\dot{p}$ percentage annual rate of change of consumer prices;
$\dot{w}-\dot{p}$ percentage annual rate of change of real hourly earnings in manufacturing;
$U$ unemployment rate ($100 \times$ number of unemployed/(number of unemployed + civilian employment)).

*Sources*: OECD Main Economic Indicators (Historical Statistics), 1960–79 and 1964–83, Paris; ILO Year Book of Statistics, 1965, 1970, 1975, 1980, Geneva; OECD Labour Force Statistics, 1957–68 and 1963–83, Paris; IMF International Financial Statistics Year Book, 1984, Washington, DC.

**Sachs's real wage gap** undoubtedly has more theoretical body as a measure of real wage rigidity than the foregoing statistical ratios. In Table 16.2 the real wage gaps in manufacturing are presented for several OECD countries. It should be mentioned that the wage gap for Japan is probably highly overestimated.[2] It can be seen in Table 16.2 that the Dutch manufacturing sector in the early 1980s showed a markedly higher real wage gap than manufacturing in France, Germany and the USA. Especially the disadvantageous difference of around 10 percentage points with the Netherlands' most important trading partner, Germany, is striking. The relatively high real wage gap in the UK also deserves attention.

*Table* 16.2 The real wage gap in manufacturing (per cent) for selected periods and years*

| *Country* | *1960–4* | *1965–9* | *1973* | *1978* | *1981* | *1982* |
|---|---|---|---|---|---|---|
| France | −0.2 | 0.0 | −0.3 | 1.5 | 1.9 | 4.4 |
| Germany | −2.2 | 0.0 | 8.0 | 9.4 | 12.2 | 8.9 |
| Japan | 0.2 | 0.0 | 9.8 | 20.3 | 19.3 | 19.5 |
| Netherlands | 1.4 | 0.0 | 6.5 | 18.3 | 24.5 | 18.0 |
| Netherlands (E) | −3.5 | 0.0 | 9.6 | 12.8 | 10.5 | 9.0 |
| UK | −2.8 | 0.0 | 3.1 | 5.3 | 19.3 | 19.0 |
| USA | 1.8 | 0.0 | 3.1 | 3.9 | 8.1 | 9.0 |

* The figures for the Netherlands include self-employed labour.
(E) Total enterprises (excluding the exploitation of natural gas) instead of manufacturing sector.
*Sources*: Sachs (1983) and own computations for the Netherlands.

At this stage of gathering information on the relative positions in wage flexibility, two comments should be made. First, the relevant wage concept for calculating the real wage gap is hourly **compensation**, instead of hourly earnings. And second, but more important for most countries, it should be stressed that the real wage gap is a somewhat ambiguous measure of real wage rigidity in the sense that it is subject to external shocks and other exogenous influences, besides the self-regulatory mechanism of the labour market.

We now turn to the simple model proposed by GJL (1983). They are concerned with the movements of average hourly **earnings** (instead of compensation) in manufacturing. Their model consists of two equations, a wage and a price equation. The wage equation is an expectations-augmented **Phillips-curve**. Nominal inertia arising from overlapping wage contracts, or from adaptive expectations of price inflation is built-in, in the form of a lagged wage inflation. The price equation is nothing more than a rewritten factor-price frontier with lagged wage adjustment. Moreover, in both equations linear homogeneity is imposed on the nominal variables.[3] GJL argue that the inverse of the coefficient of the unemployment rate in the Phillips-curve is a measure of real wage rigidity by demonstrating that this coefficient determines the cumulated unemployment change caused by the initial real shock. This is under the assumption that errors in inflation forecasts are zero in the long-run process of the economy returning to its original level of unemployment.

The measure of nominal wage rigidity is calculated as real wage rigidity times the sum of the average lag of wages on prices in the Phillips-curve equation ($AL_1$) and the average lag of prices on wages in the price equation ($AL_2$), and can be derived in an analogous way. These measures are independent of the government's policy-responses to shocks, so that the two concepts can jointly be regarded as an approximation of the institutionally-given degree of wage flexibility. The estimated values for real ($RWR$) and nominal wage rigidity ($NWR$) are presented in Table 16.3 and plotted in Figure 16.1. The very low score of Japan and Switzerland in both real and nominal wage rigidity is remarkable. The average lag is longest in the USA, making this country the most nominally rigid one.

The UK has the highest level of real wage rigidity, while the Netherlands is found in the company of other EEC member countries such as France and Belgium.

Next GJL showed in their paper, reckoning with country-specific degrees of real wage rigidity, that real shocks could generally explain the main part of the adverse development of the unemployment rate in the OECD countries after the first oil crisis. These real shocks refer to the slow-down in productivity growth and the increase in relative import prices. Differences in country performance could be explained by differences in real wage rigidity.

In a similar study for the OECD, Coe and Gagliardi (1985) used a specification for the wage equation that differs from the one used by GJL. For a number of countries they used a non-linear Phillips-term. But, more important, their specification (unlike that of GJL) forced them to distinguish between short- and long-run real wage rigidity. Their estimates for short-run real wage rigidity based on semi-annual

*Table* 16.3 Real (RWR) and nominal wage rigidity (NWR)

| *Country* | *RWR (S.E.)* | *NWR (S.E.)* | $AL_1 + AL_2$ |
|---|---|---|---|
| Austria | 0.40 (0.22) | 0.20 (0.17) | 0.51 |
| Belgium | 0.68 (0.16) | 1.12 (0.26) | 1.64 |
| Denmark | 1.48 (0.86) | 0.61 (0.56) | 0.41 |
| France | 0.51 (0.13) | 0.29 (0.17) | 0.57 |
| Germany | 1.54 (0.87) | 0.36 (0.40) | 0.23 |
| Japan | 0.13 (0.03) | 0.18 (0.06) | 1.35 |
| Netherlands | 0.49 (0.16) | 0.17 (0.15) | 0.35 |
| Norway | 1.43 (5.80) | 1.03 (4.47) | 0.72 |
| Sweden | 0.39 (0.35) | 0.22 (0.21) | 0.57 |
| Switzerland | 0.13 (0.04) | 0.09 (0.04) | 0.71 |
| UK | 2.39 (4.22) | 0.78 (1.55) | 0.32 |
| USA | 1.09 (1.14) | 3.14 (2.57) | 2.88 |
| EEC average | 1.23 | 0.52 | 0.52 |
| OECD average | 0.92 | 0.62 | 0.79 |

*Source*: GJL (1983).

*Figure* 16.1 Real wage rigidity and nominal wage rigidity

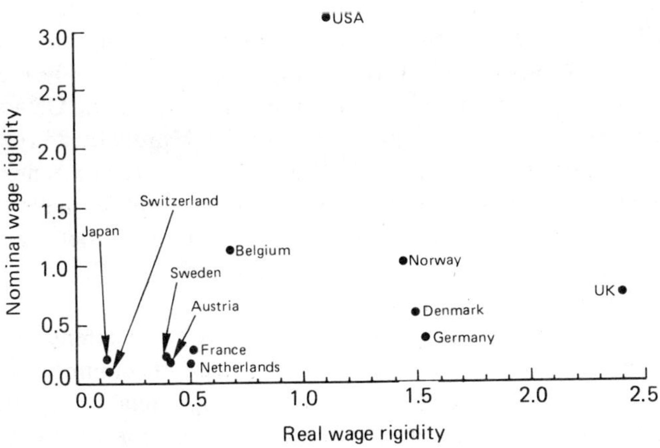


*Source*: GJL (1983)

*Figure* 16.2 Short-run real wage rigidity and unemployment

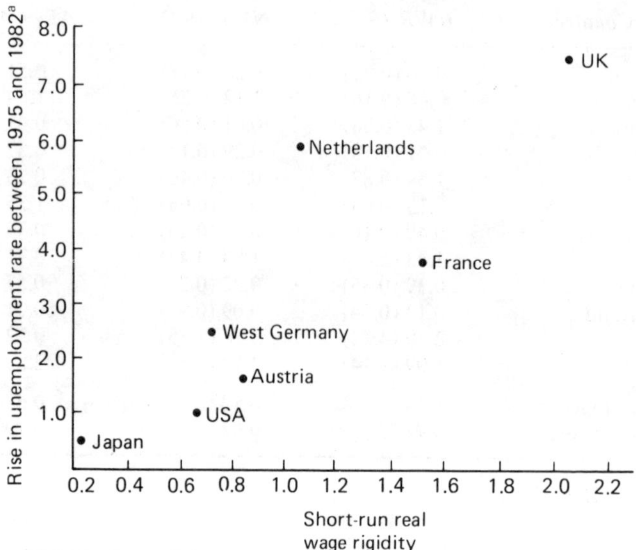


(a) Percentage points

*Source*: Coe and Gagliardi (1985)

observations are plotted in Figure 16.2. Broadly speaking these results do not differ very much from those of GJL. Our own estimations confirm this general picture.

In summary, the relative positions concerning macroeconomic wage flexibility can now in a three-polar fashion be roughly described as follows. With respect to hourly earnings Japan is probably the most flexible country in both real and nominal terms, while the USA stands out from the group of EEC member-countries, mainly by its very high level of nominal wage rigidity. The Netherlands, in earnings flexibility not differing much from the other EEC member countries, nevertheless has a conspicuously high real wage gap. The 'wedge' between compensation and earnings, which is relatively important for the Netherlands, may be one of the causes.[4]

In concluding this section we want to pay some attention to the **mesoeconomic** backgrounds of the foregoing macroeconomic measures. Care should be taken not to be tempted to superficial interpretations of the following in a flexibility-framework, because of the lack of sectoral unemployment data.

The figures in Table 16.4 are related to computations for the so-called **sectoral weighted variance (SWV)**, which is defined as:

$$SWV = \frac{\sum_{t}^{T}\sum_{i}^{J}\frac{e_{it}}{e_t}\cdot(l\dot{w}_{it}-\overline{l\dot{w}})^2}{T} \tag{16.1}$$

$$= \underbrace{\frac{1}{T}\sum_{t}^{T}\sum_{i}^{J}\left(\frac{e_{it}}{e_t}-\alpha_i\right)(l\dot{w}_{it}-l\dot{w}_t)^2}_{(1)} + \underbrace{\frac{1}{T}\sum_{t}^{T}\sum_{i}^{J}\alpha_i(l\dot{w}_{it}-l\dot{w}_t)^2}_{(2)}$$

$$+\underbrace{\frac{1}{T}\sum_{t}^{T}(l\dot{w}_t-\overline{l\dot{w}})^2}_{(3)},$$

where $lw_{it}$ and $e_{it}$ are nominal compensation per employee (per year) and employment in sector $i$ and in year $t$, $T$ determines the length of the period considered, while $J$ stands for the total number of branches. Further on $\alpha_i = 1/T\sum_t^T e_{it}/e_t$, is the average share of sector $i$ in total employment, while $l\dot{w}_t$ and $\overline{l\dot{w}}$ stand for year and period average growth of the rate of employee compensation respectively:

$$\overline{l\dot{w}} = \frac{\sum_{t}^{T} l\dot{w}_t}{T} = \frac{\sum_{t}^{T}\sum_{i}^{J}\frac{e_{it}}{e_t}\cdot l\dot{w}_{it}}{T}. \tag{16.2}$$

In equation (16.1) component (1) can be considered as the structural component of the *SWV*. Component (2) is a kind of differentiation-measure, while the third component can be entitled as a macroeconomic variance (*MV*). The results of Table 16.4 can now be interpreted in the following way. In the last column Japan, the Netherlands and Sweden stand out as countries with relatively high macro-shares in the *SWV*s, in sharp contrast to the Anglo-Saxon countries in the sample. These high macro-shares may indicate institutionally-determined strong central influences upon the wage-bargaining process in Japan, the Netherlands and Sweden.

As a logical counterpart Table 16.5 presents coefficients of variation for the period 1970-1984. This table, coupled with unemployment data, is rather suggestive. Japan and the USA have relatively high and rising coefficients of variation, and a less-than-average rise in unem-

*Table* 16.4 SWVs of (nominal) compensation per employee per year for the period 1970–83*

| *Country* | *Number of branches* | $\overline{l\dot{w}}$ | $MV = 1/T \sum_t^T (l\dot{w}_t - \overline{l\dot{w}})^2$ (3) | *SWV* (1)+(2)+(3) | $(MV/SWV) \times 100$ % |
|---|---|---|---|---|---|
| Belgium | 16 | 11.0 | 17.0 | 43.0 | 39.4 |
| Germany | 18 | 7.8 | 5.3 | 11.1 | 47.7 |
| Japan | 18 | 11.3 | 42.4 | 50.5 | 84.0 |
| Netherlands | 14 | 10.0 | 18.0 | 30.5 | 59.2 |
| Sweden | 18 | 10.4 | 12.6 | 18.0 | 70.2 |
| UK | 18 | 17.0 | 29.6 | 88.6 | 33.4 |
| USA | 18 | 8.0 | 0.9 | 2.7 | 31.0 |

* France is omitted because only earnings data were available for this country.
*Source*: OECD National Accounts (detailed tables, Vol. II), 1970–82 and 1970–83 (on tape), Paris; EUROSTAT National Accounts ESA (detailed tables), various issues, Luxemburg.

*Table* 16.5 Coefficients of variation (unweighted) of nominal hourly earnings and compensation

| *Country* | | *Number of branches* | *1970* | *1971* | *1972* | *1973* | *1974* | *1975* | *1976* | *1977* | *1978* | *1979* | *1980* | *1981* | *1982* | *1983* | *1984* |
|---|---|---|---|---|---|---|---|---|---|---|---|---|---|---|---|---|---|
| Belgium | 1 | — | — | — | — | — | — | — | — | — | — | — | — | — | — | — | — |
| | 2 | — | — | — | — | — | — | — | — | — | — | — | — | — | — | — | — |
| | 3 | 16 | 20.0 | 21.3 | 23.0 | 24.7 | 25.6 | 23.3 | 24.2 | 25.2 | 27.7 | 26.4 | 28.9 | 27.9 | 28.1 | 27.9 | — |
| France | 1 | 16 | 16.1 | 15.0 | 14.9 | 14.7 | 13.8 | 13.5 | 14.4 | 14.4 | 13.8 | 13.9 | 13.5 | 13.3 | — | — | — |
| | 2 | — | — | — | — | | — | — | — | — | — | — | — | — | — | — | — |
| | 3 | — | — | — | — | — | | — | — | — | — | — | — | — | — | — | — |
| Germany | 1 | 16 | 13.5 | 13.5 | 13.2 | 13.3 | 14.1 | 14.3 | 14.1 | 14.4 | 14.0 | 13.8 | 14.0 | 13.4 | — | — | — |
| | 2 | 8 | 18.8 | 19.1 | 18.7 | 19.5 | 19.8 | 20.6 | 20.1 | 20.5 | 20.9 | 22.0 | 22.3 | 22.5 | 22.9 | — | — |
| | 3 | 18 | 18.6 | 19.3 | 18.8 | 20.0 | 21.5 | 22.8 | 22.2 | 22.5 | 22.4 | 23.0 | 22.9 | 23.3 | — | — | — |
| Japan | 1 | — | — | — | — | — | — | — | — | — | — | — | — | — | — | — | — |
| | 2 | 11 | 25.0 | 25.7 | 25.8 | 25.1 | 25.4 | 26.0 | 26.3 | 24.5 | 24.3 | 25.5 | 24.6 | 25.5 | 28.8 | — | — |
| | 3 | 18 | 24.4 | 25.1 | 25.3 | 24.9 | 25.0 | 25.6 | 26.3 | 25.4 | 26.2 | 26.6 | 24.4 | 25.6 | 26.3 | 27.6 | — |
| Netherlands | 1 | 6 | 11.2 | 11.3 | 12.1 | 12.5 | 10.7 | 9.8 | 9.1 | 9.6 | 9.8 | 9.3 | 9.3 | 9.0 | 9.0 | 8.9 | — |
| | 2 | 8 | 21.4 | 22.5 | 22.3 | 21.1 | 21.3 | 21.6 | 21.2 | 19.4 | 19.3 | 18.7 | 17.4 | 15.0 | 14.5 | 13.2 | 12.7 |
| | 3 | 14 | 18.8 | 20.7 | 20.0 | 19.1 | 19.4 | 18.2 | 18.8 | 17.0 | 16.7 | 16.4 | 15.1 | 14.0 | 13.2 | — | — |
| Sweden | 1 | 16 | 10.0 | 9.4 | 8.8 | 9.2 | 10.1 | 9.7 | 9.3 | 8.8 | 8.6 | 8.9 | 8.7 | 8.3 | — | — | — |
| | 2 | 11 | 19.8 | 20.0 | 20.2 | 20.4 | 19.4 | 17.9 | 17.1 | 15.8 | 15.0 | 16.1 | 16.0 | 16.2 | 15.9 | — | — |
| | 3 | 18 | 17.7 | 17.5 | 17.4 | 17.6 | 17.6 | 17.2 | 16.2 | 15.3 | 14.1 | 15.0 | 14.6 | 15.2 | 15.7 | 15.6 | — |
| UK | 1 | 16 | 16.3 | 16.7 | 16.6 | 16.0 | 14.3 | 15.0 | 14.4 | 13.0 | 13.9 | 13.9 | 15.5 | 16.8 | — | — | — |
| | 2 | 10 | — | — | — | 24.7 | 25.2 | 23.3 | 20.5 | 21.4 | 21.8 | 20.9 | 20.7 | 20.1 | 20.8 | — | — |
| | 3 | 18 | 13.0 | 13.0 | 14.4 | 16.1 | 16.6 | 17.1 | 16.0 | 16.7 | 17.5 | 18.4 | 19.2 | 19.3 | — | — | — |
| USA | 1 | 16 | 17.8 | 18.9 | 20.1 | 20.5 | 21.1 | 22.0 | 23.0 | 23.8 | 24.2 | 24.2 | 24.5 | 25.3 | — | — | — |
| | 2 | 10 | 30.8 | 31.2 | 31.5 | 31.2 | 31.5 | 32.9 | 33.6 | 33.7 | 33.7 | 33.4 | 33.8 | 34.3 | 34.6 | — | — |
| | 3 | 18 | 25.3 | 25.6 | 26.2 | 26.2 | 26.9 | 28.0 | 28.6 | 28.8 | 29.0 | 29.0 | 29.3 | 29.7 | 29.7 | 29.7 | — |

*Note*: 1: hourly earnings; 2: compensation with manufacturing aggregated; 3: compensation.
*Source*: As for Table 16.4, together with Netherlands Central Bureau of Statistics (CBS) National Accounts, 1974, 1978, 1981 and 1984.

ployment. On the other hand the Netherlands combines very low and falling coefficients with a more-than-average rise of the unemployment rate in the same period. However, the examples of Belgium (high coefficients of variation, high unemployment rates) and Sweden (low coefficients of variation, low unemployment rates) prevent us from drawing any firm conclusions. It is clearly recommendable to carry out more research into suitable measures of sectoral wage flexibility.

## 16.4 AN ALTERNATIVE MEASURE OF REAL WAGE FLEXIBILITY

In section 16.2 we presented the real wage gap as a measure of disequilibrium on the labour market, while the coefficient $\beta$ from the Phillips-curve was taken as a measure of the strength of equilibrium-restoring forces. In this section we shall concentrate on labour-market influences. But we want to remedy $\beta$ for the neglect of relating actual wage adjustment to needed wage adjustment. In our opinion induced wage changes or the endogenous change of the real wage gap should be confronted with the real wage gap itself. Let us assume monotonic adjustment processes. Of course, one can imagine overshooting the target for wage formation, but we shall exclude the possibility of oscillatory movements. Define the adjustment parameter $\lambda$ as:

$$\lambda = -\frac{\Delta RWG}{RWG_{-1}} = -\frac{RWG - RWG_{-1}}{RWG_{-1}} \tag{16.3}$$

where it is to be remembered that $\Delta RWG$ represents the change of the real wage gap in response to the real wage gap itself (lagged one period). The flexibility parameter $\lambda$ is expected to have a value between zero and one, for otherwise there would be no monotonic convergence. To obtain an estimate of $\lambda$ rewrite equation (16.3) as:

$$\Delta RWG = c - \lambda RGW_{-1} \tag{16.4}$$

with the constant assumed to measure the effect of autonomous forces upon the real wage gap.

In principle, equation (16.4) can be estimated. However, data on the $RWG$ are questionable, one of the reasons being the more or less arbitrary selection of the equilibrium base period. Therefore we want to elaborate equation (16.4) in the direction of a Phillips-curve type of analysis. By definition:

$$\Delta RWG = \Delta \frac{W}{W^*} \tag{16.5}$$

$W$ denoting compensation per employee and the asterisk indicating an equilibrium value.

For wages not too far from their equilibrium value equation (16.5) can be approximated by:

$$\Delta RWG = \dot{W} - \dot{W}^* \tag{16.6}$$

A dot above a variable stands for a percentage rate of growth. Equations (16.4) and (16.6) amount to:

$$\dot{W} = c + \dot{W}^* - \lambda RWG_{-1} \tag{16.7}$$

The two explanatory variables on the right-hand side of this equation are not observed directly. Now, let us represent the equilibrium wage development by the percentage rate of inflation ($\dot{p}_c$) added to the percentage rate of growth of structural labour productivity ($\dot{x}$):[5]

$$\dot{W}^* = \dot{p}_c + \dot{x} \tag{16.8}$$

Furthermore, let us take the unemployment rate, presumably the main consequence of a high real wage gap, as a proxy for this real wage gap. As a first approximation we may write:

$$U - U_N = aRWG_{-1} + b \tag{16.9}$$

In this equation $U$ stands for the actual unemployment rate, while $U_N$ is its natural counterpart. Abstracting from the supply sensitivity for a wage change, we may interpret '$a$', the coefficient of the real wage gap variable, as (the absolute value of) the wage elasticity of labour demand.

Taking equations 16.8 and 16.9 into account we transform equation 16.7 into:

$$\dot{W} = c' + \dot{p}_c + \dot{x} - \frac{\lambda}{a}(U - U_N) \tag{16.10}$$

This equation is closely related to an equation that underlies common Phillips-curve analysis when inflation expectations are correct. In section 16.2 we saw that the coefficient of the unemployment rate (in deviation from its natural rate) in the wage equation is taken as a measure of real wage flexibility. This coefficient was called $\beta$ and it corresponds with $\lambda / a$ in equation (16.10). So:

$$\beta = \frac{\lambda}{a} \tag{16.11}$$

From a conceptual point of view we prefer as a measure of real wage flexibility the coefficient $\lambda$, the actual wage adjustment relative to the needed wage adjustment. This measure can be obtained by multiplying $\beta$, indicating the strength of labour-market influences on wage formation, with the parameter '$a$', a measure of the strength of wage influences on labour demand and on employment, demand being on the short side of the market. This closes the circle from unemployment rate to unemployment rate.

In an international comparison it appears that differences in $\beta$ are more pronounced than differences in $a$ (for example, OECD, 1985). In view of this we concentrated in section 16.3 on estimates of $\beta$, as our aim was no more than to determine the relative positions of the countries under examination. Our understanding of labour-market functioning would benefit by estimates of $\lambda$ as well.

## 16.5 CONCLUSIONS

In this paper we summarised various measures of wage flexibility, both macroeconomic and mesoeconomic. Moreover we presented our empirical findings for several OECD member-countries comparable with the Netherlands.

Measured by the variability of wages relative to the variability of unemployment, the Netherlands does not distinguish itself from the neighbouring countries. Japan and the USA seem to be more flexible countries than the European OECD area, in any case in real terms. The outlier position of Japan and, to a lesser extent, the USA, is generally confirmed by the other findings.

A closer look at the self-regulatory mechanism of the labour market as expressed by the coefficient of the unemployment rate in a Phillips-curve equation reveals that there are no salient differences between countries in real wage flexibility, the major exception being Japan. This country is characterised by a very low real wage rigidity and therefore a high real wage flexibility. In addition to this, the USA stands out by long average lags in the wage and price equations. When real shocks are coupled with a change in inflation, this provides a supplementary mechanism for real wage adjustment towards an equilibrium level. Furthermore, reckoning with country-specific degrees of real wage rigidity, real shocks could generally explain the adverse development of the unemployment rate in the OECD countries after 1973.

The real wage gap expresses the deviation of real wages from their equilibrium level. Around 1980 the Netherlands displayed a much higher real wage gap than France, Germany and the USA. Apparently, in the Netherlands the labour-market influences were too weak to counteract the adverse effects of shocks and other developments disturbing equilibrium growth.

Perhaps we should not only look at macroeconomic wage flexibility but also at mesoeconomic wage flexibility. It is shown in this paper that sectoral wage dispersion in the Netherlands, when measured by coefficients of variation, is low and falling from the middle of the 1970s onwards. This is in sharp contrast to Japan and the USA, where the coefficients of variation of sectoral wages are high and even showed a rise between 1970 and 1982. However, the empirical material is not conclusive as to the relation of mesoeconomic wage flexibility to the unemployment development in the countries considered.

## Notes

1. Sachs uses logarithms and calculates $\ln S_L^f(t) - \ln S_L^f(1965\text{–}9)$, $S_L^f$ being defined as $(W/P_v)/(V/L)^f$. Because $\ln y - \ln y_0 \approx y/y_0 - 1$, this provides a good approximation.
2. Bruno and Sachs (1985), adjusting for cyclical variations in productivity in a different way from Sachs (1983), found a 5 to 6 percentage points lower wage gap for Japan and an approximately equally higher wage gap for the European countries. The US wage gap, on the contrary, was hardly sensitive for the mode of adjusting.
3. The wage–price system actually estimated by GJL is:

$$\dot{w} = \alpha\dot{p} + (1-\alpha)\dot{w}_{-1} - \alpha\beta U + \delta t + \text{constant}$$

$$\dot{p} + (\dot{x} - 1/2s(\dot{m} + \dot{m}_{-1})) = \theta\dot{w} + (1-\theta)\dot{w}_{-1} - \gamma\dot{U} + \text{constant}$$

where $\dot{w}$ is the percentage rate of change of average hourly earnings in manufacturing, $\dot{p}$ is the percentage rate of change of consumer prices, $t$ is time (allowing for changes in the natural rate of unemployment and the target rate of real wage growth), $\dot{x}$ is the trend productivity growth rate, $s$ the share of imports in $GDP$ in 1975, and $\dot{m}$ is import price inflation minus domestic price inflation ($\dot{U}$ stands for $U - U_{-1}$). The actual measures for real and nominal wage rigidity are $1/\beta$ and $1/\beta \cdot [(1-\alpha)/\alpha + 1 - \theta]$ respectively. Both equations were estimated by $2SLS$ with instruments $\ln w_{-1}$, $\ln w_{-2}$, $\ln p_{-1}$, $\ln p_{-2}$, $t$, $U_{-1}$, $\ln GDP_{-1}$, $(\ln p + \ln m)_{-1}$, $\ln x$ and current import prices ($) divided by the world price of manufacturing exports ($). The price equation was estimated in level form with a first order autoregressive disturbance term.

4. This 'wedge' consists of social security and pension premiums paid by employers.
5. Labour productivity is adjusted for terms-of-trade losses or gains.

## References

BRUNO, M. and SACHS, J. D. (1985) *Economics of Worldwide Stagflation* (Cambridge, Mass: Harvard University Press).

COE, D. T. and GAGLIARDI, F. (1985) 'Nominal Wage Determination in Ten OECD Economies', OECD Working Paper no 19.

GORDON, R. J. (1982) 'Why US Wage and Employment Behaviour Differs from that in Britain and Japan', *Economic Journal*, 92, pp. 13–44.

GRUBB, D., JACKMAN, R. and LAYARD, R. (1983) 'Wage Rigidity and Unemployment in OECD Countries', *European Economic Review*, 21, pp. 11–39.

MALINVAUD, E. (1977) *The Theory of Unemployment Reconsidered* (Oxford: Basil Blackwell).

MALINVAUD, E. (1984) *Mass Unemployment* (Oxford: Basil Blackwell).

OECD (1985) *Employment Outlook*.

OKUN, A. M. (1981) *Prices and Quantities* (Oxford: Basil Blackwell).

SACHS, J. D. (1983) 'Real Wages and Unemployment in the OECD Countries', Brooking Papers on Economic Activity, 1, pp. 255–304.

SPRINGER, K. A., COMPAIJEN, B. and VERMAAT, A. J. (1986) 'Labour Market and Wage Flexibility' (in Dutch), OSA Working Document, Government Publishing Office, The Hague.

# 17 Rigidities and Employment in Belgium: An Econometric Analysis by Sectoral Employment Functions

A. Bayar, N. Deimezis, Y. Guillaume and D. Meulders

## INTRODUCTION

As in most industrialised countries, unemployment is at the centre of preoccupations of Belgian authorities. The Belgian rate of unemployment is one of the highest in the EEC. In 1985, it amounted to 11.6 per cent (against an EEC average of 9.9 per cent). Employment policies designed to increase labour-market flexibility are often considered as one of the possible remedies.

Flexibility is generally defined as the setting-up of policies aiming at suppressing rigidities and different kinds of factors that hinder the competitive functioning of the market and the free development of economic activity. It is a vague and complex notion which includes different and interdependent elements.

This paper is only concerned with the 'numerical flexibility' which can be defined as the possibility for firms, to adjust immediately and completely, actual employment to its desired level.[1] This is in contradiction to the attitude of firms in the 1960s, a period during which the objective of most firms was to stabilise employment in the company.

Numerical flexibility implies policies of reduction in employment in the case of recession and increased employment in the case of economic recovery. It needs many modifications in the labour legislation relative to redundancies. Numerical flexibility is favoured by partial unemployment, fixed-term contracts, overtime, subcontracting, temporary work, etc.

The objective of this study is to estimate the direct effect on employment in the manufacturing industry of an introduction of 'total' numerical flexibility into the labour market. The estimation realised on the basis of sectoral employment functions is, at this stage, a partial study, and the results are only indicative.

It only considers three aspects of the labour market:

- the link between employment and, respectively, wages, actual working time, and the speed at which employment adjusts to market conditions;
- the definition of the wage bill;
- the link between actual and agreed working time.

The interrelations between employment and other variables (prices, output, investment and the degree of production capacity utilisation, for example) have been ignored so far but will be covered at a future stage.

## 17.1 THE MODEL

### The Branch Breakdown

The model covers eight manufacturing branches, following the NACE/CLIO classification (see Table 17.1).

*Table* 17.1 Branch breakdown of manufacturing industry

| *No* | *NACE/CLIO R25 Code* | *Branch* |
|---|---|---|
| 1 | 13 | Ferrous and non-ferrous ores and metals |
| 2 | 15 | Non-metallic minerals and mineral products |
| 3 | 17 | Chemical products |
| 4 | 19, 21, 23, 25, 28 | Metal products, machinery and transport equipment |
| 5 | 36 | Food, beverages, tobacco |
| 6 | 42 | Textiles, clothing, leather and footwear |
| 7 | 48, 49 | Rubber, plastic and other manufacturing products |
| 8 | 47 | Paper and printing products |

These branches represent approximately one quarter of total employment in Belgium (see Table 17.2).

*Table* 17.2 Employment in Belgian manufacturing industries, 1966–81

| *Branch* | *Employment (thousands)* 1966 | 1974 | 1981 | *Average annual growth rate (as percentage)* 74/66 | 81/74 | 81/66 |
|---|---|---|---|---|---|---|
| 1. Metals | 85.0 | 90.7 | 60.5 | 0.81 | −5.62 | −2.24 |
| 2. Non-metallic products | 80.2 | 72.7 | 47.6 | −1.22 | −5.87 | −3.42 |
| 3. Chemicals | 75.9 | 84.5 | 79.8 | 1.35 | −0.81 | 0.33 |
| 4. Metal products | 344.5 | 394.1 | 317.9 | 1.70 | −3.02 | −0.53 |
| 5. Food, beverages, tobacco | 171.8 | 157.2 | 133.9 | −1.10 | −2.27 | −1.65 |
| 6. Textiles | 271.1 | 227.0 | 131.1 | −2.19 | −7.54 | −4.73 |
| 7. Other manufacturing | 109.7 | 118.8 | 92.2 | 1.00 | −3.56 | −1.15 |
| 8. Paper | 69.3 | 73.5 | 57.1 | 0.74 | −3.54 | −1.28 |
| Total | 1207.5 | 1218.5 | 920.1 | 0.11 | −3.93 | −1.80 |

*Source*: Bureau du Plan.

## The Model's Specification[2]

The model is based on a simple production function. For each manufacturing branch we have:

$$QP - A \cdot K \qquad (17.1a)$$

$$QP = B \cdot L^{f^*} \qquad (17.1b)$$

where:

- $QP$: Potential output, in constant prices
- $K$: Capital stock, in constant prices
- $L^{f^*}$: 'Efficient' (or 'desired') labour activity at full capacity utilisation
- $A$: Capital productivity
- $B$: Labour activity productivity

From the above, we obtain:

$$L^{f^*} = (A/B) \cdot K = C \cdot K \qquad (17.2)$$

The parameter $C$, which can be considered as a complementarity index, is treated here as a function of new investment generations, of wage part in total output and of an inverse time-trend:

$$C = Co \cdot e^{c1 \cdot Kr/K} \cdot e^{c2 \cdot CS} \cdot e^{c3 \cdot (1/t)} \tag{17.3}$$

where:

$t$: Time trend
$Kr$: Recent capital stock

$$Kr_t = K_t - K_{t-5} \tag{17.4}$$

$CS$: Wage part in total output

$$CS = (N \cdot WY \cdot DH \cdot w + SSC)/(p \cdot Q) \tag{17.5}$$

with:

$N$: Employment (number of persons)
$WY$: Worked weeks per year
$DH$: Weekly working time
$w$: Hourly wage rate, in current prices
$SSC$: Employers' social security contributions
$P$: Price index
$Q$: Output, in constant prices.

The specification of the equation 17.3 has the advantage of according increased importance to the influence of wages on employment when the wage part increases. In fact, this can easily be seen in the values of employment elasticities relative to wages, presented in Table 17.3.

The form of the trend ($1/t$ in place of the commonly used $t$) implies a progressive deceleration of exogenous productivity growth.

The relation between 'efficient' activity at full capacity utilisation and 'efficient' activity at actual capacity utilisation is a non-linear function of capacity utilisation rate:

$$L^f/L^{f^*} = (Q/QP)^d = U^d \tag{17.6}$$

*Table* 17.3 Sectoral employment elasticities

| *Branch* | *Metals* | *Non-metal* | *Chemical* | *Metal Products* | *Food* | *Textile* | *Other* | *Paper* |
|---|---|---|---|---|---|---|---|---|
| | | | | *Relative to wage rate* | | | | |
| | | | | (*a*) *Equation* (17.10) *only* | | | | |
| Short term | −0.022 | 0.000 | −0.159 | −0.356 | 0.000 | 0.000 | −0.285 | −0.080 |
| Long term | −0.071 | 0.000 | −0.474 | −1.021 | 0.000 | 0.000 | −0.560 | −0.458 |
| | | | | (*b*) *Complete model* | | | | |
| Short term | −0.021 | 0.000 | −0.137 | −0.262 | 0.000 | 0.000 | −0.222 | −0.074 |
| Long term | −0.066 | 0.000 | −0.322 | −0.505 | 0.000 | 0.000 | −0.359 | −0.314 |

where:

$L^f$: 'Efficient' (or 'desired') labour activity at actual capacity utilisation
$U$: Capacity utilisation rate

$$U = Q/QP \tag{17.7}$$

and

$$0 < d \leq 1$$

A simple adjustment mechanism links actual labour activity to actual 'efficient' activity:

$$L_t/L_{t-1} = (L^f/L_{t-1})^{\mu} \tag{17.8}$$

with $0 < \mu \leq 1$.

The parameter '$\mu$' can be considered as being an indicator of the rigidities in the labour market. When it is equal to 1 the labour-market adjustment is immediate and labour activity can be defined as totally 'flexible'.

Labour activity is defined as a non-linear relation between employment and actual working hours:

$$L = N \cdot DH^g \tag{17.9}$$

where:

$DH$: Working hours per week.

From relations (17.2), (17.3), (17.6), (17.8) and (17.9), we obtain:

$$\begin{aligned} \ln(N/N_{t-1}) = {} & \mu \cdot \ln Co + \mu \cdot c1 \cdot (Kr/K) + \mu \cdot c2 \cdot CS \\ & + \mu \cdot c3 \cdot (1/t) + \mu \cdot \ln(K/N_{t-1}) + \mu \cdot d \cdot \ln U \\ & - g \cdot \ln DH + g \cdot (1-\mu) \cdot \ln DH_{t-1} \end{aligned} \tag{17.10}$$

Estimation of the coefficients of this equation was obtained by non-linear least squares.

The model is completed by an equation relating average weekly hours to agreed weekly hours:

$$DH = h1 \cdot DHC^{h2} \cdot U^{h3} \cdot e^{h4 \cdot (1/t)} \qquad (17.11)$$

Thus, the model in its actual form consists of estimated equations (17.10) and (17.11) and identities (17.4), (17.5) and (17.7) for each one of the eight branches. At this stage, the exogenous variables are output ($Q$), potential output ($QP$), the capital stock ($K$), the agreed hours of work ($DHC$), the wage rate ($w$), the price index ($p$) and time. In other words, labour supply is exogenous and wages do not adjust to market conditions. In the case of Belgium, this assumption is acceptable in the short run.

Values of estimated coefficients are presented in Appendix 17.1. Some interesting remarks can be made on those results:

(a) The overall wage effect on labour demand is relatively small. Table 17.3 shows the sectoral employment elasticities relative to wages, which is nil in three branches and smaller than 0.5 in almost every other case.
(b) Working-time elasticities are also significantly smaller than unity. In other words, a decrease of the working-time has a limited effect on manufacturing employment.
(c) The speed of adjustments of labour activity to its desired level is on average slow, proving the presence of important rigidities in the labour market.

## SIMULATION RESULTS

This small and partial model has been used to analyse the effects of an introduction of 'total' numerical flexibility on the labour market. We assume that, as a result of policy measures already described, labour activity adjusts completely and immediately to its 'efficient' (or 'desired') level. In the model this is obtained by substituting the estimated value of the parameter '$\mu$' by 1. Applying this to the Belgian case would require fundamental modifications in the labour legislation, which at present seems a very remote possibility.

The results we present may be regarded chiefly as a counterfactual partial equilibrium analysis on the period of observation. The effects of total numerical flexibility on employment are analysed over the whole estimation period (1966 to 1981) and they are compared with the basic solution of the model.

The effects of a full and immediate adjustment (total 'numerical' flexibility) are naturally very different through time and by sector.

For the manufacturing sector as a whole, a full adjustment of employment to market conditions would have yielded only positive effects, substantial in 1969–70 and marginal in 1973–4. But for all other years during the period of 1967–81, the effect would have been negative, with 1975 as the worst year (see Table 17.4 and Figure 17.1).

By sector, the situation is not clear:

- Employment in the metals sector is less than the 'optimum' employment level for the period 1969 (1968 and 1969 saw a speedy rise in output combined with a decrease and then stagnation of employment) - 1974 (the year of historic maximum output). During the other years there was an excessively high level of employment which tended to be annulled by redundancies at the end of the period.
- In the non-metallic products branch, only the years 1975 (general recession) and 1981 (general recession, but especially in the building industry) see a level of 'desired' employment below the real level; substantial discrepancies can be seen especially in the years 1969 and 1970 (by about 8 per cent).
- In the chemical industry too, real employment is often below the level of 'desired' employment; moreover, from 1975 to 1981 only the years 1978 and 1980 (low or negative growth of production) showed an employment surplus.
- Metal products performed in the same way as the metals industry. The only difference occurred in the year 1972 (substantial deceleration in the growth of output) when employment was in surplus. Due to the large size of the labour force in this sector, the size of the discrepancy between 'adjusted' and real employment amounts to some 40 000 units (1970–5).
- The same can be observed in the textiles sector (the year 1974, which had already seen a decrease in output, showed a surplus instead of the year 1972). However, in view of the importance of the adjustment coefficient (0.67), the discrepancies are relatively slighter than in the metal products sector.
- Two other sectors also reacted in a largely similar way to total adjustment: food and the miscellaneous sector, where employment

*Table* 17.4 Manufacturing employment: simulation results by branch

| | *Base solution (thousands)* | *Simulation (difference in %)* | | *Base solution (thousands)* | *Simulation (difference in %)* |
|---|---|---|---|---|---|
| **1 Ferrous and non-ferrous metals** | | | **5 Food, beverage and tobacco** | | |
| 1967 | 83.63 | −3.37 | 1967 | 170.11 | −4.67 |
| 1968 | 81.29 | −2.31 | 1968 | 167.58 | −5.00 |
| 1969 | 81.83 | 3.33 | 1969 | 167.52 | −1.76 |
| 1970 | 83.62 | 4.30 | 1970 | 166.05 | −3.67 |
| ... | | | ... | | |
| 1974 | 89.97 | 7.92 | 1974 | 154.99 | −6.60 |
| 1975 | 86.35 | −6.61 | 1975 | 150.91 | −9.10 |
| ... | | | ... | | |
| 1980 | 63.40 | −7.13 | 1980 | 136.11 | −5.45 |
| 1981 | 61.24 | −3.20 | 1981 | 133.72 | −5.75 |
| **2 Non-metallic products** | | | **6 Textiles** | | |
| 1967 | 77.86 | 4.94 | 1967 | 256.95 | −1.00 |
| 1968 | 74.96 | 2.89 | 1968 | 245.81 | −0.41 |
| 1969 | 75.57 | 8.19 | 1969 | 248.01 | 2.18 |
| 1970 | 76.28 | 7.48 | 1970 | 248.86 | 1.49 |
| ... | | | ... | | |
| 1974 | 70.94 | 5.00 | 1974 | 225.37 | −0.71 |
| 1975 | 65.61 | −2.39 | 1975 | 204.88 | −3.77 |
| ... | | | ... | | |
| 1980 | 52.67 | 1.17 | 1980 | 140.26 | −1.52 |
| 1981 | 47.50 | −4.18 | 1981 | 130.60 | −1.89 |
| **3 Chemicals** | | | **7 Other manufacturing** | | |
| 1967 | 75.70 | 0.23 | 1967 | 110.92 | −3.60 |
| 1968 | 76.60 | 2.56 | 1968 | 111.32 | −3.69 |
| 1969 | 77.94 | 5.82 | 1969 | 114.66 | −1.55 |
| 1970 | 79.65 | 6.23 | 1970 | 114.50 | −4.17 |
| ... | | | ... | | |
| 1974 | 84.80 | 6.10 | 1974 | 118.59 | −3.66 |
| 1975 | 83.26 | −4.34 | 1975 | 110.87 | −9.33 |
| ... | | | ... | | |
| 1980 | 80.33 | −2.90 | 1980 | 96.35 | −6.18 |
| 1981 | 79.46 | −1.63 | 1981 | 93.16 | −7.16 |
| **4 Metal products** | | | **8 Paper** | | |
| 1967 | 332.88 | −3.28 | 1967 | 69.87 | −0.31 |
| 1968 | 332.03 | −0.79 | 1968 | 70.57 | −1.74 |
| 1969 | 351.72 | 6.32 | 1969 | 71.89 | 3.38 |
| 1970 | 376.34 | 6.45 | 1970 | 72.81 | 0.81 |
| ... | | | ... | | |
| 1974 | 390.31 | 1.51 | 1974 | 70.51 | −5.64 |
| 1975 | 372.93 | −4.76 | 1975 | 66.24 | −20.37 |
| ... | | | ... | | |
| 1980 | 332.57 | −2.55 | 1980 | 58.61 | −5.59 |
| 1981 | 321.54 | −3.07 | 1981 | 57.33 | −7.74 |

*Figure* 17.1 Total employment 1967–81, base solution and flexibility policy

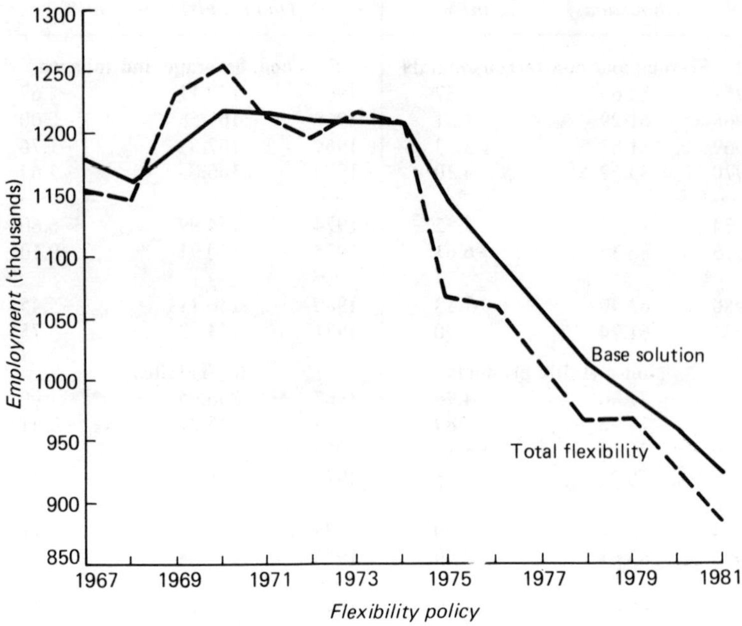


was in surplus from 1967 to 1981, the surplus reaching a relative maximum of the order of 9 per cent in 1975.

- Lastly, the paper sector almost always had an employment surplus (which could go up to 20 per cent as in 1975) except in 1969–70.

## CONCLUSION

In conclusion, even though our approach to 'numerical flexibility' policies may seem fairly simple, it does seem to confirm that in a period of relatively weak activity, as is the case in Belgium at present, the application of these type of measures may in the short term, result in a decrease of employment, contrary to what is usually claimed.[3]

A series of recent studies on the same issue, though proceeding by different methods, has reached quantitative results which are more or less comparable to ours.[4]

## Appendix 17.1

*Table* 17.A.1 Estimation results for equation (17.10)

| Coeff. | 1 | 2 | 3 | 4 | 5 | 6 | 7 | 8 |
|---|---|---|---|---|---|---|---|---|
| $\mu^* \ln Co$ | −0.7215 | −2.025 | −1.257 | −0.5842 | −1.017 | −1.558 | −1.935 | −0.599 |
| | (−0.78) | (−2.51) | (−3.85) | (−1.91) | (−1.61) | (−4.78) | (−3.09) | (−2.53) |
| $\mu^* c1$ | 0.3751 | 0.0675 | −0.1314 | −0.0174 | −0.2883 | 0.7132 | 0.1803 | −0.1309 |
| | (1.93) | (0.38) | (−1.69) | (−0.11) | (−1.09) | (2.84) | (1.63) | (−0.55) |
| $\mu^* c2$ | −0.20 | 0.00 | −0.5322 | −0.9451 | 0.00 | 0.00 | −0.6900 | −0.2825 |
| | | | (−1.71) | (−2.78) | | | (−2.05) | (−1.39) |
| $\mu^* c3$ | 0.4422 | 2.0328 | 1.1084 | 1.1505 | 0.8459 | 1.7815 | 1.5809 | 0.7039 |
| | (0.71) | (2.27) | (5.84) | (3.21) | (1.62) | (4.33) | (3.33) | (3.32) |
| $\mu$ | 0.3860 | 0.4966 | 0.20 | 0.3343 | 0.2739 | 0.6656 | 0.4143 | 0.20 |
| | (1.29) | (2.73) | | (2.84) | (1.40) | (4.06) | (2.74) | |
| $\mu^* d$ | 0.3331 | 0.4660 | 0.09 | 0.2973 | 0.1818 | 0.3769 | 0.1462 | 0.20 |
| | (7.07) | (6.17) | | (2.28) | (2.00) | (6.97) | (1.12) | |
| $g$ | 0.2248 | 0.5292 | 0.3083 | 0.3521 | 0.1194 | 0.2426 | 0.00 | 0.3051 |
| | (2.28) | (2.65) | (0.75) | (1.65) | (0.47) | (1.79) | | (1.26) |
| $Co$ | 0.1541 | 0.0170 | 0.0018 | 0.1742 | 0.0244 | 0.0963 | 0.0094 | 0.0500 |
| $c1$ | 0.9723 | 0.1360 | −0.9070 | −0.0521 | −1.0527 | 1.0714 | 0.4351 | −0.6547 |
| $c2$ | −0.5184 | 0.00 | −2.6509 | −2.8271 | 0.00 | 0.00 | −1.6655 | −1.4126 |
| $c3$ | 1.1463 | 4.0932 | 5.5418 | 3.4417 | 3.0887 | 2.6764 | 3.8159 | 3.5193 |
| $d$ | 0.8633 | 0.9383 | 0.45 | 0.8893 | 0.6637 | 0.5663 | 0.3528 | 1.00 |
| $R2$ | 0.889 | 0.915 | 0.478 | 0.916 | 0.571 | 0.967 | 0.887 | 0.809 |
| $SEE$ | 0.017 | 0.012 | 0.015 | 0.014 | 0.010 | 0.009 | 0.013 | 0.016 |
| $DW$ | 2.024 | 2.738 | 2.529 | 2.651 | 2.781 | 2.265 | 2.394 | 1.298 |

*Note*: $t$-statistics in parentheses.

*Table* 17.A.2 Estimation results for equation (17.11)

| *Branch* | log $h_1$ | $h_2$ | $h_3$ | $h_4$ | $R^2$ | *DW* |
|---|---|---|---|---|---|---|
| 1 | −0.0662<br>(−0.07) | 1.0326<br>(4.28) | 0.2554<br>(3.06) | | 0.833 | 2.059 |
| 2 | −0.1156<br>(−0.46) | 1.0179<br>(15.28) | 0.2063<br>(2.60) | | 0.958 | 1.956 |
| 3 | 2.1837<br>(6.91) | 0.3200<br>(2.77) | 0.0584<br>(1.40) | 0.2043<br>(2.19) | 0.970 | 1.811 |
| 4 | −0.9083<br>(−2.67) | 1.2297<br>(13.75) | 0.0660<br>(0.86) | | 0.958 | 1.997 |
| 5 | 0.0320<br>(0.16) | 0.9714<br>(18.27) | | | 0.960 | 1.052 |
| 6 | −0.8563<br>(−2.83) | 1.221<br>(15.27) | 0.4030<br>(5.07) | | 0.965 | 1.499 |
| 7 | −2.9541<br>(−11.06) | 1.7994<br>(25.00) | 0.0730<br>(1.09) | | 0.982 | 2.149 |
| 8 | 0.1705<br>(0.31) | 0.9514<br>(6.40) | 0.1668<br>(1.72) | | 0.842 | 0.641 |

*Note*: *t*-statistics in parentheses.

## Notes

1. Other different kinds of labour 'flexibility' are analysed in various recent studies. See, among others: Boyer (1986); Cette *et al.* (1986); Coe (1985); Drèze (1985); Grubb *et al.* (1983); Klau and Mittelstädt (1985).
2. The form of the production functions used in this model is partially based on the French model '*Copain*' (see Dehove *et al.*, 1981; and Cette, 1981). For a more detailed presentation see Deimezis (1985).
3. See, for example, OECD (1984).
4. The probable effects of a future modification of labour legislation in France promoting 'numerical' flexibility by suppressing the administrative authorisation needed to dismiss workers, have recently been tested by different authors. Their results are comparable to ours: in the short- and medium-term such a measure will lead to a decrease in employment. For more details, see GAMA (1986) pp. 77–83, Elbaum *et al.* (1986), Lebaube (1986), and Bloch (1986).

## References

BLOCH, L. (1986) *Labour Market Flexibility: An Analysis with the DMS model* (Paris: INSEE) April 1986.

BOYER, R. (1986) *La flexibilité du travail en Europe* (Paris: Ed. La Découverte).

CETTE, G. (1981) 'L'efficacité du capital productif fixe dans l'industrie entre 1959 et 1979', *Economie et Prévision*, no 50.

CETTE, G., DURAND, B. and TYL, T. (1986) 'Réorganiser le travail: une solution pour l'emploi?', *Economie et Statistique*, no 184, Janvier.

COE, D. T. (1985) 'Salaires nominaux, Taux de chômage non inflationniste et flexibilité des salaires', *Revue Economique de l'OCDE*, no 5, Automne.

DEHOVE, M. *et al.* (1981) 'Le modèle COPAIN: Comportements patrimoniaux et Intégration financière', *Economie et Prévision*, no 48.

DEIMEZIS, N. (1985) 'Analyse sectorielle de l'emploi dans l'industrie manufacturière belge: Perspectives à long terme', *Cahiers Economiques de Bruxelles*, no 106, 2ème trimestre.

DREZE, J. H. (1985) 'Work Sharing: Why? How? How not...', *Economic Papers*, Commission of the European Communities, no 42, December.

ELBAUM, M., CORNILLEAU, G. and FONTENEAU, A. (1986) 'La suppression de l'autorisation administrative de licenciement: des emplois ou des chômeurs?', *Lettre de l'OFCE*, no 31, Janvier.

GAMA (1986) 'L'économie française en 1986-88: Quelles perspectives? Quelles politiques?', *Etudes Prévisionnelles du GAMA*, no 1/86.

GRUBB, D., JACKMAN, R. and LAYARD, R. (1983) 'Wage Rigidity and Unemployment in OECD Countries', *European Economic Review*, vol. 21, no 1, March-April.

LEBAUBE, A. (1986) 'L'autorisation administrative de licenciement en question', *Le Monde*, Mardi, 11 mars, p. 40.

OECD (1984) *Employment Outlook* (Paris: OECD).

## COMMENT ON CHAPTERS 16 AND 17

**Peter de Gijsel**

The discussion of the flexibilisation of markets, especially labour markets has become very popular in recent years. One of the most intriguing problems which has arisen in this discussion is how to conceptualise and measure the flexibility of a market. The following comment will deal exclusively with this topic by answering the question as to how both chapters have tackled this problem.

The chapter by Bayar *et al.* limits the discussion to one dimension of labour-market flexibility, that is to say the speed by which firms can adapt actual labour inputs to actual 'efficient' labour input which is defined as desired labour activity at a given capacity utilisation rate. This 'numerical flexibility' is introduced by the authors through equation (17.8) where parameter $\mu$ is considered as an indicator of labour market rigidity. Following the authors, total flexibility will exist when $\mu$ equals 1, because then actual labour activity will always be equal to actual 'efficient' labour activity. In contrast, total inflexibility will exist when $\mu$ equals 0, because then employment will not change from period to period. The idea behind this flexibility measure is obvious. If firms can never adapt actual labour activity to efficient labour activity, for whatever reasons, then it is reasonable to speak of inflexibility.

By setting $\mu$ equal to 1 and thereby assuming total numerical flexibility the authors calculate employment figures for eight branches of the Belgian manufacturing industry which could have been observed if 'total flexibility' had existed during the time under investigation. Comparing these figures with employment figures being obtained as basic solutions of their empirical model, the authors come to the conclusion that more flexibility in the labour market, at least in the short run, will not lead to higher employment. This result is provocative and interesting because most authors have until now come to an opposite conclusion. Yet the problem with this result is that it rests on a theoretically ill-founded measure of flexibility.

This will become clear if one asks why rigidity in the labour market should exist, when the numerical flexibility parameter $\mu$ equals zero. This would mean that employment would not change in the current period but would remain the same as compared with labour activity in the preceding period. Now assume that actual 'efficient' labour activity is higher than actual labour activity. Must it then be concluded that labour-market rigidity exists only because firms do not adapt actual labour capacity to actual 'efficient' labour capacity?

The answer, of course, must be no, simply because this seemingly 'inefficient' behaviour of firms can be the result of firms' expectations that the capacity utilisation rate will fall in the next period. When expecting such a fall, it would be unwise for firms to adapt actual labour activity to actual 'efficient' labour activity. If expectations are taken into account it is therefore possible that a statistically low numerical flexibility parameter $\mu$ can be in accordance with the highly flexible behaviour of firms. The validity and reliability of the proposed measure of flexibility is therefore highly questionable. This result is not very surprising if one takes into account that the problem of a proper conceptualisation of labour-market flexibility has not been taken very seriously by the authors.

Some reservations should also be made with regard to some concepts of wage flexibility or wage rigidity as measures of labour-market flexibility. This topic has been discussed at length in the chapter by Compaijen and Springer, from which the following questions arise:

1. What kind of rigidity, real-wage or nominal-wage rigidity, is an appropriate indicator of the malfunctioning of the labour market?
2. How appropriate is the notion of wage-flexibility being used by the authors themselves?

Real-wage rigidity can coexist with nominal-wage flexibility or nominal-wage rigidity. Real-wage flexibility can be accompanied by nominal-wage rigidity or nominal-wage flexibility. This is well known and is of course seen by the authors. Although they mention the possibility of a simultaneous existence of real-wage rigidity and nominal-wage flexibility and *vice versa* no methodological consequences are drawn from this observation. Instead the authors prefer to rely on the idea of real-wage rigidity as an appropriate measure of wage rigidity and of the malfunctioning of the labour market without giving a justification for their approach. Yet a problem arises when wage rigidity is to be used as an indicator of the malfunctioning of the labour market as the authors do. Which type of wage rigidity should then be chosen? The answer I think will depend strongly on one's own vision on the working of a market system. This vision is quite unclear in the chapter, though I guess that the authors would explain their vision in terms of neoclassical theory.

The familiar argument which comes from the neoclassical camp is that if competition in the labour market is strong enough unemployment will always be eliminated by the wage mechanism. The adjustment process runs from a reduction in nominal wages via a reduction in real wages to more employment. Because the nominal-wage change is assumed to be always strong enough to secure a fall in the real wage it is sometimes erroneously concluded that the real wage is determined in the labour market. If this were the case, then of course real wage rigidity could be used as an indicator of the malfunctioning of the labour market. The real wage, however, is not determined in the labour market. That has always been stressed by Keynesian economists and general-equilibrium analysts. They argue correctly that in a competitive market-system goods prices are determined in the goods markets and money wages in the labour markets. The determination of real wages should therefore be regarded as a result of the working of at least these two markets. This implies that the determination of the equilibrium real wage must in fact be regarded as the result of simultaneous adjustment processes in both markets. From this point of view it must be denied that the real wage can be an indicator of the malfunctioning of the labour market.

Another argument against the use of the real wage as an indicator can also be derived from general equilibrium theory. As is well known, labour-market demand and supply do not depend on the product price and the nominal wage only, but also on other prices such as, for instance, the interest rate. Because of zero homogeneity of labour demand and supply, only relative prices are relevant. Now the choice of the *numeraire* is quite arbitrary. So although relative prices are the relevant prices in determining labour market equilibrium this does not mean that the real wage should be regarded as the relevant relative price. To draw such a conclusion would be valid only if one confined the analysis to the goods and labour market, neglecting thereby the existence of all other markets, an assumption which can hardly be defended.

Keynesian economists would not only deny real-wage rigidity as an indicator of the malfunctioning of the labour market but would go even further by arguing that also money-wage rigidity cannot be used as an indicator. There are two lines of arguments which can be distinguished. The first which was brought forward by Keynes in Chapter 17 of the *General Theory* is that money-wage rigidity can be explained as the outcome of a monetary economy, where money wages determine in a significant way the price level and thereby the exchange value of money. Because one of the essential functions of money is to be a store of value and a unit of account it can fulfil these functions only if the exchange value of money is kept stable which requires stable money wages. For the survival of a monetary economy it is therefore necessary that money wages are kept stable. To be sure, this line of argument has not been accepted by most economists, because it wrongly assumes that a functional argument in favour of system-stability will be sufficient to explain why money wages in a monetary economy can be expected to be stable. Yet the requirements for system-stability can be in conflict with the outcomes of optimising behaviour. It is therefore not surprising that a second line of argument in favour of rigid money wages has become more popular among economists who feel that Keynes was right in claiming that money wages can be expected to be sticky. The reasons are that the labour market does not work in general as the standard model of neoclassical theory suggests.

Labour markets are incomplete, which makes the existence of uncertainty a theoretical relevant problem. As the theory of implicit contracts makes clear, the situation can arise in this context that profit-maximising firms and utility-maximising workers prefer to negotiate stable money wages for several states of the world instead to agree on state dependent wages.

Even if one takes into account that the simultaneous explanation of rigid wages and involuntary unemployment raises some problems in this approach it must be recognised that in the past few years more and more economists are inclined to accept the hypothesis that rigid wages in a state of unemployment can be the outcome of profit- and utility-maximising behaviour. This hypothesis has turned out to be a fruitful research strategy having led to interesting theoretical results besides the implicit contract theory.[1] It should be clear that by taking these new developments into account the central point of the paper that real-wage rigidity can be an appropriate measure of the malfunctioning of the labour market becomes highly questionable.

A final remark on the quite unusual notion of wage-flexibility being used by the authors. As it is pointed out by the authors, from a conceptual point of view they prefer the adjustment coefficient $\lambda$ as a measure of real-wage flexibility to all other measures being discussed in their chapter. From equation (18.3) it turns out that $\lambda$ measures the speed by which the real-wage adjustment process converges monotonically to a new equilibrium. When discussing wage rigidity the authors are in fact talking about the speed of adjustment processes which secure dynamic stability in the labour market. Now wage flexibility is normally simply understood as the characteristic of wages to change when disequilibrium occurs in the labour market. How far these wage-changes lead to an equilibrium in the first instance is an open question and is dealt with by stability analysis.

It is of course quite legitimate to assume, as the authors do, dynamic stability in the labour market and to concentrate only on those wage-adjustment processes which secure dynamic stability. But why then restrict the discussion to a specific class of adjustment processes? It would have been interesting to have learned from the authors why they explicitly exclude wage-adjustment processes which can be expected to develop in a market where no auctioneer exists and uncertainty prevails.

**Note**

1. See, for example D. Gale, *Money: in Disequilibrium* (Cambridge and New York: Cambridge University Press, 1983); T. Negishi, *Microeconomic Foundations of Keynesian Macroeconomics* (Amsterdam, New York and Oxford: North-Holland Publishing Company, 1979); J. Yellen, 'Efficiency Wage Models of Unemployment', *American Economic Review Proceedings*, May 1984, 74, pp. 200–5.

# Index*


Abraham, K. 175, 176
absorption block, economic models 376–7
Addison, J. T. 168, 193 n25
aggregate demand 124–5, 197, 201, 215–16, 248–9
aggregate supply 201
agriculture 5, 371, 374, 390–1
Andrews, M. A. 351, 368
*Annual Abstract of Statistics* 148 n8
Ansar, J. 2, 60, 117, 118–20
Appels, A. C. W. 314
Arbeidskrachtentelligen 47, 53
*Arbeitslosengeld* 325, 340 n8
*Arbeitslosenhilfe* 326, 340 n8
Armstrong, H. 133, 147 n1, 147 n2, 172
Artus, P. 418
Ashenfelter, O. 10
Ashton, P. 340 n2, 341 n10, 341 n11
Atkinson, A. B. 11, 14
Aukrust, O. 232
Australian Bureau of Statistics 153

Bacon, P. 361
balance of payments, effects of employment policy 387
Balogh, T. 193 n20
bargaining, unions/employers 238
Barro, R. J. 214
Barton, M. 9
Bayar, A. 4, 439, 452
Bean, C. R. 151, 213
Belgium 6, 157, 160, 161, 289, 291, 293, 311, 420
  job-creation policies 299
  manufacturing industry 452
  numerical flexibility, modelling 440–5
  real wages 425, 428
  unemployment 439
Bellante, D. 312
benefit/income ratios 323–4
benefits 224, 323–5, 332
Bennett, A. 154
Bera, A. K. 18
Beveridge, William 187, 188, 190–1, 193 n20, 193 n26
Blank, R. 30
Blau, D. M. 44
Bloch, Laurence 5, 397, 418, 450 n4
Blundell, Richard 1, 9, 15, 16, 20, 56–8, 367
borrowing requirement, effects of employment policy 385
Bosworth, Derek 3, 150, 153, 154, 159, 198
Bowers, J. K. 150, 173
Boyer, R. 397, 450 n1
Bradley, John 5, 361, 367, 368, 369, 418, 421
British disease 5, 316
Brittain, A. 379
Brooks, S. 343
Brown, A. J. 173
Brown, C. 312
Browne, F. X. 376
Bruno, M. 423, 427 n2
Buddenberg, F. H. 173
budget balances 346
budget deficits, targets 345
Bundesanstalt für Arbeit 341 n7
Burchardt, F. A. 193 n20
Bureau du Plan, Belgium 441
Burg, H. van den 172, 173
business cycles 110, 192 n16, 287, 288, 289
  effects on unemployment 335–8


* Compiled by Richard Wright.

capacity
growth 197
underutilisation 2, 178
capacity output 101-2, 109
growth 139-41
capacity utilisation 2, 140, 142, 143-6, 147, 178, 181, 182, 374, 453
rate 102-3, 109, 110, 111, 112 n4, 112 n8
capital
productivity 115 n44
vintages 60
capital accumulation, dynamics 408
capital demand 93
capital productivity 88
capital shortage unemployment 176-7, 178, 180, 181, 182, 183, 192 n14
capital shortages 109-10, 176
capital stock 148 n7, 351
capital-labour ratio 117, 214
Casa Integrazione Guadagni 276
CBI 134-5, 140, 141, 142, 143, 144, 146
Central Bureau of Statistics, Netherlands 47, 52, 433
Central Planning Bureau 114 n32, 115 n48, 177
Cette, G. 450 n1, 450 n2
Charpin, J. M. 407, 498, 411, 412
Chesher, A. 18
Chick, Victoria 357
Chung, A. 374
Clark, K. B. 45
clay-clay model 67, 72, 73, 77, 86, 117, 394, n3, 418
Cobb-Douglas-Leontief production model 3, 67-8, 76, 120, 157, 208, 366
Coe, D. T. 428, 430, 450 n1
Cogan, J. F. 10, 30
collective agreements 311
Common Agricultural Policy 374
Compaijen, Bernard 3, 315 n3, 422, 453
competitiveness 5, 420
consumer prices 419
consumer wage rates 224, 349, 359
consumers, real wages 201-2
consumption, reduction 403
cooperative solutions, wage formation 250-1
Copain model 450 n2
Corden, W. M. 344
Cornilleau, G. 450 n4
costs
job creation policies 291
unemployment, European Community 269-79
costs/benefits, given level of unemployment 271-2
Cragg, J. G. 14, 57
Cramer, U. 172, 175
cyclical unemployment 2, 101-2, 109-11, 122-3, 177, 186, 336

David, M. H. 45
Davidson, P. 168
Davies, D. 340 n2, 341 n10, 341 n11
Davis, John 5, 315 n2, 316, 357
Dawkins, P. 151, 154
de Galan, C. 225
de Grauwe, P. 317
de Gijsel, Peter 452
de Jong, A. H. M. 86, 87, 90, 93, 101, 104, 105, 106, 108, 111, 112 n2, 112 n8, 113 n16, 113 n17, 113 n18, 113 n26, 114 n32, 114 n33, 114 n38, 114 n41, 115 n44, 115 n46
de Klerk, R. A. 177
de Menil, G. 210
de Neubourg, Chris 1, 2-3, 129, 148 n7, 150, 152, 165, 172, 173, 191 n2, 192 n16, 193 n23, 197, 198
de Regt, E. R. 117
de Wachter, Marcia 6, 281, 301 n1, 301 n2, 311, 314-15
Deaton, A. S. 14
Deaton, D. R. 150
Dehove, M. 450 n2
Deimezis, N. 4, 439, 450 n2, 452
demand, expansion 145, 147
demand constraints, output growth 140-1

demand deficiency 124–5, 307
demand deficient unemployment 125, 167–9, 172, 176, 180–1, 183, 184, 197, 273, 358
demand elasticity 351, 353
demand side, open economies 201, 207–10
demographic characteristics
  labour force 171
  women workers 18–19
den Hartog, H. 90, 101, 112 n1, 112 n5, 114 n40, 176, 394 n3
Denmark 157, 160
desired labour hoarding 98
DHSS 352
Dicks-Mireaux, L. A. 129, 173
*Digest of Social Security Statistics* 352
direct taxation 379, 382
Directorate General for Job Creation Policy 281
DMS model 5, 418
  characteristics and structure 407–8
  France 397–406
  French economy 397–400
  price determination 412
  production function 408–10
  scrapping behaviour 410–11
  unemployment determination 411–12
domestic absorption, modelling 376
double-hurdle model 14, 20, 21, 22, 23, 57
Dow, J. C. R. 129, 173
Dreze, J. H. 420, 450 n1
Driehuis, W. 173, 177, 420
Driffill, E. J. 214
Dunlop, J. T. 210
Durand, B. 450 n1
Dutch disease 316, 330
dynamic costs, unemployment 275

early retirement 275, 276, 282, 289, 293, 295–6
earnings, expected, employment and 43
economic behaviour 306
economic costs, unemployment 6, 271
economic effectiveness, job creation programmes 285–6
*Economic Trends* 145
economy, effects of real wage reduction 403–5
education 6
  employment and 43, 287, 290
  job creation and 282, 288, 290, 293–4
education programmes, employment and 287, 290
educational measures, job creation programmes 282, 288
EEC 3, 157, 216, 217
EFO-model 267
Ehrenberg, R. G. 46
elasticities of demand, Ireland 369–70
Elbaum, M. 450 n4
emigration, Ireland 361, 363, 367, 376, 391
employers, non-wage costs 331
employment
  adjustment 446–8, 454
  agriculture 374
  changes 423
  changes by sector 136–7
  manufacturing industry 404
  market sector, Western Europe 309–15
  Netherlands 86
    putty-clay model 87–101
  numerical flexibility 439
  public sector 418
  trade-off with wages 202–3
  trends 216
  women 1
employment elasticities 25–6
employment function 178–9
*Employment Gazette* 133, 138, 139
*Employment Outlook* 270
EMS 398, 405
entrepreneurs 113 n17
  behaviour 106
  expectations 90, 91, 114 n27, 117
entrepreneurship 315
  promotion 282
envy effect 232, 242, 251

equipment, scrapping 87, 93-7, 99, 110, 111, 113 n 15, 118-19, 147, 148 n7, 176, 398, 400
European Community, unemployment 269-279
European disease 5, 316-17, 330-4
EUROSTAT 432
Evans, G. J. 150, 152, 153
exchange rates 398, 405
expectations
  choice of production technique 89-90
  entrepreneurs 114 n27, 117
  formation 82-4
expectations-augmented Phillips curve 190
expenditure, household 56-7
exports
  effects of employment policy 385
  modelling 376-7

factor demand, modelling 60
factor prices, expectations 89-90
Fair, R. C. 150, 153
Fanning, C. 367
Feldstein, M. 279 n2
Fels, G. 176
female labour supply
  data appendix 31-5
  empirical model 9-13
female participation rate 394 n5
female unemployment 25-6
final demand 184-5
financial effectiveness, job creation programmes 285-6
financial strategy, medium-term 345
firm, neoclassical theory of 366-7
firms, relations with trade unions 225-6
fiscal activism 5, 364, 380-7
fiscal policy 343, 344-5
  Germany 335-6
Fisher, F. M. 155
Fitoussi, 192 n18
Fitzgerald, J. D. 368, 369
flat rate benefits 323-4
flexibility, labour usage 60-1
Flinn, C. J. 39, 54 n3
Fonteneau, A. 450 n4
forced labour hoarding 98
foreign debt, interest 382
foreign investment, Ireland 368
foreign workers, Germany 341 n16
Foster, J. I. 173
Fouquet, D. 407, 408, 411, 412
France 6, 152, 160, 269, 289, 291, 293, 295, 310, 312, 341 n11, 418, 427
  DMS model 397-406
  job creation policies 298
  real wages 425, 427, 428
  unemployment benefit 333
Franz, W. 340 n5
Fratianni, M. 317
free lunches 6, 343, 345, 350, 353, 355, 359
FREIA 109, 176
frictional unemployment 125, 128, 170-1, 177, 189, 191 n3
Friedman, M. 189, 215, 278
full employment 187-91, 193 n20, 193 n22, 343
Fuss, M. 61, 67, 68, 69, 118

Gagliardi, F. 428, 430
Gale, D. 456 n1
GAMA 450 n4
game theory, wage claims and 236-8
Garzuel, M. 327
Geary, P. T. 368
Gelauff, G. M. M. 86, 87, 90, 93, 101, 104, 105, 106, 108, 111, 112 n2, 112 n8, 113 n16, 113 n17, 113 n18, 113 n26, 114 n32, 114 n33, 114 n38, 114 n41, 115 n44, 115 n46
gender, employment and 43
general equilibrium theory 454
geographical component, structural unemployment 125, 128
Georgescu-Roegen, N. 192 n18
Germany 5, 6, 152, 157, 159, 160, 176, 269, 276, 291, 293, 308, 311, 358, 368, 427

European disease 316
job creation policies 300
natural rate of unemployment 325–30
real wages 425, 427
unemployment, effects of business cycle 335–7
Giersch, H. 317
Gilpatrick, E. G. 170, 175, 183
Gilroy, C. 312
Ginneken, W. van 327
Gleave, D. 147 n1
Goldstein, M. 376
Gompertz model 54 n2
Gomulka, J. 14
Gordon, B. D. 214
Gordon, R. A. 172, 189
Gordon, R. J. 423
Gould, J. P. 204
Gourieroux, C. 18
government agencies, hiring additional workers 353–4
government demand 219, 221
government expenditure 309
Germany 341 n13
Netherlands 333
government intervention, effects on employment 332
Great Britain *see* UK
Greece 160
Greer, J. 150
Gregory, R. G. 151, 154
gross domestic product 273, 274
gross fixed investment, manufacturing 142–3, 145
Grout, P. A. 213
Grubb, D. 424, 427 n3, 427–8, 429, 450 n1
Gruen, F. H. 177
Guillaume, Y. 4, 439, 452
Gujarati, D. 173
Gylfason, T. 231, 232, 236

Hahn, F. H. 167, 355
Hall, R. E. 171
Hallett, G. 327, 340 n8, 340 n9
Ham, John 1, 9, 10, 56–8
Hannemann, Frey and Weck 310
Hansen, B. 173
Hargreaves-Heap, S. 147 n4, 279 n3
Hartog, J. 172
Hauser, P. M. 150
Hausman, J. A. 9, 10, 11
hazard functions, transition probabilities 39–42
Heathfield, David 197
Heckman, J. J. 9, 11, 30, 39, 54 n3
Helliwell, J. F. 374, 394 n2, 394 n4
Hersoug, T. 236
Heijke H. 171
hidden unemployment 3, 150, 151, 198, 276
Hill, M. J. 167
hoarding
labour 2, 3, 97–8, 100–1, 108–9, 111, 112, 121, 152–6, 178, 192 n13, 198–9
estimates 157–61
Hoel, M. 235
Holden, K. 173
Holland *see* Netherlands
Holt, C. C. 45, 173
Honohan, P. 377
Horn, H. 214
hourly compensation 427
hourly earnings 426, 427
hours of work 153–4
House of Commons, Treasury and Civil Service Committee 278
household expenditure 14, 56–7
housing, investment 376
Hughes, G. 368
Hughes, J. J. 147 n1, 172
human capital, deterioration 275

ILO 152
imports, modelling 375
income distribution block, economic models 377–80, 392–4
income tax, marginal rates 352
industrial sector
Ireland 368
output 373
*Industrial Trends Survey* 134, 135, 140, 141, 142, 143, 144, 146
industry 5, 371, 389–90

inflation 168, 309, 318
  Scandinavian model 232
Ingham, A. 2, 60, 117, 118–20
interest, foreign debt 380, 382
International Labour Organisation 157, 426
International Monetary Fund 426
investment 98–9, 114 n30, 114 n36, 114 n31, 118–119, 120, 204–6, 273
  agriculture 374
  decisions 192 n14
  as endogenous variable 86–7
  foreign, Ireland 368
  modelling 376
  Netherlands 216–17
involuntary unemployment 166–7, 180–1, 191 n4, 350
Ireland 157, 160, 161, 418, 420
  economic modelling 370–80
  labour market, research 365–70
  unemployment 361
Irish, M. 14, 18
Italy 6, 157, 159, 160, 161, 269, 308, 333, 341 n11, 341 n12

Jackman, R. 128, 129, 424, 427 n3, 427–8, 429, 450 n1
Japan 3, 157, 160, 161, 309, 310, 312, 314, 368, 427 n2, 431, 436
  real wages 425
Jarque, C. M. 18
jealousy effect 232, 242, 251
Jenness, R. A. 172, 173
job arrivals 14
job creation policies 6, 282, 289, 293, 296–300, 311
job creation programmes 281–3
  evaluation 291–6
  evaluation criteria 283–6
  evolution 286–90
job-losses, manufacturing 136–7
Johansen, L. 113 n11, 155, 250
Junankar, P. J. 46
Junankar, P. N. 6, 269, 279 n1, 306–9

Kaldor, N. 354
Kalecki, M. 193 n20
Keenan, G. 367
Keizer, P. 263
Keynes, J. M. 166, 167, 170, 187, 191 n3, 191 n4, 191 n5, 197, 344, 355, 454, 455
Khan, M. S. 376
King, J. E. 147 n1
Klaasen, C. 171
Klau, F. 311, 313, 450 n1
Klauder, W. 142, 175
Kloek, T. 109
Klundet, T. van de 368, 394 n7
Koken, A. 312
Kooiman, P. 109
Kooreman, P. 41
Kuipers, S. K. 86, 87, 90, 101, 104, 105, 106, 108, 111, 112 n2, 112 n6, 112 n7, 112 n8, 112 n10, 113 n17, 114 n30, 114 n35, 115 n46, 115 n49, 173
Kydland, F. W. 202, 212, 344

Laan, H. B. M. van der 177
labour
  hoarding 2, 3, 97–8, 100–1, 108–9, 111, 112, 121, 152–6, 178, 192 n13, 198–9
    estimates 157–61
  marginal product 343–4
  mismatch between demand and supply 125
  supply price 346
  underutilisation 151, 161
  unit costs 400, 403
labour costs
  Netherlands 219, 220
  subsidies 6
labour demand 1, 2, 93, 101–3, 109, 115 n50, 142, 255, 318, 332
  application of vintage model 77–82
  elasticity 245–6, 419–20
  excess 129–30
  forecasts 75–6
  lack of 307
  putty-clay models 117–23
  schedules 202
  UK 63

UK manufacturing 118–20
vintage model 65–70
labour force
demographic composition 171
participation 15, 391, 394 n5
married women 16–26
voluntary withdrawal 357
labour intensity, equipment 105, 106
labour market 344, 345–6, 455
discrepancies 1
distortions 344
effectiveness, job creation programmes 285
flexibility 397, 398, 452–6
imbalances 2–3
imperfections 172, 174–5, 176, 177, 178, 180, 181, 182, 183, 185–6, 192 n15, 192 n16
individual histories 50
inflexibility 309, 311–12
influence on wage flexibility 424
Ireland, research 365–70
policies 192 n15, 381–7
small open economies 380–7
state intervention 361
stock-flow model 1–2, 38, 44–50
*Labour Market Quarterly Report* 133
labour prices, real, UK 64
labour productivity 78, 113 n17, 117, 121, 153
new equipment 106–7
labour relations, regimes 264–5
labour shortage 143
Labour Shortage Indicator, CBI 134–5
labour shortages 109
labour slack 187–91
labour supply 1
aggregate 349–50
estimates 29–31
female, empirical model 9–13
modelling 376
neoclassical model 56
reduction 282, 287, 289
traditional model 1
trends 216
labour usage, flexibility 60–1
labour utilisation 154–5
Lancaster, T. 41, 43
Laroque, G. 418
Laslett, R. A. 171, 189
Lawson, A. 351
lay-offs 14
Layard, P. R. G. 151
Layard, R. 9, 351, 424, 427 n3, 427–8, 429, 450 n1
leader-follower equilibrium, wage formation 242–4, 254, 266–7
leasing, assets 142–3
Lee, L. F. 18
leisure 307, 319
implicit price 56
Leontief functions 61, 67, 68, 77, 80, 118
lifetimes, expectations 89–90, 115 n42
likelihood ratio test 22
Lindbeck, A. 231, 232, 236, 372, 377
Linear Expenditure System 16, 17, 22
Lipsey, D. 150, 151
local governments, public expenditure 351
logit models 39
long-term unemployment 131–4, 269, 275, 289, 323
Lundberg, E. 193 n21
Luxembourg 160
Lynch, L. M. 41

McCarthy, C. 367
McDonald, I. M. 204, 210
McMahon, P. C. 366
macroeconomic policies, unemployment 5
Maddison, A. 150, 166, 167, 170, 171, 175, 177
Magnus, J. R. 419
*Main Economic Indicators* 134, 137, 144
Maks, J. A. H. 306
male participation rate 394 n5
Malinvaud, E. 184, 185, 422
Mandelbaum, K. 193 n20
Maneval, H. 172

Mangan, J. 150
Manpower Services Commission 133
manufacturing, UK 61, 118–20
manufacturing industry
  Belgium 452
    labour market flexibility 440–3
  employment 402
  UK, collapse 3, 135–46
  vintage production model 2
marginal costs 78
market clearing, wage flexibility 423
market closure 365–6, 367–8
marketed services sector 375
married women, labour force participation 16–26
Marshall, A. 192 n17
medium-term financial strategy 345
Meghir, Costas 1, 9, 15, 16, 20, 56–8
Meijers, H. 86
men, employment, stock-flow analysis 49–50
Mendix, L. 61
Mertens, D. 172, 175
Metcalf, D. 150, 151
Meulders, D. 4, 439, 452
Michel, G. 418
Micklewright, J. 11
migrant workers 276, 341 n16
Minford, Patrick 5, 315d n2, 316, 329, 340 n2, 340 n3, 341 n10, 341 n11, 351, 357, 358
minimum living standards 326
minimum wages 312
Mittelstadt, A. 311, 313, 450 n1
mixed occupational/geographical component, structural unemployment 126
Modigliani, F. 420
monetary policy, Germany 335–6
money supply, target growth rates 344–5
money wages 454–5
Monfort, A. 18
monopolistic competition 200, 204–6
Moy, J. 152
Mroz, T. 10
Muellbauer, J. 61
Muet, P. A. 407, 408, 411, 412
Mulder, C. B. 4, 200, 263–6
Murphy, A. 368
Muysken, Joan 1, 2, 86, 100, 113 n11, 113 n21, 114 n28, 114 n29, 117, 120–3, 150, 172, 173, 177, 180, 181, 182, 184, 192 n15, 192 n16

Nabli, M. K. 317
NAIRU 189–90, 192 n11
Nash-Cournot equilibrium 237, 266
*National Accounts* 157
national debt, interest payments 380
National Institute of Economic and Social Research 379
national insurance contributions, Germany 331
De Nederlandsche Bank 310
Negishi, T. 456 n1
Nelder and Mead 75
neoclassical approaches, labour market 366
neoclassical model, labour supply 56
Netherlands 6, 42, 47, 152, 157, 173, 175, 176, 291, 293, 311, 314, 419–20, 427, 431, 436
  government expenditure 333
  job creation policies 296–7
  manufacturing sector 2
  putty-clay model 87–101
    estimation 101–11
  real wages 425, 427
  unemployment 200, 201, 216, 217–18, 264
Nickell, S. J. 41, 151, 205, 351, 358, 368
nominal wages 189–90, 231, 419
  change in 423
  flexibility 453
  rigidity 424, 428
  setting 230
non-accelerating inflation rate of unemployment (NAIRU) 189–90, 192 n11

non-demand deficient
unemployment 167-9
non-tradable goods 4
non-traded sector 232
North Sea energy 333
Norway 4
wage formation 231
numerical flexibility 4, 439, 452
Belgium, modelling 440-5

obsolescence, scrapping 93, 107, 110, 113 n25
occupational component, structural unemployment 125
OECD 134, 137, 144, 148 n9, 157, 173, 175, 216, 217, 270, 277, 279 n4, 310, 312, 317, 425, 426, 428, 433, 436, 450 n3
oil prices 80
oil shock 1973 287, 288
Okun, A. M. 278, 422
Okun's law 6, 277, 278, 307-8
O'Malley, E. 368
open economies 201, 263-6
modelling 200-3, 204-16
trade unions 266-8
operating costs 80
opportunity costs 306
unemployment 274-5
Opstal, R. van 54 n3
organisational effectiveness, job creation programmes 286
Oswald, A. 210, 230, 231, 232, 236, 238
output 148 n6
constraints on growth 143-5
expectations 89-90
future losses 275
growth 139-41
industrial sector 373
loss, costs of unemployment 273-8, 307-9
Netherlands 219, 220
UK 62

Palm, F. C. 418
Palmer, D. 147 n1
Parick, A. 173
Pearson family 18
Peel, D. A. 173
per capita real gross wages 5
Perlman, R. 147 n1
Persson, T. 214
Peterson, William 6, 343, 359
Phelps, E. S. 173, 193 n25
Phillips, A. W. 151
Phillips curve 151, 189, 190, 192 n11, 319, 424, 428, 434
Pigou, A. C. 166, 167, 170, 191 n3, 193 n22
plant capacity, reduction 141-2
Ploeg, F. van der 4, 200, 214, 263-6
policies, labour market 381-7
policy measures, unemployment 1, 185-7
political costs, unemployment 6, 271
political factors, economic analysis 265
Portugal 158
Prendergast, C. 368
Prescott, E. C. 202, 212, 344
price arbitrage 420
price determination 392-3
price elasticities 120
price elasticities of demand 369-70
price expectations 66-7
price levels, anticipated 193 n24
Price, S. 46
price-setting, firms 406
prices 189-90
agriculture 374
demand indicators 359-60
determination, DMS 412
pressure on 169
private enterprises 6
private expenditure 309
private marginal product 348-9
private sector, job creation 287, 290
probit equations, participation 15
probit model 39, 42
producer wage rates 224
product wages 346-7, 349, 359
production bottlenecks 145, 146
production factors, substitution 117
production function 152-3, 154-6, 366, 441
DMS 408-10

production structure 87–9
production techniques, choice of 65–6, 88–93
productivity cycle 411
profits, increase 400
protectionism 311
public administration 375
public employees, increase, effects 382–7
public expenditure 353, 354
  local governments 351
public sector, employment 418
public sector borrowing, Ireland 361, 363, 364
purchasing power, domestic 403
putty-clay model 67, 72, 117–23, 374, 394 n3, 418
  Netherlands 87–101
    estimation 101–11
putty-putty model 67, 73, 77, 117
putty-semi-putty model 61, 67, 68, 72–4, 77, 117

quantity flexibility, labour market 422

Raaum, Oddbjorn 4, 230, 266–8
reaction functions, wage formation 240–2
real employment 216
real exchange rates 223, 320
real interest rates 22, 202, 215, 222
real labour prices, UK 64
real wage gap 423–4, 427, 434
real wages 2, 110, 113 n17, 117, 167, 176, 190, 191 n7, 192 n14, 224, 236, 247, 263, 264, 332, 338, 343–4, 359
  adjustment 357
  consumers 201–2
  decrease, effects on enterprises 400–3
  effect of unemployment 351–2
  flexibility 434–6, 453
  marginal 319
  reduction 397–400, 418
  USA 334
  variability 425–6
recession
  1979–81 136–8
  Germany 329
Record, N. 148 n9
redundancies 137–9, 147 n5
regional impact, recession 137–8, 139
registered unemployment 152
Reijher, L. 172, 175
relative wage focusing 230, 251–6, 267
relative wages 231
Renault, E. 18
reservation wages 340 n5
Rhodes, S. R. 150
Richardson, I. G. 136
Ridder, G. 41
Riese, M. 172
Rimler, J. 150
Robins, P. K. 44
Robinson, J. 167
Roper, J. 128, 129
Rose, D. E. 394 n7
Rowthorn, R. E. 354
Roy's Identity 17

Sachs, J. D. 423, 427, 427 n1, 427 n2
Sato, K. 113 n11
Scandinavian model, small open economies 372, 377
Scandinavian Model of Inflation 232
school-leavers, unemployed 294
Schumacher, E. F. 193 n20
Scott, M. 171, 189
scrapping, equipment 3, 87, 93–7, 99, 107–8, 110, 111, 113 n15, 113 n19, 117–18, 147, 148 n7, 176, 192 n14, 398, 400, 405, 406
scrapping behaviour, DMS 410–11
search time, unemployed 171, 323, 324, 334
seasonal unemployment 170, 188, 192 n10
sectoral employment, Ireland 361, 362
sectoral wages 425, 427

sectoral weighted variance, compensation rates 425, 431–4
Selody, J. G. 394 n7
service sector 312
  modelling 375
services 5, 371
shadow value, capital 214
shadow wages 56
Sheehan, P. 150
Siebert, W. S. 168, 193 n25
Simler, N. S. 172
skills 273
  loss of 275
  shortages 135
  unemployed 132, 134
small open economies, modelling 370–80
Smith, B. D. 382
Smith, R. E. 151, 154
Smith-Gavine, S. A. N. 154
Smyth, J. D. 366
social aid 5, 323, 357
  Germany 325–6
social contract 225–6
social costs, unemployment 6, 271, 278, 306–7
social factors, economic analysis 265
social innovation, job creation programmes 287, 288–9
social marginal product 348–9
social security contributions 171, 221, 223, 224, 314
Solow, R. M. 152, 204, 210, 279 n3
Somers, Yolanda 6, 281, 311, 314–15
Sorrentino, C. 152
*Sozialhilfe* 326, 340 n8
Spitznagel, E. 172, 175
Sprague, A. 340 n2, 341 n10, 341 n11
Springer, Klaas A. 3, 315 n3, 422, 453
stability tests, vintage models 74–5
Stackelberg solution 237–8
Standing, G. 167
Startz, R. 349
static costs, unemployment 274–5
Stern, N. H. 11, 14
stock-flow analysis, labour market 1–2, 38, 44–50
Stone-Geary utility function 17, 210
Stricker, P. 150
structural unemployment 100–1, 109–11, 111, 122–3, 125–6, 127–9, 146–7, 171–7, 180–1, 183, 184, 187, 189, 192 n11, 192 n15, 197
  and collapse of UK manufacturing sector 135–46
  UK 131–5
substitution, production factors 117, 120
Summers, L. H. 45
supplementary benefit 323, 326, 352
supply block, economic models 373–6, 389–91
supply capacity 405
supply constraints, output growth 140–1
supply elasticity 353
supply price, labour 346
supply side
  economy 344
  small open economies 201, 204–6
Sweden 314, 425, 431
Symons, E. 16
Symons, J. S. V. 351

taxation 5, 6, 221, 223, 224, 314, 345–6, 347–8, 359, 378
  Ireland 361, 363, 364
  lower 353
Taylor, H. 172
Taylor, Jim 3, 124, 133, 147 n1, 147 n2, 150, 152, 153, 154, 173, 197, 315 n1
technical progress 2, 67, 88–9, 102–5, 109, 114 n38, 115 n43, 115 n44, 115 n47, 120, 122, 247
technology, industrial sector 373–4
Temporary Employment Subsidy 288
temporary jobs 289

Theeuwes, Jules 1-2, 37, 54 n3, 56, 58-9
Thio, K. B. T. 177
Thirlwall, A. P. 147 n1, 168, 173, 190
time-inconsistency
  fiscal policies 344
  union behaviour 202, 210-13
Tjan, H. S. 101, 114 n40, 176
Tobit model 9-13, 19, 20, 21, 22, 23, 24, 27, 40, 57
Toker, M. 2, 60, 117, 118-20
tradable goods 4
trade unions 4-5, 200, 201, 201-2, 210-13, 230-2, 263-6, 311-12, 344, 358
  open economy 266-8
  relations with firms 225-6
traded sector 232
training 314
training programmes 288-9, 290, 293-4
transition probabilities, stock-flow analysis 38-44, 50, 58-9
Treasury 351
Trognon, A. 18
Turvey, R. 175
Tyl, T. 450 n1

U-V method, categorising unemployed 125-9, 197
UK 6, 152, 157, 161, 173, 269, 289, 291, 293, 308, 311, 312, 326, 368
  job creation policies 301
  manufacturing industry 61, 118-20
    collapse 2, 135-46
  real wages 425, 427, 428
  structural unemployment 131-5
  unemployment 124-5
UK. Family Expenditure Survey 1, 9, 11, 16, 27
UK. Treasury 351
Ulph, A. 2, 60, 117, 118-20
underemployment 150, 151, 198
underutilisation
  equipment 93, 96
  labour 3
  scrapping 107-8, 110, 113 n15, 113 n19, 115 n44, 120, 121
unemployed
  reached by job creation measures 291, 292
  U-V method of categorising 125-9
unemployment 1, 115 n50
  Belgium 439
  classification 3
  determination, DMS 411-12
  duration 39-40, 131-4
  effect on real wages 351-2
  effects of employment policy 385
  equilibrium levels 347-8
  Europe 286, 332-4
  European Community 269-79
  female 13-16, 25-6
  Germany 326-7, 329, 330, 335-7
  Ireland 361
  Keynesian 418-19
  kinds of 165-6
  link between causes and policy options 185-7
  macroeconomic policies 5
  natural rate 147 n4, 189-90, 274, 276, 316, 317, 344, 348, 358
    Germany 325-30
  Netherlands 86
  official figures 126-7
  policy measures 1
  putty-clay model 100-1
  recorded 151-2, 198
    OECD comparison 159-61
  research programme 37-8
  revised rate 156
  rise 346
  time-series relationship with vacancies 129-35
  true rate 150
  types, simultaneous definition 177-83
  UK 124-5
unemployment benefit 5, 126, 127, 193 n23, 319, 338, 340 n5, 344, 352, 357
  Europe 333
  Germany 325-6, 330
unemployment rates 47-8, 58-9

Unemployment Research Unit 147 n3
union behaviour, time-inconsistency 210–13
unionisation 318–19, 331
unskilled workers 275
US Bureau of Labor Statistics 191 n1
USA 3, 6, 157, 160, 161, 309, 310, 312, 314, 368, 427, 427 n2, 436
  real wages 425
  unemployment support 333–4
utilisation, equipment 93–7
utility functions 235, 236, 239, 255, 304
UV analysis 173–5, 177, 189, 190

vacancies 168, 172
  data 125–9
  relation with unemployment 3
  time-series relationship with unemployment 129–35
  under-recording 127
Vallet, D. 407, 408, 411, 412
Valli, V. 341 n16
variable costs 77–9
Vintaf II 176
vintage model 2, 176, 177, 192 n14
  application to labour demand 77–82
  labour demand 65–70
  results 70–7
vintages 118
  capital 60
  equipment 93–5, 114 n27
Visser, E. 301 n1, 301 n2
vocational measures, job creation programmes 282
voluntary unemployment 6, 57, 166–7, 180–1, 191 n5, 273, 276, 354, 357
voters, expectations 307

wage claims, interdependency 237
wage cost subsidies 288, 293
wage determination 393–4
wage differentials 312, 313
wage drift 251
wage elasticities 22–3
wage equation 27–9, 367–8
wage flexibility 1, 3–4, 422–3, 455–6
  international comparison 425–34
  measures 423–5
wage formation 1, 3, 4, 213–15
  cooperative solutions 250–1
  leader-follower equilibrium 242–4, 254, 266–7
  modelling 233–8, 378–80
  non-cooperative equilibria 238–42, 244–5, 252–4, 266
wage offers 349–50
wage rates 56
  labour force participation and 16
  sectoral 425
wage rigidity 61, 171, 231, 312
wage strategies, time-inconsistent 210–13
wage subsidies 354
wage-cost subsidies 282, 287, 288, 293
wages
  optimal 210–13
  pressure on 169
  trade-off with employment 202–3
Wald test 22
Walker, I. 15, 16
Ward, T. S. 354
Warren, T. S. 354
Warren, R. S. 173
Weibull distribution 58
Weiserbs, Daniel 56
Weiss, F. 176
welfare programmes, effect on labour supply 44
Wennekes, A. R. M. 86, 87, 90, 93, 101, 104, 105, 106, 108, 11, 112 n2, 112 n8, 113 n16, 113 n17, 113 n18, 113 n26, 114 n32, 114 n33, 114 n38, 114 n41, 115 n44, 115 n46
West Germany *see* Germany
Westaway, Tony 3, 150, 154, 159, 198

Windmuller, J. P. 225
*Witboek van de Commissie voor de Europese Raad* 311
Wohngeld 326
women
  employment 1
    stock-flow analysis 49–50
  unemployment 13–16
Wodden, M. 151, 154
work tests 332–3
workers, discouraged 1, 150, 152
working time
  flexibility 287, 288
  reduction 289, 290, 293
world output 368–9
world trade 201, 219, 221, 227 n7, 335–6
Worswick, G. D. N. 191 n6, 193 n20
*Yearbook of Labour Statistics* 157
Yellen, J. 456 n1
Youth Training Programmes 288–9, 290, 293–5
youth unemployment 42, 269, 275, 289, 294
youth wages, minimum 42, 43

Zabalza, A. 9
Zon, A. H. van 2, 86, 87, 90, 101, 104, 105, 106, 108, 111, 112 n2, 112 n6, 112 n7, 112 n8, 112 n10, 113 n17, 114 n30, 114 n35, 115 n46, 115 n49, 117, 120–3
Zweeden, A. F. van 225